THE NEOLITHIC CULTURES
OF THE
BRITISH ISLES

THE
NEOLITHIC CULTURES
OF THE
BRITISH ISLES

A Study of the
Stone-using Agricultural Communities of Britain
in the Second Millennium B.C.

BY

STUART PIGGOTT

Abercromby Professor of Prehistoric Archaeology in the
University of Edinburgh

CAMBRIDGE
AT THE UNIVERSITY PRESS
1954
REPRINTED
1970

Published by the Syndics of the Cambridge University Press
Bentley House, 200 Euston Road, London, N.W.1
American Branch: 32 East 57th Street, New York, N.Y. 10022

PUBLISHER'S NOTE

Cambridge University Press Library Editions are re-issues of out-of-print standard works from the Cambridge catalogue. The texts are unrevised and, apart from minor corrections, reproduce the latest published edition.

Standard Book Number: 521 07781 8

First published 1954
Reprinted 1970

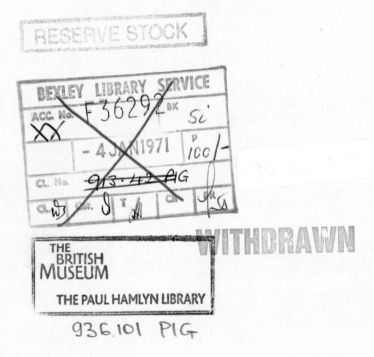
First printed in Great Britain at the University Press, Cambridge
Reprinted in Great Britain by John Dickens & Co. Ltd, Northampton

CONTENTS

northern province, *p.* 324; material equipment, *p.* 328; other settlement sites in the
northern province, *p.* 336; the southern province, *p.* 337; material equipment, *p.* 338;
the relationships of the Rinyo-Clacton culture, *p.* 343; the Ronaldsway culture, *p.* 346;
material equipment, *p.* 348; the relationships of the Ronaldsway culture, *p.* 351; the
Dorchester culture, *p.* 351; material equipment, *p.* 358; the relationships of the Dorchester culture, *p.* 361; a note on Circumpolar Stone Age elements in Shetland, *p.* 363.

FOREWORD TO NEW EDITION

THIS edition is an unaltered reprint of the original text published in 1954, which represented the state of knowledge up to 1951. In the intervening 18 years there has been a considerable accession of new primary material as the result of excavation, and perhaps even more important, fundamental new interpretations of the whole period have been made. The most important of these are outlined below, and the factual information contained in the book should now be viewed in their light.

The most striking revolution in thinking has come about since 1950 with the development of the technique of absolute dating by means of the radioactive isotope of carbon, C_{14}. Two such dates only were available for the British Neolithic in 1951 : today there are over 100 radiocarbon dates directly applicable to the Neolithic material of the British Isles, in addition to numerous determinations of such relevant natural phenomena as the palaeobotanical and climatic zones within the same period. As a result the time-scale given in 1954, containing the Neolithic cultures of the British Isles within a 500-year span from c. 2000 B.C. to c. 1500 B.C., can now be seen to be ludicrously short, and must be replaced by one running from not later than c. 3000 B.C. to an approximate terminal date still c. 1500 B.C., substantially overlapping with the Beaker cultures and the first copper (or even the earliest bronze) technology in the British Isles (Clark & Godwin 1962; Clark 1965; 1966). Not only have the C_{14} dates from these islands been internally consistent, but they are consonant with what we know, in increasing detail, to have been the general pattern of events, when ordered by radiocarbon dating, of the spread of agriculture in the Near East and Europe (Clark 1966).

Within this extended time-span, with all its implications for a lengthy development, it is now equally clear that we must vizualise the British Neolithic pottery sequence as a continuously evolving insular phenomenon and not, as in 1954, as the product first of a 'Windmill Hill Culture' and subsequently of 'Secondary Neolithic' cultures with pottery traditions of alien origins. Dr Isobel Smith has demonstrated that the 'Peterborough' group of pottery styles (Ebbsfleet, Mortlake and Fengate wares) evolve directly from the earlier 'Windmill Hill' traditions of Whitehawk, Abingdon and East Anglian (now Mildenhall types, and that the later of these (e.g. Fengate) are themselves ancestral to our Bronze Age Cinerary Urns and Food Vessels of the second millennium B.C. This essential continuity involves a rejection, or at best a drastic re-thinking of the concept of 'Secondary Neolithic' cultures in Britain as set out in 1954, though Rinyo-Clacton pottery remains stubbornly intractable in any assessment.

A broad tripartite division into Early Neolithic, from the beginnings to c. 2500 B.C.; Middle Neolithic to c. 2000 B.C.; and a final Late Neolithic seems today to provide a more satisfactory model of the assumed situation (Smith 1965; Clark *loc. cit.*)

A final point may be made in respect of the European antecedents of the Windmill Hill Culture. It has become increasingly difficult to derive all the relevant features of this culture, especially the non-megalithic long barrows, from a source among the Western European Neolithic cultures, and the suggestion of a dual origin, partly in these cultures and partly in those of broadly Funnel-Beaker affiliations on the North European Plain, has been increasingly supported by new evidence. The recognition that many 'unchambered' long barrows covered timber mortuary houses; that both barrows and chambers may have an easterly origin; and that C_{14} dates suggest that they are predominantly Early Neolithic, has in turn affected thinking on the relationships of such barrows to the long cairns in the Cotswold areas and elsewhere (Piggott 1961; 1967; Ashbee 1969; Powell 1969).

References

ASHBEE, P., 1969. *The Earthen Long Barrow in Britain* (London 1969).

CLARK, J. G. D., 1965. 'Radiocarbon dating and the expansion of farming culture from the Near East over Europe', *Proc. Prehist. Soc.* XXXI (1965), 58-73.

——, 1966. 'The Invasion Hypothesis in British Archaeology', *Antiq.* XL (1966), 172-189.

CLARK, J. G. D. & GODWIN, H., 1962. 'The Neolithic in the Cambridgeshire Fens', *Antiq.* XXXVI (1962), 10-23.

PIGGOTT, S., 1961. 'The British Neolithic Cultures in their European Setting', in Bohm, J. & de Laet, S., (ed.), *Europe à la fin de l'âge de la pierre* (Prague 1961), 557-74.

——, 1967. ' "Unchambered" Long Barrows in Neolithic Britain *Palaeohist.* XII (1967). 381-93.

POWELL, T. G. E., 1969. Ed., *Megalithic Enquiries in the West of Britain* (Liverpool 1969).

SMITH, I., 1965. *Windmill Hill and Avebury: Excavations by Alexander Keiller 1925–1939* (Oxford 1965).

——, 'Windmill Hill and its implications', *Palaeohist.* XII (1966), 469-81.

STUART PIGGOTT

The University, Edinburgh
1969

PREFACE

THE original impetus to undertake a study of the British Neolithic cultures was provided fortuitously in 1928, when, on my first excavation, I worked with Dr E. C. Curwen at The Trundle in Sussex, the first Neolithic cause-wayed camp to be dug after the recognition of the type at Windmill Hill. The interest in the period then aroused continued after the excavation, and in 1931 I published a catalogue, with commentary, of the Neolithic pottery of the British Isles. Since that time the problems of the period have continued to intrigue me, and this book is the outcome of intermittent study of the British Neolithic in the field and in museums over the past twenty years.

In its original form, the book was begun, singularly inauspiciously, in the summer of 1939, for as Tristram Shandy observed, 'when a man sits down to write a history—tho' it be but the history of *Jack Hickathrift* or *Tom Thumb*, he knows no more than his heels what lets and confounded hindrances he is to meet with in his way'. Work was resumed on it, and the earlier drafts rewritten, after the War, and in its present form it includes, with some minor exceptions, information available up to the spring of 1951.

During the preparation of the book I have examined practically all the museum material and visited a very large proportion of the field monuments described. But while much is based on first-hand study of sites and finds, such a work of synthesis must inevitably owe a large debt to other archaeologists, and the Bibliography, at the end of the volume, will indicate how much I owe to scholars in many European countries and extending in time from Sir Richard Colt Hoare in the days of the Regency to my own contemporaries.

The impersonal thanks implicit in a bibliography are, however, wholly inadequate to express the gratitude one feels to those who have played a personal part in a long-sustained piece of work. Of these, my wife has not only continuously encouraged me and offered lively and penetrating criticism to the book's great advantage, but has also undertaken the greater part of the line illustrations which form an essential accompaniment of the text. Among my colleagues, there are three to whom I owe a degree of intellectual stimulus and friendship of long standing that I find hard to measure and more difficult to repay. To Professor Gordon Childe, Professor Grahame Clark and Professor Christopher Hawkes my archaeological work and thought stand indebted at every turn, and to them I offer this small expression of my gratitude.

That portion of the book dealing with the Secondary Neolithic cultures owes much to discussions with Mr R. J. C. Atkinson, while Dr E. C. Curwen, since introducing me to Neolithic sites in 1928, has helped me at many points. During the time of the 'confounded hindrances' of 1939–45 Dr G. E. Daniel and I found opportunities of discussing the problems of the chambered tombs together, on occasion in extremely curious circumstances, and the discussions continue in more congenial settings today.

To Mr Alexander Keiller this book, and its author, owe an especial debt for his unreservedly placing at my disposal the unpublished material from Windmill Hill and Avebury, as well as for stimulating discussion during our field-work on the latter site. Mr T. G. E. Powell helped to alleviate the tedium of many a military *longueur* with conversations on Irish prehistory, and since the War we have worked together in the field on more than one occasion. Sir Lindsay Scott was always ready with illuminating and provocative comment, and Dr J. F. S. Stone has throughout the writing of the book offered valued and critical advice as well as the stimulus of his own alert approach to prehistory.

I am indebted to all the museum curators and other guardians of original material from whom I have obtained information, and to those many scholars who have helped so willingly and generously. In the British Isles I should like especially to thank Mr A. L. Armstrong, Mrs E. M. Clifford, Prof. Estyn Evans, Dr H. Godwin, Mr W. F. Grimes, Dr Elizabeth Knox, Mr E. T. Leeds, Mr Basil Megaw, Dr Frank Mitchell, Prof. Sean O'Riordain, Dr J. Raftery, Mr R. B. K. Stevenson, and Mrs Audrey Williams. On the European continent I am particularly grateful for the help I have received from Dr J. Arnal, Dr C. J. Becker, Dr Bernabo Brea, Prof. J. Brønsted, Dr V. von Gonzenbach, Major A. do Paço, Dr Gustav Schwantes and Prof. Emil Vogt.

For permission to publish redrawings of their line illustrations, or halftones from their photographs, I have to thank Mr A. L. Armstrong, Mr R. J. C. Atkinson, M. l'Abbé Breuil, Mr J. P. T. Burchell, Prof. V. G. Childe, Dr R. C. C. Clay, Mrs E. M. Clifford, Dr E. C. Curwen, Dr. G. E. Daniel, Prof. O. Davies, Prof. E. E. Evans, Miss C. Fell, Mr W. F. Grimes, Mr A. Keiller, Mr E. T. Leeds, Mr B. R. S. Megaw, Miss F. Patchett, Mr C. W. Phillips, Mr T. G. E. Powell, the late Sir W. L. Scott, Mr Hazzledine Warren, Sir Mortimer Wheeler and Mr W. E. V. Young, and the following museums or institutions: the British Museum, the National Museum of Antiquities of Scotland, the National Museum, Dublin, the Ancient Monuments Department of the Ministry of Works, the Surrey Archaeological Society and the Central Office of Information. Acknowledgement of the individual source of illustrations has been made in each instance in the body of the work.

S. P.

University of Edinburgh
   1951

INTRODUCTION

THIS book is an attempt to make a detailed study of a series of interrelated communities in prehistoric Britain at the beginning of the second millennium B.C., and is a description and discussion of the material culture of a number of groups of stone-using agriculturalists, united by trade and intercommunication and forming a recognizable entity in the archaeological record as we see it today. Conventionally, such farming communities using only stone for their tools and weapons are labelled 'Neolithic', and this time-hallowed nomenclature has been retained in the title of the book and in its text, although many of us today feel that our archaeological terminology is in serious need of revision and that such phrases as 'Neolithic' or 'Bronze Age' periods have a rather dubious validity.

The cultures described in this book are, however, sufficiently homogeneous to justify their treatment as a group. Their inception, with the arrival of immigrants from the European continent bringing the first elements of an agricultural economy to the British Isles, marks a break with the ancient hunter-fisher mode of life with its roots in the Palaeolithic, and although as we shall see the indigenous Mesolithic cultures were profoundly to influence the character of the British Neolithic, nevertheless a fresh era in British prehistory opens with the coming of the new colonists. The lower limits of the phase are less easy to define. Sporadic objects of copper or bronze are likely to have been traded into Britain while many of the cultures described in this book were flourishing with a completely stone-using economy, and it is difficult to regard the scanty metal equipment of the beaker-using population of these islands as really constituting a Bronze Age. Makers of Beaker pottery certainly arrived in Britain at a time likely to be the middle of our so-called Neolithic period, so that we cannot say that the phase ends with the arrival of the Beaker folk—indeed, those British beakers which come within the continental Bell-Beaker class (Abercromby's type *B*) might be regarded as a ceramic component of our later Neolithic cultures, though they have not been so treated in this book.

A more effective boundary seems that afforded by burial rites. Some form of collective burial, by inhumation or cremation, appears to be characteristic of all the Neolithic cultures described in this book, often finding expression in monumental chambered tombs and allied monuments. But with the beginning of what is usually classed as the Early Bronze Age in Britain, a novel rite of individual burial, often beneath a barrow or cairn, appears, and in such inhumation graves the first known metal objects in our prehistory appear also. The inhumation rite changes to cremation, but the single-grave tradition and the barrow persist until the arrival of immigrants of continental Urn-field affinities in southern England early in the first millennium B.C. to bring our Middle Bronze Age to an end and initiate a Late Bronze Age phase.

The appearance of single-grave burial, therefore, has been taken to mark the end of the British Neolithic cultures. Overlapping naturally occurs, and our final Neolithic phase is undoubtedly much influenced by traditions belonging to the single-grave immigrants reaching Britain at this time from northern Europe, burying their dead with stone battle-axes, metal tools, beakers of continental or insular types, and pots of the Food-vessel class, again of British origin. Certainly in many areas of the west and north the Neolithic traditions exemplified in the chambered tombs continued to flourish at this time, and later, so that the line dividing 'Neolithic' from 'Early Bronze Age' in the British Isles is of varying chronological significance within the first half of the second millennium B.C.

The work I have undertaken follows naturally upon the studies of the Northern Mesolithic cultures made by Professor Grahame Clark and published as *The Mesolithic Age in Britain* (1932) and *The Mesolithic Settlement of Northern Europe* (1936): for the British Isles I hope that it may serve as a sequel, carrying a detailed presentation of our prehistoric material a stage further. Professor Clark's admirably lucid presentation in his second book has led me to cast my own work into much the same form so far as the differing material allows, but it is admittedly experimental in so far as, apart from his studies, it represents the first attempt to present a detailed account of all aspects of the material culture of a complicated phase of British prehistory, rather than a treatment of a selected element such as pottery or tomb types.

Following a brief statement of the background, human and ecological, against which the British Neolithic cultures must be considered, the book is planned to fall into two broad subdivisions. In the first, the cultures within the Western Neolithic group of European prehistory are described, brought to these islands by immigrants from the Channel and Atlantic coasts of the Continent, and including those distinguished by the building of chambered megalithic tombs. These, representing as they do the first impact of agricultural economies upon Britain, may conveniently be classed as primary Neolithic in content, and their abundant archaeological material is discussed in Chapters II to IX. With the establishment of these colonies, however, there arose in many parts of Britain derivative cultures in which there is a marked resurgence of indigenous Mesolithic elements as well as contributions from Scandinavian and north European sources themselves largely of Mesolithic stock. The resultant secondary Neolithic cultures of Britain form the content of Chapters X and XI, and in the final chapter of the book the relationships of all the British Neolithic cultures is considered, within these islands and in their Continental setting, and some attempt at a relative and absolute chronology made.

Under these two main divisions cultural or regional groups have been distinguished, and under each group the treatment of the material has been made to follow the same basic pattern throughout, with numerous sub-headings to aid clarity and to assist in comparison. References to published works are made in the text by citing author and date, the works consulted being arranged alphabetically in a bibliography at the end of the book.

The illustrations, which form an essential part of the book, have been prepared with particular care to ensure that all plans and line-drawings should conform to uniform scales, conventions and techniques of draughts-manship in order to facilitate comprehension and comparison. All plans have therefore been redrawn from published or unpublished originals, and the necessarily large series of chambered-tomb plans have been reduced to a common scale of 40 ft. to 1 in. (1 : 480).[1] Complete or restored pottery forms are uniformly one-quarter full size, and other objects normally one-half. While many of the objects illustrated are well known, the opportunity has been taken of including much obscure or unpublished material, and by redrawing it is felt that objects known all too well from old and hackneyed illustrations may take on a new significance when presented afresh.

1 The source of plans or other illustrations is given in all cases except where they are from original surveys or drawings by the author.

LIST OF TEXT-FIGURES

LIST OF PLATES

between pages 8 *and* 9

PUBLISHER'S NOTE

F o r the CUPLE reprint it has been necessary to photographically reduce the size of the text matter. The reduction of the figures is now $13\frac{1}{3}\%$ greater than that indicated on the figure captions. However, the plates have been printed the same size as before and reductions mentioned in plate legends remain correct.

CHAPTER I

THE NATURAL AND HUMAN BACKGROUND OF NEOLITHIC SETTLEMENT IN THE BRITISH ISLES

THE NATURAL HISTORY

BEFORE entering upon a description of the material culture of the various groups of early agricultural colonists in Britain, it is essential to sketch an outline of the natural and human background which these colonists encountered on their arrival from the European continent in these islands. The natural background may best be considered in terms of recent geological events, of forest history and the development of the British flora, and of the fauna, terrestrial and marine, known to have existed at the time of Neolithic colonization. The human background is provided by the evidence for communities of hunter-fisher tribes already established, and largely indigenous, in the same period.

The framework within which these phenomena can best be arranged is that provided by the study of post-glacial forest history in northern Europe. This is described at greater length below, but for convenience of reference it can be noted here that a series of climatic phases has been established, each with its characteristic flora, and following one another as the ice-sheets retreated northwards after the Last Glacial period. In terms of plant-history, these have been classified into zones which may be equated in whole or in part with the older nomenclature of the climatic sequence. Thus Zones I-III comprise the Late Glacial phases (with Zone II the warmer Allerød period), IV Pre-Boreal, V–VI Boreal, VII *a* Atlantic, VII *b* Sub-Boreal, and VIII Sub-Atlantic. As we shall see, all the material described in this book can be assigned to Zones VII *a* and VII *b*, and unless other methods of sequential reckoning can be used (such as a true time-scale in solar years) the zoning system is used where possible.

Land and sea movements

The question of the insulation of Britain from the Continent, and the formation of the modern coast-line, has been discussed and summarized in several recent papers (cf. Movius, 1942, 75 ff., also Oakley, 1943; Godwin, 1945). The formation of the English Channel seems to have been an event of Late Boreal times, and Godwin has examined the evidence for a 'rapid and very extensive eustatic marine transgression affecting the shores of all countries bordering the North Sea' during Zone VI (1945, 67). This process continued and culminated in Zone VII, and in east and south Britain sub-mergence continued into at least the middle of Zone VII*b*, though in the south-west there is some evidence of local emergence continuing from Zone VI. The evidence for the relation of this movement to the formation of the north British and north Irish raised beaches has been discussed in detail by Movius (1942, Appendix VI). In Scotland the carse clays of the Firths of Forth and Clyde are deposits of this marine transgression of Zones VI–VII (Godwin has named it the 'BAT Transgression' from its appearance at the Boreal-Atlantic transition), and the so-called 25-ft. raised beach represents its counterpart in the west: the extent of the Scottish subsidence has been recently mapped by Lacaille (1948). Movius would style these beaches as 'Litorina', in reference to the Litorina Transgression of the Baltic, but the extremely complex nature of the late land-and-sea movements in the Baltic, as revealed by recent research, makes equations dangerous, though there is some reason for thinking that the Essex coast subsidence is equivalent to LG IV in Denmark (cf. summary by Troels-Smith in Mathiassen, 1943, 162; Bagge & Kjellmark, 1939, 140ff.).

In south-east England, in the Fenland and on the Essex coast, some Neolithic colonization had taken place before the last phase of marine trans-gression in Zone VII, while products of late Neolithic stone axe-factories occur in submerged peat-beds on the North Wales coast (p. 292). Evidence for the English Channel region is unfortunately scanty, and the so-called Flandrian Transgression of north France is ill-documented, though un-doubtedly of long (if intermittent) duration. But there seems good reason for assuming a late marine transgression in the region of the Scilly Islands (Daniel, 1950, 24), and much the same is suggested by the half-submerged stone circles and cremation-cemetery of Er Lannic in Brittany, evidence from the Channel Islands (J. Hawkes, 1939*a*), and from the Devon and Somerset coasts. Here at Yelland a long stone setting and a flint industry of Secondary Neolithic type (cf. p. 285 below) have been recorded from a sub-merged land-surface (Rogers, 1946), and at Brean Down, at the seaward tip of the Mendips, a *B*-beaker and a sherd of a pot-beaker of the type found on the submerged Essex coast were again found below present tide level (Dobson, 1938). On the other hand the evidence from the Somerset fens implies that there was 'no substantial transgression' after the end of Zone VI, until Romano-British times (Godwin, 1945).

On the whole then the Neolithic coastline would have approximated to that of the present, except that there may have been considerable land losses along the coastal fringe in south and south-eastern England at least: in the areas of the raised beaches the reverse applies, and old shore-lines may either be high above present high-water mark or (as in the carse-clay areas) buried beneath estuarine silt.

Climate and vegetation history

The general principles of the process whereby the sequence of post-glacial climates in northern Europe has been worked out by means of the resultant changes in forest composition, observed above all in the distinctive pollen-content of peats, are now familiar. The evidence was summarized to date by Clark (1936*a*) and Movius (1942), and the British material has been worked out in detail in a series of studies by Godwin and his colleagues referred to below. The Irish evidence has been admirably dealt with in the work of Jessen (1949) and Mitchell (1945; 1951), and in this connexion it is necessary to point out that before 1949 these workers used a notation for zoning the Irish peat deposits in accordance with Danish usage, but not in agreement with that in use in England by Godwin and others. But this latter system has now been adopted for the Irish material, and its correlation with the previous mode of zoning has been made clear. A single frame of reference is therefore now employed for all such deposits in the British Isles (Jessen, 1949, pl. xvi; Mitchell, 1951, 117). It should also be noted in passing that the peculiar conditions of the eastern English Fenlands led Godwin to adopt a series of subdivisions of Zone VII (*a–d*): these are of local significance only and should not be confused with the division into VII*a* and VII*b* used elsewhere in the British Isles.

The climatic phases with which we are concerned in this book are those of Zones VII*a* and VII*b*—the Atlantic and Sub-Boreal periods. The only Neolithic find directly related to a peat deposit of VII*a* is that at Peacock's Farm in the Fenland, where sherds of Western Neolithic pottery were found in a late Atlantic context in the Lower Peat below the Buttery Clay layer which represents a marine transgression at about the VII*a*–VII*b* transition (p. 94), but several VII*b* correlations can be established. The older Scandinavian dates for these zones were 6000 to 5000 B.C. for the end of Zone VI, and 3000 to 2500 B.C. for the VII*a*–VII*b* transition (cf. Clark, 1936*a*, 53; Jessen, 1949, pl. xvi), and available dates based on radio-active carbon are contradictory—wooden objects from what is almost certainly a VII*b* peat at Ehenside Tarn, 3014±300 B.C., and charcoal from the Stonehenge Aubrey Holes, archaeologically contemporary, 1848±275 B.C. The question of dating by archaeological means is discussed in the final chapter of the book.

VEGETATION IN ZONE VII—THE FLORA OF NEOLITHIC
BRITAIN

The evidence for the natural conditions of vegetation in Atlantic and Sub-Boreal times is based most reliably on the pollen-content of stratified peats, but in addition to this, there are the remains of actual trees and other vegetation, in natural deposits, and the charcoal resulting from natural carbonization or artificial burning on humanly occupied sites. This last evidence must be used with caution, and its limitations are discussed below. In southern England attempts to determine climatic and vegetational conditions from the occurrence of certain assemblages of land-snail species in ancient deposits have been made, and this is in turn examined at a later stage.

Evidence from peat deposits

The pollen diagrams constructed from stratified peats in many parts of the British Isles show a consistent evolution of forest assemblages parallel with that from Scandinavia despite local divergences. The majority of pollen analyses at present available are based on a count of the percentages of tree pollens, but following the lead of such Scandinavian workers as Iversen, attention has more recently been turned to the proportions of non-tree pollens as well, with extremely interesting results.

With the climatic amelioration following the Boreal phase the beginning of Zone VII is marked by a decline in the proportions of pine as a forest tree, and a corresponding increase in alder and the other constituents of the mixed oak forest, which becomes characteristic of Atlantic times (VII a). Elm is abundant in calcareous regions in VII a, and the proportion of oak increases (at least in Ireland) in VII b. The significant boundary of VII a and VII b is seen in most pollen diagrams by a marked decrease in elm (though this is less easy to detect in the Fenland series of eastern England) and a continued decrease in pine. In the Highland Zone of Britain and in Ireland there is a rise in the proportions of birch in VII b, but in some areas (e.g. the north Pennines) the occurrence of this tree is likely to be a function of height, for the high-level peats of late Atlantic date in the Pennine region indicate a landscape of 'cotton grass and sphagnum, more alder scrub and probably birch-hazel woods on the better drained slopes' on hills of up to 2000 ft. (Raistrick & Blackburn, 1932, 99).

The Fenland sequence, thanks to Godwin's work, is particularly well documented. Here in earlier Atlantic times forests of tall well-grown timber, with oak, alder and lime predominating, covered the area now fenland, but as a result either of encroaching sea or a wetter climate, or both in conjunction, the region became rapidly waterlogged and 'we can picture the Fenland as a vast tract of sedge fen much the same in extent as now... extremely inhospitable, with alder, birch and sallow forming a light canopy above an undergrowth of abundant sedge and reed'. But in later times drier conditions set in, and the fen margins were 'invaded by a large proportion of oaks, and in some places, by pines and yews'—conditions to be rudely interrupted by the marine transgression which deposited the Buttery Clay in the middle of Zone VII (Godwin, 1940, 298–9).

Artificial forest clearance

In the Breckland of East Anglia, recently a great area of open heath, Godwin has been able to demonstrate artificial forest clearance in ancient times in the most interesting manner (1944). At Hockham Mere the VII*a* pollens show a woodland of oak and alder, with smaller proportions of elm and birch, but at the VII*a*–VII*b* boundary (marked by decreasing elm) the non-tree pollens show a rapidly increasing proportion of grasses and herbs, and also plantain. This is exactly parallel with the phenomena observed in Denmark by Iversen (1941; 1949) and there associated with the first appearance of Neolithic colonists in wooded regions and the cutting or burning down of forest for agricultural clearance. A similar increase in the pollen of grasses just above the VII*a*–VII*b* transition has been noted at Carrowkeel in western Ireland (Mitchell, 1951, 199), and here again is likely to be the result of the arrival of agriculturalists in the region. Pollen-diagrams from the Somerset fens show a consistent feature at or just above the VII*a*–VII*b* transition, marked by a sudden decrease in all forest trees except birch, which shows a complementary peak: shortly after this level, the trees reassume their earlier proportions (except for the decline in elm characteristic of Zone VII*b*) (Clapham & Godwin, 1948). Now Iversen has noted that birch is a 'pioneer tree' which rapidly colonizes an area after a forest fire, and in the Danish pollen-diagrams a high proportion of birch appears in the first stage of forest regeneration after the clearance of wood-land by fire, attested for the Neolithic agriculturalists in that country (Iversen, 1949, 12). It seems possible then that the Somerset diagrams might be interpreted in terms of similar artificial clearance of local forest by fire in Neolithic times.

A preliminary examination of peat samples from the Ehenside Tarn site described on p. 295 shows high percentages of the pollens of grasses at a level probably to be equated with the beginnings of the Neolithic occupation of the site. But the Ehenside peat, apparently of Zone VII, has exceptional features which include a very high proportion of beech pollen, a tree usually represented in pollen-diagrams of this period by sparse grains, if present at all (cf. Godwin & Tansley, 1941, 120).

The problem of the south English chalk downland

The chalk downland of Wessex and Sussex, a region of early and con-tinued Neolithic occupation, constitutes a special problem in the deter-mination of its original conditions in Atlantic or Sub-Boreal times. The question has been ventilated in a controversy (Salisbury & Jane, 1940; Godwin & Tansley, 1941) in which the point at issue was the former authors' contention that the charcoal specimens from Maiden Castle indicated that 'in Neolithic times the chalk of Dorset was probably clothed with a closed plant community of woodland of the oak-hazel type'. Their opponents consider that 'no sound evidence is presented for any such belief', and bring forward evidence to show that in Neolithic times (i.e. from Late Atlantic times onward) 'many places in the Wessex downland were bare of trees', the forest taking the form of scrub and woodland patches at most, and that by Sub-Boreal times (Zone VII b) there was an increasing amount of grass-land, brought about partly by natural causes and partly by deliberate forest clearing for tillage, and by cattle grazing.

The evidence of non-marine Mollusca

The downland problem was independently approached by the late A. S. Kennard on the basis of the non-marine Mollusca found in prehistoric con-texts in southern England (summary in Cunnington, 1933; cf. also Stone, 1933 a; Kennard, 1935, and in Drew & Piggott, 1936; Wheeler, 1943, 372). In brief, he contended that this faunule represented climatic and vegetational associations obtaining locally at the time of the construction of the sites examined (for the Neolithic, these comprised causewayed camps long barrows and flint mines of the Windmill Hill culture, and other sites of late Neolithic date). There seems little doubt that the land-snails would reflect local conditions, but the question remains as to whether they can be used as a basis for generalization. Kennard, using material spread over the whole prehistoric period from Neolithic to Early Iron Age times in southern England, claimed that certain broad climatic phases were in fact indicated, and these were not incompatible with the Atlantic, Sub-Boreal and Sub-Atlantic stages of climatologists.

The land-snail assemblages from sites archaeologically assigned to Neolithic cultures fell into two groups. The first group comprised assem-blages of snails which would naturally live under conditions of heavy rainfall (and a higher water-table than today), with a fair amount of sun and winters approximating in severity to those of the present day. With this climate, the faunule implied a vegetation on the chalk downland which was either beech woodland, or 'open wood with open spaces and scrub' (Kennard in Stone, 1933 a, 240). In the face of the botanical evidence for the great rarity of beech in Neolithic times, the second alternative is to be preferred, but com-parison made with the modern land-snail assemblages from a hawthorn thicket and a juniper scrub area on the downs showed that these were dis-similar, in lacking the true damp woodland species.

Sites producing this faunule comprise causewayed camps in Wessex and Sussex (though not Maiden Castle, as we shall see below), flint mines in the latter county and at Grimes Graves, and long barrows in Dorset. An exactly comparable assemblage was also found in the tufa deposit of Blashenwell in Dorset, which is almost certainly of Late Atlantic date and contains a Tardenoisean flint industry (Clark, 1938 b): the resemblances include the occurrence of the extinct *Ena montana* at Blashenwell, Thickthorn long barrow and Easton Down flint mine, and the absence on the last site and at Blashenwell of the unbanded *Cepea hortensis*. An initial objection to the use of the land-snail assemblages from these sites is that they are almost entirely derived from ditches or mine-shafts, where damp conditions are naturally to be expected, but one must note in fairness that Kennard's second series, indicating drier conditions, also come from ditch-sites, while the Sanctuary site at Avebury (Peterborough and Beaker wares) produced this same assemblage from post-holes and shallow stone-holes.

Kennard's second type of faunule indicates conditions with less rainfall than the first (approximating to modern conditions, in fact), with open downland but with a relict-fauna proper to a scrub-covered habitat, and comparable to the modern test-series from juniper scrub in Wiltshire. The three main sites yielding this faunule are Maiden Castle, Stonehenge and Woodhenge: of the first site the land-snails indicated 'warm and fairly dry conditions, certainly not damper than today. It is not a dry chalk-down faunule, and there was probably coarse herbage' (Kennard in Wheeler, 1943, 372). There is good archaeological evidence, as we shall see, for making the sites of Woodhenge and the earliest Stonehenge approximately contemporary, and Maiden Castle might, like them, be regarded as late rather than early in the Neolithic and therefore of a somewhat different period to Windmill Hill and the long barrows at least. But against this must be set the disconcerting evidence from a pit with Woodhenge pottery near that site, at Ratfyn, which produced a faunule of Kennard's first group, indicating conditions which were 'damp with abundance of shade and little if any grassland', but with luxuriant scrub growth (Kennard in Stone, 1935 a).

It seems clear that we must use the molluscan evidence with very great care, remembering Kennard's own warning about the extremely local occurrence of land-snail assemblages (1935, 433). With this proviso, it seems reasonable to accept the evidence for damp, wooded conditions in the immediate neighbourhood of the sites which produced the first type of faunule, with locally cleared areas, and probably a drier climate, around those of the second series—the Ratfyn site would imply a similarly localized relict area of heavy scrub. Whether or not the indication of the change to drier conditions in late Neolithic times, as indicated especially by the Stonehenge and Woodhenge evidence, can be equated with the Atlantic-Sub-Boreal transition is another matter. Certainly on archaeological grounds the first type of land-snail assemblage is associated with a number of sites (causewayed camps and long barrows) which should be among the earliest Neolithic structures of southern England, and the beginning of flint mining at least should go back to the beginning of the phase. Stonehenge and Woodhenge are again late in the Neolithic sequence, and probably Maiden

Castle is relatively late as well, and although the 'wet' faunule is again found in Beaker sites, there seems some evidence that the 'dry' assemblage is characteristic of the Middle Bronze Age sites on the downland. Godwin & Tansley feel that despite the doubts felt by archaeologists as to 'the clear-cut conception of a wet Atlantic and a dry Sub-Boreal period' in England, yet 'it is certain that part at least of the Bronze Age in England was relatively dry' (1941, 121). If such climatic fluctuations did in fact take place during the later Neolithic period as defined by archaeology, the land-snails would be likely to reflect them in some measure, even though individual local conditions must render the evidence of slender value unsupported by other factors.

Other botanical evidence: carbonized wood

In their discussion of Salisbury's and Jane's conclusions on the downland flora referred to above (1940), Godwin & Tansley pointed out the inherent limitations in the use of botanical determinations from charcoals and carbonized wood in ancient hearths or other deposits to establish the character of the local flora (1941). Fuel wood may be brought long distances, and naturally carbonized worked specimens (such as hafts, etc.) may be imported: Childe suspected this with a piece of oak from Rinyo (Childe, 1948 b). Again, in coastal regions or on islands, drift-wood may play a very important part in carpentry and as fuel, and the spruce posts at Stanydale in Shetland seem certainly to be explained as drift-wood from the North American continent (see below, p. 263).

But in general, the charcoal determinations from British Neolithic sites confirm the results of pollen-analysis in a convincing manner. The constituents of the mixed oak forests predominate, and among the rarer trees one may note beech at Cissbury in Sussex, Rodmarton and Nympsfield in the Cotswolds, and Ehenside in Cumberland. The presence of gorse on downland sites such as the Trundle and Cissbury should imply open scrub, and it is also recorded from Southbourne (near Bournemouth) and Pentre Ifan in Pembrokeshire. In Ulster, gorse is again noted in Clyde-Carlingford sites, and these also have produced birch, which confirms the pollen evidence for this tree in some numbers during Zone VII b in Northern Ireland: it is again present at Clettraval in the Hebrides and in the Rinyo-Clacton sites of the Orkneys. To the occurrences of yew noted by Godwin & Tansley (1941) one may add Whitehawk, Hembury, Rodmarton and Nympsfield as Neolithic finds; the pine at Woodhenge is exceptional on a downland site and is commented upon below (p. 341) as a probable import from adjacent heathland.

PLATES

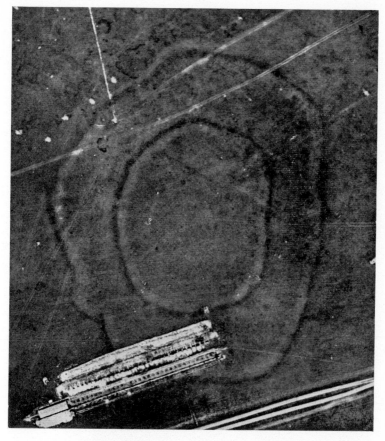

PLATE I   Air photograph of causewayed camp at Robin Hood's
Ball, Wiltshire.

(*Crown Copyright Reserved*)

PLATE IIA   Unchambered long barrow, Wor Barrow, Dorset. Excavations, 1894.
A, B, C, bedding trench of timber mortuary enclosure; D, E, F, G, quarry-ditch of barrow; H, causeway.

(After Pitt-Rivers)

PLATE IIB   Wor Barrow, detail of construction.

A, B, C, bedding trench of mortuary enclosure with packing-stones; D, wooden upright visible in section;
E, F, original turf-line, with turf-line of backing to mortuary enclosure above.

(Unpublished photo. Pitt-Rivers Mus. Farnham)

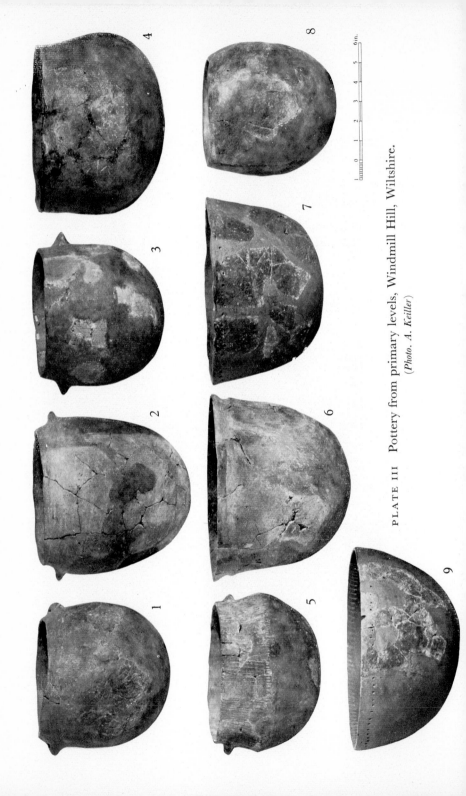

PLATE III   Pottery from primary levels, Windmill Hill, Wiltshire.

(Photo. A. Keiller)

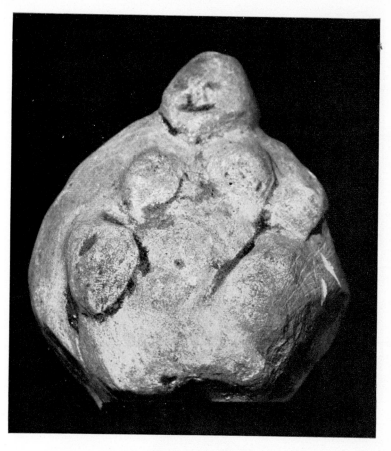

PLATE IV Chalk figurine ($4\frac{1}{4}$ in. high)
from shrine, pit 15, Grimes Graves Flint Mines.
(Photo. A. L. Armstrong)

PLATE V Clyde-Carlingford chambered cairn, Cairnholy I, Galloway.
Excavation of forecourt, 1950, with blocking half removed and stones of façade behind.

(Photo. S. Piggott)

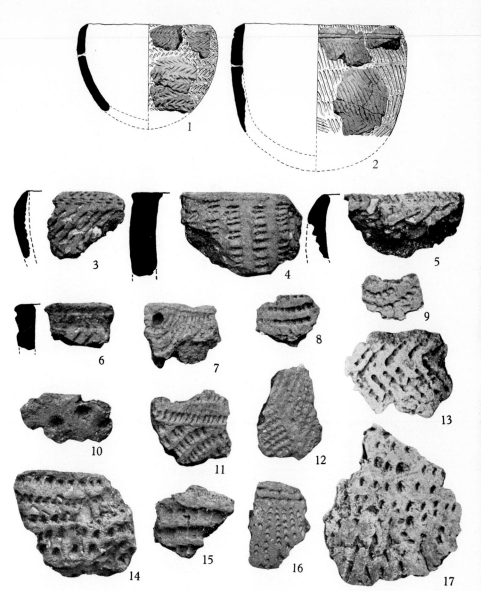

PLATE VI Boyne culture: pottery
1–3, Loughcrew; 4–13, 15–17, Carrowkeel; 14, Moytira
Scales, 1, 2, $\frac{1}{4}$; remainder $\frac{1}{2}$.
(Photos. Nat. Mus. Dublin)

PLATE VII   Boyne culture: decorated stones in passage-graves of New Grange (left) and Loughcrew (right).
(Photos. E. C. Curwen)

PLATE VIII   Hebridean chambered tombs, etc.: pottery.
1–6, Unival tomb; 7, 8, Eilean an Tighe potters' kilns. Scales in inches.

(Photos. W. L. Scott)

PLATE IX Orkney-Cromarty chambered tombs: view of stalled cairn of Midhowe.

(Photo Central Office of Information)

PLATE X   Peterborough culture: pottery.
1, Wallingford; 2, Icklingham; 3, Badshot 4, Hedsor; 5, Mortlake. Scales in inches.

(Photos. British Mus. and Surrey Arch. Soc.)

PLATE XI   Skara Brae: view of House I. (*Photo. Central Office of Information*)

PLATE XII   Rinyo-Clacton culture: pottery from Skara Brae and Rinyo. Scale $\frac{1}{2}$.

(*Photos. Nat. Mus. Antiq. Scotland*)

THE EXPLOITATION OF FOREST RESOURCES

Apart from that indirectly indicated by the constant presence of stone and flint axes on Neolithic sites, and the elaborate mining and manufacturing processes undertaken for their production, evidence for the use of the natural woodland resources by Neolithic colonists in Britain is slight or inferential. Initial forest-clearance may have largely employed burning rather than extensive tree-felling as a means, though the direct evidence as known in Denmark is at present lacking in this country. Clark has stressed the fact that in Britain Neolithic colonization was by no means confined to such areas likely to have been relatively open as the chalk downs just under discussion, and has quoted the evidence for the placing of chambered cairns in the Cotswolds and in Wales in what must have been clearings in dense woodland, and one may add to this the evidence from the Clyde-Carlingford tomb of Cairnholy in Galloway (Clark, 1945; 1947b; Piggott & Powell, 1949). The occurrence of stone-axe finds in or near rivers has more than once been commented upon, in France and in this country (Clark, 1945; Elgee, 1930, 39–40), and any large-scale distribution study emphasizes the broad relationship between axe-finds and areas of ancient woodland. Clearly then we must visualize the Neolithic settlement of Britain to have been accompanied by local, sometimes probably extensive, forest clearance by means of stone-bladed axes. The pollen evidence for this has already been noted.

Subsequent carpentry is likely to have been at least competent, and probably often more than that. The few surviving wooden objects, such as those at Ehenside, are admirably shaped with a craftsmanship by no means inferior to that seen in the comparable artifacts from the Cortaillod culture of Switzerland and its congeners in France (e.g. at the Lac du Chalain). The houses at Haldon, Clegyr Boia, Lough Gur and Ronaldsway, and even more the stone skeuomorphs at Skara Brae, show an ability to build with competence, and the timber-work structures within long barrows tell the same tale. The Henge monuments of the later Neolithic phase present a rather separate problem—such sites as Woodhenge, The Sanctuary and Arm-inghall show at least an assured handling of massive timber uprights and their setting into formal order, and if my contention that the two former structures may in fact be roofed temples is considered a possibility, the carpentry involved would be of a proportionately higher level (Piggott, 1940a). At all events massive squared and morticed beams on the submerged land-surfaces of the Essex coast are hardly later than final phases of the Neolithic in Britain. Dug-out canoes, known since early in Mesolithic times, were certainly used by the Neolithic settlers, though direct evidence is almost completely lacking.

The question of roofing materials needs comment at this point. If thatch, other than that afforded by heather or bracken, were needed, and sods were not used, the only likely natural substance would be reeds, since with primitive agriculture the straw available from cereal crops would be neither abundant nor of good quality. Fox, noting the distribution of Late Bronze Age sickles in fenland areas in southern and eastern England, has suggested the possibility of their being in effect reaping-hooks for reed-cutting, and this possibility may also apply to some of the single-piece flint sickles of the Secondary Neolithic cultures found in marshy environments.

THE FAUNA: THE WILD ANIMALS OF NEOLITHIC BRITAIN

The evidence for wild animals, birds and fishes contemporary with Neolithic occupation in this country is patchy, and inevitably selective. The material consists of the debris of meals, either the normal refuse of a settlement or that of ritual and sacramental feasts and offerings at burial places, and in either suitability for food or conformance to taboos makes for a limited choice. The flint mines have preserved some interesting incidental information on species such as bats or small rodents which have sheltered in the mine-shafts and galleries while these were open, and occasionally it has been possible to identify wild species from their bones when worked into implements.

The larger mammals

The wild ox (*Bos primigenius*) must take first place among the mammalian fauna appropriate to the woodlands of Neolithic Britain. Recorded examples in direct association with Neolithic material are confined to southern England—Windmill Hill and Knap Hill causewayed camps and Thickthorn long barrow; Easton Down flint mine; the Severn-Cotswold chambered cairns of St Nicholas and West Kennet, and probable records from Knook long barrow and Stonehenge. The Burwell Fen (Cambridgeshire) find of a skull allegedly with a flint axe embedded in the frontal bone (Fox, 1923, 14), must, it seems, be regarded with considerable suspicion.[1]

There seems a general consensus of opinion among naturalists that *Bos primigenius* became extinct during the Sub-Boreal phase—possibly as a result of the changing conditions of vegetation brought about by drier climate and increased forest clearance, although Matheson (1932) has commented on the possibilities of later survival in Wales and elsewhere. The two breeds, smaller and larger, noted at Star Carr in an early or pre-Boreal Mesolithic context have not been recognized among the available Neolithic material, though the former may have played a part in the ancestry of the long-horned domestic cattle of the Windmill Hill culture (p. 91). (Fraser & King in Clark, 1950.)

[1] I am indebted to Dr G. H. Bushnell and Mr T. C. Lethbridge for their comments on this find.

The commonest animal present as a component of food bones is certainly the red deer (*Cervus elaphus*), known from Dorset to the Orkneys in Neolithic contexts and, owing to forest conditions, usually of great size compared with the contemporary Scottish beasts. Enormous numbers of red-deer antlers were used in the flint mines as 'picks' (actually levers— see p. 80 below), and they were similarly used in digging the ditches of causewayed camps and long barrows in southern England. The remains of massive red deer in Neolithic chambered tombs on Rousay in the Orkney archipelago raises the question of importation from the Mainland island, or from the Scottish Highlands (Platt in Callander & Grant, 1935, 343). Of the other deer, the roe deer (*Capreolus capreolus*) is common in sites of the southern English Windmill Hill culture at least, and scattered elsewhere, while there is a single record of fallow deer (*Dama dama*) from the Giants Hills long barrow in Lincolnshire.

The horse (*Equus* sp.) seems likely to have been a fairly common wild animal in certain areas. Jackson (1935 *b*) has summarized the scanty southern English finds such as those at Cissbury, Grimes Graves and the Thickthorn and Winterbourne Stoke long barrows, but there are at least eight occurrences in Severn-Cotswold chambered tombs (largely on the oolite), and there are records from five such tombs in Caithness and one in Orkney: in Caithness relatively open conditions suitable for wild horses are likely to have existed under primitive conditions. The bones of presumably wild horses occur in some quantity in the Iberian chambered tombs (cf. Leisner, 1943, *passim*), and the question of such finds in relation to early domestication has been discussed by Childe (1950 *b*, ch. VII).

Remains of wild boar (*Sus scrofa*) are often not easy to distinguish from those of domesticated species, though a few large tusks are likely to belong to wild animals. In certain Secondary Neolithic graves (p. 369 below) unworked tusks of large size, or blades cut from them, appear as recurrent items in the grave-goods. The beaver (*Castor fiber*) is recorded from Grimes Graves, and teeth of this animal were found in the Secondary Neolithic burial of Howe Hill, Duggleby, E.R. Yorks. Matheson (1932) notes numerous Pleistocene occurrences and cites documentary evidence suggesting its survival in Wales at least until the sixteenth century A.D. The brown bear (*Ursus arctos*) is represented by finds at Carrowkeel, Co. Sligo and Ratfyn in Wiltshire, and less precisely dated but allegedly Neolithic finds are recorded from Denbighshire (Matheson, 1932, 28): here again survival into historic times is attested.

Mice, voles and shrews are represented in the flint mines and exceptionally elsewhere, the field mouse (*Apodemus sylvaticus*) being known from Grimes Graves, as also the field and bank voles (*Microtus agrestis hirtus* and *Clethrionomys glareolus britannicus*), the former being also recorded from the Stoke Down mine in Sussex and the latter from the causewayed camp of The

Trundle. The shrew (*Sorex araneus castaneus*) occurs at Grimes Graves, and there is one record of the Orkney vole (*Microtus orcadensis*) from the Midhowe chambered tomb on Rousay.

The bat remains from Grimes Graves are particularly interesting. Four species are represented, the Whiskered, Natterer's, Daubenton's and Bechstein's bats (*Myotis mystacimus, nattereri, daubentonii, bechsteinii*). All have at the present day a woodland and water-side habitat, and neither *mystacimus* nor *bechsteinii* is found in East Anglia, the latter being the rarest of British bats. In view of the recent condition of the Breckland, in which Grimes Graves lie—a vast region of open heathland—these woodland species go to confirm the former natural forested conditions indicated by the Hockham Mere pollen-analyses already referred to, the abundant red-deer antlers of large size used in the mining process, and finally the mines and axe-factories themselves, devoted to the production of tree-felling tools.

Reptile identifications (grass snake and toad) have been made from the Grimes Graves flint mines, and frog is recorded from Woodhenge.

Whales, seals and walrus

The exploitation of these beasts by early man has been discussed by Clark (1946; 1947*a*). Few identifications have been made in Neolithic contexts, except those of whales at Skara Brae in Orkney, and whale's bone used at Loughcrew. Mesolithic sites of Atlantic date have, however, yielded Rorqual and Blue whales stranded in the Firth of Forth, and grey and spotted seals in Oronsay, with possible Rorqual bones as well. The walrus (*Odobaenus rosmarus*) is recorded from Skara Brae.

Birds

Except for a group of chambered tombs in Orkney, Neolithic sites have yielded few recorded bird remains, and in the south of England we have only thrush, starling, blackbird and phalerope (from Chelms Combe in the Mendips and Grimes Graves in East Anglia), and an unspecified species of goose from a long barrow (Stonehenge 165) in Wiltshire.

The three Orkney sites, on the island of Rousay, have, however, produced a list of fifteen species of sea-birds comparable with though not exactly the same as the thirteen species listed from the Mesolithic sites, of Atlantic date, in Oronsay, and including the extinct Great Auk. The Rousay list, from the tombs of Midhowe, Blackhammer and Knowe of Ramsay (p. 241), is as follows:

Cormorant (*Phalacrocorax c. carbo*)	Guillemot (*Uria troile*)
Shag (*Phalacrocorax graculus*)	Gannet (*Sula bassana*)
Pink-footed Goose (*Anser brachyrhynchus*)	Buzzard (*Buteo vulgaris*)
Skua (*Stercorarius crepidatus*)	Carrion Crow (*Corvus corone*)
Great Auk (*Alca impennis*)	Falcon (*Falco peregrinus*)

Eagle (*Halaiaetus albicilla*)   Whooper Swan (*Cygnus c. cygnus*)

Bittern (*Botaurus stellaris stellaris*)   Duck sp.

Curlew (*Numenius a. aquata*)

These are presumably mainly food-birds, but Clark in discussing pre-historic bird-catching, has noted the frequent use of eagle's tail-feathers as arrow-flights among modern primitives (Clark, 1948 *b*).

Fish

The Rousay chambered tombs also produced certain fish bones, representing wrasse (*Labrus maculatus*), sea-bream (*Pagellus centrodontus*) and conger eel (*Conger conger*), while Skara Brae yielded cod (*Gadus morrhua*) and coal-fish (*G. virens*) and the Dyserth Castle site in North Wales (Secondary Neolithic, with Graig Lwyd axes) produced bones of the thorn-back ray (*Raia clavata*), known also in the Oronsay Mesolithic sites. The only record of freshwater fish is that of chub (*Leuciscus cephalus*) from a pit of the Rinyo-Clacton culture near Woodhenge in Wiltshire, within a short distance of the River Avon. Clark has recently assembled the evidence for fishing in prehistoric north-western Europe (1948 *a*), and the discovery and excavation of coastal Neolithic habitation sites would no doubt add greatly to our knowledge of the fish caught and eaten. As with the Mesolithic folk of Oronsay, the catching of wrasse, sea-bream, conger, ray and similar deep-water fish all imply line-fishing from boats.

In view of our very incomplete knowledge of the proportions of wild and domestic animal bones present on Neolithic settlement sites in this country it is impossible to assess the proportionate relation between meat obtained from tame herds and that won by hunting, in the Neolithic diet. It seems fairly certain, however, that venison at least was eaten in quite large quantities, and at all times coastal dwellers must have practised a certain amount of fishing and perhaps trapping for crabs and lobsters: river fish-traps are again a likelihood. Wild-fowling too must have contributed to the food available, though here we have virtually only the few Orcadian sites to give us evidence.

THE HUMAN POPULATION: MESOLITHIC COMMUNITIES IN BRITAIN

It is not the province of this book to describe or discuss in any detail the Mesolithic cultures of Britain in existence in Atlantic times, contemporary with the arrival of the first Neolithic colonists. These have been well served by the work of Clark (especially 1932 *a*; 1936 *a*; 1949; 1950), Movius (1942) and Rankine (1949 *a*, *b*; Clark & Rankine, 1939), together with other workers, and for our purpose it is only necessary to sketch the present state of our knowledge, particularly in connexion with the relations between these communities and those of the Neolithic immigrants.

Surviving Upper Palaeolithic strains, of Cresswellian type, seem to have contributed at least to the Early Larnian Mesolithic cultures, and perhaps to the Obanian as well, though here some sort of affiliation with the west French Azilian seems certainly to exist. The Star Carr discoveries in Yorkshire have shown that cultures of Maglemosean affinities were established in what is now eastern England at least as early as the beginning of Boreal times, and until the final severance of Britain from the European continent (and probably after), eastern England must be regarded as a westerly province of the Maglemose continuum, and probably in a less peripheral sense than the eastern fringe of the same culture in Esthonia and Russia. These Maglemose traditions in England seem to have been of great importance and to have shown considerable aptitude for survival into later prehistoric times.

Mingling with the Maglemose elements in south-eastern England, and widely scattered elsewhere in the west and north, cultures allied to the Tardenoisean can be identified, usually by means of their microlithic flint industries. While these show affinities with French and Belgian material, the Tardenoisean remains an imperfectly understood culture and is likely to remain so until settlement sites with a wide range of artifacts other than flint-work are discovered.

In the extreme north, in the Orkneys and Shetlands, traces of what Gjessing has described as the Circumpolar Stone Age cultures can be detected, with an ultimately Mesolithic ancestry but with a very long survival.

The economy of these cultural groups is throughout that of hunter-fishers, including in this term the exploitation of natural food resources by hunting, trapping, fishing, whaling, sealing and presumably some food-gathering of edible seeds and fruits. Such communities are likely to have been small, and the nature of their food-quest would entail a certain mobility at least within a cycle involving regular winter and summer camps. Actual dug-out boats of Mesolithic date are known from Scotland and from southern England, and their use is implied by the products of line-fishing on coastal midden-sites. The presence of pebbles from Cornwall or Devon in Mesolithic sites in Surrey is probably to be interpreted in terms of such seasonal wanderings rather than deliberate 'trade' (Rankine, 1949b), and comparable to the widespread use of Broom chert hand-axes in Lower Palaeolithic times. In these terms, too, the probable interchange existing between the Obanian communities in western Scotland and those on the north-east English coast is best explained.

The areas of settlement include the coasts and islands, river valleys, sand dunes and, especially in southern England, areas of sandy heath (usually greensand). In the north, summer camps were established high up in the Pennines, beyond the 1,000 ft. contour. The south-eastern English distributions have been studied in detail (e.g. Clark, 1936a, fig. 66), and the essential divergence between the Mesolithic occupation of the greensand and the Neolithic colonization of the chalk downs has been frequently commented upon (cf. p. 18 below).

The first Neolithic colonists of Britain encountered then a Mesolithic population likely to have been very small numerically, probably largely moving in seasonal migrations, having semi-permanent camps and settlements. In all respects they were in a state of culture comparable to the allied communities in Scandinavia, and probably those of western France before the advent of agriculturalists in those regions. It is difficult to detect signs of contact between the two groups—aboriginal hunter-fishers and immigrant agriculturalists—in the British Isles during what must have been the first phases of colonization in the various regions. At Glecknabae in Bute a Clyde-Carlingford chambered tomb overlay a midden of shells, undated but likely to have been a product of local Mesolithic folk, and over this a turf-line had formed before the building of the cairn (Bryce, 1904); at Thickthorn in Dorset a long barrow overlay a pit probably of Mesolithic origin, and here again sealed by a turf-line (Drew & Piggott, 1936). Neither instance really demonstrates any relationship between the two groups of cultures.

The material culture of the immigrant agriculturalists which can on various grounds be assigned to an early phase of settlement seems invariably to represent the introduction of completely novel equipment, and there are no signs that an immediate fusion took place with any Mesolithic traditions. But in various regional cultures in Britain which can be shown to belong to a later phase, elements derived from indigenous Mesolithic sources can be detected, often contributing very strikingly to the make-up and producing distinctive insular variants of Neolithic culture unknown on the Continent. Such a state of affairs is only to be expected—the introduction of a completely novel mode of living based on agriculture and stock-breeding, with its accompanying material equipment, from the European mainland, and the subsequent absorption into this of the residual elements of the old hunter-fisher traditions which it largely, but not wholly, supplanted. These Secondary Neolithic cultures, as I have called them, were to form the basis of the ensuing British Bronze Age.

This book describes the component elements of the first agricultural stone-using communities of Britain so far as they can be distinguished. Initially, it is a record of the arrival at various points of the long coastline of the British Isles of smaller or larger groups of colonists from varied regions of the Atlantic and Channel coasts of western Europe. These immigrant bands must have brought with them not only the knowledge and skills of the agriculturalist, but the actual seed corn and domesticated beasts of their flocks and herds, as well as some portable belongings—bows and arrows, spears, axes, hoes, tinder and fire-making materials—from their homeland. They would come to a land heavily forested for the most part, though open higher land would probably have caught their eyes in southern England at least while they were still well out at sea. It is likely that little or no opposition would be received from the scattered and migratory population—the land was large enough for all, and there was no competition in the two divergent ways of life of the farmer and the hunter.

Of these primary colonies our knowledge is unequal and frequently very incomplete: in the west and north practically our only evidence is that of the stone-built collective family tombs which were constructed not far from the beaches on which the first boat-loads had landed. In Wessex and Sussex our knowledge is rather more adequate, and it is likely that the relatively open conditions of the chalk downlands at the time caused these regions to be the main areas of settlement at the time of the first introduction of agriculture, as they continued to be throughout prehistory.

We can trace some evidence of the growth and spread of these communities within Britain, and then in the later phases of Neolithic culture we can see the emergence of the secondary developments in which the old hunter-fisher traditions appear blended with those of the newcomers, and the distinctively British Neolithic cultures emerge. Probably there was new settlement taking place in some part of the British Isles throughout the few centuries which seem to be spanned by the cultures we have agreed to distinguish as Neolithic, but there is no decisive break in the basic traditions. The initial arrival of the makers of Beaker pottery in England appears to have been an event in the middle phase of Neolithic development, but the appearance of single-grave burial, replacing that of the collective tomb, marks an historical moment of change. Pastoralism probably takes a dominant place in the vital economy of the people, affiliations with the west of Europe become weaker as new connexions with the Rhineland and north Europe are established, and metal comes into use for the first time. It is at this moment that we are justified in rounding off the story of the earliest agriculturalists of the British Isles.

CHAPTER II

THE SITES AND MONUMENTS OF THE WINDMILL HILL CULTURE

WITHIN an area of southern England roughly bounded on its north by a line from the Severn Estuary to the Wash, remains of an immigrant Neolithic culture occur in the form of certain field monuments and finds of characteristic objects, mainly pottery. This area approximates to the natural geographical region of the Lowland Zone of Britain as defined by Fox in his studies of early settlement in these islands; and the culture under discussion, while divisible into local groups with regional variants in pottery styles (and less often other elements of material culture), has an underlying homogeneity that justifies us in treating it as a unit (Fig. 1).

To this culture, the content of which is described in this and the next chapter, it is convenient to give the name of the *Windmill Hill culture* from the site near Avebury in north Wiltshire where in the early 1920's the existence of a Neolithic culture in Wessex, stratigraphically earlier than the Beakers, was first demonstrated. The field monuments of the culture fall into three classes, the first being the earthwork enclosures consisting normally of more than one ring of bank-and-ditch construction set concentrically, with the ditches made in a peculiar discontinuous fashion so that they are interrupted by frequent causeways of undisturbed soil. Of these *causewayed camps* as they have come to be called, Windmill Hill is one of the most important, and they are known from as far west as Devonshire, eastwards along the south coast to east Sussex, and inland to the Thames valley and the Bedfordshire chalk, with a total of at least thirteen examples. As will be seen, these sites seem not to represent villages so much as enclosures, probably for cattle, occupied seasonally. Very few actual permanent settlement sites have been identified as yet.

The second group of monuments are the *flint mines*, dug into the chalk for the extraction of suitable flint, largely for the manufacture of axes, with their attendant axe-factory sites. These mines are naturally confined to the geological areas in which flint is available in this manner, and are known from Wiltshire to Sussex and Surrey, in the Chilterns and in Norfolk.

Finally, burial monuments are represented by the well-known *long barrows*, elongated mounds of earth and rubble covering collective burials but not incorporating chambers built of stone or wood to which continuous access could be gained in the manner of collective tombs of the normal chambered cairn class. These unchambered long barrows are found in approximately the same area as the causewayed camps, though not occurring further west than Somerset. The chambered long cairns of the Cotswolds and north Wiltshire, often in the past grouped with the unchambered long barrows of Wessex and Sussex, must be regarded as a separate phenomenon, and are described in Chapter v.

THE 'CAUSEWAYED CAMPS' OF WESSEX AND SUSSEX

Introduction

As is to be expected, the distribution of the main sites of the Windmill Hill Neolithic culture in the south of England appears largely as a response to the needs of the economic system introduced by the authors of the culture, rather than by a completely servile acquiescence to the natural conditions of vegetation and landscape. Although it is obvious that in general the well-drained porous subsoils with relatively sparse woodland, so abundantly represented in our region by the chalk uplands, would tend to attract settlement rather than the tangled damp-oak forests of the clays or the undrained morasses of the larger river-valleys, yet the almost exclusive choice of the chalk for settlement, which the distribution of the sites and finds of the culture immediately suggests, was not such a simple untutored response to an inability to clear the woodland as sometimes seems to have been assumed. The disparity in distribution of Tardenoisian and Neolithic finds in Sussex, for instance, shows that the greensand, which could never have supported more than light woodland growth, although densely occupied by Tardenoisian man, was practically deserted by Neolithic folk, whose occupation was clearly concentrated on the chalk downs and the coastal plain.

This deliberate choice of the chalklands shows in itself that something more was sought than freedom from the heavily wooded and swampy regions, and, as is demonstrated below, the excavation of a group of earthwork enclosures during the past ten years has shown that the Windmill Hill culture was basically that of cattle-breeders, and that in consequence the provision of adequate pasturage was of foremost importance in determining the settlement of these people. In assessing the content of this culture, the evidence from these remarkable enclosures must be given first place, for they provide in themselves the main clue to the broader economic organization of the entire culture, in terms of which we can later discuss the remaining monuments (flint mines and long barrows), and the material equipment, and in particular examine the distinctions which can be made in local pottery types.

The earthwork enclosures about to be described[1] have produced abundant evidence of the culture of their builders in the form of pottery and the tools of stone, bone and antler, found in occupation-layers in the silting of their ditches. The problems of stratification involved are discussed at a later stage, but it may be noted here that all save one of the excavated sites

---

[1] Documentation in Appendix A, p. 382.

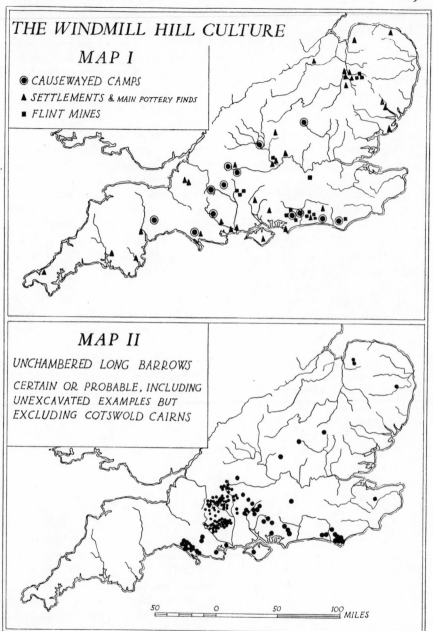

THE WINDMILL HILL CULTURE

MAP I

◎ CAUSEWAYED CAMPS
▲ SETTLEMENTS & MAIN POTTERY FINDS
■ FLINT MINES

MAP II

UNCHAMBERED LONG BARROWS

CERTAIN OR PROBABLE, INCLUDING
UNEXCAVATED EXAMPLES BUT
EXCLUDING COTSWOLD CAIRNS

50   0   50   100
MILES

Fig. 1.

(Combe Hill, Sussex) have yielded pottery of types within the European 'Western Neolithic' family, and in several instances this has been stratified below Neolithic pottery of types outside the Western group (such as Peterborough ware), and beakers characteristic of the beginning of the British Bronze Age. Combe Hill produced homogeneous pottery of a type within the Peterborough group of British Neolithic wares, stray sherds of which also occurred mixed with Western Neolithic pottery at Whitehawk, not far to the west. This raises a point of importance with regard to the origins of these enclosures outside Britain, and is discussed below.

While these smaller peculiarities of pottery styles are a valuable index to the regional differences of the tribes who inhabited southern England in Neolithic times, yet such differences must be relegated to a position of minor importance in the face of cultural traits that can be seen uniting the various groups from Sussex to Devon and northwards up to and probably beyond the Thames valley. The basic unity of the pottery tradition itself is no less significant than the occurrence in southern England of a number of earthwork enclosures of peculiar type which excavation has shown to be attributable to the Western Neolithic people. It is clear that the widespread occurrence of these enclosures, which cuts across minor distinctions of pottery styles, constitutes a unifying factor in terms of which the culture can be studied as a whole, and the purposes for which these structures were used should likewise be found to be the outcome of some common practice, economic or political.

The structures, usually known as 'causewayed camps', have been known in isolation since the beginning of the century, but were first recognized as a group and discussed in 1930. Today over a dozen examples are known, of which most have been excavated or have yielded archaeological material (Appendix A, p. 382). It was in the ditches of these causewayed camps that the first Neolithic occupation material in Britain was found and the enclosures were immediately claimed as settlements in the form of fortified camps, the earthworks of the European Michelsberg culture such as Mayen and Urmitz being cited as parallels. But as we shall indicate, an alternative explanation is more likely.

The sites

The causewayed camps are represented by ten examples which have been partially excavated, and another three sites which appear from surface indications to be of the same class. The excavated sites comprise Hembury in Devon, Maiden Castle and Hambledon Hill 'Old Camp' in Dorset, Windmill Hill, Knap Hill and Whitesheet Hill (Mere) in Wiltshire, Abingdon in Berkshire, and The Trundle, Whitehawk and Combe Hill (Eastbourne) in Sussex. The unexcavated camps whose plans and causewayed ditch systems suggest inclusion comprise Robin Hood's Ball in

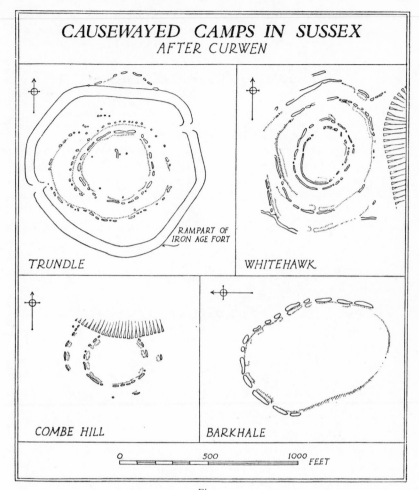

CAUSEWAYED CAMPS IN SUSSEX
AFTER CURWEN

RAMPART OF
IRON AGE FORT

TRUNDLE

WHITEHAWK

COMBE HILL

BARKHALE

0   500   1000 FEET

Fig. 2.

Wiltshire (Pl. I), Barkhale in Sussex, and Maiden Bower in Bedfordshire, where what appears to have been two segments of a causewayed ditch were accidentally discovered near the Iron Age fort on the same site in the last century, and yielded Western Neolithic sherds and a typical antler comb of Windmill Hill type[1] (Map I, Fig. 1).

[1] General description in Curwen, 1930a; for individual sites, Hembury, Liddell, 1930–35; Maiden Castle, Wheeler, 1943; Windmill Hill, Keiller, 1934, but mainly unpublished; Knap Hill, Cunnington, 1912; Abingdon, Leeds, 1927b, 1928; The Trundle, Curwen, 1929a, 1931; Whitehawk, Ross-Williamson, 1930, Curwen, 1934a, 1936; Combe Hill, Musson, 1950; Barkhale, Curwen, 1937a; Maiden Bower, W. G. Smith, 1915. Trial excavations at Hambledon Hill and Whitesheet Hill were made in 1951. (See also Appendix A.)

The situation of these enclosures is usually on rounded hill-tops, though at Abingdon the site is on the valley-gravel of the Thames. At Hembury, Maiden Castle and The Trundle, the Neolithic earthworks were later to be

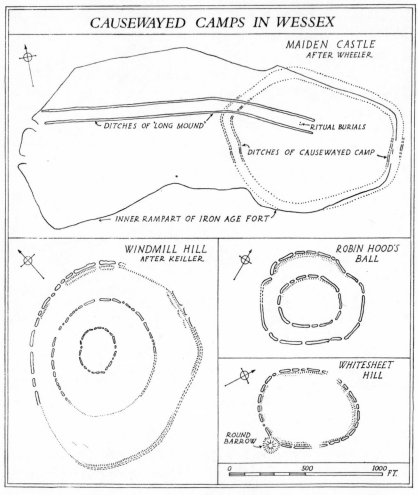

CAUSEWAYED CAMPS IN WESSEX

MAIDEN CASTLE
AFTER WHEELER

DITCHES OF 'LONG MOUND'

RITUAL BURIALS

DITCHES OF CAUSEWAYED CAMP

INNER RAMPART OF IRON AGE FORT

WINDMILL HILL
AFTER KEILLER

ROBIN HOOD'S
BALL

WHITESHEET
HILL

ROUND
BARROW

0   500   1000
FT.

Fig. 3.

overlaid by Iron Age forts. All sites are on the chalk except Abingdon, already mentioned, and Hembury, on the greensand.

The earthwork enclosures consist of from one to four oval or roughly circular ditches, broken by causeways of undisturbed soil at frequent but irregular intervals and with banks on the inner side (Figs. 2 and 3).

Advantage is frequently taken of natural slopes, and the ditches may be deficient at these points, and indeed Hembury (Fig. 5) and Abingdon constitute promontory enclosures, with a line of earthwork across the spur or

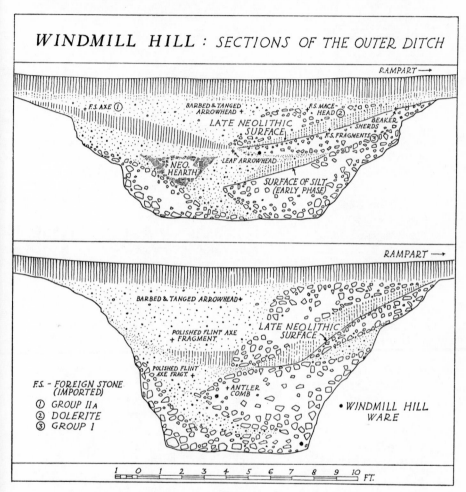

Fig. 4.

between streams. At Hambledon, spur earthworks are probably contemporary with the main site. At Knap Hill, Whitesheet Hill and Barkhale, there is a single line of ditch, and at Hambledon the main enclosure has a single line only, though the spur ditches are double. At Maiden Castle, Combe Hill and Robin Hood's Ball there are double ditches, triple at

Windmill Hill and The Trundle (where, however, the middle ditch over-laps in a spiral fashion to form four lines in places), and Whitehawk has four ditches. In size these enclosures range from Maiden Castle or Windmill Hill (both approximately 1,200 by 1,000 ft. overall) or Whitehawk (900 by 700 ft.), to Combe Hill (550 by 320 ft.) or Knap Hill (540 by 370 ft.). The innermost enclosure at Windmill Hill measures about 270 by 210 ft., and that at Whitehawk 350 by 250 ft.

The ditches and ramparts

The ditches (Fig. 4) are normally flat-bottomed, with slightly sloping sides that must have been nearly vertical when originally dug, and vary from about 3–7 ft. in depth. In any one ring depth is more or less constant, but with a tendency to increase from the innermost enclosure outwards (though at The Trundle the reverse is the case). The length of individual segments and the breadth of the intervening causeways varies considerably, and except where a causeway can be seen to have been used as an entrance, the general impression is one of gang labour in which the ditch was regarded as a rough quarry for a continuous rampart within.

Post-holes for gates have been recorded in two instances only, at Hembury (Fig. 5) and Whitehawk. At the former site, of the five causeways stripped, one 20 ft. wide was found to have four post-holes and a possible fifth that suggested a gate structure at this point. At Whitehawk, of nine causeways wholly or partially stripped, one only, in the third ditch, bore four post-holes for a somewhat similar structure, set back behind the actual line of the ditch. Here, too, were found post-holes implying some sort of palisade or timbering within the rampart, and it was noted both at this site and The Trundle that turf had been stripped from the site of the rampart before it was built, so that there was no old turf-line beneath it, and it merged confusingly with the natural chalk surface. Furthermore, the rampart material here, at The Trundle and at Maiden Castle (though there over a turf-line), was a firmly concreted mass consisting of rubble mixed with hardened chalk mud (Curwen, 1936, 66). This technique of rampart construction—compacted chalk mud and rubble over a stripped surface—is found again in such late Neolithic earthworks as that surrounding Stonehenge and the bank of the Cursus at the same site. (See below, Chapter xi.) At Hembury, in that part of a large Neolithic earthwork explored to the rear of the main line of causewayed ditches, eight post-holes of a palisade were found outside the ditch (Fig. 5).

Internal features

At Hembury alone were any traces of timber-built structures found—an oval or sub-rectangular hut 28 by 12 ft. lying within the earthwork by the gateway already described. At the end of the promontory at the same site was an occupation area with hearths, pits and scattered stones (possibly ruined walls), but nothing that could be construed as a structure. Similar pits containing occupational debris occurred sparsely at Windmill Hill, Whitehawk and Maiden Castle, but unassociated with any signs of permanent settlement. Only at Windmill Hill and Whitehawk were extensive

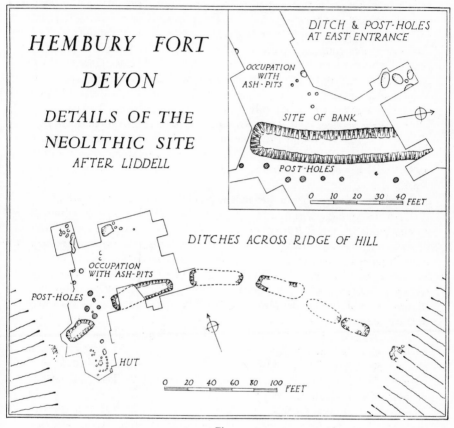

Fig. 5.

areas within the ditch system cleared; at the former site half the area within the inner ditch was stripped, revealing only one localized group of post-holes near the eastern edge. At Whitehawk, an area varying from 50 to 25 ft. in width and nearly 1,000 ft. long was stripped over the lines of all four ditches, with similarly negative results except for very sporadic pits and post-holes.

Stratification in the ditches

In all the sites save at Hembury and Knap Hill, evidence of hearths showed that the ditches were temporarily occupied even after silt had formed in them, and at the two exceptional sites occupational debris with Neolithic pottery of the Western group was present as a scatter in the filling. At Windmill Hill (Fig. 4), Maiden Castle, Knap Hill, Hambledon Hill and Whitehawk this occupation material could be stratigraphically placed as earlier than Beaker pottery: at the two former sites it was also earlier than late Neolithic pottery of the Peterborough and Groove-ware styles, and earlier than Peterborough ware at Hambledon Hill. At Whitehawk and Abingdon, Peterborough pottery was present, at the latter site as a few scraps but at the former as sherds representing several vessels, intermingled with the Western types of pottery normal to the primary occupation, but at Whitehawk not in the earliest deposits in the ditches. At Combe Hill, no Western wares occurred, but only the same stylistically early Peterborough ware of the Ebbsfleet type as was present at Whitehawk in small quantities. Furthermore, at Windmill Hill, the deep silt of the outer ditch showed a stratification in which a typological sequence of development in Western wares could be seen before the arrival of makers of Peterborough ware on the site.

At Maiden Castle the ditches of the causewayed camp, when silted and turf-grown, were cut through by the ditches and overlaid by the mound of an enormous ritual structure known as the Long Mound. The lower levels of the Long Mound ditches, however, contain Western Neolithic pottery indistinguishable from that in those of the causewayed enclosure, and in both instances stratification shows the deposits to be earlier than Peterborough ware and beakers. At Whitesheet Hill a large round barrow containing an inhumation burial, presumably of the Early Bronze Age, overlies the ditch of the causewayed camp.

This occupation in the ditches led to the identification of the causewayed enclosures as fortified village sites. Curwen (1937a, 81–90) painted a gloomy picture of the squalidly low standard of what he believed to have been a Neolithic village—his 'Brighton of Abraham's Day'—from the evidence derived from the Whitehawk excavations, and indeed if we are to imagine that our first Neolithic colonists were at such a stage of barbarism that they were unable to provide better housing accommodation than that afforded by the dank hollow of a wind-swept, half-silted ditch, the standard of life must have been low indeed. But there is no reason to suppose that the southern English Neolithic was so immeasurably inferior to those economically comparable, if culturally distinct, civilizations of the Continent, where, to mention but one site, the Danubian village of Köln-Lindenthal with its timber houses, barns and granaries stands as an objective witness to the high degree of organized village life reached by the northern European Neolithic cultures. And to look no further than our own shores, the Neolithic habitation sites at Haldon in Devon and Clegyr Boia in Pembrokeshire (with no causewayed ditches) cannot be unique in possessing, within the relatively restricted areas excavated, the post-holes of at least two large rectangular timber-built houses (p. 34 below). The familiarity of the Neolithic folk with timber construction is, as we shall see, further afforded by the earthen long barrows, in which in more than one instance upright posts were employed set either in a bedding-trench or in individual post-holes, while the dominance of the polished axe in the material equipment implies not only forest clearance, but carpentry of a sort. In the face of these facts it becomes increasingly difficult to regard the casual hearths and scattered rubbish of the causewayed enclosure ditches as representing villages of the Windmill Hill culture.

The actual nature of the occupation deposits in the ditches repays examination. In the first place it is clear that the primary purpose of the ditches cannot have been that of elongated hut-basements. At Hembury (the only causewayed enclosure producing definite evidence of internal occupation) the excavator was careful to point out that there was no evidence of any occupation in the ditches, the archaeological material from them being merely derived rubbish, and in the other sites the constant feature of the stratification is the presence of sterile primary silt at the bottom, and particularly in the bottom angles, of the ditch, with the occupational debris accumulated in the resultant trough. If the sections of ditch were then used as dwellings, the occupants cheerfully lost floor-space and exchanged a solid chalk surface for one of angular lumps of rubble by the expedient of leaving the site for at least one winter after its construction before they attempted to live there. Nor is the occupation material above the primary silt of the nature of a true hut-floor, but is largely casual rubbish with only occasional hearths, in no way suggesting anything more than temporary occupation at most. It is clear that the ditch sections remained unroofed, for there is evidence of secondary silting or rampart-slips of sterile chalk between layers of occupational debris.

At The Trundle, certain sections of the Second Ditch were found to have post-holes around the edge attributed by the excavator to the Neolithic occupation of the site, and Curwen (1931, 110–11) suggested that in fact these post-holes supported a roof and that in effect this ditch constituted a row of dwellings and was planned as such. But a re-examination of the evidence leads to the inevitable conclusion (with which the excavator now agrees) that the post-holes belong in fact to the secondary Iron Age occupation of the hill. Apart from the oval hut near the gateway at Hembury (Fig. 5) (where the occupation was otherwise mainly in the form of surface scatter and cooking-pits, with a few indeterminate post-holes, but never in the ditch) there is no evidence from the causewayed enclosures of roofed habitations. At Maiden Castle there were Neolithic pits and post-holes, but none attributable to permanent buildings (Wheeler, 1943).

This evidence would in itself suggest a short and transient occupation, but the material from the deeper ditches of such sites as Windmill Hill and Whitehawk shows a stratification of archaeological material which implies at least intermittent occupation during the whole period of the ditch's silting, and indeed the pottery types represented show a sequence which at Windmill Hill at all events has been taken to indicate that the site was occupied for many centuries. This question of stratification will be discussed later and we may merely add that, since recurrent occupation seems likely, the lack of remains of roofed shelters and the use of the open ditches for hearths and meals, suggests that it was during the drier and more genial months of the year. At Abingdon there was definite evidence recovered during excavation that the eastern part of the site had been periodically flooded, and one Neolithic pit was found to be covered by the calcareous deposit of the flood-water and another adjacent to it to have been cut through the layer; flooding was also noticed in the Hembury ditches. There is in fact actual evidence that the occupation was probably mainly in the late summer or autumn for, in addition to the evidence of the animal bones detailed below, at Windmill Hill, Hembury, Whitehawk and Maiden Castle, the shells of hazel nuts were observed in fair abundance among the carbonized wood from the occupation layers, and at Hembury crab-apples were also found.

If we abandon the idea that the causewayed enclosures represent permanent villages, and reserving for the present the question of the location of such permanent settlements, we have still to account for the presence of elaborate earthwork enclosures on the high open downs to which large numbers of the people came at intervals (possibly yearly) and almost certainly in the summer and autumn months and temporarily established themselves.

The clue to the use of the causewayed enclosures is probably provided by the character of the animal bones which occur in quantities in the occupational debris of the ditches. The overwhelming majority of these bones are those of cattle, it being possible to identify cows and bulls and a great preponderance of calves. These ox bones form the vast majority of animal remains excavated from these enclosures, pig coming second and followed by sheep or goat, and dog, with red and roe deer being represented by relatively scanty finds. The large proportion of young animals represented among the cattle is noteworthy and implies the necessity of reducing the herd at the beginning of winter owing to the practical impossibility of obtaining adequate winter feed, a practice which, of course, continued to some degree in Britain until the improved methods of agriculture of the eighteenth century. At Windmill Hill the evidence for this autumnal battue is convincing and striking—several skulls show that the animals were pole-axed by a blow with a sharp instrument over the eye (normally the right)[1] and

---

1 This method of killing is known to have been employed in the Early Bronze Age in Wiltshire and Yorkshire. *Proc. Arch. Inst. Salisbury*, 1849, 105; Mortimer, 1905, 318.

articulated joints of oxen were frequently found in the ditch silting. Further-more, the bones themselves showed flint knife-cuts at points convenient for removing the sinews from their attachments and other cuts associated with the removal of the flesh and skin were observed on such places as the frontal bones of the skulls. Here, and at other sites, a large number of the bones had been split for marrow.

This suggests an alternative explanation for the causewayed enclosures—that they were designed primarily for the purpose of impounding cattle at an annual round-up at the end of the summer, when beasts belonging to half a dozen small tribes might be brought together for purposes of identifi-cation by such means as ear-nicks, reduction by a slaughter of young animals and possibly control by castration—a practice attested in the late Neolithic in Orkney (D. M. S. Watson in Childe, 1931 b, 198–204). The large size of many of the causewayed enclosures implies co-operative effort on a fairly large scale and the conditions of agriculture at the time could certainly not have afforded the food necessary to a large permanent community living within their bounds, but these places may well have constituted centres and rallying points for large areas populated with the relatively small social units that the imperfect agriculture employed would support. It seems likely that the pasturage of herds of cattle was the main economic standby of the folk of the Windmill Hill culture rather than corn-growing, with pigs and sheep or goats forming a secondary source of subsistence, and accompanied by hunting deer and wild ox, and although we cannot visualize the precise system employed within the enclosures, nor explain the part played by the multiple ramparts, it is along some such lines that the most satisfactory solution of their purpose is to be found.

Nor does it seem that the activities of the assembled tribes stopped short at the decimation of their herds. We have to look no further than the flint mines to realize that the idea of a specialized industry was appreciated and developed by the Western Neolithic folk and the utilization of the by-products of the annual slaughter is only to be expected. The Western Neolithic culture in Britain shows no evidence of possessing the arts of spinning and weaving and although the absence of spindle-whorls or loom weights is not in itself decisive, it is more than likely that weaving was un-known or not carried on to any great extent; if so, there would be a demand for leather and skins for clothing. It is therefore probable that the newcomers would have taken over from the Mesolithic inhabitants their technique of skin preparing and as we shall see, probably also adopted actual tool types connected with it. It is to be expected that skin-dressing on a large scale would be carried out after the autumnal decimation of stock in the cause-wayed enclosures, and it can hardly be coincidence that the two dominant bone types from these sites are points or awls for boring soft material and antler-combs (Fig. 13, nos. 1, 2), the Eskimo analogues of which are used in removing the coarse hairs from the outer surface of skins. Preparation of skins and manufacture of garments sewn with the sinews that we have seen were in fact carefully removed from the carcasses seem likely to have been important features of the economy of these temporary settlements and a new supply of clothing would be all the more important with the winter months already menacing.

If such an explanation for the causewayed enclosures be accepted, a point of some importance is raised. We have seen that the social pattern implied by these sites is likely to have involved co-operative work by, and seasonal meeting-places for, a scattered population, perhaps to some extent semi-nomadic, following the herds, but almost certainly comprising relatively small family or clan units. The bearing of this upon the pottery stratification in the ditches is obvious, since this cannot be regarded as the product of a continuous evolution within a single settled community: this is discussed in Chapter III. The broad facts of, for instance, the late appearance of cord-wares of Peterborough or Ebbsfleet type at Windmill Hill and Whitehawk remain significant, representing as they do the impact of an alien culture upon that of the causewayed enclosures, and their presence in restricted areas on both the sites mentioned suggests the temporary occupation of the site by a small group of people for reasons unconnected with its original purpose. But the presence of pottery in a 'Thames-valley' style in a secondary position at Windmill Hill need not be taken to imply an absolute chronological sequence save on the site itself, but may indicate only the use of the enclosure by groups from that region some years after its first construction. At Windmill Hill, indeed, evidence for the seasonal occupation being that of scattered tribes is forthcoming in the presence of fragments of stone, and of pottery with stone grits, attributable to the Frome region, as well as the Thames-valley wares referred to. This, rather than true imports to a permanent community, may be the explanation of the imported wares at Hembury, derived from the Dartmoor region.

As we have seen, when surveying the natural conditions in southern England at the time of the arrival of the first agricultural colonists from across the Channel, the chalk hills probably carried patches at least of woodland and scrub vegetation, and in some areas forest may have been relatively dense. Clearance, whether by burning or by tree-felling, would have been necessary to provide the initial pasturage for the herds of cattle implied by the causewayed camp evidence, and once such clearings were made, they would be maintained and enlarged by the beasts themselves. The importance of the flint axe in the economy of the Windmill Hill people is shown by the large-scale factories and mines described in a later section of this chapter, and it is likely that substantial clearings would have been made in the woodland at an early stage in the colonizing process, both for pasture and for corn-growing.

As soon as the causewayed camp was recognized as a type of Neolithic earthwork enclosure in England it was observed that significant parallels to the interrupted ditch systems were to be found in the Michelsberg culture, notably at Mayen in the Eifel and Urmitz on the Rhine (Lehner, 1910; Buttler, 1938, 79). Here again is the multiplication of 'entrances' through the ditches (eleven at Mayen and no less than forty-three in the double-ditch system of the enormous camp at Urmitz), though both earthworks are reinforced by an inner palisade set in a continuous bedding trench well within the ditch system. It is worth remarking that at Urmitz the palisade was not interrupted at every break in the ditch (five entrances in it were identified and excavated and they seem roughly spaced in the proportion of 1:4 to the ditch causeways) though most of the wider of these causeways had the post-holes and sleeper-trenches of massive timber structures usually interpreted as gate-towers. Similar foundations were found on one causeway at Mayen: as we have seen such gate-posts are of very infrequent occurrence in the English sites.

However the details may differ, it is clear that some relationship must exist between the English causewayed camps and these Michelsberg earthworks: it seems, however, that the German interrupted ditch systems enclosed true settlements (as did the continuous ditch at Michelsberg itself). But in a search for origins one is faced by a chronological difficulty in that, as we shall see, the Michelsberg earthworks are later than such sites as Windmill Hill and so should be derivative from, rather than ancestral to, the English enclosures. There are at present no other types recognized which could be claimed as even distantly related with the Western culture, and a Mesolithic origin seems perhaps improbable. The only claimant for an earlier causewayed earthwork is suggested by the remarkable ditch-systems at Kothingeichendorf on the Isar near Landau (Wagner, 1928; Buttler, 1938, 10) where two sites enclosed by ditches with fairly frequent interruptions yielded Danubian I pottery in the smaller site and similar ware with Rössen and Münchshofen sherds in the larger. Whatever the exact nature of the site (Buttler has suggested that it may be some form of 'sacred' enclosure rather than a normal settlement) it should clearly antedate Mayen and Urmitz, at least in its earlier phase, though it seems difficult to postulate a Danubian origin for the causewayed camps of England and Germany. The internal timberwork of the rampart at Whitehawk detected by Curwen (1936), finds a good parallel at Fort Harrouard, where a similar construction appears to have existed, though not in the rampart (Philippe, 1927).

The fact that the causewayed camp of Combe Hill, near Eastbourne in Sussex, has been shown to have been occupied and presumably built by people using pottery not of Western Neolithic character but a form of Peterborough ware raises a very interesting point in connexion with the origins of this type of earthwork. We have already seen that Peterborough pottery belongs to a group of Secondary Neolithic cultures whose origins are partly rooted in the north European hunter-fisher traditions, and we shall see in Chapter XI that these cultures are sometimes associated with causewayed ring-ditches of a funerary or ceremonial nature. Again, in south-eastern England there is reason to suspect some absorption of local Mesolithic elements (such as techniques of skin preparation) by the intrusive agricultural colonists, and a similar mingling of agricultural and hunter-fisher strains is probably perceptible in the Michelsberg culture in Belgium and the Rhineland.

It is possible, then, that the causewayed enclosures, whether for village enclosures or as cattle corrals, are in both regions a local phenomenon due to intermixture between the intrusive agriculturalists of the Western Neolithic group and indigenous hunter-fisher peoples. We may have to distinguish between semi-defensive enclosures in stone or earthwork, well known in the Western Neolithic cultures (e.g. the Charente 'camps' of the Peu-Richard type, the Camp de Chassey or Fort Harrouard) and the peculiar modification known at present only in the Windmill Hill and the Michelsberg cultures.

OTHER SETTLEMENT SITES IN SOUTHERN BRITAIN AND WEST WALES

In the foregoing section the causewayed enclosures attributable to the Windmill Hill culture have been described. There are, however, a number of other habitation sites in southern England which belong to the Western Neolithic family and which probably or certainly also belong to the Windmill Hill culture. The evidence for such relationship is mainly that of pottery, and in the case of simple undecorated types it is sometimes unsafe to claim anything more than a kinship within the Western family. But on the whole it seems unlikely that we should assume all these scattered sites to be the product of a cultural stream or streams entirely separate from that of the causewayed camps.

In Cornwall, pottery which has claims to be a form of Hembury ware was discovered in the circular hut-foundations outside the hill-fort on Carn Brea (Patchett, 1946, 20). The vessels include carinated forms in fine ware (Fig. 9, no. 2), applied cordons, simple lugs and a 'trumpet-lug' handle, and the whole series compares in general terms with that from Hembury; and the flint industry, with leaf-arrowheads, is similarly consistent. But the finds from the similar hut sites below Legis Tor on Dartmoor are not so easy to parallel. The excavators found round-bottomed vessels *in situ* on the hearths within the huts, but flat bases also occur among the sherds now preserved from the site, and the general feeling of the pottery is that it is late, and a survival of Neolithic traditions into the Bronze Age. The small angular-section cordon of Carn Brea is here thick and heavy, and the lugs are massive rectangular features, while the ornament with square or round-toothed combs is quite foreign to Hembury ware and might suggest Beaker influence. From an examination on the ground it is clear that the settlement is of at least two periods; of the ten huts of the main group six lie within an irregular enclosing wall, three immediately outside and one actually overlain by the wall, showing it to be a later addition. To this later phase may possibly be attributed the flat-based vessels, as well as the half of a clay spindle-whorl, since there is otherwise no evidence of spinning within the Windmill Hill culture in England. Other finds from the Legis Tor huts include stone mullers and rubbing-stones, and a large axe-shaped object of stone with an unfinished perforation at the larger end that may well be a whetstone. Neolithic occupation has been suspected at various other Dartmoor hut-villages, but the evidence brought forward seems largely negative. Curwen (1927b) has suggested that certain types of settlement, characterized by huts within irregular lynchetted areas, may be Neolithic in date, and the finest (unexcavated) group of these enclosures lies on the other side of the river Plym a quarter of a mile from the Legis Tor site, on Trowlesworthy Warren. It is possible that in its original form the Legis Tor site itself consisted of similar enclosures, and it seems likely that careful excavation of the Trowles-worthy Warren site might throw much light on presumably Neolithic settlements in this region.

Coming further eastwards into Devon, a most important settlement has been identified on the exposed hill-top of Haldon, seventeen miles from Hembury Fort itself. (Willock, 1936; 1937.) The site lies at a height of nearly 800 ft., on a subsoil of flints, clay and sand which is most unfavourable to the preservation of structural remains, but nevertheless it was possible to identify the foundations of a large rectangular house nearly 25 by 16 ft. in extreme measurements, with wall footings of stones, in which were the sockets of wooden uprights. Two post-holes along the central axis suggest a gabled roof, and the entrance appears to have been at one corner of the building. Within the house two occupation layers were distinguished, separated by sterile sand, and a hearth delimited by an internal wall occupied one corner of the building (Fig. 6). Elsewhere in the occupied area sherds and flint implements occurred and occasional hearths and local concentrations of stones were recognizable, but no other buildings could be identified. The pottery compares closely with the Hembury material and includes sherds of carinated vessels, but a small flat-bottomed decorated bowl found almost complete (Fig. 9, no. 3) is without parallel and although the incised ornament, in zones of horizontal and vertical lines, might have ultimate connexions with channelled ware motifs, the resemblance to a Bronze Age 'incense-cup' may not be fortuitous. The flint industry is partly carried out in the local material, but the finer worked forms, including abundant leaf-arrowheads, are of imported Beer flint which seems to have been worked on the spot. Many rough 'flint mine' forms occur, as at Hembury, and part of a polishing stone made from a large pebble. Corn-growing is attested by a grain impression on a sherd, with similar dimensions to the Hembury wheat. What appears to be a similar open settlement has recently been identified at Hazard Hill near Totnes (Houlder, 1951).

At Clegyr Boia near St David's, Pembrokeshire, a settlement site comparable to that at Haldon has been identified, partly overlaid by an Early Iron Age or Dark Ages fort. A small roughly circular hut was found actually beneath the later defensive wall, and within the area of the fort was a rectangular house some 24 by 12 ft. built in an angle of outcropping rock, with

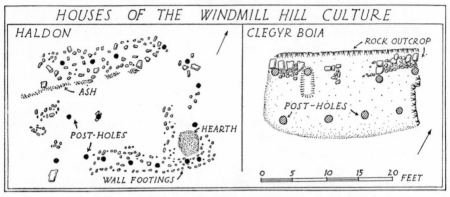

Fig. 6. (*After Willock & Williams.*)

eight post-holes in two rows and stone wall footings on one of the long sides (Fig. 6). The pottery comprised round-based bowls, mainly shouldered and with everted rims, and lugs including examples cupped on the upper side, and the whole assemblage is comparable with the material from Carn Brea and from the Lough Gur sites described below (Chapter IX), where similar rectangular houses and circular huts were found together.[1]

These west British sites are of great importance in connexion with the Lough Gur finds, and suggest the existence of a common province around the southern shores of the Irish Sea with similar traditions of pottery, and probably house-types as well. We shall see later how undecorated carinated bowls are widely distributed throughout Eire and Northern Ireland, and while the more northerly examples seem allied to those of Yorkshire, the southern group must be considered in connexion with the Cornish, Welsh and Devonshire sites just described.

1 Unpublished: referred to here by kind permission of the excavator, Mrs Audrey Williams and the Ancient Monuments Department of the Ministry of Works, who have also permitted a plan of the long house to be reproduced in advance of the publication of the excavation report.

For parallels to these sites within the Western culture, it is relatively easy to compare the circular huts of Carn Brea and Legis Tor with the dwellings of the primary settlement of El Garcel in Almeria (Childe, 1947, 259), the circular stone hut-foundations at Le Lizo in the Morbihan (Le Rouzic, 1933) or that in wood at Fort Harrouard (Philippe, 1927, Plan C). Such circular forms may be, as I have suggested elsewhere, an essentially West European house-type (Piggott, 1940a) which can be observed in Britain persisting almost unchanged into the Early Iron Age and even into medieval times.[1] But the Haldon house and the fragmentary example from Easton Down mentioned below seem to have no analogues in the more westerly areas and are closely paralleled by the Danubian II (Rössen) houses on the Goldberg in Würtemberg (Bersu, 1936) and at Aichbühl on the Federsee (Reinerth, 1929) and to some extent by Michelsberg houses (Buttler, 1938, 76–7; Childe, 1947, 283; Hawkes, 1940, 138). In the absence of the definite identification of rectangular houses in the Cortaillod culture (cf. the warning in Childe, 1947, 281) it is impossible to say whether rectangular houses are to be considered an original feature of the Western culture in Europe.

The Haldon site is easily the most important settlement of the culture in our area, excluding the camps, but in the Mendips it is interesting to note Neolithic occupation in at least two caves—at Sun Hole where a broken pottery spoon was found associated with Western Neolithic ware and beaker material (Piggott, 1936a), and at Chelm's Combe, where a Neolithic occupation level yielding two fine bowls as well as split metapodial bone points was stratified below an Early Bronze Age hearth (Clay et al. 1926). The bowls in question relate not to the Hembury-ware group to the west, but rather have affinities with Windmill Hill ware and Wiltshire types, and emphasize the connexion between Wiltshire and the Mendips across the Frome Gap in the forest strip that Crawford demonstrated with regard to the distribution of the long barrows of the two regions and give point to the pottery imports from the Frome region noted from Windmill Hill.

Occasional small habitation sites, usually represented only by pottery finds, occur on the Wessex and Sussex downs, as for instance near Avebury (Piggott, 1937b), and at Michelmersh in Hampshire (Piggott, 1934a). At Corfe Mullen on the gravels near Wimborne (Calkin & Piggott, 1938) and at New Barn Down near the Harrow Hill flint mines in Sussex (Curwen, 1934b) oval hut-basements with characteristic pottery have been found: Hembury ware, with types closely allied to Maiden Castle, was found at the former site and forms similar to Whitehawk at the latter. In the predominantly Beaker settlement near the Easton Down flint mines what appears to be part of an earlier rectangular house, represented by stake-

1 E.g. as a shepherd's hut in a fifteenth-century MS. illumination reproduced in Hartley and Elliott's *Life and Work of the People of England* (1925), Pl. 20e.

holes and a bedding-trench for the wall, was found associated with sherds which may be Neolithic. Its resemblance to Danubian house-types has been noted above.

Of particular interest is a series of sites in low-lying situations, such as those at Southbourne, Hampshire (Calkin, 1947) or in the Thames valley at Marlow, where sherds of undecorated bowls and leaf-arrowheads have been recovered from the brick-earth pits (unpublished); at Selsey in Sussex, exposed by coastal erosion and yielding developed Abingdon ware (unpublished), and on the submerged land surface of the Essex coast, where both Abingdon ware and (more abundantly) plain wares occur (Warren et al. 1936). In East Anglia indeed two strains in the local Neolithic ceramic seem present. The earlier phase, characterized by undecorated ware allied to that of Lincolnshire and Yorkshire, is represented by surface discoveries in Norfolk, Suffolk and Cambridgeshire (Appendix A), on sand islands in the Fens at Mildenhall and on gravel at Chippenham (Leaf, 1935; 1940), and by the notable discovery of typical undecorated Windmill Hill sherds stratified in the Lower Peat on the slopes of an occupied sand island at Peacock's Farm near Ely, in an Atlantic horizon, commented upon in greater detail on p. 94. The specialized form of Abingdon ware which may be called the East Anglian bowl also appears, and is known from several sites, and although direct stratigraphical evidence of succession is not yet available, it seems likely that this represents a later intrusive element from the west into the East Anglian territory.

FLINT-AXE FACTORIES AND MINES

Introduction

As we have seen at an earlier stage, there is reason to think that the authors of the Windmill Hill culture organized in south-east England, perhaps on some form of Mesolithic basis, an industrial system whereby axes of flint could be manufactured and distributed in large numbers. This mass-production of an essential tool, and the segregation of certain areas as industrial centres, represents an important economic concept. In general, the Neolithic communities form self-sufficient units dependent on trade only for comparative luxuries, the needs of daily life being supplied by the individual peasant crafts of the farmers, potters or flint-knappers within the family or village group. But the limitation of the manufacture of a necessary product to a group of specialized workers implies a system of barter or trade and of long-range communication between the factories and their buyers. The mines and factories seem unlikely to be the result of even regular seasonal visits by agricultural villagers, for not only the high degree of mining skill shown by the galleried shafts, but the individual and economic process whereby axes were flaked from the rough suggest rather the work of full-time craftsmen skilled at their task and dependent on exchange of their finished products for the corn, skins, pottery or other articles which they needed but did not themselves produce. If we are correct in so interpreting the social status of the axe manufacturers, livelihood would have depended, not on their unaided efforts to wrest an existence from nature, but on the goodwill of prospective purchasers among their fellows, and would fore-shadow the beginnings of that interdependence of the members of the community usually heralded by the introduction of the specialized craft of metal-working.

Owing to the often elaborate methods of mining employed to extract the flint from the deeper seams in the chalk, the flint mines have in name dominated over their products, and tend, it seems, to be regarded as ends rather than means. It is important to realize that the mines were in reality ancillary to the chipping-floors for which they provided the raw material, and that such well-known sites as Cissbury or Grimes Graves were in reality axe factories on an equal footing with that at Graig Lwyd, and the technique employed at one must be considered in connexion with the other.

The inclusion of the flint-axe factories[1] as a component of the Windmill Hill culture is warranted, in my opinion, by a variety of reasons. Their re-markable concentration in Sussex in the same areas as the causewayed camps, which in part at least were recipients of their wares, makes it difficult to attribute them in that region to any rival culture, especially since that hypo-thetical culture is unrepresented by any other tangible relics (Map I, Fig. 1). Again, the technique of excavation of the camp (and long barrow) ditches is identical with that employed in the mine shafts, and the tools used (as will be seen in the section dealing with bone and antler types in Chapter III) are found to be of the same types in the camps and in the mines. The curious chalk cups form a connecting link the importance of which was stressed by Clark and myself in considering the question of the date of the English mines (Clark & Piggott, 1933), and scanty pottery finds point in the same direction. When allowance is made for the inevitable disparity between the material likely to characterize cattle enclosures and mining shafts, the re-semblances still remain more striking than the differences.

The question of the date of the English flint mines was for many years a matter of heated and often acrimonious discussion following the publica-tion of R. A. Smith's paper of 1912, in which a claim was put forward for a Palaeolithic date for the mines, based solely on the typology of the rough-outs and other incidental flintwork. The attempted application of this system to Grimes Graves in particular led to a long series of excavations and conse-quent reports and commentaries by half a dozen different hands, and a pure typological method was applied to the mining system as well as to the pro-ducts. Evidence from other mines in Sussex and elsewhere was largely

1 For documentation, see Appendix A (p. 382).

ignored, and even the publication of Warren's reports on the Graig Lwyd stone-axe factory, demonstrating clearly the place of the archaic types in the stages of manufacture of the finished axe (Warren, 1919; 1922) at a site which no one ventured to claim as Palaeolithic, seemed to have no effect upon the interpretation of the precisely similar types from the Norfolk mines. The unsatisfactory state of affairs led Clark and myself to review the question briefly in 1933, when we came to the conclusion that 'all the evidence points to a Neolithic date for the main flint-mining activity in Britain' and 'its inception seems indeed to be linked with the Windmill Hill culture' (Clark & Piggott, 1933, 182). It is important to note, however, that the mining activities continued on most flint-mine sites until the Early or even Middle Bronze Age.

The necessity for mining for flint is dictated by the geology of the Upper Chalk, in which flint nodules occur in horizontal seams separated by intervals of several feet of 'dead' chalk. Furthermore, the better nodules come from the lower seams (the 'floorstone' of the Brandon miners), and this fact, once appreciated, led to the development of the galleried pits in Sussex and Norfolk. Armstrong has suggested, with every show of probability, that the first intimation of flint seams occurring below the surface at Grimes Graves was afforded by outcrops exposed by accident on the slopes of valleys in the chalk (Armstrong, 1926, 101), and Curwen (1937a, 105) has pointed to the possibility of flint nodules being found accidentally in digging the ditches of camps or long barrows.

The distribution of the mines, then, is governed by the geological occurrence of Upper Chalk (the Middle and Lower Chalk containing no flint), and they have been recognized in Sussex, Surrey, the eastern border of Wessex, the southern Chilterns and Norfolk (Map I, Fig. 1). Since they form a homogeneous group it is convenient to deal with the features they share in common in general terms, drawing attention to specific instance where necessary.

Mining procedure and types of shafts

Since, as has been indicated above, the depth of the pit was largely if not entirely determined by the depth of the desired flint seam, the types of shafts driven into the chalk vary from the shallow open-cast pits of Harrow Hill to the 30 ft. deep shafts of Pits 1 and 2 at Grimes Graves (Fig. 7). Armstrong (1926) argued that the pits at the great mining centre of Grimes Graves were worked in a sequence from the side of the valley to the top of the slope, and correlated this not only with an evolution in mining technique from 'primitive' to galleried pits, but with a time-scale beginning in the Upper Palaeolithic and ending in the Late Neolithic—an interval which on the most conservative estimate would represent at least ten thousand years of sustained activity on the site. Armstrong's view was that his 'primitive' pits, with very slight undercutting at the base in search of the flint nodules, or none at all, were the first stages in a development scheme which was the product of an evolving cultural history (Armstrong, 1926). But unfortunately it cannot be proved that these simple pits are earlier in date than those with the 'advanced' system of radiating lateral galleries to follow the flint-seam, for they occur not only at Grimes Graves, but at Easton Down (where the mining certainly flourished mainly in Beaker times), at Blackpatch, where the maximum period of activity was the Early and Middle Bronze Age, and at Church Hill, Findon, with a Beaker cremation presumably of the final phase of the Early Bronze Age actually in one of the shafts. Stoke Down, also of this 'primitive' type, yielded an upper stone of a grain-rubber, so is at least not earlier than Neolithic. In all these sites, and in the 'primitive' pit area of Grimes Graves, the required flint was obtainable at a depth of some 10–15 ft., and it was evidently less labour to dig another pit rather than adopt the somewhat precarious method of cutting galleries. The famous Spiennes section shows admirably this gradation in type in response to the depth at which the flint seam lay. (Cf. Clark & Piggott, 1933, fig. 3.)

One point to which Armstrong has drawn attention is that the tools used in his 'primitive' pits are not the familiar pick of red-deer antler, but a type made from the leg-bones of oxen and described below, p. 82. Their segregation to the particular group of pits at Grimes Graves is peculiar, though not complete—they appear with antler-picks in the partially ex-cavated Pit 8 (Armstrong, 1926)—and the hollowed red-deer tibia 'hacked and scratched' and 'other split bones artificially hollowed in the same manner' from Pit 1, gallery 15 (A. E. Peake et al. 1915, 209) seem likely to be the type in question. In any case it is difficult to regard their absence or presence as having any strict chronological significance.

The galleried shafts which form so spectacular a feature of the mines at Grimes Graves, Cissbury or Harrow Hill seem to have been adopted when the flint seam was at such a depth that a considerable amount of 'dead work' had to be done before the flint was reached. It was therefore obviously easier to excavate lateral galleries following the seam than to sink another pit, and Armstrong's contention that these mines were a late type is to some degree confirmed by the inherent probability that the easier, more accessible seams would be worked first on any given site, and, as the shafts became crowded together (for the Neolithic conception of Cretaceous geology was most likely such that the fear of the complete disappearance of the flint seam would result in successive shafts being sunk as near previous successful mines as possible), galleries would become a necessity for the economic production of the material.

The system of making the galleries has been described by Curwen and others—it is interesting to note the difference of technique between the prehistoric mines and those recently worked at Brandon, in that in the modern galleries the 'floorstone' flint is worked out by tunnelling below the seam, but was dug from above in the ancient galleries although at Spiennes the flint was sometimes worked from below (cf. R. Clarke, 1935). Sometimes, as at Harrow Hill, galleries were made to work at two levels of flint nodules, and at Easton Down an unfinished shaft showed that a similar practice was intended in at least one instance there.

Access to the shafts was in some cases by steps cut in the chalk (as in the Grimes Graves 'primitive' pits), but in the deeper pits there must have been some form of ladder, either a notched tree-trunk or a rope. Interesting confirmation of the existence of such a ladder was found at Grimes Graves, where not only the skeletons of voles, but antlers gnawed by them were found in the galleries, and Andrews concluded from this that the voles could only have reached the galleries alive by running down some form of ladder, as a direct fall from the top of the pit would certainly have killed them. (Andrews in A. E. Peake *et al.* 1915.)

The tools used in the excavation of the pits are described below in Chapter III: in addition to the bone and antler picks, marks of chipped or polished flint or stone axes were found on the walls at Grimes Graves, Pits 1 and 2 (A. E. Peake *et al.* 1915; A. E. Peake, 1916, 305), and an actual polished axe of greenstone was found in 'Greenwell's Pit' at the same site, in one of the galleries.

As a mine shaft became worked out and additional pits were dug round about, the material derived from these was apparently dumped in the disused shaft, and a certain amount of occupation material has been found among the chalk rubble thus deposited, while occasional stadia in the process of infilling gave convenient opportunities for lighting fires or eating meals in the partially filled shafts. In the galleries themselves there is no trace of occupation in the normal sense, though antler-picks and other tools are found lying about, and occasional heaps of flint chippings indicating finer flaking being carried out, but this is exceptional. In an industrial site such as a mine it is not to be wondered at that no occupation material should occur, though the 1914 excavators of Grimes Graves seemed surprised at the miners' behaviour and ventured on the bold assumption that 'it is, of course, possible that they quitted the shafts at meal-times'. It seems conceivable.

The galleries were certainly in many instances lit artificially—not only have soot-marks been observed on the roofs, but charcoal indicating burnt-out torches occurs, while the chalk cups have often been explained as lamps, one at least showing sooting on the edge from such a use.

Finds other than antler or bone picks are rare in the shaft-filling—sherds occur in certain pits, notably at Cissbury, where a fragment of a carinated bowl was found (Clark & Piggott, 1933, fig. 6), and at Grimes Graves,

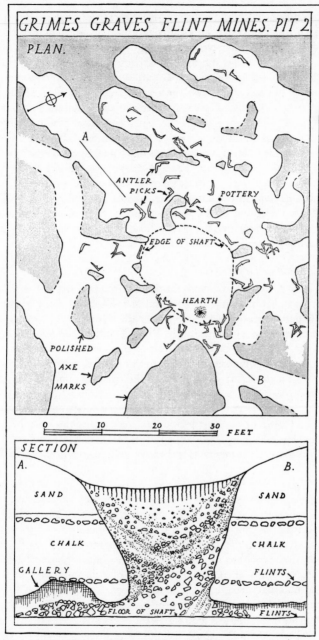

Fig. 7. (*After Armstrong.*)

where in addition to sherds of probably Western culture in Pits 1 and 2 sherds of cord-ornamented wares, probably some form of Peterborough ware, and of flat-bottomed vessels probably Early Bronze Age occurred (*ibid.* fig. 7), while in Pit 12 numerous Peterborough-ware sherds were found in an occupation site in the upper part of the filling (Armstrong, 1934). Carved pieces of chalk have also been recorded, including rounded balls, the chalk cups (at Grimes Graves not only in the galleried pits but in the 'primitive' pit, no. 4), and at Grimes Graves again a phallus (Greenwell, 1871). Scratchings on the walls were found at Grimes Graves and Cissbury, and at Harrow Hill they took the form of a 'chess-board' pattern similar to some from Whitehawk camp. Human remains were also found at Grimes Graves and Cissbury in circumstances described below (p. 49), and at Church Hill, Findon and Blackpatch, burials of Early Bronze Age date had been made in the filling of the shafts, while at the last site it was demonstrated by the excavator that even Middle Bronze Age barrows were being erected during the period of the mines' continued activity.

The ritual deposit at Grimes Graves

In Pit 15 at Grimes Graves an extraordinary ritual deposit was brought to light in 1939.[1] On a built-up pedestal of chalk blocks on the right-hand side of a gallery entrance was a carved chalk figurine of a grotesquely fat and pregnant woman 4¼ inches high (Pl. IV), and on the left side a carved chalk phallus, and chalk balls. In front of this remarkable fertility assemblage was an 'altar' composed of blocks of mined flint, arranged in triangular form and with a chalk cup at the base of the triangle opposite the goddess. Seven deer-antler picks were upon the 'altar'.

The excavator notes that Pit 15 was in fact very poor in flint deposits, and this obvious shrine of an Earth Goddess may represent an appeal to the chthonic powers for more abundant flint. At all events it constitutes one of the most dramatic documents of primitive religion in prehistoric Britain.

The chipping-floors and their products

Among the mine-shafts on all sites there appears to have been a large number of working places where the flint nodules were chipped into implements, and it is the flint types from the floors, notably those from Grimes Graves, that have been the main evidence used in the claim for a Palaeolithic date for the mines, either as a whole, or as an initial phase. The pseudo-Palaeolithic forms are, of course, the outcome of a chipping process whereby the axe was manufactured from the parent block; such objects as the rostro-carinate associated with a polished axe at Easton Down emphasize the fallacy of applying pure typology *in vacuo*.

1 I am greatly indebted to the excavator, Mr A. L. Armstrong, for providing me with details in advance of his full publication, and for permitting me to use a photograph of the figurine in Pl. IV.

It was the expressed opinion of the excavator of the Easton Down mines and floors that the whole indicates 'a celt and hand-axe industry' (Stone, 1931 *a*, 358), and the evidence from other sites points in the same direction. The abundance of material suitable for making smaller implements would obviously lead to the occasional manufacture at least of scrapers or other tools, and these do occur in the floors, but the vast bulk of the material must be interpreted as axes in the course of manufacture, or the waste from this process. Normally the floors show no stratification, save sometimes to overlap a filled-up mine-shaft, but at Grimes Graves a stratification was observed in one floor, no. 85, upon which much of the argument for a Palaeolithic date of the mining industry was based. It will be convenient to reserve discussion of this floor to the last, and to deal in general terms with the chipping-floors on all mine sites.

At Easton Down it was observed that 'Palaeolithic' forms were associated with true Neolithic-type axes on the floors, and a polished axe was found in floor B7 associated with a large 'rostro-carinate' (Stone, 1933*a*; 1935*b*). One floor (B3) was of great interest in suggesting that a regular sequence of manufacture was adopted, for one-half of the figure-of-eight shaped accumulation of material consisted of large flakes and no implements, the other of axes and much smaller chippings (Stone, 1931*b*). This suggestion of the segregation of one manufacturing stage to one floor or part of a floor has, as we shall see, important bearing on Grimes Graves. The Blackpatch floors yielded axes in all stages of manufacture and beneath Floor 2 was a cremated burial with beaker sherds, two axes and a pointed tool, while the floor was in turn overlaid by the material excavated from an adjacent shaft (Pull, 1932).

At Grimes Graves a number of floors were excavated by various hands over a period of some ten years, and the more significant finds may be detailed here. Chalk carvings included a cup from Floor 4 (Peake *et al.* 1915), and various rounded pieces and other forms from Floors 46 and 52 (Richardson, 1920; Kendall, 1920). A flake from a polished axe was found in Floor 16, and a broken polished greenstone axe in Floor 15 (A. E. Peake, 1919), while Floor 46 was evidently (like the Easton Down floor described above) devoted to an advanced stage of axe manufacture, 20 per cent of the recognizable artifacts being actual axes. The same floor produced three antler tines, and Floor 58 (Kendall, 1920) another, associated with a heap of minute flakes, indicating their use as pressure-flakers (as suggested independently by Curwen at Harrow Hill). A sherd of pottery similar in texture to those from the galleried pits, nos. 1 and 2, was found in Floor 46, and pottery was also found in Floor 16. This latter floor, however, raises difficulties. A stratification was observed in which a hearth lay upon the boulder-clay, apparently on a made chalk floor with at least one post-hole in it, regarded as belonging to a possible hut-site or wind-shelter. Beneath this hearth were found sherds of Early Bronze Age rusticated ware. In the original account of this floor (Peake, 1916, 275) the hearth and the chipping-floor were regarded as broadly contemporary, the hearth if anything being the earlier, but in a subsequent report (Peake, 1917, 412) in which the pottery is described and illustrated, this hearth is considered to be a later insertion, but no evidence for this change of opinion is given. The importance of the evidence from Floor 16 will be realized in dealing now with the stratification of the much discussed Floor 85.

This floor (Armstrong, 1922*a*; 1922*b*; 1924*b*; 1926) showed three distinct layers, distinguished as *A*, *B* and *C*. Floor 85*A* was the uppermost, and was a Late Bronze Age occupation-layer with hearth, pottery, and a pair of bronze tweezers. Beneath this, and separated by a sterile layer of sand, was 85*B*, a chipping-floor producing types indistinguishable from those from all the other floors of the site, and below this again, beneath another sand layer, was 85*C*. The flints from this lowest floor were described by Armstrong in successive reports as 'Mousterian', 'Abri Audi' and finally merely 'Upper Palaeolithic' in type, but in his original reports they had been stated to be exactly similar to the flint industry from Floors 15 and 16, the pottery and other artifacts from which have been described above. The changed opinion of the relation of the hearth to the latter floor has also been pointed out, so if flint typology is to be used at all in the determination of the age of Floor 85*C*, the evidence is certainly for a late date.

But there were further finds in the floor itself. There was a hearth, with willow charcoal, upon which was found the 'base of an earthenware vessel of about 9 in. diameter, made of coarse pottery', further sherds, two pressure-flakers of antler tines associated with minute chippings of flint, bones of horse and red deer, an arrowhead of the 'derived *petit-tranchet*' type (Armstrong, 1924*b*; Clark, 1935*a*, 52), and certain flints with naturalistic engravings of animals upon the crust. It was these remarkable pieces of art that suggested an Upper Palaeolithic date, to which the flints (or some of them) could be adjusted. The engravings are discussed in Chapter xi, where reasons are given for attributing them to the Secondary Neolithic cultures of partial Mesolithic heritage. Engraved lines upon flint crust in the same technique had been recognized previously in Floors 29 (Peake, 1919) and 16 (Peake, 1917), the latter also containing the debatable hearth and the Early Bronze Age pottery.

The products of the factories and their dispersal

The number of axes produced by the flint mines and factories must have been enormous, and it is impossible to determine the geographical limits within which they were traded. The twenty flint axes from Hembury, all of imported chalk flint, are probably to be regarded as flint-mine products; Cissbury-type axes certainly occurred at Whitehawk and Combe Hill, and in the hut at New Barn Down, but otherwise they have not been recorded in datable contexts. It is probable that most of the axes from the camps (e.g. at Windmill Hill and Maiden Castle) are ultimately of factory origin, and at the former site a few exceptionally large flakes and cores, from late in the site's occupation, seem likely to be mine products.

An important link was established by Bruce-Mitford (1938) between the factory-exports and the curious hoards of flint axes of which at least nine are known in England. He demonstrated that axes in a hoard from Peaslake (Surrey) were in all probability products from one of the Sussex factories, and he also compared the axes from these hoards to others, from sites such as Seamer Moor and Duggleby Howe, which produced axes of the type of those in a hoard at Canewdon, which in turn contained a chisel similar to that from the Bexley Heath hoard, an axe from which provides the best parallel to the polished axe from a chipping-floor at Easton Down. Seamer Moor and Duggleby Howe are funerary deposits of the northern province of the Dorchester culture, and are discussed in Chapter xi.

While holding its own in the regions of its origin, there is no evidence to show that the flint axe competed with those of stone in the regions of the west and north, but the adze of Wiltshire chert from Brecknockshire shows that occasional trade must have taken place, and the flint axe, one of a hoard of four, of which the remainder were of stone, from near Crickhowel in the same county, points in the same direction (Grimes, 1939a, 24, 25).

The Continental affinities of the British flint mines

As Clark and I showed several years ago (Clark & Piggott, 1933), the best analogies to the British flint mines are those of the Michelsberg culture in Belgium. To this observation there is little to add, save to point out that there are chronological difficulties in deriving the British from the Belgian mines, unless one assumes that flint mining in southern England was not an integral feature in the Windmill Hill culture as originally introduced from northern France. Two sites of major importance in the west, Hembury and Maiden Castle, were using axes of Cornish greenstones in addition to those of flint, and the production of axes of mined flint may be a relatively late feature in the development of the Windmill Hill culture.

THE USE OF STONE AXES (OTHER THAN FLINT) IN THE WINDMILL HILL CULTURE

As will be seen in the next chapter, there is an almost complete predominance of flint axes over those of other stones in sites attributable to the Windmill Hill culture. Two sites only, the causewayed camps of Hembury and Maiden Castle in Dorset, have yielded a large proportion of axes of igneous rocks, and of these, five from the former and six from the latter sites are of identical rock with an almost certain origin in Cornwall (Stone & Wallis, 1947).

Hembury and Maiden Castle are further linked by a distinctive pottery variant, described as Hembury ware in Chapter III, so that participation in a local west-country product is not surprising. The axes were presumably made in a factory site, as yet unidentified, but similar to those worked in Wales and the Lake District in later Neolithic times, and discussed in Chapter v. In view of the mixture of cultures at Grimes Graves the two axes of igneous rock from this site, referred to above, are likely to be attri-butable to the Secondary Neolithic cultures.

RELIGION AND THE DISPOSAL OF THE DEAD

Evidence for the spiritual culture of the Windmill Hill folk is meagre save for the long-barrow evidence, discussed below, but there are certain objects suggesting ritual employment from the settlements, and a few burials which can conveniently be described before the evidence of collective burial in unchambered long barrows is considered.

It will be seen in Chapter III that chalk carvings of phallic form have been found in the Windmill Hill culture (Fig. 14), and these, with the more direct Grimes Graves evidence, afford some evidence for fertility rites. Parallels for such representations are rare in the Neolithic cultures of the Continent, but in the Cortaillod culture are small bone objects which Vouga considered as possible statuettes[1] (1934, pl. XVIII, no. 3) but which are usually classed as pendants (von Gonzenbach, 1950, pl. II, no. 18). These may, however, be phallic, and a precise parallel to the tip of such an object, also in bone, comes from The Trundle and was regarded by the excavator as a phallus (Fig. 14, no. 11). Elsewhere, phalli seem unknown, and their presence in the Windmill Hill culture is of some importance in determining its origins. Childe has said, in discussing phalli from Troy and elsewhere, that they are symbols of an Anatolian cult strange to the Mediterranean, and their complete absence in the collective tombs of Western Europe, where ritual ornament seems to be dominated by the magic eyes of the 'dolmen goddess' may be significant, the more so since the decorative motifs of the great Western ceramic group of channelled ware have a source in common with these megalithic 'owl-face' carvings (J. Hawkes, 1939b), and the distinction of the Windmill Hill culture from this complex, which as we shall see is suggested on grounds of pottery typology, might receive support from this evidence of a differing religious background.

The figurines in chalk from Windmill Hill and Maiden Castle, (Fig. 14), described below, are best paralleled (in clay) from Fort Harrouard, but with a possibly Neolithic example from La Grotte Nicolas, Gard (Déchelette, 1908, 603), they do not seem to be known elsewhere in the French Neolithic, and the decorated Iberian idols of stone or bone belong to a separate art

---

1 Presumably in the style of the Amratian tusk-figurines (cf. Childe, 1934, pl. va).

style. The eastern Mediterranean seems the most likely area to consider for origins. The Grimes Graves figurine, however, has its best parallels in the well-known Upper Palaeolithic series.

Disposal of the dead: casual deposits

In the absence of temples and distinctive cult-objects, the most important pointer to the religious ideas of a people is to be found in the methods of burial and the attitude adopted towards the dead. From the camps comes important evidence which suggests that the bodies of the dead were not always regarded with the respect that demands burial of the corpse, but may be taken to hint strongly at cannibalism.

At Windmill Hill fragments of human bones, including the skulls of two children, were found scattered among the occupational debris in the ditches; at Whitehawk similar fragments, many of children, occurred, and at one point a remarkable collection of human bones (mainly skull fragments) representing two young males, one individual in the teens, a boy of c. twelve years and a child of c. six years, was found by a hearth, three skull fragments being charred by the fire. At Knap Hill a human lower jaw was found detached in the silt of the ditch, at Maiden Castle and at Hambledon Hill fragments of crania, and at Maiden Bower a 'broken-up human skeleton' is recorded from the ditch of the Neolithic camp. This feature is paralleled at Fort Harrouard, where Philippe (1927, 138–65) records fragmentary human bones, almost invariably skull fragments, from no less than twenty out of the thirty-seven hearths excavated, and equally divided between the Lower and Upper Neolithic horizons, and in the Cortaillod culture at Port Conty, where Vouga (1934, 53) notes the occurrence in his Lower Neolithic level of occasional scattered human remains, of which the long bones were all broken as if to extract the marrow. Cranial amulets, not the product of trephination, also occurred.

From the English flint mines, too, comes evidence of the casual disposal of the dead. Both at Cissbury (Lane-Fox, 1875) and at Grimes Graves (Peake et al. 1915) a girl's body had apparently been thrown in with the rubble filling the shaft, and the latter site also yielded fragmentary skulls and a broken fibula in the filling of two other mines (Pits 1 and 12) (Armstrong, 1934, 385). In shaft 4 at Blackpatch a lower jaw and a femur, representing two individuals, were found (Pull, 1932, 56), while finally, at Grimes Graves a 'hand-pick' of a type discussed above was found to have been made from a human femur (Armstrong, 1923, 121).

It is difficult to escape from the conclusion that the Windmill Hill folk in England, in common with their Continental relatives in the Western Neolithic, practised some form of cannibalism, utilitarian or ritual, while the abundance of skulls represented may point to its sometimes at least taking the form of head-hunting. The custom may have its roots in the

Palaeolithic, with Neanderthal examples, and probably in the Mousterian at Krapina (Déchelette, 1908, 110), in the Aurignacian at Vistonice (Childe, 1929 *a*, 14), and in the Upper Palaeolithic again in Belgium. Clark (1936 *a*, 128) quotes this last example in connexion with the fragmentary human bones found with the occupational debris in Maglemose sites which seem to point to the same conclusion, and a full study has more recently appeared on cannibalism in the Danish Stone Age (Degerbøl, 1941).

There appears to be one clear instance of ritual cannibalism in England, that of the remarkable burial in the 'Long Mound' at Maiden Castle (Wheeler, 1943). Here a mound 1,790 ft. long and 65 ft. wide, flanked by two continuous quarry-ditches, overlay the ditch of the Neolithic camp, but yielded pottery indistinguishable from that of the primary occupation. At its eastern end were found pits and post-holes and three burials on the old surface, two of children and the third a young man 'who had been systematically dismembered immediately after death. The bones bore many axe-marks, and the whole body had been cut up as by a butcher for the stew-pot. The skull had been hacked into pieces as though for the extraction of the brain but, so far as could be seen . . . all parts were present. Save where they have been hacked off, the limbs were still in articulation, as were the divided halves of the spine. The impression given . . . was that the body had been cooked and eaten' (*P.P.S.* III, 440; and Wheeler, 1943, *passim*). The problems raised by the relation of this sacrificial burial and those of the two children to the 'Long Mound' are discussed below.

Single burials

Apart from burials in earthen long barrows there are a few instances which go to show that an individual burial rite, sometimes near the dwelling-place, was practised. The first of these burials is that from Pangbourne, Berks (Piggott, 1929). This was unfortunately dug up by workmen, but the whole of the finds were rescued, consisting of the skeleton of an aged female, a deer-antler broken from the skull, ribs of deer and a pig's molar, and the fragments of a large bowl in the Abingdon style. The antler showed no obvious signs of wear, and may have been a hoe (appropriate to a woman) rather than a pick.

From the causewayed camps come a series of burials. At Windmill Hill the body of a microcephalic dwarf had been buried in the first foot or so of primary rubble of the outer ditch; the body lay on its right side, the legs were lightly flexed and the hands on the knees. There were no grave-goods. At Whitehawk two burials were found in the occupation layer of the third ditch: one, a young female, lay crouched on the left side, and was accompanied by an *Echinocorys scutatus* fossil; the other burial consisted of a young woman crouched on the right side and a child of a few weeks old, in an oval grave measuring 5 ft. by 1 ft. 6 in., surrounded by large chalk blocks.[1] There were two rough chalk pendants, half an ox radius and an *Echinocorys* fossil as grave-goods. A similar oval grave set round with chalk blocks was found containing the skeleton of a young male, 16 ft. deep in the filling of a flint-mine shaft at Cissbury (Harrison, 1876*b*). Another burial at Whitehawk lay on the old surface within the camp, and was of a middle-aged male, crouched and with several mussel-shells at his head. The skeleton of an adult male with a leaf-arrowhead in his ribs and accompanied by the skeleton of a child found in the primary filling of the Wor Barrow ditch is presumably a burial analogous to those from the camps (Pitt-Rivers, 1898, 63).

Burials within the settlement areas are known from Western Neolithic sites on the Continent—at Fort Harrouard (Philippe, 1927, 111) and in sites of the Michelsberg culture, including the type-station itself (Childe, 1929*a*, 182; Buttler, 1938, 79). They also occur in the Breton Tardenoisean at Téviec and Hoëdic (Péquart *et al.* 1937).

At Blackpatch, in addition to burials of Early and Middle Bronze Age date, Pull excavated two round barrows in the mine area which appear to be Neolithic. His Barrow 3 had been made on top of a filled-in mine-shaft before silt had formed on top of the rubble, and contained a platform of flint nodules, on which lay the skeleton of a young man crouched on the left side. Grave-goods around the body comprised a leaf-arrowhead, axes and an ovate and chopper of mine workmanship, a boar's tusk and teeth of ox and pig. There was a second skeleton by the first, a crouched female, and a cremation had been scattered over both. The barrow had been made of chalk rubble with an inner core of knapping debris. A second barrow (no. 12) had again been built on unweathered shaft-filling, and contained a crouched skeleton which had been disturbed by an intrusive burial of a brachycephalic individual, presumably of the Early Bronze Age. (Pull, 1932, 69–72.)

What may be another Neolithic interment is that from Barrow 13, Crichel Down, Dorset, where a crouched skeleton lay on a bed of flints on a natural knoll of chalk thinly covered with earth and stones. By the ribs was a leaf-arrowhead, and at the feet was a figure-of-eight hole cut in the chalk which probably held a post or posts. The significance of this post-hole will be apparent in dealing with the examples described below. (S. & C. M. Piggott, 1944.)

Two burials may now be considered together. At Whitehawk the burial of a child of *c.* seven years was found 'curled up' in a deep hole, 4 ft. deep and 2 ft. 6 in. in diameter, accompanied by a chalk slab with rough incisions. The conditions suggested to the excavators that the hole held a wooden post at the foot of which the child was buried, presumably as a foundation

---

[1] This burial in an oval grave surrounded by large stones suggests comparison with that of a dwarf in the ditch at Avebury (Gray, 1934, 145), presumably Early Bronze Age in date.

sacrifice. Something of a parallel existed on the same site, where the dismembered skeleton of a roe-deer was found at the bottom of a similar
(though shallower) post-hole in the fourth ditch, but there is also another
human burial of Neolithic date, in Dorset, which seems analogous. On
Handley Hill Pitt-Rivers excavated a pit 4 ft. deep and 8 ft. in diameter,
with a circular hole in one side of the bottom, 1 ft. 6 in. deep and 2 ft. 6 in.
in diameter. In the main pit was a disarticulated human skeleton, with
numerous fragments of a large Windmill Hill ware bowl, and the whole
arrangement suggests that a post had been set up (its base in the smaller
hole) and the burial placed beside it. (Pitt-Rivers, 1898, 49; Piggott, 1936 b.)
A somewhat analogous but incomplete burial, but without evidence of a
post, was that nearby at Rushmore Park (Pitt-Rivers, 1898, 42) where a pit
contained part of the pelvis and fragments of the femora of a small individual, associated with a chipped flint axe. These burials might possibly be
compared to the Michelsberg pit-graves (Buttler, 1938, fig. 30).

These indications that standing posts may have formed cult-objects to
the causewayed camp folk are important, both in their relation to the posts
standing at the end of certain south English long barrows and to the whole
question of foundation burials in Neolithic times, for there seems little doubt
that, if the burials in question, of humans or animals, were associated with
ritual posts, they served the purpose of foundation sacrifices of victims whose
souls were intended to hold up the posts. Such foundation sacrifices are
known in megalithic tombs, and the whole question has been discussed by
Scott (1932, 208).

COLLECTIVE BURIAL IN EARTHEN LONG BARROWS

Introduction

By far the most important group of burials associated with the Windmill
Hill culture, however, are those beneath the well-known long barrows of
Wessex, Sussex, Lincolnshire and Yorkshire.[1] These burial mounds are a
conspicuous feature of field archaeology on the chalk hills of Dorset, Wiltshire, Hampshire and Sussex, where their distribution is approximately
coincident with the causewayed camps and the flint mines (Map II,
Fig. 1), while north of the Wash, they again occur on the chalk uplands
of Lincolnshire and Yorkshire (Fig. 15). The southern English long
barrows, now under discussion, are normally elongated mounds, often
of great size and frequently between 200 and 300 ft. long, containing
collective burials grouped near one end (usually the larger, and easternmost)
and with remains of internal structures of wood or turf which in no instance
can be interpreted as the equivalent of the stone-built burial vault of the
normal long-chambered cairn of the Severn-Cotswold or Clyde-Carlingford

1 Documentation in Appendix A (p. 382).

type. There has been a tendency to include all long barrows or cairns under the general heading of megalithic monuments, but it seems likely that this indiscriminate gathering together of all long mounds associated with collective burials into one category has in fact confused the issue. As we shall see, although definitely allied one to another, the only real features linking the earthen long-barrow group with the chambered long cairns are a common elongated plan, a similarity (though by no means an identity) in the idea of communal burial, and the concentration of these burials towards one end of the structure. But the chambered-tomb practice of successive interments in one family vault to which recurrent access can be gained is not only absent but precluded by the very construction of the barrows, and evidence of the equally characteristic elaborate forecourt ritual is again missing. In fact, while the unchambered long barrows have important points in common with the chambered long cairns, these similarities must be regarded as the outcome of common ancestry rather than the derivation of the earthen barrows from megalithic long cairns—a sequence more than once put forward.

In the past the view has often been taken that the lack of stone chambers and other similar constructional features in the vast majority of southern English long barrows is due solely to the geological conditions imposed by building the monuments on chalk or gravel soils, where stone suitable for building burial chambers would be unobtainable. Such a view would imply a derivation of the earthen long barrows of Wessex and Sussex from tomb-building communities established in naturally stony areas. There could be two such areas as claimants as the homeland of the earthen long barrow, either the Severn-Cotswold region, or some megalithic culture of north-west France where the Severn-Cotswold complex itself may have had its origin.

The chronological and typological difficulties which a derivation of the earthen long barrows from the Severn-Cotswold long cairn area would involve have been pointed out more than once (e.g. Piggott, 1934 b; 1935) and are further referred to in Chapter v. The alternative explanation would be to assume that a chambered-tomb culture was introduced into southern England, represented by such coastal monuments of local sarsen as the Grey Mare and the Hell Stone in Dorset, and then to see in the remaining unchambered barrows a degeneration in areas where building stone was not available. Here again, as we shall see, the internal structure of the excavated barrows does not in fact suggest any derivation from stone-built prototypes.

A dual origin for the long barrows on the one hand, and the long-chambered cairns on the other, is more likely, with features in common due to a shared ancestry, and the evidence in fact suggests that the unchambered long barrow is a type of burial monument which is not a second-best substitute for a megalithic tomb, but is a distinct type of burial within the British branch of the Western Neolithic cultures. As we shall see, there is some reason to visualize the Wessex and Sussex earthen long barrows as in part at least deriving from similar tombs in Brittany, and reaching England in close connexion with, if not as an integral part of, the mainstream of Neolithic culture to southern Britain. In such a position, the occurrence of this type of tomb not only in the south but in such regions as Lincolnshire would take its place as part of the basic cultural elements diffused over the whole of the area of settlement.

Distribution

The main facts of the distribution of these non-megalithic long barrows have more than once been discussed (e.g. Piggott, 1935) and it has been stressed that their incidence in general terms closely follows the distribution-pattern of causewayed camps in southern England. In Sussex this virtual identity of distribution is particularly striking, and it has been used as an argument in favour of making a cultural link between the barrows and the camps. In the westerly regions around Hembury and Haldon no earthen barrows are recorded (although they may yet be discovered), but over the whole of Dorset, Wiltshire, and Hampshire, the barrows are thickly dotted, with a total of some 170 examples (Crawford, 1932). They follow the line of the chalk south-eastwards into Sussex and north-eastwards along the Chilterns to such outlying examples as Therfield Heath and that at West Rudham and other probable examples in Norfolk. In Kent, Julliberries Grave at Chilham is a barrow which excavation has shown to be of Wessex type, and it must be regarded as allied to the non-megalithic group under discussion rather than to the Medway megalithic culture which, as we shall see, forms a 'Nordic' intrusion into the southern English Neolithic cultures. The long barrow at Badshot on the western end of the Surrey Hog's Back chalk ridge may provide a link intermediate between the Wessex and Kent tombs. In southern Dorset the earthen long barrows impinge on the area of the chambered long cairns of Clyde-Carlingford derivation (The Grey Mare and her Colts) and in north Wiltshire overlap with the southern-most extension of the Cotswold long-chambered cairns, represented for instance by the West Kennet barrow.

In general the barrows are built upon the chalk uplands, although a re-markable example at Holdenhurst lay on the valley gravel of the Stour near its junction with the Avon at Christchurch, only 35 ft. above the present sea-level. While relatively isolated barrows occur, often of large size, there is a tendency to form groups which may sometimes be related to springs and natural water-sources in a similar manner to the chambered cairns of the Cotswolds, and as we have seen, there is some reason for supposing that settlements may also have existed in the valleys and at spring-heads. In Cranborne Chase the concentrations round the headwaters of the Allen and the seven barrows ringing round the great springs on Rockbourne Down, may be noted, and we shall see something similar with regard to the siting of the Lincolnshire barrows. Barrows not infrequently appear in pairs (for instance Gussage in Dorset, Barton Stacey in Hampshire, Stoughton in Sussex) in a manner comparable with both the Cotswold and the Clyde-Carlingford cairns. Like these, too, they never occur in regular cemeteries or groups. The concentration on the chalk lands of Wessex and Sussex affords an interesting contrast to the distribution of the Bronze Age round barrows in the same regions, where, as Grinsell's detailed surveys are showing with increasing emphasis, the open heathland is studded with barrows to a degree rivalling the chalk. The changed economy that has been suggested for the British Bronze Age, with the cattle-breeding so dominant in the Neolithic falling away in favour of hunting (and a consequent utilization of otherwise unproductive heathland) might perhaps be invoked to account for this difference of distribution in the tombs of the two cultures.

External features

The unchambered long barrows were first discussed as a type separate from, though allied to, the chambered long cairns, by Thurnam in his classic study of 1868, which analysed the evidence obtained from the excavations of Colt Hoare and himself. Though these excavations and their record fail lamentably to satisfy even the most moderate demands of the modern archaeologist, it is possible to extract a certain amount of detailed information which can be set in its proper place by comparison with the more recently and more satisfactorily excavated barrows, of which we can enumerate five in Wessex, one in Surrey, one in Kent and a most interesting example showing cremation at West Rudham in Norfolk. In addition the Lincolnshire barrow of Giants' Hills, Skendleby, provides valuable comparative data which may be used to illuminate the southern English group now under discussion.

In external appearance there is considerable variation in the size and proportions of the mound, which may range from nearly 400 ft. to 100 ft. or less in length, while attention should be drawn to the type of monument, represented by two examples, which may be in some way allied, already mentioned earlier in this chapter and named by Wheeler a 'bank-barrow'. At Maiden Castle the excavated example reached the fantastic length of three-quarters of a mile, and was evidently devoted to ritual performances not only directed towards simple burial.

In the normal long barrow the material of the mound was provided by flanking quarry-ditches which may sometimes continue in a U-shaped plan around one end of the mound, or even (as at Wor Barrow) form a discontinuous oval completely enclosing the inner area, the ditch being interrupted with causeways in the manner of that of a causewayed camp. Frequently the mound is sharply ridged along its axis, and tends to be higher at one end, which often has a vaguely easterly orientation. A well-marked berm is sometimes left between the inner lip of the ditch and the skirts of the mound, and in certain instances (e.g. at Thickthorn and Wor Barrow) this berm is sloping, and would appear to have been so designed to give an appearance of added height to the mound. It does not seem possible to distinguish regional types, although there is a tendency for the U-shaped ditch to occur frequently in Cranborne Chase, and the very large barrows seem confined to Wiltshire and Dorset and to be absent from Sussex.

Internal construction

The most constant feature observed within the excavated barrows is the frequent presence of an inner core of turf, forming the lower and central parts of the mound, which is otherwise of chalk rubble derived from the ditches. This turf layer presumably represents the first material stripped in making the ditches, and so far as can be judged from the unsatisfactory accounts of the early excavations, was not in these observed to take any definite form other than a central longitudinal heap, and this is confirmed by the excavations made more recently at Therfield Heath (Phillips, 1935*a*), Julliberries Grave (Jessup, 1939) and West Rudham (Hogg, 1940). The Holdenhurst barrow (Fig. 8) was found to have been constructed in its first stage of a series of roughly conical dumps of top-soil piled along the axis and later covered by the gravel from lower in the ditch.

At Thickthorn (Fig. 8) the interior turf structure was found to have been arranged in a more definite plan (Drew & Piggott, 1936). At the eastern end turf had been built up into two short parallel walls, with vertical inner faces 3 ft. high and sloping outer surfaces, which ran across the axis of the barrow near its eastern end with a space of 6 ft. between them. Within this oblong space so formed the interments were naturally expected, but nothing was found except a small heap of turf centrally placed within the enclosure, which was filled with compact chalk rubble. Elsewhere in the barrow turf was found in heaps of varying dimensions, but no similar regularity of structure was observable. Turf was also extensively employed in the Holdenhurst barrow, in the form of a built wall of sods forming a rectangular revetment to the entire mound measuring 240 by 35 ft. and unbroken by any entrance (Fig. 8 and Piggott, 1937*c*).

At Wor Barrow (Pitt-Rivers, 1898) the idea of a rectangular enclosure again found expression, but here the area was delimited by a fence of small posts set in a bedding-trench packed with flint nodules and enclosing an area 90 by 35 ft., with an entrance to the east (Fig. 8 and Pl. II). This enclosure was set well within the skirts of the mound, and cannot have originally enclosed it in the manner of the much stouter palisade of Giants' Hills described in the next chapter. Nor can it have formed the walling of a roofed chamber, as has often been suggested, as the posts are too small to take the thrust of the roof necessitated by this hypothesis. It can only have

55

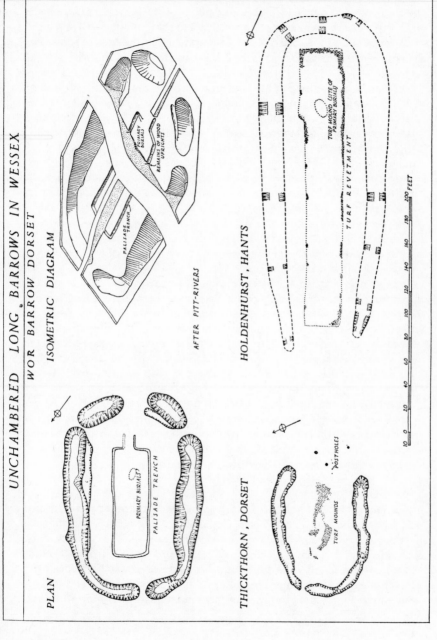

UNCHAMBERED LONG BARROWS IN WESSEX

WOR BARROW DORSET

ISOMETRIC DIAGRAM

PRIMARY BURIALS

REMAINS OF WOOD UPRIGHTS

PALISADE TRENCH

AFTER PITT-RIVERS

PLAN

PRIMARY BURIALS

PALISADE TRENCH

THICKTHORN, DORSET

TURF MOUNDS

POSTHOLES

HOLDENHURST, HANTS

TURF MOUND (SITE OF PRIMARY BURIALS)

TURF REVETMENT

10 0 20 40 60 80 100 120 140 160 180 200 FEET

Fig. 8.

constituted an open enclosure, within which the funeral ritual was enacted and the dead finally deposited beneath a mound of turves towards its eastern end. Plate II *a* is from an unpublished photograph of Pitt-Rivers's 1894 excavations and shows clearly the deliberate filling of the enclosed area, and the construction of the remainder of the barrow with more than one old turf-line.

Timber was also utilized in connexion with an important ritual feature which occurs in several barrows, namely a standing post or posts towards or at the eastern end. Post-holes implying such timber uprights were found on the causeway at Thickthorn (three) and one at Badshot (Keiller & Piggott, 1939) and within the mound at Durrington (Hoare, 1812, 170) and Wexcombe (Piggott, 1937*a*, 455). This feature was represented in stone in a barrow near Warminster, where within the mound 'at the south end was a sarsen stone five feet high, terminating almost in a point, and placed in an upright position' (Hoare, 1812, 65), and the large conical sarsen set at the south side of the entrance to the Wor Barrow enclosure may be an analogous cult object. Bowls Barrow (Wiltshire) contained a central spine of large stones, which included the well-known block of Presely 'Blue Stone' identical with those at Stonehenge.

It is possible that some of the 'ritual holes' frequently recorded from near the burials in the Wessex barrows may have been post-holes, but the majority seem to have served some other unexplained purpose connected with the funerary rites. They have been discussed by Phillips (1936) in connexion with a Lincolnshire barrow: some ten or twelve occurrences have been noted in Wessex (Thurnam, 1868, 181; Pitt-Rivers, 1898; Piggott, 1937*b*, 7) and one was found in the Kent barrow of Julliberries Grave (Jessup, 1939). The pits beneath the Thickthorn barrow are in no way connected with the foregoing, though this was not made clear in the excavation report: they were long anterior to the construction of the barrow and were sealed by a thick turf-line, while the presence in them of pine charcoal, taken in connexion with a microlith found in the turf-line nearby, suggests a Mesolithic date (Drew & Piggott, 1936).

The burials

The burials beneath the barrows are normally concentrated in a restricted area towards the higher end, usually on the old ground surface, exceptionally in graves (e.g. Cherhill 1*A*, and Warminster 6).[1] While more than one individual is usually represented, it is important to note that single skeletons were found in at least four Wiltshire barrows (Figheldean 31, Heddington 3, Warminster 6 and Winterbourne Stoke 1), while at Tilshead 2 in the same county a group of three individuals was found at one end

[1] The Wiltshire barrows are numbered according to Mrs Cunnington's list (M. E. Cunnington, 1914) where full references are given.

of the barrow and a single interment at the other. The individual skeletons are recorded as being either very considerably flexed and lying on their sides, or in a disarticulated condition compressed into a small space (e.g. Figheldean 31).

Multiple burials are the more normal feature, ranging in the recorded instances from two to twenty-five individuals. The excavation reports of Colt Hoare leave much to be desired, but he frequently records that the skeletons were 'lying promiscuously in several directions' or 'strangely huddled together' (Hoare, 1812, 102). The somewhat more precise observations and records of Thurnam, however, throw valuable light on the method of deposition of the bodies in the barrows dug by him. At Tilshead East the remains of eight individuals were packed together in a space of less than 4 ft. in diameter and 1 ft. 6 in. thick, and at Norton Bavant eighteen or more skeletons were represented by a mass of bones of the same thickness and measuring 3 by 8 ft. In both instances the phenomena present could only be explained by assuming the individuals to have been in a skeletal condition at the time of the building of the barrow, and at Norton Bavant it was noted that many limb bones were absent. But it was in his re-excavation of Boles Barrow that Thurnam obtained the clearest evidence of individuals in a dismembered and skeletal condition. Between twenty and twenty-five bodies were represented in a disordered pile of bones, and of the skulls, one had attached to it a neck vertebra cut in two, implying decapitation, while three skulls were found *in situ* resting on the lower mandible and the occiput, showing that they were separate from the body though complete with both jaws when so placed. On the other hand a lower mandible was found with the condyle encircled by a vertebra, implying that it was detached and fleshless before burial. To this evidence may be added that from Wor Barrow, where, of the six skeletons found together, three were articulated and flexed, three in a dismembered condition, and comparisons may be drawn with the Giants' Hills barrow in Lincolnshire. Pitt-Rivers (1898, 82) noted that of the six burials in Wor Barrow three were 'put in as bones and not in sequence, the limb-bones being laid out by the sides of the skulls' whereas the remainder were crouched. This arrangement is clearly seen in his photographs (*ibid*. pl. 256) and recalls the circumstances of the burials in the Lanhill megalithic chamber described below (p. 139).

In certain instances (Bratton 1, Knook 2, Tilshead 1 and 2 and Winterbourne Stoke 53) the bones were burnt or partially burnt, in a less complete manner than the typical cremation of the Middle Bronze Age. At Tilshead 2 the burning may have been performed *in situ*, for it appears that the charred bones were found on a pavement of burnt flints, as occurred at Winterbourne Stoke. Analogous flint pavements are recorded in inhumation barrows from Heytesbury 1 and Knook 2, and a floor of rammed marl was found beneath the interments in Warminster 1. In addition, cremation may have taken place at Sherrington and Murtry Hill in Somerset, but the only recently excavated long barrow with cremation rites is that at West Rudham in Norfolk (Hogg, 1940). Here, owing to the acid sandy soil, all traces of the actual bones had vanished, but the bodies appear to have been burned *in situ* on a prepared platform of gravel towards one end of the mound. Hogg has drawn attention to the similarities between this and the Wessex cremations on pavements described above, and in a valuable discussion of long-barrow cremations makes an important distinction between these 'platform cremations' and the 'flue cremations' of the Yorkshire long barrows described in Chapter IV. He points out that the presence of the platform type of cremation at West Rudham links it typologically with the Wessex rather than the Yorkshire Neolithic culture: there was no evidence from pottery or other artifacts.

A point of some interest is that in five of the barrows (Norton Bavant 13, Tilshead 2, Boyton 1, Heytesbury 1 and Knook 2), the interments were under a small cairn of stones and flints, a feature represented by a heap of turves at Wor Barrow, Heddington 3 and Holdenhurst.

Two sites may conveniently be referred to here, though they are not long barrows in the sense of the examples described above. The Winterbourne Stoke 'oval' barrow appears from Thurnam's description to have been two contiguous barrows, one covering a Beaker interment and the other a single burial with four large leaf- or lozenge-arrowheads. A similar group of flint arrowheads came from a barrow on Pistle Down, Edmonsham, Dorset, described as 'oblong', but no burial seems to have been recognized by the excavators, for the excavation was declared to be 'without any result as regards the deposit; four flint arrowheads being all that was discovered'. These two barrows, which may date in the Early Bronze Age, are mentioned here since they are frequently included in long-barrow discussion, and since the leaf-arrowheads give them some claim to be regarded as Neolithic.

To summarize the foregoing evidence, the burials in the unchambered long barrows are normally multiple, a large proportion of the skeletons being found in a disarticulated or confused condition, and others in a normal form. Some form of incomplete burning was sometimes practised, and the burials frequently lay beneath a small cairn of stones or sods towards one end of the mound. As we shall see in a subsequent section of this chapter (p. 61), the deposition of grave-goods was exceptional. The problem raised by the burials in the unchambered barrows is that the occurrence of articulated and disarticulated skeletons is similar to the circumstances in a chambered cairn, to which periodical access could be obtained, by successive burials of members of a family or dynasty, with the skeletons of the previous occupants of the tomb pushed aside in disorder to make way for the latest tenant. But in an unchambered barrow, once the great mound was cast up from the flanking quarry-ditches, access to the burial area would clearly be impossible. Two alternatives are open, the first involving re-burial, with the earlier interments being preserved in some repository other than the barrow until some reason prompted their transfer, to take their place with those most recently deceased in the tomb newly prepared for the permanent reception of them all.

There are of course good anthropological parallels for such a practice, and it is not impossible that it may have taken place in some instances. But a recent suggestion based on new structural evidence provides a second alternative which has much to recommend it, and which has the advantage of bringing unchambered long-barrow ritual into line with that normal to collective chambered tombs as a whole (Atkinson, 1951). Among the complex of ritual sites at Dorchester-on-Thames, described in detail in Chapter xi, Atkinson excavated a large rectangular enclosure delimited by a ditch which can have supplied no more than an internal bank—it was not the quarry-ditch for a long barrow, although its proportions and its Neolithic date suggested the closest affinities to such a monument. A comparable enclosure, unexcavated and now nearly obliterated by ploughing, exists on Normanton Down, Wilts, and Atkinson points out that the published plan and section of Wor Barrow in Dorset strongly suggests that this classic long barrow at some stage of its construction consisted of such an enclosure, later almost entirely destroyed in the making of the great quarry-ditch for the mound (Fig. 8).

Now we have seen that at Wor Barrow the burials, of three articulated and three disarticulated skeletons, lay under a mound of turf within a palisade enclosure of rectangular plan, later covered by the mound of the barrow. If we assume, as we may with reason, that this was a sacred funerary enclosure, we may go further, and see in the turf mound the collapsed remains of a small mortuary-house of sods within which successive burials were made from time to time, the earlier occupants being in due course packed away with the limb-bones laid out by the skulls in the manner recorded by Pitt-Rivers, and completely comparable with the practice seen in chambered tombs such as that of Lanhill (Chapter v). The curious turf structure at Thickthorn, the mound at Holdenhurst, and the less well-recorded remains of turf in the barrows excavated in the nineteenth century, would all fall into place as representatives of similar temporary mortuary-houses, as would the arrangement at Giants' Hills in Lincolnshire described in Chapter iv.

The unchambered long barrows, in fact, may have to be interpreted as without burial chambers only in so far as these were of impermanent construction and were never intended to remain open and accessible after the mound was actually thrown up. We would have to visualize the construction of a long barrow as consisting of two main events, separated by a long interval of time. The first would be the delimiting of a sacred funerary enclosure by timber, turf or a bank and ditch, or these in combination. In a small mortuary-house (or perhaps in some instances simply on the ground, without covering) the bodies of successive members of the family or clan entitled to burial in this manner would be laid successively, in the tradition of collective burial common to the chambered tombs of stone construction. Then, for some reason unknown to us, burial at this place would cease, as burial certainly ceased in a like manner in chambered tombs. The second part of the funeral ceremony would then take place, involving the piling up of the long barrow itself in such a way that the burials were rendered inviolate—the mound in fact being the counterpart of the forecourt and entrance blocking that sealed the chambered tomb after the last burials had been deposited.

It is interesting to note that age and sex vary considerably among the burials, and the few recorded instances are given in Table I:

TABLE I

Site	Adults (sex un-specified)	Males	Females	Children	Total persons
Bishops Cannings 65	.	2	.	2	4
Boyton 1	7	.	.	1	8
Heytesbury	.	20 (approx.)	.	4	24
Norton Bavant 13	.	8	5	5	18
Tilshead 7	.	3	3	2	8
Wor Barrow	.	6	.	.	6

Ritual feasts

As Thurnam originally suggested, the evidence from the excavated barrows points to some form of funeral feasts having taken place during their construction, for animal bones occur in very large numbers in the material of the mound and (as more recent excavations have shown) in the filling of the quarry-ditches. The most interesting, and by far the most frequent, are the bones of oxen, normally of the small long-horned domesticated breed described above, but occasionally those of the great wild ox, *Bos primigenius*. At Amesbury 42 it was observed that there were remains of three oxen, cut up into joints still articulated when found, and the same was found at Tilshead 5, where at least four or five animals had been present and where the remains included a skull with a cleft cervical vertebra showing that the neck had been chopped through. Skulls of seven or more oxen were found at Heytesbury 1 (Boles Barrow) under the central cairn of the barrow. At Wor Barrow Pitt-Rivers commented on the frequence of ox humeri in the ditch silting: bones split for marrow were found abundantly in the Badshot and Thickthorn ditches and at the latter site a skull of *Bos primigenius* was also found in the ditch, and vertebrae of the same species in the primary turf structure within the mound. This suggests comparisons with the skulls from the eastern end of the south ditch of the Maiden Castle Long Mound and with the exceptionally large skull, perhaps of this species, recorded by Colt Hoare from Knook. The predominance of ox in the fauna represented in these barrows shows that it must have played the dominant role in the funeral feasts that one might have supposed with a people whose interests and livelihood were so bound up with cattle-raising as we have seen reason to believe those of the Windmill Hill folk to have been.

In addition to the ox bones, those of domesticated pig, sheep and dog have been recorded from the barrows, but in insignificant proportions. Various unidentified bird bones, and even the entire skeleton of a goose (Thurnam, 1868), were also discovered in the early excavations.

Grave-goods and associated artifacts

The deposition of grave-goods seems to have been a very infrequent practice in the unchambered long barrows. At Fifield, Thurnam found a leaf-arrowhead; with the interments at Norton Bavant 13 a small bowl of Windmill Hill ware (Fig. 10, no. 2), and at Winterbourne a flaked rod of flint, which might be interpreted as phallic, with analogies in Early Bronze Age burials at Easton Down and Netheravon (*Man*, 1934, no. 51; *W.A.M.* XLIII, 490). Elsewhere artifacts associated with the barrows derive from the material of the mound or from the silt of the ditches. The scattered sherds on the old surface beneath the Wexcombe barrow, and the flint axe (to which further reference is made below) from the inner turf core of Julliberries Grave may represent ritual deposits of some kind, but the finds from the ditches can only have been casually deposited. Of these, one may note leaf-arrowheads at Thickthorn, Badshot and Wor Barrow, Hembury ware at Holdenhurst and sherds probably Windmill Hill ware at Thickthorn, and also carved chalk phalli from the last site.

The ditches at Wor Barrow, Thickthorn, Holdenhurst and Badshot provide a valuable and consistent series of stratified deposits which are in precise agreement with those of the causewayed camps, showing Western Neolithic wares below cord ornamented (Peterborough) Neolithic sherds, and, at a slightly higher level, Early Bronze Age beaker material. At Lamborough, Hants, a sherd of Peterborough ware was alleged to come from the bottom of the ditch in primary silting, but the excavation and the report are alike unsatisfactory (Grinsell, 1939, 202). In general, the evidence shows that the unchambered long barrows were being built at the same time as the causewayed camps, and before the arrival of the Peterborough folk in Wessex. The axe from Julliberries Grave allows of an important correlation between the Western and the Nordic Neolithic provinces, for it is of the thin-butted 'dolmen' type, and its presence in a non-megalithic barrow of Wessex type enables a chronological link to be made between the two cultures.

While it is perhaps difficult to bring forward conclusive proof, there seems little doubt of the cultural identity of the unchambered long barrows and the causewayed camps. The close coincidence of distribution, the occurrence in both groups of structures of identical pottery types in the same stratigraphical relationship to later Neolithic and Early Bronze Age wares, the similar technique observable in the digging of the ditches, all make it difficult to refer the enclosure and the tombs to two independent cultures, and in fact one must see in them two most significant aspects of that culture: the causewayed camps representing the basic stock-breeding and cattle-herding upon which the material economy of the whole civilization rested, the long barrow providing the evidence for the spiritual life of the people.

The origins of the earthen long barrows

For the prototypes of these tombs we must turn to western France. In the Morbihan region of Brittany there exists a group of monuments whose inconspicuous nature has led them in the past to be neglected in favour of the more striking megalithic monuments of this remarkable area, but which seem to be of importance in connexion with our long barrows (Piggott, 1937a). The structures in question consist of low elongated mounds which on excavation are found to cover a rectangular or trapezoidal enclosure of dry-stone walling or upright stones within which are a number of small stone cists beneath circular cairns, some apparently having contained bones, some ritual deposits of burnt material, pottery and implements. The pottery from the best-recorded example, one of a group at Manio near Carnac, is of undecorated Western Neolithic type comparing closely on the one hand with that of the Cortaillod culture or the earlier phase of the south French caves or the Camp de Chassey, and on the other with our Windmill Hill ware, while the cairn in question is earlier in date than the great megalithic avenues of Kermario, which run across it. Towards its eastern end is a large standing stone, and a similar stone stands just beyond the larger end of another analogous cairn nearby. The focus of interest in each of these long mounds seems to be centred on a feature situated on the main axis, which may be either an internal circular cairn of larger dimensions than the others (as at Crucuny and Manio no. 5) or an exceptional cist (as that by the standing stone in Manio no. 1).

The resemblance between this type and our English long barrows described above will be immediately apparent. The long mound covering a quadrangular enclosure, multiple burials on the axial line, often under cairns of stones (or heaps of sods which may represent collapsed temporary chambers), standing stones (or posts), frequent 'ritual deposits' in the body of the mound, the early Neolithic dating with closely related pottery—all these features in common with the allowance for the inevitable differences resulting from the change from a granite to a chalk subsoil, leave us with little doubt that the Breton long cairns of the Manio class must somehow be connected with the English unchambered long barrows, and in a position which should be ancestral. While it is possible that the English tombs derive from as yet undiscovered analogous types within the Western culture further north-east along the French coast, if in the Morbihan region we can discover the genesis of the Manio cairns themselves, and so recognize them as a type which does not necessarily form a part of the general early Neolithic complex diffused over France, but as a form of tomb with its origin in Brittany and peculiar to that region and to Britain, we shall be relieved of the difficult task of explaining the absence of this type of burial in the Western Neolithic culture outside these two areas.

Hawkes (1940, 147) has suggested a local Breton origin for the Manio cairns. He points out that the closest parallels to the cist-graves under small cairns, the burnt ritual offerings and the multiple burials are to be found in the remarkable Tardenoisian cemeteries on the islands of Téviec and Hoëdic off the Quiberon peninsula, where burials of this type occurred scattered about among the midden debris of the Mesolithic beachcombers (Péquart et al. 1937). Their enclosure within a quadrangular wall in the Manio cairns he would see as a 'refining' Neolithic influence which separated the cemetery from the village (it is noticeable that at Manio no. 1 at least nine cists lie immediately outside the northern wall of the enclosure, implying that its ritual significance had not taken on its full exclusive import) and he regards the type in consequence as representing a fusion between the native Mesolithic element and the intrusive early Neolithic economy. This suggestion seems to have much to commend it: one may note the Tardenoisian flint types from the cairns (le Rouzic, 1934, 488) and it is even possible to note certain important traits in common between the Téviec burials and those in the non-megalithic culture of Wessex. The idea of burials within the occupation areas of the causewayed camps may well be susceptible of a Mesolithic origin: the crouched posture is common to Téviec and e.g. Whitehawk, and at both sites there are burials of mothers with infants, while the burial with mussel-shells at the head from the Sussex site is, in the Téviec connexion, suspiciously Tardenoisian, though of course such Mesolithic traditions (if such they be) may well have been derived from the local Tardenoisian in south England as from that of Brittany. The multiple burials in such tombs as Téviec K immediately recall those of the long barrows, and there is yet another point, that of the funeral feasts. At Téviec, funeral ritual was centred round the red deer, appropriate to a hunter-fisher economy, and deer antlers sometimes crowned the deceased in the grave. There may be a significant similarity with the funeral feasts attested by the remains from the unchambered long barrows, where the chosen animal for the sacrament is the bull, the Neolithic herdsman's symbol of his very livelihood.

It is clear that the English barrows represent a further stage in the evolution of the type from the Manio cairns, for the scattered cist burials have vanished, and ritual appears to be analogous with that of the collective chambered tombs. But as we shall see, the long mound with its contained circular ritual structure occurs as a feature recurring in the megalithic chambered tomb complex in the Severn-Cotswold group and beyond to the head of the Irish Sea.

The precise connexions between the English unchambered long barrows and the Breton strain attested in the Hembury-ware group of pottery is not clear. The Holdenhurst barrow certainly yielded sherds of this class, and its resemblance to the Manio type cairns is relatively close. But there are many difficulties in deriving the whole of our non-megalithic culture from so far west as Brittany, and the long barrows may represent a feature originally confined to Wessex, though quickly spreading over the chalk lands to Sussex and forming an established part of the culture by the time it spread north-eastwards to Lincolnshire and the Yorkshire Wolds.

The Maiden Castle 'Long Mound' and its analogues

This enormous 'Long Mound' (Fig. 3) covering a sacrificial burial at one end has already been commented upon. No excavated parallels are known, but in the same part of Dorset are two 'bank-barrows' of 600 ft. and more long, with similar proportions to the Maiden Castle example though only a third of its length. In view of the extraordinary character of the burial it cannot be taken into consideration with the more normal long barrows, and must be regarded as a unique performance. Stone (1948) suggested that a mound existed between the ditches only at the eastern end, and for the remainder of its length it would consist of two parallel ditches in the 'Cursus' earthwork manner. Recent trial excavations by Atkinson suggest, however, that some form of mound was probably continuous throughout the length of the structure.

Collective burial under round barrows

There is some evidence for burial under round barrows with the same or a similar rite to that in the unchambered long barrows of Wessex. In Wiltshire, a round barrow at Dilton was made up of material from a ring of encircling quarry-pits and covered seven or eight disarticulated skeletons (Hoare, 1812, 54), and on Therfield Heath in Cambridgeshire a round barrow contained nine disarticulated skeletons and a bone pin (Fox, 1923, 32). The Kingston Deverill barrow (Wilts), with a cremation and a carinated bowl which may be related to Windmill Hill ware, might possibly be included here (Piggott, 1931, 141).

The unpublished excavation of the Whiteleaf Barrow in Buckinghamshire disclosed elaborate timber structures within the round mound, interpreted as a collapsed cupola-tomb and containing an incomplete human skeleton and Neolithic pottery of the East Anglian bowl class.

Long barrows and 'Cursus' earthworks

In Wessex and the Thames valley long barrows are on occasion found in intimate relation to certain extremely long and narrow bank-and-ditch enclosures, for which the name of Cursus has been accepted since its use by William Stukeley in the eighteenth century to describe the best-known example near Stonehenge. These curious monuments have been discussed by Stone (1948), and the extensive excavations at Dorchester-on-Thames, still in progress, will throw further light upon the age and affinities of Cursus enclosures, but they certainly are to be placed somewhere in the Neolithic and are conveniently described here.

The larger known examples at least have a width of about 250–350 ft. between the parallel ditches with internal banks, and these may run for a length of over five miles (as in the Dorset Cursus), over 9,000 ft. at Stonehenge, and for lesser distances elsewhere. The Stonehenge Cursus appears to be a unit, and is closed at its eastern end by a long barrow set transversely across its line, while the Dorset example is almost certainly a complex structure made up of successive additions and includes not only a long barrow set across its line but further north-east another long barrow is actually incorporated in the line of the western bank and ditch. At Dorchester one ditch of the Cursus there is similarly interrupted by a rectangular ditched area referred to above (p. 59) which is likely to have been a funerary enclosure of long-barrow affinities.

Trial excavations in the Stonehenge Cursus showed it to be contemporary with the first phase of the main monument represented by the bank, ditch and Aubrey holes: there was a fragment of sandstone from the Cosheston-Senni Beds of Milford Haven on the bottom of the ditch, and the bank, with no turf-line and a hard compacted composition, was structurally identical with that at Stonehenge. At Dorchester, sherds probably of Abingdon ware were found in the lower levels of the silt, with Peterborough ware at a higher level.

The proximity of many (though not all) Cursus enclosures to Henge monuments (cf. p. 352 below) implies that some connexion exists between the two groups of structures, and chronologically this would suggest that they come late rather than early in the Neolithic sequence as a whole. There appear to be no Continental parallels, unless the Carnac alignments be considered as in some way related. The relationship of the Cursus monuments to the 'Avenues' of earthwork (as at Stonehenge) or of standing stones (as at Avebury or Stanton Drew) is again problematical.

CHAPTER III

THE MATERIAL EQUIPMENT, ORIGINS AND RELATIONSHIPS OF THE WINDMILL HILL CULTURE

THE field monuments described in the foregoing chapter—causewayed hill-top enclosures, open settlement sites, flint mines and long barrows—have produced a relatively large quantity of artifacts in pottery, stone, bone and antler which form a consistent assemblage by which, with the monuments, we can define the Windmill Hill culture. This material culture is described below, beginning with the pottery, which is the most characteristic and distinctive element. As is well known, such flint types as axeheads or leaf-shaped arrowheads are of common occurrence in England as unassociated surface finds both within and outside the area of the Windmill Hill culture as defined above, but in general little use can be made of such finds except to emphasize the broad outline of the known areas of early human settlement in Britain. Axes of igneous rocks in southern, and to some degree in northern England and Scotland, form a separate problem discussed in Chapter x and, as we have seen, their use was extremely restricted in the Windmill Hill culture itself, and in the main their production and use was later in date. The flint axes characteristic of their settlements and produced at the factories associated with the mines cannot, in the present state of our knowledge, be arranged in any significant typology, so here only associated finds can be dealt with: the same applies to leaf-shaped arrowheads. It has not been possible to isolate any distinctive assemblage of flint or stone types in surface finds, or those otherwise unassociated with pottery or field monuments, as characteristically Windmill Hill, or even Western Neolithic, products.

The pottery associated with the Windmill Hill culture, while it presents a number of differing regional styles, yet comes as a whole within the great family of 'Western' Neolithic wares whose representatives in Britain I classed in 1932 as 'Neolithic A', as opposed to the corded wares of Scandinavian analogy then grouped as 'Neolithic B'. Subsequent work has shown that the diversity of cultural traits within the group of Western Neolithic wares is much greater than was suspected in 1932, but a generic title may still be retained to denote the large group of British Neolithic wares and cultures which derive from a common Continental background of 'Western' facies, but comprise such diverse elements as the causewayed camps and the megaliths; such divergent ceramic styles as that of Hembury and that of Beacharra. The use of alphabetical nomenclature is therefore dropped here, and my 'Neolithic A' is replaced by 'Western Neolithic'.[1] For the regional variants we may continue to use the time-hallowed system of type-station nomenclature.

The general features of the British Western Neolithic wares can be shortly summed up. The vessels are normally of well-made, dark-faced ware, with smoothed and often burnished surface, and are usually round-bottomed. Rims are frequently simple and thin, but may be slightly turned over or beaded; shoulders or carinations are not infrequent, giving rise to a series of bipartite bowl forms, but simple 'baggy' shapes are common. Lugs are frequently present, perforated or unperforated, of various forms, and in one sub-group these are developed into tubular handles. Decoration is frequently entirely absent, and when present is relatively simple and formed either by incision or grooving (in the wares derived from the French ware *à cannelure*) or by punctulations or dots. Ornament in the fine punctulated and incised style of Chassey is not represented in the British Neolithic series. The ornament is sometimes arranged in curves or panels in the Scottish series, and in straight or oblique strokes on other groups, but the herringbone or zigzag is never employed and cord-impressed patterns are normally absent.

Within this broad framework we can discuss the regional types of this pottery which occur in the Windmill Hill culture. While the culture as a whole is best named from the type-site near Avebury, it will be seen that there are a number of variants in pottery types, mainly recognizable in distinct regions. For these I propose using the names of Hembury, Windmill Hill, Abingdon, East Anglian and Whitehawk wares.

Owing to the simplicity of the basic features of the Western wares, it is difficult to evaluate the presence of simple or primitive forms in various sites of the Windmill Hill culture in south England, since they might equally well be interpreted as remnants of an original substratum of some early-established culture linking all the sites, upon which later divergent elements had been imposed, or merely as the common heritage, with a remote Continental ancestry, of each specialized culture recognized. Nevertheless it does seem possible to distinguish certain groups of pottery as early, and others as later developments from them, as well as the presence of certain features localized to restricted areas.

If we make our survey from west to east, we have the advantage of starting with a distinctive group of pottery which has been found at several sites and has well-marked features with Continental connexions. This group, which I propose calling *Hembury ware*, from the site of its first recognition in Devon, is particularly characterized by a form of developed lug or tubular

[1] In the sense of Menghin's *Westischekeramik*, and not in reference to its British distribution.

handle, frequently with expanded trumpet-shaped ends, which I described in 1932 as a 'trumpet-lug' (Fig. 9, no. 1). This type of handle occurs at the type station, at Maiden Castle and at the occupation site outside the fort on Carn Brea, Cornwall. There is a single poor example from Windmill Hill from a position (Middle Ditch VII, 3–4 ft.) which is probably primary. At Maiden Castle there appears a solid form of this lug, constituting a dumb-bell shaped projection, and there is a single example from Windmill Hill, unfortunately a surface find. Allied are double lugs, which may be solid or perforated; these occur at Hembury, Maiden Castle, Holdenhurst long

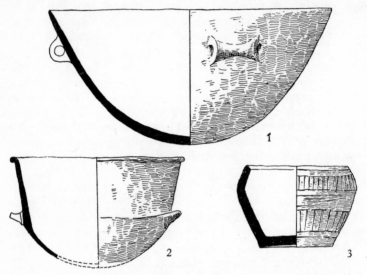

Fig. 9. Windmill Hill culture: Hembury ware. 1, Hembury; 2, Carn Brea
(*after Patchett*); 3, Haldon (*after Willock*). Scale ¼.

barrow ditch and at Windmill Hill, where the stratification of the three examples suggests that they are secondary to the site. Further features of Hembury ware are a complete lack of ornament, only one sherd from Hembury and Maiden Castle respectively showing any ornament at all, and the 'pin-prick' and shallow incisions which appear at Windmill Hill in the earliest levels are absent. The forms of the vessels include bag-shaped pots, open bowls, and, very rarely, carinated bowls (Fig. 10). At Maiden Castle was one and a possible second example of the narrow-necked amphora with globular body and upright cylindrical neck, and the same site produced a series of 'bead-rim' bowls which are paralleled in another Dorset site at Corfe Mullen. The pottery from Clegyr Boia in Pembrokeshire and Lough Gur in Eire is probably to be related to Hembury ware (p. 273).

The antecedents of the Hembury ware are interesting. The trumpet-lug

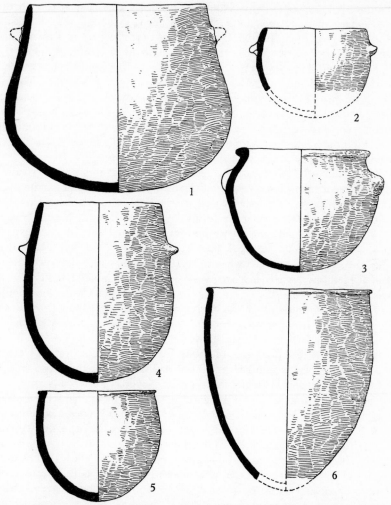

Fig. 10. Windmill Hill culture: Hembury and Windmill Hill ware. 1 and 6, Maiden Castle (*after Wheeler*); 2, Norton Bavant long barrow; 3, Chelms Combe (*after Clay*); 4, Hembury (*after Liddell*); 5, The Trundle (*after Curwen*). Scale ¼.

does not occur in the Cortaillod culture, although something resembling the notched form does (Vouga, 1934, pl. XVI, nos. 2, 5), and the necked jar or amphora is also present in Cortaillod II (von Gonzenbach, 1949, 31). Trumpet-lugs appear however with undecorated sherds at the Grotte de Saze, Gard (tubular lugs are considered a 'typical feature' of channelled ware in that region (J. Hawkes, 1939*b*, 139)) and at the Camp de Chassey

(Piggott, 1937a, 451), where they are probably to be equated with the early phase distinguished by J. Hawkes (1934), though they do occur exceptionally at Fort Harrouard (Philippe, 1937, fig. 57). In Brittany this type of lug occurs at Castellic associated with plain 'early' wares of the type of Manio (Piggott, 1937a, 452), and also at Kervilor associated with a bowl with pendent semicircles in the *cannelure* style (J. Hawkes, 1939b, 145). Its rarity in the channelled ware of Brittany suggests that it is not an integral feature of this group of pottery, and an origin in an earlier (undecorated) phase seems more probable. On the whole then it is not unlikely that Hembury ware represents a fairly early tradition which may have reached south-west England from the Brittany region.

The Maiden Castle pottery evidence suggests that this site was of later establishment than Hembury, for at the former a type of solid trumpet-lug occurred which was altogether absent at the latter site. Arguing from the sequence of precisely similar lug forms observed in Troy I–II and Thermi I–IV, where the solid type is stratigraphically as well as typologically later than the true tubular form, I have suggested (in Wheeler, 1943) that Maiden Castle was founded when the culture was in a more advanced stage than at Hembury, where in a site whose occupation extended into the Early Bronze Age, the solid-lug type never appeared. Maiden Castle then should be later in its inception than the beginning of Hembury, and a west to east movement may be suspected, which is borne out by the fact that at both sites stone axes of a distinctive Cornish greenstone were used.

The effective distribution of Hembury ware is from Cornwall to Dorset, and the sites so far recognized have been reasonably near the coast. Inland in North Dorset and Wiltshire the Western Neolithic pottery is scanty save for a few finds from long barrows and the famous site of Windmill Hill in north Wiltshire. Here the lowest levels of the camp yielded a ware which may be known as *Windmill Hill ware*, and, though allied, shows certain marked differences from that of Hembury.

At Windmill Hill the range in type is relatively small (Pl. III). The rims are invariably very simple, and the bowls show a gradation from wide shallow open vessels through more or less straight-sided bowls to deep bag-shaped pots; shallower bowls with inbent rims and similar vessels with a slightly everted or beaded lip also occur. Small cups are common, usually representing open or globular forms, rarely deep and narrow. A special class of vessel, unknown save on this site, is the globular or deep bag-shaped pot with a groove as if made by the potter's thumb immediately below the rim. Ornament occurs, even in the lowest levels, but is confined to rare carinated bowls of smaller rim than shoulder diameter, with vertical strokes lightly incised, and to punctulated ornament taking the form of a single line of 'pin-pricks' or larger impressions immediately below the rim of bowls of the normal types described above. Allied to this punctulated ornament is the row of large indentations, often perforating the wall of the pot to form a series of holes beneath the rim, which also occurs. All the types enumerated above have reason to be regarded as primary to the site, which, by reason of its deep silted-up outer ditch, provides, as we have seen, a valuable stratigraphical conspectus of the wares used by the successive occupiers of the camp. The question of the later types of ware will be considered below: for the present we must confine ourselves to the primary phase.

It is difficult to find a site which equates with the primary occupation of Windmill Hill to the same close degree as for instance Maiden Castle does to Hembury, and the nearest (except for a small series from Chelms Combe cave in the Mendips and perhaps that from Hambledon Hill) is The Trundle in west Sussex. Here, however, although the general similarity is strong, ornament is freer and more abundant, and, with the scanty material from Knap Hill, one is tempted to regard it as slightly more evolved and therefore a little later than that from Windmill Hill, although there is nothing so convincing as for instance the appearance of the solid trumpet-lugs at Maiden Castle as opposed to Hembury. The technique of ornament is the same on all sites—punctulations or holes and shallow incisions on a nearly dry pot—and it is only the relative abundance of decorated sherds that suggests a distinction. The virtual absence of shouldered forms, and the complete absence of the open carinated bowl, distinguish the site from the east Sussex camp of Whitehawk and link it to the northern Wessex region.

This Windmill Hill ware forms the closest English counterpart to the European Neolithic wares of the type of the Early Cortaillod phase, or those from south French sites such as the Narbonne and Gard caves. The bearing of this on the general question of the origins of the Windmill Hill culture is discussed later in this chapter: for the present it is sufficient to note that the same group of wares is likely to be ancestral to those of Michelsberg, where again ornament is scanty or absent. The development of decoration in southern England seems likely to be a purely insular phenomenon, though the ornament of some of the Sussex pottery certainly recalls techniques and patterns characteristic of the channelled-ware group.

At the east Sussex site of Whitehawk the evolution from the Windmill Hill stock has gone a stage further, and we encounter certain elements unknown further west. A novel form of vessel becomes dominant, a wide-mouthed carinated bowl, and ornament is applied, often lavishly, on rim, neck and shoulder. This bowl type is discussed below: it has no prototypes in the Western wares so far examined and the impression given is that we have in part an evolved form of the primitive Windmill Hill ceramic (and the evidence from that site, and others, confirms this suspicion), but in part a new tradition. It is convenient first to discuss the features assignable to the Windmill Hill style.

As has been noted above, the stratigraphy of the ditches at Windmill Hill indicates that developed forms of pottery were in use by the occupants at a period some time subsequent to the earliest deposits of typical Windmill Hill ware. Apart from the occurrence of more abundant ornament, of developed thickened rims, and the presence of carinated open bowls, the texture of the pottery itself changes from the hard gritty paste of the earlier series (with flint particles as the normal grit employed) to a softer paste with the frequent use of shell as backing. The lugs had sometimes developed into strap-handles. It has been usual to assume that evolution proceeded actually on the site at Windmill Hill, as the product of a settled community there, but, as we have seen in the previous chapter, the evidence actually suggests intermittent and probably seasonal occupation of this and other causewayed camps by neighbouring tribes, and the appearance of shell-gritted orna- mented wares could on this hypothesis equally well represent the use of the enclosure by a tribe or tribes representing a different region from those responsible for the flint-gritted Windmill Hill ware, which continues in the successive occupation levels from the beginning to the end of the site's history, associated with these shell-gritted wares under discussion and even with later intrusive types.

A clue to the direction from which these novel wares came to Windmill Hill is afforded by the large series of pottery from the causewayed camp at Abingdon in the Upper Thames valley. The Abingdon stratigraphy has already been discussed, and the use of stone axes from the Langdale factory implies a date relatively late in the southern English Neolithic sequence. Now this site produced pottery exactly similar to that from the secondary occupation at Windmill Hill: an occupation which is on that site stratified below the Peterborough ware and Beaker levels. The Abingdon site then probably began its life in what we may term Middle Neolithic times (cf. Chapter XII), and produced a pottery style which is an evolved form of Windmill Hill ware and which may indeed conveniently be named *Abingdon ware* (Fig. 11, no. 1). Here we find the rims thickened and rolled over, with abundant stroke-ornament or punctulations across them; carinated bowls in the Whitehawk style do not actually occur, although there is at least one example which is reminiscent, though coarser and heavier. The lugs are frequently developed into a strap-handle. This Abingdon ware occurs on several sites: that at Selsey in west Sussex produces sherds typologically nearer to the Thames-valley style than those from the adjacent site of The Trundle, and Maiden Bower in Bedfordshire yielded typical sherds.

Further afield there are several examples of bowls in the Abingdon style from East Anglia, and these constitute such a distinctive sub-group as to merit the title of *East Anglian ware* (Fig. 11, nos. 4, 5). The close kinship of these vessels with the Abingdon material however is so apparent as to leave no doubt that they are derived from a common source. The distinctive

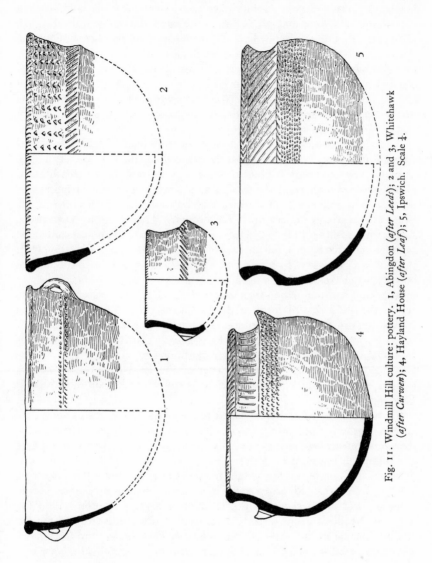

Fig. 11. Windmill Hill culture: pottery. 1, Abingdon (*after Leeds*); 2 and 3, Whitehawk (*after Curwen*); 4, Hayland House (*after Leaf*); 5, Ipswich. Scale ¼.

D

feature of the East Anglian bowls is the band of ornament below the carina-tion—a region normally undecorated even at Abingdon—and we shall see in Chapter xi that these bowls may have been a strong formative influence in determining the form and decoration of the most characteristically English form of the Peterborough bowl. It is convenient to refer to these bowls here, as they must certainly be regarded as products of the Windmill Hill culture in its developed form, and they represent in all probability the intrusion of some elements of this culture into East Anglia at a time when that region already possessed an undecorated Neolithic ceramic of its own, represented by the Peacock's Farm sherds, and allied to that of Yorkshire and even with that of Whitehawk mentioned above.

The alien tradition which we have seen combined with the developed Abingdon ware style of ornament at the east Sussex site is the use of an open carinated bowl, and this *Whitehawk ware* (Fig. 11, nos. 2, 3) is clearly allied to the whole eastern English series of such bowls, which range from Sussex through Lincolnshire to Yorkshire and beyond, but which north of the Wash are invariably undecorated. The occurrence of analogous bowls in the Michelsberg culture in Belgium led me some years ago to suggest connexion between the two regions, but chronology does not allow of a derivation from that culture. Hawkes has given fresh expression to this view, assuming the bowl-type to have been introduced into an already Western Neolithic Sussex by later drafts of population from across the sea. But there seems reason to see in the similarity of form in the two areas the influence of common Mesolithic prototypes either in actual pottery or in the leather vessels that the pottery appears to imitate. We have already discussed the possibilities of common underlying hunter-fisher traditions in England and on the Continent contributing to the character of the local Neolithic in certain regions, such as that of the Michelsberg culture and again in south-east England.

To sum up the rather complicated pottery typology outlined above, we have in southern England a series of variant styles all basically derived from the simple forms best represented in Continental Europe by the first phase at Cortaillod. The nearest pottery to this, with the least differentiation, is *Windmill Hill ware*, known from the type-site and a few other localities. Westwards of this, *Hembury ware* is a variant which may have Breton affinities, and at all events is the product of a specialization within the Western Neolithic group already developed on the Continent, and not the result of insular evolution. With the *Abingdon, East Anglian* and *Whitehawk* styles, however, we see the local development of Windmill Hill ware into characteristically English forms, and at the more easterly sites such as Whitehawk a tendency to develop an open-shouldered bowl which may owe something in its ancestry to underlying Mesolithic strains shared in common with Belgium and the Rhineland, where a parallel evolution seems to have taken place in Michelsberg pottery. The probable arrangement can best be shown by a tentative pedigree as in Table II.

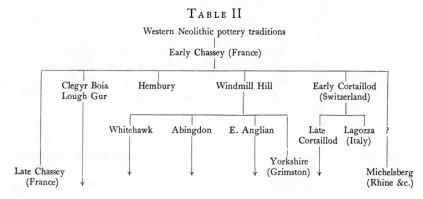

TABLE II

Western Neolithic pottery traditions

Early Chassey (France)

Clegyr Boia Lough Gur	Hembury	Windmill Hill		Early Cortaillod (Switzerland)
	Whitehawk	Abingdon	E. Anglian	Late Cortaillod Lagozza (Italy) ?
Late Chassey (France) ↓	↓	↓	Yorkshire (Grimston) ↓	Michelsberg (Rhine &c.)

Spoons

A type likely to belong to the Windmill Hill culture, though not found in association with any characteristic monument or with pottery vessels, is the *spoon* of pottery, known from sites in Sussex, Kent, the Isle of Wight and Somerset. Similar though not identical pottery spoons are known from Western Neolithic sites in Europe (e.g. in the Cortaillod culture and at Fort Harrouard, Grotte de Nermont, Camp de Chassey and elsewhere). The Hassocks (Sussex) find comprised a 'pair' of spoons of types conveniently distinguished as 'finger' and 'thumb' respectively, and a similar association occurs in exactly similar spoons from a Cotswold long cairn (p. 144). A recent find from Glenluce (1951) shows the type to be associated with Beaker material, and the Sun Hole (Mendip) find could also be in such a context. The type may in fact be a late feature in the British Neolithic series.

FLINT AND STONE

Since the main areas occupied by the Windmill Hill folk were on the chalk, flint occupies by far the largest place in the raw materials employed for tools and weapons, but at Hembury and Maiden Castle axes of both flint and igneous rocks were used by the original inhabitants of the sites. Elsewhere, as at Windmill Hill for instance, stratigraphy shows that the spread of these exotic substances to the chalk regions was relatively late in the Neolithic.

Axes: Flint

The most important implement of our culture was the hafted axe, normally in chipped or chipped and polished flint, the local product of the chalk regions in which the culture is centred. Such flint axes are widely distributed as surface finds but here we shall only deal with the types actually attributable to the Windmill Hill culture (Fig. 12). The elaborate means adopted for the mass-production of axes of flint in regular factories with attendant mines has been dealt with in Chapter 11.

Apart from Hembury, and to a less extent Windmill Hill, the flint-work from the camps themselves is normally scanty and poor in quality. Hembury yielded stone axes (described below) but also some twenty axes, chipped and polished and uniformly of opaque white flint foreign to the region and probably coming from the chalk country. At Haldon no axes were found. Maiden Castle, again producing stone axes from the primary levels, also yielded about twenty axes and adzes of chipped and polished flint.

Windmill Hill produced ten recognizable fragments of polished flint axes, and a large number of flakes struck from similar implements, from the primary layers of the ditches, and the Outer Ditch stratification made it clear that on this site the igneous stone axes were confined to the secondary occupation of the site late in the Neolithic, but at Abingdon stone axes were found in the primary occupation layers together with pieces of two polished flint axes. In Sussex, Whitehawk produced fragments of four polished and two chipped flint axes, the latter of narrow flint-mine type, and another flint-mine axe was found at Combe Hill, while in the hut-site of New Barn Down one broken polished axe and another, chipped, and obviously a product of the adjacent Harrow Hill flint mines, were found.

Typologically, there is little to be gleaned from these axes in a firm cultural context: they are all core-axes, and thin pointed butts seem normal, and the occurrence of flint-mine types at Whitehawk and New Barn Down is important. Another noteworthy feature is that the squaring of the sides of polished axes, which has in the past been claimed (on Scandinavian analogy) to be a later feature is, as Bruce-Mitford pointed out (1938, 282), a feature found on axes in primary associations at Windmill Hill, and to this may be added the presence of the type at Whitehawk and the New Barn Down hut.[1] The long barrow of Julliberries Grave in Kent produced a flint axe of the 'thin-butted' Danish type, clearly an imported object.

Axes: Stone

Of the stone axes from Hembury and Maiden Castle (Fig. 12), five from the former and six from the latter site have been petrologically determined as of identical sheared tremolite, likely to be of Cornish origin (Stone & Wallis, 1947). A single axe of a characteristic greenstone (Group IIA of the S.W. sub-committee's classification) was associated with the sheared tremolite axes (Group IVA) at Hembury: a dozen identical axes are known of which one was found in a secondary context in the Outer Ditch at Windmill Hill (Fig. 4, no. 1). There is no evidence of the exploitation of these rocks by other communities of the Windmill Hill culture. The axes from Abingdon,

---

[1] Another, re-chipped, came from the secondary silt in the Wor Barrow ditch.

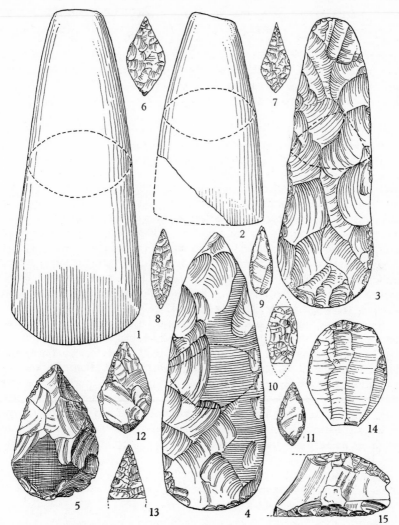

Fig. 12. Windmill Hill culture: stone and flint types. 1–4, 6, Maiden Castle (*after Wheeler*); 5, 10–13, 15, Windmill Hill; 7, Hembury (*after Liddell*); 8, Abingdon (*after Leeds*); 9, 14, Whitehawk (*after Curwen*). Scale ½.

however, are the products of the Langdale Pike factory in the Lake District (Keiller, Piggott & Wallis, 1941) which stratigraphical evidence from Windmill Hill and elsewhere shows to have been producing axes late in the Neolithic, normally associated with the Secondary Neolithic cultures. The igneous stone axes from Grimes Graves are likely to belong to a similar context (see Chapter x). All the axes detailed above are of pointed-butt form with oval section.

Pounders or hammers

Flint, sarsen and other hard stones were used, notably at Windmill Hill, and the use of sarsen for corn-rubbing stones will be dealt with under the section on agriculture.

Arrowheads

Apart from an isolated example of the *petit tranchet* from Whitehawk, the arrowheads are consistently of the leaf-shaped type (Fig. 12). At Hembury, 149 finely flaked arrowheads of local Beer flint were found, and a similarly high standard of workmanship and the use of the same flint was noticeable in the thirty-three specimens from Haldon. At Windmill Hill there are only seven complete or fragmentary arrowheads definitely assignable to the primary occupation of the site, eighteen at Maiden Castle, Whitehawk produced five, The Trundle two fragments, Hambledon Hill four, and Abingdon eleven complete and fourteen fragments. From the long barrows leaf-arrowheads are also a frequent feature. One occurred with a burial contemporary with the mining industry at Blackpatch and another in a chipping-floor at Cissbury (Pull, 1932, 70).

Again, it is difficult to read any typological significance into the material thus presented. The range of types is considerable, the forms exhibiting every variation between the long double-pointed 'laurel' form, to the round-based 'turnip' of R. A. Smith's classification (1927). At Hembury there are a number of examples showing an ogee outline, which appears to be rare elsewhere though it occurs at Maiden Castle and Carn Brea and may be a west English type, but the only generalization that can be made for the series is the negative one, that the angular lozenge form does not seem to occur. Whether this distinction is chronological or cultural it is difficult to say, but the latter seems the more probable.

Large heavy points of leaf-form, which may be javelin-heads, occur at Windmill Hill, Whitehawk, and Hembury, and must fall under the same heading as the arrowheads.

'Fabricators'

Flint tools of rod-like or D-shaped section are known from Hembury, Maiden Castle and Corfe Mullen and may constitute a distinctive west English type of uncertain use.

Scrapers

These form an important feature of the industry from the camps, but their characteristics are best defined by a series of negatives. Scrapers on the end of flakes and small thumb-scrapers do not seem normally to occur, and the shallow scale-flaking typical of Early Bronze Age technique hardly appears (although there is something like it at Whitehawk—Curwen, 1934a, 121). In general, the scrapers are rough and heavy, tending to horseshoe form, often with a large amount of cortex left on the upper face.

Knives

Knives are represented by flakes with blunted backs, but it is rarely that any more formal shape appears, and the plano-convex type is completely absent. Flakes with *bevelled edges* which may be partly the result of use occur sporadically on most sites, but in quantities at Hembury, while *serrated flakes* are comparatively rare here, though abundant elsewhere. At Abingdon, indeed, Leeds was able to say (1927b, 446) that 'practically every thin flake above 1½ in. in length and of substance and form suitable to the purpose has had one or both of its long sides chipped into minute serrations' and Curwen (1930b; 1935) has noted the frequent appearance of a narrow band of lustre on the serrated edge, which he has shown by experiment to be precisely similar to that produced by cutting wood. The diffuse lustre characteristic of true sickle-flints is, however, absent, and the question of such types in the culture is discussed below under 'Agricultural Equipment' (p. 89).

Choppers

Various rough wedge-shaped tools or choppers occur on most sites: at Hembury they were frequently made of the local chert, and sometimes appeared in pseudo-Palaeolithic forms as at the flint mines.

This meagre outfit of tools is not without interest from the viewpoint of the flint types of the Bronze Age, for it demonstrates the small part played by the Windmill Hill culture in the make-up of the subsequent industries, just as we see a similar discontinuity in the pottery styles. As we shall see, certain Early Bronze Age flint types derive from those in the Secondary Neolithic cultures, with ultimate antecedents indeed lying rather with Mesolithic forms (e.g. the *petit tranchet* derivatives and thumb-scrapers). There is no evidence of Mesolithic survivals in the flint series from the camps unless one cites the isolated *petit tranchet* from Whitehawk, although in regions where we have reason to think the camp culture less dominant than in the southern chalk, Mesolithic survivals in flint-work may appear in Neolithic contexts, as Mrs Clifford has claimed in the Cotswolds (1936, 47). Elsewhere such survival in flint-working does not appear in a Western Neolithic context. The 'Mesolithic' traits discerned by Clark (1932a, 113–14) at Grimes Graves owe their appearance to contacts with the Peterborough or allied groups within the Secondary Neolithic cultures, but not included in the Windmill Hill traditions, and the *tranchet* axe from Easton

Down (Stone, 1931 a, fig. 15) is in turn to be related to such industries as that from near Stonehenge (Laidler & Young, 1938) and in the Stourpaine and Farnham districts of Dorset, where implements with very strong Mesolithic traditions are observable, as is discussed in detail in Chapter x. The stone industry of the Windmill Hill culture is definitely intrusive in its character and clearly one of its 'Western' elements. But the recrudescence of Mesolithic types in the Early Bronze Age emphasizes how its dominance was relatively short and its influence upon the stone equipment of ensuing cultures practically negligible.

Analogues to the above types occur normally in the Western culture of the Continent: the pointed-butt axe is a universal 'Western' trait, and Vouga (1934) has shown that the variations of forms dependent on the natural pebble utilized, nullify any typological scheme evolved *in vacuo*. But the distribution of leaf-arrowheads is limited, for although known in the early Neolithic in the south of France the type is unrepresented in the Cortaillod culture or in that of the Morbihan. The significance of this unequal distribution is commented on below when dealing with the Continental affinities of the Windmill Hill culture.

BONE AND ANTLER

Implements of bone and of red-deer antler occupy a relatively large place in the range of tool types of the Windmill Hill culture, the specialized occupations of skin dressing and flint mining each producing certain characteristic forms. It is convenient to deal with the types in groups according to the work for which they were designed.

Digging and shovelling tools

Quite apart from the digging of mine-shafts, the construction of the camps and of the long barrows when on suitable soil necessitated tools for excavating and moving earth and rubble. Of these, the *antler-picks* are the best known, and are represented by finds not only from the mines, but from the ditches of the camps and of the unchambered long barrows. They are formed from a red-deer antler from which all but the brow tine has been removed, the latter forming the pick, the beam the handle. The commonly used name is to some degree misleading, for the light antlers could certainly not have been employed with the swinging blow of a modern pickaxe, and Curwen's suggestion, based on unfinished work in flint-mine galleries and the marks of battering on the butts of the picks, is that the picks were hammered into cracks in the chalk and then used to lever blocks out. (E. & E. C. Curwen, 1926, 15.) Detached *tines* also occur in the mines, but with no traces of battering on their butts to suggest that they were used as punches, and *hammers* which would have driven in the picks occur in antler. The picks

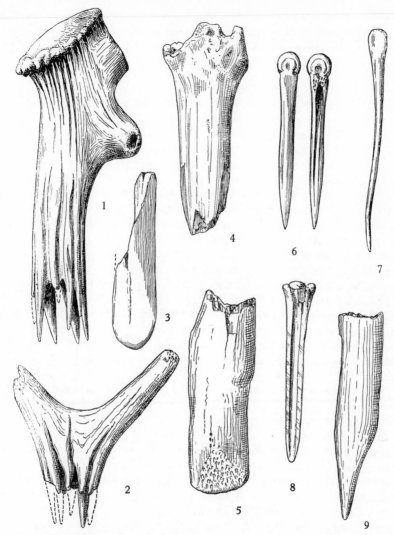

Fig. 13. Windmill Hill culture: bone and antler types. 1, 3, 6, 7, Windmill Hill; 2, Abingdon (*after Leeds*); 4, Grimes Graves (*after Armstrong*); 5, Cissbury; 8, Chelms Combe (*after Clay*); 9, Maiden Castle (*after Wheeler*). Scale ½.

are made both from naturally shed antlers, and from those derived from slain animals. At Grimes Graves two specimens bore the imprint of the miner's thumb on the chalk mud adhering to their handles. At Cissbury an antler was found 'stripped and perforated' to form a haft either for a bone or flint axe (Willett, 1872), presumably employed in the mining process.

Wedges

Wedges with shaped ends occur at Harrow Hill and at Cissbury, the latter specimen being formed from a horse metacarpal (Fig. 13, no. 5) and forming a typological link with the bone 'chisels' described below.

Bone 'hand-picks'

Grimes Graves produced an important type of digging implement described by the excavator as a 'hand-pick' (Armstrong, 1923, 121; 1924a, 187; 1934, 391). These tools appear to be unknown from other English mining sites, and their occurrence at Grimes Graves is mainly in a certain type of mine-shaft without galleries. They are strongly made from the long bones of ox (in one instance from a human femur) roughly cut across obliquely at about two-thirds the length of the bone, with the medullary cavity cleared out through the distal end (Fig. 13, no. 4). The cut end shows signs of hard wear and splintering, and picks were in some cases reunited from a mass of shattered fragments.

The affinities of these tools are likely to be with the very similar 'bone axes' of the Scandinavian Mesolithic, where the hollowed distal end is considered as a socket for a wooden haft; the bone forming a durable axe- or adze-blade exactly in the manner of a bronze socketed celt. These bone axe-heads are known from Jarlshof in Shetland (Curle, 1934) and from several Maglemose sites, though they are not of very common occurrence (Clark, 1936a, 112; Brønsted, 1938, figs. 24, 30, 34). In effect, then, the Grimes Graves examples would when hafted be the equivalents of the more normal deer-antler picks.

In the removal of excavated material we find antlers again employed as *rakes*, notably at Windmill Hill and the Harrow Hill and Easton Down mines, the tines showing distinct signs of wear, but the most important tools in this connexion are the *shovels* formed from the scapulae of deer, pig or ox, by removing the medial spine. At Harrow Hill, one was found hollowed to take an antler handle, and at Easton Down it was found that the scapulae of *Bos primigenius* had been used. Curwen has pointed out that this particular tool appears in Sussex to be confined to those mines whose *floruit* is Neolithic rather than Early Bronze Age (Curwen, 1937a, 109), but the Easton Down mines have, as we shall see, a strong persistence into the latter period. The type does not occur at Grimes Graves. The same author has followed up a curious philological by-path which leads to the conclusion that in most European languages the words for shoulder-blade and shovel have originally a single 'digging' connotation. (Curwen, 1926.)

As is only to be expected, these specialized tools are mainly represented by finds from the flint mines, and from Harrow Hill came two objects formed from antler-tines which Curwen (1927) thinks may have been *pressure-flakers* for the secondary working of the axes. Similar objects, associated with masses of minute flakes, were found at Grimes Graves, Floor 58 (Kendall, 1920) and Floor 85 C (Armstrong, 1922 a), and they appear again in an Orkney chambered tomb (p. 252). Picks and rakes, however, have been found in the ditches of the camps and long barrows, and the ditches themselves frequently show the means by which they were excavated—wedge-holes and grooving by picks at Thickthorn long barrow and pick-marked blocks of chalk at Windmill Hill and The Trundle.

Skin-dressing tools

Under this head must fall a remarkable group of antler tools usually called *antler-combs*, formed from a section of red-deer antler cut across and with the cut end grooved into a ring of teeth, which are carefully pointed and in most specimens show a high degree of polish from wear (Fig. 13, nos. 1, 2). Unfinished specimens from Windmill Hill show the process of manufacture. A series of deep longitudinal grooves was first cut into the antler by some burin technique, following the natural sulcations at intervals of about a quarter of an inch, and a groove was then made encircling the antler (and cutting across the longitudinal grooves at right angles) at the point where it was desired finally to form the end of the teeth, and the antler was then snapped across at this point. The strips of antler between the truncated grooves were then cleared of the cancellous tissue of the medullary canal on their inner sides, and sharpened into teeth. These combs appear to have been made indifferently from any part of the antler, provided that a convenient hand-grip was produced, this being normally the antler crown, or the forked junction of two tines, or tine and beam.

These combs have been found at most of the camps (at Windmill Hill and Abingdon in abundance, and also at Maiden Castle, Whitehawk and Maiden Bower), while grooved antlers which may represent unfinished examples were found in the Easton Down and Harrow Hill mines, and in the ditch of the Thickthorn long barrow. Outside the primary area of the Windmill Hill culture there is a specimen from the Thames at Hammersmith, and one from the Yorkshire Wolds mentioned below in dealing with the culture of that region.

At Abingdon, Leeds recognized a bone type which is probably to be related to the antler combs, formed of a metapodial from which one or both epiphyses had been knocked off, forming irregularly notched ends to the bone, the surface of which shows polish from handling.

The use of these combs is explained by reference to the precisely similar objects, named *kumotin*, used by the Esquimaux of Point Barrow for removing the loose coarse hair from deer-skins,[1] and this use is precisely in

---

[1] The original publication is in *Ninth Annual Report, Bureau of Ethnology* (Washington, 1887–8), 301. Attention was first drawn to them in this country by H. Ling Roth in *Studies in Primitive Looms* (1918), 139, and fig. 301, in connexion with Iron Age weaving-combs.

accordance with the other evidence for extensive skin-dressing being carried out in the camps.

Bone points

These are probably to be connected with the process of piercing skins preparatory to sewing them together with thongs or sinews. Windmill Hill produced two forms, one a carefully polished bone pin (which may be a dress fastening or hair-pin) (Fig. 13, no. 7) and the other a stouter awl formed from a split bone, frequently a sheep's metapodial. The first type is comparable with the Dorchester pins described in Chapter xi, and the split-bone type is characteristic, being recorded from The Trundle, Whitehawk, Abingdon and from the inhabited cave at Chelms Combe (Fig. 13, nos. 6, 8).

An interesting though rare type is the bone *chisel* or *gouge*, made from a split bone ground to a smooth transverse edge. Childe (1931 *b*, 121) has connected similar types with skinning operations and we have a single example from the camps (Windmill Hill: Fig. 13, no. 3). There are examples from chambered tombs, one from a Lincolnshire unchambered long barrow, and the type survives into the Early Bronze Age.

The analogies of these bone types are interesting. The specialized mining equipment, as might be expected, is almost completely duplicated in the Continental mines, with the exception of the scapula-shovels, although these appear to have been used in the Aichbühl culture at the type-station and at Riedschachen (Curwen, 1926, 38, quoting Reinerth *in litt.*). Other implements made from scapulae with cut-down spines occur, however, in the Cortaillod culture at Port Conty (Vouga, 1934, pl. vi, nos. 16, 22), and scapula-shovels may exist unrecognized in the culture. In England they are present in late Neolithic context at Woodhenge (Cunnington, 1929, 108). In the Cortaillod culture (Vouga, 1934, pl. vii) and at Fort Harrouard (Philippe, 1927, pls. xxvii, xxviii) it is interesting to see the occurrence of antler-picks of various types which can be paralleled in English and Belgian mines.

With regard to the antler-combs, it seems probable that these may be a type of ultimately hunter-fisher origin. Bone combs (though of a different type) occur in the Ertebølle culture, and a persistence of this type into Michelsberg contexts at certain sites has been noted (e.g. Bodman—Buttler, 1938, pl. 21). That antler-combs of the type under discussion may have existed, if not originated, in the northern hunter-fisher cultures is suggested by the stray find of a comb identical in type to the English Neolithic examples at Höckendorf near Kiel, which Schwantes would attribute to late Mesolithic times (Schwantes, 1934, fig. 143 and *in litt.* 1939). Futhermore, identical combs occur again in the Michelsberg culture at Spiennes, which suggests that they are as much a Mesolithic borrowing in the culture there as the Ertebølle type combs in other regions. Their appearance in our southern and eastern Neolithic, and in the causewayed camps, would then equate with the adoption of Mesolithic methods of skin-dressing and leather working that we have seen reason to suspect.

The bone points are simple forms without very distinctive features, and the split metapodial type which appears at Ertebølle (Clark, 1936a, 151; Ekholm, 1927, pl. 15) also occurs in the Cortaillod culture (Vouga, 1934, pl. vi, no. 6), in the lower horizon at The Pinnacle, and at Er Yoh (J. Hawkes, 1939a, 166).

The bone chisels again have no really good Mesolithic antecedents, but are recognized in the retarded 'bone cultures' of Norway and Finland (Childe, 1931b, 122) and become common in Scandinavia in Passage-grave times. The type occurs in the Cortaillod culture (Vouga, 1934, pl. vi, nos. 11, 12, 19) with channelled ware at Peu-Richard, Charente Inférieure (St Germain Mus.) and in Chassey contexts at Fort Harrouard (Philippe, 1927, pl. xxix) and in Brittany and Jersey (J. Hawkes, 1939a, 166). These specifically Western Neolithic parallels, and the occurrence of the same type in British megalithic tombs, suggests that it may be regarded as one of the intrusive elements in the Western culture as it arrived in England.

MISCELLANEOUS SMALL OBJECTS OF CHALK AND OTHER STONES: ORNAMENTS, ETC.

The soft chalk rock offered itself as a material peculiarly fit for carving with flint tools, and certain types were produced in the camps and flint mines which could only evolve in such a geological setting.

Perforated blocks

Such blocks, of various sizes, were probably used as weights: one at Whitehawk weighed 32 lb., and another large specimen was found at The Trundle—one smaller piece from the same site might be an unfinished pendant, and there is also an oval perforated piece of chalk superficially resembling a small 'mace-head'. At Cissbury four pear-shaped perforated chalk lumps were found in a shaft filling (Willett, 1872). The perforations are all of hour-glass type, and afford the only examples of stone-perforating in the Windmill Hill culture.

Chalk cups

These curious objects form a distinctive type in the Windmill Hill culture, and are common to the camps and the mines (Fig. 14, nos. 5, 6). They occur in primary associations at Windmill Hill, Whitehawk and The Trundle, and as surface finds at Knap Hill and New Barn Down, and were found in the mines at Cissbury, Lavant (Curwen, 1937a, 129) and Grimes Graves. Their use is doubtful, but the suggestion that they were used as blubber-lamps at least in the mines receives support from the fact that a

Cissbury example shows sooting on the edge. Shallow pottery vessels in the Ertebølle culture have been interpreted as lamps by Mathiassen (Clark, 1936a, 152).

Chalk balls

Carefully carved chalk balls, from one to two inches in diameter, have been found at Windmill Hill and Grimes Graves. Their purpose is unknown, though their presence with a phallus in the fertility group at Grimes Graves Pit 15 suggests a sexual significance.

It will be convenient to treat the remaining chalk and stone types under collective headings, as follows:

Personal ornaments

In the very scanty series available we may first notice *pendants* of chalk, usually rough lumps perforated at one end (as at Windmill Hill, and with Whitehawk burial no. II), or better finished into subrectangular form (Windmill Hill) (Fig. 14, no. 7). From the latter site came also a decorated fragment, probably an unfinished pendant, discussed under 'Art' below.

Beads &c.

Beads do not occur in chalk, although the spherical chalk sponge-fossils *Coscinopora (porosphaera) globularis*, which have a natural perforation, may have been utilized (cf. Curwen, 1929a, 66). From Hembury, however, comes a bead of steatite, apparently originally tubular but later broken and rebored transversely. In its original form it is paralleled by steatite beads in the Cortaillod culture (Vouga, 1934, pl. xvii, no. 17), and it must be regarded as an imported object. Hembury also yielded a large oval bead of shale, which is of great interest, being paralleled at Windmill Hill, and in two chambered long cairns in the Cotswolds discussed in a later chapter. Exploitation of the Kimmeridge shale deposits, exposed by coastal erosion, is obviously to be expected, and this receives confirmation in the form of an unfinished bead, unquestionably of Kimmeridge shale, from a Neolithic pit at Maiden Castle.

Indirect evidence of the existence of necklaces of small globular beads about 4 mm. in diameter, of some unknown substance but possibly seeds, is afforded, as I pointed out (1934a), by the impressions on a vessel from Michelmersh, Hants, and probably also on a sherd from Whitehawk (Curwen, 1934a, 116).

A small bone object from The Trundle (Fig. 14, no. 11) seems likely to be the tip of a 'pendant' of a common Cortaillod type (cf. von Gonzenbach, 1949, pl. 11, no. 18) rather than a phallic representation as suggested by the excavator (Curwen, 1929a).

Other non-utilitarian chalk carvings are dealt with in the section on 'Art'.

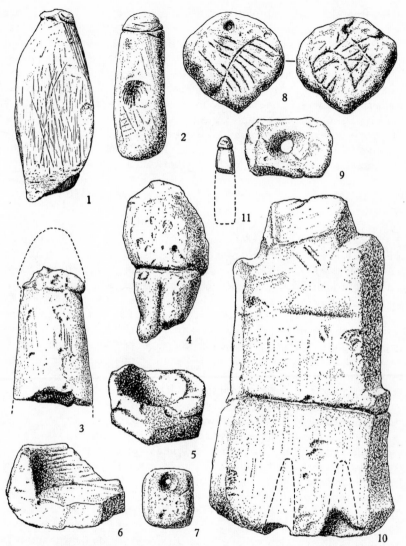

Fig. 14. Windmill Hill culture: chalk and bone (no. 11) carvings. 1, 3, Thickthorn long barrow; 2, 4, 7, 8, Windmill Hill; 5, Knap Hill; 6, 9, 11, The Trundle (*after Curwen*); 10, Maiden Castle (*after Wheeler*). Scale ½.

ART[1]

Apart from that employed by the potter, decorative or representational art is extremely rare in the Windmill Hill culture. Decoration of bone objects is quite unknown, and the manifestations that lay claim to inclusion in so grandiose a heading are confined to a few incised lines upon lumps of chalk. There are several series of roughly parallel and straight incisions from the mines—where they have been interpreted as tallies—and from the camps, while at Harrow Hill mine and at Whitehawk a reticulated pattern of lines crossing at right angles occurs.[2] And by the side of these essays in linear design the carving from Windmill Hill (probably a pendant with unfinished perforation) stands out by reason not only of its bifacial decoration, but by the combination of intersecting straight lines with a curvilinear element on one side (Fig. 14, no. 8). The ornament on this object invites comparison with Irish megalithic carvings of Breuil's *Hommes-sapins* class (Breuil, 1934, 296), the Breton examples interpreted along the same lines by Mahr (1930; 1937, 59), or those on rock surfaces at Traprain Law (Edwards, 1935).

In contrast to the linear abstracts described above, chalk carving in the round was employed to produce naturalistic representations of the male generative organ (Fig. 14, nos. 1–3) at Windmill Hill, Grimes Graves, Thickthorn long barrow and possibly at the Blackpatch mine (Drew & Piggott, 1936, 86–7). Three figurines have been found, from Windmill Hill, Maiden Castle and Grimes Graves (Fig. 14, nos. 4, 10; Pl. IV). The first is incomplete or unfinished, and is a fairly naturalistic representation of human thighs with an apparent belt above, while the second is now a headless and armless torso of conventionalized angular form (suggesting a skirted figure) with two holes at its base for the insertion of legs. The Grimes Graves carving (p. 42) is a naturalistic rendering of an obese and pregnant woman recalling Upper Palaeolithic examples (Pl. IV).

The scratching of the surface of a block with an irregular serrated flake, causing a characteristic grooved surface, occurs at Windmill Hill, Thickthorn and Harrow Hill, and from The Trundle comes an enigmatic object consisting of a large block of chalk, 10½ in. by 7 in. and 2–3 in. thick, which has been cut on one side into a semicircular notch 3 in. across, perhaps half a circular perforation. On one face the edge of this opening has been defined by a ridge, by means of scraping the surrounding chalk away by a flint implement in such a manner as to produce a series of radiating grooves which look deliberate in intention. The use of this object is unknown, and it is difficult to suggest parallels, although I have tentatively suggested (in Curwen, 1931, 144) the radiate carvings of, for example, Ile Longue in the Breton megalithic series.

1 The naturalistic engravings on flint crust from Grimes Graves are discussed on p. 282.
2 Cf. the engraving on stone from Lindø (Winther, 1926, pp. 37–8).

AGRICULTURAL EQUIPMENT AND CEREALS

Equipment

Evidence for the practice of agriculture in the Windmill Hill culture is consistent, if meagre. *Grain-rubbers* or 'saucer-querns' of sandstone, distinguished by Curwen (1937*b*; 1938, 35) from the true saddle-querns on the grounds of an irregular or circular grinding movement rather than a to-and-fro motion of the upper stone have been found in the camps at Windmill Hill, Whitehawk, The Trundle, Hambledon Hill and Hembury, and from the New Barn Down hut and from Stoke Down flint mine. The querns from Maiden Castle, classed by Wheeler as 'saddle-querns' (1943), appear equally to belong to this type. *Sickle-flints*, characterized by the diffused lustre on their edges (cf. Curwen, 1930*b*; 1935; and above, p. 79) have appeared at only one site, Windmill Hill, where two examples have been found and are considered by Curwen[1] to have been in all probability part of composite sickles with straight hafts in the manner of certain predynastic Fayum specimens. An analogous sickle-flint from the top-soil above a mine shaft at Cissbury has been cited as having possible connexion with the Windmill Hill culture (Curwen, 1938, 32) but the evidence seems insufficient to warrant its inclusion.

Cereal remains

Actual grain has survived in carbonized form at Hembury, and grain impressions on sherds have been identified from the Windmill Hill culture sites of Haldon, Maiden Castle, Whitehawk and Abingdon (Jessen & Helbaek, 1944).[2] The Hembury grain was identified by Percival as a form of *Triticum vulgare*, and the Haldon impressions appear to be similar. Wheats of the *dicoccum* or *monococcum*, and of the *vulgare* or *compactum* forms, were noted at Maiden Castle, and Emmer (*dicoccum*) was definitely identified at this site and at Abingdon. Barley impressions at Maiden Castle included both naked and hulled grains of *Hordeum*, and naked barley was also identified at Whitehawk.

DOMESTICATED ANIMALS

Together with agriculture, the domestication of animals forms one of the main traits distinctive of 'Neolithic' civilization, and it is in the Windmill Hill culture that we have the fullest evidence of animal domestication in Neolithic Britain. From the camps (and to a minor degree from the flint mines and long barrows) we have a large amount of skeletal material showing

[1] *In litt.* December 1938.
[2] It should be noted that Helbaek's investigation of British Neolithic material did not include that from Windmill Hill, nor from any of the south-west English museums: cf. his list of museums examined in Jessen & Helbaek (1944, 16–17). His survey was completed in 1952.

that the authors of the culture arrived in England with the full complement of domesticated species normal to the Western Neolithic cultures of the Continent—oxen, sheep, goats, pigs and dogs—and these animals must have been actually imported to south England from across the Channel. Though the dog was domesticated in the late Mesolithic forest cultures of Scandinavia and in the Tardenoisian of Téviec, there is no evidence of its presence here in pre-Neolithic times, and of the remaining species there can be no question of their being domesticated *de novo* in Britain from feral stock. This prompted Peake (1937, 64; 1938) to assume, in opposition to the consensus of opinion, the late existence of some form of land-bridge across the Straits of Dover over which these cattle could be herded; it is, however, hardly possible, in analogous circumstances, to invoke a land-bridge to account for the presence of domesticated cattle in Orkney in the late Neolithic, and we clearly must visualize in both instances the transport of calves in boats.

The determination of the precise breeds of domestic animals in the Windmill Hill culture, and their correlation with those from Continental Neolithic sites, has not been worked out in the detail one could wish, though Watson's and Jackson's work, particularly on the cattle, has already produced informative, if sometimes confusing results. Since the oxen constitute the main crux, it will be convenient first to deal briefly with the other four animals.

The *sheep* is often not distinguishable from *goat* in the absence of horned skulls: a small breed of goat was, however, recognized at Windmill Hill and Whitehawk. The sheep appears to be identical with the 'Turbary Sheep' of the Swiss Neolithic (*Ovis aries palustris* Rüt.), which Hilzheimer (1936) derives from the Asiatic Mouflon, and considers to be represented today by the long-tailed Drenthe breed of Dutch heath-sheep.

The *pig* occurs fairly frequently, and is a small form which Jackson (1929, 69) finds to agree with the Swiss Neolithic breed (*Sus scrofa palustris* Rüt.), which in England persisted into the Early Iron Age.

The *dog* again appears to be identical with the Swiss *Canis familiaris palustris* Rüt., and is a small breed considered by Jackson as of large fox-terrier type. The prehistoric dog has been found by Dahr (1937) to preserve primitive cranial and mandibular features: he considers the race completely homogeneous in Mesolithic and Neolithic times and to have originated in a Pleistocene species of dingo type, stressing the small size and unspecialized form of the teeth as points against derivation from large carnivore-toothed animals of the wolf species to which most writers (e.g. Hilzheimer, 1932) normally refer. The dog remains from the Mesolithic site at Téviec were referable to *Canis familiaris palustris*.

The *oxen* of the Windmill Hill culture are at once the most important and the most difficult species to assess. Jackson first demonstrated that the ox represented at Woodhenge in the Early Bronze Age was not that usually classed as *Bos longifrons* Owen or *Bos brachyceros* Rütimeyer, and known from many English Iron Age sites, but a small large-horned breed (both sexes being horned) with horn-cores closely comparable with Rütimeyer's *Primigenius*-race of the Swiss Neolithic (Jackson, 1929). Subsequent excavations showed that this particular breed was normal to the Neolithic camps, and it became possible to speak of a 'Neolithic ox'. The true *longifrons* type has not been recorded in any true Neolithic contexts, but Jackson (in Stone, 1933 *a*, 235) has recognized bones of a slender-boned ox, probably of *longifrons* type, in Beaker contexts, suggesting that the breed made its first appearance in England at this time. The Skara Brae late Neolithic cattle described by Watson (in Childe, 1931 *b*, 198–202) appear to be a breed distinct from either the 'Neolithic ox' or *Bos longifrons* (cf. p. 336).

Despite the evidence detailed above, Bryner Jones would include the whole series under the term *Bos longifrons* or *brachyceros*, although admitting the tendency to a long-horned form in the Neolithic which would be explicable in his view by assuming that all prehistoric and modern breeds of cattle in Britain probably derive from 'a mixed stock, the result of a cross between the descendants of *Bos primigenius* and a small, slightly-built race derived from the same primitive stock as *Bos primigenius* itself' (J. B. Jones, 1934), the long horns inherited from the *primigenius* stock characterizing the early hybrid forms. The recent recognition of two breeds of wild oxen in Britain during pre-Boreal or Boreal times, one smaller than *Bos primigenius*, may be significant in this context (Fraser & King in Clark, 1950).

There is no evidence of the domestication of the *horse* in the Windmill Hill culture, the few bones that have been found being presumably attributable to wild breeds. (Cf. p. 11 and list of occurrences in Jackson, 1935 *b*.)

SUMMARY—THE MAIN FEATURES OF THE WINDMILL HILL CULTURE

The material described in the foregoing chapter combines to give a fairly convincing presentation of the culture as a whole. The material equipment, with a fair range of stone and bone types and a notable pottery series, presents us at once with a civilization formally 'Neolithic': ignorant of the use of metals but with an economy adapted to the primitive forms of agriculture attested by the presence of grain-rubbers (though not apparently the true saddle-quern) and sickle-flints as well as the actual grain and the bones of domestic flocks and herds. Flint arrowheads and the bones and antlers of deer and other feral types show that hunting still played a part in the make-up of the cultural pattern, though it had clearly lost the dominant status it had enjoyed, in the face of this intrusive agricultural economy which, in Britain as elsewhere in Europe, impinged upon the old hunting cultures.

The dominance of the axe, of chipped or ground and polished flint, in the stone equipment, suggests that forest clearance was an important problem which confronted the first Neolithic colonists and was in some measure answered by this tool for timber-felling.

The field monuments and sites of occupation and burial belonging to the culture combine with the portable equipment to give solidity to the picture. As we have seen, save for a few poor sites, we have not as yet identified permanent settlements attributable to the Windmill Hill people, but that such must exist, still undiscovered, is implied not only by the occasional finds of such houses as that at Haldon but by a consideration of the implications of the other aspects of the material and spiritual culture which are of a nature which preclude them from being the manifestations of a nomadic tradition of life. The not inconsiderable part played by corn-growing in their agricultural economy implies a settled existence at least from seed-time to harvest, the deposition of multiple burials in the same family tomb must result from tribes made by economic reasons to remain in one locality for several generations, and the elaborate and evolving pottery styles are surely to be equated with local traditions of craftsmanship established in distinct regions by permanent communities. The flint mines again must represent stable and organized units systematically exploiting select areas of chalk over long periods of time, while the causewayed camps themselves seem best interpreted as communal constructions which formed permanent rallying-points for several small scattered communities at a certain time of the year.

It is in fact these enclosures which give the clue to a part at least of the pattern of life of the Windmill Hill culture of south England. Though the settlements are probably to be sought in the main in the lightly wooded valleys by the streams or at the spring-heads, grazing for the herds of cattle which formed the basis of existence of our Neolithic people could only be found on the more lightly wooded or open chalk uplands, and in search of good feed the herds would have to wander far and wide. The lack of winter fodder would have made reduction of the herds an economic necessity each autumn, while a periodic round-up of stock was equally vital when the herds of half a dozen tribes may have wandered together over the common pasturage. A seasonal rhythm of life was therefore dictated, and in the Early Iron Age of Wessex and Sussex Bersu demonstrated just such a rhythmic sequence consequent upon a developed corn-growing economy, with a seasonal resort to farmsteads on the hills with threshing places and granaries, and in the causewayed camps we can see much the same pulse beating in a civilization of herdsmen. Up on the high pastures these enclosures would serve as the centres for the autumn round-up of stock—the several entrances reflecting the peaceful movement of cattle driven in from all round into the enclosure rather than the heroic egress of warriors as from hundred-gated Thebes, as Lehner would have it. The concentric ditches may have served as boundaries to different herds when sorted out and identified, and temporary radial divisions may well have been set up.

And there, for some days or weeks, the tribes from round about would camp, roasting joints of veal in the lee of the enclosure banks, milking cows into the bowls carried up from the village, perhaps making cheese. To the men would doubtless fall the tasks of the cow-boy and the butcher, but to the women the preparation of the skins of the calves and the tougher hides of the grown animals and the conversion of some into new leather clothing against the coming winter. For there is no evidence of the practice of the crafts of the weaver in the British Neolithic, though known in the ancestral cultures of the Continent, and as a result the hunter's craft of skin dressing seems still to have remained an important feature of our Neolithic economy, so that we may with every show of probability see in it an inheritance taken over from the Mesolithic hunter-fisher traditions. Nor is it impossible that not only were the techniques of skin dressing taken over from the Mesolithic folk in the abstract, but that by intermarriage the invading Neolithic chieftains not infrequently acquired a wife who was a leather-worker skilled in the ancient crafts of her own people.

It is impossible to estimate the number of people using a causewayed enclosure in any one season, but it need not have been large. The occupational debris in the ditches is sometimes fairly dense, but the enclosures certainly had a long life and the material could all have been deposited by a small number of people successively returning over a long period of years.

The status of the flint mines is uncertain. The mines and chipping-floors could have been worked periodically by members of farming or hunter-fisher groups, perhaps largely of the Secondary Neolithic cultures, though the skill and accomplished technique displayed in the economical mass-production of axes not less than in the actual mining reflect a body of men as specialized in their training and employment as the metal-worker, and we cannot altogether dismiss the alternative of a specialized mining class relying for their subsistence on the agriculturalists and for their mining tools on the hunters of deer for whom they manufactured an essential tool which could therefore be used as an article of barter. The importance of such a non-food-producing unit within a primitive society hardly needs stressing. It presumably implies an agricultural economy sufficiently satisfactory to provide a small surplus outside the needs of the farmer and his dependants, a surplus which can be used as a medium of exchange for other products. The immense number of red-deer antlers at Grimes Graves must reflect hunting in this area on a far larger scale than in the Wessex or Sussex regions, and this may in part be due to the strong Mesolithic element which we have seen unites the flint-miners of the Continent and of England, while the widespread dispersal of the products of the mines and axe-factories presupposes regular routes between the settlements along which the traders could make their way, and the existence of such routes is further attested by the spread of pottery styles from one region to another.

Apart from the elaborate funeral ceremonies attested by the long barrows and their burials, the spiritual culture of the communities is ill represented by the scanty cult objects recovered from the camps or mines. The phallic representations, however, would belong better to the magic of stockbreeders than to that of cultivators, and it is conceivable that the standing stones or posts of the barrows may have been endowed with phallic attributes. The remnants of funeral feasts from the barrows clearly represent an ox-cult, but the collective tombs have an added significance in the culture, for they must be products of units with a fair degree of permanence of habitation in a given region. Only in such communities can the phenomena implicit in these tombs arise—the elaborate, probably communal, construction of the barrows no less than the nature of the burials themselves, which clearly represent members of a family. The variation in age and sex among the interments shows that the right to burial in such elaborate fashion was hereditary and dynastic rather than that of the elected rulers: the privilege was obtained by a right of kinship which applied indifferently to women and young children in addition to the men. This same use of family tombs by members of a ruling caste who could command the labour for their manufacture is of course spread throughout the areas in which megalithic tombs were built, and we shall see later how large a proportion of the available wealth of the community in the form of labour was expended on these grandiose sepulchres in the west and north of Britain. But wherever they occur, such collective burials, representing generations of the local ruling house, can only have been possible in a community whose economic system allowed the continued existence of a clan or tribe for some length of time in one place.

Relative chronology in Britain

This culture, the salient characteristics of which I have sketched above, is relatively well tied down within chronological limits by stratigraphical evidence within the area of settlement. It is fortunately possible to relate the Windmill Hill culture to the natural geological sequence. At Peacock's Farm we have in the Fenland the culture (represented by typical unornamented sherds) stratified in the Lower Peat above a late Tardenoisian flint industry, and separated from it by 2 ft. of compressed peat deposits. Furthermore, the Tardenoisian is here climatically in a Boreal horizon at the end of Zone VI, with a pollen-spectrum dominated by *Pinus*, and the Western Neolithic sherds are in an Atlantic peat of Zone VII *a*, with *Quercus* taking its place as the characteristic forest tree, while the entire Lower Peat is earlier than the land subsidence represented in the Fens by the semi-marine deposit of the Buttery Clay (approximately at the Zone VII *a*–VII *b* transition), above which appears the Upper Peat, with an Early Bronze Age horizon in its lowest part (Zone VII *b*), characterized by type *A* beakers. The Windmill Hill pottery from the old land surface of the Essex coast must similarly be dated before the same subsidence as that of the Fenland, which here submerged the land below present high-tide level, though it is impossible here to make any stratigraphical distinction between the pottery finds and those of later Neolithic and *B*-beaker type from the same surface. Another Fenland find enables us to limit the horizon of the Peacock's Farm Neolithic occupation a little more precisely, for in a position equating with the base of the Buttery Clay at Upware (Zone VII *a*–VII *b* transition), a stone axe petrologically identified as a product of the Graig Lwyd axe factory has been found. The production of these axes was a late Neolithic phenomenon, and in Wessex they are stratigraphically later than the primary occupation at Windmill Hill, so the corresponding Neolithic culture in the Fens is similarly earlier than the arrival of North Welsh axes, associated with the Secondary Neolithic cultures, in that region.

Now the evidence from artificially accumulated deposits in Sussex and Wessex, in the silting of the ditches of the camps or long barrows, is completely in agreement with that from the natural sequence of the Fens and the Essex coast. The effective occupation of Whitehawk had ceased by Beaker times: Beaker sherds were similarly stratified only in the uppermost levels of the ditches of Windmill Hill, Knap Hill, Maiden Castle, Hambledon Hill, Wor Barrow, Thickthorn, Holdenhurst and Badshot long barrows, and in the cave deposits of Chelms Combe. But the stratigraphical priority of the Western culture not only to the beakers, but to Peterborough ware, was established at all these sites save at Whitehawk (where an overlap with an early phase (Ebbsfleet ware) was established), and Chelms Combe where Peterborough occupation was absent, while at Windmill Hill, as we have seen, Graig Lwyd axes likewise make their appearance for the first time in the Peterborough horizon, satisfactorily confirming the Fen stratigraphy. There is then consistent evidence of the priority in Wessex of the Windmill Hill culture over the arrival in that region of the makers of Peterborough ware—a westward movement which might be due in part to the land subsidence in East Anglia and in part to the arrival on those coasts of the first Beaker settlers—and if so, it would give that phase as a general *terminus ad quem* for the Windmill Hill culture in southern England. At Avebury, stratigraphical priority of Peterborough ware over *B i* beakers was established on the Kennet Avenue, but it was associated with *A* beakers in the West Kennet long barrow, so that in this region at all events the distinction may be cultural rather than chronological.

At Whitehawk, Peterborough ware, in the typologically early Ebbsfleet stage, instead of appearing on the scene after the effective abandonment of the site by its original builders, as elsewhere, is present mingling with the developed Western Neolithic wares. Here there seems to be genuine cultural mixing, but this need not necessarily be equated with a particularly late date for the abandonment of the site, for the Combe Hill evidence, with Ebbsfleet ware primary in the causewayed camp, shows that Neolithic folk of cultures outside those of the Western group were living side by side with the Windmill Hill colonists at an early date. At Easton Down in Wiltshire fusion seems also to have taken place (Stone, 1933 a), but here the flint mines would account for an understandable mixing of cultures and of their survival into Early Bronze Age times. At Abingdon the typologically late pottery is associated with a few scraps of Peterborough ware as well as axes of Langdale rocks proper to that phase of the Neolithic.

It is significant that the Peterborough ware and Beaker material from the causewayed camps described above is restricted to small concentrations which suggest only the use of the deserted ditches as convenient shelters by occasional herdsmen, with nothing to imply that the practice of intensive cattle-raising in which the enclosures played the part of corrals and stock-yards was still in being. Indeed, the ditch-filling normally exhibits in section a relatively sterile accumulation of slow silt below the later Neolithic and Early Bronze Age deposits, showing that the economic system that produced the camps had become outworn, the enclosures deserted in the face of a changed pattern of existence. At two sites, however, continuous survival into the Early Bronze Age seems to have taken place, and significantly enough both sites depart from the normal causewayed camp tradition as we have described it, and have some claim to have been the sites of settlements in a more permanent sense. At Abingdon, the earthwork on the gravel between the two streams seems to have sheltered hut-sites behind it, and here as we have seen the Neolithic culture appears to have survived sufficiently long to acquire late Neolithic and even Early Bronze Age types of flint tools (Langdale stone axes, and a single-piece flint sickle of Secondary Neolithic type, and a lanceolate Beaker dagger). At Hembury, where definite habitation areas and even remains of wooden huts were found, and occupation was lacking in the ditches, barbed-and-tanged arrowheads (and perhaps a possible sickle-blade) imply late survival which the pottery would not otherwise suggest. The simple life of a Neolithic settlement would continue into the Early Bronze Age unchanged, while the highly individual system of cattle-herding implied by the causewayed camps would tend to succumb to the inevitable danger of impermanence latent in specialization and fail to survive changes of population and ideas.

At Maiden Castle, too, Western Neolithic occupants continued to live on or near the site after the causewayed enclosure was deserted, and indeed built across its silted ditches the fantastic ritual structure of the Long Mound, but the pottery from this is indistinguishable from that of the earlier site. The trepanned skull from the sacrificial burial in this Mound might be used as an indication of relative date, for as I have suggested (Piggott, 1940*b*) it might well in fact be coeval with that from a *B*-beaker burial at Crichel not far away.

As we shall see in Chapter v, approximate contemporaneity existed between the Windmill Hill culture and that of the Cotswold-Severn long cairns, where again stratigraphical evidence shows them to have received their last interments at a time when Peterborough ware was in use in the region.

To sum up, we have in the Windmill Hill culture one which the evidence from the area of settlement shows to have made its appearance in Atlantic times, but earlier than the land subsidence and consequent marine transgression which deposited the Buttery Clay over the Lower Peat in the Fens and submerged the Essex coast sites; a subsidence which in archaeological terms seems to have intervened between the arrival of the *B*- and *A*-beaker people in eastern England. By this time, our Neolithic cultures of Western derivation appear to be dwindling, with the cattle enclosures deserted, and the villages adjusting themselves to the new ways of life brought in by the Early Bronze Age colonists from the Low Countries. But this is only a lower limit for the culture, and for an initial date for the introduction of this agricultural colonization to southern England we must look across the Channel and try to discern its origins, and its place among the Neolithic cultures of the European mainland.

The origins of the culture

While the pottery types make it abundantly clear that the Windmill Hill culture is a member of the great Western family, the difficulties of a more precise definition of its immediate origins and antecedents on the Continent are scarcely less today than they were twenty years ago, when Childe in his classic paper (1931*d*) laid the foundations of our knowledge of the place of British Neolithic cultures in West European prehistory. Since that time, subsequent work has materially clarified the position with regard to the general sequence of Neolithic pottery styles in France and Iberia and the bearing of this on the chambered tombs in the west and north, yet while many points have been cleared up, the origin of the British Windmill Hill culture is by no means clear.

The characteristic pottery of the Windmill Hill and Hembury types, with its simple baggy forms and lack of ornament, is clearly related to that of the earlier phase of Cortaillod, known also in south France, where the stratigraphy shows that this plain ware was relatively soon superseded by decorated types of the channelled ware and Chassey groups (J. Hawkes, 1934, 1939*b*; Brea, 1949; von Gonzenbach, 1949; Sandars, 1950). Of these, practically no influence can be detected on Windmill Hill ware, and it is necessary to assume that makers of pottery allied to that of the early Cortaillod culture and the earliest Neolithic levels of the south French caves either reached our shores before the later French Neolithic ceramic styles had come into being, or came by routes which precluded contact. At all events our south English Windmill Hill culture must belong to a relatively early stage in the story of Neolithic Western Europe. In general terms this seems clear enough, but we encounter difficulties when we attempt a more precise statement of the relationship between our Windmill Hill culture and that of the European continent, and seek there for a region as a likely point of departure for the bearers of the culture across the Channel.

There seems to have been a spread of early Neolithic culture from Languedoc north-westwards at least as far as the Dordogne, while in the Morbihan there are sites geographically nearer to our shores. In our more westerly sites we have in Hembury ware a class of pottery to which parallels in details such as the 'trumpet-lug' occur specifically in Brittany (though such lugs occur also in Burgundy and south France), and in that region there appear structures that could be claimed as ancestors for the un-chambered long barrows. There might then be a case for the derivation of the Windmill Hill culture from Armorica, as a prolongation of the same movement that brought the early Neolithic culture to that region from south France. But, as Childe originally pointed out, the virtually complete absence of the leaf-arrowhead in the Breton Neolithic may make it difficult to see a purely Armorican origin even for such sites as Carn Brea, Haldon or in particular Hembury, where the 150 leaf-arrowheads as against two barbed-and-tanged examples presumably point to alien influences. Again, the dis-tribution of the long barrows and of Hembury ware is not concordant, and the rectangular house as exemplified at Haldon or Clegyr Boia may be a type foreign to south-western Europe, while the antler combs, the most typical feature of the bone industry of the causewayed camps, have no analogues in south or south-western French Neolithic cultures, and the causewayed enclosures are similarly unidentified in those areas. On the whole then it seems difficult to make a case for a Breton origin for our Windmill Hill culture as a whole, though Hembury ware, and that from Clegyr Boia and Lough Gur may not be unconnected.

In the Michelsberg culture, and particularly the local variety displayed in Belgium, we find parallels to certain of the English features absent from the Breton province. Causewayed earthworks (surrounding settlements) occur in the lower Rhine, and the house plan of the culture is rectangular and allied to types which most closely resemble the Haldon structure; there is a certain correspondence in pottery forms, notably between the carinated bowls of east Sussex and Yorkshire and those of the Belgian Michelsberg, the English antler-combs are precisely paralleled in the same region, similar techniques of mining and flint-working are common to both areas, and leaf-arrowheads are a common feature in Belgium. But apart from the chronological difficulties inherent in the relatively late date of the Michels-berg culture, the similarities we have seen between it and the Windmill Hill culture extend only to a general resemblance in a single rather unspecialized type of pottery bowl—such characteristic forms as the baking-plate for instance (at Fort Harrouard in a late 'Chassey' context and present at Chassey, Campigny and Catenoy unstratified) and many other Michelsberg forms being absent from the English series, nor are such forms as antler sleeves for hafting axes known on this side of the Channel. And anything approaching long barrows or their analogues is completely unknown in Michelsberg, while the specialized features of Hembury ware are equally far to seek. In short, we have certain similarities, but nothing to warrant derivation of one from the other culture.

We are left with the possibility of a middle course, with an origin for our culture in the region of north France intermediate between Belgium and Brittany. Here information is scanty, except for certain sites in the Paris region and in Oise. Yet there seems to have been an early spread of Cortaillod ware north-eastwards from the upper Rhône at least as far as the valley of the Yonne in the neighbourhood of Auxerre (Grotte de Nermont) and a further extension from these limestone hills towards the open country of the Artois chalk is not impossible. Field-work in Normandy and the Pas-de-Calais may yet reveal settlements of this early Neolithic culture, and there is some evidence even of long barrows, for the Manio type is known to extend outside the Morbihan at least as far as Île-et-Vilaine, while there are frequent, if vague, references in French archaeological literature to *buttes allongées* and similar types of barrows along the northern littoral.

The French evidence suggests that promontory forts may constitute a distinctive form of defended settlement within the Western Neolithic cultures (e.g. Fort Harrouard, Catenoy and the Camp de Récoux in Charente), and it is noteworthy that Hembury, the English site most comparable to these, has evidence of more permanent occupation than any other causewayed camp: Abingdon, too, may be comparable.

The probable Breton features in Hembury ware may be explained by some sort of influence from that region, but that even in the west of England the cultural elements were mixed is shown by the Armorican pottery styles occurring in a causewayed earthwork and a rectangular house, both having their nearest analogues in Rhenish Neolithic cultures, and associated with the typically north Gaulish leaf-arrowheads. That there is a Breton strain in the long barrows seems probable, but their adoption may not necessarily be an altogether original feature of the Neolithic culture as originally intro-duced from northern France, for the individual burials from the camps imply a tradition certainly distinct from and perhaps earlier than the communal interments in long mounds. The thin-butted flint axe of Danish 'dolmen' type from the Julliberries Grave long barrow in Kent shows that unchambered long barrows were contemporary with this phase in Denmark.

As for the similarities inherent in both the Michelsberg and the eastern English cultures, Hawkes has suggested that these may result from later drafts of Michelsberg colonists impinging on an already established Neolithic culture in Sussex and further north-east (C. Hawkes, 1940, ch. v). But were this the case, the absence of any really specific Michelsberg pottery forms makes a derivation for the carinated bowls of eastern England from such a source very difficult. The genuine but relatively unspecialized similarities which do exist between the pottery of the two regions seem more the simultaneous but independent outcome of an early common tradition asserting itself on both sides of the Channel than the result of the later interaction of mature styles, and it seems likely that the unifying link is to be found in a late Mesolithic continuum which included both areas within its ambit, and which imparted a common distinctive tinge to the intrusive agricultural cultures which mingled with and adopted something of the old hunting economy, and it is indeed possible to suggest the relative quota which each culture contributed in forming our south English Neolithic.

As innovations from the Western Neolithic cultures we must recognize all those traits which go to make up the culture of a typical 'Neolithic' economy—the stockbreeding, corn-growing and pottery-making carried on in relatively permanent village communities by individual or communal enterprise, and the careful deposition of the dead in imposing family tombs. But there are other elements in the culture which can better be traced to a Mesolithic source. While there is no evidence that flint mining started in pre-Neolithic times and Childe has recently stressed its Western Neolithic antecedents (Childe, 1940, 38), there is a strong suspicion, if nothing more, that Mesolithic man had learned to exploit the deposits in the Upper Chalk. The causewayed camps, on the evidence of Combe Hill and the causewayed ditches of the Dorchester culture ritual sites, may themselves have an origin outside the Western Neolithic group of cultures, and again be related to north European hunter-fisher traditions. And in the skin-dressing and leather working as practised in these camps we may well see a Mesolithic craft taken over by a Neolithic folk who had either lost the art of spinning and weaving known in the Cortaillod culture or who for some reason did not practise it extensively, or at all. The antler-comb, so distinctive a type fossil of our culture, has, as we have seen, claims to be regarded as having an origin outside the Western Neolithic world, and in addition to the European evidence, the fact that the combs are exactly matched in modern Esquimaux contexts among the skin-dressing tools of the Point Barrow group, may be significant in view of the place of Esquimaux culture within the Circumpolar Stone Age.

In assessing the proportions of new and old, of intrusive Neolithic and established Mesolithic ideas which made up the Windmill Hill culture and gave it that individuality by which it can be recognized from the other Neolithic cultures of Europe, we find the elements which were blended together from the intrusive agricultural and from the local hunter-fisher economies were the inevitable result of an unconscious selection of qualities necessary for the formation of a culture peculiarly adapted to its situation and needs. The newcomers, as they moved over France from the south, brought the herds of the open grasslands, the traditions of pastoralists and farmers, and the accomplished arts of the potter and the weaver. But by the time they had pressed northwards, climate and country had changed from that of their relatives and forebears. Gone were the sultry *garrigues* of Languedoc, the sunny limestone slopes of Burgundy were left behind, and the dark-green masses of the Wessex downs loomed sullen in the moist chill air above the swampy river valleys. To survive, to lead a possible life, one must adapt, and learn from the old inhabitants how to trick the winter and make the best of the strange land, to make warm leather clothes and to mine flint for wood-cutting axes since suitable stone no longer lay near to hand. It was this adaptiveness that gave the culture its strength to establish foothold in an alien land.

CHAPTER IV

THE EXPANSION OF THE WINDMILL HILL CULTURE

F ROM the area of primary settlement discussed above it is possible to see a spread of the Windmill Hill culture into regions beyond the chalk massif of Wessex and its Sussex prolongation. Geographical considerations would appear to limit any dispersal of population northwards from this region to two main regions—the relatively thinly wooded Cotswold oolite to the north-west, and along the line of the Icknield Way by the Chilterns to the Cambridge chalk and the Norfolk breckland. Beyond lies the area now the Fens, and northwards again the chalk wolds of Lincolnshire and Yorkshire—a region eminently suitable for settlement by the Windmill Hill herdsmen, and one which we shall see was certainly reached by them.

But the lines of connexion between the southern and the north-eastern provinces are not definite. The Jurassic ridge affords the natural highway between the Cotswolds and Yorkshire, yet, as the evidence discussed below indicates, this was not the main corridor along which the cultural elements passed northwards from the south (although some connexion was probably established by this route). The pottery which forms the main evidence for the Yorkshire Neolithic is definitely a part of that easterly group of wares characterized by open carinated bowls which, as we have seen, occur in East Sussex and East Anglia. Connexions must have existed either across the Fenland, which the botanical evidence suggests was forested, but not impassable marshland, in early Neolithic times, or by means of coastal sea-ways, and we can trace certain probable connexions between Wessex and East Anglia at least by the Icknield Way route. Whatever the precise means of intercommunication we must regard the Yorkshire Neolithic as more closely allied to the east Sussex area than to Wessex.

In the Cotswolds, as we shall see in Chapter v, Neolithic communities building chambered long cairns for collective burial were establishing themselves via the Bristol Channel at a time probably in the main contemporary with the Windmill Hill settlement of Wessex. Some contact is likely to have existed between these two allied groups but the evidence is rathe1 inconclusive: for the present we are concerned with the spread of the Windmill Hill culture to Lincolnshire and Yorkshire. Here, on the chalk wolds and to some extent on the limestone hills of north-east Yorkshire, considerable traces of Neolithic occupation remain. The presence on the Yorkshire wolds of long barrows which seemed likely to be allied, in some instances at least, to the Wessex series, had been known since the researches of Greenwell and of Mortimer at the end of the last century, while the later discovery and excavation of similar monuments in Lincolnshire by Phillips rendered the isolation of the Yorkshire group less complete and gave the culture a welcome southward extension. My own work on Neolithic pottery (Piggott, 1931) indicated, as Leeds had suggested some years before, the possibility of a large Neolithic ceramic series from Yorkshire, which Newbigin's exhaustive survey (1937) confirmed and classified. The general facies of the culture thus revealed has given an impression of an extensive, though retarded, occupation, the Yorkshire Neolithic province in conse-quence being sometimes regarded as a dead end which the English Neo-lithic cultures reached as a late offshoot from primary occupation areas, and there, mingling with Bronze Age elements, dwindled into obscurity.

It is true that much of the Yorkshire Neolithic pottery is found associated with late Neolithic and Early Bronze Age types, and it is clear that survival took place here to a degree unknown in other regions. But a critical examina-tion of the evidence from Yorkshire and from further north indicates that the concept of this region as a cul-de-sac, colonized only at a late stage of the English Neolithic, is erroneous. It is in fact possible to identify an early phase in the Yorkshire Neolithic both on the grounds of the pottery typology itself and of the associations in which it is found, a phase whose early dating is independently confirmed by evidence outside Yorkshire, which indeed suggests that the Yorkshire Wolds lay on the line of a cultural movement which, spreading northwards, passed beyond Yorkshire over the Pennines to the head of the Irish Sea.

THE SITES AND MONUMENTS OF THE CULTURE IN LINCOLNSHIRE AND YORKSHIRE

The evidence for the Windmill Hill culture in England north of the Wash is almost entirely confined to burial monuments—mainly long barrows, but some consisting of collective burials under a round mound. No causewayed camps are known, and the evidence of settlements is scanty. Considerable interplay seems to have existed between the Windmill Hill culture and others within the Secondary Neolithic group, and it is not always possible to make sharp distinctions of culture in certain sites where elements from both sources are present, and this chapter must be taken in conjunction with the evidence discussed in Chapter xi for the northern province of the Dorchester culture.

LONG BARROWS

In Yorkshire and Lincolnshire some forty long barrows have been recorded, the majority being on the chalk wolds and on the limestone hills north of the Vale of Pickering (Fig. 15, Map IV). Of these, fifteen in Yorkshire and one in Lincolnshire have been excavated, though since only the Lincolnshire barrow of Giants' Hills has been examined by modern technique, we have a somewhat incomplete and confusing excavation record to work on.[1] The barrows are usually scattered, though pairs close together sometimes occur, as in the singular examples at Rudstone, and at Giants' Hills and Deadmen's Graves in Lincolnshire. Phillips has noted in the latter county the siting of barrows on the edges of valleys and at the heads of streams, as we have seen was common in Dorset.

The internal structure of the excavated barrows immediately divides them into two distinct types, for while some covered inhumations more or less in the Wessex manner, others contained multiple cremations, apparently carried out *in situ* along a narrow area on the axis of the barrow and at one end. No significant difference of distribution can be observed on the strength of the excavated examples.

Inhumation long barrows: internal construction

The Giants' Hill barrow (Fig. 16) being the only example in our region of which we have a full record of internal structure, it will be well to describe this in some detail, considering at the same time parallels from Yorkshire where such evidence has been recorded (Phillips, 1936). The barrow was found to cover a rectangular system of timber uprights 200 by 40 ft., spaced about 5 ft. apart along the sides, and at the east end taking the form of a façade formed by a closely-set revetment of massive half-logs, split side inwards, supported in a bedding-trench of shallow crescentic plan. Eight post-holes across the west end of the barrow, which might be taken as a termination of the post-system at this point, are considered by the excavator rather to relate to the eight individuals buried in the tomb and to have held posts of a special ritual purpose. There was no trace of any entrance, actual or ritual, through the façade, and 25 ft. within was a large oval pit, filled with clean chalk rubble and piled over with a conical mound of occupation soil containing much organic matter, sherds and flint flakes, and enclosed on three sides by a light hurdle-work fence. Traces of a somewhat similar fence, of heavier construction and axial to the barrow and with offsets to the south, was found throughout the western half of the barrow.

Certain of these features have been recorded in inhumation long barrows in Yorkshire. It is clear, as Phillips pointed out, that at Hanging Grimston (M 110)[2] was a revetment trench analogous to that at Giants' Hills, though here supporting a façade not crescentic but tending to a cuspidal form, with a central feature which may have been a large post-hole. The standing post surround is not elsewhere recorded, but in the most interesting barrow at Gilling (G ccxxxiii)[2] (built of sand and containing no recognizable inter-

---

1 Greenwell (1877); Mortimer (1905); Phillips (1933 *a, b*; 1936).
2 References thus—M 110—refer to the numbers of barrows in Mortimer (1905); thus—G ccxxxiii—to those in Greenwell (1877).

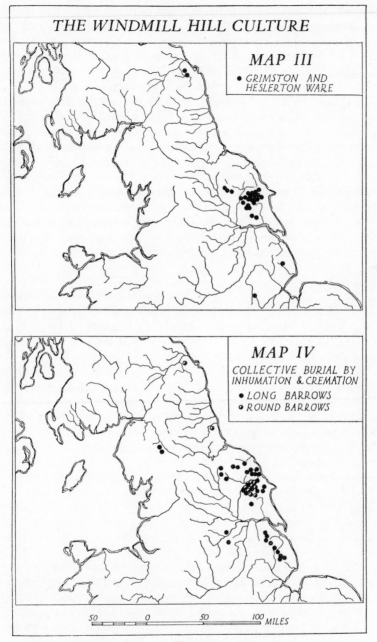

THE WINDMILL HILL CULTURE

MAP III
• GRIMSTON AND
  HESLERTON WARE

MAP IV
COLLECTIVE BURIAL BY
INHUMATION & CREMATION
• LONG BARROWS
◦ ROUND BARROWS

50   0   50   100 MILES

Fig. 15.

ments, which seem likely to have been inhumations destroyed by the acid soil as at Holdenhurst) parallel lines of sandstone walling were found 10 ft. inside the edges of the barrow apparently enclosing a trapezoid of uncertain length, but having widths of 27 and 41 ft. No details are recorded by Greenwell of either end of this enclosure.

'Ritual' holes occur also at Kilham (G ccxxxiv) and at Helperthorpe (M 'A'), and at Hanging Grimston in the same relative position to the façade bedding-trench as at Giants' Hills. The conical deposit of occupation-soil suggests possible comparisons with the feature in the limestone-built barrow on Seamer Moor, where inhumation may have been practised (and cremation in the usual Yorkshire style certainly was not) (Londesborough, 1848). Here the only deposit found was not of the Windmill Hill culture, but consisted of a circular cairn within the long barrow, on top of which burning had taken place and a ritual deposit of flint axes, arrowheads and knives, all types belonging to the Dorchester culture, had been placed unburnt. Within the cairn were two 'masses' of human bones which may have been the primary interments. This site is further discussed in Chapter xi.

Burials

At Giants' Hills the burials were found to be 30 ft. from the eastern façade of the barrow on a narrow pavement of chalk slabs 9½ by 3½ ft. set at right angles to the axis and on its southern side. Along the western side ran a vestigial wall of boulders, and it was observed that in the construction of the barrow the platform has been partly built round with a bank of loam and occupation soil open to the north. On the pavement were skeletons representing eight individuals, of which three were disjointed and broken and obviously anterior to the remainder, which were articulated—an arrangement recalling that in Wor Barrow (p. 57). Interesting and important observations were made as regards the earlier skeletons—it was noted that many of the bones were weathered, and inside one of the skulls of this series was found an egg-case of helicoid snail of a type which lays eggs only in the open, and never underground. This, and the absence of the carnivorous *Cecilioides acicula* in this skull (though present elsewhere), suggests that the bones had been exposed to relatively open-air conditions for some time prior to burial. Cave (in Phillips, 1936) is of the opinion that the individuals (comprising an adult male, five women and a child) may well have been members of one family.

At the other sites, the evidence is scanty. In the Cropton barrow various interments, some apparently articulated and others not, were found in 'graves' in the old surface, at Kilham at least nine articulated interments were found scattered along the axis of the mound on the old surface, and at Over Silton the disarticulated remains of at least five individuals were found in a limited area at the east end of the mound with something of a cairn of

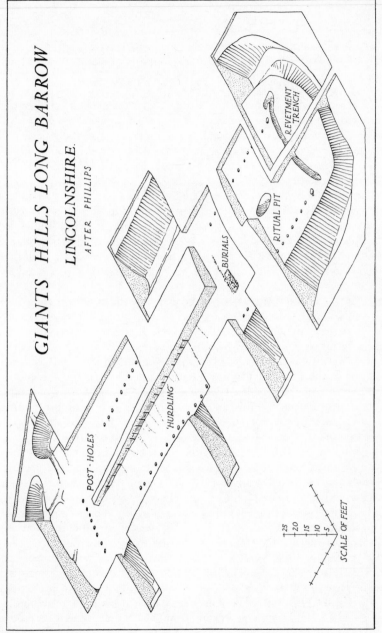

GIANTS HILLS LONG BARROW

LINCOLNSHIRE.

AFTER PHILLIPS

POST-HOLES

'HURDLING'

BURIALS

RITUAL PIT

REVETMENT
TRENCH

SCALE OF FEET

25
20
15
10
5

Fig. 16.

stones over them. At Rudston (G LXVI) any primary interment had been disturbed by intrusive Beaker burials, and at Gilling as we have seen the soil was destructive of bone. At Hanging Grimston no interments appear to have been found, and at Helperthorpe a single cremation, which can hardly have been the primary burial, was found in one of the 'ritual' pits.

Ritual and grave-goods

There seems little evidence of the ritual feasts of oxen attested by the remains in Wessex: at Hanging Grimston a pig cult seems more likely, as jaws representing at least twenty animals were found in one deposit, and in the ritual hole behind the façade a pig scapula was found set on end. The deposit of flints on the top of the burnt cairn at Seamer Moor is unique, but is of the Dorchester culture (p. 356).

The grave-goods, or objects associated with the primary construction of the barrows, are scanty—the characteristic shouldered bowls described below being found at Hanging Grimston, Kilham and (in a slightly modified and softened form) at Giants' Hills. A leaf-arrowhead is reported from one of the interments beneath the Cropton barrow, and five were found in the Seamer Moor deposit, but this as we have seen was not of the Windmill Hill culture.

Despite the very scanty material, and certain local features exhibited, there seems no reasonable doubt that these inhumation long barrows relate fairly closely to those of Wessex. Such features as disarticulated skeletons, burial-pavements, small internal cairns, ritual pits and timber construction in the form of free-standing posts or those set in bedding-trenches are all paralleled in the southern English long barrows, as we saw in Chapter II, and a spread from the chalk lands seems likely, yet the strain is not pure. The façades of Giants' Hills and Hanging Grimston, and the internal wall at Gilling, might suggest influences from the chambered long cairns of the Cotswolds, via the Jurassic outcrop. A bowl of typically 'Abingdon' shell-gritted ware from Great Ponton in south Lincolnshire (Phillips, 1935 b), actually on the Jurassic itself, points the way, and the presence of similar shell-backed ware among the Giants' Hills sherds may be significant. The cuspidal form of the Hanging Grimston façade is distinctly reminiscent of the Cotswolds, and though it has been suggested that the crescentic form of the Giants' Hills façade may echo that of the Northern Irish horned cairns, the degenerate horns of certain typologically late Cotswold barrows (e.g. West Tump or Eyford) have in fact a similarly flat crescentic plan. The absence of any entrance through the timber façades favours such a derivation rather than from Irish horned cairn prototypes, and the Giants' Hills burials on their transverse platform may relate to such features as the elongated lateral chamber at West Tump. The posts around the barrow recall the peristalith at West Kennet, which is unparalleled elsewhere in the Severn-Cotswold group, and may even be of *A*-beaker age, while the interior hurdlework was pertinently compared by the excavator with the similar stone walls at Uley and Randwick in the Cotswolds. Furthermore, the ritual pits (and at Giants' Hills the conical heap of soil) behind the façade on the axial line, and even more the cairn at Seamer Moor with its ritual significance, may be related to the Notgrove 'rotunda'.

Yet this last feature, as I have shown, has early prototypes in the Manio cairns of Brittany, and the walling at Gilling may be compared with that in turf at Holdenhurst, the late date suggested by the copying of the façades of degenerate Cotswold type at Hanging Grimston and Giants' Hills is at variance with the pottery evidence for earlier settlement in Yorkshire. It seems necessary therefore to assume unchambered long barrow culture in Yorkshire perhaps later receiving ideas from the Cotswolds. And at Giants' Hills there is evidence of late date, for sherds of *B*-beakers occurred in the body of the mound (though *A*-beaker material occurred high up in the ditch silting). It is significant, as we shall see below, that the pottery from this barrow, while still significantly the typologically early Grimston ware, nevertheless shows softened profiles which point to the subsequent Yorkshire degeneration into Heslerton ware, and the similarities adduced above between the plan of the Giants' Hills façade and the very latest of the Cotswold series would conform with the late date enforced by the beaker sherds. The typologically earlier bowls of Grimston and Kilham should then antedate *B*-beakers in north-east England, and with them are to be placed the simple inhumation barrows. Secondary burials in these barrows of beaker (G LXVI) and food-vessel (G CCXXXIV, G CCXXXIII) date go to support this view.

There is practically no evidence for funeral ritual save at Giants' Hills, and here the association of articulated and disarticulated skeletons with a partial turf wall around them does suggest the provision of a temporary mortuary-house on the spot in the manner suggested for the Wessex examples, and the above-ground carnivorous snail would point in this direction. The wooden structure, however, seems less likely to be a free-standing fence as at Wor Barrow than an adjunct to the mound, and belonging to the period of construction of the latter.

Cremation long barrows

At least six long barrows in Yorkshire, and a single example in Westmorland, belong to a well-defined group in which cremation of multiple burials was apparently carried out actually within the barrow during its construction. The type is remarkably uniform: at one end of the barrow a narrow trench, 3–4 ft. wide and up to 30 ft. long, appears to have been left during the construction of the mound, and along this trench remains of dismembered skeletons were piled (as many as twenty-six individuals were represented at

Market Weighton) and in some way calcined, together with the loose stones and rubble on top of them. The exact method of firing, whereby this trench became a crematorium, is not clear—Greenwell's excavation accounts, on which we have to rely, are far from patterns of lucidity, but he himself was convinced, as were his workmen from practical experience in lime-burning, that such a process was actually carried out. Childe has suggested (1940, 63) that this burning was the accidental result of purificatory fires setting light to a wooden chamber, but in the absence of definite evidence of such from a modern excavation the suggestion should I feel be treated with reserve, though, as he points out, the evidence of horizontal timbers in M 81 (a crematorium in a round barrow) might be suggestive.

At five barrows, holes or short transverse trenches were found beneath or at the outer end of this crematorium trench, and Greenwell thought they had assisted in the firing process in some way, by producing draughts, but they may also be allied to the 'ritual' pits already mentioned. At Westow (G ccxxiii) the burnt skeletons lay on a paving recalling the 'platform cremations' in Wessex long barrows, or the pavement of Giants' Hills, and above them the limestone slabs were piled in such a way as to form a rough overlapping 'roofing' to the deposit. In all instances it was observed that the burning was most intense at the outer end of the trench, decreasing inwards, the innermost bones being sometimes quite unburnt.

At Rudstone (G ccxxi) the cremation trench terminated against a circular stone cairn within the barrow, and at Raiset Pike (Westmorland) against a standing stone 6 ft. high (though not projecting from the mound, which was here 10 ft. in height). Other incidental features revealed were internal walling, of uncertain extent, at G ccxxi and G ccxxv, and a small cist of stones covering a deposit of a human jaw and ox-bones at G ccxxvi. Very scanty pottery finds comprise sherds of hard dark ware probably to be allied to the Grimston rather than to the Heslerton class, and at G ccxxvi a cord-ornamented sherd of food-vessel type appears to have been primary.

The remarkable type of burial presented by these barrows is not easy to parallel. As we have seen, cremations existed in certain Wessex long barrows, and the type is known as far north-east as West Rudham in Norfolk, with some evidence of burning in situ in more than one instance, but the formalized Yorkshire trench-cremation seems a local product. Features such as internal cairns or standing stones and internal walling suggest comparison with the Manio cairns of Brittany and with the south of England again, especially the Cotswolds, though some at least of these elements recur in the Hiberno-Scottish long cairns of the Clyde-Carlingford culture, with which the Yorkshire Neolithic was in contact. But there is some reason to regard just those features as original ancestral elements in the long-cairn cultures which persisted from Brittany to the Cotswolds, and from the Isle of Man to Yorkshire, where their presence need show no more than a common parentage for a part of the Neolithic culture displayed there.

In Ireland, however, more conclusive evidence of intercommunication between Ulster and Yorkshire is afforded by the Clyde-Carlingford cairn at Dunloy, where behind the crescentic façade and the single-segment chamber is a crematorium-trench of Yorkshire type, paved, and with three pits beneath it containing sherds of shouldered bowls (cf. Chapter VI). Such a cultural fusion is striking and proportionately significant, but it is clear that the cremation trench idea is foreign to the Clyde-Carlingford culture, and as much an introduction from Yorkshire as the pottery that accompanies it. It should be noted that the narrow elongated form of the cremation trench in Yorkshire long barrows may be aptly compared with the series of segmented cists in the Clyde-Carlingford tombs, and if this form is not dictated by practical reasons associated with the actual firing of the deposit it might be possible to see in the Yorkshire cremation long barrows evidence of reflex from the north-west, where cremation of some kind is well attested in many instances in the segmented cist cairns both in Ireland and in Scotland, though as Hogg has pointed out, the Wessex and Norfolk cremations must be taken into account.

ROUND BARROWS

Peculiar to Yorkshire are a large number of burials of varying types under round barrows, but associated with pottery and other grave-goods of Neolithic types, and not in graves of megalithic form. Some of these (e.g. the notable barrow of Duggleby Howe (M 273)) do not belong to the Windmill Hill culture, but come within the Secondary Neolithic group (Chapter XI). The shape of the covering mound itself suggests connexion either with single-grave burial traditions of Early Bronze Age date or from rare but analogous burials of the late Neolithic, and the collateral evidence from the grave-goods indicates that in general these tombs date from a later phase than the earlier at least of the long barrows in the same region. The rites represented may be divided into three groups, each having counterparts in the long barrows—multiple inhumations of mainly disarticulated skeletons, burials of one or two individuals, and finally multiple cremations burnt *in situ*.

Multiple inhumations

This rite is represented in some five barrows, including M 275, with ten skeletons lying on a pavement of chalk slabs and associated with leaf-arrowheads, and M 18, with six dismembered skeletons again with leaf-arrowheads and also with Neolithic bowls. In three barrows (G VII, G VIII and G LVII) similar multiple burials occurred (in the first barrow eight and in the second and third five, in the last on a pavement of slabs) but also under the same mound and apparently contemporary were more than one single crouched inhumation. Grave-goods included Heslerton ware, leaf-arrows, food-vessels and beakers, with nothing to show any difference of date. And that multiple dismembered burials persisted into purely Early Bronze Age contexts is shown by such interments as those in M 99 (with a V-bored jet button) and in M C 51, with beakers, while burial pavements in the Neolithic style also appear in M C 69, with thirteen skeletons and food-vessels, and in M 32, with a single food-vessel inhumation.

The presence of burials of one (G 111) or two (M 94 and M 230) crouched inhumations with Neolithic pottery and leaf-arrowheads could be interpreted as evidence of single-grave influence, but such single burials as those under at least four long barrows in Wiltshire show that such a custom is not peculiar to the Yorkshire Neolithic.

Multiple cremations

Multiple cremation burials in elongated trenches in the local long-barrow style and associated with Neolithic material are known from at least one barrow directly associated with Neolithic pottery in Yorkshire (M 81—demonstrably pre-Beaker) and (not in a trench formation) at Ford in Northumberland (G clxxxviii). The trench crematorium under a round barrow persisted into later times on the Wolds: those in barrows M 277 and M C 34 are not directly dated and may well be Neolithic, but in M 80 such a trench was later than a Beaker burial and in M 224 probably contemporary with a plano-convex knife, which may be of Food-vessel age though as we shall see a late Neolithic date is quite possible. An undated crematorium trench was found under a round barrow at Copt Hill, Houghton-le-Spring, Durham, which comes into the same series and affords some link between the Yorkshire province and the Ford barrow mentioned above.

Under two barrows (G vi and M 254) Neolithic pottery was found with occupational debris in a narrow longitudinal trench the purpose of which remains obscure, though in neither instance does it seem explicable as a crematorium. It is conceivable that these trenches represent elements of a causewayed earthwork overlaid by later barrows.

HABITATION SITES

In addition to the burials described above, certain Yorkshire barrows have been found to cover areas containing Neolithic pottery and other objects, but not strictly associated with a burial. In G xxiii, G xlii, G xlvii and G lxi extensive deposits of dark soil, full of organic material, charcoal, bone and pottery fragments and some flints were found on the old surface, and were by Greenwell interpreted as domestic debris. In the light of the

evidence of the ritual heap of occupation soil at Giants' Hills this interpretation seems a convincing one, and comparison may be made with
occupation deposits of Beaker date beneath round barrows (e.g. Reffley
Wood, Norfolk, and Chippenham, Cambs). This occupation soil may either
have been brought from a settlement site at some distance away, as the
Giants' Hills deposit seems to have been, or it is possible that the barrows
may have been built actually on the sites of destroyed huts.

Unequivocal evidence of a dwelling covered by a round barrow was however found at Kemp Howe (M 209) where, eccentric to a round barrow in
which no primary interment was found, was a deep oblong excavation in
the solid chalk with sloping passage approach, a raised 'dais' at the far end
and a narrow bench along one side. Remains of a central row of wood posts
to support a ridge roof were found down the centre (Piggott, 1935, fig. 7).
From the filling, in which it was possible to distinguish the collapsed and
burnt remains of roof timbers, came fragments of bowls of Grimston ware.
Such hut burials might be of importance, as Hawkes claimed, in connexion
with the similar practice in the Michelsberg culture. The actual house type
of Kemp Howe is of interest. Hemp's interpretation of it as a rock-cut
burial chamber with Balearic Bronze Age affinities is unconvincing, but in
its semi-subterranean form it does seem to have connexion, however remote,
with the Palaeolithic dwellings of the East Gravettian culture in Russia,
and seems distinctly a type suited to sub-arctic conditions and to be allied
to the semi-underground dwellings within the Circumpolar Stone Age
(G. Gjessing, 1944). At all events Kemp Howe represents a most interesting
local house-type which, while it may have pre-Neolithic origins, certainly
persisted into the Middle Bronze Age (e.g. under a barrow with a cinerary
urn in M 241) and even into the Iron Age of Yorkshire (in Holderness with
ware allied to that from Scarborough: Man, 1910, 86).

Other habitation sites are virtually absent in our region: an important
piece of evidence with regard to their probable location is supplied by
Kennard's remarks on the occupation soil from the ritual deposits at Giants'
Hills (in Phillips, 1936), for he found it to contain mollusca suggesting
much damper conditions than the assemblage from elsewhere in the barrow,
and consequently urged that it was probably brought to the barrow from
lower ground. This may suggest that, as I indicated with the primary settlements in the south of England, the permanent settlements of the Windmill
Hill culture are likely to have been near water in relatively low-lying situations in the more lightly wooded valleys between the chalk hills, and in this
connexion Elgee's remarks on the lowland distribution of polished stone
axes in north-east Yorkshire are significant (Elgee, 1930, 38–9).

Outside Yorkshire, scattered finds of characteristic pottery indicate
settlement sites of the culture or its derivatives as far away as Easterton of
Roseisle in north-east Scotland, where oval pits, perhaps hut-basements,

were found, and again on the sand dunes of the Wigtown coast in Luce Bay and in Ulster, where they are referred to again in Chapter VI. Similar pottery occurred at one of the most interesting Neolithic sites in Britain, the lakeside settlement of Ehenside Tarn, near Egremont in Cumberland. But here the dominant elements are not of the Windmill Hill culture, but of people making and using Langdale Pike axes and having strong hunter-fisher affinities. It is therefore described in Chapter X.

MATERIAL EQUIPMENT

Pottery

Newbigin's work on the Yorkshire Neolithic pottery excavated by Green-well and Mortimer established the existence of over 130 vessels whose profiles were sufficiently complete to be capable of classification, and she was able to place this material in two main categories, for, with the exception of 25 per cent. aberrant types, the remainder fell into two groups—of 15 per cent. fine carinated bowls typified by those from the Hanging Grimston long barrow and which may conveniently be called *Grimston ware*,[1] and of 60 per cent. vessels of coarser ware with a softened S-profile or simple open form, usually with a rolled rim, typified by the pot from Greenwell's Heslerton VI barrow and consequently referred to here as *Heslerton ware*. She pointed out that the latter class seemed to be a degeneration from the former, but emphasized the impossibility of making a hard and fast distinction in many cases, since the types of profile merge imperceptibly into one another (Fig. 17).

Nevertheless, it is possible to separate certain vessels with some confidence as belonging to our Grimston ware class, the criteria being fineness of texture, excellence of technique and sharpness of profile. To this relatively well-defined class belong in addition to the Grimston bowls (N. 41)[2] those from Kilham (N. 4), Garton Slack (N. 19), Cowlam (N. 16), Ganton (N. 6–9) and possibly Huggate (N. 31), and sherds from a barrow at Ford, Northumberland (G CLXXXVIII). The Kemp Howe bowls (N. 17), while not strictly in this group, seem closely allied, and the same may be said of the pottery from Giants' Hills, Lincolnshire. In all these vessels save the last-named two sites, the form is an open shallow bowl with an everted rim with slightly beaded edge and a shoulder marked by a carination which at Kilham takes on a characteristic stepped form. The ware is good, hard and thin, and the impression given is certainly not that of a late or decadent product. Associations are likewise significant, for the Grimston and Kilham vessels come from long barrows covering inhumations and of a type certainly

---

1 The restricted use of the term here must not be confused with Menghin's *Grimstonkeramik*, which he used to comprise all the 'Western' Neolithic wares in Britain.

2 Numbers in brackets thus (N. 41) refer to the catalogue of Yorkshire Neolithic pottery in Newbigin, 1937.

far nearer to south English tombs than to the cremation long barrows around them and apparently peculiar to the north, while the Garton Slack bowl was associated with an antler-comb, characteristic as we have seen of the primary Windmill Hill culture; the Northumberland sherds however were in a

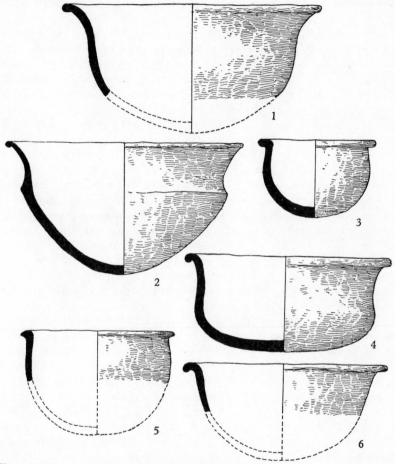

Fig. 17. Grimston and Heslerton ware in Lincolnshire and Yorkshire. 1, Giants' Hills long barrow (*after Phillips*); 2, Hanging Grimston; 3, Towthorpe; 4, Heslerton; 5, 6, Cowlam. Scale ¼.

crematory group under a round barrow. The Giants' Hills material is from an inhumation long barrow with Wessex analogues, though probably dating from *B*-beaker times. The remainder occur in association with Heslerton ware or in contexts not explicitly earlier than the bulk of the Yorkshire material. But the associations at the four sites mentioned seem too consistent and striking to dismiss as fortuitous, and their importance is strengthened by the fact that in no case has Heslerton ware, to all appearance derivative from the Grimston style, been found in a context which can be attributed to a culture associated closely with that of the primary settlement area of the Windmill Hill culture, and is frequently found with distinctively late types of stone implements and pottery.

While the internal evidence alone suggests an early date for this group of pottery, comparisons with actual ceramic material outside Yorkshire confirm it. The bowls belong to the class of carinated vessels which I have already shown to be characteristic of south-east England (Whitehawk ware) and which I have suggested may be influenced by underlying Mesolithic traditions in that region. At Whitehawk similar bowls (though here ornamented under the influence of Thames-valley styles) occur in a causewayed camp stratified below *B*-beaker: in a similar horizon are the Essex finds, while analogous pottery at Peacock's Farm, Ely, was in a peat deposit which should be early in the Neolithic and certainly well pre-Beaker. In Sussex again the type (undecorated) is associated with flint mining at New Barn Down and at Cissbury—at the latter site with a stepped shoulder which foreshadows that of Kilham, and the distribution is continued in unassociated forms on the edge of the Fens and in Norfolk. If the main Neolithic colonization of Yorkshire took place from the south, as seems likely, an early date for the inception of Grimston ware in the Wolds seems more than probable. But there is further evidence to consider, which not only supports the dating suggested but gives a clue to the true nature of the Yorkshire Neolithic culture as a whole.

For vessels clearly intimately allied to or derived from Grimston ware are known from regions to the north and north-west of Yorkshire, characteristic bowls being recorded from sites in Northumberland, the Moray Firth, Cumberland, Galloway, the Isle of Man, and finally, and most abundantly, in Northern Ireland, and sporadically even further south. This Ulster Neolithic pottery style will be discussed fully below in connexion with the megalithic tombs with which it is there intimately bound up, but its essentials must be summarized here. It is characterized by shouldered bowls of plain thin ware which as Evans and Hawkes have emphasized, are of frankly Yorkshire types, the carinations of which are of the stepped 'Kilham' form and which evolve into highly keeled types. These forms are also in some instances demonstrably anterior to the appearance in Northern Ireland of the Neolithic decorated Beacharra ware, so it is necessary to assume a fairly early implantation of the culture from Yorkshire, the relative stage of its departure being that marked by the appearance of the Kilham type of shoulder. And since the further evolution of this shoulder (without any degeneration of the ware) as observable in Ireland, does not also take place in Yorkshire, we must presume that the main force of the culture had but a transient though not inconsiderable effect on the Wold dwellers, and passed on to the north-west, leaving in Yorkshire the degenerate, thick, soft-profiled Heslerton ware as a local imitation of the fine wares of the original Neolithic arrivals in the region. In fact, the Yorkshire Neolithic represents not a Dead Sea into which the dregs of the Windmill Hill culture eventually trickled and stagnated, but a backwater formed on the course of an important and early stream of cultural movement from the south to the north-west.

It might be objected that this cultural movement assumed on the strength of pottery styles could in fact be reversed, and Yorkshire made the recipient of shouldered bowls from a Northern Irish source. Carinated vessels in the Breton Neolithic and at Hembury, Haldon and Carn Brea in south-west England and again at Clegyr Boia in Pembrokeshire, as well as at Lough Gur, Co. Limerick, might be cited as prototypes, and indeed evidence of Hiberno-Scottish influence on the Yorkshire Neolithic does in fact exist— for instance the monument of Hedon Howe near Langton comprises a series of radially placed septal-slab chambers in the manner of Dunan Mor in Arran, while Newbigin has shown that certain decoration on later Neolithic pottery in Yorkshire may well be derived from Irish sources. But the difficulty would remain of accounting for the shouldered bowls of the south-east, themselves securely dated to a phase as early as Hembury itself, or earlier, unless one were to assume two routes, eastern and western, along which identical types of carinated bowls were diffused.

The carinated bowls which have formed the key-note of the foregoing argument are probably not the only types which may be assigned to the Grimston ware class, though the most distinctive. Simple open bowls of good ware with a hooked rim, often with finger-tip rippling across it, may belong to this early phase, though direct evidence is lacking save for their association with shouldered bowls at Easterton of Roseisle in Moray. Lugs are not recorded, though very sparsely known in Heslerton ware. Certain carinated vessels with neck diameter less than the carination are known, and may possibly represent influence from the Beacharra ware of south-west Scotland.

Heslerton ware, while including a variety of coarse pastes, is frequently characterized by a distinctive light corky fabric which Newbigin has shown to endure in Yorkshire into the Bronze Age and even beyond. Forms are either the S-profiled bowl of the type site or simple forms with more or less rolled or thickened rims. Lugs, both perforated and solid, are known from two or three pots, but are clearly exceptional. The associations of this ware have been noted above in dealing with the actual sites: it does not occur in the inhumation long barrows nor in typical form from the cremation type, and is mainly associated with round-barrow interments, sometimes mixed with Grimston ware.

Leaf-arrowheads

Leaf-arrowheads of flint are recorded from both long and round barrows. From the former, that from Cropton is lost, and the five from Seamer Moor (associated with objects of the Dorchester culture) are of elongated lozenge form, similar to those from four round-barrow burials (M 230, M 18, M 275 and M 273), where again they sometimes occurred in groups—of six from M 18 and of three from M 275. A simpler rounded form occurred at Ford (G CLXXXVIII) in Northumberland and in the septal cists at Hedon Howe.

Typologically, these lozenge arrowheads are late. The form does not occur in the primary settlements, and their shape, no less than their occurrence in groups prompts comparison with those from the 'oval barrows' of Winterbourne Stoke and Edmonsham in Wessex (p. 58). The type may be susceptible of explanation as due to Irish influence: it occurs in the Bann culture and is present in the Clontygora long-horned cairn and in a related form at Clady Halliday.

Bone and antler

Bone and antler artifacts attributable to the Windmill Hill culture in Lincolnshire and Yorkshire are scanty: an *antler-comb* precisely similar to south English types was, however, found with a bowl of Grimston ware in a hole under M C 37 in conditions which, *pace* Newbigin, seem to be domestic rather than sepulchral. A *bone pin* of simple type which may be compared with one form at Windmill Hill comes from a long barrow (G CCXXII), but even here it may be related rather to forms typical of the Dorchester culture and found in our area at Duggleby Howe. From Giants' Hills comes a bone *polisher* or *chisel*, with good parallels in the Cotswolds, and from Windmill Hill.

SUMMARY

The main features of the Windmill Hill culture in its areas of secondary colonization in the north-east of England and beyond have been discussed by Childe (1940) and Hawkes (1940). The former, while recognizing the essential kinship of the Yorkshire pottery with that of East Anglia and Sussex, tentatively derived the long barrows from the Clyde-Carlingford cairns and the Neolithic round-barrow burials from the chambered tombs of the Boyne with their round cairns, while the latter pointed out that the cremation idea is likely to have reached Ulster with the shouldered bowls and hints that the whole complex, including the long barrows, may derive from south England and thence move to Ireland on the lines I have indicated. Hawkes further stressed the ceramic similarities between eastern England and the Michelsberg culture, which he accounts for by suggesting a relatively late movement from Belgium, bringing with it carinated bowls, cremation and hut-burial.

As will have been seen, I am in favour of a somewhat different explanation for the pottery similarities, which I would see as the outcome of underlying cultural unity in earlier times. As for the cremation idea in the Belgian Michelsberg culture, the sites usually quoted in support of this (Gastuche and Boitsfort) seem to me unconvincing, the latter site in particular being surely explicable (as Childe suggested some years ago) as a hill-fort rather than as a cremation cemetery, while house-burial, though significant to some extent, need not after all be regarded as the monopoly of the Michelsberg culture.

From the evidence detailed in the foregoing pages, I think it is possible to draw some general conclusions with regard to the Neolithic of Yorkshire and its allied regions which, while differing in some points of detail from the views just quoted, are in marked agreement in most respects. The significant factor is the essential unity of the pottery style, from the Lincoln-shire Wolds to the Cumberland coast and beyond, and its clear connexion with the Windmill Hill culture of the south-east of England. The structure of the culture is not, in the absence of sufficient evidence from habitation sites, possible to assess in the same way as that of the primary settlement area of Wessex and Sussex, but the antler-combs from Garton Slack hint at the same skin-dressing processes as in the causewayed camps of the south, and stable communities are presupposed by the common burials, presumably those of the local ruling families.

Connexion must have originally existed between the Sussex-East Anglia region and the Lincolnshire-Yorkshire Wolds across the Fens. Godwin has shown (1940) that in late Atlantic times the Fenland was sufficiently dry to support a forest growth of tall timber with high canopy, and we have concrete evidence of Neolithic settlement within this forest area on the less heavily overgrown sandhills. The trackways of Mesolithic hunters must have crossed this forest, linking the chalk lands of Norfolk to those of southern Lincolnshire, and along these the bearers of the Windmill Hill culture have moved northwards to find fresh pastures, thus forming a cultural continuum over the whole of eastern Britain. The deterioration of the Fenland conditions which Godwin shows to have occurred in later Neolithic times, when the whole area became a great sedge fen with dense marginal woods, would sever connexions between the Wolds and East Anglia, and subsequent traffic could only reach it from regions further west.

Connexions with the south and the south-west of England seem to have been established along two lines—from the Wessex chalk-lands via the Icknield Way and from the Cotswolds along the Jurassic belt. It is possible that the original Neolithic culture of the Lincolnshire-Yorkshire Wolds may not have included long barrows as a part of its make-up, but that these are due to movements into that area from the south and south-west. If the long barrows of our region contain, as I have suggested, at least two strains in their make-up, then the duality of their character would be the outcome of the double lines of connexion. Along the Icknield Way route one might see the earlier move of unchambered barrows from Wessex, that on Therfield Heath and those in Norfolk being intermediates. Hogg has stressed the Wessex rather than the Yorkshire affinities of his 'platform cremation' rite in the West Rudham barrow, and the cremation idea itself in Yorkshire might then be derived from the south.

The changing conditions of the Fenland implied by the palaeo-botanical evidence would serve to throw the cross-fen route into disuse in later Neolithic times, and connexion with the south could satisfactorily exist only by means of the Jurassic belt, and a later movement of ideas up the Jurassic from the Cotswolds might be invoked, as we have seen, to account for such features as the timber-built façades at Giants' Hills and Hanging Grimston, and perhaps for other internal features. The absence of any entrance through these wooden crescentic façades to my mind argues strongly against their derivation from the Clyde-Carlingford cairns, where degeneration never took the form of loss of function of the entrance to the chamber from the forecourt as it did in the Cotswolds. But that some Irish influence might have been exerted upon the Yorkshire and Westmorland barrows is not impossible, and in view of Hogg's observations it may be that the flue cremations are the result of a later interaction between platform cremations and the idea of the elongated burial chamber of the Clyde-Carlingford cairn.

It is interesting to note, in parenthesis, that the connexions between Yorkshire and the south of England were definitely in existence in the Bronze Age on the lines suggested above. The Wessex culture of the Early Bronze Age reached Yorkshire via the Icknield Way and Norfolk, degenerate but characteristic products even appearing as far north as Northumberland, and there may well have been some movement up the Jurassic as a reflex of the undoubted move of the Food-vessel culture southwards both by this highway and into the Fenland. Even in the Iron Age the same pattern persists, for Hawkes and Ward Perkins have shown how the Marnian invaders pressed northwards from their landing places in Sussex to establish themselves in Yorkshire, with subsequent interaction along the Jurassic with the cultures of the south-west. And the character of the Ulster Iron Age as shown by its archaeology and reflected in the early legends makes it relatively certain that it was the result of a cultural movement from Yorkshire which would have followed in the tracks of the Windmill Hill colonists of two millennia before.

The spread from Yorkshire to Cumberland is a most important feature of the migration of the Windmill Hill culture to Ireland. As well as the pottery in the Ehenside settlement, the excavated long barrow with cremation-trench at Crosby Garrett in Westmorland and the unexcavated example at Sampson's Bratfull go to indicate fairly widespread penetration and settlement of the region, which is likely to have constituted the embarkation point for Ireland. The connexion thus established between Ireland and Yorkshire is of course the precursor of an overland route from the Atlantic coasts to Scandinavia in Early Bronze Age times, and it is not improbable that it was used as such in the Neolithic, as we shall see when we later discuss the megalithic tombs, and consider such Yorkshire monuments as the septal-slab cist of Hedon Howe on the Wolds in connexion with the gallery-graves of the north-west. It does seem possible that such a route was already established by local hunter-fisher groups by the time of the arrival of the Windmill Hill culture in Yorkshire, and, in fact, that the existence of such a connexion made possible the spread of the culture to the north-west.

In Yorkshire, as we have seen, the relatively lightly forested chalk would have attracted the Neolithic farmers, and their culture was there firmly established well into the Early Bronze Age. The most noticeable feature of this lingering Neolithic culture is the adoption of burial under a round mound. Such a practice is not unknown elsewhere in the Windmill Hill culture: there seem to have been Wessex examples (p. 64), as well as the round barrow containing communal burials in the Yorkshire style, significantly situated on Therfield Heath (Fox, 1923, 32), while the Soldiers' Grave, Frocester, in the Cotswolds, shows a similar rite under a round cairn (p. 147). Childe's derivation from the Boyne cairns is difficult to accept: if one is to search so far afield one might point rather to such round cairns as that of Castellic in Brittany, apparently belonging to the earliest Neolithic phase there, as more likely claimants for ancestors. But as we shall see in Chapter xi, round barrows covering single graves occur late in the Neolithic, and in general it seems likely that the earlier round barrows of this type, and those of both food-vessel and beaker makers, who must have been contemporary with some at least of the Yorkshire Windmill Hill culture round-barrow burials, provide the explanation for the change in outward structure of these communal tombs. The initial force of the culture was spent, and had largely passed on into Ireland, and the remnants, out of touch now with the old centres of their civilization, would be in a condition to adapt and adopt ideas from the newcomers who were so rapidly growing in numbers and prestige among them.

CHAPTER V

THE NEOLITHIC COLONIZATION OF THE
WEST AND NORTH: CHAMBERED TOMBS
AND THEIR BUILDERS

INTRODUCTION: THE PROBLEMS OF THE BRITISH
CHAMBERED TOMBS

I N Chapters II–IV of this book it has been possible in some degree to reconstruct a tentative outline of the economy of the Neolithic civilization of
southern England and its extensions to the east and north-east, since a
relatively large amount of material from habitation sites is available to
supplement the scanty finds from the graves, and the few inferences to be
drawn from the tombs themselves. But if from this we have been able to
outline a possible history for our first farming settlements, in the regions
into which we now enter, any reconstruction of unwritten history can no
longer be based on several aspects of a culture, but must rely almost entirely
on the evidence of tomb architecture and grave-goods. Habitation sites in
our region which can be called Neolithic are scanty, and mainly ill-explored
and worse recorded, and any coherent knowledge of the events of our period
in the west and north of Britain must be derived from the frequently equi-
vocal, always unsatisfactory sources afforded by a series of structures built
as the outcome of a complicated funeral ritual which, while having basic
elements common to all its manifestations, clearly included sects and heresies
which expressed themselves in variations of tomb architecture of bewildering
complexity.

These collective tombs, with chambers built of large blocks of stone, or
with walling of small horizontally laid slabs, form the main content of
Chapters V–IX. Their enduring substance, their size, and their immediate
suggestion of a vigorous architectural tradition, primitive in its use of great
stone masses but accomplished in their combination into an often imposing
structure, has made them the best-known prehistoric antiquities of the
British Isles, and since the eighteenth century they have been the source of
much fantastic speculation and misguided theorizing. And even now, with
their cultural significance and their archaeological background fairly well
established, the megalithic chambered tombs form source-material which
must be handled with care. The excavations of the last decade have brought
home to us the fact that deductions drawn from an unexcavated monument
of this class may often be not only incomplete, but dangerously misleading.
From comparisons of the plans of unexcavated or partly ruined tombs

elaborate typological schemes and theories may be devised, but these in many instances may have only the purely academic interest of an ingenious supposition based on inadequate premisses. So far as possible I have based my discussion and conclusions in the following chapters on the excavated tombs, relating them to unexcavated examples only when really distinctive architectural features seem to warrant their inclusion in one or other of the main typological groups into which the megalithic tombs can be divided. Such inclusion seems warranted when the distribution of any given type is discussed, and, if accepted with the proviso that subsequent excavation may alter the tentative conclusions expressed, is not likely to be misleading.

The mention here of the varying types of megalithic collective tombs leads to the necessity of making a distinction here with regard to the use of the term 'culture', all too loosely employed in archaeological diction, as applied to the varying regional types of tombs in the British Isles. Probably the word 'culture' should be employed to define the collective and tangible outcome (pot-making, house-planning, tomb-building) of the material and spiritual traditions of a group of people. In primitive, mobile, hunting economies, cultural traits are spread undifferentiated over a large area, but with the acquisition of a more stable existence slightly varying traditions crystallize and acquire distinctive features which reflect adjustments and specializations of the basic economy to fit local conditions and the individual way of life of separate communities. In such a sense we can distinguish, among the Neolithic farming communities, such regional cultures as those of Cortaillod, Windmill Hill, or Michelsberg, each presenting to the archaeologist a large series of objects and sites which together form the material expression of the regional groups of peoples within the wide area of the Western Neolithic culture. But with the megalithic tombs, forming at best a single, accidentally durable, aspect of cultures which are otherwise only imperfectly represented (if at all) by the grave-goods within them, the use of the term 'culture' to denote a regional type of religious monument carries a far more limited implication.

To define a local culture in terms of its chambered tombs may be no more than indicating the boundaries of a sect, for, as Childe phrased it in this connexion, 'the galvanized iron mission chapel in a new suburb may be called a degeneration of the cruciform parish church built of stone; it is not necessarily either later in date or less orthodox than the mother church'. But with these reservations, it is nevertheless necessary to divide the variant forms of megalithic tombs in Britain into certain main typological or regional groups before they can be studied in any systematic manner. In Scotland and Northern Ireland there is fortunately a relatively large amount of exact data available to form a sound basis for study, and here it is possible to equate more than one type of tomb with distinctive pottery styles and so come nearer to defining local cultures with some confidence.

Before proceeding to examine the British evidence for the spread and settlement of communities building chambered tombs along our western seaboard, we must briefly consider certain problems of nomenclature and classification. Between 1939 and 1942 the whole question of the colonization of Britain and northern Europe by chambered-tomb builders was discussed with vigour and even acerbity by the main protagonists in its study, Childe, Hawkes, Daniel, Forde and Scott, in a series of books and papers, and a summary of this controversy is an essential preliminary to our examination of the British material.

We may conveniently begin with Childe's résumé of the subject in its European setting (Childe, 1947, 316). He distinguished two strains of megalithic tradition (not entirely for the first time, since the division had been implied by various writers before) characterized as *passage-graves* and *gallery-graves* on a typological distinction of plan, suggested that the earliest tombs in Britain were likely to be certain structures of the gallery-grave series in western Scotland and Northern Ireland, and regarded the chambered cairns of the Cotswold-Severn area as also probably of gallery-grave affinities. These views he had amplified in detail for the British Isles (Childe, 1940, 46 ff.); passage-graves, having a clear structural distinction between the burial chamber and a narrow corridor of approach, were seen as the primary form with ultimate ancestors in the eastern Mediterranean, and early implanted in southern Spain, but 'the first great schism had perhaps taken place already in the western Mediterranean' and while orthodoxy prevailed in Almeria, the gallery-grave schismatics were establishing themselves in the Gulf of Lions and the Pyrenees, soon to find their way to western Scotland, where the 'tradition of the megalithic cist in its purest form', normally a long rectangle in plan with no structural distinction of passage, was to be established. These gallery-graves, Childe pointed out, were usually contained in long cairns, in contradistinction to the passage-graves beneath round mounds, and he considered it 'likely that the long mound and long cist were brought from south France together' to Britain. He classified the British tombs into three main groups, the first being *long cists* or *gallery-graves*, with representatives in the Clyde-Carlingford area (west Scotland and Northern Ireland), the Severn Estuary and Cotswolds, and other regions in Ireland, Shetland and Kent. His second group, *unchambered long barrows and collective tombs*, we have already considered in dealing with the Windmill Hill culture in southern and eastern England, and his third, *passage-graves*, comprised those of the Boyne group in Ireland, the Pentland (Caithness and Orkney) and Beauly (Moray) groups in Scotland, and 'entrance-graves' in Scilly and South Ireland. He considered that 'there is no megalithic culture defined by equipment and ornaments, common to all megalithic tombs', and referred the building of the tombs to a 'spiritual aristocracy of "divine" chiefs'. The two strains of passage-graves and gallery-graves were seen as mingling in the Hebrides, Orkneys and Caithness to produce hybrid monuments.

In the same year as this study an independent review of the problem was published by C. Hawkes (1940, 167ff.). Accepting the dual nature of the chambered tombs in Europe, he advanced a novel explanation of the genesis of the gallery-grave in a fusion of the Almerian cist-burials with the collective tombs of passage-grave tradition in south Spain, and with Childe saw a spread from southern France via the Catalan sites and those in the Basque provinces to the Clyde-Carlingford area, but considered that the essential tomb element which was transmitted was that of a 'minimal' single cist. The long mound associated with gallery-graves he regarded as marking the 'graves of adventurers of Breton connexion', and some at least of the Cotswold cairns as 'genuine megalithic gallery-graves'. Like Childe, he saw fusion of passage-grave and gallery-grave strains in north-west Scotland.

As will be seen, it was the gallery-graves that were constituting the main element in the discussion of origins, no one disputing the derivation of such tombs as New Grange or Maes Howe from the passage-grave types in Iberia, despite local peculiarities of plan. The Cotswold chambered cairns formed the centre of a controversy which involved the distinction between passage-graves and gallery-graves, for Daniel (1937b; 1939b) had classed these as members of the gallery-grave family and found convincing prototypes for these transepted gallery-graves, as he styled them, in west French tombs around the mouth of the Loire and in Brittany. His two papers provoked a rejoinder from Forde (1940) who disputed all his conclusions, interpreted the west French tombs and their derivatives as transepted *passage-graves*, and finally swept away all tombs previously classed as gallery-graves except perhaps the S.O.M. and Swedish long cists, relegating them to the position of degenerate descendants from 'the one basic form of collective-tomb style in western Europe', the passage-grave: in fact our alleged gallery-graves were merely 'a number of collateral descendants of "passage-graves" which lack spacious terminal chambers'.

In the following year Daniel (1941) published a detailed survey of the whole question of the dual character of the chambered-tomb colonization of Europe, pointing out at the beginning that Forde was practically *contra mundum* in his denial of at least two main streams in the process of the diffusion of megalithic tombs. He then followed with an elaborate and over-ingenious classification, based on variations in tomb-plans, of the extant monuments from the western Mediterranean to Scandinavia under the two main heads of passage-graves and gallery-graves. In general terms his scheme in reference to Britain (re-stated in Daniel, 1950) agreed fairly well with that of Childe (1940), though the Irish gallery-graves were split up into a large number of typological sub-varieties and he assigned primacy of position in the Scottish series of passage-graves to the Clava cairns of the

Moray, rather than to the Caithness monuments as Childe preferred. In north-west Scotland he considered 'the traditions of passage-graves and gallery-graves seem so inextricably mixed that morphological analysis is impossible' (p. 44) and held that the movement of people that brought the tombs from the continent of Europe to Britain and beyond was that of colonization and not that of the propagators of a religion alone.

His reference to the mixture of cultures in the Hebrides was taken up by Scott (1942) with especial reference to three chambered tombs he had excavated in Skye and North Uist. One of these, Clettraval, which had been considered by Childe and Daniel as showing a noteworthy fusion of passage-grave and gallery-grave elements, Scott considered as 'passage-grave in the significant sense that a chamber, approached by a passage, provided for burials...despite the fact that its long, segmented passage links it as regards methods of construction with the gallery-graves of the Clyde'. This really seems to be much the same as Childe's and Daniel's interpretations, differing only in the conception of what constitute 'elements' in megalithic tomb architecture and funerary ritual, but the pottery sequence in these North Uist tombs, and that from the Eilean an Tighe potters' workshop on the same island, seemed to Scott to throw 'some measure of doubt on the two-stream theory of the typology of chamber tombs or at least on the priority in time of the gallery-grave over the passage-grave which is usually associated with it'. He found the pottery sequence to be so analogous to that in southern France that he suggested the possibility of continuous contacts between the Hebrides and Languedoc throughout the Neolithic, and ended with a plea that the classification of megalithic cultures should not be made on pure typology of tomb-plans, 'but from consideration of all relevant cultural traits in the regions and periods concerned'. This conclusion one whole-heartedly endorses, regretting only that in so many areas 'relevant cultural traits' other than the tombs themselves are absent or inadequately recorded, and urging that some typological scheme which does not seek to be too inclusive or all-embracing is really essential as a working hypothesis in order to arrange the mass of material in some sort of a framework within which its features can be described with convenience.

The arrangement which I have adopted here for discussing the regions of settlement of chambered-tomb builders in Britain is fundamentally that of Childe and Daniel with minor variations: the latter has adopted (1950) a more detailed subdivision of the English and Welsh material, based on regional groups, than I have found it necessary to make here. A basic dual division into passage-grave and gallery-grave series seems an essential, for however ambiguous may be the ancestry of many degenerate monuments, some difference in origin is obviously necessary to explain such divergent conceptions of tomb architecture as displayed at New Grange and at East Bennan, or that of the Clava *tholoi* and that of the Severn-Cotswold long cairns, linked as they are by the common practice of collective burial in stone-built vaults and little else. Within the two main families the tomb-types, and in some instances other associated cultural traits such as pottery types, form themselves into regional groups, or natural areas within which distinctive variant cultures seem established. Of these, ten main provinces seem recognizable, with in some instances subdivisions where variations in tomb form justify this. In addition to these main areas of megalithic colonization in the west and north of Britain (which, whatever the exact components, must all derive from European cultures scattered along the western seaboard from Portugal to Normandy), there is a regional group of megalithic tombs in Kent which seem likely to be representatives of a secondary colonization from the megalithic areas of Holland and North Germany.

Our scheme for a classification of the megalithic cultures of Britain on a basis of tomb typology, associated elements of material culture, and regional distribution, works out as follows:

Gallery-graves and their probable derivatives

Regional Groups:
(1) The Severn-Cotswold long cairns.
(2) The Clyde-Carlingford Culture of West Scotland and North Ireland.
(3) The Irish galleries and derivative 'dolmens'.
(4) Miscellaneous local groups, including long cairns.

Passage-graves and their probable derivatives

Regional groups:
(1) The Boyne culture of Ireland.
(2) The Hebridean passage-graves.
(3) The Orkney-Cromarty tombs of north Scotland.
(4) The Clava passage-graves of Scotland.
(5) The Shetland group.
(6) The Scilly-Tramore culture of south-east Ireland and Scillies-west Cornwall.
(7) Miscellaneous local groups.

In view of the controversy outlined above, a few words of justification are necessary for the grouping adopted, and the order in which the various regional groups are treated. To anticipate, it may be said that there is some weight of evidence for classing the Severn-Cotswold cairns and the Clyde-Carlingford culture among the earliest of the chambered-tomb groups of west Britain. It is convenient to deal with the former group immediately after the description of the Windmill Hill culture in the two previous chapters, since Wessex and the Cotswolds are adjacent regions and contact between the two communities—Windmill Hill folk and Cotswold cairn builders—is likely to have existed. In the Clyde-Carlingford culture too, contacts with that of Windmill Hill as represented in Yorkshire is almost certainly represented by pottery and other features.

About the passage-graves there is likely to be less dispute. The Boyne culture has a marked insular individuality with, as will be shown, many features which link it with British Bronze Age communities at least in its later stages. The passage-graves of the Clava Group have little or no direct evidence of date relative to those of other regions except the typologically early form of the actual corbelled tombs. In the Hebrides Scott's excavations have fortunately related at least three tombs to a pottery sequence consistent in all and able to be correlated with that of the Clyde-Carlingford culture. Links with the Hebridean pottery sequence are also found in the large group of tombs on both sides of the Pentland Firth, where are also found local eccentricities evolved in isolation but based on early structural features of tomb construction, but the remarkable Shetland group is a distinct unit with consistent plan. Finally, the Scilly-Tramore group consists of a very homogeneous group of tombs concentrated in two areas, one on each side of St George's Channel, without any distinctive connexions with other Neolithic cultures in these regions. Their position within the passage-grave derivatives has been disputed, but quite apart from formal architectural considerations they fall more reasonably into this setting within the British series of derivatives.

In the regional groups the tombs have necessarily to be taken as the main criteria for defining the cultural area on a map, as it is not always possible to associate tomb types with other elements of material culture such as pottery, and habitation sites are relatively rare. Where these occur they are, however, discussed after the tombs and their grave-goods have been described, and such correlations made between the settlements and the tombs as is possible.

Within these areas the information recorded by field work or excavation varies profoundly in quality and extent: knowledge of the Clyde-Carlingford culture is fortunately soundly based on Bryce's pioneer work and the later excavations of Evans and Davies, while Clifford and Grimes have produced the classic excavated sites in the Severn-Cotswold area, and the Ordnance Survey, Grimes, Hencken and Daniel have clarified the Welsh and English distributions. Of the hundred or so great passage-graves of the Boyne culture none has been excavated according to modern standards, and most of the Caithness tombs were dug in the last century. Ireland, with the exception of the work already referred to in Ulster and a few restricted regional surveys in Eire, is still without a critical map of its vast number of chambered tombs, and while most of the passage-graves of the Boyne culture are adequately recorded, the derivative gallery-graves and other allied forms which make up the bulk of the material in Eire have never been worked on since the days of Borlase. In Scotland, however, the work of Childe and of the Royal Commission on Ancient Monuments has rendered the general distribution-pattern reliable and there is a long series of excavations culminating in Scott's work in the Hebrides, where precise observation of stratigraphy has been made for the first time in Scottish chambered tombs. The comparatively few tombs of the Scilly-Tramore culture have been well served by the work of Bonsor, Hencken, Powell, J. Hawkes, and O'Neil.

It is however possible to digest and correlate the available material and to produce a provisional picture, using the results of the recent scientific excavations as a criterion against which less precisely recorded information can be tested and interpreted. It may be remarked in passing that the actual date of an excavation need not be an index to its relative reliability, and we should not dismiss too summarily the work of the nineteenth-century workers such as Wood-Martin or Anderson, whose accounts often contain objective observations which can be illuminating when interpreted by the modern excavations carried out on scientific lines.

The literature of the British chambered tombs is very scattered and includes a large number of individual authors. I have given at the beginning of each section dealing with a regional group a list of the main references which should cover practically every tomb dealt with in that section, and reserved individual bibliographical references in the text for special points or for authors not included in the general list. The English and Welsh chambered tombs have been listed with full references by Daniel (1950), and the existence of his study has led me to devote greater space to the Scottish and Irish sites which have not hitherto been studied as a group. Inevitably there has been some overlapping with Daniel's work in my treatment of the chambered-tomb groups in England and Wales, but it is hoped that a difference of approach renders the two surveys complementary.

THE REGIONAL GROUPS: THE SEVERN-COTSWOLD
CHAMBERED CAIRNS

Introduction

Since the end of the nineteenth century, the 'long barrows of the Cotswolds' have been one of the best-known groups of British chambered tombs, and the classic work of Crawford (1925) gave precision to the individual culture they were seen to represent. But for some years after their definition as a group, the issue was confused by what we can now see to be a mistaken inclusion of these tombs within the same group as the earthen long barrows of Wessex and Sussex, and their recognition as a class of monument related to the chambered cairns series of the western seaboard was not clearly stated until Grimes made his studies of Welsh megalithic monuments (1936 a) and of the Brecknockshire long cairns in particular (1936 b). In 1937 Daniel, describing a tomb of this group in Gower, discussed the seventy or so cairns that could be included in the same typological series on both sides of the Bristol Channel and proposed the term 'Severn-Cotswold Group' as a reasonable geographical label, analogous to that of Clyde-Carlingford (Daniel, 1937 b, 80; 1950, with full bibliography).

The chambered cairns in question, while showing considerable variation in detail, nevertheless all consist of collective tombs within long mounds or cairns with elaborate revetments or peristaliths along its edge, which normally follows a straight-sided trapezoid or approaches a rectangle in plan. In the typologically early forms access to the burial chamber is gained through an entrance set between incurving walls at the broader end of the cairn; in derivative examples the chambers may open from the long sides of the structure. Grave-goods are not very abundant, but are consistent within the whole group.

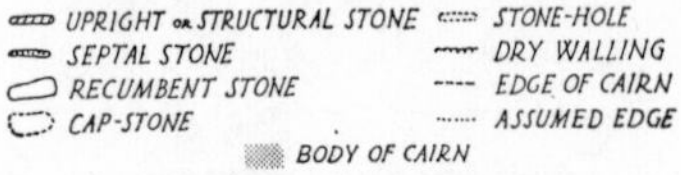

Fig. 18. Conventional symbols used on plans of chambered tombs.

UPRIGHT or STRUCTURAL STONE
SEPTAL STONE
RECUMBENT STONE
CAP-STONE
STONE-HOLE
DRY WALLING
EDGE OF CAIRN
ASSUMED EDGE
BODY OF CAIRN

The distribution of these tombs (Fig. 19) shows that four main regions were settled from the shores of the Bristol Channel and the Severn estuary. Along the coastal plain from Gower to Monmouthshire are scattered ten tombs, and on the opposite side of the river the main concentration of thirty or so tombs is on the Cotswold Hills and thence on to the northern edge of the chalk massif in Berkshire and probably to North Wiltshire, though the chambered tombs there may be related to inland penetration from the more southerly area of primary colonization, in Somerset. In the Black Mountains of Brecknockshire a group of a dozen tombs imply penetration up the valley of the Usk, but seem likely to represent secondary colonization from the Cotswolds rather than direct from the coast.

The Cotswolds, Wiltshire and Somerset tombs lie for the most part on ridges or uplands of the Jurassic oolite or the chalk; no doubt, as we have seen, wooded at this time, though hardly with heavy oakwood. But several of the coastal sites in Wales, and more strikingly the Black Mountain cairns, lie in valleys that must have been among thick oak forest under natural conditions, their siting recalling the Galloway group of tombs in the Clyde-Carlingford region. At Swell, Gatcombe and Avening in the Cotswolds the cairns are grouped round springs, though not in the actual valleys. A curious feature (reminiscent of Galloway and also of Wessex long barrows) is the grouping of cairns in pairs (Ffostyll, Hazleton, Eyford and Newclose, Poles Wood North and South for instance) from 70 to 500 yards apart.

Cairns and their plans

While preserving a notable uniformity of essential plan over the whole area of settlement, there is nevertheless a considerable range in length and proportions. Daniel has drawn attention to this (1937*b*, 83 n.), and has contrasted such enormous mounds as those at East and West Kennet in North Wiltshire, 350 and 340 ft. long respectively, with such sites as Parc le Breos Cwm (90 ft.) or the large series of Cotswold cairns varying from 100 to

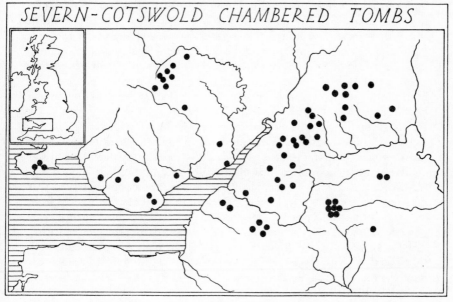

Fig. 19. (*After Daniel.*)

175 ft. in length. The North Wiltshire group of tombs has, however, many individual characteristics, and a length of about 100 ft. is probably representative of the remainder of the Severn-Cotswold sites.

The building material is local: oolite and other Jurassic rocks in the Cotswolds, limestone in some Somerset cairns, Old Red Sandstone in Brecknockshire. In the Berkshire and North Wiltshire tombs, the body of the mound is made of chalk rubble derived from flanking ditches in the manner of the 'unchambered' long barrows described in Chapter II, while structural elements of chambers, façades or peristaliths are made of local Tertiary sarsen blocks with a consequent influence on architectural modes in these regions. But in the tombs at West Kennet and Walker's Hill in North Wiltshire at least, oolite and coral rag for dry-stone walling was imported from the Calne region, eight miles to the west.

Thanks to a notable series of excavations, beginning with the remarkable pioneer work of John Ward at Tinkinswood (Ward, 1916), followed by Mrs Clifford at Notgrove and Nympsfield (Clifford, 1937; 1938) and elsewhere in the Cotswolds, and by Grimes at Ty Isaf in Brecknockshire (Grimes, 1939*b*), we have a considerable body of reliable and detailed evidence for the construction of the Severn-Cotswold cairns, in the light of which we can often utilize the earlier excavation reports (Fig. 20).

Evidence for any preparation of the ground on which the cairn was to be built seems confined to patches of burning suggesting clearance of vegetation, and, although at Notgrove and Nympsfield a thicker clay layer beneath the cairn than around it at first suggested deliberate deposition, the geological evidence is against this and the difference of thickness is more likely to be the result of the preservation of the clay from subsequent denudation when the surrounding land became tilled or grazed as open pasture.[1] At both these sites, however, it appeared that a shallow marking-out trench had been made to indicate the outline of the cairn, and at Notgrove and Ty Isaf small marking-out stones set on edge were also found.

It is clear that considerable attention was paid to the formal shape of the cairn, which, except in the sarsen-built tombs already mentioned, was demarcated by one or more lines of carefully built dry walling bonded into the cairn material on its inner side. There seems little doubt, however, that these walls were, almost simultaneously with their building, obscured from sight by deliberately placed 'extra-revetment' material piled against their outer face, and their function was purely ritual. It is probable, however, that the walling at the entrance to the burial chamber was exposed during the funerals at least, though at Ty Isaf the walls outlining the forecourt area were themselves ritual performances made on top of the blocking material.

At Wayland's Smithy, and at least seven tombs in the Avebury region, monumental peristaliths of standing sarsen stones probably originally linked by panels of dry-walling surrounded the mound. At Wayland's Smithy, a buried sarsen revetment bonded back into the chalk rubble mound was found behind and more or less parallel to the line of the peristalith.

The plans of the cairns, as demarcated by these walls or peristaliths, is consistently straight-sided, tapering slightly towards the far end (which is squared or even, as at Nympsfield, slightly concave), behind the burial chamber if this is set in the wider end as in the typologically earlier examples. The walls curve inwards to form a forecourt between two 'horns' to such chambers, and a degeneration series can be observed in which, though the chambers become multiple and entered from the sides of the cairn, and the functional entrance dwindles to a ritual 'false portal', the original trapezoid outline is never completely lost.

1 Cf. the similar circumstances obtaining under a Bronze Age cairn at Cairnpapple, West Lothian (Piggott, 1950).

SEVERN – COTSWOLD CHAMBERED TOMBS

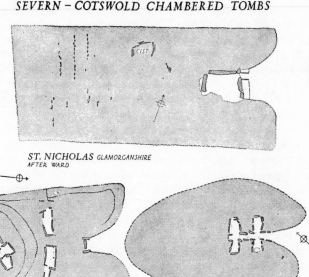

ST. NICHOLAS GLAMORGANSHIRE
AFTER WARD

TY ISAF BRECKNOCKSHIRE
AFTER GRIMES

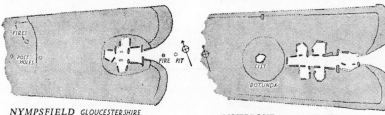

PARC LE BREOS·CWM GOWER
AFTER DANIEL

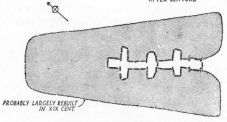

NYMPSFIELD GLOUCESTERSHIRE
AFTER CLIFFORD

NOTGROVE GLOUCESTERSHIRE
AFTER CLIFFORD

STONEY LITTLETON SOMERSET

Fig. 20.

The burial chambers

Within these cairns are set the burial chambers, and a primary division can be made between terminal and lateral disposition. There seems little doubt that terminally chambered cairns are the earliest within the series, and these can be divided into three main groups on the evidence of their plans. The first, and most important, is the transepted gallery of Daniel's terminology (1937 *b*, 84), represented by nine tombs, two on the coastal plain of Gower, three in the Cotswolds, one in Brecknockshire, two in Somerset and one in Berkshire. As will be seen, convincing parallels to this tomb-plan can be found in western France, and its builders must have formed the most significant component in the initial colonization of the area under review. Further examples may be revealed as the result of excavation, since the nature of the transepted gallery at Ty Isaf was unrecognizable before Grimes' work on the site.

Heston Brake represents the sole convincing example of another type of chamber, a simple parallel-sided gallery, and there are a few examples of smallish rectangular chambers such as those at Tinkinswood, Randwick or Manton Down. The degenerate laterally chambered tombs show various eccentricities of chamber form, sometimes entirely built in dry-stone walling, and finally becoming small closed cists within the cairn. West Kennet presents a problem. The chamber with its long passage approach does at first suggest a fairly normal plan within the passage-grave group, as indeed do the lateral chambers at Belas Knap, for instance. But Mr Grimes has suggested to me (*in litt.* 1947) that a pair of transepts may have been missed by Thurnam in his excavations of 1859 and that the plan could have re-sembled Wayland's Smithy with the addition of these.

The chambers are normally built of orthostats with dry walling between, and forming a slight degree of corbelling to carry cap-stones. At Stoney Littleton in Somerset, however (Fig. 21), the great gallery with its three pairs of transeptal chambers has a corbelled barrel-vault carried out in a manner recalling Carn Ban in Arran (Fig. 24), and corbelling was used for the roofs of two of the lateral chambers at Belas Knap, and at the Cow Common long cairn there seems to have been a small chamber entirely of *tholos* construction.

The evidence of excavation has shown that, as might have been expected, the chambers were built first, and the cairn then made around them. At Nympsfield, the cairn immediately around the transepted gallery was built as a self-contained oval structure itself buried in the general cairn mass, and at Ty Isaf a much more elaborate circular construction was built around the transepted chamber there. The significance of such constructions is dis-cussed at a later stage.

Paving of the chamber floor, wholly or in part, was noted at Notgrove

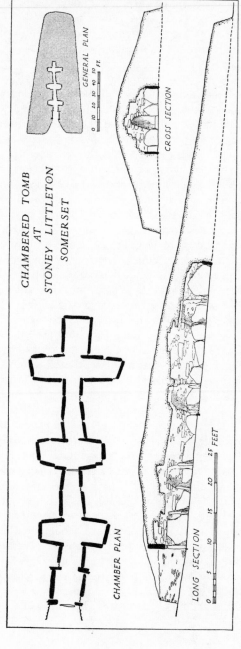

CHAMBERED TOMB
AT
STONEY LITTLETON
SOMERSET

GENERAL PLAN

0 10 20 30 40 50 FT.

CROSS SECTION

CHAMBER PLAN

LONG SECTION

0 5 10 15 20 25 FEET

Fig. 21.

and Ty Isaf and in the terminal chamber at Belas Knap. At Rodmarton two lateral chambers were constructed on ground-level in the normal way, but access to them was gained by a flight of carefully built stone steps from a point over 3 ft. higher in the cairn material.

Entrances: portals, false portals and port-holes

The entrance to the burial chamber in the Severn-Cotswold tombs is normally unelaborated, though the unique gallery at Heston Brake has two asymmetrical portal stones, one 5 ft. and the other 3 ft. high, and both standing higher than the remaining stones of the gallery, recalling Clyde-Carlingford examples. But in most tombs the revetment walls are curved in to make a forecourt or façade, of types described below, and not infrequently a characteristic form of degeneration takes place, whereby a 'false portal' is constructed of two jamb-stones and an intermediate slab, set H-wise, but backing on to the solid material of the cairn. This H-plan setting is sometimes graced with a lintel, and the whole may be a massive and impressive structure, as at Lugbury or The Devil's Den, where the denuded stones form a conspicuous monument of the type claimed as a 'dolmen' in the last century. Final degeneration involves not only lack of a functional entrance, but even the false portal vanishes, and a shallow curve of dry walling is the only relic of the forecourt and entrance. In such false portal and more devolved tombs, the burial chambers are set laterally.

At Rodmarton, Avening and Nempnett Thrubwell, and probably at Belas Knap and Lanhill, the chamber entrance was formed by a 'port-hole' made by hollowing the edges of two adjacent slabs to form an oval hole through which it is just possible to gain access to the burial chamber, or (as seems to have been the case in the now-destroyed Nempnett Thrubwell tomb) by perforating a single slab to produce the same effect. This type of entrance is very widely known among chambered tombs in Europe and elsewhere, and by Childe (1948 a) has been regarded as a 'highly specialized trait suitable for defining a generalized "megalithic" culture if one exists', contrary to the view of Daniel (Clifford & Daniel, 1940), who regards the port-hole entrance as only 'one of the many devices for restricting and demarcating the entrance of tombs' available to the collective-tomb builders, though the most striking. For the present we may notice the technical aspect of the manufacture of the hollowed stones at Rodmarton, as observed by Mrs Clifford. 'Flakes were removed to produce the general shape' of the half-porthole at the edge of the slab, and on the upper part 'the flake scars remain untouched, but lower down, where the semicircular holes are cut and a finer finish desired, the stones were brought to a smooth surface by rubbing down and pounding' (Clifford & Daniel, 1940, 139).

Forecourts and their blocking

The space between the incurving walls leading to the entrance to the burial chamber, where this is a terminal feature, was clearly the focus of considerable ritual before and during the funeral ceremonies, as discussed below. The forecourt area at Wayland's Smithy and West Kennet, and probably in several other now destroyed north Wiltshire tombs, lay in front of a straight façade of orthostats, presumably with dry-walling between them, and in the absence of excavation of any of these sites we have no knowledge of its features or its blocking, if such existed. But among the Severn-Cotswold tombs as a group, a forecourt marked by deeply incurving walls is normal, with a depth of some 12 or 15 ft., at the narrow inner end of which lies the entrance or false portal. At Ty Isaf, the forecourt walls were as false as the portal, in that they were built not as original features, but as 'dummies' erected on the material of the cairn (Grimes, 1939 b, 125).

At Tinkinswood, Notgrove and Nympsfield the forecourt was found on excavation to have been deliberately filled up with a 'blocking' which must have rendered access to the chamber impossible by normal means after its deposition: a feature which seems to be common if not universal among all types of chambered tombs in Britain. At Notgrove the forecourt area had been roughly paved, and there were various ritual hearths and deposits described below, while the blocking material, which extended beyond the end of the reveted 'horns' of the cairn, could be distinguished as of different stone from that with which the cairn itself was constructed—an upper rather than a lower bed of Stonesfield slate, less compact and more shelly than that used elsewhere. At Nympsfield there were again traces of ritual fires on the old surface of the forecourt.

A feature at Tinkinswood not apparently represented elsewhere in the Severn-Cotswold tombs is a closing-slab which was found flat in front of the entrance to the tomb but which fitted the opening in such a way as to suggest that it was intended to serve as a 'door'. Whether it did in fact act in this manner during some part of the funeral ritual is of course unknown, but it is curious that it was prone before the forecourt blocking was built up. At Tinkinswood a deposit of potsherds was found on the old surface beneath the blocking, as at Notgrove and Nympsfield.

The blocking material itself does not appear, in any of the recorded instances, to have been so massive, or so carefully built up, as for instance at Cairnholy I in the Clyde-Carlingford area described below. But it was not a random tip of stone rubble, and in it were not only deposits of pottery, flint implements, etc., but fragmentary human skeletons representing more than one individual; human remains again were placed on the lintel of the false portal at Belas Knap.

Internal structures other than burial chambers

At Notgrove the excavations revealed a very remarkable feature which may well have existed in other cairns less thoroughly examined. Immediately behind the transepted burial chamber was a circular drum-shaped structure built of stones with carefully made, slightly battered, dry-stone walling enclosing it, 23 ft. in diameter and 2 ft. 6 in. high. Centrally within this was a closed stone cist, polygonal and about 4 ft. across, originally roofed with flat slabs and containing the skeleton of an adult male; bones of a girl were found on top of the structure. It could be established that this 'rotunda' was the first element of the eventual structure to be erected on the site. This 'rotunda' suggests comparison with the oval construction enclosing the chamber at Nympsfield, and still more with the extraordinary double-walled structure of similar character, slightly oval and approximately 40 ft. in diameter, enclosing the transepted chamber in the rear end of the Ty Isaf cairn. In Belas Knap, too, the nineteenth-century excavators discovered a roughly built circular structure only 7 ft. across, with burnt material within it, more or less central to the structure of the cairn, and this may represent the final degeneration of the same idea.

In the Tinkinswood cairn was a large irregularly built 'cist' within the cairn near its northern side: it contained some animal bones, and human bones were found around it. This is comparable with the similar though smaller structure in the Clyde-Carlingford cairn of Ballyalton.

Two Severn-Cotswold cairns have large standing stones set within them near the broader end. That at Tinglestone has not been excavated, and the stone is now 6 ft. above the surface of the cairn, but at Lyneham nineteenth-century excavations showed the stone to have had an original height of 10 ft. 6 in. and to have stood in a stone-hole 3 ft. deep. The excavations did not however contribute in any way to a real understanding of the structures within the cairn, nor the relation of the standing stone to these.

The typological sequence

It is possible to perceive two or more strains of typological development or degeneration in the Severn-Cotswold cairns, but it must be stressed at the outset that any such scheme is unsupported by collateral evidence of grave-goods or other finds. Among the most 'degenerate' tombs are those of Eyford and Poles Wood South; the former had sherds of a beaker almost certainly of Class B in a secondary context, and the latter not only a beaker (lost) but a bowl of Peterborough ware from similarly secondary positions. So even these tombs are earlier than the late Neolithic or Early Bronze Age in the Cotswolds, and yet Peterborough pottery came from the blocking at the typologically 'early' tombs of Notgrove and Nympsfield. These last finds, even though presumably related to the final use of the chamber for burial, at least show that the original tomb ritual was still being performed, and the tradition was by no means dead, at that time. On the whole then one can only say that all typological variants must lie within the same archaeological period.

The complexity of these lines of devolution has been stressed by Grimes when discussing them with wise restraint (Grimes, 1939*b*, 136). Loss of function of the entrance, with the consequent development of the false portal, marks one such line, though, as at Ty Isaf, the main transepted chamber may be moved to a position near the rear of the tomb, with an oblique lateral entrance and an enclosing rotunda-like structure. In other cairns side-chambers may form the only burial-places, following a breaking-up process similar to that perceptible in the Clyde-Carlingford area with the appearance of such tombs as The Caves of Kilhern or Dranandrow in Galloway, or Cuff Hill in Ayrshire. In such cairns as that of Eyford, entirely built in dry-walling and with closed cists within the revetment wall, we are closely approaching the Manio type of tomb which on other grounds we have suggested may form a prototype rather than a devolution of the chambered long cairns of Clyde-Carlingford and southern England. Such resemblances only serve to stress the dangers of the purely typological approach to such monuments.

Burials and funeral ritual

In all Severn-Cotswold tombs for which we have information burials have been collective, and all by inhumation if we except a rather unsatisfactory record of cremation from Temple Farm (Lukis, 1866). At Luckington, Nympsfield, Randwick, Rodmarton and Tinkinswood, however, charring of some bones was noted, as if by ritual purificatory fires. The number of recorded burials ranges from three or four (Walker's Hill) to forty-eight (Tinkinswood); six tombs have yielded over twenty burials in various parts of the monument, and nine between ten and twenty. The recorded information is set out for convenience in Table III, which indicates the total number of burials known from each tomb, whether in chambers or in other positions such as among the blocking stones, etc. Figures for sexes (frequently not recorded) give proportions of 49 per cent males, 29 per cent females, 21·5 per cent children and 0·5 per cent infants out of the total where these details are available, and we may compare the figures of 69 per cent male, 5 per cent female, and 26 per cent children from the few recorded burials in the unchambered long barrows of Wessex.

Earlier excavators had frequently noticed the great crowding of skeletons in the chambers, which were sometimes obviously too small to have contained all the bodies had they been deposited at one time and as intact corpses. The discovery of an untouched lateral burial chamber in the Lanhill cairn in recent years gave an opportunity of studying the problem of the deposition of the burials afresh, and it was clear that in this instance, and by inference elsewhere in the Severn-Cotswold tombs, the burials had been successive and spread over a relatively long period of time, so that earlier burials could be packed away in a skeletal condition to make room for each newcomer (Keiller & Piggott, 1938). It seems likely that this method of burial, so well documented from Mycenaean tombs and also recognized in Scandinavia, was that generally employed in British chambered tombs, and further examples of the practice will be noted in later chapters. In our area, as well as the explicit evidence from Lanhill, the earlier excavation reports imply that it occurred at Uley, Belas Knap, Poles Wood South and Nempnett Thrubwell, and it can reasonably be inferred in the remaining tombs.

TABLE III. *Interments in Severn-Cotswold chambered tombs*

Site	Unidentified	Male	Female	Children	Infants	Total
Belas Knap	13	6	2	1	.	22
Bown Hill	.	2	2	2	.	6
Eyford	.	7	5	1	.	13
Ffostyll S.	9+	.	.	.	.	9+
Lanhill	.	13	4	2	.	19
Little Lodge	.	5	1	2–3	.	8–9
Luckington	.	6	3	2	.	11
Lugbury	4	13	3	6	.	26
Norns Tump	11	.	.	.	.	11
Notgrove	1	3	2	2	1	9
Nympsfield	20	.	.	.	.	20
Parc Cwm	21	.	.	3	.	24
Pen y Wrylod	12	.	.	.	.	12
Poles Wood E.	19	.	.	.	.	19
Poles Wood S.	12	.	.	.	.	12
Randwick	4+	.	.	.	.	4+
Rodmarton	.	6–7	3–4	3	.	12–14
Tinkinswood	.	16	21	8	3	48
Ty Isaf	26	2	.	4	1	33
Uley	14	.	1	.	.	15
Walker's Hill	3–4	.	.	.	.	3–4
Waylands S.	8	.	.	.	.	8
West Kennet	.	5	.	.	1	6
West Tump	23	.	1	.	1	25
	200–201 +	84–85	48–49	36–37	7	375–379 +

There is some evidence from Nympsfield for the deposition of small groups of bones in divisions partitioned off within the main chambers by small slabs in a manner known in certain Scottish passage-graves, and at Rodmarton small 'pockets' of bones were found, and some human finger-bones seemed actually to have been pushed in between the stones of the dry-walling. At West Kennet the fragments of an infant's skull of about one year were found in the narrow gap between two stones of the chamber wall, together with three flint-flakes and a heap of sherds, in a manner comparable with deposits noted by Scott at Rudh'an Dunain (Scott, 1932).

The general practice seems to have been to leave the burial chamber after the final burial without any filling, though at West Kennet 2 ft. of chalk rubble covered the skeletons, above which was a layer of 'blackish sooty, and greasy-looking matter' containing flint flakes and animal bones and suggesting some form of offerings (Thurnam, 1861). At Lanhill the last burial was lightly covered with earth, but the rest of the bones at the back of the chamber were uncovered. Grave-goods were relatively frequently deposited with the dead, though many chambers contained nothing but the burials, but pottery (usually in sherds), bone and flint tools, arrowheads, axes and ornaments occur and are discussed below.

Crawford (1925) drew attention to the curious evidence from Belas Knap suggesting that several of the skulls had been dealt heavy blows before death, or at least while the bones were still green, and he made the practical suggestion that a joint investigation by a police surgeon and an anatomist would constitute the best approach to the subject. It has already been touched on in connexion with the skulls from some unchambered long barrows, but the necessary type of investigation has not yet taken place.

The physical type represented in the Severn-Cotswold cairns is consistently the gracile long-headed form common to all British Neolithic sites. At Lanhill a detailed examination of the skeletons was made with interesting results, and it was possible to show that the nine individuals were members of one particular family group, recognizable not only by the striking similarities in features, but also in the presence of the rare Wormian ossicles in seven of the nine skulls. This is, of course, of considerable importance in any reconstruction of the social structure of the communities building the collective tombs, and receives confirmation from other British and European skeletal groups from similar burial chambers. Other evidence obtained from the relatively few detailed anatomical reports on material from Severn-Cotswold tombs includes that of frequent osteo-arthritis (Lanhill), a low incidence of dental caries but a very high percentage of 'dirt pyorrhoea' (Nympsfield), and the presence of supernumerary and maloccluded molars (Lanhill). A curious feature recognized in two Severn-Cotswold burials, at Luckington and Nympsfield, is the inward bending of the fifth metatarsal bone of the foot, a condition precisely similar to that induced by the pressure of the strap of constantly-worn sandals (Cameron in Passmore, 1933; Faucett in Clifford, 1938). This condition has again been recognized in a fifth metatarsal from the chambered tomb of the Déhus in Guernsey, and the wearing of sandals by at least Iberian members of the Western Neolithic group is attested by those surviving in esparto grass from the Cueva de los Murcielagos, and the model stone and ivory ritual sandals from chambered tombs in South Spain and Portugal.[1] On

1 For Déhus, Cameron in Collum, 1933, 93; Cueva de los Murcielagos, Serra, 1925; Almizaraque and Los Millares, Leisner, 1943, 470; Alapraia (Portugal), Jalhay and do Paço, 1941, fig. 20.

the whole there seems reason to accept the English evidence as strongly in favour of sandal-wearing among the Neolithic population of the Severn-Cotswold area at least.

One skull, from Bisley, has upon it the scars of an unfinished trepanning operation, a circular groove having been cut through the outer table and down into the spongy diploë, though the inner table is still intact and the roundel has not been completely excised. There are no details of its discovery, and it may not be primary to the cairn. Although post-mortem trepanning is known in the Windmill Hill culture at Maiden Castle, true ante-mortem operations are only known on four other English skulls of which one is certainly and the other probably of Beaker date (Crichel and Eynsham: Piggott, 1940*b*). The practice is common in several Neolithic and Early Metal Age cultures of the Continent and seems to have no restricted cultural significance.

We have already noted the use of the forecourt in front of the entrance as a focus of ritual—at Notgrove and Nympsfield, where this area was carefully excavated, hearths and deposits of human and animal bones, sherds and ornaments such as beads, were found on the old surface and in the blocking material. This recalls the similar features in the Clyde-Carlingford tombs described in Chapter VI, though the blocking seems nowhere in the Severn-Cotswold area to have been so massive as at Cairnholy I. Nor is there evidence of the exact point in the obviously long funerary ritual at which the blocking was finally deposited, though it is significant that at both Notgrove and Nympsfield Peterborough ware was found in the blocking, but nowhere in primary associations in either tomb. This does suggest that either relatively temporary blockings were removed and replaced at every funeral during the active period of use of the burial chamber, or that the blocking was carried out only at the end of some fairly long stadium in the construction of the cairn in its final form, up to which time free access could be gained to the forecourt and a temporary closure made of the actual chamber entrance. In this connexion the stone slab at Tinkinswood may be significant, and could be interpreted as the temporary means of closing the entrance to the chamber until the final blocking was constructed.

Evidence of ritual fires and burning in the forecourts or elsewhere has been recorded from nine Cotswold tombs (Clifford, 1950).

MATERIAL EQUIPMENT[1]

Pottery

Pottery of the Western Neolithic group of wares has been found in twelve tombs in primary associations, though in few instances was it present as more than small sherds. At Ty Isaf, however, at least one bowl could be restored (Fig. 22, no. 2), and the kinship of the sherds there to the couple

---

1 The grave-goods from the Cotswold tombs only are listed and discussed in Clifford (1950).

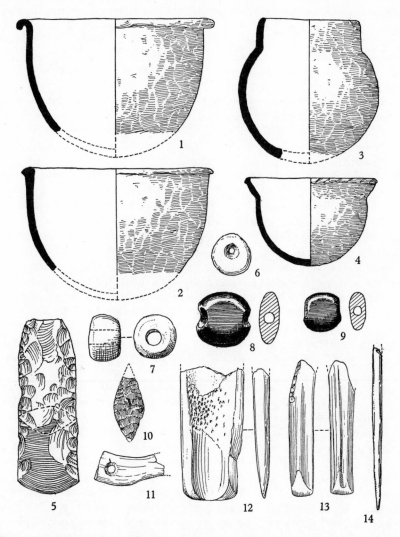

Fig. 22. Severn-Cotswold culture: pottery, stone and bone types. 1, 9, Eyford (*after Clifford*); 2, 5, 6, 14, Ty Isaf (*after Grimes*); 3, 4, 8, Notgrove (*after Clifford*); 7, West Kennet; 10, West Tump; 11, Uley; 12, Poles Wood East (*after Clifford*); 13, Temple Bottom. Scales: 1–4, ¼; remainder, ½.

from Parc Cwm was apparent. The simple little bowls from Lanhill and Poles Wood East have no really significant features except perhaps the shell grit at the former site, but Eyford produced a large fragment (Fig. 22, no. 1) comparable in general terms to the Ty Isaf material and still more to that from Tinkinswood, while Nympsfield produced two vessels (Fig. 23, nos. 3, 4) that could be restored but which have no very precise analogies within the area.

But on the whole we are justified in regarding the finds as representing a homogeneous group. The wares are dark and often leathery, the forms mainly simple bowls with thickened, rolled or hooked rims. One Nympsfield pot is globular with a vertical neck, and the other has nicks along the everted rim. Otherwise decoration is absent except for a faint rippling made with the finger-tips over the thickened rims at Ty Isaf and Parc Cwm.

While recognizably within the Western Neolithic group, the pottery is not identical with Windmill Hill ware in Wessex. It has certain affinities with Abingdon ware, however, in rim forms and the use of shell grit and perhaps in the rippling, but these features are shared equally with pottery from beyond the area of primary settlement of the Windmill Hill culture in Yorkshire or even Scotland. On the whole then, while we cannot regard it as derived from Wessex at an early phase of the Windmill Hill colonization, it might well be the product of a parallel tradition with common roots in western France, with some probability of give-and-take with the Abingdon and similar wares of the Upper Thames valley and further north. The pottery spoons from Nether Swell (Leeds, 1927a), with their exact parallels in Sussex, may imply similar contacts with other areas of the Windmill Hill culture.

In the blocking at Notgrove and Nympsfield, and near the surface of the cairn material at Poles Wood South, pottery of the Peterborough class, described in Chapter XI below, was found. In the first two instances at least it implies continued use of the burial chambers until the arrival in the Cotswolds of the makers of this ware, presumably as in Wessex an event late in the Neolithic, and this is referred to again when dealing with the Peterborough folk in detail. But at West Kennet, large quantities of Peterborough pottery, together with sherds of Class *A* beakers, were found in primary contexts with the burials in the chamber, with no evidence of any phase associated with Western Neolithic wares. Short of assuming a total clearance of the contents of the chamber before the deposition of these burials at West Kennet, one must assume them to be primary and to imply the construction of the tomb at a very late date, within the Early Bronze Age. Such clearance is not in fact impossible, and it has been demonstrated in certain Scandinavian chambered tombs at least, but until there has been complete excavation of West Kennet, with its forecourt, the evidence from Thurnam's excavations of 1859 must be used with reserve.

Flint and other stone objects

Axes of chipped and polished flint are represented by one complete implement (Fig. 22, no. 5) and the butt-end of a second from Ty Isaf, the complete example coming from one of the burial chambers. At Rodmarton the nineteenth-century excavators found a 'polished greenstone fragment' presumably of an axe, but this has since been lost. It would constitute the sole piece of evidence for linking the Severn-Cotswold tombs with the use of stone (rather than flint) axes in southern England.

Leaf arrowheads of flint are known from Notgrove, Nympsfield, Rodmarton, Tinkinswood, Ty Isaf, Walker's Hill and West Tump (Fig. 22, no. 10). The types vary from the long 'willow-leaves' of Rodmarton to the angular outline of one from Ty Isaf and another from Notgrove. The abundance of leaf-arrowheads as surface finds in the Cotswolds has often been commented upon (Crawford, 1925, 7).

Serrated flakes which might have been saws or possibly sickle-flints are recorded from Belas Knap and West Kennet.

Polished-edge knives are represented by a single example from West Kennet. The type has been mentioned earlier in connexion with Clyde-Carlingford and other finds, and is discussed fully in Chapters x and xi in connexion with the Secondary Neolithic cultures of which it is typical.

A *stone whetstone*, of Pennant Sandstone probably from the valley of the Somerset Avon, was found at West Kennet. It need not necessarily have been for sharpening metal objects, but in view of its association with *A*-beaker sherds, this possibility cannot be ruled out. Another whetstone (broken) was found at Bisley.

Stone or flint hammer-stones occurred at Belas Knap, Bisley, Rodmarton, and West Kennet, and a similar object came from the Temple Farm chamber.

Stone discs ranging in size from 2 in. to nearly 5 in. in diameter, made from the local thin-bedded rock and chipped (or in one instance also ground) into shape round the edge, were found at Ty Isaf, where ten came from various locations in the chambers and cairn material. Their use is unknown, but parallels can be quoted from the Clyde-Carlingford area and elsewhere in Scotland.

Haematite fragments at Nympsfield and Rodmarton and *quartz* at Rodmarton both seem likely to have been imported to the Cotswolds from the Iron Acton region, some twenty miles away to the south-west.

In examining the significance of these finds, we can immediately perceive that the West Kennet assemblage is anomalous and unrelated to other finds in the Severn-Cotswold group of tombs. The pottery of Peterborough and Beaker types in primary contexts, the polished-edge knife, the whetstone and probably the absence of leaf-arrowheads in an otherwise richly furnished tomb, all serve to mark off this site as exceptional, linked to the others solely by the architectural character of the tomb.

The remaining stone objects form a consistent enough group, comparable in general lines with that of the Clyde-Carlingford tombs—leaf-arrowheads, axes, and the curious stone discs, paralleled at Cairnholy I, Ballynamona, Pant y Saer and at Clettraval, a tomb having marked affinities with the Clyde-Carlingford group, if not itself a member of it. As we shall see in considering the other elements of the material equipment represented in the Severn-Cotswold tombs, connexions with the Windmill Hill culture are generalized rather than specific, though the Wessex chalk-lands must have been the source of much if not all the flint used in the Cotswolds and Welsh marches.

Bone objects

The most frequent type represented in the Severn-Cotswold tombs is the *chisel* or 'scoop' made by polishing the edge of a split animal bone (or exceptionally a horse's tooth) to form a smooth rounded wedge, a tool known from Belas Knap, Bown Hill, Notgrove, Poles Wood East, Rodmarton and Temple Farm (Fig. 22, nos. 12, 13). Rough bone *points* are known from Nympsfield and Notgrove, and a simple oval-section *pin* from Ty Isaf (Fig. 22, no. 14). From Uley and Belas Knap come *perforated boar's tusk* fragments (perhaps of pendants) (Fig. 22, no. 11).

Little can be said of these tools except the 'chisels', already commented on in connexion with the single example from Windmill Hill and another from the Giants' Hills long barrow in Lincolnshire. Their relative abundance in the Severn-Cotswold tombs contrasts with their rarity in the Windmill Hill culture.

Beads and pendants

Two large oval beads of shale or inferior jet were found, at Notgrove and Eyford respectively (Fig. 22, nos. 8, 9), and the former site also produced a small bone bead, and half a small bone ring probably a form of bead or pendant. A single large stone bead, of oblate spherical form, was found at West Kennet (Fig. 22, no. 7). Two bone tubes from Rodmarton seem best explicable as large cylinder-beads, and from Nympsfield came a shell of the dog-whelk (*Nucella lapillus*) rubbed smooth and perforated for suspension. Ty Isaf produced a small sandstone pendant of more or less circular form with eccentric perforation (Fig. 22, no. 6).

The shale beads are of some interest in view of the relative scarcity of such objects in the British Neolithic, though there was one unfinished example from Maiden Castle in an early context, one from Hembury, another from Windmill Hill and a fourth from Cairnholy I. If the material of the Cotswold beads is Kimmeridge shale, it would point to trade contacts at least with Dorset.

Art

At the Ty Illtyd cairn in Brecknockshire, three uprights of the visible chamber have a number of incised designs upon them, consisting of small cruciform figures either enclosed within diamond-shaped outlines or with small hollows at the ends of the arms. Crawford, who gives an excellent photograph of them (Crawford, 1925, 64) is in favour of regarding them as medieval Christian symbols and draws attention to the association of the cairn with St Illtyd. Breuil, on the other hand accepts the signs as prehistoric, and compares them with such stylized human forms as those on the Clonfinlough stone (Breuil, 1934, 290). Both views are possible and the question must remain an open one.

Domesticated animals

A considerable number of animal bones have been recovered and reported upon from the Severn-Cotswold tombs, and the wild forms represented have already received comment in Chapter 1. Of domesticated breeds, *ox* predominates, with identifications from fourteen sites, closely followed by *pig* from thirteen tombs, though some of these may well be wild boars. *Sheep* or *goat* is represented in eight instances, and *dog* in four—at Nympsfield it was possible to distinguish two breeds of dog, one the size of a Scottish deer-hound, the other of a collie or terrier build (Bate in Clifford, 1938). There is no evidence that the horse (known from eight sites) was domesticated, and its presence as a feral type has already been commented on.

COLLECTIVE BURIAL UNDER A ROUND CAIRN

A single monument, the Soldiers' Grave near the Nympsfield long cairn, represents the collective burial tradition in the Cotswolds under a very curious form. A circular cairn 56 ft. in diameter and probably originally about 8 ft. high, with a kerb on the downhill side, covered a very large rock-cut pit, lined with very well built dry walling. The grave thus formed was boat-shaped, 11 ft. long and 4 ft. 6 in. wide at the square end, curving symmetrically into a point at the other, and 3 ft. 9 in. deep. The cairn had been plundered but the evidence suggested that this grave had been roofed with flat slabs, and within it there still remained the bones of not less than twenty-eight individuals, with a possible maximum of forty-four, with charring noticeable on one or two fragments. Ox, pig, and dog bones were also present, and a few sherds of unornamented ware, probably of the Early Bronze Age (Clifford, 1938).

This remarkable tomb is without parallel, and although the pottery suggests a post-Neolithic date, the rite of collective burial links it to the tombs previously discussed and merits its inclusion here.

USE OF TOMBS IN THE BRONZE AGE

The only evidence suggesting use of the burial chambers in the Early Bronze Age comes from Tinkinswood, where *B*-beaker sherds were found with the inhumations and sherds of Western Neolithic ware mixed in the chamber. It is possible that in this instance access to the chamber had been gained from one side, found ruined by Ward in his excavations, and that the bones did not in fact represent the final deposits accompanying burials brought in through the doorway over the forecourt. West Kennet, of course, did produce *A*-beaker sherds in a primary context, but the unique character of the deposits in this tomb has already been commented upon.

At Eyford, Poles Wood South and Ty Isaf, beaker sherds (Class *B* at Eyford, *A* at Ty Isaf, and unknown at Poles Wood) were found in secondary contexts unassociated with burials: at Ty Isaf Grimes noted that the sherds could only have come into the position in which they were found after disturbance of the chamber.

On the whole therefore the use of the burial chambers in the Severn-Cotswold cairns seems to have ceased by the time of the local advent of beaker-makers.

A PROBABLE OUTPOST OF THE SEVERN-COTSWOLD TOMBS
IN NORTH WALES

While the chambered cairns under discussion have been shown to have, on the whole, a relatively compact distribution in the lands around the Severn estuary, there are nevertheless two chambered cairns in North Wales, over 100 miles north-west of even the Brecknock group, that typologically have claims to be connected with the Severn-Cotswold group, though Daniel (1950) would consider them as independent of it, and related to the other long cairns of Gwynedd. It is, however, convenient to refer to them here.

One of these, at Capel Garmon (Llanrwst), has been excavated, and the plan is known in detail. The characteristic wedge-shaped outline enclosed by the revetment wall, buried within the cairn, no less than the incurving horns with forecourt and false portal, seem to link it unambiguously with the Cotswolds, and the T-shaped chamber entered from the side of the mound can be seen, following the Ty Isaf discoveries, to be in origin a transepted gallery (Hemp, 1927; Grimes, 1936*a*; 1939*b*). The finds were scanty, but included a sherd of Western Neolithic ware and scraps of beakers which may have been deposited before the final blocking of the passage-approach to the burial chambers.

Not far from Capel Garmon, an unexcavated tomb, Maen Pebyll, shows the characteristics of a more or less rectangular cairn, with horns, forecourt and an apparently rectangular chamber in the Maes y Felin or Randwick manner. Again these peculiarities of plan can best be explained by refer-ence to the Cotswold-Severn region (Grimes, 1936 a).

The two chambered cairns constitute a first-class problem. Despite extensive field-work, no intermediate examples between Denbighshire and Brecknockshire can be traced; but unless one assumes a remarkable sea-voyage from the Bristol Channel to the North Wales coast, the connexion between the two areas must have been overland. I have suggested elsewhere that the trade in stone axes from the factory site at Graig Lwyd in North Wales to Wessex may be connected, but direct evidence is lacking (Keiller, Piggott & Wallis, 1941).

RELATIONSHIP OF THE SEVERN-COTSWOLD TOMBS

In any attempt to assess the relationships of the chambered cairns described in this chapter two regions have strong claims for consideration—that of the Windmill Hill culture in Wessex, and that of the Clyde-Carlingford tombs in the west and north-west of Britain. Features shared with the unchambered long barrows of the Windmill Hill culture are the practice of collective burial, and the almost exclusive inhumation rite, within and at one end of long mounds of more or less regularly defined rectangular or straight-sided forms. The placing of these mounds on ridges, and their not infrequent occurrence in pairs, are again features in common to both regions, but the siting of such cairns as those of Brecknockshire, in valleys among thick oakwood, is something very unlike the Wessex long-barrow tradition. With these long barrows and with the settlements, however, the use of pottery, almost entirely undecorated, within the Western Neolithic family, is a link, as is also that of leaf-arrowheads and axes of flint. The shale beads from two Cotswold sites and three in Wessex are again a rather specialized feature shared by both regions. But with the exception of these beads, the common features mentioned are none of them very specific, and are hardly more than products of a common ancestry within the Western Neolithic cultures as a whole.

When we turn to the Clyde-Carlingford group of chambered cairns we find perhaps rather more detailed points of comparison. The trapezoidal cairn, with its revetment of dry-stone walling or orthostats, and the gallery-type burial chamber at the broad end, are virtually identical in the two regions, though the chambers are normally different in their detailed plans. The forecourt, with its attendant ritual and elaborate blocking, is again a common feature, though the hollow crescent of Clyde-Carlingford con-trasts with the funnel-shaped forecourt of the Severn-Cotswold group. But a significant link is the typological devolution whereby the broad end of the cairn loses its pre-eminent function, and lateral chambers are made along the sides—the plans of The Caves of Kilhern or Dranandrow in Galloway, or Cuff Hill in Ayrshire, are startlingly like Lugbury or

Rodmarton. On the whole then, despite the contrast between the plans of the segmented chambers of Clyde-Carlingford and the transepted galleries of the Severn-Cotswold tombs, the structural features of the two groups are remarkably similar. Siting, too, agrees in both regions, with the use either of ridges or of valleys among the oakwood, and the occasional placings of cairns in pairs.

But there is a contrast in the burial rite—equally divided between cremation and inhumation in Scotland and almost wholly cremation in Ireland and the Isle of Man, but inhumation only in the Severn-Cotswold area. But again, in both regions there is Western Neolithic ware and leaf-arrowheads, though the pottery similarities are generalized rather than specific. The shale or jet bead from Cairnholy I might be yet another link.

On the whole, then, comparison with the Windmill Hill and Clyde-Carlingford areas leaves us with much the same impression in each instance—generalized resemblances within the Western Neolithic family, with one or two specific links suggesting something more than remote ancestral kinship. Of the two, perhaps the connexions with Clyde-Carlingford might be thought a little closer than those with Windmill Hill. But in neither case are we dealing with the derivation of one set of traditions from another, but rather a kinship close enough to suggest that a common origin on the European continent lies not so far away in time or space.

When we turn to the Continent one feature at least of the Severn-Cotswold chambered cairns can be recognized within a relatively restricted area. The transepted galleries, as Daniel (1939*b*) has shown, have good parallels among a group of tombs in the Morbihan and around the mouth of the Loire, typified by Keriaval in the former area and Herbignac in the latter, and to this group he has given the name of the Retz culture. Apart from the fact that these tombs have elongated cairns, we know nothing of their detailed form, but it must be remembered that the trapezoid cairn with dry-walled revetment does occur in the Morbihan in the Manio group of tombs, and may well lie concealed beneath the unexcavated mounds of the Retz group. One might also point to a possible parallel for the standing stones at Gatcombe and Lyneham in that in the Manio cairn beneath the Kermario avenues. Something resembling the Notgrove closed cist behind the burial chamber seems to have existed in the Tumulus de Bernet, Gironde.

There seems little doubt, furthermore, that the long cairn with terminal burial chamber is by no means so rare a form in western France as the accessible published records would suggest. The Charente and Deux-Sèvres region is likely to yield some surprises, as Daniel's preliminary fieldwork has already shown—the chambered long cairn at Bougon in the latter department is a case in point. Here the cairn is 225 ft. long, 85 ft. wide at one end and 52 ft. wide at the other, where a dry-wall revetment can be seen outlining 15 ft. of straight side and turning at right angles to form a squared end in the Cotswold manner. At the wider end of the cairn is a ruined burial chamber under an enormous capstone 20 ft. across. A similar group of chambered long and round cairns at St Martin-la-Rivière, Vienne, might also be cited, but here (as at Bougon) the occurrence of much pottery of S.O.M. type makes it difficult to regard these long cairns as ancestral to those of the Cotswolds. But the type may well have earlier origins in western France.

With regard to the grave-goods, leaf-arrowheads are, as we have seen, rare in Brittany, though not infrequent in Charente in sites of the Peu Richard culture, where bone chisels also occur. The pottery of course is not directly comparable, though of Western Neolithic stock. On the whole, though, there seems a likelihood that the origin of the builders of the Severn-Cotswold tombs lies in western France, probably round the mouth of the Loire or between there and the Île de Rè. We have seen that there is some reason to think that the origins of the Windmill Hill culture may lie to the north-east of the Armorican peninsula, and that the Clyde-Carlingford segmented galleries suggest affinities with the western end of the Pyrenees, so that the Severn-Cotswold tombs would derive from an intermediate point along the west French sea-board.

Such a west-to-east series—Clyde-Carlingford, Severn-Cotswold, Windmill Hill—seems on the whole likely enough, explicable as emigrations to the corresponding regions of Britain from points along the shores of the Bay of Biscay. The underlying similarities within the Western Neolithic traditions would belong to the ancestral French stock (perhaps represented in the earlier levels in the south French caves), and the cultural divergencies, already marked in western France, would become accentuated by the separation and isolation of the various colonies established in this country, the peculiarities of the terrain encountered, and perhaps also contact with indigenous cultures.

CHAPTER VI

THE CLYDE-CARLINGFORD CULTURE IN WESTERN SCOTLAND AND NORTHERN IRELAND

INTRODUCTION

A group of megalithic tombs showing remarkable uniformity of type has been recognized in south-west Scotland since the work of Bryce at the beginning of this century: since then Childe has given precision to the definition, and in more recent years the excavations of Evans and Davies in Northern Ireland have established the existence there of a large group of very closely allied monuments. Outliers in Eire, in Wales and in the Isle of Man show the culture responsible for these tombs to be centred on the head of the Irish Sea, and derivatives as far away as Yorkshire and Derbyshire and perhaps even in Cornwall and Wessex show that secondary colonization extended over a wide field. The area of the main settlements of the Clyde-Carlingford culture is shown in the map, Fig. 23, where the distribution of characteristic tomb type shows that northwards colonization spread to the neighbourhood of Oban on the coast and inland to Loch Earn in Perthshire, with the main centres of the culture in the islands of Arran and Bute and southwards in Galloway. In Ireland the main concentration is around Carlingford Lough near Dundalk, and inland they spread westwards to Fermanagh and even Sligo, and northwards into Tyrone and along the coastal areas of Co. Down and Co. Antrim. An important group of tombs in the Isle of Man warrants inclusion in the area of primary colonization.[1]

Within this area the tombs show a considerable variation in type, but all have features uniting them into a group sufficiently homogeneous to be discussed as a unit, and in the ensuing pages evidence from the whole of this area is considered together. In a later section various scattered tombs outside this group, but sharing the distinctive features peculiar to it, are described as a diffuse region of secondary colonization which extends to southern Eire, Wales, Derbyshire and other regions remote from the primary settlements.

---

[1] The bibliography of these sites is very large; Ulster excavations of 1932–1941 in *Ulster Journ. Arch.* VI (1943), 4–6; Arran, Bute and Kintyre, Bryce (1902, 1903, 1904, 1909); Galloway, Piggott & Powell (1949); other Scottish sites, Childe (1934*b*); Isle of Man, Megaw (1938); Creevykeel, Hencken (1939); other Sligo tombs, Piggott & Powell (1947). Points of individual importance are documented in the text.

The background in the area of primary settlement

The natural conditions of the coastal regions of the Highland Zone in Atlantic times have been discussed in the first chapter: Childe has shown how the distribution of the tombs in south-west Scotland reflects not only the use of natural landing-places such as Luce and Wigtown Bays, the south coast of Arran and the shores of Loch Fyne, but the choice of raised-

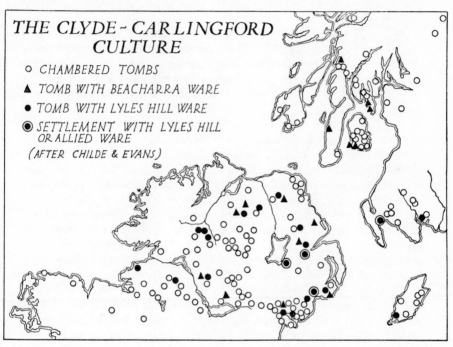

Fig. 23.

beach platforms or alluvial gravels adjacent to such shores, with their lighter vegetation offering less resistance to the stone-equipped colonists than the heavily wooded boulder clays, though many of the tombs must have been built in artificial clearings in woodland. The builders of the Clyde-Carlingford tombs must have arrived in a region supporting only the most meagre and scattered Mesolithic population, descendants of the Obanian and allied groups of hunter-fishers who left their traces on Oronsay and in Kirkcudbright. Movius (1940) has shown that there is no evidence for human occupation in north-east Ireland before late Boreal times, and the main Mesolithic horizon for this region lies in the Atlantic climatic phase, with various epi-Mesolithic cultures, including those of the sand-hills and the well-known Bann culture, which he has suggested represents a surviving

Mesolithic fishing economy, belonging to late Atlantic or sub-Boreal times and contemporary with the agricultural settlements of the megalithic builders (cf. Chapters x and xi). Characteristic flint types show the Bann culture to be well represented in the Isle of Man, though not in Scotland, and the total Mesolithic population at the head of the Irish Sea must have been exiguous, migratory, and unlikely to offer any effective opposition to new arrivals with cultural traditions alien to, though in no way conflicting with, their own.

Negligible though the local hunter-fisher element must have been, we have to consider the possibility of pre-existing agriculturalists in the region. We have seen in Chapter IV that the pottery evidence strongly suggests a spread of population from the Yorkshire Wolds to Northern Ireland at a stage of the British sequence which appears to have been fairly early, and it is obviously necessary to attempt some sort of equation between the arrival of these folk and that of the builders of the Clyde-Carlingford tombs coming up the western seaways. Now, as will be shown below, the distribution of the shouldered bowls allied to Yorkshire forms in our region is interesting: they occur widely scattered in Northern Ireland both in burial monuments and in habitation sites, similar bowls have also been found in Galloway and in the Isle of Man, but there is a complete absence of this type in the Bute-Arran region (where the relatively abundant pottery from the gallery-graves is all quite dissimilar). This strongly suggests that the newcomers from eastern Britain found, on their arrival at the North Channel, the territory now south-west Scotland already in the possession of Neolithic colonists burying their dead in gallery-graves, but Ireland as yet unoccupied by any people liable to offer opposition to new settlers. As I shall show, there is considerable evidence to support this supposition that a Neolithic culture of east British derivation was established in Ulster about the same time as the gallery-grave builders found their way to Northern Ireland, there to take an exceptionally strong hold.

The distribution and relationship of the tombs

The essential features common to the whole group of gallery-graves under discussion (Figs. 24–26) are based on an oblong or rectangular roofed burial-chamber with the sides of orthostatic blocks. Roofing may take the form of a corbelled barrel-vault or flat cap-stones resting more or less directly on the walling slabs, while the chamber is normally divided into compartments by a slab or series of slabs set transversely and only reaching to about half the height of the orthostats: in its minimal form the septal slab may be set across the entrance, and the outer compartment scarcely exists or is merged into the portal, if such exists. (In most Irish tombs the septal slabs are flanked by jamb-stones, or these latter only may exist, the slab being omitted.) The chamber may, however, be closed at both ends: a low

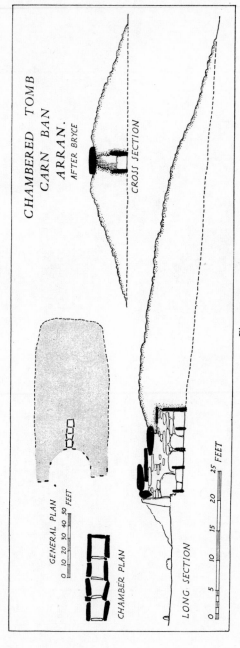

CHAMBERED TOMB
CARN BAN
ARRAN.
AFTER BRYCE

CROSS SECTION

GENERAL PLAN
0 10 20 30 40 50 FEET

CHAMBER PLAN

LONG SECTION

0   5   10   15   20   25 FEET

Fig. 24.

156

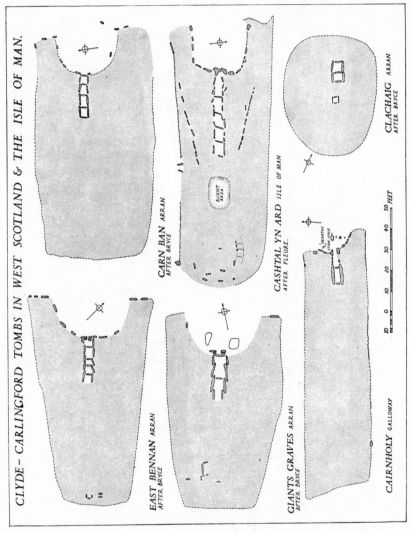

CLYDE – CARLINGFORD TOMBS IN WEST SCOTLAND & THE ISLE OF MAN.

CARN BAN ARRAN
AFTER BRYCE

CASHTAL YN ARD ISLE OF MAN
AFTER FLEURE.

CLACHAIG ARRAN.
AFTER BRYCE

EAST BENNAN ARRAN
AFTER BRYCE

GIANTS GRAVES ARRAN
AFTER BRYCE

CAIRNHOLY GALLOWAY

Fig. 25.

septal at one end and an upright of full height at the other, and exceptionally, as at Cairnholy, the rear portion of the chamber may be completely cut off from the outer. When there is a definite entrance this is frequently marked by two large flanking portal stones, which may form the innermost members of a façade of orthostats which may be flat or concave in plan and which may form one end of a long cairn or part of the periphery of a round mound. These covering mounds may vary from round through oval to elongated or trapezoid, and may have a peristalith of standing stones. There is a frequent tendency for a mound to cover more than one cist, usually of 'minimal' type, and there is marked preference for orthostatic and slab construction rather than the use of dry-stone walling, though this may be employed in conjunction with uprights in a 'post-and-panel' technique.

It will be immediately apparent that there are considerable variations within the main group, but the similarities far outweigh the differences, and the homogeneity of the family over the whole area is quite clear. This distribution presents several interesting features, particularly when examined in conjunction with the sub-types of tomb. In general terms, the focus of the segmented gallery distribution is the head of the Irish Sea, and one typological distinction is immediately apparent—the Irish tombs, and those in the Isle of Man, are exclusively of the elaborate type with elongated mound and crescentic façade which, although present in Scotland, is of comparatively rare occurrence compared with the simpler forms of chambers which may be covered by long or oval cairns.

The distribution in Scotland shows a marked concentration in Arran and Bute, where the most common type is the 'minimal' chamber of two or three segments, without façades but frequently with twin portal stones. This type also occurs in the second area of Scottish concentration, in Galloway, and common to both regions is a curious type in which three segmented chambers are set radially under a roughly circular cairn. Neither of these types seems to have been distinguished in Ireland.

Façades of orthostats take two forms, flat and crescentic. The former probably occurs on one or two tombs in Arran and on hybrid tombs in the Hebrides, but the latter occurs in various forms in Argyll, Arran and in Galloway, usually with a regular trapezoidal mound in the Irish style.

In Northern Ireland, the tombs, which are all variations and evolutions from the segmented chamber with long mound and crescentic façade, show a primary focus in the region of Carlingford Lough, with some coastwise colonization in eastern Down and Antrim, but the main cultural movement seems to have been inland through Armagh and Monaghan to Tyrone, Fermanagh and Sligo, where the derivative 'lobster-claw' type evolved from the closing-up of the crescentic façade. In Man, too, the tombs have the elongated mound and crescentic façade.

This variation in the sub-types of the tombs, reflected to some extent in

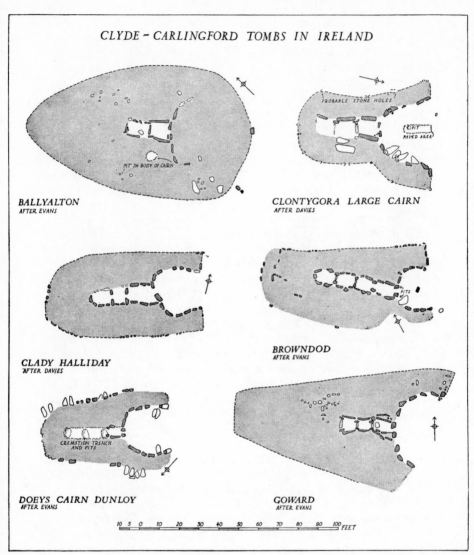

CLYDE ~ CARLINGFORD TOMBS IN IRELAND

BALLYALTON
AFTER EVANS

CLONTYGORA LARGE CAIRN
AFTER DAVIES

CLADY HALLIDAY
AFTER DAVIES

BROWNDOD
AFTER EVANS

DOEYS CAIRN DUNLOY
AFTER EVANS

GOWARD
AFTER EVANS

Fig. 26.

their differential distribution, must either be the outcome of the arrival of several groups of colonists from the Continent, each with a variant form of tomb plan, or of an evolutionary or devolutionary series, from a more or less standard imported prototype, developing in the Hiberno-Scottish areas of primary settlement. Such development would take time and need not be assumed as taking place untouched by further influences either direct from the Continent or from other cultures in Britain. This question is discussed later in the chapter.

THE CAIRNS AND THEIR PLANS

The tombs as a whole fall into fairly well defined types. A simple segmented chamber may be set in an oval cairn as at Clachaig or the cairn may be irregularly elongated as are many on Arran, but with the entrance marked by portal stones as at Cairnholy II. Rectangularity of outline is observable at Dunan Beag and at Cairnholy I in Galloway, and Monyquil, Arran, in all cairns with remains of a peristalith of upright slabs. The façades which remain are of two main types, flat or crescentic, and are discussed below. They take their place at one end of the elongated cairn, which with the crescentic façades in Scotland, Ireland and Man take on a trapezoid outline frequently demarcated by a peristalith. Dry-walling is used at Cashtal yn Ard and Cairnholy I combined with orthostats, and in certain Irish tombs (e.g. Clady Halliday and Dunloy) the hinder end of the cairn is rounded instead of angular. In both Ireland and Scotland abnormalities occur such as chambers and crescentic façades at both ends of a long mound (e.g. Aghanaglack and Carnanbane) or double chambers only as at Ballyrenan (Co. Tyrone), and at Dunan Beag, Carnbaan (Bute) and probably Glenrickard. The 'lobster-claw' cairns of Co. Sligo and the adjacent regions preserve the trapezoid mound with revetment at Creevykeel, the type site, and in this form the façade is brought round the forecourt in two 'claws' to enclose an oval open court opening at one end through the wide end of the cairn and at the other into the chamber. Two sites in Argyll have small segmented cists with crescentic façades under circular cairns.

In all the foregoing types the chambers are oblong and subdivided by septal slabs into anything up to five compartments, but the underlying idea of multiple chambers is given expression in cairns covering more than one separate megalithic cist, sometimes arranged radially, as at Dunan Mor and Cairnderry, and probably at Glecknabae (where a third chamber seems likely to have existed in that part of the cairn now destroyed). In other tombs (e.g. Kindrochat, Caves of Kilhern and Dranandrow in Galloway, Cuff Hill and Darvel in Ayrshire, and perhaps Port St Mary in Man) the arrangement of the cists is at the end and along the sides of an elongated cairn in a manner comparable to the long cairns of the Cotswolds described in Chapter v. The remarkable site at Mull Hill, Isle of Man, must be taken into consideration when dealing with multiple-cist structures: here within a circular bank of earth and stones having two opposed entrances in the Early Bronze Age 'Henge' tradition were six T-shaped groups of two chambers and a passage opening to the outside, typologically of Clyde-Carlingford derivation.

Of the construction of the actual cairns little enough can be said. In Ireland a clay floor was found to be of frequent occurrence beneath the cairn: this was, however, noticeably absent at Creevykeel, where the cairn was observed to have been built direct on to the turf, nor was it present in Cairnholy I and II, but here the surface was burnt in patches, probably the result of clearing woodland by fire. At Ballyalton a roughly dry-walled cist or 'pit' was found in the cairn material, containing a ritual deposit of sherds and burnt matter. The orthostats of peristalith, façade or chamber were set up in relatively shallow sockets, with packing-stones to wedge them into position.

The frequent presence of the trapezoid cairn, with its carefully demarcated outline, is a type which we have seen occurring in the early Neolithic cairns of Manio in the Morbihan and reproduced in a modified form in Wessex and Yorkshire (Gilling East long barrow, with its converging dry-stone revetment walls, is particularly relevant) and we shall find it especially characteristic of the Severn-Cotswold long cairns. The occurrence of such a specialized type in Brittany, the Cotswolds, north Britain and Ireland can hardly be fortuitous, and we shall return to consider its implications in relation to other structural features below.

The burial chambers

The chambers are normally of rectangular plan, in which large flat slabs are used with a minimal employment of dry-stone walling. There is a tendency in Ireland for certain chambers in tombs which appear (by any typological arrangement) to be late, to become oval in plan and to be constructed of smaller stones than the massive flat slabs forming the angular chambers typical of Scotland and of some Irish monuments.

The septal slab which forms the most distinctive structural feature common to practically the whole group, is a stone set transversely across the chamber but only reaching to half of its height or less—e.g. at Carn Ban (Arran), which retains its original roofing, the height from the floor is some 8 ft., whereas the septals are less than 3 ft. high (Fig. 24): similar proportions are observable at Clachaig. In the typical form of 'segmented gallery' a number of such slabs divide the chamber into a series of compartments, in Scotland normally with walls formed of a single slab often set overlapping in such a way that the segments appear in plan to fit into one another telescope fashion (e.g. Giants' Graves and Monamore, Arran). At both the

Cairnholy cairns the rear of the two segments of the chamber were cut off not by septals but by slabs rising to the full height of the roof: Cairnholy I had a subdivision of the outer compartment by a sill only a few inches in height, and similar sills constituted the 'septals' at Dranandrow. In Scotland (and at Cashtal yn Ard) the septal slabs are set with the ends flush with the side stones of the gallery, but in Ireland Ballyalton is the only example of this construction, elsewhere the septals being flanked by upright jamb-stones, and this arrangement is also found in the chambers of the Mull Hill Circle. In Ireland a further development leads to the septal slab being omitted in certain tombs, the jambs remaining to form the only divisions between the chambers.

An example of the 'porthole' entrance occurs in the tomb known as 'King Orry's Grave' in Man, with two adjacent upright stones having their inner edges hollowed in a manner which recurs in the Cotswold cairns (Clifford & Daniel, 1940). A hollow on the upper edge of a septal slab suggestive of an incipient 'porthole' has been noted by Childe (Childe & Graham, 1943) at Ardmarnock in Argyll, and we shall see it again in an outlier of the Clyde-Carlingford group in Cheshire. The perforated single stone type of 'porthole' has been identified in a tomb with façade at Corracloona, Co. Leitrim (Davies & Evans, 1943).

Details of the roofing of the galleries and cists is available in a few examples, such as Carn Ban, with a partial barrel-vault formed by corbelling and capped by large slabs, and evidence of similar corbelling has been recognized in Ireland in two or three tombs. Capstones resting either directly on the uprights or with a dry walling to make them level still remain in Scotland at Cairnholy II and other sites.

The floor of the chambers was roughly paved or cobbled in such Irish tombs as Browndod and Dunloy, at Cairnholy I and probably II, and in at least two sites (Ballyalton and Clady Halliday) paving seems to have separated successive layers of funeral deposits.

The tomb of Nether Largie excavated by Greenwell (1866—plan of chamber in M. Mitchell, 1930, but with wrong scales) is an exceedingly interesting example of what appears to be a fusion of gallery-grave and passage-grave traditions. A large gallery of four segments was covered by a circular cairn 130 ft. in diameter: the northern end of the gallery was almost closed by two large portal stones set close together. Burials were found in the two innermost (southern) compartments, of cremations with Neolithic pottery and barbed arrowheads, stratified below inhumations with beakers. The third segment contained fragments of inhumations only and the fourth and outermost 'had a wall of small flat stones built up on each side to a height of about 2 ft. 7 in., having a space 2 ft. 2 in. wide in the centre'—in fact converting the outer segment into a short 'ritual' passage. This construction, coupled with the use of the innermost two segments only for the original burials (the third segment seeming to function as an antechamber), indicates a convincing mixture of burial traditions.

Cremation trenches

Two examples of cremation burials in the Yorkshire manner in the Clyde-Carlingford province occur in cairns whose other features link them with the segmented gallery complex. At Dunloy in Co. Antrim a single chamber, with jambs but no septal slab, opened on to a crescentic forecourt, but at its rear end two further jambs framed an opening into a long dry-walled trench with a thick charcoal layer above paving, beneath which were found three pits containing burnt matter. Cremated human bones were found on the pavement and in one pit, and the whole structure showed signs of fire. At Ballafyle in the Isle of Man a short cairn with crescentic façade and dry-walled revetment contained no megalithic structure, but had along the axial line an elongated area of intensely burnt material and the remains of cremated bones apparently burnt *in situ*. At the degenerate site of Well Glass Spring, Largantea, cremation *in situ* had taken place (Herring, 1938 *b*) and the pit at Killaghy, Co. Antrim, adjacent to one containing Neolithic sherds, might be related (Evans, 1940*c*).

These cremation trenches are closely paralleled by the arrangement of the Yorkshire cremation flues described in the preceding chapter, a representative of which type is known from as far west as Cumberland, and the Irish and Manx examples constitute a most important link, in addition to that provided by the shouldered bowls, for the close cultural contacts between the regions to the east and the west of the Pennines, and stress the complexity of the traits which combine to make up the Clyde-Carlingford culture.

It is convenient at this point to mention the burnt mass of material found behind the chambers in the Cashtal yn Ard monument. Here was an area 20 by 12 ft. and 4 ft. high consisting of burnt stone and charcoal, and having at the centre a built platform. No burnt bones were, however, identified and the unsatisfactory report on the excavations does not make the structure at all clear (Fleure & Neely, 1936).

The entrance-portals

Although in many Scottish tombs there is no special feature at the entrance to the chamber (e.g. Monyquil, Cragabus, Dunan Beag and Dunan Mor), a feature frequent in this region and constant in Ireland is the provision of massive portal stones set close to and at right angles to the lateral slabs forming the walls of the chamber. These portals may be of considerable, though sometimes disparate, height and frequently they are set so close together that the 'entrance' between them is reduced to a merely symbolic aperture a foot or less across. A septal slab may run across the entrance immediately inside the portals, thus further diminishing the opening (e.g. Glecknabae, Bickers Houses, Clontygora Large Cairn) or this may be omitted (Monamore, Michael's Grave, Goward, Cashtal yn Ard). Where crescentic façades occur, the portals normally form the innermost members of the orthostats of the forecourt setting, but at Cashtal yn Ard, however, the portals are set within the two highest orthostats of the façade.

Façades and forecourts

A further step in the elaboration of the entrance to the tomb, a constructional development which may be the outcome of a corresponding increase in ritual importance for this part of the monument (and while a frequent feature in Scotland, is almost invariably found in Ireland), is a façade of orthostats fronting the cairn and having as its central feature the opening of the gallery with its flanking portals. Such façades may be crescentic, or less frequently almost straight in plan.

A funnel-shaped forecourt approach may have existed at Monyquil, in Arran, and certainly did at Balix in Co. Tyrone, but the most frequent forecourt type, completely dominant in Ireland with the exception mentioned, is the concave or crescentic façade, from which the term 'horned cairn' frequently used in the past for these tombs is derived. In Scotland, eight good examples of the crescentic façade have been recognized, and to these one must add the Baroile and Gartnagreanoch tombs as degenerate examples under small circular cairns. There is also a patently degenerate example at Auchoish, where neither chamber nor even ritual entrance graces the centre of the deeply incurved façade. These eleven examples of tombs with the crescentic façade constitute only a small proportion of the Clyde-Carlingford tombs of the Clyde-Solway area, but in Ireland this feature in varying forms of evolution or degeneration is constant.

The crescentic forecourt typically presents an approximately semi-circular area recessed into the wider end of a long cairn, with the façade formed by orthostats ascending in height to the portals and originally linked by dry-stone walling in a 'post and panel' technique, and the degree of concavity varying from a shallow arc to more than half the full circle. In Scotland, Carn Ban (Arran) preserves a single stone on the same circumference as the façade, suggesting to Hawkes an original completely circular enclosure at the entrance to the tomb, of which the façade recessed into the body of the cairn formed one half, and free-standing stones the other. In Ireland a series can be traced in which a progressive concavity of the façade is seen to be accompanied by an obvious degeneration of the chamber and its segmentation until the 'lobster-claw' type is reached, with the forecourt area completely closed save for a narrow entrance, as at Creevykeel.

The forecourts flanked by these façades were, as will be seen when discussing the burial ritual, the focus of the main funeral ceremonies before the deposition of the blocking: structurally we may, however, notice the frequent paving or cobbling of the area (e.g. Cashtal yn Ard, Dunloy) or the provision of a paved path to the entrance (Clontygora Large Cairn) and the placing of a standing stone in front of the entrance either in the centre of the forecourt, as at Browndod, or beyond it, as at Ballyalton and Cairnholy I. At Clontygora Large Cairn a 'ritual pit' which may have been a stone-hole was found in the centre of the forecourt and small pits containing sherds flanked the entrance at Browndod, while hearths were found in the forecourt area at Cairnholy I and several Irish sites.

The typological sequence

Any deductions drawn from the pure typology of tomb-plans must be used with the greatest caution, and the lines of evolution or devolution of the Clyde-Carlingford tombs are particularly confused. The problem seems simpler in Ireland than in Scotland, for in the former region there seems little reasonable doubt that there is a progressive degeneration-series beginning with tombs having fairly flat façades, and of slab-built construction (such as Ballyalton), and then continuing with increasingly deep forecourts and a tendency for the chambers to become oval rather than rectangular in plan, and to be built of less slab-like orthostats. In some, too, the septal stones are omitted, though their jambs remain. The final forms include such eccentricities as the 'lobster-claw' type with enclosed forecourt (Creevykeel and other tombs in Sligo), or double-ended variants. Interaction is likely to have taken place with other forms of gallery-graves in Ulster, and these are discussed in Chapter ix.

In Scotland, however, development seems to have taken place along different lines. In Galloway and in Ayrshire one can trace a series curiously analogous to the Cotswold degeneration described in Chapter v, where façades seem to be omitted, and several small chambers are set along the edges of the cairn as well as that at one end. At Cairnholy in this region, however, we have two cairns within 500 yd. of one another, one with a fine façade and a forecourt elaborately blocked after the funeral rite, and the other with portals but no façade or forecourt ritual, and the evidence from excavation shows them to be broadly contemporary. The relationship therefore of the tombs with façades and forecourts, and those having none (as many in Arran, Bute and Kintyre), is obscure: while it is possible that the latter are degenerations, they may in fact be earlier, or there may be two strains present in the original colonizing of the region. At all events, evolution did not proceed along the Irish lines, and there are no tombs indicating any approach to the 'lobster-claw' form of forecourt with the façade enclosing more than half a circle. The whole question is further discussed in the last section of the chapter.

THE BURIALS AND FUNERAL RITUAL

The method of deposition of the bodies comprised both inhumation and cremation. In Scotland, of the eighteen or so tombs yielding evidence of the rite, the proportion of one to the other was almost exactly equal, but in Ireland, of those tombs where the rite could be observed only one (Ballyalton) and just possibly one degenerate example (Ballyedmond) had inhumed bodies, and the rest contained cremations. Following the normal collective tomb tradition, interments would presumably have been successive and often spread over some considerable period of time: at Clachaig in a chamber only 10 by 5 ft., and divided in half by the septal, were bones representing fourteen persons, and the arrangement of the long bones at the sides and the skulls in the corners of the compartments shows the periodic packing away of earlier burials in a skeletal condition to make room for a newcomer, as so often observed in chambered tombs in this country and elsewhere. At Torlin bones of six adults and a child were found similarly placed and, in dealing later with the finds of pottery, we shall see that evidence of successive deposits of grave-goods comes from more than one tomb in Scotland and Ireland.

The only available figures for interments (all from Arran and Bute tombs) are given in Table IV.

TABLE IV

Site	Adult	Child	Total
Dunan Beag	3	.	3
Clachaig	12	2	14
Torlin	6	1	7

In Ireland remains of five or six cremated adults occupied one pit of the cremation trench at Dunloy, but the double monument of Aghanaglack contained nothing but the cremations of two young children. It seems likely that some of the human remains showing burning in these tombs (e.g. Clady Halliday) may owe their condition to scorching from ritual fires rather than from deliberate cremation upon a pyre. The distinction, however, between the presence of inhumation in Scotland and its virtually complete absence in Ireland is important, and that the single Irish inhumation grave should be that of Ballyalton, which on typological grounds stands nearest to the Scottish series, is proportionately interesting and suggestive.

Deposits of animal bones have also been found in the chambers yielding inhumations: the Scottish evidence comprises the domesticated ox, pig, sheep or goat, and dog, and Ballyalton produced a similar range of species. At Goward was found a series of deposits of ox-bones in the chamber filling with the appearance of their being ritual deposits, but there is reason to think that these are not contemporary. Feral types are confined to otter, birds and fish from Torlin, and a dubious record of deer from Ballyalton. These records of domesticated animals are important in indicating that the tomb-builders were agriculturalists, presumably introducing their stock to the areas of settlement for the first time.

Evidence of funeral ritual outside the actual burial chamber itself is best provided by the excavated forecourt of Cairnholy I, in the light of which the less extensively explored Irish sites can be interpreted (Pl. V). In this Galloway tomb, there was a shallow asymmetric façade of eight stones, the two innermost (and tallest) forming the portals of the burial chamber. In the forecourt area, a hearth near the north portal had scattered by it the sherds of a shallow Neolithic bowl and a flake of Arran pitchstone: this had been covered by a clean earth spread, and four other fires lit, either at this time or later in different places in the forecourt area. A sixth hearth covered a filled-up stone-hole on the outer edge of the forecourt, on the axial line of the cairn, showing the standing stone to have been removed at an early stage.

Over these hearths was a very massive and deliberately built blocking, in which was set a closing stone against the entrance between the portals, and in and at the base of which were deposits of pottery, a jet bead and a mass of the shells of edible molluscs. Pottery at the base of the blocking was of the same late Neolithic type (Peterborough ware) as that accompanying what must have been the final burials in the chamber, showing that the blocking was not placed in position until after this time. The total thickness of the blocking was over 3 ft. at its maximum. If the hearths each represent a fire lighted at the time of a funeral, one could suggest that there had been six burials made in the tomb, which on a twenty-year generation would give it a life of a century or so. It will be seen that evidence from the Hebrides discussed in Chapter VII, leads to a similar conclusion for two chambered tombs there.

Similar features were observable in the excavated Irish forecourts. Blocking was present in all instances. At Hanging Thorn as at Cairnholy I sherds occurred in compact groups, suggesting separate or successive cere-monies of libation and deposition of the broken pot. At the same site was also a hearth, and these again occurred at most of the other sites, including Creevykeel. At the latter site were votive deposits of stone axes at the entrance to the court and to the chamber, and at Dunloy similar deposits of axes were made in the material sealing the entrance after the final burial, while at Ballyalton a ritual deposit of flint axes, scrapers and flakes, and a large stone bead (or perhaps a spindle-whorl, as described by the excavator) were found in the stone-hole of a destroyed upright of the façade. In addition to the central standing stone in the forecourt at Ballyalton and Browndod, the entrance to the chamber of the latter was flanked by two small regularly cut circular pits containing sherds, while another similar hole was placed on the outer edge of the forecourt area. Holes that may have been stone-holes were found at Clady Halliday, Clontygora (large), and Mourne Park.

The blocking of the entrance after the final burial took variant forms—at Goward and Ballyalton a transverse bank of stones was piled in front of the entrance across the forecourt, and at Clady Halliday and Dunloy the fore-court appears to have been left clear and loose stones used as the entrance blocking, but in other instances it seems likely that the entire forecourt was more or less filled in. At Creevykeel the court was apparently left open.

MATERIAL EQUIPMENT

Pottery

The types of pottery found in the Clyde-Carlingford tombs and at one or two allied settlement sites in the same region can be divided conveniently into two main groups—one characterized by distinctive unornamented shouldered round-bottomed bowls which I propose calling *Lyles Hill ware*; and another which has already been distinguished, largely on the grounds of its highly finished ornamented bowls, as *Beacharra ware*, within which subvarieties are apparent. Both these come within the Western Neolithic province in style and origin and, though one variety of Beacharra ware shows contact with alien cord-ornamented wares, the Western Neolithic elements are still well characterized even in the vessels which employ these novel motifs and techniques.

Lyles Hill ware. In describing the Grimston ware class of pottery from Yorkshire, it was seen that forms so similar to this as to suggest close con-nexion were found in Northern Ireland. There are some fifteen or twenty sites, mainly chambered tombs but including settlements (as for instance Dundrum (Hassé, 1894), Dunmurry (Whelan, 1938) and Lyles Hill (E. E. Evans, 1940*b*)) which have produced a very homogeneous ware, found in great abundance at the last site, which therefore provides an appro-priate name for the pottery as a class. Its main features are its good fabric, dark faced and with a smoothed surface which may be almost burnished to a leathery texture and which can be built up into thin-walled vessels; its normal lack of ornament save for a rippling of the surface with the finger-tips often carried over the rim, which is usually of a simple thin or rolled form; approximately hemispherical bases above which a shoulder, which may be exaggerated and applied as a separate strip of clay, breaks the profile to a concave neck which may be considerably flared-out in the more graceful versions of the form; and finally an almost complete lack of lugs or handles (Fig. 27, no. 9). These features, as will have been seen, might as well apply to the bowls from Kilham or Hanging Grimston in Yorkshire: in Northern Ireland the ware is spread across the country westwards from Carlingford Lough to Sligo in tombs of every sub-type of the gallery-with-forecourt series and cannot be dissociated from the spread of the tombs themselves but must be considered as an integral part of the Carlingford culture at the time of its territorial expansion in Ulster. Outside the area of these tombs similar pottery is known as far afield as Co. Cork and Co. Limerick, but this is more likely to be of an independent (if allied) origin, with affinities in south-west England and west Wales.

In western Scotland, however, Lyles Hill ware is absent from the Arran, Bute and Argyll tombs though occurring as a single bowl in the blocking at Cairnholy I, in the last phase of the tomb's use. Elsewhere in Scotland it is known from several sporadic finds, none from chambered tombs, scattered from Luce Bay in Wigtownshire to Easterton of Roseisle in Moray-shire (Callander, 1929 with refs.). In the Isle of Man, this pottery occurs abundantly in the curious monument of Mull Hill, which may be allied to that of Dun Ruadh in Tyrone, both showing a mixture of 'Henge' elements with cists of Clyde-Carlingford derivation (O. Davies, 1937b). The sherds from Cashtal yn Ard are not distinctive enough to be regarded as anything other than 'Western' in the broadest sense (Piggott, 1931).

In Northern Ireland, Lyles Hill ware occurs in Clyde-Carlingford tombs showing every gradation of evolving or devolving plan, but it does not appear in those tombs with Early Bronze Age grave-goods and unseg-mented chambers such as Giant's Grave (Lougash), Cloghnagalla Boviel, or Largantea.

We must presumably admit a long survival of Lyles Hill ware through-out the derivation of the Clyde-Carlingford culture in Ulster, but an upper limit for its appearance is fortunately provided by the evidence of successive deposits of burials and their accompanying grave-goods as recovered by excavation in several tombs. Wherever a stratigraphical relationship can be established with Beacharra ware, Lyles Hill ware is never found to be subse-quent in order of deposition and in several instances there are reasons for supposing it not only to be contemporary, but actually stratigraphically earlier.

At Ballyalton, Lyles Hill ware was found under the paving in the outer of the two segments of the chamber, and in pits in the floor of the inner, and again in a 'cist' containing a ritual deposit in the cairn material, closed and contemporary with the building of the monument. Above the paving in the chamber were found sherds representing a bowl with panelled ornament likely to be a derivative from the Beacharra series. At Clontygora Large Cairn sherds of Lyles Hill ware were found in the yellow clay floor wherever it survived undisturbed: sherds of a Beacharra pot were found in disturbed soil and might have been secondary, but not conclusively so. At Dunloy, however, a most interesting stratification was observed. Here, it will be remembered, a single-segment chamber joined on to a cremation trench of more or less Yorkshire type: sherds of Lyles Hill ware were found not only on the old surface under the body of the cairn but in pits in this

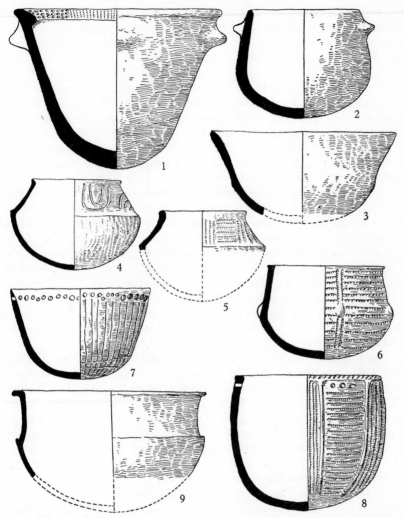

Fig. 27. Clyde-Carlingford culture: pottery. 1, 4, Beacharra; 2, Sliddery; 3, Cairnholy; 5, near Larne; 6, Ballyalton (*after Evans*); 9, Browndod (*after Evans*); 7, 8, Dunloy (*after Evans*). Scale ¼.

cremation trench and on or in the floor of the chamber. In this chamber a secondary funerary deposit of four vessels (A–D of the original account) had been made at a slightly higher level, including derivative or late Beacharra forms, while slightly lower were sherds of a fairly typical Beacharra bowl (E) with whipped cord ornament. The Dunloy evidence suggests therefore that at this site Lyles Hill ware was contemporary with

G

the original building of the cairn and its crematorium trench, probably earlier than a Beacharra bowl deposited in its outer chamber, and certainly earlier than vessels derived from the Beacharra style, and allied to the 'Sandhill' type of ware.

At Hanging Thorn the various ritual deposits in the forecourt area comprise at least three of Lyles Hill ware, ranging in position from near the portal to a central area of charcoal deposit, while the two Beacharra pots were found beyond this, at the furthest point from the portal and on the chord of the forecourt arc. It is possible that these deposits were successive, with the outermost the latest. At other sites yielding both Beacharra and Lyles Hill ware, such as Carnanbane and Ballyreagh (both tombs late on any reckoning) there is no evidence of relative date available.

To summarize, then, Lyles Hill ware occurs associated with the Clyde-Carlingford tombs in Northern Ireland, and its main area of distribution is approximately co-terminous with these tombs. Except at Cairnholy I, it does not occur associated with chambered tombs in Scotland,[1] but is represented by scattered and scanty finds from Wigtownshire to the Moray Firth. It occurs in a late monument with Irish antecedents in the Isle of Man. Its appearance in Northern Ireland may antedate the arrival there of pottery of the Beacharra class, but it had a very long life, persisting at least to the local Early Bronze Age in the more remote parts of Ulster, often associated with an evolved tomb-type. At Cairnholy I it belongs to the last phase of the cairn's use.

The origins of this pottery may be looked for in two directions. The first alternative is to derive it from the Yorkshire Neolithic wares which it closely resembles and so see in Lyles Hill ware an ultimate origin in the Windmill Hill culture of south-eastern England. The second alternative is to regard it as introduced to Northern Ireland from further south in Eire, or direct from a Continental source, either by the builders of the Clyde-Carlingford tombs or by a separate group of colonists, its resemblance to the Yorkshire pottery being the result of an ultimate common ancestry. The question is further discussed at a later stage.

Beacharra ware. The existence of a distinctive pottery style associated with the Scottish Clyde-Carlingford tombs was recognized by Bryce, its first discoverer, who, in the light of the then available evidence, fully appreciated its relationship with pottery found in chambered tombs in Iberia, Brittany and the Pyrenees and pointed out the probable significance of this with regard to the Neolithic colonization of western Britain, and to the Clyde mouth in particular (Bryce, 1902). His arguments, which anticipated much of the results of recent research, were somewhat lost sight of until Childe thirty years later restated the case in his definitive study of British Neolithic pottery in its European setting (Childe, 1931 d) and upon

---

1 Though Easterton of Roseisle has been claimed as the site of a destroyed long cairn.

this foundation J. Hawkes (1939b) was able to work out the relationship of the west Scottish Neolithic wares in fuller detail.

With the abundant material now available we can see that the pottery from the Clyde-Carlingford tombs in Scotland and Ireland, even after the separation of Lyles Hill ware, still contains a number of recognizable variants. But it seems safer to group all these as subdivisions within a general grouping of Beacharra ware than to create separate classes each perhaps containing only two or three pots. Only further excavation and observation of exact stratigraphy in tomb deposits will enable us to determine whether these multiple but allied strains really represent significant divisions in the cultural or chronological sense.

Into the first sub-group, which may be called *Beacharra A*, come vessels of simple Western Neolithic style which could be matched equally at Cortaillod or Windmill Hill, and which could be taken to represent an early phase of colonization in south-west Scotland, for such vessels are not present in the Irish tombs (Fig. 27, nos. 1–3). From three tombs in Arran (Clachaig, Torlin and Sliddery (Fig. 27, no. 2)) come unornamented bag-shaped round-bottomed pots with simple rims and unperforated lugs, and a similar vessel was associated with the earliest deposit in a chambered tomb in the Hebrides which will be described in a later chapter. Scott, discussing this latter example, considers that such vessels do in fact occupy, in the west Scottish Neolithic pottery series, precisely the place their analogues do in the stratified deposits of south and west France: that of the earliest Neolithic ware from the region (Scott, 1942). Stratigraphy however does not permit us in the other Scottish tombs to separate these lugged bowls chronologically from the ornamented carinated forms, though they may well at least represent a survival of an earlier phase. At Beacharra itself was a large lugged pot with elaborate ornamented rim (Fig. 27, no 1), and other graves in Galloway, Arran and Bute have produced vessels of simple unornamented ware, while at Cairnholy I a shallow bowl was stratigraphically the earliest deposit (Fig. 27, no. 3). A more developed type of flattened or thickened rim also appears, as at Glecknabae, Bute, and the bowl from Nether Largie, and this feature recurs in the Hebridean passage-grave province (Fig. 35, no. 5). At Nether Largie, the finger-tip rippling over the body suggests comparison with the Grimston-Lyles Hill class of ware.

The most distinctive type of Beacharra ware is, however, the decorated carinated bowls, with a rim of less diameter than the shoulder and with ornament in shallow channelling or incision. These may be classed as *Beacharra B*. The distribution of the channelled and incised patterns is not confined to the west Scottish area of segmented galleries—for they form a very important feature of the pottery of the Hebridean passage-grave culture, while no less than nine sites in Ulster have yielded such vessels or derivatives, all save one being from gallery-and-forecourt tombs of types within the variations of the Irish manifestations of the Clyde-Carlingford culture.

At the type-site (a segmented chamber without portals or façade on the west coast of Kintyre) were found six vessels, three of which are carinated bowls with channelled or incised ornament (Fig. 27, no. 4) and the remainder heavier deep pots with little or no ornament. In Ireland, similar bowls are known from Hanging Thorn (vessels 'A 1 ', 'A 2 '), Tamnyrankin (vessel 'O'), Ballyreagh (vessel 'M'), Clontygora (vessel 'O'), Carrick East (vessel 'D') and Carnanbane (unornamented: vessel 1). At the site known for some time as 'Larne' (cf. Piggott & Childe, 1932) typical sherds with vertical channels occur. This latter site has since been identified by Evans (1940a) as one or more gallery-graves of a type not directly allied to the Clyde-Carlingford monuments, at Goakstown and Dunteige, Co. Antrim, excavated in the last century: the type of tomb is discussed later in this chapter (p. 190 below), but the Beacharra ware is best included here, with the name 'Larne' retained for convenience of reference since the exact monument and circumstances of finding cannot now be recovered.

On the foregoing vessels, the ornament is arranged either as horizontal or vertical zones of channelling or incision, or in panels of these alternating. At Beacharra itself one bowl has a series of multiple semicircles in channelled technique (Fig. 27, no. 4). Such ornament and technique is, as we shall see, characteristic of a mass of French and Iberian Neolithic or early metal age wares, but we also find in the area of the Clyde-Carlingford culture bowls of similar form and with similarly arranged ornament to those just described, but in a technique of impressed twisted or whipped cord in a manner totally foreign to the Western Neolithic tradition, and these form a third group, *Beacharra C*. Clachaig (Arran) produced a beautiful little Beacharra bowl with panel ornament in fine whipped cord technique, and in Ireland similar sherds appeared in the 'Larne' site (Fig. 27, 5) as well as at Dunloy (vessel 'E'), where curved line ornament strongly recalling that of the type-site was executed in this technique. A fine twisted cord line is used to produce panel ornament on a vessel from 'Larne', and curved patterns in very fine twisted cord impression occur on sherds from Dunloy (Sherd 'H') and Lyles Hill, and in whipped cord from Ticloy (Evans & Watson, 1942). At Ballyalton was a vessel ('G') with panel ornament in a coarse imitation of whipped cord (Fig. 27, no. 6), and as we shall see in Chapter VII, this forms a link with vessels of Loughcrew ware from the Boyne culture passage-graves.

This use of cord ornament on Beacharra ware leads us to a consideration of one of a group of four vessels ('A'–'D') which formed a secondary deposit in the chamber at Dunloy. Two of these ('C' and 'D') were undecorated rather globular pots, a third ('B') was an open bowl with decoration of vertical incised lines and a row of holes below the rim (Fig. 27, no. 7), and the fourth ('A') (Fig. 27, no. 8) was a large bag-shaped vessel with panels of vertical and horizontal lines in whipped cord technique, separated by raised vertical ribs very much in the manner of the (incised) pattern on the Ballyreagh bowl. These vessels suggest yet another variant of Beacharra ware, and when we turn to the 'Larne' group of sherds we find numerous examples of cord ornament on vessels, and the same may be said for sherds from Tamnyrankin or Carrick East which repeat motifs (e.g. crescentic 'maggots') known from 'Larne'. And in the Sandhill wares, which have no known connexion with chambered tombs, we again encounter whipped and twisted cord motifs which link with this subgroup of the Beacharra bowls just described, and the same relationship must exist in the pottery previously described as 'Peterborough ware' from Lough Enagh and Island MacHugh, really itself of 'Sandhill' type (see p. 317 below).

It is clear therefore that we have two distinct phases in the decorated Beacharra ware (types B and C)—that with channelled and incised ornament which in technique and motifs is closely related to a large series of western European Neolithic wares, and that in which similar motifs are executed in twisted and whipped cord techniques absolutely foreign to these European regions, though of course well known in the north and east. These cord-ornamented Beacharra pots are found in a very restricted area of Ulster and in Bute and must represent a local phenomenon in which the Sandhill wares, and those of Island MacHugh and Lough Enagh, are likely to be involved. Their significance in the general picture of the Clyde-Carlingford culture is discussed in a later section.

Peterborough ware. Sherds of Peterborough ware were found at Cairnholy I accompanying the final burials in the chamber, associated with a plano-convex knife, *B*-beaker sherds, and probably the jadeite axe fragment. Similar sherds occurred at the base of the forecourt blocking. A single sherd of what appears to be *Rinyo I ware* comes from Tormore in Arran (p. 346).

Flint and other stones

Axes of chipped flint or ground stone were present among the gravegoods or ritual deposits of six tombs of the Clyde-Carlingford culture: one of the two Scottish examples, from Clachaig, is a large stone axe over 8 in. in length, but the Irish examples are usually rather smaller. At Ballyalton were two poorly chipped flint axes from a hoard of flint artifacts containing in addition to the axes a chopper, a saw, thirty-nine flakes and a flint nodule. The Large Cairn at Clontygora produced a ground stone adze with one flat face, apparently of epidiorite, and of the two stone axes at Creevykeel one was small and finely polished suggesting to the excavator a metal prototype. Typologically there is little to be said about the variant forms included in the tools enumerated above, and no significant comparisons can be made. At Dunloy two well-made polished stone axes (Fig. 28, nos. 1, 2) were found in the entrance blocking, one at least of which was of the porcellanite of Tievebulliagh in County Antrim, a site where an open axe-factory had been identified by Knowles (1903) and is discussed in Chapter x. Its products are known to have been exported as far afield as Gloucestershire, Dorset and Kent (Keiller, Piggott & Wallis, 1941).

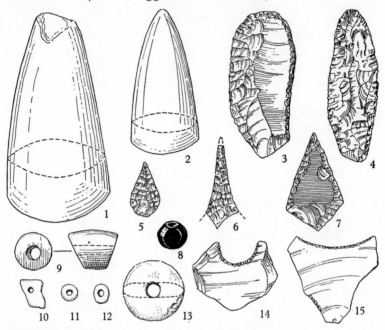

Fig. 28. Clyde-Carlingford culture: stone and flint types. 1, 2, 9, 15, Dunloy (*after Evans*); 3, Torlin; 4, 8, Cairnholy; 5, Sliddery; 6, 7, Clontygora (*after Davies*); 10–12, Lyles Hill (*after Evans*); 13, Ballyalton (*after Evans*); 14, Tamnyrankin. Scale ½.

At Cairnholy I, probably but not certainly associated with the Peter-borough and *B*-beaker sherds, was found an abraded fragment of a large ceremonial axe of pyroxene jadeite with high glassy polish. About fifty axes of similar stones have been found in Britain, but the Cairnholy specimen is the only one in any archaeological context (Piggott & Powell, 1949, 138, with map). Petrologically, the source of the Cairnholy axe is almost certainly Brittany, and its significance is commented on below.

Leaf-arrowheads of flint occur fairly abundantly to a total of some twenty-five specimens from half as many tombs (Giants' Graves, Arran, Sliddery (Fig. 28, no. 5), Cairnholy I and II, and Kindrochat in Scotland; Ballyalton, Clontygora Large and Small Cairns (Fig. 28, no. 6), Clady Halliday, Doey's Cairn, Carnanbane, Tamnyrankin, Aghanaglack, Ballyrenan and Creevy-keel in Ireland, and Mull Hill in the Isle of Man). The types vary between the various forms of leaf- and lozenge-shaped outlines which could occur in Britain in almost any region of the Windmill Hill culture, but at Clontygora Large Cairn is the angular lozenge form with slightly concave sides which occurs in the Yorkshire Neolithic series, while at Clady Halliday is another lozenge-shaped specimen with polishing on the face in a well-known Irish and Iberian manner (Fig. 28, no. 7). *Barbed* arrowheads are known only from the Nethei Largie tomb (a Clyde-Carlingford–passage-grave hybrid) stratified however below Beaker buiials.

Plano-convex flint knives have been found at Tormore, Sliddery, Torlin (Fig. 28, no. 3), Dunan Mor, Clachaig and Giants' Graves, in Arran; Cairnholy I (Fig. 28, no. 4) and II in Galloway; in Ulster at Dunloy, Tamnyrankin, Carnanbane and Creevykeel; and at Mull Hill in the Isle of Man. At Cairnholy I the knife was associated with the latest burials in the tomb, with Peterborough and *B*-beaker sherds, but the type has every claim to be considered an integral feature of the Clyde-Carlingford culture, though as we shall see it also occurs in the Pentland Firth group of tombs and in cultures outside the Western Neolithic group. It is of course best known in the Food-vessel culture of the Bronze Age, but several of the Clyde-Carlingford examples retain surface cortex on the upper face in a manner unknown in the Bronze Age specimens.

Long flint knives with polished edge. This, as we shall see, is a form typical of the Secondary Neolithic cultures (e.g. Ronaldsway, Rinyo and Peterborough), but one example is known from a Clyde-Carlingford tomb, at Tormore. This type again recurs in the Pentland Firth province in passage-graves.

Hollow scrapers or *concave saws* of flint, usually with very fine serrations on the curved scraping edge, are a peculiarity of the Ulster tombs (Fig. 28, nos. 14, 15), where they occur in almost all excavations, and they were found at Mull Hill and Cashtal yn Ard in the Isle of Man. The type had long been known from surface finds in Ireland, and does not seem to have affinities outside that area. It does not occur in the Scottish tombs.

Perforated stone mace-heads. At Tormore there was found, in association with a flint knife with polished edge and two of plano-convex type, a small well-finished mace-head with straight cylindrical perforation. Similar mace-heads come from Caithness and Orkney chambered tombs, and, with their antler prototypes, are characteristic of the Rinyo-Clacton and Dorchester cultures. Its association at Tormore with a polished-edge knife and a fragment of pottery of Rinyo I type, also typical of these cultures, is significant.

Stone beads, etc. Several of the Ulster tombs have produced various bead forms in stone (or in one instance, at Dunloy, in bone), and a large jet bead was found at Cairnholy I (Fig. 28, no. 8). The types are not very significant in the main—a plain disc-bead (but perhaps as thought by the excavator a

spindle-whorl) from Ballyalton (Fig. 28, no. 13), a small stone ring from
Clady Halliday, and a perforated object either a large bead or a pendant
from Clonlum Small Cairn do not offer much scope for typological com-
parison, but the cylindrical serpentine bead from Dunloy, with the ends
cut obliquely (Fig. 28, no. 9), and the small serpentine beads from Lyles
Hill (Fig. 28, nos. 10–12) may be more significant. The disc-beads from
Mull Hill, Creevykeel and Ballyrenan have, it is true, British Early Bronze
Age parallels, and at the last site were collared biconical beads aptly compared by Hencken (1939, p. 79) to those in a Beaker context at Cruden in
Aberdeenshire, but the disc type may well have earlier antecedents.

Jet belt-fastener. From Beacharra came a jet object known as a 'slider'
or belt-fastener, found 'not at the bottom of the cist, but comparatively
near the surface, though below the level of the transverse slab' (Bryce, 1902,
105), and therefore secondary to the six pots already mentioned. It is a type
belonging to the Secondary Neolithic cultures, and almost certainly to be
associated with Peterborough ware, with which it was found in a Dorset
barrow, and in the Gop Cave in North Wales: it also accompanied a burial
earlier than another with a *B*-beaker in Oxfordshire, and is further discussed
in Chapter XI.

Objects of pitchstone. Flakes of characteristic Corriegills (Arran) pitchstone were found in five Arran tombs, in two in Bute and in one in Galloway
(Cairnholy I). The use of this rock as an adjunct to the beach-pebble flint
upon which the cairn-builders would otherwise be dependent for flaked
tools is interesting, and clearly some local trade was involved in western
Scotland between the various Clyde-Carlingford settlements. (Mann, 1918.)

Stone discs, ranging from 2 to 4 in. across and chipped or ground into
shape were found at Ballynamona (one), Cairnholy I (two) and Pant-y-Saer
in Anglesey (two). They may be compared with those from Ty Isaf in the
Severn-Cotswold group.

Clay balls. Two clay balls about ¾ in. in diameter, were found at Creevykeel. They have parallels (in stone) in the Boyne tombs, and in the Rinyo
and Dorchester cultures.

Art

Apart from pottery decoration, the only evidence of ornamental design
on the part of the builders of the Clyde-Carlingford tombs consists of two
examples of incised stones. The more elaborate example comes from the
monument on Lyles Hill, where the outer surface of the sill-stone of the
'false portal' has a delicately engraved pattern of chevrons and triangles,
while at the Goward cairn a loose slab had a somewhat similar engraved
lozenge pattern. Evans (1940*b*) has pointed out the distinctive character
of this ornament which dissociates it from the 'pecked' and usually curvilinear technique of the ornament on the stones of the Boyne passage-graves,

and compares it with similar ornament from Skara Brae. It is also comparable with the incised plaques at Ronaldsway, and Iberian parallels are also to be found.

Cereals

Sherds from Dunloy, examined by Helbaek (Jessen & Helbaek, 1944), contained impressions of the grains of small spelt (*Triticum monococcum*), Emmer wheat (*T. dicoccum*) and of others of *monococcum-dicoccum* type. The occurrence of small spelt grain-impressions is of great interest, since its Neolithic distribution stretches from central Europe into Denmark, with its furthest western occurrence in Belgium. The probable Danish connexions of some of the Dunloy pots may be significant in this regard. A single identification of a wheat-grain impression is recorded from Mull Hill (Hyde in Megaw, 1939).

USE OF TOMBS IN THE BRONZE AGE

There is evidence from Scotland and Ireland that the tombs of the Clyde-Carlingford culture continued in use until and after the arrival in those areas of the makers of beakers usually associated with the beginning of the Metal Age in Britain and the practice of separate burial. At both Cairnholy I and II the later deposits in the chambers include *B*-beaker fragments, deposited as broken sherds in the Neolithic tradition, and not as complete pots. At Nether Largie in Argyll, in the innermost compartment of the segmented gallery, two layers of burials were distinguishable, the lower being a black deposit on the floor, with cremated bones and Neolithic pottery. Above and on this layer had been built a small secondary cist in one corner of the gallery, and unburnt human bones and Beaker sherds also occurred at this level, almost certainly derived from a disturbed burial formerly in the cist. These two layers were again clearly marked in the next segment, where the upper yielded remains of three beakers, one a fine vessel of Mitchell's *CB* class (Greenwell, 1866). In the tomb at Kilchoan in Argyll (Mapleton, 1866) a sequence of burial deposits was observed in which a lower black layer with burnt bones was covered by an upper loose deposit with unburnt bones and a sherd probably of a food-vessel. At Cairnholy I the rear portion of the burial chamber had been re-used in the Bronze Age for a Food-vessel interment with an inserted cup-and-ring marked stone.

In the tombs of Arran and Bute the evidence for any sequence of burials is uncertain except at Clachaig, where the cairn contained a secondary cist with a Food-vessel inhumation. But the Beaker or allied sherds from Giants' Graves, Dunan Mor and Glecknabae, and these and a terminal of a crescentic jet necklace from Dunan Beag, were found in conditions comparable with the Beaker sherds at Cairnholy, and imply a mixture of Neolithic and

Beaker elements in the population entitled to bury in the tomb. The secondary cists built up against the façades at Gartnagreanoch and Cashtal yn Ard are presumably Early Bronze Age but did not yield definite evidence.

In Ulster there seems no clear indication of Bronze Age re-use of the tombs, but a group of galleries or derivatives (e.g. Clogherny Meenerrigal, Loughash and Loughash Cashelbane, Cloghnagalla and Largantea) have produced grave-goods exclusively of Beaker or other Early Bronze Age cultures, while the 'double' tomb of Aghanaglack produced in one of its chambers a burial with barbed and tanged arrowheads and cord-ornamented sherds presumably of this date.

HABITATION SITES

Settlements which can be attributed to the Clyde-Carlingford culture within the area of the distribution of its characteristic tombs are very few. The site on Lyles Hill itself is unfortunately published only in Evans's preliminary note (1940*b*), and excavation has been centred on the cairn on the hill. The enclosing rampart however, which trial trenches have shown to be contemporary with the shouldered bowls I have named after the site, encloses an area of 13 acres (comparable with such large causewayed camps as Windmill Hill or Whitehawk) and consists of an irregularly circular but continuous bank with no ditch. Within this are habitation areas and the cairn to which reference has already been made. Axes of Tievebulliagh stone appear to have been contemporary with the pottery. Lyles Hill ware has also been found in surface habitations such as those at Dunmurry, and in sand-dunes at Dundrum and at Glenluce in Galloway. A site at Rothesay, Bute, produced pottery allied to those forms of Beacharra ware with developed rims such as are seen in the tombs at Nether Largie or Gleck-nabae and again occur in the Hebridean passage-grave culture, but the dominant culture was that of Rinyo-Skara Brae type and it is more fully discussed in Chapter XI.

At Carnanbane, Co. Londonderry, Evans found underlying the east end of the cairn and forecourt an area of scorched earth and charcoal measuring 45 ft. by at least 25 ft. and containing eleven holes, some probably hearths but others almost certainly post-holes. The dark earth layer over this area contained sherds and burnt flints and 'moulded lumps of potters' clay' which may be burnt daub. He would regard this as the result of ritual performances at the time of the construction of the tomb and does 'not think that the evidence can be interpreted as the result of normal habitation' (Evans, 1939, 12). It seems, however, possible that this may be an instance of the erection of a tomb over the dwelling of the dead man, whose pottery had included Lyles Hill ware and an unornamented bowl of good Beacharra form.

OUTLYING COLONIES OF THE CLYDE-CARLINGFORD CULTURE[1]

Beyond the area of primary and intensive settlement in south-west Scotland and Northern Ireland just discussed, there are various chambered tombs occurring singly or in groups along the shores of the Irish Sea and in the English Channel which show kinship with the Clyde-Carlingford tombs.

On the coast at Ballynamona Lower in Co. Waterford, Powell (1938 b) excavated an isolated small tomb of Clyde-Carlingford type, with a fore-court of orthostats and a short chamber divided into two by an orthostat of full height blocking three-quarters of the width, leaving a narrow entrance with a sill to one side, and a low septal with jamb-stones at the entrance. There was a hearth in the forecourt and finds comprised a stone disc and sherds of a highly ornamented bowl which seems to relate to the Sandhill wares.

Another and even more isolated monument is The Grey Mare and Her Colts on the Dorset coast near Portesham, consisting of a small oval cairn with a simple rectangular chamber and the remains of a peristalith and of a forecourt setting of massive orthostats set in a shallow arc originally about 35 ft. across (Piggott, 1946 a).

These two monuments serve to show the furthest extremities of the Clyde-Carlingford culture, but in Wales, Grimes's field-work has shown the existence of colonies of settlers developing local fashions in chambered tombs of Clyde-Carlingford derivation.[2]

In Anglesey, the Trefignath tomb near Holyhead is a segmented gallery with large portals completely in the west Scottish manner, and the ruined remains of similar portalled galleries exist at Ty'n Drifol and Trefor, while derivative portalled chambers in long cairns (Grimes's 'North-western Long Cairns') are found on the mainland in Carnarvonshire and Merionethshire, where they are typified at Gwern Einion. Three excavated chambered tombs in Anglesey have features relating them to Clyde-Carlingford types. The first is a large 'polygonal dolmen' at Lligwy, in which a 'kind of paving of flat stones' was noticed, above and below which human bones and sherds were found. This pottery (Piggott, 1933) included a sherd with *cardium* ornament similar to that on local Anglesey Beaker sherds, found above the paving, and three sherds with channelled ornament in the Beacharra-Hebridean manner, from an unlocated level.

The Pant y Saer tomb, excavated by Scott (1933), consisted of a rect-angular cist-like chamber of massive orthostats set in a pit cut in the solid limestone, surrounded by the remains of a cairn with a shallow curved façade to the north-west and straight converging lateral walls, all of dry

1 Bibliography for England and Wales in Daniel (1950).
2 Where other references are not given, the Welsh monuments described below are documented in Grimes (1936 a) and Daniel (1950).

walling with one or two orthostats. The burials comprised the bones of no less than thirty-six adults, three adolescents, six children, and nine full-term foetuses—a total of fifty-four persons—associated with leaf-arrowheads and unornamented Neolithic pottery with thickened rims which could be fairly well matched in Beacharra contexts in south-west Scotland. Secondary burials in an inserted cist had been associated with sherds of an *A* beaker. Although actual access to the tomb for successive burials was over the western 'horn' of the monument, the plan as a whole with its façade, 'horns' and straight-walled sides, relates it to the gallery-and-forecourt monuments we have been discussing.

Bryn yr Hen Bobl (Hemp, 1936) has a small nearly rectangular chamber opening straight on to the forecourt of a very large kidney-shaped mound, 130 ft. across with its outer edge defined by at least one and occasionally two or more dry-stone walls. The entrance to the chamber is blocked by a large slab which probably originally completely filled the opening to cap-stone level and which has two natural 'porthole' perforations which have probably been trimmed and which certainly seem likely to have dictated the choice of the stone for its purpose. Such a chamber is unlike anything in the passage-grave series and may be related to Clyde-Carlingford forms, but the round mound suggests contact with local communities of the Boyne culture. The Bryn yr Hen Bobl plan is further complicated by the remark-able, built 'terrace' bounded by dry walling and running for no less than 330 ft. from the south side of the mound, with which it was structurally bonded.

Remains of about twenty individuals, of both sexes and including small children, were found in the chamber, and the cairn and terrace apparently overlaid an occupation floor with pottery of Western types as well as Peter-borough ware, flints including *petit-tranchet* derivatives, and axes of Graig Lwyd stone (cf. p. 292).

In Pembrokeshire three chambered tombs can be related to the series under discussion. At Pentre Ifan and Garn Turne (Grimes, 1932) are chambers with forecourt settings of orthostats, the former having partial analogies at least with the plans of Ballynamona Lower and The Grey Mare while the latter, with its deep funnel-shaped approach, is perhaps more com-parable to that at Bryn yr Hen Bobl. The long sides of the chamber at Pentre Ifan (Grimes, 1948) were found never to have been closed by ortho-stats, there being only a rough dry-wall foundation, and it was further found that the whole chamber was set in a pit dug in the solid ground, as at Pant y Saer, and Grimes thinks that at Pentre Ifan access must have been gained to the chamber from one or other of the unwalled sides since, as at the Anglesey site and at The Grey Mare, entrance from the façade is impossible owing to orthostats rising to full height. The façade (probably about 20 ft. across) had consisted of four stones only, two on each side of the portal, and the forecourt area was tightly packed with cairn material. Sockets for peristalith stones showed that the cairn was originally about 130 ft. long and 56 ft. wide. A sherd of a vessel of undecorated pottery of Western Neolithic type, probably allied to that from Clegyr Boia and Carn Brea, and a small triangular flint arrowhead were found.

The Pembrokeshire monument of Cerrig y Gof, where five massive rectangular chambers are set in a roughly radial arrangement in a nearly circular cairn, seems comparable to the round cairns with radial cists as at Dunan Mor in Arran and Cairnderry in Galloway. At Hedon Howe in Yorkshire a barrow containing one central and four radial cists, one apparently with a septal slab at its outer end, seems also related. It contained Grimston ware and a leaf-arrowhead, and there were secondary burials, one with a beaker and one with a food-vessel. (Mortimer, 1905, 346.)

There is one monument in Cheshire which is clearly an outlying member of the Clyde-Carlingford group. This segmented gallery with forecourt is known as The Bridestones and has been recognized as a notable antiquity since the eighteenth century (Phillips, 1933 *b*; Dunlop, 1939). In its present much-ruined condition it comprises a large gallery divided into two compartments by a slab now broken and bearing the lower half of a 'porthole' opening. There is another massive septal slab across the entrance, and three stones still standing of the crescentic forecourt setting. Excavations in 1939 brought to light a flat slab and a spread of charcoal just beyond the chord of the forecourt arc.

THE RELATIONSHIPS AND CHRONOLOGY OF THE CLYDE-CARLINGFORD CULTURE

So far as the typology of the tomb plans goes, the presence of jamb-stones to the septals in Ireland and their total absence in Scotland, suggests that Arran and Bute, and the valleys of the Luce and Cree in Galloway, were the areas of primary colonization. In the Irish series a clear degeneration sequence can be observed whereby the septals become omitted and the jambs alone remain: had Scotland been colonized from Ulster therefore the tombs should either show jambs and septals (if an early move) or jambs only (if made at a later stage). A reverse process is in fact implied, with a segmented gallery-grave having septals without jambs introduced from the European continent (where this plan is in fact found, but not the Irish arrangement) to west Scotland. Ulster may have been colonized direct or from Scotland, with Ballyalton as one of the earliest tombs by reason of its close adherence to the Scottish type of segmentation.

There is no evidence from the tomb typology to show the relationship in south-west Scotland of the long segmented gallery with crescentic forecourt of the East Bennan type to the tombs without façades such as Torlin or

Cairnholy II, though in Galloway a degeneration-series can be seen, ending in cairns with multiple lateral chambers, which occur again in Perthshire and Ayrshire. In Ireland there is little doubt about the development, with the dropping of septals and slab-cist construction in favour of oval chambers separated by jambs, and the progressive elaboration of the forecourt until it attains the exaggerated plan of the 'lobster-claw' monuments of the west. A different line of degeneration may produce the undivided galleries which have Early Bronze Age grave-goods, or these may be another group allied to Daniel's 'Loire Galleries'.

The funeral rites, with inhumations occurring in numbers equal to the cremations in Scotland, but absent in Ireland save for the one instance of Ballyalton, might argue for multiple strains in the original colonists. No significant correlation can be made between burial rite and tomb type in Scotland. Cremation occurs in other Scottish tombs, but not in the Cotswolds.

Typologically, the Clyde-Carlingford tombs must be related in some way to the Severn-Cotswold cairns, with which they share the trapezoid mound, the ritual forecourt, and in Galloway and Ayrshire at least, a parallel devolutionary series. On the other hand the long cairn and the crescentic forecourt appear again on both sides of the Pentland Firth, though (as in the Cotswolds) the burial chambers have quite different plans from the Clyde-Carlingford examples.

The evidence of the grave-goods suggests that the restricted distribution of Lyles Hill ware, of probable Yorkshire derivation, may imply that the makers of this pottery colonized Ireland and probably Man from the north English coast, but avoided western Scotland since it was already occupied by people of a Neolithic culture who are likely to have been the builders of the Clyde-Carlingford tombs in that region. The bowl of Lyles Hill ware stratigraphically related to the latest phase of the tomb's use at Cairnholy I is significant. In Ulster Lyles Hill ware and the chambered tombs seem in origin fundamentally distinct, with the pottery probably partly related to similar wares in Eire (e.g. Lough Gur), and the virtual failure of the pottery to spread into the Scottish area of colonization at a later date, contrasts with Beacharra ware, more probably an integral part of the culture of the tomb-builders as brought from the Continent, which is common to Ulster and the Clyde estuary.

The plain pots of Beacharra A which are likely to be an integral and early feature of this group of wares occur in Scotland in simple segmented cists without façades, and from a similar tomb come the decorated bowls of the type-site, while at Cairnholy I the primary pottery deposit was a plain shallow bowl. The traditions of Beacharra ware were firmly established further north in the Hebrides associated with chambered tombs which architecturally show Clyde-Carlingford contacts. In Ulster, the vessel from

Clontygora Large Cairn seems typologically early, but it is in Northern Ireland that we presumably have to look for the origins of a later style (Beacharra C) in which the motifs originally executed in channelling or incision are carried out in impressed whipped or twisted cord techniques. This is certainly related to Sandhill wares, the antecedents of which lie in the same Scandinavian contexts as those of Peterborough ware, without being identical with them.

The unornamented vessels of Beacharra A (often with lugs) are of forms which could be paralleled in Windmill Hill ware or in almost any province of the Western Neolithic cultures. The carinated and decorated pots of phase B, however, are more distinctive, and in Britain the only analogies outside the Clyde-Carlingford area are the Hebridean series, in which the ornament and its techniques are seen, though not the forms, and an isolated unornamented vessel of the characteristic carinated form from the Holden-hurst long barrow in Hampshire. As we shall see, the channelled and incised ornaments have good Continental analogues; somewhat similar ornament at The Trundle causewayed camp in Sussex (Curwen, 1929a, pl. VIII, 2) may possibly have a common origin with that of Beacharra.

Most curious though are the vessels of Beacharra C style, with their use of fine whipped or twisted cord technique to produce patterns in the incised and channelled traditions. What little can be gleaned from the pottery of the so-called Sandhill culture, with which Beacharra C ware must be considered, is discussed in Chapter XI, but the main point to stress here is that it is distinctively different from Peterborough ware even though it may sometimes share motifs (such as the looped cord impression). Some of the Beacharra C pots, like sherds from Sandhill sites, seem to show a really marked relationship with Scandinavian vessels of the early passage-grave period, and this point is referred to again in the last section of this chapter.

Of grave-goods other than pottery, few show any distinctive connexions with other British Neolithic cultures. The ceremonially deposited axe of Tievebulliagh stone at Dunloy is important, as we shall see below, in helping to relate the Clyde-Carlingford sequence to natural bog stratigraphy in Ireland and beyond; the jadeite fragment from Cairnholy I, while a member of a large class of ceremonial axes widely scattered over Britain, and probably (as this) mainly of Breton origin, is the only example in an archaeological context. The trade contacts implicit in these axes suggest comparison with other stone axes, of identical rock, known from Wessex, Jersey and Brittany (p. 300 below). Leaf-arrowheads are the types common to all British Neolithic cultures, though the example with polished faces from Clontygora is a form restricted to Ireland but elsewhere only known from surface finds, though characteristic of the Portuguese chambered tombs. The barbed arrowheads from Nether Largie should indicate Bronze Age contacts. The plano-convex knives seem likely to be a distinctive product of the culture (though that at Cairnholy I was found with Peterborough and *B*-beaker sherds), but occur also in Orkney-Cromarty passage-graves and in the Secondary Neolithic cultures. To these cultures must be attributed the perforated stone mace-head and polished-edge flint knife found in association in the Tormore chamber: a knife of this type was associated with Peterborough pottery and axes of Graig Lwyd and Langdale origin in Yorkshire. The few beads give us little indication of relationships, though the stone discs from Cairnholy I and Ballynamona should be compared with those from Pant y Saer in Anglesey and Ty Isaf in the Severn-Cotswold group of chambered cairns.

Chronologically, we can proceed a little further. Apart from the evidence of the culture's European origins discussed in the last section of this chapter, it is difficult to find evidence for the beginnings of the Clyde-Carlingford culture in Britain. The plans of the cairns, with their trapezoid form and ritual forecourts, suggest a broad contemporaneity with the similarly planned Severn-Cotswold group—these as we know are themselves roughly contemporary with the Windmill Hill culture of Wessex, and both are earlier than the arrival of makers of Peterborough pottery in the south and south-west of England: in the Severn-Cotswold tombs such pottery appears in the final blocking of the forecourts. On the other hand, the cremation-trench at Dunloy must be connected with the Yorkshire cremation-barrows which should be derivative from, and therefore later than, the south English Windmill Hill series, so we may expect some fairly long duration for the Ulster culture.

Dunloy contributes further important evidence for dating the period of the final use of the tombs. An axe deposited in the ceremonial blocking of the forecourt—the final act before the cessation of the tomb's use—is a product of a factory at Tievebulliagh, described in Chapter x, and here such axes could be related to bog stratigraphy by Jessen (1949, 142). Both sites were shown to date from the base of his Zone VII*b*, or the VII*a*/VII*b* transition, which is in fact the transition from Atlantic to Sub-Boreal climatic conditions. As we shall see, there is reason to believe that the stone-axe factories of late Neolithic times, of which Tievebulliagh is one, worked for a limited duration only, and their products can therefore be used with some confidence as indicating a chronological horizon. Now in Somerset, Peterborough pottery was related to bog stratigraphy on Meare Heath (Godwin, 1941), where it could be assigned to Zone VII, and again at Upware in the Fenland an axe from the Graig Lwyd factory (whose products reached Wessex, Anglesey and Yorkshire at least, contemporaneously with Peterborough ware) could be related to Godwin's Zone VII*b*/VII*c*—approximately contemporary with Tievebulliagh and Meare. With this Dunloy evidence can be taken the presence of Peterborough pottery with the last burials and in the final blocking at Cairnholy I. The end of the Clyde-

Carlingford culture then, and the cessation of burial in its collective tombs, comes with the appearance of makers of Peterborough pottery in the region, as in the Cotswolds. And that these two events were broadly contemporary is suggested by the collateral evidence of the products of the axe factories, and their relation to bog stratigraphy. The Tormore finds would be appropriate to this same chronological horizon.

The bearing of this upon the pottery sequence is of importance. At Dunloy, as we have seen, Lyles Hill ware was found associated with the cremation trench in the primary deposits, and the Beacharra C pottery was later, broadly contemporary with the Tievebulliagh axe or a little earlier. So a fairly early date is given for the arrival of the makers of Lyles Hill pottery in Ulster, though its long survival is shown not only by the north-west Irish evidence already commented on, but by the presence of a bowl of this ware in the blocking of Cairnholy I, where it must be contemporary with Peterborough ware and B-beakers. Its presence at Ehenside Tarn with Langdale Pike axes and sherds of Peterborough ware is consistent with this.

If Beacharra C ware is to be dated to a period shortly after the Zone VII a/VII b transition, the A and B phases should be earlier, and so overlap with the Severn-Cotswold cairns, and probably the Windmill Hill culture too. At Beacharra itself, the six A and B ware pots forming the primary deposits were stratigraphically earlier than a jet belt-fastener of a type having significant associations with Peterborough ware and allied late Neolithic cultures. The stratification recorded by Scott from the Hebrides and discussed in Chapter VIII confirms this early dating for the A and B wares in the Clyde-Carlingford tombs. At Nether Largie, in a tomb which appears to combine Clyde-Carlingford and Passage-grave traditions, it is noteworthy that barbed arrowheads, normal to Early Bronze Age contexts, were found with the primary deposits, thus suggesting a late date for the tomb which the typology would support.

The European relationships of the Clyde-Carlingford culture

It remains for us to analyse the Continental affinities of our Clyde-Carlingford culture, which as we have seen must be regarded as an intrusive sea-borne complex established at the head of the Irish Sea. The typology of the tomb-plans is the first line of approach, though it must be used with caution. On this evidence, Davies has made claims for contact between Ulster and Sardinia; Childe has pointed to significant parallels in the Pyrenees; Scott has looked to Languedoc, Daniel to the Loire. There are three main structural elements significant to our enquiry—the parallel-sided burial chamber which may be divided internally by septal slabs or jambs; the setting of this 'gallery' within a long cairn whose length is not merely a strict function of the proportions of the chamber; and the frequent presence of a forecourt marked by a façade at the entrance to the chamber.

As Childe first demonstrated, strong architectural resemblances to the Clyde-Carlingford chambers are to be found among the Pyrenean chambered tombs of Catalonia and the Basque provinces, where specific features such as segmentation with septal slabs occur, in such sites as Puig Rodo and La Halliade. Going further afield we can point to a similarity, though not identity, of structure in the south French gallery-graves, in the rock-cut tombs and stone-built navetas of the Balearics, and the famous Giants' Graves of Sardinia, while in South Italy the Apulian gallery-graves are an outpost of south French derivation, presenting striking parallels even to the use of segmentation by sills or septals at Corato. (Childe, 1947, 235; Gervasio, 1913.)

The form of the cairn in the Clyde-Carlingford culture ranged from short oval mounds enclosing simple burial chambers such as Torlin or Clachaig to such examples as East Bennan, with a 20 ft. gallery in a mound which stretches back 80 ft. from the forecourt. In the Catalonian tombs the cairn is, where recoverable, circular, but long cairns are by no means uncommon in western France and in such areas as the Aveyron and elsewhere, in the Balearics, in Sardinia and Apulia.

In Brittany, not only are there long cairns of undifferentiated plan, but the Manio type accurately reproduces the trapezoidal plan characteristic of many of the Clyde-Carlingford cairns and those of the Severn-Cotswold group. As we have seen, these Manio cairns may be related to the long barrows of Wessex and Sussex and their derivatives, and there is evidence for placing them early in the Breton Neolithic.

The most striking structural feature characteristic of the Clyde-Carlingford tombs is the crescentic façade. This is unknown in the tombs otherwise comparable with those of the Clyde-Carlingford culture in the Pyrenees and elsewhere, occurring only in the famous series of crescentic forecourts and 'horns' which grace the Sardinian Giants' Tombs, while a modified version occurs on some navetas in Majorca. Eastwards in the Mediterranean the Maltese 'temples' share the same feature, where as Ward Perkins has shown (1942) Temple 3 at Hal Tarxien is essentially an elaboration of a tomb with crescentic façade and oval cairn, not really very far removed from the navetas of the Sardinian graves, and suggestive of some common set of origins. Certain of the Sicilian rock-cut tombs (e.g. Cava Lavinaro and Cava Lazzara) have semicircular façades with carved pilasters replacing orthostats. In the great Almerian passage-grave cemeteries a forecourt setting of stones is found at the entrance in a few examples, all in circular cairns (Los Millares, no. 20; Almizaraque, no. 1; Los Avejos, no. 2; Rambla de la Tejera 3), but it does not give the impression of an integral or essential part of the structure. (G. & V. Leisner, 1943, 287–8.)

It seems impossible therefore to derive the combination of façades, rectangular (sometimes segmented) chambers, and long cairns (sometimes trapezoidal) from any one European source. However, the chambers and long cairns certainly occur together in west France, and the trapezoid outline may well be concealed beneath the cairns where a search for a peristalith has never been made—such a buried dry-stone revetment certainly exists at Bougon in Charente. The sporadic appearance of crescentic façades in the Mediterranean, scattered from Sicily to south Spain and combined indifferently with tombs of diverse ground-plans, may indicate that this architectural setting for forecourt ritual is a latent element in the chambered tomb complex at large which may be locally developed or locally ignored. In the Cotswold tombs indeed the forecourt lies between 'horns' convex and not concave on their inner faces, as in passage-graves such as Bryn Celli Ddu and others.

We must therefore consider the possibility that the crescentic façades of the Clyde-Carlingford tombs may be the result of local evolution (as perhaps are the Cotswold forecourts), following the regional development of certain funerary ceremonies that needed the façade as a necessary ritual adjunct. We have seen that in the Scottish tombs it is impossible to make any chronological distinction between tombs with and tombs without façades, and certainly nothing indicates that the latter are late in the general series; in Ireland the development is clearly from a relatively small and flat façade (as at Ballyalton) to elaborate and deep arrangements culminating in the 'lobster-claw' forms. If the plain lugged bowls of Beacharra A ware from Trolin and Sliddery in Arran are really earlier than the decorated ware of type B, as Scott suggests on the Hebridean evidence, it is noteworthy that they come from chambers without façades as did indeed the B ware vessels at Beacharra itself, and we may have to regard the primary tomb form as the short segmented chamber set in an oval cairn, perhaps with portal stones, but without a monumental façade. This type of tomb certainly comes nearest to the west French and Pyrenean series, and while some shallow-façade tombs may also represent an original type introduced from the Continent, by far the greater part of the development seems likely to have taken place locally, both in Scotland and Ireland.

While the simpler forms of Beacharra A ware are difficult to classify within the general Western Neolithic province, they would find their best parallels in the earlier Cortaillod culture of western Europe, represented in the south and centre of France, in the Dordogne, and in Brittany. But the incised and channelled wares have precise analogues widely distributed in coastal sites from the mouth of the Rhône to that of the Tagus, and again (less precisely) in Charente and Deux-Sèvres and in Brittany. Stratigraphically, ornamented wares of this type appear in settlement sites in the south of France later than the plain lugged pots of Cortaillod type, and seem to be associated with the introduction of bell-beakers and tanged copper daggers into the region at such sites as Fontbouïsse (Sandars, 1950), which suggests a Spanish source, and Mrs Hawkes's study of the designs used on these wares (J. Hawkes, 1939 *b*) has shown that they must originate in such representations of the human face as appear on the 'idols' and pottery of Los Millares. Comparable pottery to that of south France, and using the same motifs (including the pendant semicircle) common to that area and to the Beacharra B ware, is known from a series of habitation sites in Portugal around the mouth of the Tagus, and here in one instance, at Senhora da Luz, Rio Maior, it appears to be stratigraphically earlier than bell-beakers (Belem Museum, unpublished). In Charente and Deux-Sèvres the comparable pottery from habitation sites (such as that on the Île d'Oléron and the numerous sites in the Peu Richard region) and from a chambered tomb at Availles-sur-Chizé, while recognizably a member of the same family, shows strongly marked local peculiarities which render it far less like the Beacharra B wares than those from Portugal or Provence, though a lug somewhat comparable to Charente forms was found at Clontygora Large Cairn. The Breton pottery of this group (e.g. the well-known pots from Conguel) is, however, again quite similar to the Scottish material.

There is little doubt therefore that the Beacharra B ware shares a common origin with that from the various sites mentioned above, and its presence in Britain is the result of a prolongation of the coasting ventures that took its makers along the Atlantic seaboard from Portugal to Brittany. In none of these areas is it possible to show any association of this type of pottery with chambered tombs that might be ancestral to the Clyde-Carlingford series, except a sherd with incised semicircles from the segmented gallery of Puig Rodo in Catalonia (Pericot, 1950, 61), and we are left with the possibility that two separate but allied strains of colonization may be involved. Further field-work and excavation in western France might go far to clarifying this problem.

The problem of the cord-ornamented wares of Beacharra C involves that of the Sandhill wares from coastal sites in Ulster, and will be further discussed in this connexion (Chapter xi). But it must be noted that close parallels to the panelled arrangement of vertical and horizontal lines in whipped cord technique occur in Danish Neolithic pottery of the early Passage-grave period. Vessels such as those from Mogenstrup (Brønsted, 1938, 187) or Trammose (Ekholm, 1927, pl. 78 *a*) of this phase, or funnel-beakers of late Dolmen-period date (Brønsted, 1938, fig. 102 *b*) really show surprisingly close stylistic affinities with the Dunloy vessel, which also has the raised ribs common on Dolmen-period pots. Again, the bowl from Dunloy with holes beneath the rim and vertical incisions below, strongly recalls the bowl from Ettrup (Brønsted, 1934) with similar holes but the vertical lines in whipped cord. Mrs Hawkes has even suggested that the tiny half-circle of whipped cord on the fragmentary Dunloy bowl E may possibly represent part of an 'eye' pattern in the Scandinavian manner, as for instance on pots from the Swedish passage-grave of Vestra Hoby (Forssander, 1936, 49). Childe emphasized this similarity between Irish and Danish pottery styles when discussing the 'Larne' pottery (Piggott & Childe, 1932), pointing out that, although broad similarities existed, the Irish ornament could not be derived from the British Peterborough style.

We can only note these close parallels between Ulster and Denmark (with which the occurrence of the impressions of grains of small spelt at Dunloy may perhaps be considered), while emphasizing the complete lack of any intermediate links in for instance the chambered tomb culture of the Pentland Firth and Orcadian region. A cross-country route from the Clyde-Carlingford region to the east coast between the Forth and Humber is always a possibility, though here again evidence (apart from the connexion of Hedon Howe with septal-slab tombs) is lacking.

The remaining grave-goods have little to offer as indications of foreign affinities except possibly the Clontygora arrowhead, with polishing on the faces in a manner known in the Palmella tombs in Portugal. More precise indication of trade at least with western France is afforded by the fragment of a ceremonial jadeite axe from Cairnholy I, petrologically almost certainly of Breton origin. The chevron and triangle ornament on the Lyles Hill stone is comparable with similar incised patterns at Gavr' Inis in Brittany (M. & S. J. Péquart & Le Rouzic, 1927, pl. 133, no. 30) and those painted on the wall of a Portuguese passage-grave, the Pedra Coberta (Leisner, 1934, pl. 10). The incised plaques of schist also show similar designs. But none of these comparisons takes us further in deciding on the exact region of origin of the Clyde-Carlingford culture, or of any of its essential components, beyond the fact that it is likely to lie on the Atlantic coasts between Portugal and Brittany, with a probability that it was centred on the western end of the Pyrenees.

OTHER CHAMBERED TOMBS OF GALLERY-GRAVE DERIVATION IN IRELAND

Introduction

Any treatment of the Irish chambered tombs outside those of the Clyde-Carlingford culture described above, or the passage-graves of the Boyne culture to be described in Chapter VII, is vitiated at the outset by the absence of any comprehensive survey of the enormous mass of material since that of Borlase (1897), which itself leaves very much to be desired. He estimated the total number of chambered tombs in Eire and Northern Ireland to be about nine hundred, and while he was frequently uncritical in acceptance of bogus sites, there have been more than enough recent discoveries to redress the balance, and a total of 1,000 tombs would probably not be far off the mark. Even after subtracting the Clyde-Carlingford and Boyne culture sites, the remaining bulk would be sufficiently large, and may be compared with the 215 chambered tombs listed by Daniel (1950) for England and Wales, and the 357 in Scotland (Childe, 1946, 99).

The vast majority of the residual Irish sites seem probably or certainly to consist of members of the Gallery-grave class of tomb, or the so-called 'dolmens' derivative from it. Attempts to classify the material on typological lines have been made by Daniel (1941) and by de Valera (in O'Riordain, 1946), and various regional surveys have been made which clarify local distributions (e.g. Powell, 1941a; Hartnett, 1940; Piggott & Powell, 1947). While variants undoubtedly exist, and may after detailed field-work be found to have some significance, for our present purposes it is sufficient to use de Valera's simplified classification. With the removal of the Clyde-Carlingford series already discussed at length in this chapter, we are left with a group of miscellaneous gallery-graves including those classed as 'wedge tombs' by Evans, and on the evidence of excavation of those in Tyrone and Londonderry very late in the sequence; a second group of massive structures, also wedge-shaped, and typified by the Labbacallee site; and a third rather indeterminate group of 'portal-dolmens' and those of rectangular plan (if these exist as a class, which de Valera doubts). Discussion here will be limited to excavated examples, of which we have several in the Londonderry-Tyrone group, though Labbacallee stands alone as an excavated example of its class.

Bronze Age gallery-graves in Londonderry and Tyrone, and their congeners

In Northern Ireland a distinctive type of chambered tomb within the Gallery-grave class has been recognized which is not a member of the Clyde-Carlingford group, and is best represented by sites in Co. Tyrone—Loughash Giants' Graves and Cashelbane (Davies, 1939c; Davies & Mullin, 1940), Clogherny Meenerrigal (Davies, 1939a)—and Co. Londonderry—Well Glass Spring, Largantea (Herring, 1938b) and Cloghnagalla (Herring & May, 1940). These tombs share the characteristics of a gallery with antechamber opening on to a straight façade and enclosed in an elongated D-shaped cairn with kerb averaging 20–30 ft. long. At Clogherny Meenerrigal a free-standing stone circle about 50 ft. in diameter encircles the whole cairn, the area between being paved.

Burial ritual is that of cremation, one person only being represented at Cloghnagalla, but six adults, a youth and an infant being identified at Largantea. At Loughash Cashelbane, it was thought that one skull was brachycephalic, of the so-called 'Beaker' type.

The grave-goods from these sites are consistent in showing that the tombs cannot be called 'Neolithic' except in so far as they indicate the collective burial rite and formalized tomb architecture persisting into the full Bronze Age. *Beakers* were found at Largantea and both the Loughash sites, at Cashelbane with Food-vessel pottery and at Giants' Graves with encrusted urn and other flat-based sherds; at Cloghnagalla were cord-ornamented sherds probably of the Bronze Age. *Barbed and tanged flint arrowheads* from Cloghnagalla, Clogherny Meenerrigal, Loughash Cashelbane and Kilhoyle are again consistent, and contrast with the leaf-arrows typical of the Clyde-Carlingford tombs, and the *bronze blade* from Loughash Giants' Graves, the *tanged bronze blade* from Largantea, and the *copper ring* also from Giants' Graves emphasize the non-Neolithic character of the sites. At Giants' Graves there was also a fragment of a mould for casting a bronze palstave of Middle or Late Bronze Age type apparently contemporary with the final blocking.

The Moylisha tomb and comparable sites

A group of tombs which in plan should belong to some variant of the gallery-grave group is typified by an excavated site at Moylisha, Co. Wicklow (O'h-Iceadha, 1946). Here the burial rite was cremation, but there was no pottery in primary contexts, though stone discs occurred. In the base of the cairn two halves of a stone mould for casting bronze spearheads with socket and loops were found 'firmly embedded' and were regarded as primary by the excavator. Tombs of similar plan in Ulster include those of Goakstown and Dunteige, from which it seems the 'Larne' group of pottery of Beacharra C type was obtained in the nineteenth century (p. 172 above).

Massive gallery-graves of the Labbacallee type

In all the Munster counties except Waterford, and westwards at least as far as the Aran Islands, it has been noted that tombs of a consistent type show 'a remarkable coincidence with the occurrence of certain lighter soils mainly on the Upper Limestone and Old Red Sandstone' (de Valera in O'Riordain, 1946). Of these tombs, two have been excavated, at Lough Gur and Labbacallee, Co. Cork, and the latter site has been published (Leask & Price, 1936). The oblong burial chamber was enclosed in a very massive wedge-shaped construction 40 ft. long, 11 ft. across its narrow (western) end and twice this width at the east. An outer kerb to the south suggested to the excavators that the whole structure had originally been enclosed in a covering cairn.

The rectangular chamber had at its western end a closed square compartment to which access could not have been gained after its construction save from the top. In it was found a disarticulated skeleton, with the skull and cervical vertebrae missing, and a rough bone pin: it was suggested with reason that the skeleton may have been buried in a bag fastened by this. With the human bones were charred bones of pig, ox and sheep, and also a human cremation which appeared to have been inserted at the same time as the remainder of the deposit.

In the main chamber there was considerable evidence of disturbance in the Early Iron Age, but of the original deposits there survived the remains of three individuals, all disarticulated, and a skull which corresponded in 'sex, age and state of preservation' with the headless (female) skeleton in the closed compartment. With the bones were some sherds of thin pottery with incised herring-bone ornament for which no precise parallels are forthcoming. The female skull proved to be brachycephalic, of the type normally found in the Middle Bronze Age cists of Ireland, sometimes accompanied by food-vessels (Martin, 1935, 88; and in Leask & Price, 1936).

The scanty evidence from Labbacallee is very little to use as a basis for deductions, but the brachycephalic skull may be significant in connexion with that reported from Loughash Cashelbane. The vast number of gallery-graves and 'dolmens' in Eire and Northern Ireland must, almost of necessity, be spread over some fairly long period of time, and they may well represent a tradition which persisted well into the Bronze Age, side by side with the new modes of single-grave burial in earth graves or cists usually associated with food-vessels and cinerary urns.

Rock-cut tomb

The site known as St Kevin's Bed, Glendalough, has been interpreted as a rock-cut tomb, with its analogy in the Dwarfie Stane in Orkney (Hemp, 1937; O'Neil, 1947; cf. p. 245 below).

CHAPTER VII

PASSAGE-GRAVE BUILDERS IN IRELAND: THE BOYNE CULTURE

INTRODUCTION

WHATEVER the origins and affiliations of the British tombs within the gallery-grave family, there can be no feeling of unfamiliarity when we come to the passage-graves of Ireland which have been classed as the Boyne culture (or better, Boyne group of tombs). Here are passage-graves of classic form, obvious members of the Western European family of collective tombs that includes Los Millares, Alcala, Île Longue and La Hougue Bie, and represented in Ireland by such internationally famous monuments as New Grange. The tombs number over 130, mainly grouped in four main cemeteries but with a wide scatter of isolated examples in southern and north-eastern Ireland and at least two in Wales (Fig. 29). From the group that includes New Grange, near the banks of the River Boyne, Powell has classed these tombs together as the Boyne type. (Powell, 1938 a, with bibliography.)

The distribution of the four great cairn-cemeteries of Brugh na Boinne (New Grange) (Coffey, 1912), Loughcrew (Conwell, 1867), Carrowkeel (Macalister *et al.* 1912) and Carrowmore (Wood-Martin, 1888), and a newly identified group of tombs at Fourknocks, is in a line running north-westwards from the neighbourhood of Drogheda on the east coast to Sligo on the west and, as we shall see, there is some reason to regard this line as indicating a process of colonization westwards from original points of entry on the east coast of Ireland. Of these published cemeteries, although the New Grange region (with three tombs) is relatively low-lying, along the banks of the Boyne, Loughcrew (twenty-four tombs) is on a dominating ridge, Carrowkeel (fourteen tombs) on a tremendous bare limestone scarp over 1,000 ft. above sea-level, and Carrowmore (sixty-three tombs) on an elevated upland, with its outliers on Knocknarea crowning a great bluff which towers above the Atlantic. The isolated cairns of the group, too, are normally on hill-tops, such as that on Tibradden Hill above Dublin, or on Belmore Mountain or Baltinglass Hill, where the chambered cairn is on a mountain summit 1,258 ft. above sea-level. This use of hill-tops, and the frequent grouping into cemeteries, serves immediately to distinguish the Boyne tombs from those of the gallery-grave type, where we have noted in Chapters V and VI the preference for the lower slopes or actual valleys for the siting of these tombs. The Brugh na Boinne cemetery must have been originally in thick woodland, but the mountain-top cemeteries and isolated cairns are likely

to have stood in open country. The Anglesey tombs of this group, Bryn
Celli Ddu and Barcloddiad y Gawres, are both in low country where
boulder-clay makes primitive woodland inevitable (Daniel, 1950, 186).

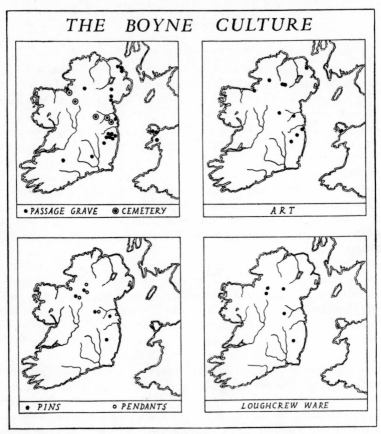

Fig. 29.

CAIRNS AND THEIR PLANS

With the exception of two anomalous long cairns at New Grange and
Carrowkeel respectively, all the Boyne group of passage-graves are contained within circular cairns (Fig. 30). The diameter of the cairns varies,
from over 250 ft. at New Grange to 40 ft. or even less at Carrowmore, and
the average size decreases in the four cemeteries from east to west—280 to
200 ft. at New Grange, 170 to 50 ft. at Loughcrew, 100 to 50 ft. at Carrowkeel, and 40 to 30 ft. at Carrowmore (though Knocknarea 7 is 95 ft. in

195

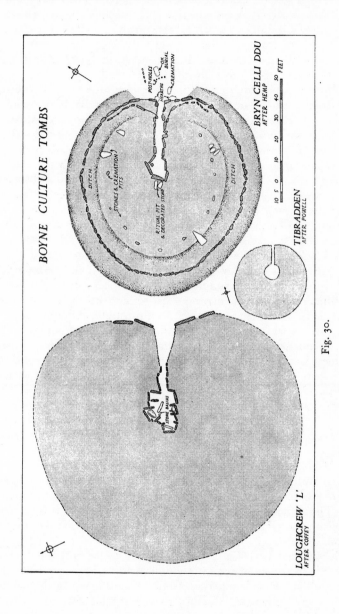

Fig. 30.

diameter). The isolated cairns tend to be of relatively small diameter (Cross 45 ft., Tibradden 50 ft., Carnanmore 85 ft., Seefin 85 ft., Bryn Celli Ddu 90 ft.). All these figures are within the range of comparable chambered tombs in western Europe—Romeral and La Hougue Bie 180 ft., Kercado 100 ft., Île Longue 80 ft., Los Millares 30–40 ft.—except for the giants of New Grange (250 ft.) and Dowth (280 ft.).

Owing to unsatisfactory excavations we have little or no knowledge of the structural features of the Boyne cairns save at Baltinglass and Bryn Celli Ddu (Walshe, 1941; Hemp, 1930). Elsewhere, excavations have merely taken the form of removing the human skeletal material and grave-goods from the burial chambers, frequently with quite inadequate records of the circumstances of their deposition. But it seems likely that some form of kerb of large blocks was normal at the base of the cairn, and sometimes this was duplicated by an inner ring of stones (Carrowkeel H and many Carrowmore cairns). In some instances, notably at Dowth and New Grange, the kerbstones were decorated with incised and carved patterns. At Bryn Celli Ddu (Fig. 30) the kerbstones, which were joined by dry-walling, were set up in a large circular ditch, 15 ft. wide and over 5 ft. deep, which was then refilled with stones and clay so that only the tops of the kerbstones were visible. Inside this ditch was a horseshoe setting consisting of twelve holes (some containing stones of varying sizes, set either upright or deliberately inclined), one stone that had always been prostrate, and a group of small stones: these were arranged so that diameters drawn from one stone to another all crossed at a central point immediately behind the burial chamber where there was a ritual deposit to be described later. In four of these holes were deposits of human bones—complete cremations of young persons by two holes, and single cremated bones (cochlea and tibia fragment) by the remainder. The whole horseshoe setting was of course completely buried beneath the superincumbent cairn once it had been constructed, and it invites comparison with certain 'Henge Monuments' described in Chapter xi.

The Baltinglass cairn proved to contain a complex series of kerbs and chambers which are difficult to disentangle, though clearly at least two phases of reconstruction and enlargement of an original structure are represented. The sequence is discussed below, and it is sufficient here to note that a completely buried kerb had two decorated stones and that the latest phase had plain stones.

Baltinglass and Bryn Celli Ddu again provide the only information we have on the treatment of the surface on which the cairn was built. In the former site there were large areas of burnt clay suggesting the lighting of ritual fires, and on them were found carbonized grains of wheat, oak charcoal and carbonized hazel nuts. A stone axe found under the cairn again suggests a ritual deposit. At Bryn Celli Ddu, a deliberately laid floor of purple clay covered the area within the ditch holding the kerbstones, and traces of burning were frequent upon it.

At New Grange the cairn stands within a free-standing stone circle, originally of thirty-six massive stones, with a diameter of some 330 ft., and it is possible that a similar circle surrounded Bryn Celli Ddu, where it would have had an estimated diameter of 160 ft.

The burial chambers

Within these cairns the burial chamber is set more or less centrally, usually however rather short of the true centre, with a narrow passage approach leading out to the kerb. Broadly speaking, these chambers can be divided into three main types, which may have a certain chronological significance though direct evidence, as so often, is lacking.

The first type consists of chambers of small size, usually about 10–12 ft. in internal diameter, set in proportionately small cairns of 50 ft. or less overall diameter. These chambers are either built entirely of dry-walling as a true corbelled *tholos* from floor to roof, and are circular, or they are polygonal with orthostatic walling and a corbelled roof. The passage approach is normally something under 20 ft. long, and may be roofed with capstones. Examples are Tibradden (Fig. 30) or Slieve Gullion (*tholoi*) or Carnanmore (orthostats and corbelled roof) or Bryn Celli Ddu (orthostats and corbels-and-capstones roof). Decorative art engraved upon the stones is rare and naturally demands some form of orthostat for its application—it is present for instance at Carnanmore and Bryn Celli Ddu.

The second type includes the enormous structures of New Grange and Dowth, and the majority of the cairns in the Loughcrew (Fig. 30) and Carrowkeel cemeteries. The chamber at Slieve Gullion had a smaller cell opening from it, and this plan is again followed in the southern chamber within the Dowth cairn, while typically the chamber is either cruciform, with a terminal and two side cells opening from the main chamber, or more elaborately 'transepted' as at Carrowkeel F, with two pairs of side cells and a terminal cell which have dwarfed the central area from which they open into a vestige of a chamber. Constructionally, these chambers are normally walled by orthostats but with high corbelled roofs, though at New Grange the entire structure of chamber and passage is of elaborate dry-walled masonry, in front of which the orthostats stand without performing any architectural function. In the Brugh na Boinne, Fourknocks, and the Loughcrew cemeteries these tombs have a great display of engraved designs upon the stones of peristalith, passage and chamber, and the New Grange technique of construction shows that the internal orthostats there were evidently regarded largely as convenient vehicles for a display of this art, and were furthermore carefully dressed by hammering with mauls to a flat surface, as at Stonehenge. Among the outlying tombs of this type one may mention Belmore Mountain (Fermanagh), Seefin (Wicklow) or Knock-narea 7 (Sligo), and in Anglesey, Barcloddiad y Gawres.

The third type is best represented at Carrowmore, and there, within small cairns about 40 ft. in diameter, occur degenerate cruciform chambers (e.g. Carrowmore 27 and 63) which can be followed into the simpler form of polygonal chamber of orthostats, with no corbelling, in such tombs as nos. 3, 7 and 56. There is no decorative engraving of orthostats. It is probable that some outlying examples such as Shantavny Irish (Tyrone) should also be included in this group.

In addition to this series, there are certain eccentric chamber-plans such as the northern chamber in the Dowth cairn, where an additional L-shaped pair of cells open out from one corner of a lateral cell in a normal cruciform plan, or Carrowkeel H, where the chamber is scarcely differentiated from the passage and the whole is curved in plan, recalling the Breton *allées coudées*. And there are certain other tombs which, while features such as decorated stones link them to the series under discussion, are nevertheless of distinct types outside the range of Boyne plans. These are discussed separately later in this chapter.

The three main types of plan within the Boyne group cover between them by far the greater number of the relevant tombs and can be used as a sound basis of differentiation. *Type I*, the simple *tholoi* or polygonal chambers with corbelled roofs, comes nearest to the basic type of chambered tomb in Iberia (Los Millares, Alcala, Pavia) or in western France (Île Longue, La Sergenté in Jersey), and is significantly present in Scotland (Rudh' an Dunain, Skye, the Clava tombs). It has therefore good claims to be representative of an early movement of colonization from Iberia-Brittany to Ireland and Scotland. *Type II*, the cruciform chambers with associated stone-engraving in great profusion, seem specifically Irish in their elaboration and detail, with Maes Howe in Orkney as their nearest architectural representative outside their own country. *Type III* forms a degeneration series not dissimilar in many respects from that observable among the Clava tombs to be described in Chapter ix, and could hardly be regarded as anything but late in any postulated sequence.

When we come to examine the material equipment of the tomb-builders, as represented by grave-goods, we shall see that little or no help towards settling the architectural sequence can be gained from this material, which is almost entirely derived from type II chambers. But there is one site which shows in itself a structural sequence, and this must be discussed in detail.

The Baltinglass cairn is the only monument of the Boyne group in Ireland where the structure has been examined by excavation and, as already mentioned, it was found to be composite. There were two main burial chambers, one of which, Walshe's II, clearly belonged to a cairn with kerb about 65 ft. in diameter. Two kerbstones and two orthostats of the cruci-form chamber have engravings upon them, including spirals, and there were fragments of pottery of the type normally associated with such tombs as Loughcrew and Carrowkeel, together with cremated bones in the chamber. This element, then, would constitute a typical tomb of our type II. After an interval sufficient for the incised kerbstone to become weathered, a crescent-shaped enlargement was added to the cairn on north, east and west, with a new kerb having a diameter of some 85 ft., and probably associated with the remains of a much-ruined but probably cruciform chamber (Walshe's III).

Within this crescentic enlargement on the north was the second main burial chamber, Walshe's I. It was a small well-built almost circular structure, some 7 ft. in diameter, with a passage 12 ft. long and had a corbelled roof. On each side of the entrance there stretched the remains of a kerb of which nine stones in all remained, set on an arc indicating a circle of 40 ft. diameter, and buried under the crescentic enlargement. The inner kerb (surrounding Walshe's Chamber II) was broken at the point where its line would have cut across Chamber I and there was no continuation of the arc under this earlier cairn. There were no finds except a single flint scraper in Chamber I, but one stone of the arc had a double oval incised on it.

Walshe's sequence assumes that Chamber I was later than the cairn containing Chamber II, and he does not recognize the arc of stones as the possible remains of a kerb of a 40 ft. diameter cairn enclosing Chamber I, partly demolished in the building of the Chamber II cairn, which would then be a later addition. There seems no evidence to run counter to this suggestion, which is here put forward with all reserve. If we could regard the sequence at Baltinglass to have been a small corbelled chamber within a cairn with a diameter of 40 ft., later incorporated within a cairn with cruciform chamber 65 ft. in diameter, and still later both structures enlarged to the 85-ft. diameter cairn of the final phase, we should have a sequence in accordance with the presumptive evidence from the tomb types over the whole area of settlement. But the evidence is not decisive enough to be more than suggestive.

Passages and minor details: entrances and forecourts

In the Baltinglass cairn just described, the passage to Chamber I opens direct from the kerb without any incurving, and this was probably the case at New Grange, but at Loughcrew L and T, Bryn Celli Ddu and probably also at Knocklea (Newenham, 1837), there was an incurving of the side walls so as to form a slight funnel-shaped forecourt. At most sites (notably at Carrowkeel) no attempt was made by the excavators to examine the junction of passage to kerb. At Bryn Celli Ddu lateral recesses and a raised roofing-slab marked a ritual 'antechamber' at the outer end of the passage.

At Dowth, Loughcrew and Carrowkeel, and in such outlying tombs as Belmore Mountain and Baltinglass, a frequent feature is the setting of stone sills across the passage at intervals, and across the entrances to the lateral and terminal cells in the cruciform chambers. These sills do not rise to the height of the septal slabs of the Clyde-Carlingford galleries, and they have good Iberian ancestors in Spain and Portugal. They are more frequent in tombs of type II than in the other two classes, being absent for instance in the type I tombs of Bryn Celli Ddu or Tibradden, and also at New Grange. At Bryn Celli Ddu there were curious low 'benches' of thin slab walling in clay along the passage walls.

In the chamber of this tomb, and at Carrowkeel F, are upright standing stones with no structural function, and there is evidence that a standing stone was originally set on the summit of the cairn at New Grange. Centrally placed standing stones are a common feature at Los Millares, where however they normally appear to have been functional as roof-supports, and at Kercado in Brittany there is a good parallel for a stone set on top of the cairn in the New Grange manner.

A most remarkable feature of the Irish chambers of type II (New Grange, Loughcrew F, H, L, T, and W, Baltinglass III and Knockingen) and a few of type I (Baltinglass I, Slieve Gullion) is the occurrence of large shallow stone basins often filling the greater part of the floor of the cells. In some instances at least these basins seem to have held the cremated burials. Here again Iberian parallels suggest themselves.

In some chambers a partitioning-off of the floor into small compartments by light stone slabs has been noted (Carrowkeel B and K) and at Tibradden a centrally placed stone cist contained a food-vessel which need not necessarily be a secondary insertion. Similar partitioning has been recorded from Iberia, at Mont Ubé in Jersey and in Scottish tombs.

The forecourt area has been excavated in one tomb only, that of Bryn Celli Ddu (Fig. 30). Here Hemp found a most interesting ritual deposit of the crouched skeleton of an ox set nearly centrally to the entrance, flanked by small stone settings and with a line of five post-holes running across between the burial and the entrance to the passage. This entrance was flanked by two paved hearths, in front of one of which was the cremation of an adult set in a hollow scooped in the old surface. Over all these features extended the blocking of the entrance, comparable to that described at Cairnholy I, Notgrove and Nympsfield, in Chapters v and vi.

This same tomb, thanks to its almost total excavation, provided evidence for a most extraordinary feature, central to the cairn and immediately behind the actual burial chamber. Here it was found that a pit had been dug into the old surface, 5 ft. across and nearly the same in depth, in which fires had then been lit, scorching the sides. In the bottom were placed a deposit of a few fragments of charcoal and a cremated human right ear-bone, together

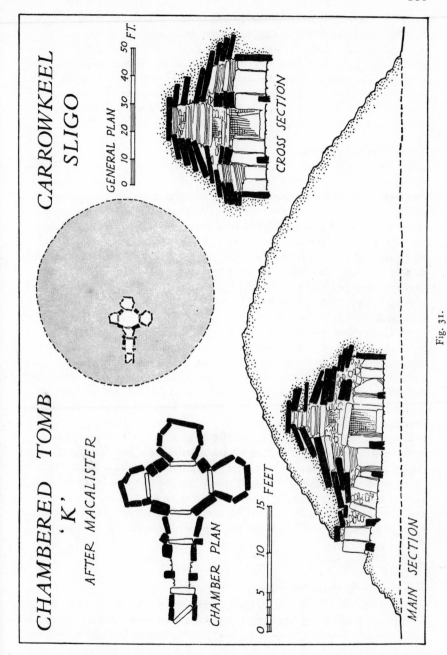

CARROWKEEL
SLIGO

CHAMBERED TOMB
'K'
AFTER MACALISTER

GENERAL PLAN

0 10 20 30 40 50 FT.

CROSS SECTION

CHAMBER PLAN

0   5   10   15 FEET

MAIN SECTION

Fig. 31.

with fragments of unburnt hazel wood. The pit had then been carefully filled so as to leave a hollow basin sunk into the central clay filling, which was then covered by a large flat slab of stone. By the side of this stone was then laid another stone, elaborately decorated with spiral, zigzag and curvilinear carvings. The whole of this curious deposit had been covered by the maximum height of the cairn, and against it was abutted the rear stone of the chamber wall. It is possibly comparable in ritual function to the 'rotunda' feature described in the Notgrove cairn in the Cotswolds in Chapter v.

Burials and funeral ritual

In few of the tombs has excavation been sufficiently careful to reveal details of the actual burial deposits where these were more or less intact. In many of the chambers disturbances or complete robbing had taken place, and all evidence consequently destroyed. But the burial rite seems certainly to have been predominantly that of cremation, of which instances are known from twenty-seven tombs. From seven of these tombs inhumations are also recorded, but in two instances at least these seem certainly secondary, and in only one tomb certainly, and in a second doubtfully, was inhumation the only rite recorded. At Fourknocks I the burials (in the side chambers and passage only) were approximately two-thirds cremated and one third inhumed.

At Carrowkeel and Loughcrew at least the cremated bones formed a layer upon the floor of the chamber up to 6 in. thick in more than one instance, or the cremations were heaped on to flat stones or placed in the shallow stone basins. With the burnt bones, sherds of pottery, bone pins and other objects, stone beads and pendants, were deposited unburnt.

We have a brief anatomical report upon the Carrowkeel bone fragments, though no statistical analysis was made tomb by tomb, the material from all excavated chambers being reported upon *en masse*. There was a preponderance of males, though at least twelve females were identified, and some infantile and foetal bones. There were no senile specimens, and many under twenty-five. It was further noted that the bone fragments indicated individuals of exceptional height, the males averaging 5 ft. 9 in. to 5 ft. 5 in., and the females 5 ft. 5 in. to 5 ft. (Alexander Macalister in Macalister *et al.* 1912). At Fourknocks I, the burials represented over 100 individuals.

Pottery from the Boyne tombs: Loughcrew ware

In several of the tombs at Loughcrew and Carrowkeel, and also at Baltinglass, pottery of a characteristic type has been found, at the two former sites in some quantity. None was found in Fourknocks I. It seems to have been deposited in fragments, one tomb at Loughcrew (R2) having over

150 sherds associated with the cremated interments, and it is not easy to reconstruct the original form of the vessels, though this can be done with some fair probability in a couple of instances. In addition to the sherds from the Boyne passage-graves there are two complete bowls, one from Lislea, Co. Monaghan, and the other from Dunagore Moat, Co. Antrim, which can be seen to belong to the same general class of ware: the Dunagore pot was found in vaguely recorded circumstances which suggest that it might have come from some form of chambered tomb. Finally, a single sherd of the same ware was found in a massive closed cist at Moytira, Co. Sligo, associated with a well-known group of Beaker sherds. An appropriate name for the whole group of pottery is Loughcrew ware (Pl. VI).

The actual texture of the ware is in all instances coarse, but surprisingly uniform: it is fairly hard, but flaky, with large grit, and ranges from light reddish to ashy grey and a cindery white. In at least two pots (Loughcrew and Lislea) it can be seen that the technique of manufacture was by over-lapped rings or coils of clay.

The complete vessels from Dunagore and Lislea, and the reconstructed forms from Loughcrew (Pl. VI, nos. 1, 2), are all of them simple small bowls, with the depth approximately equal to the diameter, and with rims slightly bevelled or inbent. There is no evidence among the extant sherds of any flat bases, and thickened round bottoms seem likely in all instances. The rims are either simple and slightly thinned out or bevelled externally, as in the pots just described, or massive and flat-topped, as at Carrowkeel and Baltinglass.

Ornament is profuse but unsophisticated and often haphazard, and executed in a variety of techniques. Simple jabs with a point or with a rounded instrument (perhaps sometimes a finger-tip) (Pl. VI, no. 10), are made either vertically or obliquely on the surface of the pot; simple rather shallow incision is common; and the 'stab-and-drag' line made by a point applied with intermittent pressure in tracing a groove is also frequent (Pl. VI, no. 16). Coarse square hyphenations sometimes probably made with a broad-toothed comb occur (Pl. VI, no. 9): there is a single example of an impressed line of twisted cord (Dunagore), and there are varieties of coarse imitations of whipped cord, sometimes made with a finger-nail.

These techniques are used to build up rough patterns, the stabbing for instance sometimes being applied haphazard, or in lines. The incisions occur in vertical or horizontal parallel lines, obliquely or in zigzags. On one pot (Lislea) the ornament, in lightly impressed coarse square hyphenation, is arranged in six panels of horizontal lines separated by double vertical elements. A sherd from Carrowkeel has a series of pendent arcs in coarse hyphenation around a deep circular pit, and vaguely curved lines in similar technique can be seen on other sherds (Pl. VI, nos. 7, 9).

It is clear that the features of Loughcrew ware described above are in no way typical of the Western group of Neolithic pottery as a whole, though certain elements, such as the panelled ornament at Lislea, and the pendent arcs at Carrowkeel, recall Beacharra B and C wares. Furthermore, certain vessels with stab-and-drag motifs, and with oblique incisions, have good parallels among the pottery from the west and north Scottish tombs and domestic sites, which has itself close affinities with some forms of Beacharra ware. It cannot therefore be regarded as entirely *sui generis*, and its more detailed relationships within the Hiberno-Scottish Neolithic series is discussed below.

Other pottery: food-vessels in primary contexts

As well as the Loughcrew ware just described, there are certain other pottery finds to be noticed. At Carrowkeel K an intact food-vessel of a type normally attributed to the British Middle Bronze Age was found standing on the floor of a good cruciform chamber of type II, and must have been placed in this position at a time when access to the chamber for funerary or ritual purposes was still possible. While it may be the last object to be deposited, it is primary in the sense that it could not have come to this position after the use of the passage-grave for successive collective burials had ceased unless elaborate measures had been taken to unblock the entrance. In the same cemetery, Cairn O contained a degenerate closed megalithic chamber of type III similar to some at Carrowmore, and this again contained a Bronze Age food-vessel. This implies use of the cemetery-area for building a cairn with a closed chamber at the tail-end of the passage-grave tradition, but still within it. The lower limits of the use of the Carrowkeel cemetery must therefore be brought within the Food-vessel period.

At Belmore Mountain, however, the two Food-vessel burials from the cairn were in cists secondary to the actual passage-grave, and secondary Food-vessel burials again occurred at Fourknocks I. The situation at the *tholos* of Tibradden is ambiguous, where the cist containing a food-vessel was placed centrally on the floor of the chamber, which must at least have been accessible and with its roof intact at the time of its deposition. The cist, however, might be taken as evidence of a secondary burial rather than the latest of the original series. From Carrowmore 27 came a sherd (now lost) which from an illustration might have been a sherd of food-vessel with 'false-relief' pattern, but the circumstances of finding are not clear.

On the whole then the evidence suggests that some of the Boyne Group of passage-graves were open for burial within the chamber in the traditional manner at a time when food-vessels were in use in Ireland. The chronological inferences to be drawn from this will be discussed later.

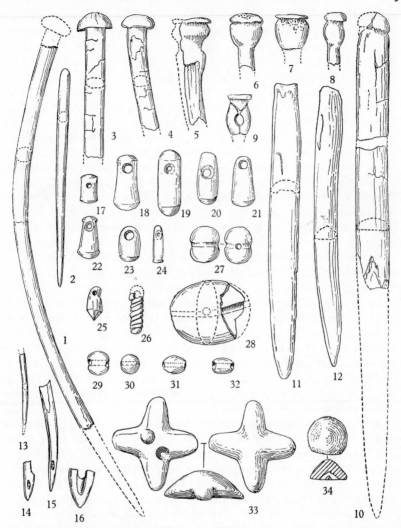

Fig. 32. Boyne culture: bone and stone types. 1, 3–6, 10–12, 14–16, 18, 21, 23, 24, 26, 30, 31, Carrowkeel; 2, 19, 20, 22, Loughcrew; 7, 17, 27, 28, Feenagh Beg; 8, 9, 13, 25, 29, 32, 34, Carrowmore; 33, Dowth. Scale ½.

Pins and needles of bone and antler

Among the most remarkable objects found in the Boyne tombs is the large series of pins of bone or antler, often of enormous size (Fig. 32, no. 10) —one from Carrowmore 15 must have been over 16 in. long when intact. Such pins occur at Loughcrew, Carrowkeel, Carrowmore, Baltinglass,

Fourknocks I and a site, probably a destroyed passage-grave, at Feenagh Beg in Co. Leitrim. They are usually made of red-deer antler (as at Loughcrew and Carrowmore: Frazer, 1896) but at Carrowkeel one was made of a tibia of *Bos longifrons*, one from that of a red deer, and another from the fibula of a bear (Scharff in Macalister *et al.* 1912).

These pins may be classified into three main types. *Type I, mushroom-headed pins*, include the largest known specimens, and have a sturdy shaft with a domed or mushroom-shaped head of slightly greater diameter (Fig. 32, nos. 3, 4). These are known from Loughcrew, Carrowkeel and Carrowmore. *Type II, poppy-headed pins*, have the head formed of a flattened or slightly domed disc, below which is a bulbous swelling, the whole resembling the seed-case of a poppy. These occur at Carrowkeel, Feenagh Beg and Carrowmore, one from the last site being perforated vertically and transversely (Fig. 32, nos. 5–9). *Type III, skewer-pins*, are represented by fragments of slender, finely made pins of circular section and while no heads survive it may be presumed on analogy that these would have been simple and rounded: a variant from Baltinglass has an oval knobbed head, and the other sites producing fragments are Loughcrew, Carrowkeel, and Carrowmore (Fig. 32, nos. 2, 13).

From Carrowkeel come one or two large bone or antler points of flattened cross-section which may constitute a fourth type, or may be variant forms of type I or type II with the heads missing (Fig. 32, nos. 11, 12), and from Fourknocks I a pin with zigzag incised ornament on the head. From the Carrowkeel cemetery also come curious broken objects perforated near the point, and presumably to be classified as some form of *needle* (Fig. 32, nos. 14–16), and a more normal form perforated near the head is represented at Carrowmore and Baltinglass.

As a group, these pins and needles form a unique assemblage, the large size being especially remarkable. Macalister suggested that some at least may have been used to pin together a bag of leather or fabric containing the cremated bones of the burial, and this view has much to recommend it. As we shall see, skewer-pins of our type III were probably used for the same purpose in the Dorchester culture, and an isolated type I pin occurred in the Ronaldsway culture of the Isle of Man (Chapter XI), again associated with cremation burial. Pins of type II are unknown elsewhere in the British Isles, but they do occur in an Early Metal Age context in Portugal.

Stone beads and pendants

Beads of various forms have been found in almost all Boyne tombs in which the grave-goods have survived at all (Loughcrew, Carrowkeel, Carrowmore, Fourknocks I, Belmore Mountain, Feenagh Beg and a site at Patrickstown, Co. Meath (Macalister *et al.* 1912), and at Bryn Celli Ddu). The stones utilized include limestone, steatite, serpentine, jasper and carnelian. One bead of 'transparent greenish glass' was found in cairn R2 at Loughcrew (Frazer, 1896, 342).

The commonest form is that of subconical barrel beads (Beck, 1927), usually small, and known from Carrowkeel, Carrowmore, Loughcrew and Patrickstown. From Bryn Celli Ddu comes a stubby flattened barrel bead with large perforation, and from Feenagh Beg a large flattened oblate oval example. The same site also produced several grooved globular beads of a type not known elsewhere, and at Carrowmore 27 was a broken stone ring-bead with an internal diameter of nearly one inch (Fig. 32, nos. 27–32). Small ring or disc-beads are also known from Carrowkeel and Belmore Mountain.

The *pendants* of the Boyne tombs are among the most remarkable and consistent articles of grave furniture, occurring at Loughcrew, Carrowkeel, Carrowmore, Belmore Mountain, Knockingen and Feenagh Beg. They may be divided into four main types, of which type I is by far the commonest, being represented at all the sites mentioned above, except Carrowmore.

Type I—pestle-shaped. Within this class come various forms of pendant, but all approximate in shape to miniature perforated stone pestles or subconical 'mace-heads', of types originating in the Secondary Neolithic cultures and persisting into the British Early and Middle Bronze Age. These variants are scarcely distinct enough to warrant formal subdivision, but one can note a difference between cylindrical forms (Loughcrew) and those with a truncated conical outline (Loughcrew and Carrowkeel) sometimes with concave sides (Carrowkeel and Feenagh Beg) (Fig. 32, nos. 17–24). These same two sites also produce a stubby, rounded form, again occurring at Belmore Mountain, which also yielded a form with grooving round the lower end, comparable with one from Carrowkeel where the grooving is emphasized by a slight enlargement of the end.

Type II—rock-crystal drops. Two examples are known, from Loughcrew and Carrowmore respectively, of a natural quartz crystal perforated so that the resultant object approximates in outline to a type I pendant (Fig. 32, no. 25).

Type III—segmented. A single cylindrical stone pendant from Carrowkeel G has oblique grooves cut around it to produce a roughly segmented effect (Fig. 32, no. 26).

Type IV—triangular. This again is represented by a single example from Belmore Mountain (now lost). It appears to have been a small flattish equilateral triangle perforated near one angle.

Type V—tooth-pendant. At Belmore Mountain was a single perforated tooth, apparently an incisor of an unidentified animal.

These pendants form a series without parallel in the British Isles, except for strikingly similar type I pendants (of amber) in the Wessex Bronze Age culture, the implications of which are discussed below. Actual stone mace-heads of comparable type have, however, been found, as we have seen, in a Clyde-Carlingford tomb, and others occur in north Scottish passage-graves and in Secondary Neolithic cultures. The segmented treatment of type III is common on pin-heads and other objects in Iberian chambered tombs.

V-*bored buttons*

Two examples of stone buttons with V-boring are known from Boyne tombs, but neither is certainly primary. In Carrowmore 49, a ruined chamber of uncertain plan, cremated bones were found under a paving, and above this two inhumations (possible male and female) were accompanied by an unburnt steatite V-bored conical button of normal western European type (Wood-Martin, 1888); this suggests a secondary burial (Fig. 32, no. 34). At Dowth, the chamber had been disturbed in early medieval times and probably at other times as well; there was evidence of both cremation and inhumation, and among the miscellaneous objects recovered was a large cruciform stone button (Fig. 32, no. 33) with V-perforation, which might have been associated with the primary interments (Coffey, 1912).

Stone balls

Carefully made stone balls, with an average diameter of about one inch, have been found at Loughcrew, Carrowkeel and Feenagh Beg. Parallels are available from Skara Brae, Rinyo, and other sites discussed in Chapter xi, and there is also one example from the Creevykeel long cairn in Co. Sligo (Chapter vi). Their use and significance are unknown.

Other stone objects

A complete *stone axe* was found at Baltinglass, and a chip of a polished *flint axe* comes from Loughcrew. The same cemetery produced one flint *leaf-arrowhead*, and another *barbed and tanged* example; a *petit-tranchet derivative* arrowhead came from an unlocated find-spot at Bryn Celli Ddu.

ART

A very distinctive feature of the Boyne culture, and probably that by which it is best known, is the elaborate ornament carved on the faces of many of the uprights and roofing slabs in the Boyne group itself, at Fourknocks, at Loughcrew, and sporadically elsewhere. In the Carrowkeel cemetery, such ornament is completely absent, and at Carrowmore slight traces of simple patterns have alone been detected; the passage-graves of Baltinglass, Seefin, Carnanmore and Knockmany have one or more ornamented stones apiece, while two stones of an abnormal tomb at Seskilgreen have decoration in the same style. A somewhat similar grave at Clover Hill has again ornamented stones, but in a distinctive style which lies outside the main series, and there are one or two detached stones from various sites which have decoration belonging to the typical Boyne series or allied groups discussed later.

Techniques

Where necessary, the surfaces of stones to be ornamented appear to have been dressed flat with mauls, in a manner normal to the ancient Orient and seen in Britain again at Stonehenge (E. H. Stone, 1924, ch. v). At New Grange, such globular or hemispherical granite mauls form part of the cairn material together with local boulders, and others seem to have been found near the entrance in early excavations. At Knowth, Macalister's excavations produced 'eight or ten spheroidal balls of granite, of about the size and shape of footballs' among the debris outside the kerb (Macalister, 1943, 139), which must surely be such mauls, comparable to those used at Stonehenge, and a further comparison in technique between the two sites may be made in the 'ripple' dressing of several of the Stonehenge stones and that on a New Grange stone illustrated by Coffey (1912, fig. 16).

Coffey also drew attention to the curious treatment of his stone no. 19 in the same tomb, in which some of the incised ornament has been obliterated by tooling which suggested to him the use of a metal chisel. 'The chisel has been driven sideways', he wrote, 'and the marks are quite different' from the normal 'picked' or battered technique.[1] 'They are about three-quarters of an inch long by half an inch broad, and in each cut the marks left by the gapped edge of the chisel are quite distinct... the surface of this stone is not very hard, and a bronze tool may have been capable of removing it' (Coffey, 1912, 37).

The ornament itself has been carried out by two main methods, the first (and rarer) being *incision* or graving, in the manner of Upper Palaeolithic mural engraving. The great mass of the patterns however has been formed by *pecking* a line or surface with some form of punch, producing a softer and usually broader line than incision, and also capable of roughening an area for decorative purposes. The pecked lines have frequently been rubbed smooth after their initial execution, but no tools have survived to show the precise process employed.

At Bryn Celli Ddu, there is a single spiral cut on a stone of the chamber wall, and of this Hemp writes: 'It appears to have been cut by a tool having a straight chisel-edge about an inch and a quarter long, which was probably held in position and hammered into the stone, hence the curves of the spiral are somewhat irregular, being composed of a succession of straight or almost straight cuts' (Hemp, 1930, 186). This is reminiscent of the chisel-dressing at New Grange claimed by Coffey and referred to above.

[1] This maul-battering technique was noted by Hemp at the Boyne-culture tomb of Bryn Celli Ddu in Anglesey (Hemp, 1930, 186 and pl. xlv, fig. 2).

Breuil (1934, summarizing earlier papers) has discussed these techniques at length, and has built up a chronological scheme upon them. His first and earliest group is that of engraved patterns: he notes that at Dowth pecked triangles (of his fourth group) cut into engraved ornament on one stone. His second and third groups are of curvilinear figures executed in either slender or wide and deep pecked lines, and his fourth and latest is that of rectilinear patterns in pecked technique. Such rectilinear patterns, he thinks, can be shown to avoid or fit into curvilinear designs of his second and third groups. This sequence has met with little support; it was tacitly ignored by Mahr in his illuminating discussion of Irish megalithic art (1937, 354ff.), and Powell (1938 a) points out that it is in part 'based on a faulty sequence of tomb-types'. It seems in fact quite unnecessary to separate curvilinear and rectilinear designs in this arbitrary manner and, as we shall see, precisely this combination of patterns recurs in Iberia in contexts where they are inescapably contemporary. Of course there is no necessity to assume that all the ornament on any one stone or at any one site was executed as a single act, but on the other hand it does not seem feasible to construct a convincing chronology, applicable to the whole series over Ireland, on the lines attempted by Breuil.

Disposition of ornament

The most frequent place for a display of ornament is on the passage and chamber walls of the passage-grave. As Powell has pointed out (1938 a, 243), at New Grange 'the chamber and passage roofs are sprung from dry-walling in front of which stand megalithic slabs of no structural significance'. As in many other Irish tombs these orthostats evidently exist to supply a suitable surface for the depiction of 'art'. The roof, or at least the uppermost slab closing the corbelled vault, may also be decorated, and at New Grange one such slab shows a feature seen elsewhere: the partial covering of a design by constructional features, showing that the decoration (as might be expected) was executed before the stone was incorporated in the architecture of the tomb. At Bryn Celli Ddu the main effort in such decoration has been expended on the two faces and edge of a slab which had been buried in a pit before the construction of the cairn and was thereafter totally invisible. (Cf. p. 196 above.)

The massive kerbstones of the cairns covering the passage-graves of New Grange, Dowth and Knowth are in some instances decorated—two at New Grange, at least five at Dowth, and a great number at Knowth. At Baltinglass three kerbstones were ornamented, and at least one at Loughcrew—the famous Hag's Chair. At New Grange there is the exceptional feature of a highly decorated sillstone, and an ornamented lintel above the entrance.

It is convenient to refer here to the curious grave at Seskilgreen, containing decorated stones in the Boyne style. The site is in Co. Tyrone, and consisted of an egg-shaped enclosure of small boulders, 10 ft. 10 in. by 7 ft. 5 in. internal dimensions, and open at the small end. There was no cairn, and the enclosure was filled level, and on excavation produced a cremated interment near the larger end and by the two main ornamented stones, and, not far away, a shaft-hole stone battle-axe of a type well known

Fig. 33. Boyne culture: art motifs (*based on Breuil*).

from single-grave inhumations and some cremation burials in Britain (R. A. Smith, 1926), and from a Scottish find, apparently in a chambered long cairn (see p. 252 below).

The motifs employed

The study of the Boyne-culture art is hampered in all its aspects by the lack of a systematic *corpus* of the whole series of decorated stones, but the task of classification on broad lines has been undertaken by Breuil in a notable paper (1934, with full references to sites).[1] Even if we do not accept

1 The newly discovered Fourknocks site is not included in the following discussion.

the chronological assumptions of Breuil's scheme, his grouping of significant motifs has an objective value of its own, and is used as a basis here.
Simplifying his detailed series of variants, it seems possible to define twelve
main groups (with simple cup-marks forming a thirteenth), and within these
groups subdivisions can be made, bringing the total of thirty-nine variants
(Fig. 33).

1. *Face-motifs*. A point of fundamental importance established by Breuil
was the recognition that a large number of motifs in the Irish series were
more or less distorted or derived versions of a human face in which the eyes
were depicted as the dominant feature. As we shall see, a great number of
the group 2 motifs are in effect 'detached eyes' from face-motifs, but the
recognizable schematized faces may be divided into

    a.   Combined multiple circles or arcs;
    b.   Combined multiple spirals;
    c.   Eyes-and-eyebrow and/or nose motifs.

2. *Circles*. These are common, and may be divided into

    a.   Single circles;
    b.   Multiple circles;
    c.   Circles with central dot, and
    d.   Gapped or incomplete circles.

3. *Rayed circles* are sufficiently distinctive to merit a separate group,
divided into

    a.   Single circle with radii and/or dots inside;
    b.   Double circles with rays between;
    c.   Circle with 'flower' pattern;
    d.   Circles with filled-cross pattern;
    e.   Circle with external rays;
    f.   Dot with rays;
    g.   Asterisk;
    h.   Circle with external arc of rays.

4. *Crosses* are typologically related to group 3f and g, and may be

    a.   Simple;
    b.   Petal-shaped.

5. *Spirals* are peculiarly characteristic of Irish passage-grave art, as

    a.   Single;
    b.   Double (really face-symbols of type 1 b), and
    c.   Triple spirals.

6. *Arcs* are again common motifs allied to circles, and may be

    a.   Single;
    b.   Multiple, and
    c.   Rayed.

7. *Ovals* are distinctive and often elaborate motifs, often with internal features within their outline distinguishing them as

    a. Vertebrate;

    b. Striped;

    c. Rayed, and

    d. Relief-carved.

8. *Scalloped outlines* are rare but distinctive, and without subdivisions: they represent, in fact, multiple 'face' motifs joined together.

9. *Hurdle-patterns* composed of horizontal lines in groups, separated or crossed by verticals, are difficult to classify, but we can recognize

    a. Vertebrates;

    b. Miscellaneous hurdling, and

    c. Comb-shaped or pectiform groups.

10. *Fir-trees* or patterns like schematized ferns, divided into

    a. Those with central line, and

    b. Those without central line.

11. *Zigzags* are a simple and common motif, either

    a. Angular, or

    b. Rounded or meander-like.

12. *Triangles and lozenges* may be grouped together, as lozenges may result from opposed triangles, executed in

    a. Outline;

    b. Solid pecked areas, or

    c. Relief outline.

13. *Cup-marks* are not uncommon, and are invariably without encircling rings: the cup-and-ring motif is distinctively alien to the Boyne-culture art.

In addition to these groups and variants of motifs within what may be called the 'classical' Boyne-culture art, there are other styles in stone decoration in Ireland which cannot be related to any specific type of monument, save in one instance. At Clover Hill, Co. Sligo, a small grave of the Seskilgreen type exists, four stones of which are decorated with pecked curvilinear designs, and while one stone has ornament of group 2 c, the remaining three stones have patterns in a distinctive style which, while it may well derive from Boyne-culture art, nevertheless constitutes a separate entity.

The distribution of the motifs

The occurrence of the main motifs enumerated above is summarized in Table V, which lists the Boyne-culture tombs containing ornament as well as a few detached stones which have claims for inclusion. The recognizable face-motifs of group 1 are nowhere very common, though there are notable examples at New Grange (Pl. VII), Knowth and Knockmany. Group 2 (circles) is very common, with Loughcrew producing, in the closely allied group 3 (rayed circles) certain distinctive forms not found elsewhere, and the related group 4 (crosses) seems again peculiar to this cemetery (Pl. VII).

TABLE V. *The occurrence of motifs in Boyne-culture tombs and on allied decorative stones*

Sites	Motifs						
	1	2	3	4	5	6	7
Baltinglass	.	.	.	.	a	.	a?
Bryn Celli Ddu	.	.	.	.	a	.	.
Carnanmore	.	b	.	.	a	a	.
Carrowmore	.	.	.	.	.	.	.
Castle Archdale	a	b, c, d	.	.	a	b	.
Deerpark, Sligo	a	b	.	.	a	b	.
Dowth	.	a, b	b, f	.	a	b	.
Dun Laoghaire	.	b	.	.	a	b, c	.
Knockmany	c	b, c	d	.	.	b, c	.
Knowth	a	a, b, d	c	.	a	a, b	.
Loughcrew	a	a, b, c	a, b, c, e, f, g, h	a, b	a, b	a, b	a, b, c
New Grange	a, b	a, b	.	.	a, b, c	b	d
Seefin	.	.	.	.	.	.	.
Seskilgreen (grave)	a	b	.	.	.	.	.
Seskilgreen (stone)	.	b	f	.	b?	.	.

Sites	Motifs					
	8	9	10	11	12	13
Baltinglass	.	.	.	.	.	.
Bryn Celli Ddu	?	.	.	b	.	.
Carnanmore	.	.	.	b	.	.
Carrowmore	.	.	.	.	a ?, b?	.
Castle Archdale	.	.	.	a	a	×
Deerpark, Sligo	.	.	.	.	a	.
Dowth	.	a	.	a, b	.	×
Dun Laoghaire	.	.	.	a, b	.	.
Knockmany	.	.	.	a, b	a	×
Knowth	.	b	a	a, b	a, b	×
Loughcrew	.	a, b, c	a, b	a, b	a	×
New Grange	×	c	a	a, b	a, b, c	.
Seefin	.	c	.	.	.	.
Seskilgreen (grave)	.	.	.	.	a	.
Seskilgreen (stone)	.	.	.	.	.	×

Spirals (group 5) are widely distributed, with the finest examples at New Grange, including the unique 5 c (triple spiral). Arc patterns, usually multiple (6 b), are frequent, but the oval patterns of groups 7 a, b and c are confined to Loughcrew (with a single doubtful example at Baltinglass), while the relief ovals (7 d) are peculiar to New Grange, where, too, the scalloped outlines of group 8 are alone found, unless we may recognize a variant form on the 'pattern stone' at Bryn Celli Ddu. Loughcrew again abounds in group 9 motifs, some of which are in fact related to the 'verte-brate ovals' of group 7a, and the so-called 'boat symbols', as Breuil and others have realized, must come under the group 9c classification. Breuil's 'fir-tree men' of group 10 are again more common at Loughcrew than else-where, but the variant zigzag patterns, 11a and 11b, are frequent every-where. Lozenge patterns of group 12a may result, as at Loughcrew, from simple intersecting oblique lines, but it is at New Grange that the 'solid' triangles and lozenges of 12b are most frequent, and the recticulate lozenge pattern in relief (12c) is found here alone. Cup-marks (group 13) appear sporadically, but are never very important.

Despite the characteristic individuality which distinguished, for instance, the Loughcrew school of symbolists from those working on New Grange, there is nevertheless a real homogeneity throughout the whole series which permits us to identify a Boyne-culture art-style common to over a dozen Irish sites and also represented in the notable outlying tomb in Anglesey, Bryn Celli Ddu. This art-style is distinguishable from that of Clover Hill, mentioned above, and its congeners, and again from that typified by the Clonfinlough stone, as well as from what MacWhite (1946) has defined as the Galician style of rock-engraving. But it is important to note that the Boyne style of ornament has also been found in two instances on the cist-covers of individual graves of the Irish Bronze Age—at Moylough, Co. Sligo, pattern of group 6a (single arcs) in a cist containing a cremation and a halberd of O'Riordain's type 5, and at Ballinvally, Co. Meath, ornament of group 2b on a similar cist with a cremation and a food-vessel (MacWhite, 1946, with refs.). Perhaps the curious Seskilgreen grave should more properly be included here, but it is not clear whether we are really dealing with the survival of Boyne-culture art into a period later than the passage-graves, or whether we should not rather regard Seskilgreen, Moylough and Ballinvally as approximately contemporary with the collective tombs, though themselves representing the single-grave traditions which were to dominate in the full Bronze Age. And as we shall see below, the characteristic Boyne-culture face-motif appears not only on pottery at Skara Brae but on the well-known chalk 'drums' from Folkton in Yorkshire.

The symbolism and origins of the style

Interpretation of a symbolic art belonging to a culture the magico-religious beliefs of which are wholly unknown save by inference may be extremely dangerous, but consideration of the Boyne-culture art-style in its relationship to comparable expressions among approximately contem-porary groups of collective tomb-builders in western Europe does lead to certain conclusions which seem reasonably founded in fact.

A point of fundamental significance is Breuil's recognition that 'certain concentric or spiral ornaments like a pair of spectacles are almost undoubtedly derived from the human face', and that these face-motifs (my group 1 ornament) relate the Irish decorated stones to Iberian representations of the human face and body which, though highly schematized, are still quite recognizably anthropomorphic (Breuil, 1934, 311). Mahr independently drew attention to the motifs of my group 7, a–c, relating these ovals with internal 'vertebrate' or striped patterns to analogous forms in such Breton carvings as those at Pierres Plates, and both to schematized versions of the human face and body. He further 'wondered why nobody ever troubled to say in plain words that [certain stones at New Grange] show exactly the same pattern as the anthropomorphic Portuguese schist idols', and felt that the bulk of the patterns were to be derived 'from distant prototypes in the shape of menhir-statues' (Mahr, 1937, 354, 360). Jacquetta Hawkes then took the matter a stage further when she demonstrated that a uniform set of symbols, including the human figure, stags and sun-patterns, linked the Irish carvings not only with carved and painted designs in Iberia and south and western Europe, but also with the patterns incised on certain pottery vessels in these regions and in the British Clyde-Carlingford culture already described (Beacharra B and C wares; Chapter VI above). (J. Hawkes, 1939 b.)

It would of course be dangerous to derive the whole repertoire of the Boyne-culture art from a single source, and both Breuil and Mrs Hawkes have emphasized that simple schematized patterns such as circles or zigzags may derive from eyes or suns; a row of sitting men or an idol's hair. And there is little doubt that in the form in which we see the art-style in Ireland, or in such comparable carvings in Brittany as the Gavr' Inis tomb, the various motifs have lost any coherence as a formal pattern, and are scattered about on the surface of the stone in confusion; only rarely do related items, such as the pair of eyes, retain their original relationship. But it is worthwhile pointing out that the best parallels for the whole set of motifs, curvilinear and angular, combined in one coherent pattern, are to be found on the Continent in one region only, on the 'idols' of stone or bone, and on the symbol-ornamented pottery, of south Spain and the Algarve.

The Portuguese schist plaque-idols to which Mahr drew attention certainly contain much of the triangle and lozenge ornament found for instance at New Grange, but the circular eye-motifs are exceedingly rare on these objects. (For a study of Portuguese schist plaques, see G. & V. Leisner, 1951.) But the south Spanish cylindrical idols, and their counterparts in Algarve and Badajoz, do present very real parallels to the Irish repertoire of patterns. This is most marked in the hoard of thirty bone 'idols' found with a stone ritual sandal in a burnt building (a shrine?) of the Almizaraque settlement, which show just the peculiar Irish combination of circular and arc-shaped motifs (face-symbols) with an elaborate patterning of lozenges, triangles and zigzags on the 'body' of the idol. (Leisner, 1943, pls. 92–4.) Leisner compares certain of these idols with reduplicated 'eyes' to Breton carvings such as those in the Pierres Plates tomb already referred to (M. & S. J. Péquart & Le Rouzic, 1927, pl. 88), but the resemblance to the Irish series is even more marked, and becomes particularly striking in the developed rubbings of the patterns in Leisner's plate 94. On the symbol-ornamented pottery, too, the association of circular eye-motifs with zig-zags and filled triangles, together with stags whose horns are schematizing towards 'fir-tree' symbols, strongly recalls the Boyne-culture patterns. In these Iberian examples the patterns are coherent, in Ireland they have broken up into their constituent elements, but the repertoire of motifs is essentially the same in both regions. Certain Portuguese rock-carvings contain motifs very reminiscent of Boyne art: Cardozo (1950) has compared patterns at Monte da Saia with New Grange and, one may add, motifs of type 4b at Loughcrew. The Monte de Eiro stone (Oporto Mus.) is very reminiscent of that at Bryn Celli Ddu (Piggott, 1948).

For one characteristic element in the Irish series, the spiral, there is, however, no parallel in these southern Iberian objects. For this motif Mahr looked ultimately to Malta; MacWhite to North Africa and the Canary Islands, with predynastic Egypt in the background (1946, 67). Coffey had looked to Mycenaean Greece, and with the recognition of the contem-poraneity of part at least of the Boyne culture with that of the Wessex Bronze Age with its close Mycenaean contacts, his view should be given reconsideration. In the south Spanish paintings spirals appear, though in five sites only, one being a triple spiral in the New Grange manner (Mac-White, 1946; Mahr, 1937, 356), and they are present on one Breton site, the Gavr' Inis tomb (M. & S. J. Péquart & Le Rouzic, 1927, pls. 119, 120, 124, 130), and on Portuguese rock-carvings at Monte da Saia (Barcelos) (Cardozo, 1950, fig. 40) and Monte de Eiro. MacWhite has discussed their occurrence in Britain outside the Boyne tombs, and it is worthwhile drawing particular attention to two finds. A well-known sherd from Skara Brae (Pl. XII, 4) seems to have come from a pot originally decorated with a pair of spirals flanking lozenge-shaped elements in such a way as to make a convincing 'face-motif' in the manner of, for instance, that on a kerbstone at New Grange (Coffey, 1912, fig. 59), and the rectilinear engraved orna-ment on stones from the Orkney site, one exactly paralleled at Gavr' Inis, must be borne in mind: the matter is further discussed in Chapter xi.

The second instance of Boyne-culture ornament (with spirals) in an alien setting is that of the three so-called chalk 'drums' from Folkton, E.R. Yorks (Greenwell, 1890, pls. I, II). These objects are in fact squat cylinder-idols of frankly Iberian type, each highly ornamented with patterns in-cluding a face-motif which on one takes the form of small double-spirals set above a lozenge—a variant which is in effect, as Breuil pointed out, the 'horned lozenge' of Seskilgreen. In their multiple-circle, zigzag, triangle and lozenge patterns these Folkton idols again come within the Boyne art-style, while the star-pattern on the top of one links them to certain food-vessels of Irish type, similarly decorated on the base. The Folkton idols were in a grave under a round barrow, contemporary with or perhaps later than inhumations with a *C* beaker. The lozenge and triangle patterns of the Boyne-culture art, and exceptionally other motifs as well, occur on the decorated copper or bronze axes of Irish origin but with a wide distribution in the British Isles and beyond, and their resemblance to the Iberian plaques has also been noted (Megaw & Hardy, 1938).

To sum up, the Boyne-culture art is closely related to that employed upon the anthropomorphic idols of southern Iberia which are themselves a product of the Los Millares culture (Leisner's Stages II and III). The spiral motifs, of uncertain origin, link the Boyne art to that of Gavr' Inis in the Morbihan, and the decoration on the stones of this tomb does in fact come nearest in style to the Irish series of all the Breton group. In Britain, the appearance of related but not identical motifs on Beacharra ware within the Clyde-Carlingford culture must be regarded as the result of a common employment of magical patterns prevalent in Iberia and south and west France, but the face-motifs at Skara Brae and on the Folkton idols should indicate specific connexions, and the Ronaldsway-culture plaques, with incised angular ornament, should again be brought into a fairly close relationship. (Cf. p. 350 below.)

AGRICULTURE AND DOMESTIC ANIMALS

Direct evidence of cereal cultivation in the Boyne culture is provided by the grains of carbonized wheat from the old surface beneath the Baltinglass tomb (Walshe, 1941), and Mitchell has recently drawn attention to the evidence for forest clearance and the growth of grasses or cereals contained in the Carrowkeel peats (1951). Bones of domestic ox were found at Carrowkeel, allegedly of *Bos longifrons* (Macalister *et al.* 1912, 337), and an ox skull was found in the material of Cairn D at Loughcrew (Conwell, 1867).

USE OF THE TOMBS IN THE EARLY IRON AGE

The nineteenth-century excavations of Cairn H at Loughcrew produced a large number of worked bone objects, many of them ornamented with engraved designs characteristic of the Early Iron Age art-style of about the first centuries B.C.–A.D. (Tempest, 1949). These had been interpreted as evidence for the re-use of the tomb as a shelter and workshop at this time—there are many instances of such use among the Irish chambered tombs, especially for metal-working (cf. Piggott & Powell, 1949). But in 1943 the cairn was re-excavated by Raftery, whose report has not yet appeared: in newspaper articles, however, and in a paper communicated to the International Congress at Zürich in 1950, he has claimed that further examples of the decorated bones found by him are in primary contexts in the body of the cairn, and that we must therefore regard the tomb as dating in its entirety from the Early Iron Age. Discussion is obviously premature pending the full report on the excavations. (O'Riordain, 1946, 164.)

THE RELATIONSHIPS OF THE BOYNE TOMBS IN BRITAIN

While the Boyne tombs readily fall into place within the British family of passage-graves as a whole, it is not easy to find precise parallels for their specialized plans and architectural features outside Ireland, at least for tombs of types II and III. The relatively unspecialized forms (often with the *tholos* vault) of type I can of course be compared to such Scottish groups as those of the Clava series, or the Hebridean passage-graves of the type of Rudh' an Dunain or Barpa Langass. Maes Howe in Orkney alone shows some affinities to the cruciform planning of type II, but it is a highly individual structure without really close parallels anywhere.

Interesting contacts can, however, be shown to exist in the decorative art. MacWhite has shown that it is possible to separate two styles in Irish rock-carvings, the Galician and the Passage-grave (or Boyne-culture) groups (MacWhite, 1946). Now while the majority of carvings upon natural rock surfaces in Britain relate to the Galician series, there are certain significant examples in such contexts, or on the stones of burial cists, that show a use of Boyne-culture traditions either by themselves or combined with Galician elements. Such an interplay of art styles must mean that the Passage-grave style was a living thing when these carvings were made. As examples of almost pure Passage-grave art on natural rocks, MacWhite notes stones at the Braid Hills, Edinburgh, and at Maughanby in Cumberland, while spirals almost certainly of similar derivation occur in about twenty instances, mainly concentrated between the Forth and the Solway.

Boyne-style ornament including 'eye-and-eyebrow' motifs occurs in an Orkney chambered tomb on the Holm of Papa Westray, and a stone from Eday carved with spirals may also have come from a chambered tomb (R.C.A.M.(S), 1946, no. 225), while we have seen that the double-spiral face-motif appears on pottery at Skara Brae. At Catterline, Kincardineshire, a stone over a cist containing a Beaker burial was decorated in pure Passage-grave style, including a spiral, and at Carnwath, Lanarkshire, another Beaker cist had a cover-stone decorated in the Passage-grave manner. The majority of cists in north Britain having decorated cover-slabs contain food-vessels, and the style of ornament suggests a mixture of Galician and Passage-grave styles, but in Ireland, as we have seen, two cist-burials had Passage-grave decoration, and the Seskilgreen grave contained a stone battle-axe of single-grave affiliations. The Folkton chalk idols, of Iberian type with Boyne-culture ornament, have again been mentioned as of Beaker or later date. In general, then, the evidence of the rock-carving motifs suggests that the Passage-grave style in Ireland was in part at least con-temporary with beakers, food-vessels, and such metal weapons as halberds and flat axes, and also probably with some passage-graves in the Orkneys, and some part of the Skara Brae culture. It is important to notice that at the Clyde-Carlingford tomb of Cairnholy I, a secondary burial with a decorated stone and fragments of a food-vessel had taken place in the rear chamber of the monument, and similar carvings on a detached slab there, and on an upright of the unexcavated tomb of Mid-Gleniron I in Wigtownshire, are therefore likely to be secondary. But the food-vessels in the Boyne tombs are primary at least in the sense that access could still be gained to the chamber in the normal collective tomb manner when they were deposited.

The grave-goods from the Boyne tombs enable certain correlations to be made in a rather more precise manner. We have seen that there is good reason to think that pottery of Loughcrew ware type derives from the Beacharra C style exemplified by such vessels as that from Browndod, and should therefore be later in the main than this group, which can be broadly equated with the beginnings of the Beaker period, and climatically, with the beginning of Zone VIIb. At Moytira in Sligo, a sherd of Loughcrew ware was associated with fragments of British Bi-beakers in a cist-grave, and the technique of ornament on other sherds from the Loughcrew cairns is, as Childe pointed out, paralleled in the Hebrides (on wares derivative from Beacharra B) and in Unstan ware in Orkney. (Childe, 1935b.)

The remarkable bone or antler pins are hard to parallel, though probable analogies to the type III pins exist at Skara Brae and in the Dorchester-culture sites. The mushroom-headed pins of type I occur again in an un-published grave at Lough Gur, Co. Limerick, and in a smaller form, with one burial of the Ronaldsway culture at Ballateare in the Isle of Man: the decorated plaques of the culture are also apposite here.

For the mace-shaped pendants there are, as stressed by Childe (1940, 68), striking parallels in the Wessex culture of the south English Bronze Age, where precisely similar pendants appear, though made in amber. Elsewhere they seem without parallels, though the actual mace-heads of pestle form from which they seem to be copied appear in chambered tombs of the Orkney-Cromarty group and have origins in the Rinyo and Dorchester cultures of the Secondary Neolithic, continuing into the Bronze Age. It may be noted at this point that the appearance of these pendants in the Wessex culture would agree with the use of Passage-grave ornament on the cover-stone of the Moylough cist, since contemporaneity between the Irish halberds and the Wessex culture can be established, and indeed the substratum of the culture is that of the food-vessels. The glass bead from Loughcrew R2 may well be primary, and comparable with others in British Bronze Age contexts.

The final type to which attention may be drawn is the series of stone balls from tombs of the Boyne culture, that occur again in the late 'lobster-claw' cairn of the Clyde-Carlingford culture at Creevykeel, Co. Sligo, in the Rinyo-Clacton culture in Orkney, and in such south English sites of the Dorchester culture as the first phase of Stonehenge. The *petit-tranchet* derivative arrow-head from Bryn Celli Ddu would also be appropriate in such a context.

The evidence taken as a whole suggests that the Boyne culture, at least in the mature form seen in the type II tombs and their contents, does not go back much earlier than the appearance of beaker-makers in north-western Britain and Ireland, and certainly runs parallel for some time with the Food-vessel culture, usually regarded as representing the British Middle Bronze Age. Some Hebridean and Orcadian passage-graves may be more or less contemporary, and links with cultures of the Rinyo-Ronaldsway-Dorchester group are the earliest contacts we can trace. The Wessex culture is one in which fairly direct Continental links can be established, and in terms of absolute chronology its beginnings can hardly be before the middle of the second millennium B.C. In short, the Boyne tombs may represent a culture which is only 'Neolithic' in so far as metal was not buried with the dead, for it certainly seems contemporary with other communities enjoying the full use of copper and bronze.

THE CONTINENTAL AFFINITIES OF THE BOYNE TOMBS

The position of the Boyne tombs in the general west European series is not easy to define. The cruciform chambers of type II certainly seem to be an Irish development from the use of small terminal or lateral chambers at Los Millares, Romeral, Alcala and other sites, and La Hougue Bie in Jersey approaches most closely to this variant of plan. The stone basins suggest connexions with Iberian examples such as that at Castraz, Ciudad Rodrigo, or the rectangular example at Matarubilla, but the carved ornament on the orthostats and capstones in the Brugh na Boinne and Loughcrew groups, and in outlying examples, point rather to Brittany (M. & S. J. Péquart & Le Rouzic, 1927), though some of the patterns are comparable with those painted on the walls of tombs such as Pedra Coberta (Coruña) or others in Portugal, mainly concentrated in the valleys of the Mondago and the Douro (Leisner, 1934). (The former existence of painted ornament in British passage-graves is a possibility that must be kept in mind when discussing distributions.) Portugal or Brittany, or both, with possible Channel Island contributions, are the most likely regions in which to place the architectural origins of the Boyne passage-graves, and indeed the same applies to all the British regional groups.

The cremation rite, like the Loughcrew pottery, seems to be of local origin. We shall see that cremation is common in the British Neolithic cultures of the Ronaldsway-Dorchester group, with which some part of the period covered by the use of the Boyne tombs must be contemporary, and it is probably a secondary and relatively late feature in the Clyde-Carlingford culture due to absorption of local ideas, perhaps with ultimate hunter-fisher origins. There is in fact nothing distinctively Iberian or Breton in the grave-goods of the Boyne tombs except for the pins of type II, with the 'poppy' type of head. Good parallels for such pins do exist in the Palmella culture site of Vila Nova de San Pedro in Portugal (Jalhay & do Paço, 1945) associated with bell-beaker pottery and copper tools, but they seem other-wise unknown. The segmented pendant from Carrowkeel G has fairly close affinities to such specimens as those from Monte de la Barsella, Alicante (Dominguez, 1929).

But on the whole the Boyne passage-graves, like those of the Orkneys and probably most of those of the Hebrides, present the contrast of marked architectural affinities with chambered tombs in Iberia and Brittany, with an almost complete absence of any other elements of material culture that can be derived from these regions. The absence of the bell-beaker in parti-cular is noticeable, and of other types linking Iberia and Brittany, such as calläis beads. The contrast with the Clyde-Carlingford tombs, in which an intrusive pottery type of Franco-Iberian origin accompanies the first appearance in Scotland of collective chambered tombs with a probably similar place of origin, is marked. It is probable that the almost complete adoption by the builders of the Boyne tombs of local traditions in pottery and other elements of material culture, and the rite of cremation, is due to the fact that they arrived in areas where Neolithic agricultural communities were already strongly established, and that we have in fact a set of cir-cumstances parallel to those in Denmark, where the material culture represented by the grave-goods of the passage-graves can very clearly be seen to be merely a development of a pre-existing and long-established Neolithic tradition.

CHAPTER VIII

THE COLONIZATION OF THE HIGHLANDS AND ISLANDS: CHAMBERED-TOMB BUILDERS IN THE HEBRIDEAN AND ORKNEY-CROMARTY REGIONS

INTRODUCTION

OUTSIDE the area of the distinctive Clyde-Carlingford collective tombs described in Chapter VI, the great majority of Scottish chambered cairns have architectural features which bring them within the passage-grave class of conventional typology. Such tombs are found to form regional groups united by peculiarities of plan and to some extent by common grave-goods, and there is evidence that the communities building the local variants in scattered areas were in touch with one another at least by trade and probably by actual interchanges of population. This communication must have been effected mainly by coastal seaways, and there is further evidence of the use of rivers and lochs, notably as trans-peninsular routes avoiding rough passages round promontories.

We can distinguish four main areas of settlement, each marked by distinctive tomb types. The first of these is that of the *Hebrides*, including a few scattered sites on the mainland as far south as the entrance to the Firth of Lorne and continuing northwards through the Outer Isles to Lewis. The *Orkney-Cromarty* group of tombs covers a long coastal area extending from the Orkney Islands and the north coast of Caithness southwards down the east coast of Scotland to the north side of the Moray Firth; the *Shetland* tombs form a distinctive group confined to these islands, lying 50 miles north of the Orkneys; and the *Clava* group comprises a compact series of chambered tombs concentrated on the south side of the Moray Firth. Outside these areas of concentration, comprising between them something over 200 tombs, there are various scattered sites of passage-grave type, including some in Galloway, and a relatively large number of long cairns without distinctive structural features which may or may not contain chambers and which occur not only in the areas of colonization indicated above, but sporadically in eastern Scotland in Aberdeenshire and elsewhere, occurring as far south as Berwickshire and Dumfries, and over the border in Northumberland. It is interesting to notice that tombs of the so-called 'dolmen' type, such as those of Ireland or Cornwall, do not occur in Scotland —a fact likely to be related to the probable derivation of 'dolmens' from tombs of the gallery-grave group rather than from passage-graves in Britain (Daniel, 1937a).

Excavation has mainly been concentrated in the Orkney-Cromarty group, though here only one tomb south of Caithness has been examined. In Caithness and Orkney, however, some thirty sites have been excavated, but of these excavations only about a third were conducted in recent years: in the Hebrides on the other hand, though only three excavations of chambered tombs have taken place, they have all been of a high standard and provided extremely important stratigraphical information, amplified by work by their excavator on a Neolithic pottery kiln in North Uist (Scott, 1932; 1934; 1935; 1948a). The Shetland tombs remain unexcavated, as do those of the Clava group, but among outlying sites the Bargrennan passage-grave was excavated in 1949 (Piggott & Powell, 1949).

Since excavation has virtually been confined to the tombs in the Hebridean and Orkney-Cromarty groups, it is convenient to take these two groups first, reserving the unexcavated groups to a more cursory survey, in Chapter IX, after the detailed evidence from the excavated sites has been considered here.

THE HEBRIDEAN GROUP OF CHAMBERED TOMBS

Distribution

We have already seen that the Nether Largie cairn (Crinan) combines elements of Clyde-Carlingford and passage-grave architecture (a segmented burial chamber with ritual passage only, under a round cairn), and this site forms, with a couple of others near, the north-western outpost of the Clyde-Carlingford area, on an important trans-peninsular route linking the mouth of the Clyde with the Sound of Jura and the Firth of Lorne, and so with the main Western Approaches up the Atlantic coasts of Britain. In the Firth of Lorne itself, at the mouth of Loch Etive, is at least one passage-grave, that of Achnacree, constituting the southernmost known settlement in the Hebridean region. The main weight of settlement is, however, in the Outer Isles, especially in Barra, Benbecula, and South and North Uist, with a notable concentration of some 15 tombs in the last island. Eight or nine tombs in Skye, mainly in the south, and a half-dozen in Harris and Lewis together complete the picture.[1]

This clearly represents a simple seaborne colonization from the south, following, as regards the Outer Isles, the west coasts with their favourable landing-places rather than the forbidding rocky shores of the Minch.

Cairns and their plans

Some diversity of cairn form can be seen even in unexcavated sites, and excavation would probably show more variations. There are four unex-

[1] Bibliography in R.C.A.M.(S), 1928 (with map); Scott (1932; 1934; 1935; 1948a); M. E. C. Mitchell (1933).

cavated long cairns, two in Skye and two in North Uist, which may possibly have had crescentic forecourts in the 'horned cairn' manner, and the Clettraval tomb (North Uist), though much robbed in the Early Iron Age, retained nearly 100 ft. of straight revetment on its south side,[1] inclining inwards towards the axial line at the far end of the cairn and joining a flat façade at the other—as Scott points out, the cairn must have been wedge-shaped in plan (Scott, 1935) and so comparable with Clyde-Carlingford sites (Fig. 34). As we shall see, the peculiar chamber plan again emphasizes this connexion.

Normally, however, the cairns approximate to a circular form, though the 50-ft. wide flat façade at Unival gives the cairn a nearly square plan, and at Rudh' an Dunain the cairn is more or less kidney shaped with a deep crescentic façade (Fig. 34). Barpa Langass and Achnacree are good examples of circular cairns: at the former site it is noteworthy that the cairn has been built on an artificially levelled platform in the hill-slope, in a manner comparable with certain Orcadian tombs such as that on Wideford Hill.

The cairns are not grouped in cemeteries and are mainly on the slopes of hills, though two sites in North Uist stand on rock now below high-water mark. Outlying standing stones occur near cairns (e.g. Unival), and the Callanish cairn is within and forms an integral part of the great stone circle with cruciform 'avenue' settings on the site.

Chambers, passages and forecourts

Both Barpa Langass and Rudh' an Dunain have polygonal or oval chambers with relatively short passage approaches and are roofed with capstones carried on orthostats and dry-walling; these tombs approach nearest to what Daniel & Powell (1949) would class as 'primary' passage-graves having strong similarities with Continental forms. Rudh' an Dunain has sills across the passage in the manner of the Boyne tombs or those of Alcala: Unival has a polygonal chamber and very short passage approach. Achnacree has a long passage leading to a fine chamber, rectangular in plan and with a corbelled vault closed by a single capstone in the manner of the Camster type of round cairn in the Orkney-Cromarty group, but behind this there open out two further chambers without corbelling and roofed by large slabs. The curious little cairn within the Callanish circle in Lewis contains a chamber (now roofless) with projecting side stones recalling again the Camster type of tomb mentioned above. Within the chambers at Clettraval and Unival was found evidence of subdivisions made with small slabs, at Unival forming a definite cist or box.

The Clettraval chamber can only be interpreted as a structural hybrid between the Passage-grave and the Clyde-Carlingford architectural traditions.

---

[1] A stretch of revetment additional to that recorded in Scott (1935) was found in 1947 during the excavation of the Early Iron Age house which overlay it (Scott, 1948*b*, 47).

The passage and chamber elements are merged into an irregular slab-built structure enlarging at its inner end, and divided by septal slabs into five compartments. Burials were found in the three innermost and in the outermost compartments (the fifth was largely destroyed) and in the penultimate com-

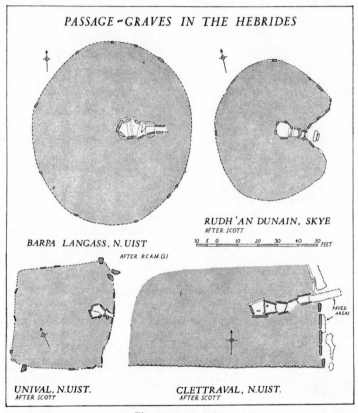

PASSAGE-GRAVES IN THE HEBRIDES

BARPA LANGASS, N. UIST
AFTER R.C.A.M.(S)

RUDH 'AN DUNAIN, SKYE
AFTER SCOTT

UNIVAL, N.UIST.
AFTER SCOTT

CLETTRAVAL, N.UIST.
AFTER SCOTT

Fig. 34.

partment was a standing stone. Half a dozen further unexcavated sites in North Uist and Boreray appear to have similarly segmented chambers in the Clyde-Carlingford manner.

The forecourt areas of tombs have only been examined at Rudh' an Dunain, Clettraval and Unival. At the first site, there was found a pair of prostrate stones laid across the axis of the entrance, but no trace of burning or other ritual: at Clettraval a narrow paved path ran up to the entrance through the flat façade. White quartz fragments were found scattered at Rudh' an Dunain in the forecourt and round the peristalith, and similar pieces were found in the chambers at Achnacree.

Burials, funeral ritual and stratification

In the three tombs for which we have information, the burial rite was by inhumation, and in two of these (Clettraval and Unival) it was possible to show that the bones had been scorched by ritual fire or hot charcoal, in a manner comparable to some Orcadian burials noted below. The meticulous excavation of the Unival tomb (Scott, 1948 *a*) enabled the full detail of the funerary ritual on that site to be worked out, and this is probably to be taken as typical.

Burials took place in the 'cist' or partitioned-off part of the chamber already referred to, and the first burial was presumably placed here with a couple of pots holding food offerings (analysis of the residual content of the pots suggested this). At each subsequent funeral the body would have been cleared out, and the longer and larger bones piled against the chamber wall with the offering-pots or their larger fragments: the smaller debris of bones and sherds were shovelled out on to the chamber floor. The burial was then deposited in the newly cleared cist, with its attendant pots, and probably further pots with their contents were placed by the chamber wall in some instances. After an interval of time sufficient for the corpse to become practically a skeleton, the remains were scorched by throwing hot charcoal on them—a fire would not have burned in the chamber, and since the last burial in the cist, intact when excavated, was thus charred, it follows that this burning was not a sacring act performed at each funeral on the remains of the previous occupant of the cist, but was subsequent. By the time the final burial came to be inserted at Unival, however, debris and accumulated soil fallen in from the roof had rendered access to the chamber from the passage impossible, so that the last corpse deposited was an unscorched inhumation laid on the earth that now covered cist and previous burials, and inserted by removing some walling from beneath the capstone.

This final burial recalls the entry from the side of the chamber which we have shown probably occurred at such sites as Pant y Saer, Pentre Ifan and the Grey Mare and her Colts: Scott compares the use of the opening in the vault at Alapraia and Palmella, and we may now add the even more comparable evidence from the passage-graves of Hérault excavated by Arnal (1949).

It seems probable that there were four or five burials made in the Unival tomb, and if there was a normal allocation of two pots to each burial, this would agree with the Clettraval evidence, where there were two pots in each of the intact segments, and four in the chamber, stratigraphically divisible into two groups, making a total of four or five interments once again. In this context the Beacharra pots, similarly in pairs, may be noted. Estimating a generation under primitive conditions as about twenty years, this would indicate a duration of about a century or so for the tombs in question, which would agree well enough with the similar length of time assigned to Cairnholy I on the grounds of the six funerary fires in the forecourt.

This recognition of a burial sequence in the pottery deposits results in a stratification in which a typological development can be observed in the Neolithic pottery at Unival and to a less extent at Clettraval, with narrow and globular forms being replaced by wider or hemispherical vessels, and the simple rims becoming thickened or flattened. At Unival, pot 51 is in fact a vessel in the Rinyo I style of the Orkneys (Chapter xi) made in fine paste, and belongs to group 4 in the tomb, with five other pots of local types. Group 6 (the final burial) contains fragments of an actual (unornamented) B beaker and sherds of a probable Rinyo II pot, and a pumice pendant in the form of a metal axe.

At Clettraval, it could be demonstrated that of two deposits in the chamber one with a plain lugged pot of Beacharra A form was the earlier, and later burials had beaker sherds with them: this stratification of Neolithic ware below Beaker was repeated at Rudh' an Dunain. In all instances the Beaker burials had been made while the tomb was still accessible for burials in the normal collective tomb manner, even if as at Unival the rite was slightly modified and the means of access unconventional.

MATERIAL EQUIPMENT

Pottery

Our knowledge of the pottery from the Hebridean tombs is almost entirely based on the large series excavated by Scott from the Clettraval and Unival tombs in North Uist, three pots from Achnacree, two from Rudh' an Dunain in Skye, and a couple of sherds from Barpa Langass. The potters' kilns on Eilean an Tighe in North Uist, also excavated by Scott, have not been published, though certain sherds and a restored bowl are illustrated in J. Hawkes (1939, pl. 11a and pl. v), while earlier finds are illustrated by Callander (1929, fig. 53).

The Achnacree and Rudh' an Dunain material (Fig. 35, nos. 5, 6) can be recognized as related to such bowls from the Clyde-Carlingford province as that from Nether Largie, with overhanging or bevelled rims and, at Achnacree as at Largie, finger-tip fluting in the Yorkshire manner on undecorated vessels. Such pots have been included in the Beacharra A group, though they probably represent a distinct subdivision of it.

The North Uist material forms a consistent series in which, thanks to Scott's admirable excavations, we have an opportunity of correlating stylistic with stratigraphical data. The heavy bevelled rims of the Achnacree-Largie type are absent, and instead we have a group of bag-shaped or carinated forms with simple or sometimes flat-topped rims. The stratification at Clettraval suggests that the earliest burial was accompanied by a large un-

decorated lugged pot of the Torlin-Sliddery class and a small carinated bowl
with channelled ornament in the Beacharra B manner (Fig. 35, nos. 1, 3),
and this would be in agreement with the Clyde-Carlingford contacts implicit
in the architecture of the tomb itself. But while in general the North Uist
wares, with their incised and channelled ornament, are clearly related to

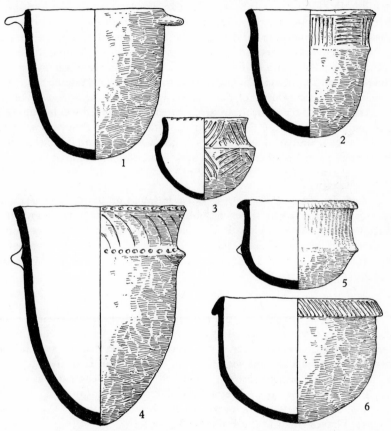

Fig. 35. Hebridean chambered tombs: pottery. 1–4, Clettraval (*after Scott*);
5, Achnacree; 6, Rudh' an Dunain (*after Scott*). Scale ¼.

those of Beacharra B, and to the south French or Portuguese antecedents
of such wares, they form a distinctive local group too specialized to be
classed as Beacharra B themselves.

The forms (Pl. VIII) range from deep bag-shaped or pointed-base vessels
to shallow bowls; carinations are never accentuated and are often absent or
minimized. Lugs are present on decorated pots from Clettraval, but absent
at Unival (Fig. 35, no. 4). The technique of ornament is that of incision or

channelling, with a notable absence of the stab-and-drag techniques of the Unstan ware of the Orkneys. The arrangement of vertical and horizontal zones of pattern, and the alternating panels of 'hurdle' design, are those of the western European Neolithic group shared with Beacharra B, and the best examples of these patterns may belong to the earlier vessels in the tomb stratigraphy (Fig. 35, no. 2). At Eilean an Tighe, it was possible to show that a shallow bowl of a type exactly matched, in profile and decoration, at Unstan and Midhowe in Orkney (Pl. VIII, no. 8 and Fig. 40, no. 3), was late in the sequence at that site, and at Unival the fourth group of funerary deposits included a cup of Rinyo I ware, so that an overlap between the Hebridean and the Orcadian chambered-tomb cultures is established, with some evidence for priority of the former, which the close similarity of its pottery to the western European group already mentioned would support. The couple of sherds from Barpa Langass, with channelled chevron pattern, would be comparable to several pots in the Clettraval and Unival series, and pottery from Loughcrew, as we have seen, is again comparable.

Stone and flint

A *barbed-and-tanged flint arrowhead* was found at Barpa Langass, and *scrapers, flakes and points* of beach-pebble flint and quartz at this tomb and at Rudh' an Dunain and Unival. Two *stone balls* were found in the forecourt at Clettraval, and another in the chamber at Unival. *Pumice* fragments were found at Rudh' an Dunain and Clettraval, at the latter site worn by rubbing.

Pendants

Two pendants are known from the Hebridean tombs, one being a mica disc 1·3 in. in diameter, pierced by two holes set together at the edge, from Barpa Langass, and the other a very remarkable pumice pendant in the form of a metal axe, found with the final burial in the Unival tomb, and 1·5 in. long in its present (broken) condition. Scott has compared it with a very similar pendant from a Breton S.O.M. cist at Kerlescan, and one may note that its shape is much nearer to the Breton flat metal axes of the 'Dagger Graves' than to the Hiberno-British series.

RELATIONSHIPS OF THE HEBRIDEAN CULTURE

So far as the tomb architecture goes, it is impossible to deny the existence of two strains in the known Hebridean sites, though as Scott has urged (1942; 1948 a) there is every likelihood that the funeral rites performed in the variant forms of tomb were practically the same. Nevertheless, Clettraval with its trapezoidal long cairn and segmented burial chamber shares little save the fundamental idea of a stone-built tomb for collective burial with the polygonal chamber with its passage approach beneath a circular mound at Rudh' an Dunain or Barpa Langass, and the fact that the two traditions represented by the planning of these divergent monuments do appear, in many regions of Britain, to have resulted in communities building one type to the exclusion of the other, must imply that there was a significance attached to specific forms of architecture in these communities. In the Hebrides one sees these strains combining, and indeed the Unival tomb may have elements from both traditions embodied in its formal plan, and again in the Orkney-Cromarty group of tombs this Gallery-grave–Passage-grave interaction can be perceived.

The pottery from Eilean an Tighe, and from the tombs of Unival and Clettraval, and probably that from Rudh' an Dunain and Barpa Langass, is closely related to the Beacharra A and B groups of the Clyde-Carlingford culture already described. The channelled and incised patterns of west French or Iberian derivation are seen developing along distinctive insular lines, as might be expected, but the links with Clyde-Carlingford might well be seen to be greater had we a larger series of vessels from the latter culture, and especially material from settlement areas. The little Beacharra bowls, with their high finish, may constitute a specific type consecrated to funeral use and so less characteristic than appears at first sight. There is then an overlap between the Hebridean culture and that of Clyde-Carlingford, established at a time before the appearance of the cord-ornamented vessels of Beacharra C, and the evidence of the plain lugged bowl of Beacharra A type from the earliest burial at Clettraval, and the use of lugs on decorated vessels, as at Beacharra itself, suggests that this tomb, employing the architectural modes of Clyde-Carlingford, is earlier than Unival, in which Passage-grave elements predominate, and in which such lugged ware is absent. An early settlement of the Hebrides, centred on North Uist, and represented by tombs of the Clettraval type, would seem likely: it may derive from the Clyde-Carlingford area, or it may represent fresh drafts of Continental immigrants from the common stock.

The fact that the Hebridean pottery appears to be unaffected by the innovations of cord-ornament marking the Beacharra C phase in Ulster and Bute suggests that if Scandinavian contacts are to be invoked to account for this technique, they would have been likely to have been established along some route or routes in which the Hebrides were not included—the Great Glen or some other overland route linking the west coasts of Britain with those of the east suggests itself.

The stone balls from Clettraval and Unival suggest comparison with those of the Boyne culture of Ireland (and pottery from Loughcrew may also be connected with North Uist styles) and they appear in Rinyo-Clacton contexts in Orkney, while the Rinyo I pot from Unival (no. 51) links a late phase in the tomb's history with an early point in the Orcadian Secondary Neolithic sequence, and should also be contemporary with the Tormore grave-group (p. 173 above): the Eilean an Tighe stratification further shows that the shallow bowl of Unstan type is a late development in North Uist, and therefore gives an approximate relative position to those chambered tombs containing this type of pottery in Orkney—they should overlap with a late phase of the Hebridean sequence. These contacts between the Hebrides and the Orkney-Cromarty regions must have taken place along the western seaways, but petrological examination of the grit in the pottery from the two areas showed that, however striking the similarities of form and ornament in the two areas, we were not concerned with an actual trade in pots, but with local developments resulting from potters accustomed to Hebridean traditions settling in Orkney (Scott & Phemister, 1942).

The wider chronological correlations of the Hebridean material made by Scott (1948 a) are discussed in detail in Chapter XII, and for the present it is sufficient to note that Pot 51 at Unival is quite likely to be contemporary with the relatively advanced Wessex Bronze Age culture, while the axe-pendant with the final burial of this tomb, apparently copying a Breton and not a Hiberno-British type of copper or bronze axe, would again be approximately contemporary. This Breton contact is interesting in view of the same source for the jadeite axe-fragment from Cairnholy I in the Clyde-Carlingford area, and indeed a jadeite axe-pendant with a probable Breton origin (though not in this instance copying a metal tool) is known from Dorset (Piggott & Powell, 1949). Contacts between the Hebrides and west France must have existed at least in trade, and perhaps in direct colonization by groups of settlers, building in either the gallery-grave or passage-grave traditions of collective tomb architecture.

THE ORKNEY-CROMARTY GROUP OF CHAMBERED TOMBS

Distribution

The north-west coasts of Scotland from Skye to Cape Wrath are for the greater part rocky and inhospitable, and do not invite landings by primitive colonists seeking to establish agricultural communities. But from the valley of the Naver, midway between Cape Wrath and Dunnet Head in Caithness, there is evidence in the form of chambered tombs for such colonization of the relatively flat coastal strip round the Caithness promontory and down the east coast to Cromarty Firth, the Black Isle, and the head of the Great Glen opening into the Moray Firth. The Orkney islands, separated from Caithness by the 10-miles wide Pentland Firth, offer, with the exception of the island of Hoy, an archipelago of low-lying islands with good landings and sheltered inland waters, and here again a large number of chambered tombs denote settlement (Fig. 36).

Throughout this large area the 130 or so recorded tombs[1] show sufficient

1 Bibliography in R.C.A.M.(S), (1911 a, b; 1946); Childe (1944); Anderson (1866; 1868; 1886).

architectural similarities to justify one in considering the colonization to have a certain homogeneity, although at least three main variants of tomb-structure occur. One of these variants is in fact confined to the Orkneys,

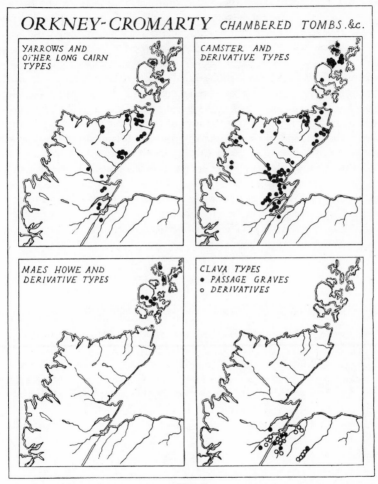

ORKNEY-CROMARTY *CHAMBERED TOMBS.&c.*

YARROWS AND OTHER LONG CAIRN TYPES

CAMSTER AND DERIVATIVE TYPES

MAES HOWE AND DERIVATIVE TYPES

CLAVA TYPES
- *PASSAGE GRAVES*
- *DERIVATIVES*

Fig. 36.

but the other two have representatives both in the archipelago and on the mainland.

This distribution could be the result of the use of the two routes, either exclusively one or the other, or a combination of both. The first would continue the Western Approaches up the Atlantic coasts beyond the Hebridean area of colonization already described, to make landfalls along the north

I

coast of the mainland and in the Orkneys, and thence down the east coast to the Moray Firth. The second would utilize the natural highway of the Great Glen, stretching for some 80 miles north-east from the Firth of Lorne on the west coast to the Moray Firth on the east and affording a series of lochs for water transport. From the head of the Great Glen in the neighbourhood of Inverness, colonization could spread northwards by coasting voyages to Sutherland and Caithness, and ultimately to the Orkneys: as we shall see, typology makes it clear that a large number of Orcadian tombs must be derivatives from Caithness forms, so that a proportion of its colonists must have come from the Scottish mainland whichever route was used. The Great Glen was almost certainly the route whereby the builders of the Clava group of chambered cairns, lying to the south of the Moray Firth with a complementary distribution to the Cromarty group on the north, reached eastern Scotland from the Western Approaches, and it was quite clearly used as a trade-route linking the earliest copper and bronze working centres in the Hiberno-Scottish region.

A brief examination of the main variants in tomb-types within the Orkney-Cromarty group will help to clarify the problem of the routes of colonization (Figs. 37–9). Where distinctive features are recognizable, the sites in general fall into three classes—

(i) Chambered long cairns of the *Yarrows* type.
(ii) Chambered round cairns of the *Camster* type, with derivatives which include the *Stalled Cairns* of Orkney.
(iii) Chambered round cairns of the *Maes Howe* type.

These three types are described and discussed in detail in a later section, but for the present we may note that the *Yarrows* cairns have Clyde-Carlingford affinities in their elongated form and crescentic façades, and the lack of the latter feature in the Hebridean sites such as Clettraval might argue for the use of a route which was distinct from that colonizing the Hebrides, and so might be through the Great Glen, though the Western Approaches are by no means ruled out, especially since their concentration is in Strathnaver and Caithness, with a couple in Orkney. Their chambers, however, are of specifically Camster type, which must indicate hybridization of some kind. Though long cairns are known from the Black Isle and Cromarty regions, none seems certainly to show the characteristic crescentic façade of the typical Yarrows form.

The *Camster* tombs of type ii are the most widely distributed in the area under consideration, from the northern shores of the Moray Firth (where as we have seen they are mutually exclusive to the Clava type of tomb) and thence up the coastal strip of Sutherland and Caithness. Their derivatives in Orkney, which include as the ultimate form the long 'Stalled Cairn' type, as we shall see, are mostly concentrated in the islands of Rousay and

235

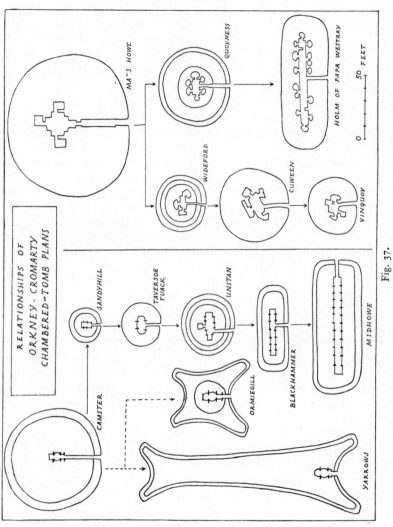

RELATIONSHIPS OF
ORKNEY - CROMARTY
CHAMBERED-TOMB PLANS

MA'S HOWE

QUOYNESS

HOLM OF PAPA WESTRAY

0   50 FEET

WIDEFORD

CUWEEN

VINQUOY

SANDYHILL

TAVERSOE TUACK

UNSTAN

BLACKHAMMER

MIDHOWE

CAMSTER

ORMIEGILL

YARROWS

Fig. 37.

Eday, and their distribution suggests an entrance to the archipelago from the east through Stronsay Firth. The Camster type has in fact the best claim to be the product of a colonizing movement up the Great Glen and thence northwards up the east coast of Scotland.

The tombs of the types derived from *Maes Howe* are specifically Orcadian in their distribution, and are concentrated on the island of Mainland, where the region of Stromness suggests itself as the port of entry. The tomb type has certain affinities with Boyne tombs of type ii, and the western sea routes seem likely to have been used by their makers. There is, incidentally, no evidence for colonization round Scapa Flow, still less of the use of the dangerous waters of the Pentland Firth. But there is good evidence from tomb-distribution for the use of a trans-peninsular route between Thurso and Wick, using the small rivers named after these two places, which would avoid the Firth.

On the whole therefore the available evidence suggests that the Great Glen route was most probably used by the builders of the Camster type of chambered cairn, and perhaps by those of the Yarrows type as well; the Western Approaches were almost certainly used by the Maes Howe colonists, and perhaps more probably than the Great Glen by the builders of the Yarrows tombs, with their Clyde-Carlingford affiliations. As we shall see, the evidence of pottery shows that contacts between the Orkneys and the Hebrides were certainly maintained during the period of use of the Camster tombs at least, and the unique Callanish tomb has certain architectural features suggesting comparison with Camster type chambers.

The tombs are not grouped into cemeteries in the manner of the Boyne group, or those of the Clava type, although the small-scale maps on which the Orkney tombs are usually crowded may suggest this. It has been suggested for instance that we might regard the tombs of Maes Howe, Cuween, Wideford and Quanterness as constituting such a cemetery (Daniel & Powell, 1949), but these (together with the so-called Ring of Bookan, which can now be recognized as a much wrecked site of the same type) are in fact strung out across a tract of country over 9 miles long. The Rousay tombs are spaced round the edge of the arable land of the island in a manner which forcibly suggests, as Childe pointed out (1942), family tombs belonging to individual crofting settlements. But at Yarrows there is something of a concentration of the four 'short' cairns dug by Rhind (Anderson, 1886, 254), and long cairns in pairs (as in the Clyde-Carlingford and the Severn-Cotswold groups) occur there and at Rhinavie.

Detailed description: tombs of the Yarrows type

Within the area of settlement described above, one group of chambered tombs stands out as a distinctive variant owing to its use of a long cairn greatly in excess of the length necessary to cover the actual burial chamber,

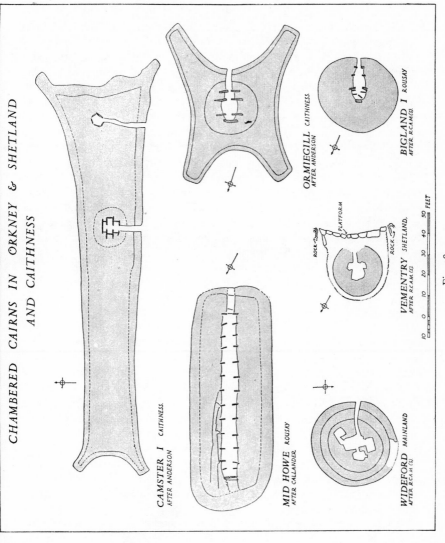

CHAMBERED CAIRNS IN ORKNEY & SHETLAND AND CAITHNESS

CAMSTER I CAITHNESS
AFTER ANDERSON

ORMIEGILL CAITHNESS
AFTER ANDERSON

BIGLAND I ROUSAY
AFTER R.C.A.M (3).

PLATFORM

ROCK   ROCK

VEMENTRY SHETLAND.
AFTER R.C.A.M (3)

10 0 10 20 30 40 50 FEET

MID HOWE ROUSAY
AFTER CALLANDER

WIDEFORD MAINLAND
AFTER R.C.A.M (3)

Fig. 38.

which is normally situated at one end only and opens on to a crescentic façade: the rear end of the cairn is narrower and frequently echoes in its plan the entrance façade on a smaller scale. These 'horned cairns' as they have been known since the nineteenth-century definition of the type, have in the essential features of their planning immediately recognizable links with tombs within the gallery-grave group described above in Chapters v and vi from the Severn-Cotswold and Clyde-Carlingford areas—the cairn in which the burial chamber occupies only a fraction of the total length, the more or less trapezoid plan, and the provision of a ritual forecourt setting in the form of a monumental façade (Fig. 38). But they differ in two important respects—the chambers are architecturally indistinguishable from those found beneath round cairns of the Camster type described below and are formally passage-graves, while the duplication of the 'horns' at the rear end is without parallel except in functionally double-ended cairns in the Clyde-Carlingford culture such as Aghanaglack in Co. Fermanagh (Davies, 1939 d), though possibly a prototype could be seen in the slightly concave rear end of the cairn at Nympsfield (Clifford, 1938). Another individual feature within the Orkney-Cromarty region is the 'short horned cairn', in which the two crescentic façades are 'telescoped' into a structure nearly as broad as it is long, as at Ormiegill (Fig. 38).

Tombs of this type can be recognized on the mainland in Caithness and Sutherland, and a possible example (Kinrive) may exist in Easter Ross (Childe, 1944), while there are three in Orkney (Knowe of Lairo, Head of Work and Burray). Constructional details are available from nine long cairns and three of the 'short' type. The lengths of the former range from the larger Yarrows cairn (240 ft.) to Head of Work or Heathercro (150 ft.), and the short variants are approximately 65 to 55 ft. long. Where excavation has been carried out, double dry-stone revetments to the cairn seem normal (both Yarrows cairns, Camster Long, Lairo and the two short variants at Ormiegill and Garrywhin), and orthostatic peristaliths exist at Rhinavie and Tulach an t-Sionnach (Caithness). At Lairo diagonal decorative walling paralleled in the stalled cairns described below was found.

The chambers open through a short passage on to the forecourt between the crescentic 'horns' except at Camster Long, where there are two chambers opening on to one side of the cairn, but none at the wide end. The chambers are constructed on precisely the same plan as those in our type ii (Camster), cairns, with two or three pairs of slabs on edge projecting into the passage or chamber in such a manner as to reduce the span of corbelled roofing and also to divide the sides of the chamber into a series of bays or stalls. In Camster Long, however, the second of the two chambers is a rather irregular corbelled tunnel, with no such features nor structural distinction between passage and chamber. The other chamber was of normal type, and excavation showed it to be surrounded by a circular revetment completely hidden

239

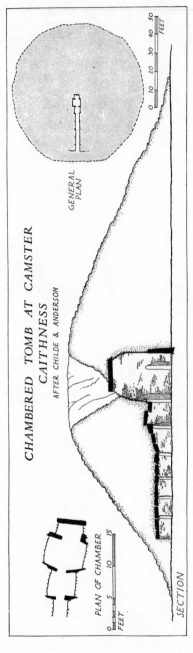

CHAMBERED TOMB AT CAMSTER
CAITHNESS
AFTER CHILDE & ANDERSON

GENERAL PLAN

PLAN OF CHAMBER

SECTION

Fig. 39.

in the cairn, and the same feature was observed in the short cairns of Garrywhin and Ormiegill (Fig. 38): the 'oval construction' round the Nympsfield chamber may be comparable. At Lairo the corbelling was carried up to the fantastic height of 14 ft. over a very narrow chamber in a manner reminiscent of somewhat similar corbelling technique in the Maes Howe group of tombs described below.

This Yarrows type of cairn constitutes a problem in origins, since two distinctive traditions seem to be embodied in the architecture of the tombs, one related to the Clyde-Carlingford (and to a less extent, the Severn-Cotswold) groups of tombs within the gallery-grave class, and the other to the local passage-graves of the Camster type. Neither distribution nor grave-goods help to clarify this problem, as both merely strengthen the connexion between the Yarrows and the Camster classes of tomb.

Tombs of the Camster type

Within a few hundred yards of the long cairn at Camster mentioned above is a magnificent chambered round cairn which may serve as typical of our second tomb-type within the Orkney-Cromarty province (Fig. 39). The characteristic basic form is that of a passage-grave within a circular cairn, the chamber having the structural peculiarities already described in the Yarrows type with the distinctive pairs of slabs projecting inwards from the walls. The range of the type is wide, extending from such sites as Camster itself, with its fine corbelled chamber, southwards to such sites as Kinbrace Burn and Carn Liath, Torboll, in Sutherland, or Ballachnecore and Contin Mains in Easter Ross. In the more southerly examples the chamber plan tends to be rectangular, probably on account of the type of stone available for building, but some corbelling exists even in Easter Ross. In the Orkneys, the form is represented by such tombs as that at Bigland on Rousay or Sandyhill Smithy, Eday, and by a series of derivatives peculiar to the islands and described separately below.

A single, and frequently a double, revetment wall round the cairn has been recorded in excavated tombs of this class, but no orthostatic peristaliths seem to have existed. At Achany in Sutherland a crescentic forecourt of orthostats recalling that in the Rudh' an Dunain passage-grave in Skye seems to exist, but the site has not been excavated. Cairn diameters range from 75 ft. (Camster) to 35 ft. (Kinbrace Burn) or even 28 ft. (Sandyhill Smithy).

Architecturally, the finest corbelled chambers occur in Caithness, where the local flagstone is especially suitable for construction of this kind. Camster itself has a vault rising at least 10 ft. above the floor of the chamber, with a single roof-slab in the manner of Achnacree, and if such corbelling as distinct from capstones supported on a few courses of oversailing dry-walling is to be considered an early feature in the typological sequence, and not merely the result of the differing local stone, it would suggest that Caithness was early colonized (whether from the west or by the Great Glen route), with a subsequent spread of population down the coasts to Sutherland and Cromarty. Side-chambers occur only once, in the small Kenny's Cairn in Caithness, where a single small cell opens from one side of the main chamber. A group of four small tombs of the Camster type at Yarrows shows an individual local development in which the number of the pairs of projecting side-stones within the chamber increases in number, with the consequent elongation of the chamber and, in one site, a resultant elongation of the covering cairn into an oval 55 by 40 ft. We shall see that in Orkney the same tendency was carried to even greater lengths.

Cup-marks

One walling-stone at Contin Mains (Childe, 1944) has three very large cup-marks on its upper edge. It is possible that their presence is to be accounted for by contact with the traditions of the Clava tombs, geographically adjacent and frequently decorated with cup-marks.

Camster tomb derivatives in the Orkneys

We have seen that at Bigland, Rousay, is a small tomb of the Camster type, with a subrectangular chamber with three pairs of projecting slabs within a small cairn with double revetment wall (R.C.A.M.(S), 1946, no. 565) (Fig. 38), and there is a similar site at Sandyhill, Eday (Calder, 1938). At Huntersquoy in the same island, in an extraordinary monument further described below, the upper of two superimposed chambers in a round cairn shows that same plan, while the lower shows a typological development, again seen in both chambers in a comparable monument at Taversoe Tuack in Rousay, where the passage enters an oval chamber with two pairs of projecting stones from the side and not the end, thus producing a T-shaped plan. This tendency to lateral elongation is still more marked in the Unstan tomb on Mainland,[1] where an oval chamber is entered asymmetrically from one side and has four pairs of projecting stones, forming ten bays or 'stalls', and a rear cell opening off the main chamber. The tomb of Blackhammer in Rousay provides the essential link between Unstan, with a circular cairn, and the classic series of 'Stalled Cairns' of elongated plan so characteristic of the island of Rousay. Blackhammer measures 70 by 25 ft., with the entrance from the side of the subrectangular cairn, but in the dozen or more stalled cairns in Rousay and elsewhere, the entrance is at one end, and the cairn may be up to 100 ft. long or more, as at Midhowe (Fig. 38; Pl. IX). In all these evolved forms, the pairs of lateral orthostats (which may

---

[1] The spelling of this site has recently been altered by the Ordnance Survey to *Onston*, but the nineteenth-century form is so well established in archaeological literature that it should remain in use.

partition off as many as twenty-eight bays or stalls, as in the Knowe of Ramsay) remain to perform the same function of reducing the span of the corbelled vault as they do in such tombs as Camster itself.

There seems then no reasonable doubt that the long-stalled cairns of Orkney are not 'long cairns' in the same sense as those of the Yarrows group, or those of the Severn-Cotswold and Clyde-Carlingford series—their length is entirely a function of the immensely elongated chamber they have to cover, instead of stretching away as a solid mass of stones behind a small chamber occupying only a fraction of their total length. We have seen that in the small group of oval Camster-type cairns at Yarrows such elongation of chamber and cairn was indeed beginning, though the extreme development was to be confined to Orkney. The distribution of the tombs of Camster and derivative types in the archipelago is, with the single exception of Unstan, outside the island of Mainland and mostly concentrated in Rousay and Eday, and colonization from Caithness by a route coasting eastwards and entering sheltered waters by Stronsay Firth seems very likely. The three Yarrows type cairns in Orkney (Lairo, Head of Work and Burray) may well owe their origin to the same movement of colonization.

It is interesting to observe that a parallel development of a laterally elongated chamber producing a T-shaped plan can be traced in Orkney among tombs of the Maes Howe type described below, while the same phenomenon is strikingly seen in the development of passage-graves in Denmark.

It remains to comment on certain details of structure in these peculiarly Orcadian derivatives of the Camster type of chambered cairn. Reference has already been made to the eccentric monuments of Taversoe Tuack and Huntersquoy, where in each instance, beneath a circular cairn with dry-stone revetment, passage-and-chamber elements appear at two levels, the upper chamber having as its floor the capstones of the lower, the passage approaches being from opposite sides of the cairn. In both sites the lower structure is formed by facing a rock-cut pit with stonework, and while the slope of the ground allows of access on the downhill side to the lower chamber at Taversoe Tuack, it was found necessary at Huntersquoy to cut a *dromos* approach outside the cairn boundary. At the former site a covered 'drain' runs out from the lower entrance, however, and at its outer end is a miniature subterranean chamber, only 5 by 3 ft., containing a deposit of three pots, but no interments. The whole structure at Taversoe Tuack stands on a rough more or less circular platform of stones, and at Huntersquoy there was a prepared clay floor under the cairn, with clay brought from five miles away.

In the long-stalled cairns of the Blackhammer-Midhowe type, decorative herring-bone walling was observed in the two sites named, and we have seen that it also occurred in the Yarrows type cairn of the Knowe of Lairo in Rousay. Double revetments to the cairn appear normal to the long-stalled type, and in the circular cairn at Unstan three concentric revetment walls existed in a manner comparable with the Wideford Hill cairn of the Maes Howe type described below. At Unstan, too, short lengths of walls pro-jected more or less radially at four points on the circumference, and similar unexplained wall footings run out from the long-stalled cairns of Midhowe and Rowiegar and elsewhere.

At Midhowe there was some not absolutely conclusive evidence for an 'upper storey' for part at least of the chamber, in the Huntersquoy manner, but normally the roofing seems to have been a corbelled barrel-vault culminating in a series of large slabs. At Blackhammer at least, well-built blocking of the entrance passage after the final funerals was still intact, and in Camster (Round) the entire 20 ft. of the passage was blocked. In a cairn on the Calf of Eday there was a remarkable arrangement whereby a normal stalled chamber 20 ft. long, with entrance at one end, occupied half of the cairn, and an oval chamber of normal Camster type was set obliquely in the body of the cairn behind it, with no functional entrance. Structurally the two elements were bounded into a single cairn with continuous revetment. Here again was a clay floor from the same source as that at Huntersquoy.

On the whole these Orcadian abnormalities seem the result of local development without outside contacts. But the double chambers with opposed entrances are paralleled (on one level only) in such sites as the Water of Deugh cairn in Galloway or that at Five Wells in Derbyshire, and the multiplication of bays or 'stalls' may be a parallel evolution to the increase in the number of segments in a Clyde-Carlingford tomb or of lateral cells in the Maes Howe derivatives described later. Just as the basic rites of collective burial persist through all the typological variations of gallery-graves and passage-graves, so certain other concepts may have had a uni-versal validity, though expressed in a diversity of architectural modes in the various areas of colonization.

Tombs of the Maes Howe type

Of the chambered tombs in Orkney which can be related to the magni-ficent structure of Maes Howe, five (including the prototype) are on the island of Mainland, and three on the islands of Eday, Lady, and the Holm of Papa Westray respectively. The type or its derivatives is unknown outside Orkney.

Maes Howe stands alone in the series as unquestionably the most accomplished as a work of architecture, executed to a scale and with a sophistication difficult to parallel in Britain. Beneath a cairn 115 ft. in diameter and 24 ft. high is a corbelled chamber of impressive dimensions described below, but the cairn is further remarkable in standing within an oval area 250 by 200 ft. surrounded by a ditch 45 ft. across. Such a feature ancillary to a chambered cairn is unique save for one other monument, which stands some two miles away and is known as the Ring of Bookan. Here a ditch of similar proportions to that at Maes Howe encloses an area 146 by 134 ft., within which are the last vestiges of a cairn containing some form of megalithic structure now practically entirely removed for building purposes, but almost certainly originally a passage-grave of the Maes Howe type.[1]

To return to Maes Howe itself, the entrance passage is 36 ft. long and leads to a chamber 15 ft. square. Immediately inside the entrance door-checks is a recess in the wall for the reception of a massive closing-block, which now occupies it.[2] The inner half of the passage had monolithic walls, floor and roof, formed of enormous slabs of flagstone some 18 ft. long. The chamber is square, with angle buttresses forming squinches to the vaulting: the walls are vertical for nearly 5 ft., and are then brought into a four-sided corbelled vault still surviving to a height of over 12 ft. and probably originally about 15 ft. high to its apex. The evenly-splitting flagstone has made it possible for the builders to carry out the work to a high pitch of exactitude and has allowed of the introduction of such sophisticated refinements as the use of slabs with their outer edges at a slightly obtuse angle to their horizontal faces in the corbelling, so that the vaulting mounts in a smooth curve and not in steps: the slabs used in the upright parts of the walls are rectilinear in section.

From the three sides of the chamber not occupied by the entrance there open rectangular cells at a higher level than the floor: each has been closed by a massive block which now lies on the chamber floor. When in place, the openings would have been difficult to detect.

The assured competence and mastery over the building material shown at Maes Howe mark it out as a monument comparable in prehistoric Britain only to Stonehenge in its individual handling of an architectural problem. In both monuments a contemporary existing conception—that of a chambered tomb or that of a stone circle—has been used to produce a super-lative monument that by its originality of execution is lifted out of its class into a unique position.

With Maes Howe as the archetype, one can trace two lines of development among the six other tombs of related plan (the plan of the Ring of Bookan chamber would not be recoverable without excavation) (Fig. 37). The first group consists of the cairns of Cuween (the older spelling is Kewing) Hill and Wideford Hill on Mainland, and Vinquoy on Eday; the second, of the tombs of Quanterness, Quoyness and that on the Holm of Papa Westray. A destroyed site near the ruined church on Eday (R.C.A.M.(S), 1946, no. 225) might, from a description, have been of the same type as this last.

---

1 The Ring of Bookan has not previously been recognized as the remains of a tomb of Maes Howe type, but field work in 1949 left the writer with little doubt of its nature.

2 Unaccountably omitted by the Ancient Monuments Commission on their plan and section, though correctly shown by Farrer in his drawings of 1862 (Farrer, 1862, pl. IV).

In the first series the sequence from Maes Howe can be followed through Wideford to Cuween and thence to Vinquoy, and is marked by a progressive breaking-up of the symmetrical plan of the prototype, the central chamber losing its rectangular plan and becoming dwarfed by or merged in the side-chambers, which retain their angularity of plan. The second series of derivatives runs through the tombs of Quanterness and Quoyness to the eccentric monument on the Holm of Papa Westray. The chamber retains its rectangularity, but the side-chambers increase in number and become rounded in plan. With this increase (six at Quoyness and no less than fourteen at Holm of Papa Westray) it became necessary in the latter tomb to build a long cairn, 140 ft. long, entered from the side. Functionally, this development is a parallel to that of the Unstan-Blackhammer types described above.

In all the tombs, a high standard of drystone walling and corbelled vaulting is continued, and there is a tendency to build high narrow chimney-like vaults—at Wideford for instance rising to a height of over 8 ft. above a chamber only 4 ft. wide. The presence of similar vaulting in the Yarrows type cairn of the Knowe of Lairo on Rousay suggests contact with these Maes Howe traditions. At Wideford and Quoyness the cairn is elaborately built with a series of three revetment walls (as at Unstan), and at Quoyness there is some evidence that there may have been a platform extending beyond the cairn rather in the Taversoe Tuack manner. Presumably these concentric walls were intended to be visible in a series of ascending circular terraces when the tombs were originally built, as Leisner has suggested was the case in certain Los Millares examples (Leisner, 1943). At Wideford and Cuween the cairns have been built on levelled platforms cut back into the solid rock of the hillside.

This Maes Howe series is centred on the island of Mainland, and it is interesting to note that the most aberrant forms (Quoyness and the Holm of Papa Westray site) are on the other islands of the archipelago. There are no comparable monuments on the Scottish mainland, and they can hardly be other than the products of some individual community coming to Orkney, probably by the Western Approaches.

Rock-cut tomb

On the island of Hoy is an isolated example of a rock-cut tomb, unique in Britain (except for the possible analogue at Glendalough mentioned above) and with its nearest structural parallels in Iberia or in Marne. In an isolated sandstone mass, known as The Dwarfie Stane, about 28 by 14 by 6 ft., a short passage leads into the side of an oval chamber (or pair of cells) approximately 9 by 5 ft. and 3 ft. high. A massive closing-block which would fit the passage entrance lies outside.

The affinities of this remarkable monument must in part lie with the recurrent tendency in Neolithic western Europe to excavate a chambered tomb for collective burials in the solid rock, rather than to build it above ground but beneath a cairn—Sicily, Sardinia, the Balearics, south Spain, Portugal and the Marne all have examples of this alternative technique. But it is worth remembering that locally the lower chambers in the double tombs of Taversoe Tuack and Huntersquoy are in fact rock-cut, though lined with walling and roofed by capstones, and that the plan of these chambers approximates to that of the Dwarfie Stane.

Art

In the Maes Howe derivative tomb on the Holm of Papa Westray are two groups of engravings, more or less in the manner of those of the Boyne culture, and including 'eyebrow and eye' motifs which look strikingly Iberian. The destroyed site near the ruined church on Eday, which might have been a similar monument, produced a stone with engraved spirals and other curvilinear patterns which again link with the Irish series. A stone with cup-and-ring carving from Pickaquoy comes from an indeterminate structure, not certainly a chambered tomb, and one may note in passing the 'footprints' pecked on a stone at South Ronaldsay, which might be comparable with Breton and Danish examples.

Burials and funeral ritual

Burials both by inhumation and cremation probably occur throughout the Orkney-Cromarty region, though evidence from excavation is not available for the Easter Ross and Black Isle group of tombs. In the Orkney-Caithness-Sutherland area, however, we find that Yarrows type cairns have yielded evidence of inhumation in four instances and cremation in four: one tomb (Ormiegill) seems to have contained both burnt and unburnt bodies. In tombs of the Camster type it is interesting to find the six tombs with cremations are all on the Scottish mainland, while the derivatives of the stalled-cairn class in Orkney have produced eight tombs with inhumations. In three or four of these some bones showed signs of burning, or the grave-goods were burnt, but there was no regular cremation and the circumstances suggest rather scorching from purificatory fires. In the three tombs of the Maes Howe group for which evidence is available, the rite was inhumation.

The cremation burials were found thickly strewn in a burnt layer on the floor of the chamber (as for instance at Camster and at Kenny's Cairn, where there was a foot-thick layer of 'ashes' and burnt human and animal bones). At Taversoe Tuack and in many of the stalled cairns such as Midhowe, the inhumation burials were laid on built 'benches' against the walls, or on paving in the 'stalls'. In Quoyness, a Maes Mowe derivative, the skeletons were in pits below the level of the floor. There are few details available of the age and sex, or even the actual number of individuals represented in the tombs, but the relevant figures known are given in Table VI. The physical characteristics appear to have been, in most instances, those of the gracile dolichocephalic 'Mediterranean' type, but brachycephalic and dolichocephalic skulls occurred together at Cuween and Quoyness.

TABLE VI

Site	Adults	Children	Infants	Total
Type i tombs				
Acaidh	1	.	.	1
Burray	10	.	.	10
Type ii tombs				
Dounreay	5	.	.	5
Holm of P.W.	6	.	.	6
Midhowe	17	6	2	25
Ramsay	3	.	.	3
Taversoe Tuack	3	.	.	3
Type iii tombs				
Cuween	7	.	.	7
Quoyness	12–15	.	.	12–15

Funeral feasts: wild and domestic animals

In almost all instances bones of animals, frequently those of birds, and occasionally those of fish, were found with the burials in contexts suggesting funeral feasts or offerings of food. The most remarkable of these finds are those recorded in detail from the recently excavated stalled cairns, as for instance the bones representing more than fourteen red deer at the Knowe of Ramsay, one of great size and with the bones split for marrow and charred, or the remains of thirty-six animals of the same species at the Knowe of Yarso. At the stalled cairn on the Holm of Papa Westray (R.C.A.M.(S), 1946, no. 545) at least twelve pairs of red-deer antlers were found. The wild animals from these tombs have been discussed in their general ecological setting in Chapter 1 but it is interesting to see the part played by hunting in the lives of the tomb-builders, while the bones of water-birds (and one egg-shell), and those of fish, show that fowling and fishing were among their activities. The massive red-deer remains, if strictly local, would imply wooded conditions in the now almost treeless Orkneys, but the horse bones from five sites in Caithness and one in Orkney (Unstan) suggest more open conditions. The venison and antlers may have been imported from the Scottish mainland.

In addition to wild animals, domestic species of ox, sheep or goat, pig and dog have been recorded from the Caithness and Orkney tombs, and most presumably these must have been imported at the time of colonization. Some curious ritual, perhaps connected with hunting ceremonies, is suggested by the carefully deposited dog skulls in two tombs—seven at Burray and no less than twenty-four in the Maes Howe type tomb on Cuween Hill.

MATERIAL EQUIPMENT

Pottery

Although there are records of the finding of pottery in at least fourteen or fifteen tombs in the Orkney-Cromarty province, little survives except that from the more recent excavations in Orkney, and a few finds from earlier excavations there and in Caithness. The disappearance of the 'extremely numerous' sherds from Ormiegill (Anderson, 1868) or those from Garrywhin, where 'an immense number of flint chips, and fragments of pottery' were found (*ibid.*) is the more to be regretted since it reduces the available pottery from the Yarrows type of tomb to the small fragments from the Knowe of Lairo, though it was found in the sites mentioned, and in one of the Yarrows cairns. Such descriptions as exist, however, are consistent in referring to sherds of thin hard dark ware, belonging to round-based pots with sparse ornament incised or made with the finger-nail or more usually with none at all, and this would agree with the Lairo sherds. While it is dangerous to argue from rather imprecise descriptions of pottery now lost, it does seem reasonable to assume that the type i tombs were characterized by some form of simple Western Neolithic ware, with some decorated sherds perhaps related to the Unstan ware described below.

The bulk of the surviving pottery, however, all from Orkney sites of Camster derivative type except that from Kenny's Cairn in Caithness, can best be classed as *Unstan ware* from the thirty or so vessels found in that tomb. Two main forms can be distinguished, the first consisting of plain unornamented round-bottomed bowls, straight sided or incurved and with simple undeveloped rims (Fig. 40, nos. 4, 5), or bowls in which a carinated form is produced by an applied fillet or cordon. Lugs do not appear.

The second, and more characteristic form, is that of a shallow open bowl with a vertical collar which is usually ornamented, either in channelled or in stab-and-drag technique, in oblique or horizontal lines, or combinations of both (including panels of alternating horizontal and vertical strokes), and, most distinctively, in a zone of hatched triangles (Fig. 40, nos. 1–3). The affinities of this pottery are quite clearly with that of the Hebrides, especially the products of the Eilean an Tighe potters' workshop. A bowl from Midhowe, ornamented in channelled technique, is extremely close to Eilean an Tighe forms, as is another from Unstan, and a bowl from the Sandyhill Smithy tomb, hemispherical and with a bevelled rim, has oblique shallow strokes again in a typically Hebridean fashion. In fact, so striking were the similarities that an investigation of the petrological content of the grit used in tempering the clay was made with a series of Hebridean and Orcadian sherds, with a view to determining whether actual pots were exported from North Uist to the Orkneys, but the results showed that all vessels in both areas were of local clay (Scott & Phemister, 1942). Nevertheless, some quite close contacts must have existed, or an actual migration of pot-makers may be involved.

The distribution of Unstan ware as at present known is almost confined to the Orkneys. The sherds from Kenny's Cairn in Caithness seem likely to be variants within this group, but the finger-nail rustication on some sherds may denote Secondary Neolithic contacts, and from Anderson's description those from Camster Round may also be included (Anderson,

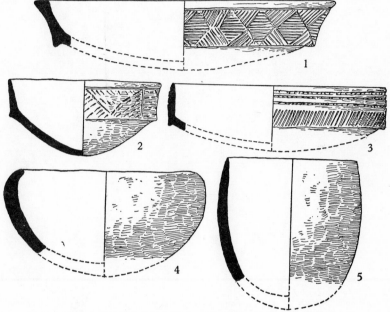

Fig. 40. Orkney chambered tombs: pottery. 1, 4, 5, Unstan; 2, Taversoe Tuack; 3, Midhowe. Scale ¼.

1866, 450). But the chance finds of isolated sherds at Skitten, Caithness, and even as far south as Urquhart, Elgin, suggest that its range may be much wider (Stevenson, 1946). It seems unlikely that the characteristic decorated forms at least can have been present in the lost groups from the type i tombs, since they would immediately call for comment, and no pottery of any kind is reported from the type iii cairns. We can therefore regard Unstan ware as distinctively Orcadian, and likely to be associated with the builders of the type ii tombs and their derivatives. Its Hebridean features point to contacts by the western sea-routes, but the stab-and-drag techniques are alien to the Western Neolithic traditions and, as in Loughcrew ware, suggest Secondary Neolithic contacts.

In one, and possibly in two tombs, Beaker pottery was found in primary contexts—that is, it was associated with burials made in the normal collective tomb manner, and not as secondary interments. At the 'short horned' cairn of Lower Dounreay sherds of a cord-ornamented beaker of class *B* were found associated with plain dark Neolithic sherds with primary interments, while later burials in an inserted cist had *A*- or *C*-beaker sherds with them (Edwards, 1929). In the similar cairn of Acaidh in Sutherland was a single sherd of what is probably a beaker of uncertain type (Curle, 1910).

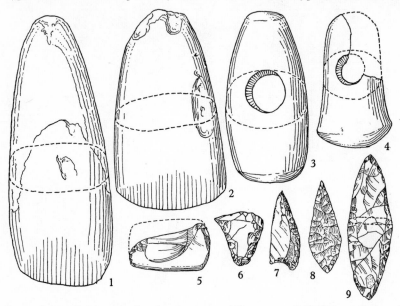

Fig. 41. Orkney-Cromarty chambered tombs: stone and flint types. 1, Calf of Eday; 2, Knowe of Lairo; 3, 7, Ormiegill; 4, Taversoe Tuack; 5, 8, Unstan; 6, Camster; 9, Midhowe. Scale ½.

Material equipment in flint and stone

Axes of stone, wholly or partially ground, come from the Knowe of Lairo, Huntersquoy, Blackhammer, two Camster derivative cairns of the Calf of Eday (one producing two axes), and from Lower Dounreay. These are small tools, ranging from 6½ to 3 in. in length, all with flattened oval cross-section and moderately pointed butts, and all appear to be of local stone, and are similar to those from Skara Brae (Fig. 41, nos. 1, 2). No flint axes are known.

Perforated mace-heads are known from Ormiegill in Caithness and Taversoe Tuack in Orkney (Fig. 41, nos. 3, 4). The first is pestle-shaped and nearly circular in section, and the second subcylindrical and somewhat flatter. Both have straight circular perforations. The Tormore mace-head from a Clyde-Carlingford tomb in Arran is comparable with that from

Ormiegill, and the Taversoe Tuack example suggests the prototypes that should lie behind the Boyne culture mace-head pendants. As we shall see, perforated mace-heads are typical of the Secondary Neolithic cultures.

Shaft-hole battle-axe. At Breckigo near Yarrows Anderson described 'a chambered cairn, which seems to have been of large size, long, and possibly horned', which had been destroyed (1868, 501). From it was recovered a stone shaft-hole battle-axe, of a type well-known from Early Bronze Age single-grave burials in England (R. A. Smith, 1926), and a stone cup (below, p. 252). While it is possible to regard either or both these finds as representing secondary burials, they may equally well be primary deposits in the chamber. A similar battle-axe came from the Seskilgreen grave in Ireland, the stones of which were decorated in the Boyne-culture art-style.

Spiked stone objects. From the Maes Howe derivative tomb of Quoyness came two carved stone objects of unknown purpose but closely comparable with similar objects from Skara Brae discussed in Chapter xi. One is a three-spiked object probably hafted as some form of ceremonial mace-head (Fig. 53, no. 2), and the other a cylindrical stone deeply notched at the ends to form two pairs of spikes. Both are of local flagstone.

Arrowheads: leaf-shaped. Leaf-arrowheads of flint are recorded from Garrywhin (three), Taversoe Tuack (two), the Knowe of Yarso (two), Calf of Eday (two) and Unstan (four) (Fig. 41, no. 8). These last are the finest, most of the others being small 'turnip'-shaped specimens. One of the Calf of Eday arrowheads has been made from a fragment of a polished knife.

Arrowheads: petit-tranchet derivatives. Of these arrowheads, first defined by Clark (1935a) and now recognized as typical of the Secondary Neolithic cultures, one comes from Camster Round (Clark's type Ci), and three from Ormiegill (types D, G and I) (Fig. 41, nos. 6, 7).

Arrowheads: barbed-and-tanged. In the primary deposits of the Yarso stalled cairn, together with two leaf-arrowheads and a number of other flint implements, were two small tanged arrowheads, one with distinct and the other with rudimentary barbs. At Unstan, a barbed-and-tanged arrowhead was found in the blocking of the passage, and so could be interpreted as belonging to the final period of use of the tomb.

Knives: plano-convex. Small knives of the plano-convex type were found in the Yarso, Midhowe and Blackhammer stalled cairns of the Camster derivative group (Fig. 41, no. 9). They may be compared to others already described in Clyde-Carlingford tombs, and are known in the Secondary Neolithic cultures.

Knives: with polished edges. Knives of this type, known from Rinyo and Skara Brae, come from Unstan (Fig. 41, no. 5), Ormiegill and Camster Round—in the two latter instances significantly associated with *petit-tranchet* derivative arrowheads—and a leaf-arrowhead at Calf of Eday was made from a fragment of such a knife. It will be remembered that a polished-edge knife was found at Tormore with a mace-head comparable to that from Ormiegill.

Miscellaneous stone objects. At Unstan was found a flaked flint rod of the *fabricator* type, known from the Secondary Neolithic cultures of England and perhaps also represented at Rinyo (Childe, 1939, fig. 8, no. 12). Several *scrapers* and flint flakes were found at Yarso, Unstan, Blackhammer and the Calf of Eday.

In the Camster type tomb at Kinbrace Burn, Sutherland, a 'pierced heart-shaped amulet of polished serpentine' was found, formerly in the Duke of Sutherland's collection at Dunrobin Castle but not now traceable (R.C.A.M.(S), 1911 *a*, no. 372), and in the long cairn at Breckigo, Yarrows, a curious fluted *stone cup* with decorated base was said to have been found with the stone battle-axe mentioned above (Anderson, 1870, 502, fig. 7). The Kinbrace Burn 'amulet' sounds like an axe-amulet of Breton type, and the Breckigo cup looks like a stone version of a Bronze Age 'incense-cup'.

Material equipment in bone and antler

Comparatively few bone or antler objects come from the Orkney-Cromarty tombs. At Lower Dounreay was an *ox phalange* with a cylindrical bored perforation. Similar perforated phalanges are known in Maglemose contexts (Clark, 1936 *a*, 111) and occurred at Jarlshof (p. 364), and at Lindø in a Passage-grave period settlement (Winther, 1926, 45). From Kenny's Cairn came a bone '*chisel*' of typical Rinyo-Skara Brae type. Five *pointed bone tools* from Yarso are comparable with the B 3 type at Skara Brae and all may be pressure-flakers comparable with the antler tines from the flint-mines referred to above in Chapter III. Their association at Yarso with a large number of flint implements and flakes may be significant. Finally, the Quoyness tomb produced a large *pin*, 7 in. long (Fig. 55, no. 3) with a lateral bulb, a peculiarly Skara Brae type and associated at Quoyness with the equally characteristic spiked stone objects described above.

CEREALS

Evidence of cereals is provided by an impression of a grain of hulled barley (*Hordeum* sp.) on a sherd from Unstan and another of naked barley on one from Eday (Jessen & Helbaek, 1944).

RE-USE OF TOMBS IN THE EARLY BRONZE AGE

In at least three sites evidence of inserted burials of Early Bronze Age type has been recorded. At Lower Dounreay, a secondary inhumation cist had been contrived in the chamber, and the associated scraps of beaker seem to be of type *A* or *C* (*B*-type sherds were found with the primary interments in the same tomb). In one of the Yarrows long cairns was found a similar secondary cist built in an angle of the chamber, containing a necklace of minute lignite disc-beads and 'an urn, apparently about 6 or 7 in. high . . . an everted rim and . . . ornamented by parallel bands of twisted thong pattern', almost certainly a cord-ornamented B-type beaker (Anderson, 1868, 497). At Taversoe Tuack, 9–12 in. above the floor of the passage leading to the upper chamber, was a deposit of disc-beads similar to those from Yarrows, with a small pumice pendant, and presumably also of the Beaker culture.

These examples show that, whatever the absolute chronological status of beakers in Caithness and Orkney may be, the Yarrows long cairn and the Camster derivative of Taversoe Tuack were constructed before the local arrival of beaker-makers, and that at Lower Dounreay pottery of Beaker type was being used by those burying in the 'short horned' tomb there in the traditional manner, as well as by subsequent cist-builders. The B-beaker sherds at Cairnholy in the Clyde-Carlingford group show a similar state of affairs.

THE QUESTION OF THE MAES HOWE 'TREASURE'

As is well known, the Maes Howe tomb was broken into through the corbelled vault by Vikings in the 1150's, who left records of their depredations in a series of Runic inscriptions on the walls of the chamber (R.C.A.M.(S), 1946, 309–13; Dickins, 1930). Viking legends were persistent in attributing hoards of treasure to all ancient mounds, and 'howe-breaking' was a recognized relaxation from the more strenuous occupation of piracy, with a similar hope of reward. Whether in fact any precious metal was recovered by the majority of these operations is unknown, but at Maes Howe the inscriptions that deal with the treasure are remarkably categorical, the relevant statements (in Bruce Dickins's translation) running thus

> It is true what I say, that treasure was carried off in the course of three nights.
> Treasure was carried off before those Crusaders broke into the howe.   (xiii-xiv)
>
> Away to the north-west is a great treasure hidden.   (xix)
>
> A long time ago was a great treasure hidden here.
> Lucky will he be who can find the great fortune.
> Hákon single-handed bore treasure from this howe.   (xx)

While it is of course possible to dismiss these as wishful thinking or as localized fantasies based on a long-standing and widespread folk-tale, nevertheless the possibility of the original grave-goods in the great Maes Howe chamber including a proportion of gold objects cannot be summarily dismissed. The older conception of the chambered tombs as the product of strictly 'Neolithic' communities, in contact only with similarly stone-using cultures, rendered this hard doctrine in the past, but with the recognition of the probable contemporaneity of many such tombs with metal-using communities elsewhere in Britain, the possibility that the architectural magnificence of Maes Howe was reflected in equally splendid grave-goods must be admitted. Gold was buried with the cremated body in the cist-grave beneath a cairn at the Knowes of Trotty, not far from Maes Howe, and we shall see there is reason for regarding the two tombs as not far removed in time from one another.

The architectural features of the tombs in the Orkney-Cromarty group show three main strains. The long cairns with crescentic façades of the Yarrows type have external features which can only be paralleled in the Clyde-Carlingford series, though they cover burial chambers of forms alien to that group and belonging to the local Camster type of passage-grave within a round cairn. Whether the features in question imply affinities with or derivation from the Clyde-Carlingford culture, or whether they represent a parallel colonization from a common Continental stock cannot be resolved, but if the connexion is with Clyde-Carlingford, it is unlikely to have reached Caithness via settlements in the Hebrides. As we have seen, there is a choice of two routes, an eastern and a western, by which the builders of the Yarrows cairns could have reached the north.

The Camster type of passage-grave is unlikely, in view of its lack of cruciform planning, to have derived from the Boyne culture in its mature form, and on the whole it seems more reasonable to suppose it to be again the product of an allied group of colonists, probably from west France or Iberia, who made their way up the Great Glen route and thence to the northeast coast. In view of the complementary distribution of the Camster type tombs in Easter Ross, and the Clava tombs of the Nairn region, it seems likely that the two areas were settled at different times, the later arrivals finding one side only of the Moray Firth available for colonization, but without excavation it is impossible to attribute priority to either group.

The Maes Howe group of tombs in the Orkneys, however, may, in view of their cruciform planning, have some relationship to the Boyne tombs of type ii and to such Continental sites as La Hougue Bie in Jersey, but derivation from Ireland is on the whole unlikely. The Ibero-Hibernian art motifs at the Holm of Papa Westray and from Eday are important indications as to the affiliations of these tombs, and the rock-cut tomb of the Dwarfie Stane again might be regarded as a fairly direct link with Iberia; the western sea-routes seem the obvious line of approach for colonists with such traditions.

But on the other hand Maes Howe itself, and the now ruined tomb of the Ring of Bookan, both have a feature virtually unknown elsewhere in association with chambered tombs, and that is a large encircling ditch.[1] Such ditches are specifically products of soft subsoils, and would be impossible to dig in most areas of settlement of chambered-tomb builders in western Europe, and in Orkney it is impossible to dissociate them altogether from that of the Boyne-culture tomb of Bryn Celli Ddu (p. 196), and from the encircling ditches of the 'Henge monuments' of the Ring of Brodgar and the Stones of Stenness, which lie between Maes Howe and Bookan. And these in turn suggest relationship with the 'disc barrows' of the same restricted area (Bookan and Vola—R.C.A.M.(S), 1946, nos. 709 and 889), which are suspiciously similar to those of Wessex; the amber space-plate necklace found with the gold discs in the Knowes of Trotty is itself specifically of Wessex type, and the barrow in which it was found stands on a platform in a manner very reminiscent of Wessex bell-barrows. Without going so far as to describe either Maes Howe or the Ring of Bookan as a bell-barrow there may nevertheless be an underlying element of organic connexion in formal planning between the Orkney and the Wessex tombs, first hinted at by Hemp (1934, 413).

The evidence of the grave-goods from the tombs shows, in Unstan ware, unambiguous contacts between the Orkneys and the Hebrides, at a stage relatively late in the local development of pottery styles in the latter area, and the stab-and-drag technique may be connected with the similar methods employed in decorating some of the Loughcrew ware vessels in the Boyne culture. We have seen that there is a possibility that some of the tombs, the Yarrows type among them, may have contained plain dark pottery which need not be of the Unstan group, and it is conceivable that this ware (now lost) might be related to the type of bowl known from Easterton of Roseisle, Burghead, on the south side of the Moray Firth, which has affinities with the Yorkshire Neolithic bowls of Windmill Hill derivation. (See below, Chapter ix.)

The most interesting points of contact, however, are between the chambered tombs and various characteristic elements of the Secondary Neolithic group of cultures. No Rinyo ware actually occurs in the tombs, but in the Maes Howe derivative site of Quoyness were two spiked stone objects and a bone pin of types peculiar to Skara Brae, thus establishing approximate contemporaneity between tomb and settlement. The perforated stone mace-heads from Ormiegill and Taversoe Tuack (and perhaps the bone object from Lower Dounreay) are paralleled in a late phase of Rinyo and unstratified at Skara Brae, and these are types associated elsewhere (for instance in Yorkshire and Derbyshire) with flint implements of the Secondary Neolithic 'light industry' such as polished-edge knives and *petit-tranchet* derivatives which themselves occur in Ormiegill, Camster Round and

---

[1] A ditch has been reported as surrounding the Achnacree tomb (R. Angus Smith, 1872), but it appears to be a natural feature (Mitchell, 1933).

Unstan. The perforated mace-head and polished-edge knife from the Tormore tomb in the Clyde-Carlingford province must indicate a settler from the Orkney-Cromarty region in Arran, his approach having presumably been down the Great Glen, and the group establishes a chronological overlap between the two cultures at some point in their duration. Similar polished-edge knives have been found, as we shall see in Chapter x, associated with Peterborough pottery in Wales and Yorkshire, in the latter instance with fragments of axes from both the Great Langdale and the Graig Lwyd factories, so that the Ormiegill-Camster-Unstan series of tomb groups should fall into the general period of the use of these factories, and in eastern Scotland be contemporary with the cremation-cemetery of Period I at Cairnpapple Hill, where similar axe fragments and Rinyo type pins serve to clinch the argument.

The presence of these stone and bone types in the Orkney-Cromarty chambered tombs can only indicate the adoption by certain of the tomb-builders of elements in a culture already existing in the region, since the distribution of the Secondary Neolithic types in question (mace-heads, polished-edge knives and *petit-tranchet* derivatives) is far wider in eastern and southern England than any form of chambered tomb. With these elements is likely to go the cremation rite, which is characteristic of the Dorchester and Ronaldsway cultures but generally speaking foreign to the collective-tomb builders. The Boyne culture seems to show a similar adoption of a local pottery style (Loughcrew ware, derived from Beacharra C) and perhaps here too the cremation rite was indigenous, while in Denmark the adoption of a local Neolithic culture by the makers of the passage-graves is very clearly seen.

The chronological position of the Secondary Neolithic cultures is discussed in Chapters x and xi, and some part of their duration must overlap with the use of copper and bronze by other communities in Britain. The persistence of a 'Neolithic' economy is likely to have been more pronounced in the Orkney-Cromarty region than, say, in Wessex, where trade contacts with the European continent were easier to establish and maintain, and the Orkney-Cromarty chambered tombs must in part at least be contemporary with the earlier Bronze Age of southern England, though on the whole dating from before the local arrival of beaker-makers in the extreme north. If the Breckigo battle-axe be accepted as primary in a chambered cairn of Yarrows type, such an overlap would indeed be demonstrated, for the axe is of a type known from single-grave burial with *A*-beakers and food-vessels. The similar axe from Seskilgreen (above, p. 211) would strengthen the case for the broad contemporaneity of the Orkney-Cromarty tombs with those of the Boyne culture.

CHAPTER IX

MISCELLANEOUS CHAMBERED-TOMB GROUPS AND OTHER RELATED SITES IN THE BRITISH ISLES

INTRODUCTION

FOLLOWING the detailed discussion, in Chapters v–viii, of those regional groups of chambered tombs where there is a sufficient amount of evidence from excavation to relate tombs and grave-goods as expressions of a characteristic culture, it is necessary to review, in less detail, various regions where chambered tombs occur but have largely to be considered as architectural phenomena unrelated to the other elements of material culture of their builders. In Scotland, the Clava and the Shetland groups are here described, while for England and Wales, Daniel's survey (1950) provides a fully documented account of the relevant material, which is therefore considered here in outline only. Of his nine regional groups of chambered tombs (Daniel, 1950, 52), his group I (Anglesey) has largely been dealt with under the Boyne culture in Chapter vii; his group 3 (Severn-Cotswold) in Chapter v; his groups 5 (Manx) and 7 (Gwynedd) mainly under the Clyde-Carlingford culture in Chapter vi. There remain for consideration in the present chapter his groups 2 (Scilly), 4 (Medway), and 6, 8 and 9, subdivisions of his Irish Sea group. Since Daniel has concentrated on the tomb architecture, attention here is more or less confined to excavated tombs, and in addition there is a brief discussion of the problems presented by the long cairns (with or without visible traces of chambers) of north Britain.

Outside the chambered-tomb groups, the opportunity is taken of including in this rather miscellaneous chapter certain habitation sites and burials in the British Isles which merit inclusion in any discussion of the cultures of Western Neolithic derivation, even if their precise place among these cultures cannot at the moment be evaluated. Much of this chapter is necessarily provisional to a degree beyond even the tentative nature of the whole book, and in many instances must be a statement of problems rather than an indication of a coherent pattern.

THE CLAVA GROUP OF CHAMBERED TOMBS

At the north-east end of the Great Glen, on the south side of the Moray Firth, is a group of chambered cairns of distinctive type having a distribution mutually exclusive to the southernmost members of the Orkney-Cromarty group of tombs described in Chapter viii. From the finest examples at Balnuaran of Clava, the group has usually been called the Clava Group, and though Childe at one time suggested the less apposite name of the Beauly group (1940), he later reverted to the older nomenclature (1944).[1]

The group as usually defined comprises about thirty cairns in three main regions—six round the Beauly Firth north of the River Ness, sixteen or more (allowing for ruined sites) by the sides of the rivers in Strath Dores and Strath Nairn, and five at least in Strath Spey. There appears to be a small outlying example in Aberdeenshire. But in each of these regions two types of plan can be recognized, only the first being a corbelled passage-grave beneath a circular cairn, and the second a similar cairn enclosing a circular enclosure without any passage approach or entrance, and too large to be roofed over by corbelling or other stone construction. The second type is more numerous (about two-thirds of the total), and certainly appears to be derived from the first, so that we have a very small group of seven or eight passage-graves with their local degenerations. At Clava at least the tombs are near enough to one another to constitute a cemetery, while here and in most other instances the cairns are placed on comparatively low-lying level ground near a river. Apart from the virtually negative results of clearing out the passage and chamber of one ruined site in Strath Spey, and a rather unsatisfactory record of a find in one of the Balnuaran tombs over a century ago, we have only the evidence of the tomb architecture to discuss, though this has points of remarkable interest.

Detailed description: type I (Balnuaran type)

Of these typical passage-graves, a total of seven, with a probability of two others, can be recognized in the group—Cairn Urnan and Corrimony north of the River Ness; Balnuaran N.E. and S.W., Leys, Croftcroy and Kinchyle in Strath Dores and Strath Nairn, and Avielochan East, with probably its intact western neighbour, in Strath Spey (Fig. 42). The cairns have a peristalith of massive boulders and range in diameter from 58 ft. (Balnuaran S.W.) to 40 ft. (Avielochan East), and except at Avielochan, cairns are surrounded by a circle of about eight or twelve free-standing stones ranging in diameter from 100 ft. at Balnuaran S.W. to 66 ft. at Cairn Urnan. In these free-standing circles the stones are usually tall slabs, and there is a tendency for the highest stones to be on the arc facing the entrance to the tomb.

The chambers are set centrally, and are circular, with an average diameter of some 12 ft., and a narrow passage approach; the construction is normally orthostatic at ground level with corbelling above the tops of the uprights. Such corbelling survives to a height of over 8 ft. above the floor of the chamber in the Balnuaran tombs, and the cairn at Corrimony is from 8 to 10 ft. high and covers a corbelled chamber of similar proportions. At

1 Described in Beaton (1882); Jolly (1882); Fraser (1884); Cash (1906; 1910); Childe (1944).

Avielochan massive dry-stone walling without real orthostats seems to have been employed throughout. What appears to be an outlier is the Milduan cairn, on the slope of the Tap o' Noth, Aberdeenshire, which is 25 ft. in diameter, with remains of a circular dry-built chamber about 6 ft. in diameter, with an approach passage some 10 ft. long.[1]

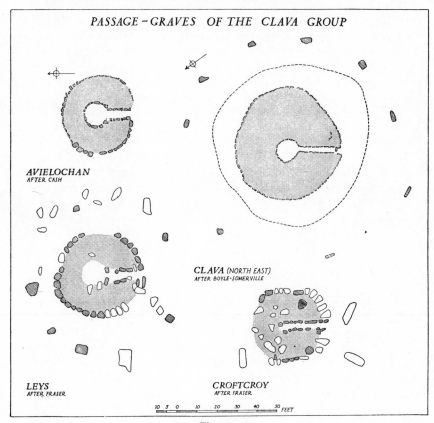

PASSAGE – GRAVES OF THE CLAVA GROUP

AVIELOCHAN
AFTER CASH

CLAVA (NORTH EAST)
AFTER BOYLE-SOMERVILLE

LEYS
AFTER FRASER

CROFTCROY
AFTER FRASER

10 5 0   10   20   30   40   50 FEET

Fig. 42.

Type II (Gask type)

The majority of the cairns in the Clava group (about twenty sites) are of a curious form which is usually considered to derive from the type I passage-graves just described. The free-standing stone circle, enclosing the round cairn with massive peristalith, is still retained, though the size is increased—cairn diameters range from 88 ft. (Gask) to 49 ft. (Daviot), and

[1] Excavated in 1952 by Mr R. J. C. Atkinson. The site had been cleared out in the nineteenth century and no finds survived.

free-standing circles from 126 ft. to 94 ft. in the same two sites. But within the cairn, instead of a chamber and passage, there is a circular area bounded by a kerb of stones averaging some 20 ft. across and clearly never roofed by any method of stone building. It is uncertain whether this inner area was originally completely covered by cairn material, or whether it was a visible feature in a low platform of stones: by inference this area was intended or used for burials, but no recorded excavations have taken place in these type II monuments. At one site (Balnuaran centre) narrow radial cause-ways of cobbles run out from the cairn peristalith to a stone of the enclosing circle at three irregularly distributed points in the circumference.

While a derivation of type II from type I is *a priori* a reasonable hypothesis, one must not exclude the possibility of there being an original dual division in the architectural traditions of the builders of the Clava tombs for, as Daniel has pointed out (1950), our type II monuments do strikingly recall the (apparently unroofed) circular collective graves which G. & V. Leisner (1943) place at the beginnings of their Almerian sequence. In north-east Scotland, however, we can certainly trace a devolution from our type II cairns into the well-known Recumbent Stone circles of Aberdeenshire and Kincardineshire, which within a monumental circle of standing stones retain a cairn with a central circular area containing evidence of cremation burial in the Beaker period or later: the frequent cup-marks on the stones of these circles are, as we shall see, another link with the Clava cairns.

Cup-marks

On the stones of at least nine Clava cairns of both types I and II are artificial 'cup-marks' worked by pecking or pounding the surface. In one or two instances pairs of cups are joined by 'gutters' or short grooves, but there are no 'cup-and-ring' markings. (Jolly, 1882.) Similar cup-marks occur in north-east Scotland on many Recumbent Stone circles (Ritchie, 1918), and on the capstones of two megalithic burial chambers in Wales (Grimes, 1936a).

Finds

Two discoveries of artifacts only are recorded from the Clava tombs. At Avielochan East 'a piece of a jet bracelet, flat on the inside, convex on the outer surface, originally about 2½ in. diameter' was found 'in the passage at about half its depth' (Cash, 1910). At Balnuaran S.W. a deposit was found, apparently in a pit 18 in. deep in the centre of the chamber floor, filled with clay containing cremated bones and two pots, which appear from the surviving illustration (Lauder, 1830) to have been Late Bronze Age vessels of the 'flat-rimmed' class, similar to those from secondary deposits in the Recumbent Stone circles of Old Keig (Childe, 1934c) and Loanhead of Daviot (Kilbride-Jones, 1935). The Avielochan armlet fragments may be compared with a similar object from Old Keig (Childe, 1934 c, 390), and both finds suggest re-use of the tombs at the end of the Bronze Age in a manner similar to the circumstances obtaining in the two Recumbent Stone circles mentioned above. (See also Addendum, p. 275.)

Relationships of the Clava tombs

While constituting an extremely distinctive group, the type I tombs of the Clava series at least fall into place as typical passage-graves of a kind which should be early in the architectural sequence. In the British Isles, the nearest comparable tombs are those of type I in the Boyne culture, such as Tibradden, Co. Dublin, or Cross, Co. Antrim, while at Shantavny Irish, Co. Tyrone, a similar tomb has a cup-marked stone in its passage (E. E. Evans, 1940 a, 247). The free-standing stone circle is of course paralleled at New Grange.

These tombs come within the group of 'primary' passage-graves as defined by Daniel & Powell (1949), and such tombs as Avielochan are strikingly similar to Iberian examples such as those at Los Millares itself, in Portugal at Monge and Barro (Correia, 1921, fig. 58), or in Jersey at La Sergenté (J. Hawkes, 1939 a). Their structural dissimilarity from the remainder of the Scottish chambered tombs, and their complementary distribution *vis-à-vis* the Orkney-Cromarty group, serve to emphasize their individuality, and they must represent settlement on the south side of the Moray Firth made directly from some west French or Iberian source. The line of approach seems most likely to have been up the Great Glen from the Firth of Lorne (though Daniel & Powell (1949) have suggested the possibility of an east-coast landing after a journey up the English Channel). But the Great Glen route is by far the more probable, and it seems not unlikely that with the Clava group of chambered cairns we should link the arrival of the builders of the first passage-graves in Denmark. The earliest copper and bronze objects traded from Ireland to Scandinavia (e.g. halberds and flat axes) seem to have been taken along two main routes in north Britain, of which that up the Great Glen was the more important: there is a marked concentration of halberd finds in the area of the Clava tombs and, as is well known, the distribution-pattern of passage-graves in Denmark is coincident with those of imported axes and halberds. It seems likely that the building of passage-graves and the bronze implement trade in the two regions—the Moray Firth and Denmark—are two events in a continual sequence, and indeed may not be widely separated in time.

If our equation between the cord-ornamented pottery of Beacharra C and that of the early passage-grave period of Denmark holds good, the Clava tombs of type I, if in an ancestral position to the comparable tombs in Denmark, would approximately overlap with the middle or latter part of the Clyde-Carlingford culture. At all events, the complementary distribution of the Clava and the Orkney-Cromarty groups implies a difference in time between the establishment of colonists in the two areas, and the former may well be the earlier.

CHAMBERED TOMBS IN SHETLAND

A curious group of chambered tombs in the Shetland Islands has become known as a result of the work of the Royal Commission on Ancient Monuments for Scotland (Bryce, 1940; R.C.A.M.(S), 1946). With the exception of one ruined site, on Ronas Hill, which may have Orcadian affinities, the remaining fifteen sites are tombs of one type, which, as Bryce pointed out in his initial primary publication of the group, is 'not simply a degenerate Orkney or Caithness monument, but a variety of chamber tomb developed independently in Shetland by people with traditions of their own' (Bryce, 1940, 36).

On account of their characteristic plan, Bryce described these tombs as 'heel-shaped', which aptly indicates the features of shallow curved façade and oval cairn common to the group.

Typology

The tombs are normally of very massive stone construction, with orthostats used only exceptionally for the chambers and passages, as for instance at Mangaster. Their plans, as Bryce recognized, bring them within the passage-grave class, and two main forms can be seen. The first, or *Punds Water type*, consists of a cruciform chamber with passage approach which opens from a slightly concave façade, the remainder of the covering cairn being oval or heel-shaped in plan: other examples are the tombs of Mangaster and Turdale Water, and probably other ruined sites. At Vementry, the chamber and passage is contained within a circular cairn 26 ft. in diameter, set on a heel-shaped platform with a façade 36 ft. overall (Fig. 38): at Punds Water the façade is 50 ft. across, and at Mangaster only 16 ft. All the chambers are ruined, but must have been wholly or partially corbelled.

The second type, represented at *Muckle Heog*, retains the general heel-shaped outline of the cairn, with curved façade, but the chamber with passage approach is absent, and its place is taken by closed cists within the cairn: the façade has become functionless. The cairns on the Hill of Dale and at Gillaburn appear to be of this type, as well as some probable ruined sites.

Burials, etc.

The only evidence comes from one of the Muckle Heog sites, where an unsatisfactory, second-hand account of the middle of the last century reports the finding of human bones and steatite urns, presumably of Bronze

Age type. But this cannot be used with any confidence to indicate primary or secondary burials of this date in the cairn. The ruined structure known as The Benie Hoose, which may have been a chambered cairn of the type under discussion, has yielded an apparently Neolithic sherd of Unstan type as well as later material, but here again no close relationship of finds to structure can be established.

Analogies

While the tombs are themselves without parallels in the British Isles, the cruciform chambers suggest ultimate connexions with Ireland or Orkney, and the curved façade can hardly be entirely dissociated from some sort of relationship with those of the Clyde-Carlingford tombs, or those of the Yarrows group in the Orkney-Cromarty region. In the Mediterranean, both the Balearic navetas and the Maltese sites are in essentials comparable, but such comparisons have probably no more validity than a recognition of the essential unity of the collective-tomb tradition in western Europe where certain ritual elements—chambers, passages, façades, forecourts—recur in various combinations in almost every area colonized by the builders of these tombs.

The Stanydale 'Temple'

A brief note is necessary in connexion with a structure in Shetland related architecturally to the heel-shaped cairns just described, at Stanydale, Sandsting. This remarkable building is oval in plan, with a shallow crescentic forecourt, and the very massive wall encloses an area 40 by 22 ft., with a series of six shallow recesses and a narrow entrance leading out through the curved façade. Two large post-holes containing the carbonized butts of posts at least 10 in. in diameter show that a timber ridge-roof was employed: the posts were of spruce, and carbonized remains of this and pine-wood were found on the floor. Pottery includes large flat-based storage vessels, and probable B-beaker fragments. (Calder, 1951.)

The large size and massive proportions of the building suggested a public building rather than a normal house to the excavator, and in view of the similarity of the plan to that of the chambered cairns of Shetland a religious purpose is surmised. The presence of spruce timbers is extraordinary, and it was calculated that a total of some 2,500 lineal feet of timber would be required to make a reasonable roof, with individual posts and purlins of 20–25 ft. long. Spruce is not recorded as a native tree in Scotland, and driftwood seems the only probable explanation, despite the large quantity and heavy scantling required. The known trends of ocean currents would suggest an origin in North America. (Scott, 1951 a.)

THE SCILLY-TRAMORE GROUP OF CHAMBERED TOMBS

A group of chambered tombs of individual type in the Isles of Scilly and in the extreme west of Cornwall has been recognized for many years, and Hencken (1932) brought the relevant evidence together in a basic study. More recently, an analogous group of tombs of identical type has been distinguished by Powell (1941 *c*) in the Tramore region of southern Ireland, near Waterford. It is therefore convenient to regard the two groups as constituting a *Scilly-Tramore group* of collective tombs, representing colonization of the two sides of the Irish Sea, about 160 miles apart (Daniel & Powell, 1949).

By far the greatest number of these tombs lie in the Scilly Isles, where at least fifty have been recorded: Daniel (1950) considers that only four sites in west Cornwall can justifiably be included in the group, and Powell has listed five in the Tramore area, all within an area of some 9 by 3 miles. Of these sixty or so sites, five have been excavated in Scilly (Hencken, 1932) and two in Tramore (J. Hawkes, 1941; Powell, 1941 *b*).

The great concentration in the Scillies has been the subject of much discussion, and there is some general agreement on the likelihood of the archipelago being, at the time of the building of the tombs, substantially one island about 10 by 7 miles in size, with a coastline approximating to the present 10-fathom line. This point has already been mentioned in Chapter I, but it should be noted here that the alleged submerged field-walls often quoted as a point in favour of comparatively recent subsidence seem in fact more likely to be those of medieval fish-weirs (cf. Goodwin, 1946. with editorial comment *ad fin.*).

Typology

The tombs are very homogeneous in plan, consisting of a circular cairn with massive kerb, averaging 20 to 40 ft. in diameter but with extremes from 75 ft. down to as little as 10 ft. 6 in. The chamber and passage (which have lost any structural distinction), usually tend to occupy more than half the diameter of the cairn. At St Mary's no. 2 the cairn appears to stand on some form of circular platform with its own kerb, and there was material beyond the kerb at Harristown (Fig. 43).

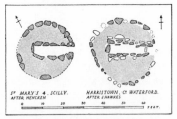

Fig. 43. Tomb plans, Scilly-Tramore group.

The detailed typology has been set out by Daniel (1950, 61–4); the chamber opens direct from the kerb without incurving, and may be parallel-sided, wider at the far end, or coffin-shaped in plan, with massive orthostats and capstones. Daniel regards these plans as derivative from the passage-grave series, and this seems probable, but it should be noted that with the exception of one or two isolated sites such as the White Cairn of Bargrennan in Galloway (Piggott & Powell, 1949) the line of devolution is not represented elsewhere in Britain, though familiar on the Continent. At Carriglong and Gugh no. 1, the entrance was closed by a flat slab.

Burials and funeral ritual

At Carriglong it was found that, after the erection of the orthostats of kerb and chamber, a fire was made on the old surface in the eastern angle of these structures, burning the faces of the stones and obviously preceding the building of the cairn. At this site too, scattered charcoal was noted on the floor of the chamber, and this was also the case at Harristown, where it was interpreted by the excavator as being probably the result of strewing burning branches on the floor, perhaps as a ritual purification.

The burials were by cremation in the two Tramore and two Scilly sites where the rite was recorded, but in one of these (Gugh 1) there were two layers of burial deposits, the lower with unburnt bones and the upper with cremations (Hencken, 1933). Pottery was found in fragments (Carriglong, St Mary's 1 and 2), or as complete pots (Gugh 1, covering cremations, St Mary's 1). At Gugh 1 and St Mary's 2, sherds of pots were found outside the entrance to the tomb.

Material equipment: pottery

It should be said straight away that, with the possible exception of a single sherd from St Mary's 2, none of the pottery from the Scilly-Tramore tombs belongs or is related to any group of Neolithic wares of the British Isles, nor of west France-Iberia. The sherds from Carriglong seem certainly to be those of food-vessels, while the Scillonian material, from St Mary's 1 and 2, Gugh 1 and Knackyboy, seems to be of Middle or even Late Bronze Age date. The commonest forms are biconical flat-based pots, sometimes with lugs or handles, with cord or coarse hyphenated ornament, and as Hencken pointed out (1932, 21) their affinities lie with Cornish cinerary urns of the Bronze Age—in fact they would all come within Miss Patchett's groups B–F, and even G, covering the west English Middle and Late Bronze Age (Patchett, 1946). Pots identical with those from the Scilly chambered tombs (and perhaps themselves from such a tomb) were found on the island of St Martin with a bronze dagger. A single sherd (now lost) from St Mary's 2 has been taken to be a fragment of a round-based bowl of Western Neolithic type, but it stands alone.

Bone

The only bone objects recorded are the points from Gugh 1, which have no useful parallels.

K

Stone

At Harristown a small perforated stone plaque was found, either a pendant or possibly a whetstone, and flint scrapers were found at Carriglong. Built into the flooring of a Scilly tomb, Samson 5, was the rider of a saddle-quern (Hencken, 1933): it is of the long oval form associated with true saddle-querns, and not the rounded shape of the grain-rubbers which, as Curwen has noted (1937 b), are characteristic of such English Neolithic sites as the causewayed camps (cf. above, p. 89). It may be compared with the lower stone of a saddle-quern found structurally embedded in the chambered tomb of La Hougue Bie in Jersey (Rybot, Nicolle *et al.* 1925).

Bronze

Associated with cremated burials at Gugh 1 was a small fragment of bronze, probably a rectangular-section awl. It was found on analysis to have a very low tin content (Hencken, 1933).

Faience and glass beads

Nine beads were obtained from recent excavations in the Knackyboy cairn, one of faience and eight of glass. The faience bead is a worn specimen of the 'star' type with a reddish core and blue glaze, known in Middle or even Late Bronze Age contexts in Britain (Beck & Stone, 1936). The glass beads may best be compared with those in Scottish Late Bronze Age hoards of the middle of the first millennium B.C., and the glass bead from Loughcrew should also be noted (p. 207).

Conclusions and relationships

The virtual identity of tomb-plan in the two areas justifies us in regarding the Tramore and the Scilly-west Cornish groups as representing parallel colonizing enterprises made by people of common origin at the southern end of the Irish Sea approaches. For the origin of the type, Hencken looked to Brittany, and this has been followed in more detail by Daniel (1950, 148–9), though Mrs Hawkes (1941) has pointed out the very comparable tombs in Catalonia at such sites as Puig Roig or Cova d'en Daina (Pericot, 1950, 41–3).

Whatever the precise origins, the Scilly-Tramore tombs must fall very late in the British series. One cannot dismiss all the grave-goods as secondary or intrusive, and it is improbable that no primary objects comparable with those from one or another group of British chambered tombs should have survived. As we have seen, the Scillonian pottery must be related to that of the latter part of the Cornish Bronze Age, and the glass and faience beads emphasize this dating within the second half of the second millennium B.C. With such a date the Carriglong sherds with false-relief would agree. If the Cornish sites of Carn Gluze and Tregaseal were to be included as relatives at least of the

Scilly group, this dating would be strengthened, for Carn Gluze produced sherds of actual Cornish Middle Bronze Age handled urns, and a complete bucket-shaped pot of Late Bronze Age type (Hencken, 1932, pl. vi, no. 7; cf. Patchett, 1946). And the Tregaseal chambered cairn, with its cremation with a whetstone, is difficult to dissociate from the Breton 'dagger-graves' of similar construction and contents (Piggott, 1938), themselves not likely to be earlier than the middle of the second millennium B.C.

THE DERBYSHIRE GROUP OF CHAMBERED TOMBS

A group of tombs on the Derbyshire moors comprise some curious structures, and not all are included by Daniel in his catalogue of chambered tombs (Daniel, 1950, 83–6). The site of Ringham Low, near Monyash (Bateman, 1848, 103; 1861, 93) seems, if Bateman's schematic plan can be trusted, to have been a long cairn about 160 ft. long, oriented north and south and with the southern end wider and suggesting in the published plan the possibility of at least vestigial 'horns' or a crescentic façade of some kind. Within the cairn were found five chambers which were either closed megalithic cists or, at least in the structures numbered 2 and 3 by Bateman, open-ended galleries with apparently septal slabs. Some of the chambers were paved, others not, and all yielded human bones—no. 1 contained bones of ten adults and two children with dolichocephalic skulls, bones of ox, horse and dog, and three leaf-arrowheads. Two more arrowheads were found in another chamber with two skeletons (arrowheads illustrated in Smith, 1927, fig. 10), and a bone pin was found with four skeletons in another chamber. The whole arrangement of chambers in the long cairn suggests a degenerate cairn of the type of Dranandrow in Kirkcudbright (Edwards, 1923), The Caves of Kilhern at New Luce in Wigtownshire or Cuff Hill, Ayrshire (p. 159), though Phillips (1933b) would regard the elongated form of the cairn as the result of successive accumulations round an original round cairn with chamber.

A much-ruined site at Harborough Rocks near Brassington was excavated by John Ward at the end of the last century (Ward, 1890; Daniel, 1950, 183). The chamber here was little more than a paved area at the small end of a funnel-shaped stone setting which seems to preserve the memory of a forecourt comparable with that of Bryn yr Hen Bobl or even of Garn Turne: the cairn originally enclosing it was probably round and the whole site may be susceptible of derivation from the chambered round cairns of passage-grave type within the Boyne culture or its extensions in Anglesey. At least sixteen dolichocephalic individuals were represented at Harborough Rocks, associated with broken leaf-shaped arrowheads.

The chambered tomb at Five Wells near Taddington, also excavated by Ward (1901; Daniel, 1950, 85) should certainly be classed with the monuments of passage-grave derivation on account of its circular cairn and chambers with passage approach. The cairn was found to have a very well built dry-stone wall around its base, forming a rough circle some 50 ft. in diameter, and breaking this wall at two diametrically opposite points were the passages leading to a pair of paved chambers which occupied the central part of the cairn with only 5 ft. between their back walls. Bateman had dug into this cairn in the last century and had found bones representing more than twelve individuals and a 'flint arrow-point' (Bateman, 1848, 91), and Ward recovered from the debris in the chambers and passages the point of a leaf-arrowhead, a plano-convex flint knife, and two sherds of pottery one of which may be Peterborough ware or Food-vessel to judge from the description of a now lost sherd, and the other, also lost, seems very likely to be from a thin-lipped bowl of Grimston ware or some allied fabric within the Western Neolithic ceramic group. A barbed-and-tanged flint arrowhead was found in the surface material of the cairn, and a secondary cist with a crouched burial was found to have been built against the retaining wall of the cairn at one point.

A close parallel for this tomb seems to be the similarly double-chambered cairn at The Water of Deugh, Kirkcudbright (Curle, 1930), though the principle of chambers backing on to one another is of course implicit in the long-cairn series where pairs of lateral chambers are similarly placed along the cairn (Dranandrow, already cited, is a good example of this arrangement). The grave-goods, coming as they do from disturbed material, give us little clue to possible affinities, but the sherd of Peterborough ware or Food-vessel might be taken with the plano-convex knife as indicative of later re-use of the chambers, the leaf-arrowhead and sherd of Western Neolithic pottery being appropriate to the original structure.

The great chambered cairn of Mininglow, Ballidon (Daniel, 1950, 86) must, in its intact condition, have been an impressive monument, but spoliation beginning with the Romans and culminating with Bateman's diggings in the last century have sadly wrecked the site. Phillips (1933b) has presented a synthesis based on Bateman's accounts and his own personal observations: the cairn is not less than 120 ft. in diameter, and was enclosed by a circular wall in the manner of Five Wells and contained at least two chambers approached by passages leading in from the periphery. Remains of these two chambers are still identifiable together with three closed cists of large stones with massive capstones. The chambers, to judge from Ward's plans, are comparable in plan with those in the Five Wells cairn but appear to have sills or septals across the entrances.

The remaining Derbyshire tombs which can claim inclusion in the megalithic series are the ruined chamber of Green Low (Daniel, 1950, 85) and a structure at Long Low, Wetton. The early accounts of the latter are conveniently summarized in Phillips (1933b); a cairn 90 ft. in diameter contained a stone cist built on a megalithic scale in which were the skeletal remains of thirteen individuals and three leaf-arrowheads. To this had been added a dry-built stone structure consisting of a narrow 'ridge' running for 220 yd. south-westwards, where it ended in a smaller cairn which had been built as an integral part of its termination. Cremations were found in the 'ridge' and in the second cairn. Further comment on this 'most eccentric' structure (to use Phillips's phrase) seems hardly possible, though there may be some connexion between the Long Low 'ridge' and the 'terrace' at Bryn yr Hen Bobl.

These Derbyshire chambered tombs seem certainly to be the result of mixed elements of megalithic tradition coming in from the west coast. Some of these elements as we have seen may relate to the gallery-grave architectural complex—chamber plans, and probably the lay-out of the whole monument at Ringham Low—but the circular reveted cairns and the passage approaches at Five Wells and Mininglow suggest the Boyne culture or some allied group.

THE MEDWAY GROUP OF CHAMBERED TOMBS

Of these well-known tombs, centred on the Medway valley in Kent, and described with plans and full references in Daniel (1950), there is little to say. They appear to have had rectangular chambers, and Daniel's suggestion that the remaining stones at Kit's Coty House represent, not a 'false portal' in the Severn-Cotswold manner, but the last remnant of such a squarish chamber, has much to recommend it. Here there were traces of a long mound, and this survives at Addington, with massive orthostats along its edge, and in shorter form at Coldrum, with large slabs now fallen prone similarly placed.

There has been no adequate excavation, but from Coldrum bones representing twenty-two inhumations were recovered, together with a sherd of pottery, probably Western Neolithic. It was noted that the skulls showed family resemblances in the manner of those at Lanhill (p. 141 above).

This group has for long been considered as likely to be of north German or Dutch origin, and the tomb-plans certainly find better parallels in those areas than in Britain. But there is no direct evidence other than this architectural similarity, and unless the untouched site of Addington were to provide material in the form of pottery or other significant grave-goods to substantiate the claim, the problem is likely to remain unresolved.

MISCELLANEOUS CHAMBERED TOMBS IN WALES
AND THE WEST OF ENGLAND

There remain a few sites, documented by Daniel (1950), which have not been considered and which deserve brief mention. For instance, he notes two probable passage-grave sites, now ruined, in Pembrokeshire

(Longhouse and Burton) which may belong to the Boyne group discussed in Chapter VII. Tombs with forecourts in his Gwynedd and Dyfed groups such as Garn Turne, Pentre Ifan and The Grey Mare and her Colts have been dealt with under the outlying colonies of the Clyde-Carlingford culture in Chapter VI, and the same applies to allied tombs such as Pant y Saer, Bryn yr Hen Bobl and Cerrig y Gof.

But his *Penwith group* includes certain important monuments of the class usually called 'Dolmens', notably those of Lanyon and Zennor Quoits, Chun and Pawton, which should be noticed. These, as Hencken (1932) saw, are products of the Gallery-grave traditions of tomb architecture, and are to be related to certain monuments in Eire of the same derivation. At Zennor, an unsatisfactory excavation produced, below a paving in the outer segment of the chamber, sherds of cord-ornamented and plain pottery, and a whetstone similar to that from the Middle Bronze Age tomb of Tregaseal (Patchett, 1946). While these objects, all likely to be of Bronze Age date, might be considered as secondary, the evidence detailed above from Scilly suggests that some at least of the Penwith tombs may also have been constructed while the Middle Bronze Age was flourishing in other parts of England.

In his discussion of chambered long cairns in North Wales Daniel (1950, 86–93, 150) draws attention to such sites as Tyddyn Bleiddyn, Dyffryn and Rhiw, and raises the question of their relationship to the long cairns of the Clyde-Carlingford culture on the one hand (represented in his survey mainly by the Manx sites), and to the Severn-Cotswold cairns on the other. He would prefer to dissociate the Capel Garmon and Maen Pebyll cairns from the Severn-Cotswold group despite their typological resemblances, and group them with the general run of north Welsh long cairns: I have included them as an appendix to Chapter V, but it is possible that they are in fact unconnected with the southern group. However that may be, it raises the whole question of the status of chambered and unchambered long cairns in the Highland Zone of Britain, and following Daniel's Welsh group, one may conveniently consider north British examples.

LONG CAIRNS IN NORTH BRITAIN

There are some fifteen or so long cairns recorded from Yorkshire to Banff-shire which cannot be regarded as related to any group of chambered tombs, save in the sense that there is a generic western European homogeneity. In a few, small chambers or large cists can be seen, but in others there is no trace of such features, or they may be entirely hidden. To this series would belong the cairns of Bradley Moor, W.R., Yorks (Raistrick, 1932; Butter-field, 1939), Samson's Bratfull in Cumberland (Daniel, 1950, 183), and those of the Devil's Lapful and Bellshiel Law in Northumberland (Newbigin,

1936); across the Border those of the Mutiny Stones in Berwickshire (Craw, 1925) and at Kirshope in Roxburghshire, the cairns of Fleuchlarg, Capenoch, Clonfeckle, Stidding and Windy Edge in Dumfriesshire (R.C.A.M.(S), 1920, nos. 47, 249, 329, 351, 415), those at Gourdon in Kincardineshire (Callander, 1924) and at Gamrie, Banffshire (Callander, 1925), and those of Cloghill, Knapperty and Balnagowan, Aberdeenshire (Callander, 1925, 1929; Simpson, 1944).

It is likely that this list is very incomplete, but even in its present tentative form it does suggest an interesting distribution of such cairns, almost entirely complementary to that of the chambered tombs of the Clyde-Carlingford and other north British groups, and in Scotland confined to the Lowlands and the eastern coastal fringes of the Highland massif. The evidence from the excavated sites, Bradley Moor, Bellshiel Law and Mutiny Stones, is wholly inconclusive; at the first site a cist contained an unaccompanied skeleton, at the second an inhumation-grave with a worked flint flake was found within the rough kerb at the wider eastern end, and at the last a stretch of walling was found which could not be interpreted satisfactorily. It seems difficult to associate the Dumfriesshire sites with the Clyde-Carlingford tombs of Galloway, as was done by Childe (1934b), and the north-east Scottish sites are even more remote from any such congeners. One may suggest as a possibility that these long cairns may possibly be the counterparts, in stony country, of the unchambered long barrows of England, extending northwards to Yorkshire and to Raisett Pike in Westmorland, and that their presence in eastern Scotland is to be associated with finds of pottery with Yorkshire affinities such as those from Falkirk and Easterton of Roseisle, Morayshire (Callander, 1929). It has been suggested that the latter find was from a destroyed long cairn, but the evidence is by no means satisfactory (cf. p. 272 below). The East Finnercy (Aberdeenshire) Western Neolithic pottery was from a round cairn of uncertain type (Simpson, 1944, 20).

MISCELLANEOUS SITES IN BRITAIN

There are a few traces of habitation sites in Britain, represented by occupation deposits with sherds and stone implements, which appear to belong to the Western Neolithic culture-group but which cannot be more precisely placed. The occupation-scatter of small sherds and flints including leaf-arrowheads beneath the Iron Age fort at Ffridd Faldwyn, Montgomeryshire comes into this rather vague group (O'Neil, 1942), and this site seems to have some affinities with the Clegyr Boia site in Pembrokeshire, and perhaps also with finds of pottery and stone and flint implements at Gwaenysgor and Dyserth Castle in Flintshire or in the Rhos Ddigre cave in the same county (Glenn, 1914; 1915; 1935). But the Gwaenysgor and

Dyserth sites also contain products of the Graig Lwyd axe-factory, linking them with the site underlying the Bryn yr Hen Bobl cairn in Anglesey (above, p. 180), and with the Secondary Neolithic cultures associated with such axe-factories described below in Chapter x, so discussion of these interesting sites is more conveniently postponed.

In Scotland there are a few east-coast sites with finds of Western Neolithic pottery, stretching from Roslin near Edinburgh (Stevenson, 1950), and Falkirk near the Forth to East Finnercy (Aberdeenshire), Granton-on-Spey, and Easterton of Roseisle (Morayshire) (Callander, 1929; Simpson, 1937; 1944, 20). The Falkirk, Granton and Easterton finds are of fine dark-ware bowls with everted rims and 'finger-tip fluting' in the Yorkshire or Lyles Hill manner; Roslin is a simple bowl and the East Finnercy sherds are round-based, with lugs. At Easterton one sherd had an impression of a grain of naked barley (Jessen & Helbaek, 1944). The affinities of these scattered finds are far from clear, though one might tentatively connect them with the long cairns described on p. 271 above. But in Morayshire it is at present impossible to disentangle the Neolithic strains implicit in the finds from the Urquhart (Elgin) region described below in Chapter VIII, which may include a Western element allied to the Yorkshire culture as well as contacts with Caithness and Orkney perceptible in the finds commented on when discussing the Orkney-Cromarty group of collective tombs.

A curious find from Knappers, near Glasgow, appears to have consisted of a cremated burial with a bowl of simple Western Neolithic type and a flint plano-convex knife (Mackay, 1950), which may be compared with the find from Killaghy, Co. Armagh (Evans, 1940c). Another west-coast site, that at Rothesay, Bute, is described below in Chapter xi, owing to the presence of Rinyo ware in it, but some sherds belong to Western Neolithic traditions.

LOUGH GUR, AND MISCELLANEOUS BURIAL SITES IN IRELAND

Lough Gur

A habitation site of great importance in Ireland is that near the shores of Lough Gur, Co. Limerick, though the full publication of O'Riordain's long campaign of excavation has not yet appeared, and we must rely on summary accounts (O'Riordain, 1946). But the main facts of the Knockadoon sites seem clear: habitations, with houses which are both circular, with walls framed on close-set poles, or rectangular, up to 26 by 18 ft. in dimensions, with stone footings and two interior rows of posts supporting the roof. Above these foundations are accumulated deposits up to 1 m. thick, in which, while there is no precise demarcation of layers, a consistent stratigraphy can nevertheless be observed.

The lowest levels contain sherds of round-based carinated bowls, with slightly thickened or rolled rims, with strong resemblances to the Carn Brea, Clegyr Boia, or Hembury material, though also similar in general appearance to Lyles Hill ware. With this pottery is a certain proportion of club-shaped and ornamented rim forms comparable with those from the 'Sandhill cultures' described below; and from the first, but increasing into the upper levels, are heavy, coarse, flat-based pots with more or less generic similarities to those of the Rinyo-Clacton and Ronaldsway cultures in Britain or the Horgen and S.O.M. groups of the Continent. In the upper layers, too, are sherds of beakers, many of which are of B-class vessels, not infrequently with a cordon below the rim. A perforated stone hammer also comes from this horizon.

In the lower layers are also leaf and lozenge arrowheads and stone axes, and also flat asymmetrical serpentine beads which have good parallels at Lyles Hill.

In considering the chronological horizon of the early Lough Gur finds, it is important to note that the beaker sherds seem on the whole to be of excellent fabric and very comparable to south English vessels—they cannot be considered late and degenerate, and an effective contrast is provided by the beakers from the tombs of the Largantea type described in Chapter VI. Sherds similar to those from Lough Gur were found at Rockbarton Bog, near the Knockadoon site, stratified in peat at a point 'before the end of Zone VI' (Mitchell & O'Riordain, 1942)—i.e. before the end of Zone VII b in Jessen's final classification (Jessen, 1949). The junction of Zones VII a and VII b approximates to the position of the Western Neolithic pottery at Peacock's Farm in the English Fenland and, as we shall see, there is evidence in Northern Ireland for equating some part at least of the Bann culture, and some Sandhill pottery, with a horizon similar to that of the Rockbarton beaker sherds. The beginnings of Lough Gur should therefore lie early in Zone VII b at least.

The affinities of the culture are, however, obscure. The carinated bowls and the serpentine beads might link it with Lyles Hill and the north Irish series of Lyles Hill ware, itself probably to be connected with that of Yorkshire. But it is difficult to assume a spread from a restricted source in Ulster to Limerick and other sites in Eire, for the pottery is known from many scattered sites, including Feltrim Hill and Drimnagh (Co. Dublin); Ballon, Co. Carlow (O'Riordain, 1946); and Kilgreany, Co. Waterford (Movius, 1935). We must be prepared to admit the possibility of a multiple origin for the plain carinated bowls in Ireland and west Britain, with some likelihood of traffic up and down the Irish Sea, possibly from some as yet unidentified Continental source, and the Carn Brea and Clegyr Boia sites in Cornwall and Pembrokeshire respectively are apposite. The occurrence of the coarse flat-based ware, as we shall see in Chapter XI, is to be related to the widespread appearance of such rough ceramics as a part of the slackening of primary Neolithic ceramic traditions and the re-emergence of native elements in the latter part of the period.

Miscellaneous burials in Ireland

It is convenient to group here certain burials, all very imperfectly understood, which have, however, some claims for inclusion in a survey of the Irish Neolithic. The first of these is represented by a very low barrow at Rathjordan, Co. Limerick, about 40 ft. in diameter and within a ditch, excavated by O'Riordain (1947), and found to cover a pit containing a carinated pot of Lough Gur type, two quartz points and a few cremated animal bones. Similar barrows have also been recorded in the same district, but excavation has yielded no certain evidence of date (MacDermott, 1949 a, b).

Two cist-burials recently discovered have produced pots of Neolithic affiliations, at least. At Linkardstown, Co. Carlow, a sub-megalithic polygonal cist, within a clay mound with a kerb of stones, contained an inhumation burial with a stone axe and the sherds of several pots (O'Riordain, 1946). One, which has been restored, is round-based with a hammerhead or bevelled rim and hollow neck, and is decorated with incised ornament comprising zones of 'ladder-pattern' with groups of vertical strokes below on the upper part of the pot, and similar ornament arranged in radial panels on the broad rim. Other sherds of reddish micaceous ware have incised horizontal and diagonal strokes in the Loughcrew-Unstan manner, and one sherd has an arched motif on it; other fragments of red flaky ware have deep stabs and grooves, and are again comparable with some from Carrowkeel and Loughcrew.

At Rath, Co. Wicklow a pot found in a sand-pit is similar in profile to the restored Linkardstown bowl, with parallel lines of fine whipped cord ornament on the rim and incised zones on the body. From a long cist with two compartments in the same pit came a bowl with four lugs and closely set horizontal lines in fine whipped cord technique (real or imitation) and on the round base a quadripartite design within a circle. (O'Riordain, 1946.)

All these pots seem to have some affinities with the Sandhill and Beacharra C wares, or with that of Loughcrew, but their detailed relationship and significance are not easy to assess.

A very remarkable burial at Drimnagh, Co. Dublin, was fortunately excavated and published with exemplary care and with abundant detail by Kilbride-Jones (1939). The sequence was very complex, and is here summarized to the exclusion of many details. A central cist of irregular shape contained a crouched inhumation of an adult male (with a cephalic index of about 78), accompanied by a unique hanging-bowl with four perforations at the shoulder and elaborate decoration by incision and raised ribs forming a cruciform pattern: the vessel is without precise analogies, though there may be Sandhill contacts perceptible. The cist was covered by a small cairn, itself beneath a mound some 72 ft. in diameter and 10 ft. high, consisting of sods and the remains of burnt alder logs, surviving up to 8 ft. long and set radially in such a manner as to suggest that they, with the turf, had originally constituted a conical hut built over the burial and ritually burnt. On the surface of this mound were a couple of sherds of plain (Lyles Hill type) ware, and charred grains of barley were identified. The barrow had later, in the middle or Late Bronze Age, been enlarged with an additional covering mound.

The extraordinary features of the Drimnagh burial merely indicate how inadequate our knowledge of much of the Irish Neolithic still remains. Here one can do no more than record the known facts, in the hope that future work may before long set them in their true perspective and relationship.

Addendum: The Clava Cairns

Since this book has been set up in type, excavations in three cairns of the Clava Group have been carried out by the writer (1952). All were type I (Balnuaran) sites and at Corrimony complete excavation showed that there had been no grave-goods, and a central crouched burial on the floor of the corbelled chamber, under a layer of stone slabs, survived only as stains in the soil. An eroded and burnt bone pin was found at the entrance blocking, and white quartz had been strewn around the kerb. Trial excavations in the areas of the largely destroyed chambers of two other cairns of the same type, at Leys (Fig. 42) and at Kinchyle of Dores, produced only scattered cremated bones in disturbed soil.

CHAPTER X

THE SECONDARY NEOLITHIC CULTURES:
THE FLINT AND STONE INDUSTRIES

INTRODUCTION

THE variant cultures which have been described in Chapters II to IX are all recognizably members of the relatively well-defined group of Western Neolithic cultures, which can be traced on the European continent in Switzerland, France and the Iberian Peninsula in forms which, while differing in detail, can be seen to be closely related among themselves, and also to the British material. Although the latter has marked insular characteristics, nevertheless in recurrent features of tomb architecture, pottery and stone types, and to some degree settlements, the Western cultures can be seen as members of the general family, and in Britain at least can be recognized as representing intrusive agricultural colonies established in areas previously uninhabited, or at most populated by a small number of hunter-fisher groups. Little interchange of traditions between these mutually complementary groups seems to have taken place on the whole, though the Windmill Hill culture seems to contain certain elements derived from hunter-fisher economies either here or on the Continent, and some give-and-take can be seen in such regions as Northern Ireland.

But among the cultures which in Britain can be shown to be distinct from and in some cases to antedate, on the whole, the invasions of the single-grave Beaker folk who in conventional terminology usher in the Bronze Age, is a homogeneous series which is in part contemporary with the Western Neolithic groups already mentioned, but in part can be shown stratigraphically to follow them. The unfamiliarity of the classification which is to be set out in the following pages necessitates some form of introduction to those British Neolithic cultures which are not clearly defined as members of the Western Neolithic group, but which have a distinctive character of their own. In the past certain aspects of these cultures have been recognized, notably the pottery styles represented by Peterborough ware and Grooved ware, but the associated elements such as the stone and bone industries, which unite these and other manifestations into a surprisingly homogeneous group, have not hitherto been defined.

It is proposed to group the cultures in question as *Secondary Neolithic cultures*, for reasons which will emerge as the definition proceeds. They are known largely from chance finds of pottery or stone tools, though some very important settlement sites, burials and ritual monuments are known. They are formally 'Neolithic' cultures in that they show no direct evidence for the knowledge of metals; flint is used abundantly, but there is also an extensive use of stone axes and adzes produced at recognizable factory-sites. These stone tools persist and recur as a continuum throughout the variant cultures which may be distinguished, partly on the grounds of differing pottery types, and it seems likely in fact that such pottery distinctions may be less important than the underlying homogeneity in other elements of material culture. Though there is some overlap in Sussex and Wessex, and again in northern Scotland, between these cultures and those of the Western Neolithic group, the sites tend to have a mutually exclusive distribution— in eastern Britain and in coastal or riverine sites as against the predominantly upland areas favoured by the Western Neolithic colonists.

The essential characteristics which unite this group of cultures are those whose origins lie in the native Mesolithic cultures of northern Europe, and of Britain in particular. The survival of Mesolithic traditions in flint-work has of course long been recognized, and Movius drew attention to certain assemblages of stone types 'the roots of which can be traced directly to Mesolithic antecedents in Northern and Western Europe but...which developed during Neolithic times and persisted in certain regions as long as flint and stone tools were used' (1942, 212). To this assemblage Movius, following French traditional usage, applied the word 'Campignian', and it was in this sense that Clark had already remarked, in connexion with the flint mines, that 'the "Campignian" style of flint-work...persisted as long as flint-axe production itself' (1936, 161).

But the use of the word 'Campignian' has, unfortunately, very serious drawbacks. In French usage and orthodox archaeological teaching, *le Campignien* is a culture chronologically and culturally intermediate between the Mesolithic and the true Neolithic—between *Maglemosien* and *Roben-hausien*—(though the type-site is by no means early in the French Neolithic itself).[1] Movius of course recognized that neither the French nor the British material could properly be interpreted in this way—'whatever else it is, the Campignian is not Late Mesolithic or Proto-Neolithic', he wrote, and re-defined his own use of the word as descriptive of 'a basic substratum or heritage from the Mesolithic which forms an important and highly specialized aspect of those Western European cultures which continued to use flint and stone tools after the introduction of agriculture' (Movius, 1942, 238–9). It seems, however, preferable to drop the ambiguous term 'Campignian', and to use instead the phrase 'Secondary Neolithic' for those cultures which contain this Mesolithic heritage.

In Britain it is possible to relate this stone-working tradition to the group of cultures under discussion, and it is in fact this common tradition which

[1] The Campigny site is approximately parallel with Fort Harrouard I, with decorated Chassey ware and baking-plates of Michelsberg derivation: 'Campignian' tranchet axes and picks are common in Fort Harrouard I and II (Childe, 1931 a, 47; 1947, 296).

forms their uniting substratum. Such cultures may properly be regarded as Secondary Neolithic in the sense that they represent the assimilation of Neolithic elements (presumably including some form of agriculture) by the indigenous hunter-fisher Mesolithic population after the first impact of the intrusive immigrants in the entrance phase of colonization, and also in many instances the cultures can be shown stratigraphically to be later than sites and monuments of the primary Western Neolithic cultures. It is not surprising that the primary Neolithic settlements in a newly colonized region should preserve the intrusive elements in the new culture virtually intact, and that in the course of time there should be a re-emergence of local Mesolithic traditions, forming composite cultures owing something to both old and new ideas.

This is not the place to pursue this matter beyond Britain, but it may be remarked in passing that the concept of Secondary Neolithic cultures of this kind may well prove applicable to parts at least of the European continent, where intrusive agricultural communities established themselves among people with vigorous hunter-fisher traditions. The Scandinavian phenomenon of the persistence of hunter-fisher economies side-by-side with those of the intrusive agriculturalists has long won recognition, but the blending of traditions is not quite parallel to this. We have seen how the Campignian industry appears in a relatively late phase of the North French Neolithic, while the cultures of Seine-Oise-Marne in France, and that of Horgen in Switzerland, again seem to represent the absorption of certain Neolithic traditions by local Mesolithic groups, and the same may be said in part at least of the Michelsberg culture. We shall note in Britain the significant decay of the tradition of fine pottery-making, so characteristic of the earlier Western Neolithic cultures, in the Secondary Neolithic cultures which follow them, with the appearance of coarse flat-based pots and often plastic ornament or surface roughening, at such sites as Rinyo, Lough Gur or Ronaldsway, and the suggested comparisons between pots from these sites and those from the Horgen-S.O.M. cultures may denote nothing but a common degeneration and breakdown of a good early tradition in ceramics —the phenomenon which Sprockhoff in a different context described as that of *kümmerkeramik*—a lowest common denominator of bad, coarse wares (Sprockhoff, 1942, 18). In Britain and in Holland the 'rusticated ware' and that of the 'pot-beakers' may again stand in the same relationship to the fine early Beaker-pottery tradition, as may the south Spanish 'cave pottery' with its encrusted patterns. Such ceramic degeneration need imply no more than the increased use of containers of other materials (e.g. leather or basketry), and it would be wrong to argue any diminution in the vigour or originality of the later Neolithic cultures on these grounds.

In the ensuing section of this book then we shall be dealing with Neolithic cultures which contain elements whose origins lie outside the Western

Neolithic group of cultures, and are on the whole likely to be of indigenous Mesolithic ancestry or form part of the continuum of Circumpolar Stone Age cultures defined by Gjessing (G. Gjessing, 1944). These elements permeate all the variant and regional forms and give them an underlying unity, the differentiation being usually that of a pottery type. This leads to a difficulty in nomenclature: can one define a 'Peterborough culture' from a style of pottery associated with stone types only in a relatively few instances, or from chance finds of sherds, when the stone types all recur in other contexts in the British Secondary Neolithic cultures? It seems logical therefore to deal with the flint and stone industries which form the essential substratum first, and then to examine the evidence for the recognition of individual regional or cultural groups within this general framework.

The material can reasonably be classified as follows:

A. *The stone industries.* These are wider in range and contain more significant types than we can recognize in the Western Neolithic cultures, and may be subdivided into

1. The non-Western types in the products of the flint mines and flint-axe factories already described in Chapter II in their Western Neolithic aspect.

2. A heavy flint industry allied to that from the mines in some respects, with *tranchet* axes and picks. This approximates to the French Campignian flint industries, and is represented in the Cushendun-Glenarm series in Northern Ireland, and by many English surface finds (Fig. 44).

3. A light flint industry which is perhaps integral with no. 2 above, though frequently found distinct from it. It includes such types as the *petit-tranchet* derivative arrowheads, polished knives, probably single-piece sickles, and may include small flake-axes with *tranchet* edges. It is known in surface finds from Dartmoor to the Moray Firth, and from a few settlement and burial sites.

4. The products of axe-factories of igneous rocks with known centres of manufacture in Wales, Westmorland, Northern Ireland, Cornwall, and probably elsewhere.

Of these industries, nos. 3 and 4 interpenetrate the regional or cultural groups almost completely, nos. 1 and 2 not so clearly.

B. *The regional or cultural groups*

1. *The Peterborough culture*, characterized by the well-known type of pottery having affinities with the pit-comb and corded wares of Scandinavia, and stone tools of A3 and A4, and occurring in the Thames valley and southern and eastern England.

2. *The Bann and Sandhill cultures* of Northern Ireland, with local communities of hunter-fishers adopting pottery-making, including cord-ornamented wares having affinities to that of Peterborough.

3. *The Rinyo-Clacton culture.* Defined originally by 'Grooved ware' (Warren *et al.* 1936), the culture has a curious distribution, mainly concentrated in two separate areas, one in south-east England and the other in the Orkneys, though intermediate sites are now being discovered. The stone industry is of A3 and A4, with, in the north, distinctive types

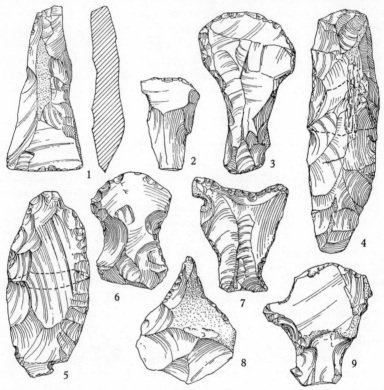

Fig. 44. Secondary Neolithic flint industries in Wessex: 1, 2, 4–8, Stourpaine; 3, 9, King Barrow Ridge (*after Laidler & Young*). Scale ¼.

related to the Circumpolar group, and there are many bone and stone types peculiar to the culture, though with affinities outside. Settlement sites and ritual monuments are known.

4. *The Ronaldsway culture.* Confined to the Isle of Man, with coarse pottery probably derivative from local Western Neolithic of the Beacharra group, and stone tools of A3 type. Settlements and a cremation-cemetery are known.

5. *The Dorchester culture.* There is a residuum of cultures known from south and east Britain with no distinctive pottery but sharing other charac-

teristics, including certain bone and stone types common to A 3 and A 4, and B 1, B 2 and B 3; cremation cemeteries; ritual monuments of Henge type; certain individual burials. The name (from the Dorchester-on-Thames sites) is not altogether satisfactory but may stand pending further clarification of what may be a complex of cultures.

In this chapter the stone industries are described, and in Chapter xi, the regional or cultural groups.

NON-WESTERN ELEMENTS IN THE FLINT-MINE INDUSTRIES

The general features of the flint-axe factories based on mining in the southern English chalk have been described in Chapter ii, where it was shown that the main impetus behind the development of this industry must have been that of the Western Neolithic colonists, for the essential product was the chipped or polished axe of Western ancestry. But it was indicated that other cultural elements were perceptible in the flint mines, and that these could be connected with surviving Mesolithic traditions.

The now extinct controversy on the date of the flint mining at Grimes Graves and other sites, touched on in Chapter ii, was largely prompted by the appearance of techniques and types among the workshop debris which recalled Palaeolithic forms, but 'Campignian' affinities were also hesitatingly referred to by the English controversialists, and more specifically recognized by such Continental scholars as Åberg. Clark, reviewing the evidence in 1932, drew attention to 'elements of an earlier industrial tradition of Late Mesolithic character' and cited as a parallel a surface flint site at Great Melton in Suffolk, which seems to be in fact representative of the 'heavy' flint industry referred to above under A 2, and comparable with the Cushendun-Glenarm sites in Co. Antrim. (Clark, 1932 a, 113; cf. Clark & Piggott, 1933.)

Apart from techniques of Palaeolithic ancestry, recalling for instance that of Levallois, more specifically Mesolithic types in the flint mines include the sporadic appearance of *tranchet* axes at Grimes Graves, Easton Down and Stoke Down, and some pick forms; on the Continent, Spiennes provides much the same assemblage within the 'Campignian' range of types. The *petit-tranchet* derivative arrowhead from Floor 8 5 at Grimes Graves is a form typical of the 'light' flint industry of A 3 above, and the greenstone axes from other Grimes Graves sites may well be related to the active exploitation of such material characteristic of the Secondary Neolithic cultures. Grimes Graves, too, produced Peterborough pottery, which occurred in a modified form at the Easton Down settlement adjacent to the mines, and a flint axe of specifically flint-mine type occurred in a Peterborough hut-site at Winterbourne Dauntsey not far away (Stone, 1934). The type of flint axe found in certain burials of the Dorchester culture in north England

(Duggleby, Seamer and Liffs Low) is again that of the mine products, especially those of the southern English hoards referred to in Chapter II above, and these may well represent trade northwards from the flint-mine areas.

A remarkable find at Grimes Graves seems once more related to Mesolithic traditions. It has already been mentioned (p. 44) that Floor 85 C produced certain engravings on flint crust which included naturalistic designs, one of a browsing deer, and others of cervid heads, originally regarded as Upper Palaeolithic in date. But these are equally well, or better, to be compared with the Arctic art-style engravings of Scandinavia, as suggested by Kendrick (1925, 164) and Burkitt (1926, 174); Clark regards this style as Mesolithic in origins but with its main period contemporary with the southern Scandinavian chambered tombs. The fine scratched technique of the Grimes Graves engravings may also be compared to that of the geometric patterns on stone at Graig Lwyd and Skara Brae within the Secondary Neolithic cultures.

We therefore seem justified in recognizing a considerable element of Mesolithic ancestry in the flint mines and their associated working floors. What this may mean in terms of actual human individuals or communities is less easy to assess, but the long heritage of flint-working within the Mesolithic world, with its roots stretching back into the Palaeolithic, would render it likely that the specialized skills of the northern European flint-workers would constitute a valuable asset when the demand for large-scale production of axes was initiated by the arrival of the first agricultural communities in these regions. Traditionally, the axe of the earlier Western Neolithic communities in Europe was not of flint, but of stone, but with the spread of these peoples on to the chalk lands of north France, Belgium and southern England, flint alone would be readily available. We have seen reason to believe that the Windmill Hill culture (like that of Michelsberg) incorporated certain elements of indigenous Mesolithic ancestry unconnected with flint-working, and it seems that to this we should add an important share in the technique of axe-production in the flint mines and their working-floors.

THE HEAVY FLINT INDUSTRIES

Apart from three sites in Northern Ireland, the flint industries under review are known in Britain almost exclusively from surface finds, where, however, a sufficiently large number of types have been found in recurrent association to enable us to recognize in them close affinities with the European flint industries classed as Campignian, and as we have seen (p. 277), this led Movius to use this designation for the Irish series he was engaged in defining. The main types which are referable to the group are various types of picks (including the 'Thames Pick' form) and of *tranchet* axes or adzes, including the 'fish-tail scrapers' of Northern Ireland which are in fact small flake-axes; scrapers on blades or with tangs; waisted scrapers and adzes; borers; rare burins; Y-shaped tools perhaps hollow scrapers; discoidal or large lanceolate knives; and occasional *petit-tranchet* forms (Fig. 44).

No general study of the distribution of these types in association has been made for Britain, but such assemblages seem to be especially common in East Anglia, where the Great Melton site (Clarke & Halls, 1918) has already been referred to (p. 281), and where connexion with the flint-mining industries is almost inevitable. It seems probable that the occupation floor with the surviving remains of wind-breaks of oak and hazel found below a thick layer of natural deposits in Bolton's Brickyard, Ipswich, and claimed to be of Palaeolithic age, should be attributed to a similar context in view of the two *tranchet* axes found: the remainder of the industry (including a chipped implement of igneous rock) is less distinctive but not inconsistent with such an attribution (Reid Moir, 1926). Zeuner has since shown that the superincumbent deposits represent comparatively recent hill-wash probably resulting from early forest clearance and agriculture (Zeuner, 1950).

In southern and south-west England these industries have been recognized in the Farnham, Durweston and Stourpaine regions (Dorset); in Wiltshire, near Avebury and again near Stonehenge (Laidler & Young, 1938), and as far west as Sidmouth (E. E. Smith, 1947): at the two last sites polished discoidal knives were found, of a type discussed below (p. 285), and the Avebury site yielded an axe of Great Langdale rock, though of course in surface finds direct association cannot be proved.

The tools of the 'Thames Pick' class constitute a special problem. Their name indicates one region of their maximum abundance in south-east England, and in Sussex Curwen has noted that the distribution of the type 'corresponds with that of the Neolithic rather than the Mesolithic population, for it is practically confined to the chalk areas' (Curwen, 1937 a, 141), though it does not occur in the causewayed camps. The antecedents of such picks, as has long been recognized, are to be found in what Clark regards as 'the British counterpart of the Ertebølle culture of Denmark', the Lower Halstow culture known from sites in north Kent, where an assemblage consisting of such picks, *tranchet* flake axes, scrapers, burins and a microlithic element has been found in two floors overlain by peat in part, and by marsh clay (Clark, 1932 a, 63–5; 1936 a, 158–60).

The pollen evidence showed the Halstow sites to be in a botanical horizon dominated by oakwoods, and so certainly post-Boreal in date, and Clark (1936 a, 158) claims that of the two floors, the southerly 'demonstrated that the floors were earlier than a flint industry, including leaf arrowheads, and probably of Neolithic age'. But the original excavator made it clear that the hearths of the south site 'rested upon the surface of the London Clay and were covered by strata, similar both in composition and sequence to those of the northern site', and that while the northern site contained an industry purely Mesolithic in type, in the southern site the finds 'represent two cultures', one being Mesolithic and exactly comparable to that of the north site, and the other comprising leaf-arrowheads, awls, and finely worked scrapers, one of the latter having a polished edge (Burchell, 1925, 217). Later he says that these latter flints 'occur on that part of the "floor" outside the perimeter of the peat area and are covered by "land wash"' (1925, 291), but it seems difficult to dissociate them from a broad contemporaneity with the industry of Mesolithic type, the more so since the polished-edge scraper is a type characteristic of the light flint industry of the Secondary Neolithic cultures already referred to, and discussed below (p.286). Such an interpretation of the Halstow sites in no way affects their essential character which, as in the Ertebølle culture, is that of a Mesolithic tradition surviving side by side with the early settlements of intrusive agriculturalists.

The distribution of tanged scrapers and the curious Y-shaped implements suggests that Yorkshire should be included within the province of the heavy industries under consideration (Bowler-Kelly, 1935), and recent finds on Flamborough Head confirm this, and stress the Irish connexions.[1] There is no evidence of the further spread of such industries into Scotland (although, as we shall see, the light industries of A 3 are well represented there). But in Northern Ireland, Movius has described assemblages of flint implements from three main sites, Cushendun and Glenarm in Co. Antrim, and Rough Island in Co. Down, which fall into the group discussed (Movius, 1942, 214–22). Here the types include small flake-axes, Y-shaped implements, points, scrapers, borers and *petit-tranchet* arrowheads. At Cushendun this industry appears in horizon 4 of the sequence, which has been assigned to the Zone VII a/VII b transition by Jessen (1949, 137), and at Glenarm it overlies a Late Larnian industry on a storm beach formed during the Late Atlantic period (Movius, 1942, 131)—a position which should approximately equate with that at Cushendun—and a similar situation was present at Rough Island. Here leaf-arrowheads occurred together with flake-axes, but there is no necessity to regard the site as later than Cushendun or Glenarm on this account: it is rather to be regarded as indication of contact between cultures of predominantly Mesolithic ancestry and those of intrusive Neolithic character, comparable with the Bann and Sandhill cultures described below. The possible links between Yorkshire and Ulster implicit in these flint industries may not be unconnected with the similar relationships of Lyles Hill ware.

1   I am much indebted to Mr John Moore for information in advance of publication.

THE LIGHT FLINT INDUSTRIES

Under this not altogether satisfactory heading we may consider certain assemblages of flint implements which, like those of the heavy industries described above, have been found frequently as surface finds and less often in archaeological or stratigraphical contexts which show them to form an integral part of the British Secondary Neolithic cultures. Associations are, in point of fact, more frequent and more satisfactory than those of the types discussed in the foregoing section. The main types which we can identify are first, and most consistently, arrowheads of the various subgroups of the *petit-tranchet* derivative class (Clark, 1935 a); small blade-knives with polished edges and faces, allied to the discoidal polished knives (Clark, 1929) which are themselves probably also to be included; scrapers with polished edges, again allied to the foregoing; plano-convex knives similar to those later to be characteristic of the Food-vessel culture of the Bronze Age (Clark, 1932 c); flaked rods of the 'fabricator' class, and single-piece sickles (Clark, 1932 b).

In addition, there are the less distinctive narrow axes or chisels similar to those from the flint-axe hoards described in Chapter III, disc-scrapers, bifacially flaked points and fine serrated flakes which are not sickle-teeth, all of which have some claim for inclusion. There is no evidence that the barbed-and-tanged arrowhead can be included as a component of this assemblage, but leaf-shaped arrowheads of forms indistinguishable from those in the Western cultures are found. Although not a part of the flint industry, the occurrence of perforated mace-heads in several instances in association with the foregoing types should be mentioned here.

No comprehensive survey of the distribution of these types as surface finds has yet been made, but apart from the associated finds listed by Clark (1935 a), the *petit-tranchet* derivative arrowhead seems to occur as far west as Dartmoor and from Pembrokeshire and Glamorganshire in south Wales, and Anglesey in the north (Grimes, 1939 a, 144, 146, 156). It is frequent in southern and eastern England and is found on the Jurassic ridge at Duston and Hunsbury (Northants). Its northern English distribution includes Yorkshire and Derbyshire, and in Scotland it is found at many sites in the southern Lowlands, north-eastwards to the Moray Firth, and beyond to Caithness and Orkney. This approximates to the range of other types which have been mapped—discoidal polished knives (Clark, 1929) and single-piece sickles (though these do not extend so far northwards; *ibid.* 1932 c)—and the polished blade-knives seem to have much the same distribution, including Caithness and Orkney (cf. Chapter VIII above).

These distributions are not very significant, except in so far as they indicate a predominantly eastern trend, and also a notable homogeneity from south to north Britain. The *petit-tranchet* derivative arrowheads are explicitly Mesolithic in ancestry, but in their evolved forms represent peculiarly insular forms unknown in Scandinavia or elsewhere in northern Europe, although something approaching them can be seen in the flint industry of the Omalian of Belgium (Hamal-Nandrin, Servais & Louis, 1936, fig. 29) and of the Danubian in Alsace (Sauer, 1949, fig. 4), which must contain a large proportion of Mesolithic derivatives. The polishing of the edges of scrapers, and of the edges or faces of knives, is a very curious feature which might tentatively be connected with a bone-working technique proper to Mesolithic traditions: indeed, certain bone objects from Skara Brae closely resemble the Scottish and north English polished flint knife-blades (Childe, 1931 b, bone type B i). But nothing strictly comparable is known from Scandinavia, though the smaller polished transverse arrowheads of the Danish Island Single-Grave culture are products of the same technique (Becker, 1940). Large blades, often of Grand Pressigny flint, with polish on the convex face, are not infrequent in the Zone-beaker cultures of Holland, Belgium, and the Lower Rhine (Bursch, 1928; 1936; Mariën, 1948; Holwerda, 1912; Rademacher, 1925; Stampfuss, 1929, 87), where these seem likely to be related to western Early Bronze Age forms such as the flint daggers from the south of France polished on the flake surface and imitating tanged copper examples (Sandars, 1950). Our British polished knives (and especially the discoidal type) must again be considered an insular development.

The single-piece sickles, however, as Clark has pointed out (in Warren et al. 1936) have good parallels in Holland, and less precise analogues in the Altheim-Mondsee cultures of Early Bronze Age date (Clark, 1932 b; Childe, 1947, 290), which can hardly be regarded as ancestral. Gjessing has included curved flint knives of related forms in his Circumpolar Stone Age, and we may be dealing with derivatives from this province within the various local Neolithic cultures.

Of the remaining types—'fabricators' and plano-convex knives—it may be remarked that both are largely characteristic of the British Middle Bronze Age, with its Food-vessel and Cinerary-urn pottery, which developed after the first impetus of the Beaker invasions had died away, and which had its roots in pre-Beaker cultures of the Secondary Neolithic group, where the cord-ornamented wares of the Peterborough group contributed much to subsequent pottery styles. As with the pottery, so with certain flint forms the same ancient tradition survived. There is good evidence for regarding a large proportion of 'fabricators' as strike-a-lights used with pyrites to produce a spark.

In addition to sites which have produced one or more of the foregoing flint types associated with other elements of pottery, bone-work, etc., and which are discussed in the next chapter, it should be mentioned that surface finds from several regions have shown that significant assemblages of a large proportion of the types enumerated do occur, without any apparent admixture of extraneous forms. The Duston site in Northamptonshire is an excellent English example of this (Northampton Mus.; unpublished), while in Scotland such assemblages as those of Overhowden and Airhouse in Berwickshire (Callander, 1928), or at Urquhart near Elgin (Morrison, 1871), repeat the familiar collocation of flint types in concentrated groups, which presumably indicate the more durable elements from habitation sites of one or other of the cultural groups described in Chapter xi. The flint assemblage from the submerged land-surface of the Essex coast (Warren *et al.* 1936) may again belong to the Rinyo-Clacton, the Peterborough or (less probably) to *B*-class beaker people at that site, or be common to all.

THE AXE-FACTORIES OF IGNEOUS STONES

Introduction

As we have seen in Chapter iii, a limited amount of exploitation of igneous rock sources for axe-blades was undertaken by the Windmill Hill culture, or at least by those western communities using Hembury ware. At Hembury itself and at Maiden Castle axes of probable Cornish origin occur in primary contexts, and petrologically identical specimens are known as stray finds in Cornwall and Somerset. At Maiden Castle, such axes are stratigraphically earlier than occupation layers with Peterborough and Beaker pottery. Apart from these two sites, however, there is no evidence of the use of materials other than flint for axes in the Windmill Hill culture, but at the type-site numerous fragments of axes of rocks geologically foreign to the region were found in horizons stratigraphically later than the primary occupation of the site and characterized by the presence of Peterborough and Beaker pottery.

The petrological examination of these Windmill Hill axes in the 1920's eventually led to a large-scale investigation undertaken by the South-Western Group of Museums, which set up a sub-committee in 1936 to examine all stone axes and similar tools not made of flint, and likely to be of Neolithic or Bronze Age date, within the English counties of Cornwall, Devon, Somerset, Gloucestershire, Wiltshire and Dorset; Hampshire and Sussex material was later included. The result of this sub-committee's work has been to place our knowledge of the use of igneous rocks in the southern English Neolithic on an assured foundation, and it has enabled us to review earlier evidence in a new light, especially with regard to 'factories' for the large-scale manufacture of axes in a manner comparable with the flint mines and their related working sites.[1]

1 The sub-committee has generously placed at my disposal the material shortly to be published in their Third Report, in advance of publication. The two previous reports are referred to as Keiller, Piggott & Wallis (1941); Stone & Wallis (1947).

The existence of such factories had in fact been recognized since the beginning of the century, and the identification of the sites on Tievebulliagh Mountain in Co. Antrim by Knowles (Movius, 1942, 222–7 with refs.). This was followed by Warren's discovery of the Graig Lwyd site in North Wales in 1919 (Warren, 1919; 1921; 1922), and about the same time a very small chipping site was found at Stake Pass, Great Langdale, in the Lake District. The South-Western sub-committee's work indicated, at an early stage, that the number of exports made of Great Langdale rock far exceeded the capacity of the Stake Pass site, and in 1947–8 the main factory area was in fact discovered, on the Great Langdale screes below the Pike of Stickle (Bunch & Fell, 1949). A factory in Cornwall still remains to be identified as the source of the sub-committee's group I, of which numerous axes are known from southern England, while a large proportion of the axes examined either fall into very small groups or are unique examples of various igneous rocks, all with a probable general origin in western Britain from Cornwall to Cumberland. These are briefly discussed below, after a consideration of the known factories. Of the products of these known or suspected factories, none has been found in a Primary Neolithic context in southern England, except the sub-committee's groups II A and IV mentioned above, but in many instances they occur in contexts stratigraphically later, frequently in association with recognizable elements of the Secondary Neolithic cultures as outlined above.

The Tievebulliagh axe factories

The sites. The Tievebulliagh factory-sites are widely scattered in Ballyemon Glen near Cushendall in Co. Antrim, and include sites near the summit of Tievebulliagh Mountain, and again in the Glendun and Glengariff regions (the evidence is summarized in Movius, 1942). The rock employed is a porcellanite which occurs in screes, but has not been traced as an outcrop (Keiller, Piggott & Wallis, 1941, 64) and a similar rock occurs on Rathlin Island at Brockley, with a small local axe-making industry based upon it. It was possible to establish the relationship of part of the working floor on Tievebulliagh Mountain to the natural stratigraphy, and it was found to be at the base of a peat with pine stumps which indicated wooded conditions, with mixed oak forest on the lower slopes of the hill, and lay within Zone VII*b* (Jessen, 1949, 142).

The industry. As in the other sites to be discussed, the rock was used predominantly for the manufacture of axes, mainly from cores though a few flake axes of *tranchet* type were recognized. The axes were flaked or chipped on the spot in large quantities (Knowles found at least 2,500 axes in a more or less finished chipped state). Polished examples were very rare, and no sandstone rubbers were found, though the material would have been locally available. Some of the axe rough-outs were indistinguishable from 'pick' forms, and a certain number of flake tools such as scrapers and points had been made from workshop waste, and hammer-stones were found. The axe in its final chipped form is of pointed-oval section, with a thin rounded or slightly pointed butt.

Exports. Axes which appear to be products of the Tievebulliagh or related sites are common in Northern Ireland, though no petrological survey has been made there. Petrology has however confirmed the presence of the material in Dumbartonshire in west Scotland, and as far away as Gloucestershire and Kent, while in Northern Ireland axes probably of this stone have been found in archaeological contexts in four instances.

At Cushendun, deposit A above the Litorina beach comprised the flint assemblage already mentioned under the Heavy Flint Industries, with flake-axes and a *petit tranchet*, and also Tievebulliagh axes, and at Ballynagard on Rathlin Island a similar industry was associated with axes of the local Rockley porcellanite and a sherd probably of Western Neolithic pottery. This sherd has a rim similar to others from the site on Lyles Hill described in Chapter vi, in which the shouldered bowls of Lyles Hill ware predominate, and here again Tievebulliagh axes were found (E. E. Evans, 1940*b*, 12). Finally, an axe probably of Tievebulliagh origin was found in the blocking of the forecourt in the chambered cairn of Dunloy, of the Clyde-Carlingford culture (Chapter vi). Here the blocking should be not earlier than the final burials in the chamber, which were accompanied by bowls of Beacharra C ware, with whipped cord ornament. In general, then, the activities of the Tievebulliagh factories overlapped with the Clyde-Carlingford culture in Ulster, though perhaps not with its earliest phase.

The Graig Lwyd axe-factory

The Graig Lwyd factory-site lay on the slopes of Penmaenmawr Mountain in North Wales, and is now largely destroyed by the extensive modern quarries on the summit or buried beneath their waste tips. The rock used in the axe manufacture, an augite granophyre, was worked from the scree, and no natural stratigraphy was recoverable, though Warren found evidence of boggy conditions, and hazel nuts indicating autumn occupation, under a flaking floor in an area now dry (Warren, 1919; 1921; 1922). It is likely that other flaking sites exist in the Penmaenmawr Mountain region, and one has recently been found 2½ miles to the south-west at Carreg Fawr.

The industry. The technique of axe-manufacture at Graig Lwyd was studied in great detail by Warren, who based his comments on an estimated three tons of material! He was able to show that the industry was specifically directed towards the production of pointed-butt or thin-butt axes, though in the process of flaking from the original block of scree a whole series of pseudo-Palaeolithic forms and techniques could be observed, with 'innumerable "Levallois" flakes' (1921, 194). He felt strongly that the techniques employed were those of flint-flaking transferred to the Graig Lwyd rock, and was tempted to connect the exploitation of the site with the arrival of axe-makers accustomed to the flint-mine traditions of south-east England.

The finished, or apparently finished forms at Graig Lwyd include thin-butted axes approximating to but not identical with those from Tievebulliagh, elongated axe and chisel forms, double-ended axes, picks, adzes (some flake-adzes, but not of true *tranchet* type), and polished axes, of which a few broken specimens were found (Fig. 46, nos. 1–3). No rubbing-stones were found, but a few battered nodules of the local rock had served as hammer-stones. A fragment of a perforated mace-head of Graig Lwyd rock was found at Windmill Hill, Avebury, but no other example has been recorded.

The engraved plaque. In his Floor B, Warren found and published a roughly oval plaque of stone, 5·2 by 3·4 in. across, which he claimed was decorated with a very finely incised pattern of lines and hatched triangles (Warren, 1921, fig. 21). The artificial character of this design was accepted by Breuil (1934) and Hawkes (1941), but Grimes, apparently influenced by geological opinion, relegated it, in the official Museum Catalogue, to the dubious position of a 'plaque with supposed incised ornament' (1939*a*, 134), and there has therefore since been some general hesitation in accepting it (cf. Bruce & Megaw, 1947, 12).

A recent re-examination of this Graig Lwyd plaque leaves no doubt in my mind of the human origin of the design on the naturally smooth surface of the stone (Fig. 46, no. 7). It is executed in extremely fine scratching, and the surface of the plaque has received damage in ancient times, but subsequent to the engraving. Warren's published drawing over-emphasizes the lines, but shows their general disposition, forming a series of hatched triangles pendant from a double line: it is probable that the pattern was continued in multiple lozenges, and there are other similar finely scratched lines in groups elsewhere on the smooth area. The back is plain except for some artificial tool-cuts which look almost metallic in character.

Both the nature and the technique of the design link the Graig Lwyd plaque with other examples of a similar art-style in Northern Ireland and in Scotland. The Lyles Hill stone has already been commented upon (Chapter VI) and its resemblance to engravings from the Rinyo-Clacton site of Skara Brae noted; the plaques from the diatomite in Co. Antrim, probably of the Bann culture, should also be quoted (below, p. 317), and we shall see that in the Ronaldsway culture somewhat similar finely engraved stone plaques also occur. Breuil and Hawkes have stressed the Iberian connexions of such objects, and of the patterns scratched on them, but it is worthwhile bearing in mind that such simple motifs as hatched triangles and lozenges are not wholly distinctive of an Iberian art-style, and occur frequently, and in finely scratched techniques, in the northern European

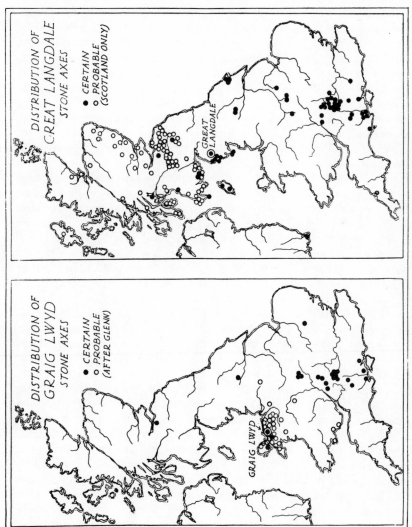

DISTRIBUTION OF
CRAIG LWYD
STONE AXES

● CERTAIN
○ PROBABLE
(AFTER GLENN)

GRAIG LWYD

DISTRIBUTION OF
GREAT LANGDALE
STONE AXES

● CERTAIN
○ PROBABLE
(SCOTLAND ONLY)

GREAT
LANGDALE

Fig. 45.

Maglemose culture (Clark, 1936 *a*, 172; Mathiassen, 1943, figs. 12, 50, 70). In view of the Mesolithic ancestry of much in our Secondary Neolithic cultures, these latter comparisons should be given due weight.

Exports. A preliminary list and distribution-map of Graig Lwyd axes, based almost entirely on macroscopic identifications, was published by Glenn (1935), and since that date new petrological determinations have appeared (Keiller, Piggott & Wallis, 1941; Stone & Wallis, 1947). These reliable identifications show a marked concentration, in southern England, within the north Wilts-Cotswold area, with outliers on Southampton water, in the Cambridgeshire Fens, in Yorkshire and West Lothian (Fig. 45). The precise status of a group of axes of identical stone closely comparable with that of Graig Lwyd, from Worcestershire, Hampshire, Jersey and Brittany, is not yet established: they may be products of an outlying factory in the Penmaenmawr region, or alternatively of French origin.

Axes of Graig Lwyd stone have been found in association with natural deposits in two instances. At Upware in the Cambridgeshire Fens, an axe was found at a level equating with a position 'just below the presumed horizon of the base of the fen clay' of the Peacock's Farm section: the Upware axe was in Zone VII, but at a higher level than the Windmill Hill pottery from Peacock's Farm, which was found (again in Zone VII peat) two feet below the base of the fen clay (Clark, Godwin & Clifford, 1935). More than one axe macroscopically identified as of Graig Lwyd manufacture has been found at the base of the Upper Peat on the foreshore at Rhyl in North Wales, but here the evidence is not decisive, although the percentages of *Tilia* and *Pinus* pollen suggest a 'sub-Boreal or Atlantic date' for this peat, and for that of the Lower bed, separated from the Upper by *Scrobicularia* clay. (Neaverson, 1936; Bibby 1940.) Such a position would approximate to a Zone VII horizon.

In considering the numerous associations of Graig Lwyd axes with other archaeological material, it is convenient first to note briefly those with Secondary Neolithic cultures which are further discussed in Chapter xi. At Bryn yr Hen Bobl in Anglesey, North Deighton in Yorkshire, Windmill Hill and the Avebury Avenue site in Wiltshire, the axes or fragments were found with Peterborough pottery and flint types of the light industry defined above; at Windmill Hill and North Deighton fragments of axes from the Great Langdale factory described below were also found, and a less close association of the products of the two factories with a cremation-cemetery of the Dorchester culture occurred at Cairnpapple Hill, West Lothian, while in pits near Woodhenge a broken Graig Lwyd axe was found with pottery of the Rinyo-Clacton culture and *petit-tranchet* derivative arrowheads.

There remains for further comment a group of four sites in North Wales, none of them very far from the factory site. At the Bryn Llwyn site at

Gwaenysgor, Flintshire, Glenn excavated an occupation site which included a roughly paved area 30 by 40 ft. which may have been a house-foundation or working floor, on which were fifty hammer-stones, flints, pottery, sea-shells, charcoal and a Graig Lwyd axe and fragments of others. Other similar occupation material was widely scattered: it included fifteen flint leaf-arrowheads, scrapers (some made from polished axes), a stone spindle-whorl, a grain-rubber and a piece of a perforated mace-head. Animal bones included ox, sheep and pig (Glenn, 1914; 1935). The pottery appears to be some form of Western Neolithic ware, though the finger-tip ornament and cabled rims are very unusual, and suggest comparison with pottery from Ebbsfleet (Burchell & Piggott, 1939), and it is possible that it may belong to some group within the Secondary Neolithic cultures.

The Dyserth Castle site (Glenn, 1915; 1935) has a remarkable stratified sequence, in which the Lower Prehistoric layer contained Graig Lwyd axes and flakes, potsherds, flint flakes and leaf-arrowheads, hammer and anvil stones, a possible grain-rubber, bone beads and a perforated metatarsal pendant. The bones comprised horse, ox, sheep or goat, pig, dog and red deer. Above this was the Upper Prehistoric layer, of Middle Bronze Age date with barbed flint arrowheads, plano-convex knives, bone pins and two pairs of bronze ear-rings of the type found with a Food-vessel burial at Goodmanham, Yorks. (Greenwell, 1877, barrow cxv.) Above this again were Roman and Medieval levels. The pottery from Dyserth is similar to that from Gwaenysgor, but less distinctive.

At Rhos Ddigre Cave in Denbighshire a polished Graig Lwyd axe seems to have been associated with some form of collective burial, with sherds of an apparently Western Neolithic bowl and others which may be Peterborough ware, and in the north-west cave at Gop, Flintshire, a chipped Graig Lwyd axe was again found associated with burials and small implements in flint and chert, claimed to be in a microlithic tradition (Glenn, 1935). In the larger Gop cave, as we shall see below, important burials of Secondary Neolithic culture were found, with Peterborough pottery and other objects.

The Great Langdale axe-factory

The sites. We have already seen how this factory was identified after the initial discovery of a small flaking-site at Stake Pass near the Langdale Pikes in Westmorland. At least two more small sites of similar type are now known on the high ground in this area, but the main factory is based on the boulders and screes south of the Pike of Stickle in Great Langdale (Bunch & Fell, 1949; Keiller, Piggott & Wallis, 1941; Stone & Wallis, 1947). The material is an epidotized tuff of intermediate basic composition, but variants of silicified rhyolitic rocks on the site were also employed. Two flakes of rock found on the screes may constitute variants of local material or have an origin in Pembrokeshire.

The industry. The products of the factory were predominantly axes, and at present there is no evidence that they were polished on the site. The axes have thin or pointed butts, in general agreeing with the Graig Lwyd forms, and four adzes made from large flakes have been recorded (Fig. 46, no. 4). A hammer-stone of granite from the glacial drift, which must have been humanly carried to the site, has also been found.

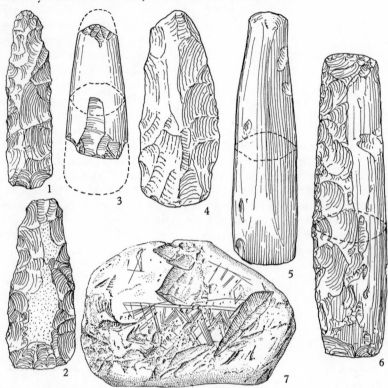

Fig. 46. Axe-factory rough-outs and axes. 1–3, Graig Lwyd (*after Warren*); 4, Great Langdale (*after Bunch & Fell*); 5, 6, Ehenside Tarn (*after Darbishire*). Scale ¼. 7, Decorated plaque, Graig Lwyd. Scale ½.

Exports. The identifications made up to 1949 have been listed and mapped (Bunch & Fell, 1949), with thirty sites ranging from Clydeside to Bournemouth. Within the area of the South-Western sub-committee's investigations, none has been identified west of a line from Gloucestershire to Weymouth, nor eastwards into Sussex—the main concentration is in the Middle Thames-Cotswolds-Avebury regions, and down the Wiltshire Avon (Fig. 45). Outside this area of systematic survey sites include the Isle of Man and Yorkshire, with four in the Scottish Lowlands. A macroscopic examination, however, suggests that about 100 axes from Scotland are of Great Langdale origin, occurring mainly in the south-east but straggling up into Aberdeenshire, and with a secondary concentration in the Dumfries-Galloway-Clyde mouth area,[1] and a similar survey suggests that probably one-third of the known stone axes from the Isle of Man are again from the same factory. Further petrological examination may well show the factory's output to be enormous, and to include such regions as Yorkshire, where finds of axes of 'Borrowdale ash' have been numerous in the past.

Some evidence exists for the finishing and polishing of the Great Langdale axes away from the factory, perhaps in the Low Furness-Cartmel area, and the Ehenside Tarn site described below seems certainly directly linked with the factory site. A characteristic feature of the finished axes is a slight squaring of the sides, and sometimes a curious thinning of the butt (as seen for instance at Ehenside itself).

At Windmill Hill, North Deighton and Cairnpapple Hill, fragments of Great Langdale axes were found in association with those of Graig Lwyd, as mentioned above, and at Abingdon, Berks, a Great Langdale axe occurred in a Neolithic settlement which, while basically of the Windmill Hill culture (cf. Chapter 11 above), also contained a few Peterborough sherds, a flint single-piece sickle of the type included in the light industry of the Secondary Neolithic cultures listed earlier in this chapter, and a piece of a flint dagger of Beaker type (Leeds, 1928). But the most important site associated with the Great Langdale industry is that of Ehenside Tarn in Cumberland, which is best considered here in detail.

The Ehenside Tarn site. This remarkable site was discovered in the 1870's in the course of draining a small lake near the Ehen river, south of St Bees (Darbishire, 1874). Along the edge of the lake was found a series of hearths with occupation debris, mainly in and at the base of a 'forest bed' of peat and decayed vegetable remains. From the original excellently objective report we find the stratification to have been as follows:

6. Recent vegetable debris on tarn bottom, 1 ft. thick.
5. 'Forest bed', with leaves, branches and stems of trees (oak and beech predominating, with birch, hazel and alder, honeysuckle and *Osmunda regalis*). This layer contained the human occupation debris to its base, and was 3–4 ft. thick.
4. 'Leaf bed' with no large vegetable remains, 3–4 ft. thick.
3. *Sphagnum* bed of uncertain thickness.
2. Lake bed of fine grey sand, resting on
1. Undisturbed marl.

1 I am indebted to Mr F. W. Anderson of the Geological Survey, and Mr R. B. K. Stevenson, Keeper of the National Museum of Antiquities of Scotland, for permission to reproduce this unpublished information on my map, Fig. 45.

The common occurrence of beech is remarkable, and was confirmed by many of the wooden artifacts noted below, and it implies a very different forest composition from that around Lake Windermere, less than 25 miles away, where the Zone VII pollen was notable for its 'complete absence of *Fagus* and *Carpinus*' (Pennington, 1947).

A recent preliminary examination of peat samples obtained from a field drain at Ehenside in March 1951 confirms the macroscopic observations made in the 1870's, and I am indebted to Dr Elizabeth Knox for permission to refer to her unpublished analysis of these samples. The *Sphagnum*-bed contains up to 30 per cent *Sphagnum* spores, together with those of *Osmunda* and *Polypodium*, with tree pollens of *Betula*, *Alnus*, *Salix*, *Fagus* and *Pinus* in decreasing order, and some of *Ericaceae*. In the Leaf bed there is a very high percentage of *Fagus* (40 per cent), an almost complete regression of *Corylus*, and a high proportion of *Gramineae*, together with some pollen grains of *Plantago* and *Myriophyllum*, and some probable fungal spores. *Fagus* declines to 20 per cent in the Forest bed, *Corylus* increases, and the *Gramineae* pollen is absent. A few spores of *Polypodium* and *Sphagnum* are present, and actual logs of *Betula* and *Salix* were identified.

Apart from the high proportion of beech pollen, the spectra of the Leaf and Forest beds suggest the probability of a Zone VII horizon. The pollen of grasses and plantain in the Leaf bed should imply cultivation in the neighbourhood of the site at the time of its formation. It is possible that the 'Forest bed' was an artificial brushwood platform as at Star Carr.

A wood sample from the old excavations was used to obtain an age-estimate based on the breakdown of radio-active Carbon (C_{14}), and the surprisingly high figure of 3014 ± 300 B.C. was obtained—a date at variance with any estimate based on archaeological evidence (Childe, 1950c).

The finds: stone. *Axes* petrologically identified as of Great Langdale origin were found, some of great size and either chipped, or partially or completely polished, and one was still in its original haft of beech-wood (Fig. 46, nos. 5, 6; Fig. 47, no. 6). The polishing had been carried out on sandstone and gritstone *grinders and rubbers*, and there was also a *saucer-quern* of Red Sandstone. (A rotary quern from the site must be related to some sherds of Roman pottery, and be a later intrusion.) The finished axes had slightly squared sides and narrowed butts.

Wood. The most remarkable feature of the site was the abundance of wooden objects. Two *axe-hafts* were found, one made from a beech-root and still retaining the axe (Fig. 47, no. 6): the haft is perforated below a re-curved club-like end, and the lower part of the shaft is missing. The wood at the head had been finished by facets ground across the grain, and tool-marks ran spirally round the shaft. Three *clubs* of flattened section (Fig. 47, nos. 3, 4) (one of them of beech) and fragments of two other hafts, had been made by a similar combination of cutting and grinding in facets to the axe-haft, and one fragment probably of a club had a finely executed lattice-pattern incised upon it. A *dug-out canoe* seems to have been found at or near the site, and a *paddle* with a blade 1 ft. long was recovered.

A fragment of a shallow wooden *bowl*, some 6–8 in. in diameter, was found in the 'leaf-bed', and a curved oak object, probably a *throwing-stick*, was

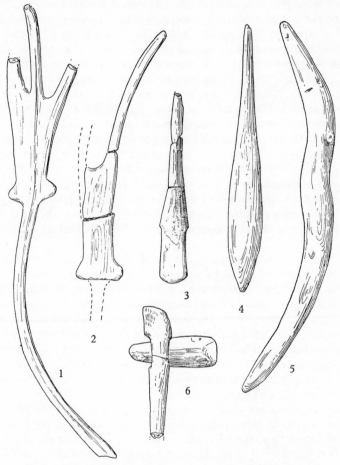

Fig. 47. Ehenside Tarn: wooden objects (*after Darbishire*). Scale ⅛.

found lying at the base of the 'forest-bed' (Fig. 47, no. 5). Finally, two remarkable objects with prongs up to 10 in. long at the end of a shaft surviving for 2½ ft., seem likely to have been *fish-spears* (Fig. 47, nos. 1, 2).

Pottery. Much pottery was found, though little survives. Enough remains, however, to show that two classes were represented, carinated bowls of good lustrous black ware of the Lyles Hill or Yorkshire Wold class, and heavier, coarser bowls with a carination and zones of ornament of bird-bone impressions (see p. 309 below), of Peterborough type (Piggott, 1931, figs. 7, 22).

Affinities. The cultural admixture implied by the pottery from Ehenside does not make it easy to interpret the affinities of the other objects from the site, and the virtual absence of wooden objects in British Neolithic cultures makes comparison here peculiarly difficult. The hafting of British stone axes has been discussed by Coghlan (1943), and the Ehenside axe-hafts may be compared with the club-shaped series known from such Neolithic sites in Switzerland as Robenhausen, Niederwyl and Wangen (Munro, 1890, figs. 24, 26, 27), though here the haft is very massive and the relatively small axe-blade set in an antler sleeve. Similar club-shaped hafts are known from Maguires Bridge, Co. Fermanagh, and Co. Monaghan in Ireland, but that from Solway Moss is a much lighter affair (Evans, 1897, 151 ff.), and Coghlan classes Ehenside as slot-hafted. The re-curving of the Ehenside haft beyond the blade was compared by Evans with the representations of hafted axes in Breton chambered tombs (e.g. Mané Kérioned and Table des Marchands—M. & S. J. Péquart & le Rouzic, 1927, pls. 37 and 41), and may possibly be a western European form: the hafts known from Scandinavia certainly do not show this feature (Becker, 1945; 1947; 1949).

Clubs are an obvious enough form of weapon and have been discussed by Mahr (1937, esp. 314–19): light clubs or throwing-sticks are known from the Mesolithic at Holmegard, while there are a whole series from the Swiss Lakes, from sites such as Robenhausen, Wangen, Luscherz, Schaffis and Sempach (Keller, 1878, pls. XI, XII, XXI; 218, 443), but no useful comparisons can be drawn from what must have been a common type wherever wood was available. The throwing-stick is, however, more distinctive, and the best parallels come from the Ertebølle site of Braband Sø (Clark, 1936 *a*, 149), and an object published as a hoe by Vouga (1934, pl. IX, 6) seems more likely to be such a weapon.

Dug-out canoes and their paddles are already known in the Mesolithic, and there was a paddle from the submerged land-surface of the Essex coast associated with Secondary Neolithic material (Warren *et al.* 1936). One from Port-Conthy can be attributed to the Cortaillod culture (von Gonzenbach, 1949, 57). Wooden bowls are common in this culture, in Switzerland and at the Lac de Chalain, and in later Neolithic contexts as well. Childe (1931 *c*) has noted the presence of a small wooden bowl from Maglemose.

The curious objects interpreted as fish-spears have a good parallel from an undated bog-find near Armagh in Ireland (Wilde, 1857–61, 206) and a three-pronged wooden fish-spear of Mesolithic date is reported from Russia (Dmitriev, 1934). The importance of fish-spearing in the economy of northern Mesolithic man has been demonstrated by Clark (1948 *a*), and it is clearly likely to have continued to be of some importance throughout prehistory: pike were the usual quarry, and these may well have been available in Ehenside Tarn. Presumably the wooden prongs would have been pointed or barbed, or have such points attached to them, though none survives. The Armagh spears have bluntly pointed prongs.

The ornamented fragment of wood from Ehenside, with a finely incised reticulate pattern, is worth comment. The technique and the pattern are known in the northern Mesolithic (Clark, 1936, motif U), but it is difficult to suggest Neolithic parallels, though the fine incisions of the stone engravings from Graig Lwyd or Ronaldsway might be considered similar. The faceting of the axe-haft and clubs may be compared with that of antler mace-heads in the Dorchester culture (p. 360 below).

But any interpretation of the Ehenside Tarn site is rendered unsatisfactory by the virtual absence of any wooden artifacts from the British Neolithic, or indeed, with the exception of the lake-sites of Switzerland and France, from the entire range of Western Neolithic cultures. Comparisons made with Mesolithic cultures in northern Europe, where wood has survived in many instances, may be misleading, but yet such types as the fish-spears and the throwing-stick, and perhaps the incised ornament, do seem suggestive of a hunter-fisher element which, as we have seen, would not be out of place in a Secondary Neolithic site in Britain.

AXE-FACTORIES IN CORNWALL, ETC.

The work of the sub-committee of the South-Western Group of Museums already referred to has resulted in the identification of a number of axes of Cornish origin. Precise comparisons can be made in a few instances, indicating that the manufacture of axes was carried out near St Ives, at Balstone Down, Callington, and at Trenow, Marazion, and the exports from these sites not only reached Wessex, but have been found as far afield as Bridlington in Yorkshire and an unrecorded find-spot in northern Scotland. None has, however, been found in an archaeological context.

The most important series, however, is that provisionally classed by the sub-committee as group I, and comprising 11 per cent of the total implements examined (over 700 in 1951). While the greenstone cannot be exactly matched, it is very near to that forming outcrops between Penzance and Mousehole, and outside Wessex the products of the factory are concentrated in this area of Cornwall. The types produced were very varied, and as well as axe-heads of normal Neolithic types included perforated battle-axes and mace-heads, and polishers or mullers of various forms. Axes or fragments have been found in secondary contexts at Windmill Hill, and as surface finds at the West Kennet Avenue and Stonehenge. A muller was found in the round barrow of Upton Lovel no. 4 in Wiltshire, associated with another of group III*a*, a rock allied to that from Trenow, and we shall see below (p. 355) that the burials in this barrow are related to those of the Secondary Neolithic Dorchester culture.

Groups II*a* and IV*a* remained unassigned to precise localities, though undoubtedly of Cornish origin: the latter group includes the majority of the foreign stone axes at Hembury and Maiden Castle, but a group II*a* axe was also found at Hembury, and another in a secondary context at Windmill Hill near the group I specimen already mentioned, and a dolerite mace-head of uncertain origin (Fig. 4, nos. 1, 2), implying that contact with the Cornish axe-factories was not established until a late stage of the site's occupation.

There remain two anomalous groups for consideration. A series of five axes from Wessex, Jersey and Carnac in Brittany have an identical composition very similar to that of the Graig Lwyd augite-granophyre, but the source of origin of this group VII*a* cannot at present be established, and clearly more work in northern and western France should be undertaken in this connexion. But whatever the actual source of the rock, the evidence of trade contacts between the three regions is of great interest, and may be related to that connected with the jadeite axes already mentioned in Chapter IV.

At Great Langdale, two flakes of rock were found on the screes which were at first regarded as variants of the local material, and classed as groups VIII and XI. Several axes of these rocks are known, three being secondary at Windmill Hill, and it has recently been suggested (Morey, 1950) that they are in fact products of a factory exploiting the Lanvirn series in the Mountjoy region of Pembrokeshire. No actual factory site has been identified.

THE USE OF PRESELY STONE

Since 1923 the source of the Blue Stones of Stonehenge has been known to lie in the Presely Mountains of Pembrokeshire (Thomas, 1923), and among the rocks which comprise the Stonehenge monoliths one is a unique and easily recognized ophitic dolerite, conveniently named Preselite. It has more recently been recognized that implements of this rock were traded far beyond Pembrokeshire, and the matter has recently been discussed by Stone (1950). Two complete axes of this rock had been identified by Keiller (1936), one from Carclinty Bog, Co. Antrim, and the other from the same county, but unlocated; Stone, as a result of the work of the South-Western sub-committee, lists axes from Maiden Castle (unstratified), Bournemouth, Stockton (Wilts), near the West Kennet chambered barrow, and (a fragment) from the upper levels at Windmill Hill. The last find comes from the same general horizon as Graig Lwyd and Great Langdale fragments, Peterborough pottery and Beaker sherds, and is subsequent to the primary occupation of the site. As we have seen, a Graig Lwyd fragment from Windmill Hill comes from a perforated mace-head, and Stone records perforated mace-heads, or shaft-hole battle-axes of the type usually associated with the *A*-beaker complex, made of Preselite and coming from Sidmouth and Fyfield Bavant (Wilts), as well as five from Wales already listed by Grimes (1939 *a*, 61). To these finds, and those at Stonehenge itself, one must add the block of Preselite from the long barrow of Bowls Barrow, Wilts, referred to in Chapter II.

These recent identifications serve to render less isolated the fact of the transport of the Presely stones to Stonehenge, though by no means minimizing the magnitude of that operation. Evidently some contact between Wiltshire and Presely existed before the obsolescence of the stone axe-blade of Neolithic type, and continued into the Beaker period. The South-Western sub-committee's work suggests that a wide diversity of stone (likely to have been glacial pebbles in large part) was employed for shaft-hole axes of Beaker type. Apart from the few mace-heads already mentioned from Scotland in Neolithic contexts, and others in the Secondary Neolithic cultures to be described in Chapter XI, the use of shaft-hole implements, and in particular of battle-axes of various forms, seems in the main to be associated with Beaker people in this country. The virtual absence of such implements among the exports from the axe-factories in itself strongly suggests that they had ceased effective production by the time of this event, or that if they continued to be worked, there was no trade between them and the newly arrived immigrants.

302

CHAPTER XI

THE REGIONAL COMMUNITIES OF THE SECONDARY NEOLITHIC CULTURES

INTRODUCTION

I N the preceding chapter we have seen that there is reason to believe that there existed in Britain a complex group of Neolithic cultures characterized by elements which in origin lie outside the Western Neolithic traditions of Europe, and which in many instances seem to have their roots in the Northern European Mesolithic cultures. To this complex the name of Secondary Neolithic has been given, and it has been shown that certain stone types persist and permeate all its regional manifestations. But within this general framework it is possible to recognize certain variants which can be distinguished by individual pottery styles, stone and bone types, or forms of ritual and domestic architecture. Of these, those classified as the Peterborough, the Rinyo-Clacton, the Ronaldsway and the Sandhill cultures are at least separated by three recognizable styles of pottery, but the fourth, the Dorchester culture, is more vaguely defined and may prove, in the light of further evidence, to be itself capable of subdivision.

The use of the word 'culture', in its accepted archaeological meaning, should be confined to an aggregate of associated elements of material culture recognizable in the archaeological record and, as we have already noticed in dealing with the chambered tombs for collective burial, to use a single element (such as a tomb-type or a pottery style) to define a 'culture' may be very misleading. This problem of nomenclature is especially acute in the Secondary Neolithic cultures under discussion, for as we shall see the substratum of stone and bone types common to all variants leaves pottery as almost the only distinguishing criterion in certain instances: this is most obviously the case in the first of our subdivisions, that of Peterborough. However, it is felt that with the reservations made above, we may continue to use 'Peterborough culture' as a convenient label.

THE PETERBOROUGH·CULTURE

The class of British Neolithic pottery named from a settlement site at Peterborough in eastern England was in fact the first group of pottery earlier than the Bronze Age to be defined in this country, in R. A. Smith's classic paper of 1910. Fifteen years later Kendrick (1925) recognized the existence of another ceramic, that within the western European group, and he, following Smith, pointed out certain north European affinities of the Peterborough class of ware. This essential duality of the British Neolithic cultures was demonstrated in greater detail by Leeds (1927 b), following Menghin, and, in respect of the pottery, by myself (Piggott, 1931): we can now see that Peterborough pottery is distinctive of only one variant within a group of Secondary Neolithic cultures.

The features of this class of pottery are described in greater detail below, but a brief indication of its salient characteristics may conveniently be given here. It is normally a coarse fabric, made up into heavy round-based vessels which in the majority of instances have a thickened rim above a cavetto neck and marked shoulder. Ornament is profuse, usually upon the upper two-thirds of the pot, especially the rim and shoulder, and is usually of impressed twisted or whipped cord in various forms, finger-nail rustication and stamped impressions from the articular ends of the leg-bones of birds and small mammals, a shell-edge or a comb. Rows of pits are common, often in the hollow of the neck, and herring-bone and cross-hatched motifs are frequent (Fig. 49 and Pl. X).

All the foregoing features serve sharply to differentiate Peterborough ware (or its Ebbsfleet variant described below) from pottery within the Western Neolithic group, and from the time of its first definition it has been seen that similarities existed between it and the great groups of cord-ornamented and pit-comb wares of northern Europe and, in part, of the entire Circumpolar Stone Age as defined by Gjessing. The nature of this relationship is discussed later.

Distribution.

Pottery of Peterborough type has been found in some eighty localities in Britain, ranging from the Firth of Forth and Galloway in the north, southwards to the English Channel. But the main concentration is in the Thames valley and thence into the Cotswolds, and the headwaters of the River Kennet at Avebury; while there are outliers in Somerset its distribution effectively ends in Dorset in the west, but extends along the Channel coast to Sussex and Kent. There are a few finds in East Anglia, and northwards in Yorkshire and the Scottish Lowlands, while there are sporadic finds in North Wales likely to be attributed to the axe-factory activities of Graig Lwyd (Fig. 48). In Ireland it is unknown, but as we shall see, the Sandhill wares represent a parallel development, and share many motifs and techniques of ornament in common with Peterborough ware.

The great majority of the finds have been stray, and many come from river-valleys or coastal dune areas. In one instance, at Meare Heath, Somerset, sherds of a Peterborough pot were found in a peat-bog at a point just above the Zone VII a–VII b junction (Gray, 1936; Godwin, 1941), and sherds also occurred on the Essex coast submerged land-surface at Clacton

(Warren *et al.* 1936). At Ebbsfleet, sherds were found beneath a peaty alluvium containing a high percentage of alder, with hazel, lime and birch in descending proportions (Burchell & Piggott, 1939). In a few instances definite habitation sites have been identified, and these are described below.

Settlement sites

Very little is known of the settlements of the makers of Peterborough pottery. The details of the type-site (Abbott, 1910) are hardly more precise than those of Grovehurst (Kent)[1] in the 1870's (Payne, 1880), but at both localities there appear to have been large shallow circular hollows, some 10–12 ft. in diameter and 2–3 ft. deep, containing occupation material and, at Grovehurst, remains of clay daub from wattle-work. At Winterbourne Dauntsey (Wilts) small shallow pits 4 ft. in diameter and 10 in. deep were found, one surrounded by eight stake-holes forming a rough circle 7½ ft. in diameter (Stone, 1934). The site on the line of the West Kennet Avenue at Avebury had no recognizable post-holes in the Combe Rock subsoil, but two pits were found, certainly not for habitation and perhaps, as argued by Stone (Stone & Young, 1948), of ritual significance, and several carefully made circular clay-lined hearths in which had been deposited unburnt objects such as broken Graig Lwyd axes. These peculiar features suggest comparison with the 'ritual hearths' and the axe-offerings from the Langeland settlements of the Passage-grave period at Blandebjerg and Troldebjerg (Winther, 1943, 25–30), and indeed the significance of the Kennet Avenue site is by no means clear.

At Combe Hill, Eastbourne, Peterborough pottery, of the Ebbsfleet variety, was found as the primary material in a small causewayed camp (Musson, 1950), and a few sherds were mixed with Western Neolithic pottery at Whitehawk. But at Windmill Hill, Maiden Castle and Hambledon Hill, the Peterborough pottery was secondary to the causewayed earthworks, and unassociated with any structures. In the predominantly Beaker-culture settlement near the Easton Down flint mines, sherds of Peterborough ware occurred, and again at Grimes Graves. Coastal sites, such as Glenluce Sands, Hedderwick or Clacton, again showed no trace of structures directly referable to the makers of the Peterborough sherds found there.

Peterborough sherds, and other objects of the Secondary Neolithic cultures, have been found in situations suggesting the collection of material from a nearby settlement below or in the material of round barrows at such sites as Niton in the Isle of Wight, Battlegore in Somerset, or North Deighton in Yorkshire. At the last site the associated material included leaf-shaped flint arrowheads and part of a polished-edge knife, as well as fragments of stone axes from the Graig Lwyd and the Great Langdale factories. At

---

[1] I formerly assigned the pottery from Grovehurst to the Windmill Hill group (Piggott, 1931) but its affinities must in fact lie with Peterborough ware (see p. 308 below).

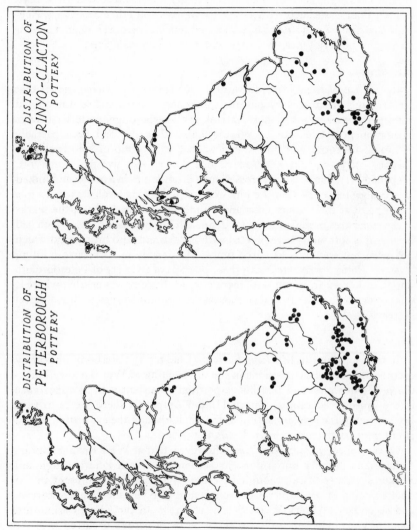

DISTRIBUTION OF
RINYO-CLACTON
POTTERY

DISTRIBUTION OF
PETERBOROUGH
POTTERY

Fig. 48.

Battlegore, a polished-edge knife and a *petit-tranchet* derivative were also found. As we have seen, Peterborough pottery was again found (with Western Neolithic sherds), in Anglesey under the chambered cairn of Bryn yr Hen Bobl, associated with Graig Lwyd axes and other Secondary Neolithic material. At the Ehenside Tarn settlement there was again a similar mixture of pottery types, this time with Great Langdale axes.

Pit-fall traps

Recent excavations in south-western Scotland (1951) have shown that the trapping of animals by pit-falls containing pointed stakes was carried out by the makers of a local variant of Peterborough pottery at Mye Plantation near Glenluce in Wigtownshire. The site had been partially excavated in 1902, and interpreted as that of a group of 'pit-dwellings' (Mann, 1903), and the new excavations showed that five pits, some 7 ft. deep, had been dug in a line across a small promontory in a marsh and linked by a timber fence. Within the pits were set numerous birch stakes cut to a sharp point at their upper ends and bluntly shaped at the base, the marks of the stone axes used being clearly defined. The sides of the pits (which had been dug in soft sand) were reveted with hazel wands and brushwood which had been renewed at least three times, presumably in successive hunting seasons. Pottery associated with these pits was of a variety of Peterborough ware also known from the settlement sites on Luce Sands nearby, where it was associated with *B*-beaker sherds and stratified below Food-vessel pottery.[1]

Burials

In the southern English *Long Barrows* (Chapter 11), Peterborough pottery occurred in secondary positions in the ditch silting at Wor Barrow, Thickthorn, Holdenhurst and Badshot: a position consistent with its appearance in the causewayed camps. But at Hinton Ampner a sherd seems to have been found in the primary silting of the ditch, though the excavation record is not very satisfactory (Grinsell, 1939, 15, 202).

Of the collective *chambered tombs*, however, that at West Kennet appears to have had primary burial deposits accompanied with Peterborough and Beaker sherds (p. 144), though Peterborough pottery was present in the final blocking of the Severn-Cotswold tombs of Nympsfield and Notgrove, and secondary at Poles Wood South (p. 142). In the Clyde-Carlingford tomb of Cairnholy I in Galloway, Peterborough pottery occurred with the final burials and under the blocking in the forecourt.

Two collective burials, however, seem distinctively of the Peterborough culture: both are small chambers or large cists built within natural caves,

1 I am indebted to Mr R. J. C. Atkinson and Mr P. R. Ritchie for information in advance of publication.

the roof of which forms the covering. The burials in the Gop Cave, Prestatyn are included by Daniel (1950, 46) in his group of sub-megalithic tombs, and in the chamber were the bones of at least fourteen individuals which the excavator considered to have been buried successively. Of five skulls which could be measured, three were dolichocephalic and two brachycephalic. With the burials were sherds of two Peterborough bowls, a flint knife polished on the edge and both faces, and two jet objects of the 'belt-slider' class. The Church Dale, Derbyshire, site was similar in construction (Harris, 1938), and contained two disarticulated skeletons, sherds of two Peterborough pots, flint flakes and a *petit-tranchet* derivative arrowhead. A similar burial, though without grave-goods, is reported from another Derbyshire site, Ash Tree Cave near Whitwell.

At least one burial under a round barrow has good claims to be included in the Peterborough culture. Barrow 26 on Handley Down, Dorset, was surrounded by a circular ditch 40 ft. in diameter, broken by an entrance causeway, and contained a fragmentary central inhumation and another, 8 ft. off-centre, with a jet 'belt-slider' at the hip. Sherds of Peterborough pottery were found in the mound of the barrow and in the ditch silting, where it was stratified below a sherd of a class *B* beaker (Pitt-Rivers, 1898, 140).

The association of Peterborough pottery with jet 'belt-sliders' is discussed below, and it suggests that the inhumations under round barrows in Yorkshire accompanied only by such objects should in fact be assigned to some aspect of the Secondary Neolithic cultures (Mortimer, 1905; Greenwell, 1877), and the Linch Hill burials, mentioned again under the Dorchester culture and accompanied by such a slider and a polished flint knife and earlier than a *B*-beaker burial, must certainly be related (Grimes, 1944). But the recurrence of the stone types only in these burials, unaccompanied by pottery, underlines the difficulty of separating the component variants within the general Secondary Neolithic group: one certainly cannot bring them within the Peterborough group on the existing evidence, and I have therefore assigned them rather to the loosely defined Dorchester culture discussed in the final section of this chapter.

Ritual structures

Peterborough pottery occurred on two sites, Dorchester I and The Sanctuary on Overton Hill, which can only be classed as ritual, consisting in essentials of circular areas either delimited by ditches and including groups of pits, or (as at The Sanctuary) consisting of timber and stone structures which seem to represent in part a much-reconstructed circular wooden building (Cunnington, 1931; Piggott, 1940a). Such structures are discussed as a group under the Dorchester culture below. At The Sanctuary the Peterborough sherds were associated with those of *B*-beakers.

MATERIAL EQUIPMENT

Pottery

The pottery by which the Peterborough culture is distinguished can now be seen to fall into two or three subgroups, but there are nevertheless certain features common to the whole series. In general, the ware is heavy and coarse, though in the Ebbsfleet class the standard is noticeably higher; flint grit is frequent, and the ware has a characteristic flakiness in fracture. Pots of at least the coarser fabrics can be seen to have been built up by the coil or ring method, each ring being smeared down on to the rounded upper edge of that beneath. Most of the vessels seem to have rounded bases, though these are not infrequently flattened by the sheer weight of the pot before complete drying and firing, and some are nearly conical, or made as a deliberate flat base of small diameter. The features of the ware as known in 1931 are fully described in Piggott, 1932 *b*, but subdivisions can now be recognized.

Of these, the most characteristic is *Ebbsfleet ware* (Fig. 49), named from the Kent site where it was first discovered (Burchell & Piggott, 1939), and since recognized at Dorchester-on-Thames, the submerged land-surface of the Essex coast (Warren *et al.* 1936, fig. 3, 4), Windmill Hill in Wiltshire, Combe Hill and Whitehawk in Sussex (Musson, 1950; Curwen, 1934*a*; 1936), and Maiden Castle in Dorset (Wheeler, 1943, fig. 34, no. 118). The ware is usually good and the walls of the pots thin, while decoration is relatively restrained and the rims simple: at least one pot from Ebbsfleet has a profile strongly resembling a funnel-beaker. There seems to be a group of unornamented, or practically unornamented, vessels, carinated or with weak rounded shoulders, best represented at the type-site.

Twisted or whipped cord ornament appears at Windmill Hill, Combe Hill and Whitehawk, and once at Ebbsfleet itself, but more common are incised patterns, of which a lattice is the most frequent. Oblique incisions, and finger-nail impressions (often on top of the rim) are also common, and rows of impressed dots or dimples, and pits (usually made with the finger-tip) in the neck of the vessel. It is possible that one should include in this group the pots with a row of holes under the rim such as those from Grovehurst and Stevenston Sands, Ardeer (Ayrshire).

There is at present no evidence for placing this ware in stratigraphical relationship with other aspects of the Peterborough culture. At Windmill Hill, Ebbsfleet and Mortlake ware were both secondary to the main occupation, but at Whitehawk, although some of the Ebbsfleet ware sherds were apparently secondary, others were 'intimately associated with the primary occupation of the Camp' (Piggott in Curwen, 1934*a*, 118), while at Combe Hill such pottery was not only primary but the only ware found. In east Sussex at least then it is approximately contemporary with the construction and use of the causewayed camps of the Windmill Hill culture.

The typical Peterborough or *Mortlake ware* (Pl. X), as originally defined from the type-site and certain bowls from the Thames at Mortlake and elsewhere, is represented by more or less hemispherical or more rarely conical vessels, with a deep cavetto neck above a carination, and a thickened rim, angular and often bevelled in section. Decoration is abundant and closely

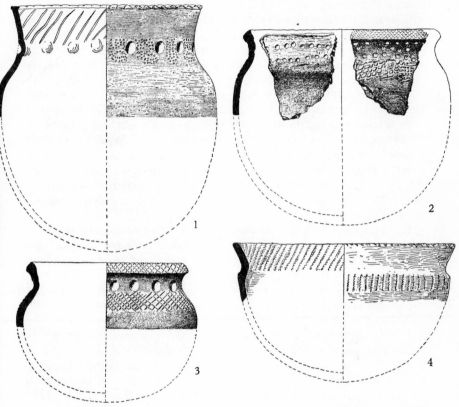

Fig. 49. Ebbsfleet ware. 1–3, Ebbsfleet (*after Burchell*); 4, Combe Hill. Scale ¼.

set, tending, however, to be absent from the lower third of the pot, and includes twisted or whipped cord, with 'maggot' patterns formed by impressing a short length of straight or curved cord. These 'maggots' are also produced, with other impressed patterns, by using the articular ends of the leg-bones of birds and small mammals, as Miss Liddell demonstrated (1929): less frequently a comb or a *cardium* shell edge is used to produce a similar effect. The elements of the patterns are usually arranged in herring-bone or zigzag zones, sometimes in horizontal lines and occasionally in multiple arcs which may be formed by impressed cord, bird-bone (or possibly by a string of small vertebrae—at Badshot: Keiller & Piggott, 1939), or by the finger-nail. Pits made with the finger-tip, or with the tip of a conical shell, occur in the hollow neck. Exceptional deep baggy vessels occur, as that from Icklingham (Pl. X, no. 2).

As we saw in Chapter III, the features of carination, hollow neck and thickened rim, together with the disposition of the ornament, are so strikingly similar in these Peterborough or Mortlake bowls, and in the series of Windmill Hill culture vessels classed as East Anglian bowls, that connexions between the two cultures seem inevitable. When we come to consider the Continental affinities of the Peterborough culture we shall see that Mortlake ware is more characteristically insular and specifically British than Ebbsfleet ware, which is more recognizably related to certain north European pottery types: if we regard Ebbsfleet as the earlier, as there is some reason for doing, the developed Mortlake type might well be the result of the adoption of certain elements from the evolved Western Neolithic wares of southern England represented by the Abingdon and East Anglian styles. Stratification is consistent in placing Mortlake ware after the abandonment of the causewayed camps and the construction of long barrows in Wessex at least, so such a sequence would be consistent with the evidence as we know it at present.

It is convenient to mention here two vessels which seem to be related to the Mortlake series just described: a small shallow undecorated saucer-like object from Iver, Buckinghamshire (Lacaille, 1937), and an oval saucer from Harmondsworth, both found associated with Mortlake ware. The latter in particular recalls the Ertebølle vessels which Mathiassen has convincingly interpreted as blubber-lamps (Clark, 1936a, 152), and it is likely that both should be classed as likely to have served for this purpose.

It seems likely that we may recognize a northern variety of pottery within the Peterborough culture when the abundant material from Glenluce Sands in Wigtownshire has been fully analysed and published (Callander, 1929). Pottery from this region, and again from Hedderwick in East Lothian, and probably, too, such finds as those from Ford Castle, and Scremerston Hill, Northumberland, while sharing many features with Mortlake ware, nevertheless have significant points of difference. It is premature to distinguish 'Glenluce ware' at the present stage, but the existence of such a local type is inherently probable.

Flint and stone

Axes. Flint axes were found at Combe Hill, Grovehurst, and Winterbourne Dauntsey: here and at Combe Hill the axes were flint-mine products. Stone axes from the Graig Lwyd factory occurred at Bryn yr Hen Bobl (with others of local rock) and at the Kennet Avenue site and North Deighton (in the latter with Great Langdale exports). Great Langdale axes at Ehenside

Tarn were associated with pottery which included Peterborough sherds of some kind, but the associations at Windmill Hill (Graig Lwyd and Great Langdale) and Abingdon (Great Langdale) were not precise. At Grovehurst was one, probably two, axes of undetermined igneous rock, and there was a flint *pick* from the same site. There was a small *tranchet axe* from the Kennet Avenue.

Polished-edge knives occurred at the Kennet Avenue site, at North Deighton, Battlegore, and in the Gop burial, while in the West Kennet chambered tomb was a *polished-edge scraper* of related form. Both types are characteristic of the light flint industry of the Secondary Neolithic cultures described above (p. 285).

Single-piece curved sickle. Three complete or fragmentary specimens came from Grovehurst, but there are no direct Peterborough associations for those on the submerged land-surface of the Essex coast or that at Abingdon.

Leaf-shaped arrowheads. This type, indistinguishable from those found in Western Neolithic contexts, is known from Grovehurst, Combe Hill, Winterbourne Dauntsey, North Deighton and Bryn yr Hen Bobl in Peterborough contexts. The association at the type-site is not clear.

Petit-tranchet derivative arrowheads. Variants of the series classified by Clark (1935 a) were abundant in the Kennet Avenue site and occurred at The Sanctuary as well as in the Church Dale burial and probably associated (like the polished-edge knife) at Battlegore. The Peterborough associations at Dorchester Site I and on the Essex coast are not direct.

Serrated flakes were recognized at Grovehurst, Peterborough and the Kennet Avenue site, and may have been present elsewhere.

Jet or lignite 'belt-sliders'. In the Gop Cave burials, and in Handley Down, barrow 26, cylindrical jet objects with rounded ends and a transverse oval perforation were found, associated with Peterborough pottery, in the latter instance at the hip of the skeleton (Fig. 63, no. 2): in the burial with a polished flint knife at Linch Hill already referred to, one was found in a similar position, and another again at the hip of an otherwise unaccompanied inhumation under a barrow at Thixendale, E.R. Yorks, which had Food-vessel and Cinerary-urn secondaries (Mortimer, 1905, 127). The use of the objects as some form of belt-fastener seems then reasonably certain. In addition to the finds mentioned, they are known from three further barrows in E.R. Yorks, all without significant associations (Mortimer, 1905, 73, 177; Greenwell, 1877, 34), from a secondary position in the Beacharra chambered cairn (p. 176 above), and similarly secondary in the silt of the Giants' Hills long barrow in Lincolnshire (Phillips, 1936, 71). Stray finds have been recorded from Newbury, Berkshire, from Berwickshire, and from the Isle of Skye (Thurnam, 1870, 513). It has been customary to regard these objects as belonging to the British Bronze Age, but there is in fact no direct evidence for such a date, and the Peterborough (and the Linch Hill) associations are convincing for placing their origin within the Secondary Neolithic cultures, even if they survived later.

Miscellaneous. Among significant stone objects one may note *balls* at Bryn yr Hen Bobl, comparable with those of the Boyne culture or with Rinyo-Clacton; a *grain-rubber* at Combe Hill; and fragments of Niedermendig *lava* from the Andernach region at the Kennet Avenue site and at The Sanctuary, Avebury. These latter finds are particularly important as an indication of trade contacts with the Lower Rhine region, though at The Sanctuary the mixture of Beaker pottery with Peterborough renders the relationship less certain, especially since this stone was used by Beaker folk in the Rhineland.

THE RELATIONSHIPS OF THE PETERBOROUGH CULTURE

So far as its material equipment is concerned, apart from pottery, we have seen that the Peterborough 'culture' consists of a selection of types from the common stock of the Secondary Neolithic cultures at large, in which local Mesolithic traditions certainly played a large part. But the pottery is something distinctive, and when it was first recognized as a class by R. A. Smith he noted certain similarities, especially in the pit-ornament, between it and the south Swedish 'dwelling-place' wares, and suggested the possibility that Peterborough ware represented a province of a widely diffused culture 'that occupied the extreme north of Europe, possibly extending into Asia' (R. A. Smith, 1910). Twenty years later Childe was able with more precision to demonstrate that it had features sufficient 'to connect it unambiguously with an extensive ceramic family to which the name Baltic might be attached', though he showed that the same pottery could be traced eastwards to the Urals and beyond, and emphasized that 'we can point to no strictly parallel combination (of motifs) east of the North Sea the direct transplantation whereof might account for the Peterborough culture' (Childe, 1931 *a*).

Reviewing the situation, Hawkes stressed the fact that the relationship between British Peterborough pottery and that of the Baltic was 'not one of exact identity, but a vague general family feeling', and suggested that some common ancestry on both sides of the North Sea was responsible for this, and the culture and its pottery 'should find its starting-point in the Mesolithic' (C. Hawkes, 1937).

We have seen how the stone industry associated with Peterborough pottery is in fact of Mesolithic ancestry in the main, and that the underlying continuity of the cultures ultimately derived from that of Maglemose is inevitable in view of the former land-connexions between eastern England and southern Scandinavia, with regional differences no less naturally emphasized by the subsequent marine transgression and the separation of the two regions. In Scandinavia, not only has the long survival of the hunter-fisher economies side by side with those of immigrant farmers been abundantly demonstrated, but the elements within the 'dwelling-place' pottery styles can now be seen to fall into at least two main groups.

Of these, one is that of the cord-ornamented wares the techniques of which Rosenberg (1931) discussed in detail and showed to belong to a huge province stretching from south Russia to the Baltic and the White Sea. Certain aspects of this widely diffused style have been clarified by Becker's work on the funnel-beakers of Denmark and northern Europe generally, which in his group B and subsequent developments use cord-ornament (Becker, 1948; 1949)—we can recognize for instance that the pottery of the first and third settlements of 'dwelling-place' folk at Siretorp in Blekinge (south Sweden) is of his C style (Bagge & Kjellmark, 1939). Becker has identified ten sites of this culture in south Sweden, and the 'dolmen' pottery of the later funnel-beaker phase, with abundant cord-ornament, again occurs in 'dwelling-place' sites.

In his study of the chronology of 'dwelling-place' pottery in Finland, Europaeus (1930) showed that in the earliest wares, his style I, twisted and whipped cord ornament was present as an ornamental technique, in addition to shallow grooving, incision, some stamped ornament and a sparing use of pits set below the rim. But in his styles II and III, with their subdivisions, the pottery shows a dominant use of comb-stamps, incisions and frequent pits in zones or chevrons over the whole body of the pot, and this 'pit-comb ware' is characteristic of most of the Finnish sites (cf. Ailio, 1909) and those in Sweden and Norway (Ekholm, 1927; Bagge & Kjellmark, 1939, with refs.; Gjessing, 1944; 1945). It occurs in the last (fourth) settlement at Siretorp.

This comb- and pit-ornamented ware has recently been set in its wider relationship by Gjessing (1944), who shows it to be an element in what he has defined as the Circumpolar Stone Age, stretching from Norway to North America. Throughout this region, mainly coastal but with penetration by rivers into the hinterland at many points, a great uniformity of culture can be observed, and this is particularly noticeable in the pit-comb pottery—Janse (1932) brought this home by publishing a striking photograph of sherds from a site in the State of Maine in the U.S.A. for comparison with Swedish 'dwelling-place' finds. Gjessing stresses that 'as an arctic culture the Baltic Stone Age is quite peripheral, the arctic elements being mixed with others of different origin' (1942, 495), and we have seen this in the pottery styles discussed above, but he also recognizes that Peterborough pottery should be brought into the Circumpolar series in a similar relationship (1944, 65). It must be emphasized that the concept of a Circumpolar Stone Age is cultural and not chronological, having its roots in the Mesolithic but surviving into recent times among, for instance, the Eskimos.

Of the British pottery, the thin rims and relatively weak shoulders of the

Ebbsfleet group come nearer to the profiles of the Scandinavian pottery than those of the Mortlake style, but we have seen reason to believe that this characteristically British form seems likely to have evolved as a result of contacts with the makers of the developed Windmill Hill pottery of the Abingdon and East Anglian bowl styles. But even at Ebbsfleet or Combe Hill there is a similarity without identity, and elements from both the cord-ornamented funnel-beakers and from the pit-comb wares are already mixed, though one bowl from Combe Hill (Fig. 49, no. 4) with cord ornament on and inside the rim, and again in a series of short vertical strokes over the rounded shoulder, comes very near to being an actual funnel-beaker, and one Ebbsfleet vessel has a profile recalling funnel-beaker forms (Fig. 49, no. 1) (e.g. Bagge & Kjellmark, 1939, pl. 56). The deep baggy form of the Icklingham pot is paralleled in pit-comb vessels from Finland (Nordman, 1922, 15).

Childe (1932) selected as especially distinctive motifs the crescentic 'maggot' pattern and the multiple arcs of impressed cord, both of which occur, as he showed, on pottery from Hammeren on Bornholm, which is now included by Becker in his C group of funnel-beakers, and similar corded arcs occur in the same phase at Kristrup Mølle (Becker, 1948, 63, 161) and again at Siretorp, with whipped cord 'maggots' in the Peterborough style, in the Upper S-layer, which also contains sherds of collared flasks of 'dolmen' type (Bagge & Kjellmark, 1939, pls. 55, 60). From the pit-comb wares the pits appear to be the main contribution, in the neck-groove in a manner comparable to those of Europaeus's style II (Europaeus, 1930, Abb. 50, 53, 6061; Ailio, 1909, Abb. 62), and the use of 'bird-bone' and similar stamps to produce a short dentated groove is in effect the counter-part of the broad-toothed comb-stamp of northern Europe.

We may also note the use of lattice incisions, common on the pit-comb ware and not infrequent in Britain (Lacaille, 1937; Burchell & Piggott, 1939); and the conical form of certain vessels such as that from Ford (Northumberland) or (with a small flat base) those from Peterborough and Wandsworth (Piggott, 1931; Leeds, 1922) must be related to similar types in the pit-comb series. The plain pottery with a row of holes beneath the rim (as at Grovehurst) presumably reflects the pit-comb element in the complex, though similarly placed holes do occur in funnel-beakers (e.g. Schwantes, 1934, fig. 158; Becker, 1948, pl. vii, no. 2).

It is clear that we cannot separate the component elements in Peterborough pottery to the same degree that is possible in Scandinavia, and we must regard the distinction between the two main contributory groups—funnel-beakers and pit-comb ware—as becoming increasingly blurred as we cross the North Sea, with the resultant production of a characteristically British type, comparable with the analogous mixed style seen in certain sherds from the Lower Rhine (Kersten, 1938). Whatever the strength of the underlying Mesolithic tradition in the two areas may have been, however, it is difficult to regard the British material, with its mixed ancestry, as representing a completely local evolution parallel to that in Scandinavia and within the ambit of Gjessing's Circumpolar Stone Age, since then the pit-comb element would surely have predominated or have been exclusively present. The funnel-beaker contribution relates it to a specific stage in the evolution of this north European pottery form, since the earlier types do not have the characteristic cord ornament, and whatever may be the earliest date of pit-comb ware in north Europe, its persistence even to the dawn of the historical period is clear.

It looks then as if we must regard the appearance of Peterborough pottery (in all its forms) as an indication of settlement in south-east England by people arriving by sea from Scandinavia and sharing with the late Mesolithic inhabitants they encountered on arrival a common ancestry and many common traditions in stone and bone working. It hardly seems possible to derive the British material from that of the Lower Rhine already mentioned, and parallel development in both areas from a common Scandinavian source seems more likely. The makers of pit-comb ware seem largely to have maintained a hunter-fisher economy, though even in Scandinavia there is some evidence of agriculture (saucer-querns from Vivastemåla, for example; Bagge, 1941), and the single-piece sickles related to the curved knives included by Gjessing as a Circumpolar type, if not used for other purposes than harvesting, such as reed-cutting, would imply the growing of cereals. But the necessary recognition of funnel-beaker elements in Peterborough ware makes some practice of agriculture almost inevitable, since the makers of these pots were agriculturalists from their earliest known stage in northern Europe (Becker, 1948; Childe, 1949).

The chronological setting of this event is fortunately fairly well documented. In Britain, the Whitehawk evidence shows that early Peterborough pottery of the Ebbsfleet type (as yet uninfluenced by local Windmill Hill styles in east England) was being made in east Sussex in at least the later phases of the use of the causewayed camps there: at Combe Hill it is in fact the only pottery found. In Wessex, pottery mainly of the Mortlake style (developed apparently under the influence of the late phase of Windmill Hill ware represented by the East Anglian bowls), appears after the desertion of the causewayed camps and long barrows by their original builders: in Somerset it is present, in terms of the natural climatic sequence, just above the Zone VII a–VII b junction. The Scandinavian evidence would place the C funnel-beakers as the product of a non-megalithic culture flourishing before the full-length inhumations in massive cists known in the past as 'dolmens', and the presence of a thin-butted flint axe appropriate to this period, found in the mound of a long barrow of the Windmill Hill culture in Kent (cf. p. 61 above) would be in agreement with such a date for the appearance of the makers of Peterborough pottery in England. The place in the climatic sequence for this phase would be early in Zone VIII of the Danish sequence, and before the LG IV marine transgression (Troels-Smith in Mathiassen, 1943, 162; Bagge & Kjellmark, 1939, 140ff.), and Jessen (1949) equates the Danish Zone VII–VIII junction with that of Zones VII a and VII b of the British sequence, so that a general agreement between the Danish and Somerset evidence seems established. And if the submerged surface of the Essex coast is to be regarded as the result of a marine transgression equivalent to LG IV, the presence of Peterborough sherds in the Ebbsfleet style upon it would again indicate approximate contemporaneity between the beginnings of the English Peterborough culture and the Danish phase C of the funnel-beaker series.

SECONDARY NEOLITHIC CULTURES IN IRELAND

The so-called 'Campignian' stone industries in Ireland have already been dealt with under the general head of Heavy Stone Industries within the Secondary Neolithic group, but there remain certain better-defined local cultures which are conveniently discussed here, since the Sandhill cultures are distinguished by cord-ornamented wares which have certain affinities with those of Peterborough, and indeed the sites on Rough Island, Lough Enagh, and on Island MacHugh, have been classed by their excavator as of the Peterborough culture.

THE BANN CULTURE

In his discussion of post-Larnian developments in Northern Ireland, Movius (1942, 213) divides the material, as we have seen, into two groups: (a) Campignian, of Mesolithic origin but originating outside Ireland, and (b) the epi-Mesolithic cultures of the Bann and Sandhill type, of indigenous origin. The 'Campignian' cultures, associated with axe-factories in certain instances, have already been discussed, but it is convenient to consider the Bann and Sandhill cultures of Northern Ireland here. The Bann culture (Movius, 1942, 239–52) is centred in the valley of the Lower Bann, though the characteristic product of the 'Bann point' is known from other parts of Ireland and in the Isle of Man (O'Riordain, 1946; Clark, 1935 b, 74). The excavated site at Newferry, Co. Londonderry, produced hearths and a culture layer in Diatomite deposits which could be assigned to Zone VII b of the post-glacial sequence (Jessen, 1949).

Pottery

Sherds of a single vessel, probably round-based, with a cordoned rim and lugs, and scored ornament, are of Beacharra and Sandhill affinities, a fairly good parallel to the rim-section coming from the lower Neolithic level at Rough Island, Lough Enagh (Davies, 1941).

Stone

Flint. The well-known 'Bann point' was represented at Newferry by primary flakes with trimmed butts, but the tanged form was not present, though widely known from other Diatomite deposits. Other types included trimmed points, triangular-section 'fabricator' tools, and scrapers.

Other stones. Small basalt axes and a polisher were found. This equipment can be amplified from other sites and casual finds—the points are frequently found in groups of from six to ten, and well-worked leaf-shaped lance-heads occur, one from Derrytagh North being found in the VII*b* zone of the peat (Jessen, 1949, 117). Huge stone axes up to 17 in. long are also known, and heavy bone points may also belong to the culture. But among the most interesting objects referable to the Bann culture are the two stone plaques, from the Diatomite at Culbane, and from somewhere in Co. Antrim, which, as Hawkes has pointed out (C. Hawkes, 1941), are allied to the schist plaques of Iberia which are themselves highly schematized representations of the human figure, and associated with the collective tombs of Portugal. Reference has been made to these plaques in connexion with the decorative art of the Boyne culture, and their presence in the Diatomite provides a cultural and chronological link between the two cultures.

This rather unsatisfactory name has come into use for certain types of pottery which frequently occur in the coastal dune sites of Northern Ireland, where they are usually mixed with other sherds, flint, stone and metal objects ranging from the Neolithic to the Early Christian period. Movius has summarized the material with a full bibliography (1942, 252; also May & Batty, 1948), but pending a full corpus of material, much of which is unpublished, it is difficult to make an analysis of types and ornament. But some of the Sandhill types do occur at Lough Gur, and at two stratified sites described below, while, as we have seen, much of the Sandhill pottery has close affinities to Beacharra C ware (above, p. 173). Movius concludes that the sandhills themselves represent relict areas of impoverished communities— 'as a group', he says, 'they suggest a continuum of Late Larnian tradition which was influenced by that particular culture which was dominant in the vicinity at any given time' (1942, 252).

The use of cord ornament on the Sandhill wares (Fig. 50) has led to comparisons being made with the Peterborough ware of England, discussed above, and some underlying affinities are certainly present. As we have seen in discussing the Beacharra C pottery, and especially the group of sherds from the 'Larne' site (Gallery-graves in the Goakstown-Dunteige area), there appears to be some Scandinavian contact distinct from that implicit in the funnel-beaker and pit-comb ware affinities of Peterborough ware—in fact, as Childe has said, 'The techniques and motifs on the... pottery from Larne... should be regarded as derived from the Baltic... while Peterborough ware would have come from the same quarter... by a rather different route'. (Piggott & Childe, 1932.) The same group of motifs and techniques appear on the Sandhill pottery, and on that from two Northern Irish sites where stratification was obtained.

The first of these, that on Rough Island, Lough Enagh (Davies, 1941), showed a stratification as follows:

(1) Lowest level; sherds not frequent, and less frequently ornamented than in layer (2) above, and on the whole dissimilar from these. Round-based bowls, one ribbed rim recalling that from Newferry. Flint hollow scrapers and four Bann points.

(2) Main Neolithic occupation with pottery of Sandhill types, with hammer-head rim and grooved neck, and lugs not uncommonly present. Comparisons could be made with Sandhill sherds from Dundrum (Hewson, 1938).

(3) Bronze Age level with late cordoned urn of Pollacorragune-Knockast type, and possibly sherds of an unornamented beaker of degenerate type (cf. Largantea).

Davies notes that the presence of lugs was unusual if the pottery was to be regarded as of Peterborough type: they are a Western feature and are common on Sandhill sites.

The Island MacHugh site, Co. Tyrone (Davies, 1950), included timberwork of crannog type in each level, but the remains in the Neolithic level were too fragmentary to interpret, though both vertical piles and horizontal logs were present. The stratification here was as follows:

(1) Lowest layer, equivalent to Rough Island (2), with Sandhill type pottery some with long lines of fine whipped or twisted cord, sometimes in panels of alternate vertical and horizontal groups; crescentic 'maggot' impressions. Flints comprised hollow scrapers, leaf and lozenge arrowheads, and flakes. One piece of stone allied to that from Tievebulliagh.

(2) Above this, with some evidence of tree growth after the Neolithic phase, were wooden structures and artifacts of the Late Bronze Age, with a pot comparable in general terms to that from Rough Island.

The palaeobotanical examination of the peat made by Mitchell (in Davies, 1950, 3–6) showed that the Neolithic occupation was shortly before the end of Zone VIIb, overlapping with the Newferry Diatomite and approximately contemporary with the Rockbarton beaker sherds.

This evidence, then, suggests that some part of the Sandhill culture at least falls comparatively late in the Irish Neolithic, a position which would be confirmed by its affinities with Beacharra C ware. It seems likely that a real distinction should however be made between the pottery of Beacharra C and that of Rough Island-Island MacHugh-Sandhill class, on the grounds that in the former alone are the finely made carinated bowls which have their origins in the Western Neolithic forms of Beacharra C. The Sandhill wares show, however, in general profiles and other features (e.g. lugs and handles)

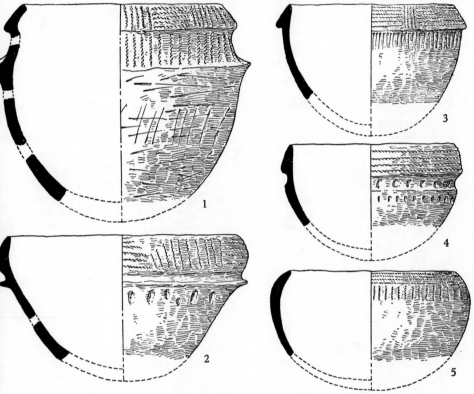

Fig. 50. Sandhill wares. 1, 2, Island MacHugh (*after Davies*); 3, 5, Dundrum; 4, Rough Island (*after Davies*). Scale ¼.

which also derive from Western Neolithic forms, and the heavy bevelled rims which bear a superficial resemblance to those of some Mortlake style bowls seem in fact to be coarse versions of forms present in the Scottish chambered tombs such as Rudh' an Dunain, Nether Largie, Achnacree, etc. (Callander, 1929, fig. 30 for sections), and we shall notice a parallel devolution in the rims of Ronaldsway ware.

The motifs employed on the Sandhill wares are in the main those of Beacharra C, with impressed twisted or whipped cord as the main decorative technique. Multiple horizontal cord lines at the rim, with a 'fringe' of short vertical impressions below, is a common motif, with the 'hurdle-pattern' of panels of horizontal and vertical lines, and simple or crescentic 'maggot' patterns of twisted cord. Whipped cord is used in long continuous lines rather than in short strokes.

The relationships of the Sandhill wares

While the use of twisted and whipped-cord ornament offers immediate comparison with Peterborough pottery, the Sandhill wares have nevertheless marked points of dissimilarity with this style. The virtual absence of pits below the rim or in other parts of the pots, and of any form of comb-ornament, seems to indicate at once that the pit-comb wares of the Circumpolar Stone Age can play no part in its make-up. The use of the hurdle-motif is again foreign to Peterborough, as is that of whipped-cord impressions in long continuous lines. Bird-bone ornament, which in Peterborough ware represents the comb-stamp element, is absent in the Sandhill pottery.

Yet, as Childe pointed out in 1932, the ornament on the 'Larne' pottery, which includes almost all the Sandhill motifs, must reflect Scandinavian contacts, and these contacts, he felt, should be not later than the beginning of the Passage-grave period in Denmark (Piggott & Childe, 1932). When we turn to the evidence reviewed in connexion with Peterborough ware, we can now see that the combination of motifs present in the Sandhill pottery but absent in Peterborough ware is exactly those that, although they begin to appear in phase C of Becker's funnel-beaker series, continue in the pottery of the 'dolmens'. We may note in detail the very characteristic rim design of horizontal lines with a fringe of vertical strokes, executed in twisted cord, on C-group funnel-beakers (Becker, 1948, pl. IV, no. 1; Bagge & Kjellmark, 1939, pl. 58), and on pots of the same phase, hurdle pattern and even crescentic 'maggots' (Becker, 1948, figs. 35, 39; pl. V, no. 2). Long lines of whipped-cord patterns are one of the most characteristic forms of ornament on 'dolmen' pottery, where perforated handles also appear (cf. Hewson, 1936, pot from Murlough Bay with fine whipped-cord lines and handle), and in discussing the Beacharra C ware from Dunloy attention has been drawn to the raised ribs on pot A, comparable with those on 'dolmen' pottery, and the Danish Early Passage-grave affinities of pot B.

It looks, then, as if the Beacharra C style, and that of the Sandhill pottery, represents a period of Scandinavian contact slightly later than that responsible for Peterborough pottery, and one which did not include contributions from the makers of pit-comb wares. In the Scandinavian sequence this would be in the period of the 'dolmen' graves, or at the beginning of the first collective tombs of the Passage-grave group, and in terms of climatic history near the middle of the Danish zone VIII, at the maximum of the fourth Litorina transgression. It may be significant to recall, in this connexion, that while Peterborough pottery from Somerset could be assigned to a position early in the British Zone VII *b* (equivalent to the Danish Zone VIII), the settlement of makers of Sandhill pottery at Island MacHugh belonged to the latter half of VII *b*.

The question of the route whereby contacts could be established between Ulster and Denmark has already been touched on in Chapter vi, in connexion with Beacharra C ware, and we may here draw attention to cord-ornamented wares from the East Riding of Yorkshire which do not seem to be typical of any known variety of Peterborough ware, but which do suggest links with Sandhill pottery (Newbigin, 1937, 199–202). Some routes across northern England seem likely, perhaps not unconnected with those which brought Irish axes and halberds of copper and bronze to Scandinavia at the dawn of the Bronze Age.

A NOTE ON SCANDINAVIAN POTTERY FINDS IN EASTERN ENGLAND

In connexion with the evidence for contacts with Scandinavian pottery styles discussed above, attention should be drawn to two finds of actual Danish Neolithic sherds in eastern England. The first, believed to be from the Durham coast between West Hartlepool and Seaton Carew, was described in detail by Childe (1932 *c*), who showed the eight sherds to range in type from the 'dolmen' period through that of the Passage-graves. But Trechmann (1936, 168) has cast doubts upon the authenticity of the find, which belonged to a nineteenth-century collection of antiquities, and the representative nature of the group raises the suspicion of the sherds being a genuine Scandinavian type-series acquired in the last century and accidentally attributed to a find-spot in a midden which otherwise only produced Roman objects. The original description of the site, in 1883, makes no mention of these sherds.

The second find consists of three sherds of Danish Passage-grave pottery found 'in a field near Orpington', Kent, in about 1880, and now in Maidstone Museum (Cook, 1937). These may again be strays from a Victorian collection of antiquities, but perhaps have a slightly better claim as an ancient import than the Durham sherds.

Fragments of a large biconical vessel from Brantham, Suffolk, have been compared to Danish Passage-grave types, but although it is not easy to suggest parallels for the pot in question, it does not seem likely that there is any real connexion (R. A. Smith, 1925).

THE RINYO-CLACTON CULTURE

Introduction

In 1936 it was recognized that a group of very individual pottery from the submerged land-surface of the Essex coast at Clacton (Warren *et al.* 1936) could be related to that already published from the Wiltshire site of

Woodhenge (Cunnington, 1929), and also to that from a settlement site in Orkney at Skara Brae (Childe, 1931 b). A total of some twenty sites producing similar pottery was then listed, and indicated two provinces—one centred in Orkney, with a few sites elsewhere in Scotland, and the other in southern England south of the Wash. Nearly double the original number of sites are now known, but the distinction of two areas, a southern and a northern, without intermediate sites, still remains, with the greater number of finds from southern England. This pottery, discussed at length below, was originally described as Grooved ware (Piggott in Warren *et al.* 1936), but it is now proposed to drop this title and to refer to the ware, with the other elements of material equipment now recognizable, as that of the Rinyo-Clacton culture. The Rinyo site (in Orkney) has been chosen to form part of the name rather than the original Skara Brae settlement, since here stratigraphy was first clearly distinguished by Childe (1939; 1948 b).

The pottery by which the culture was first identified is distinguished by its lack of cord ornament or of pit-comb techniques, and is therefore clearly separated from the Peterborough group. But the associated stone types include many characteristic of the Secondary Neolithic light industries in flint, and in the northern province there are contributions from the Circumpolar Stone Age repertoire of stone tools. Bone types, again, link the Rinyo-Clacton culture with other regional groups within the Secondary Neolithic complex, such as the Dorchester culture described below. The known sites include settlements such as those at Skara Brae and Rinyo, and on the submerged land-surface of the Essex coast; ritual monuments within the 'Henge' group (Woodhenge and other sites) and probably ritual pits (Ratfyn, etc.). The pottery is present in a chambered tomb (Unival) as a late deposit, is associated with Peterborough ware in two or three instances, is secondary at Windmill Hill and Maiden Castle, broadly contemporary with beakers at Woodhenge, and earlier than a *C* beaker at Rinyo itself.

Distribution

The northern sites comprise two main and at least one subsidiary settlement in Orkney, and the pottery appears in such coastal sand-dune regions as Hedderwick, Gullane and Glenluce, near Glasgow and in Bute. In the south, sites are concentrated in Wessex, the Middle Thames, and the Cotswold area, with Maiden Castle in Dorset as the furthest south-westerly occurrence, and again in East Anglia, with a site in northern Kent. Intermediate sites have now been recognized near Scarborough and at Scunthorpe (Lincs), but in view of the virtual distinction between the two main areas of settlement, it is convenient to consider them separately. (Fig. 48.)

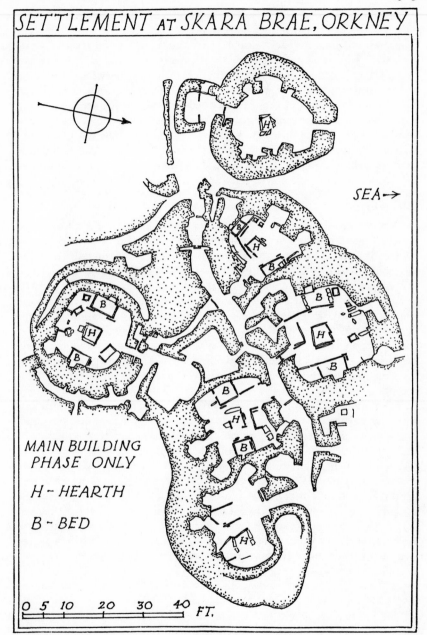

MAIN BUILDING
PHASE ONLY

H - HEARTH

B - BED

SETTLEMENT AT SKARA BRAE, ORKNEY

SEA →

0 5 10   20   30   40 FT.

Fig. 51.

The most outstanding sites of the whole culture are the remarkable settle-ments at Skara Brae in Mainland, and Rinyo on Rousay, in the Orcadian archipelago. These are unique in northern Europe in preserving in detail the structural arrangements of the houses of Neolithic communities owing to the use of stone for many of the purposes—bed-frames, shelves, etc.—normally involving wood, and so forming an enduring element in the archaeological record. Skara Brae is the better preserved of the two sites, but it presents virtual structural identity with Rinyo, and in the ensuing account features described should be taken as common to both settlements unless otherwise specified. All points are documented in Childe, 1931 b, 1939 and 1948 b.

The settlements—building material and lay-out

The houses and much of their furniture are made of the local flagstone which at Skara Brae lies in easily-split laminar masses on the sea-shore, and at Rinyo is available from adjacent outcrops. It is this fissile quality in the flagstone that made possible its use instead of wooden planks for fittings, and of course enabled a high standard of walling and corbelling to be attained in the settlements. The Skara Brae settlement (Fig. 51) lies on the present beach at Skail Bay, and that of Rinyo on a hill-slope within 1,000 yd. of the sea and near a stream, with one 'stalled cairn' within 300 yd. and another 200 yd. further off. At both sites there appears to have been some degree of occupational refuse on the original land-surface before the present constructions began, and both sites show a long history of alteration and reconstruction.

The individual houses, of types to be described below, were grouped into a closely knit complex linked by narrow passages or lanes; at Skara Brae eight houses survive of the main building period, and at Rinyo the size of the settlement is undetermined, though apparently fairly large in extent. Despite frequent rebuilding and re-occupation the material culture of the inhabitants remained fundamentally unchanged, though, as we shall see, certain changes in pottery types can be perceived during the history of the settlements. From the first, it appears that the houses were at least backed up by deliberate deposits of midden material, and in the later stages at Skara Brae this debris had accumulated, and blown sand had collected, to a degree that finally made the settlement virtually subterranean, with the houses con-nected by narrow roofed passages.

The houses

The standard type of house is internally a square with rounded corners measuring some 15–20 ft. across, entered by a single doorway and having a central stone-edged square hearth on which peat was burnt as fuel

(Fig. 52; Pl. XI). The doorways may have elaborate bar-holes, in some instances communicating with a cell in the wall thickness: walls were usually double-faced with fine horizontally coursed flagstones, and internally they

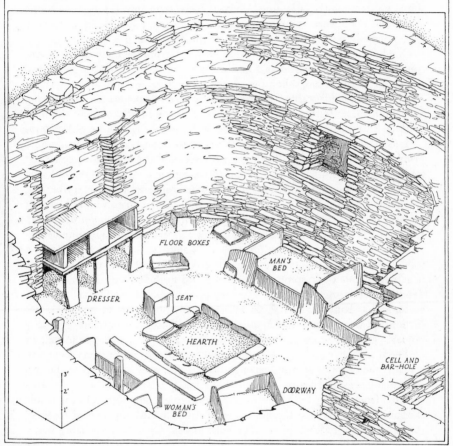

SKARA BRAE HOUSE 7. ISOMETRIC VIEW.

FLOOR BOXES

MAN'S
BED

DRESSER   SEAT

HEARTH

CELL AND
BAR-HOLE

3'

2'

DOORWAY

1'

WOMAN'S
BED

Fig. 52. (*After Childe.*)

begin to oversail almost from floor-level, and stand to a maximum height of 10 ft. To right and left of the entrance are slab-framed beds, some retaining 'bed-posts' at the outer corners formed by narrow upright flagstones. In the earliest phase at Skara Brae, and at Rinyo, these beds are recessed slightly into the walls, but in the later periods of the former site they are not, and it was noted by Childe that of the two beds, that on the right of the door on entering was the longer (6 ft. 6 in. compared with 5 ft. 2 in. in Skara Brae house 1), and on recent Hebridean analogies this may be regarded as the man's bed. Opposite the door was a 'dresser' of slab shelves, in one instance at least with a pot still standing on a shelf when the site was excavated. Keeping-places and cells were contrived in the walls, and small rectangular slab-lined 'boxes' were sunk into the floor. Drains under the floor were sometimes found, paved over, but the house floors were normally not paved, though the connecting passages were.

One house at Skara Brae (no. 8) was detached from the main complex and contained a central hearth, but neither beds nor dresser, and it may have been some form of workshop (as suggested by Childe), or a small byre.

At Rinyo a remarkable feature found in more than one hut was a clay oven built on a stone slab against the hearth, the most complete example being 1 ft. 3 in. square inside, with the walls surviving to a height of 9 in.

The original method of roofing these houses constitutes a considerable problem. Complete corbelling is improbable, and the amount of collapsed stone within the huts is not sufficient to warrant such a structure while the most obvious solution, that of a sod or thatched roof supported on timbering, has usually been ruled out on the grounds of the assumed absence of tree growth in the Orkneys at the beginning of the second millennium B.C. In house 1 at Skara Brae the jaw-bones of a whale were found in nineteenth-century excavations in such a position as to suggest they had fallen from a roof framework, and such use of whale's bones is not unlikely. But there is actual evidence for some sort of woodland both at Skara Brae, where a deposit early in the settlement's history produced alder and hazel twigs or roots, and at Rinyo, where there were not only post-holes in house G, but carbonized wood representing alder, birch, willow, pine, oak and probably poplar. Even if some of this wood were imported as tool hafts, etc., or gathered as drift-wood, in the manner likely at Stanydale (p. 263) there still remains the quite large number of stone and flint axes known from the two settlements (some twenty specimens all told), which can hardly be dissociated from timber-felling and wood-working of some sort. On the whole then it seems likely that the houses were covered with low conical roofs, of sods and rough thatch supported on such pieces of wood or of whale's bones as could be collected. Childe noted how at Skara Brae the roofs must have projected above the general midden surface in the last stages of the settlement, for evidence of surface occupation was around, but not over, the actual house-sites.

Stratification

While the culture at both the Orkney settlements remained fundamentally unchanged from first to last, Skara Brae was rebuilt at least four times in part, and at Rinyo also there was much rebuilding and structural alteration. At the former site it was noted that there was a re-occupation after the final ruin of the houses and their partial burial in drifted sand, with a significant change in the economy of the inhabitants indicated by the high proportion of red-deer bones and shellfish in their midden material, in contrast to the predominant sheep and ox bones of the main period of settlement.

As regards material equipment, the only significant changes that can be seen in the sequence of deposits is in the pottery, and this is consistent on the two sites. At Skara Brae the pottery was divided into three stylistic classes, A, B and C, of which C (incised patterns) and B (incised and relief patterns) were confined to the first two periods on the site, while class A, with relief patterns only, persisted from the beginning to the end of the occupation. At Rinyo, more precise stratigraphical information could be obtained, though the lowest levels were only explored in trial holes, with the following results:

Rinyo II. Pottery of Skara Brae 'A' class (Pl. XII, nos. 6–10, 12), with fragments of a type *C* beaker in the latest phase of the site, and undecorated pots.

Rinyo I. Pottery of Skara Brae 'B' and 'C' classes (Pl. XII, nos. 1–5, 11), with a single sherd of comb-ornamented ware.

'*Pre-Rinyo*'. Plain sherds with textures and rim forms approximating to pottery from the Orcadian chambered cairns.

This stratification is further discussed below in connexion with the detailed description of the pottery.

The economy of the settlements

The settlements were those of people engaged in breeding sheep and cattle, the latter of a distinctive type not known elsewhere in prehistoric Britain, but there is no evidence whatever of corn-growing. Wild animals and birds eaten comprise red-deer, though not in large numbers, and a few sea-fowl; cod and coal-fish, crabs and shellfish such as limpets were also eaten, but there is surprisingly little evidence of seals or whales. Fish-bones were ground to meal.

Both cod and coal-fish are bottom-feeders and imply line-fishing from boats (cf. Clark, 1948 *a*), but no fish-hooks or gorges are known from the culture.

Burials

At Skara Brae two probably ritual foundation burials of old mesaticephalic females were found in a cist beneath the wall of house 7, and a secondary (dolichocephalic) female burial was found in the re-occupation phase. In the chambered tomb of Quoyness in Orkney were stone and bone objects characteristic of the Rinyo-Clacton culture, there was a pot in the Rinyo I style from the Unival tomb in the Hebrides, and a sherd from Tormore in Arran.

MATERIAL EQUIPMENT

Pottery

As we have seen above, a consistent stratified sequence at Skara Brae and Rinyo shows that the pottery of the culture can be divided into two main phases, and Scott (1948 a) has suggested that these may conveniently be known as Rinyo I and Rinyo II (Pl. XII). At this site, Rinyo I appears to have been preceded, or to be perhaps contemporary with, plain wares which approximate to what we have described as Unstan ware when dealing with the Orkney chambered tombs (Chapter VIII). The pottery of both Rinyo I and II, however, is distinguished from this by its ornament, and by its flat bases.

In Rinyo I three main types of pottery can be distinguished, of which (a) comprises grooved and incised wares, usually of thinner and better fabric than the other sub-types. Patterns include triangular or lozenge panels filled with dots or stabs, and outlines by incisions or grooves; and the remarkable sherd with spiral ornament from period II at Skara Brae, already referred to in connexion with the Boyne culture (Chapter VII), comes into this group (Pl. XII, nos. 1–4). Type (b) comprises pots ornamented with applied bands which are themselves transversely incised or stabbed (Pl. XII, nos. 5–8), and (c) pots (usually heavier and coarser than the (b) type) have often elaborate relief-moulded ornament which may be present inside the rim as well as on the outside of the pot, but without the incision or stabbing of type (b) (Pl. XII, nos. 9, 10, 12).

In the Rinyo II phase the (a) and (b) wares drop out, and the relief-moulded wares of (c) predominate, together with (d) coarse, unornamented pots with flat bases. Little is known of the form of the pots of the (a)-(c) types, but they appear to be consistently flat-based with vertical or slightly sloping sides.

This pottery is distinguished from all the British Neolithic wares previously discussed by the presence of flat bases, while the absence of cord ornament emphatically dissociates it from wares within the Peterborough group. While a full discussion must be postponed until the analogous southern English material is described, it may be noted here that Scott's view, that Rinyo I pottery should be considered as a coarse provincial version of French or Iberian late Neolithic wares (in France represented by the so-called Chassey style of incision and punctured ornament made before baking), seems to have more to recommend it than derivation from Beaker and allied wares in Holland, as suggested in the original definition of 'Grooved ware' (Scott, 1948 a; Piggott in Warren et al. 1936). This problem is dealt with in greater detail later, but again it should be stressed that the appearance of coarse flat-bottomed vessels, often with roughly incised or applied ornament, seems to be a recurrent feature of the later Neolithic cultures of western Europe (notably in the Horgen and S.O.M. types), and that this phenomenon of *kümmerkeramik* need imply no more than parallel modifications of earlier pottery traditions partly at least owing to the incorporation of local aboriginal elements which may have included vessels of wood, leather or basketry. The applied plastic ornament of much of the Rinyo-Clacton pottery, with its strong suggestion of rope and network, may (as in comparable wares from the European continent) represent a skeuomorph of such perishable substances: the use of some form of vegetable fibre mats in the culture is indeed attested at Rinyo by a faint impression on a pot-base.

Within the northern British province of the Rinyo-Clacton culture, certain points of contact with other regions and cultures can be established. A vessel in the Rinyo I style accompanied burials in the final phase of the Unival chambered tomb in the Hebrides, there was a sherd from Tormore, and there should be an approximate equation between what is almost certainly a double-spiral pattern on a Rinyo I sherd from Skara Brae and the similar motifs in the rock-cut art of the Boyne culture, as noted above in Chapter VII. If on Rousay the earliest level at Rinyo is to be equated with the typologically late 'stalled cairns', derived from the Camster type of burial chamber in that island, the Boyne-style ornament on the equally late derivative of the Maes Howe type of tomb on the Holm of Papa Westray would be in an approximate context. And at Rinyo the later phase of Rinyo II was associated with a *C* class beaker, which in Orkney is hardly likely to have been among the earliest of its type.

Vessels of stone and whale-bone

Massive stone bowls or mortars (one found containing crushed fish-bones) were common at Skara Brae, as well as small stone cups which appear to imitate those of whalebone. Large vessels (one with a cover) were carved from the dorsal vertebrae of whales, and small cups fashioned from the caudal segments were frequently used to contain ochre pigment.

Stone

Tools of flint and chert. A single flint *axe* from Skara Brae is finely polished with thin section and squared sides, recalling Danish 'thin-butted' forms, and is presumably of imported flint (Fig. 53, no. 4); beach-pebble flint was used locally at Skara Brae and Rinyo for *polished-edge knives* (Fig. 53, no. 7) (one from each site); *knives* which merge into the thicker 'fabricator' form, with side trimming (Fig. 53, no. 10); small button *scrapers*; and a fragment probably of a re-worked triangular *arrowhead* at Rinyo.

M

Tools, etc., of stone. The stone industry from the Orkney settlements includes some most remarkable types, some virtually unique but others which are related to forms known within the Circumpolar Stone Age as defined by

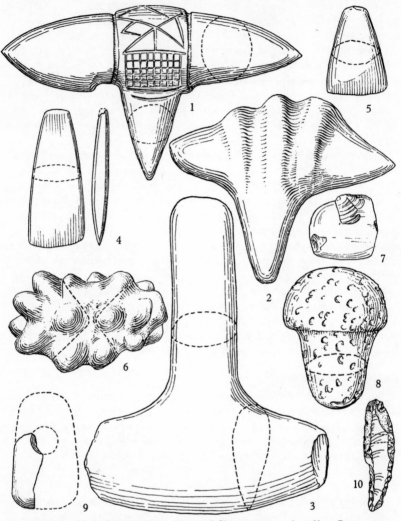

Fig. 53. Rinyo-Clacton culture: stone and flint types. 1, 3–6, 9, Skara Brae; 2, Quoyness; 7, 10, Rinyo; 8, Rousay. Scale ½.

Gjessing (G. Gjessing, 1942; 1944; 1945). These latter are practically without parallel in the British Isles, though partial analogies exist in the slate industries of Shetland (see p. 363 below).

Axes. From Skara Brae fourteen stone axe- or adze-blades have been recorded, and four from Rinyo. These are often very small and subtriangular in shape (Fig. 53, no. 5), and what may possibly be a single antler sleeve for hafting an adze-blade comes from the former site; it is, however, more probably a mace-head.

Handled tools. Into this category we may place the flagstone 'hatchet' (Fig. 53, no. 3) and a rough-out for a similar implement from Skara Brae. Childe pointed out the north European affinities of these, and they would come within the class of 'boot-shaped' tools described by Gjessing (1944), with a Circumpolar range.

Spiked tools. Certain spike-shaped tools from Skara Brae have a hafting-groove which indicates that they must have been bound transversely to the handle to form a T-shaped implement (Childe, 1931 *b*, pl. xli, nos. 4, 5). This presumption is confirmed by the existence of two objects, one from Skara Brae (Fig. 53, no. 1) and the other from the Quoyness chambered tomb (Fig. 53, no. 2), which represent double-spiked objects with their binding represented as a skeuomorph in stone-carving, as Anderson realized when publishing the Quoyness example: the haft is not represented, but a third spike projects from the base of the object in such a manner as to fit into a hollowed handle of wood or (more probably) of bone. Such a fastening could hardly be secure enough for a functional tool, and both objects must be regarded as coming within the class of ritual or ceremonial maces. Good parallels are afforded by the stone representations of adze-blades bound transversely to their shafts from Palmella, Cascais, Carenque and other sites in Portugal (Childe, 1947, 269; do Paço, 1942; Heleno, 1933; de Vasconcelos, 1922), and the spiked mace-heads of the Maglemose culture (Clark, 1936*a*, 105) must also be noted. Single-spiked knob-shaped implements come from Skara Brae and Rousay, and have Northern Stone Age parallels, as Childe pointed out.

Perforated mace-heads. Fragments of stone mace-heads approximating to the Taversoe Tuack or Ormiegill type came from Skara Brae (Fig. 53, no. 9) and Rinyo respectively; they were not stratified finds but there seems no reason to dissociate them from some phase of the settlements. In con-nexion with these one may note the concentration of such mace-heads in Orkney, almost invariably broken and particularly found in the Maes Howe-Stenness region (Callander, 1931).

A second mace-head from Skara Brae has a biconical perforation and is roughly carved into a series of knobs (Fig. 53, no. 6). There is a somewhat similar example from the Isle of Man (Cowley Coll., Manx Museum; un-located), and probably certain Norwegian types are related (e.g. H. Gjessing, 1920, fig. 130, from Garborg).

Knobbed and spiked objects. Under this heading we may group some very curious carved stone objects without perforations and of basically spherical or less frequently ellipsoid form. A very elaborate spiked and grooved ellipsoid from Skara Brae has a parallel from Evie (on Mainland), and a simpler form was found with the spiked mace-head in the Quoyness chambered tomb (Anderson, 1886, 286): these may have been bound on to the end of a shaft to form some sort of mace-head. But stone balls, either perfectly smooth in the manner of those from the Boyne culture and else-where, already referred to, or carved into knobs or spikes, are not only known in the Orkney settlements but in their distinctive knobbed form have a wide distribution in eastern Scotland, where over 120 are known as un-associated finds, with a concentration in Aberdeenshire. Outlying strays are known from Cumberland and Ulster. Childe has discussed and mapped these objects (Childe, 1931 *b*, 102) and their association with the Rinyo-Clacton culture in Orkney must mean that their origins at least belong to this phase, even if the type had a long survival. Such well-known carved balls with spiral motifs, such as that from Towie in Aberdeenshire, should, like the spiral on the Rinyo I pot referred to above, show connexions with the art of the Boyne culture.

The use, practical or ritual, of these balls is unknown, but they may have been bound on to shafts in some manner to form mace-heads: as their weights fall into a purely random series, they cannot be interpreted in this manner.

Miscellaneous stone objects. A very common and simple type of knife used in the Orkney settlements was formed by splitting a beach pebble to a suitable edge, and flagstone slabs roughly chipped to form club-like imple-ments have parallels in Shetland. A flagstone implement with coarsely serrated edge might again be related to smaller serrated tools from Shetland.

Bone and antler

Skara Brae produced a large series of tools made of animal or bird bones and from red-deer antler, and these have been fully discussed by Childe (1931 *b*), who stressed the relationship with bone types of the north European plain having Maglemose antecedents.

Bone adzes. Heavy tools made from ox metapodials cut obliquely to an adze-edge and perforated with a transverse hole below the remaining articular end of the bone are a common type at Skara Brae (Fig. 54, no. 1). They have good Maglemose parallels (Clark, 1936*a*, 111–12), and functionally related adzes made from elk antler occur at Star Carr, Seamer, in a Zone IV (pre-Boreal) context. In the same region of Yorkshire similar adzes occurred in quantity in a 'Lake-dwelling' of uncertain date at Ulrome near Holderness. The account of the find is extremely confused but the adzes, made from the metapodials of oxen larger than those of *Bos longifrons* and some possibly from bones of *Bos primigenius*, were found on the lower of two timber platforms with flint implements, while the upper structure appears to have yielded a Late Bronze spear-head. Another similar bone adze is known from the River Thames at London (Smith, 1911). Clark (1947a) has suggested that these tools were blubber-mattocks used on the carcasses of stranded whales.

Chisels. Various forms of chisel-ended bone tools (Fig. 54, no. 3), made from metapodials of ox or sheep, from birds' leg-bones and from a bovid lower jaw again relate in the main to Maglemose forms or their descendants in north Europe.

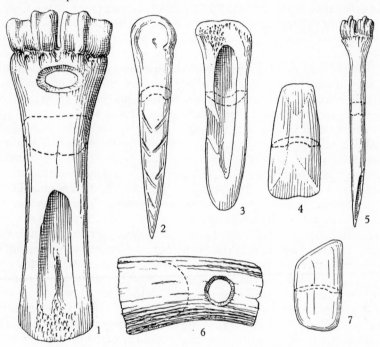

Fig. 54. Rinyo-Clacton culture: bone and antler types, Skara Brae. Scale ¼.

Perforated antler mace-head or axe sleeve. A single example from Skara Brae of an object with cylindrical perforation and hollow interior (Fig. 54, no. 6), made from the base of a red-deer antler, has usually been regarded as a 'sleeve' for hafting a small axe (in this instance actually as an adze-blade). Such a type could be of Maglemose origin but it seems very possible that the internal tissue has decayed and the object is really a mace-head with parallels in the Dorchester culture (Clark, 1936a, 112).

Points and awls. Bone points, usually made from small metapodials (Fig. 54, no. 5), were very common at Skara Brae, and are of the simple form which occurs in Mesolithic and also in Western Neolithic contexts.

Some are decorated with deeply incised chevrons (Fig. 54, no. 2), recalling those on a Mesolithic antler-axe from the River Thames and a tine from Romsey, Hampshire (Smith, 1934).

Polished blades. A curious but common type at Skara Brae is the small polished bone flake, more or less sub-rectangular in outline, with a strong resemblance to the polished-edge knives of the Secondary Neolithic cultures, to which indeed it may well be related in function (Fig. 54, nos. 4, 7).

Scapula-shovels. The use of ox scapulae for shovels, as in the flint mines and other sites of the Windmill Hill culture, is seen in the Rinyo-Clacton culture both at Skara Brae and at Woodhenge in the southern province.

Pins

Pins of bone, antler and probably cetacean ivory form a very interesting item in the material equipment of the northern province of the Rinyo-Clacton culture. Three main types may be distinguished, of which type i has been denominated a *skewer-pin* by Atkinson. These are finely made pins of cylindrical section, slender but not of great size, with domed or slightly conical heads (Fig. 55, nos. 4, 5) and not only occur at Skara Brae but in many sites of the Dorchester culture described below. Type ii is related to these and may be called *bulbed pins*, having a lateral bulb worked on the shaft, which may be perforated (Fig. 55, nos. 2, 3, 6, 7). These occur not only at Skara Brae but in the Quoyness chambered tomb, and in the Dorchester culture. The third group is a small one of *giant pins*, up to 9½ in. long, with spatulate heads (Fig. 55, nos. 1, 7), which certainly seem related to the similarly large pins in the Boyne culture (Chapter VII). In point of fact, certain type ii pins are of very large size, and one elaborate specimen (Fig. 55, no. 7) has a carved head which, as Scott has pointed out (1948 *a*), must be a coarse copy of the pins with cylindrical ribbed heads common in the Iberian chambered tombs (G. & V. Leisner, 1943, 1, 450) and represented by a fragment found with a food-vessel in Co. Galway (Chitty, 1935). The spatulate heads of the type iii pins might also be compared with examples from Vila Nova de San Pedro in Portugal (Jalhay & do Paço, 1945, pl. XVI, nos. 18, 19).

Three *perforated bone points* from Skara Brae (Fig. 55, no. 9) have been described as needles, but they resemble points from Woodhenge and the Dorchester culture which appear to be pendants or necklace elements (p. 360).

Beads and pendants

Beads of *stone* at Skara Brae are confined to a few barrel-shaped specimens, but *bone* beads, either of barrel form and made by cutting up a hollow bone into segments, or as simple disc-beads, are common: the barrel types are often massive (Fig. 55, nos. 13, 14). Other beads were made by cutting sections from the roots of animal teeth, utilizing the pulp-cavity as a perforation, or from walrus and narwhal ivory. *Pendants* occur, either made by perforating actual teeth (ox and Killer whale are represented) or by carving tooth-shaped pendants from whale or walrus ivory. Boars' tusk pendants are present, but rare (Fig. 55, nos. 10–12, 15).

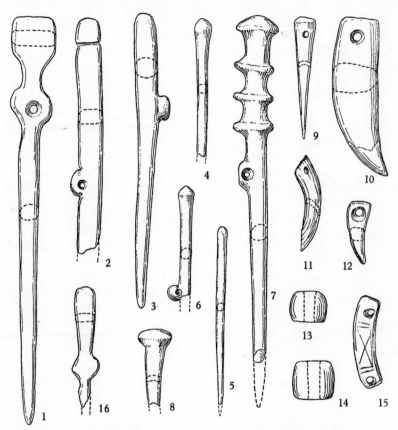

Fig. 55. Rinyo-Clacton culture: bone and ivory pins, pendants and beads.
All Skara Brae except no. 3, from Quoyness. Scale ¼.

Art

Apart from the incised bone points noted above, decorative art at Skara Brae is confined to incised (and rarely pecked) patterns on stone. These range from quite large compositions on stone slabs to finely engraved ornament on a small polished stone plaque (possibly a knife), and the motifs employed are based on zigzags, triangles, chevrons and lozenges, with cross-hatching or 'shading' on occasion. Outside Skara Brae the only parallel in Orkney would seem to be the decorated slab from inhumation cist burials at Brodgar (Marwick, 1926), but in general relationships exist with the few examples of art in the Clyde-Carlingford culture, and with that on the stone plaques from Graig Lwyd and Ronaldsway.

Matting

Faint impressions of some form of woven *mat* (probably of coiled construction) occur on the base of a pot from Rinyo and are the only evidence of such material in the British Neolithic cultures (Childe, 1948 b; Henshall, 1951).

Domesticated animals

Bones of domesticated animals were abundant at Skara Brae, and have been studied by Watson (in Childe, 1931 b; 1932 d). *Ox* is most numerous, with evidence of pole-axing and the slaughter of young animals in the manner already described in the Windmill Hill culture (p. 28), though the pole-axing seemed to have been performed with a 'blunt and heavy hammer', rather than by the pointed tool-used at Windmill Hill. The breed was uniform, but totally different from either *Bos longifrons* as known from Scottish Iron Age sites or from the southern English Neolithic breed, being noteworthy for the strongly contrasted male and female skulls and for the presence of the polled skulls of bullocks. Watson stressed how the breed was unlike other known oxen in prehistoric Britain, 'differing from all of them amongst other things in the marked sexual dimorphism of the horn-cores'. It is clear that the breed must have been introduced into Orkney by sea as a part of the original culture of the Rinyo-Clacton colonists in the northern province, but it is interesting to note that the breed of ox from southern English sites of the same culture is not that of Skara Brae, but the ox with large horns in both the male and female, present also in the Windmill Hill culture.

Sheep were numerically equal in importance to oxen at Skara Brae, and were of the slender Soay type with massive horns. There was no evidence of the winter slaughter of young animals, and their abundance contrasts with their small proportions relative to oxen in the southern English Neolithic sites. *Pig* was very rare, and not certainly domesticated.

OTHER SETTLEMENT SITES IN THE NORTHERN PROVINCE

Sites outside Orkney producing pottery of the Rinyo-Clacton style are confined to coastal or sand-dune surface areas such as those at Glenluce or Hedderwick (Callander, 1929; Stevenson, 1946); a small site with Rinyo I sherds at Knappers near Glasgow, and the settlement at Townhead, Rothesay, Bute, where Rinyo I sherds were associated with others having the heavy bevelled rims of types associated with Beacharra ware and one with a complex ladder pattern recalling that on sherds from Linkardstown, Co. Carlow (p. 274). Some indeterminate post-hole structure existed at Rothesay, and a stone axe, a saddle-quern and rider, and charred grains of wheat and hazel-nuts were also found (Marshall, 1930).

THE SOUTHERN PROVINCE

Distribution

Sites producing pottery of the Rinyo-Clacton culture in southern England have a main concentration in a relatively narrow belt stretching from the English Channel between Weymouth and Christchurch northwards to the Middle Thames and the Cotswolds, and there is a scatter of sites in East Anglia (Fig. 48). But the most northerly site there (Orton Longueville near Peterborough) is separated from the most southerly Scottish site (Glenluce) by 250 miles, and the intervening area of England and Wales is a blank with the exception of the Scunthorpe (Lincolnshire) and Wykeham (Scarborough) finds.

Habitation sites

No settlements are well documented: on the submerged land-surface of the Essex coast at Clacton there were 'pits' or 'cooking-holes' containing burnt stones, flint implements and pottery, but it was not possible to assign any of the timber structures observed on the same land-surface to any specific archaeological horizon (Warren *et al.* 1936). In Wessex and East Anglia typical pottery and associated artifacts have frequently been found in various forms of pits or holes which may be domestic, though Stone has recently made a case for regarding these pits as non-utilitarian, and 'ritual' in a sense which would relate them to some of the certainly ritual monuments described below (Stone and Young, 1948, to their list add that near Cambridge; Frere, 1943).

Ritual monuments

The first site where a form of Rinyo-Clacton ware was distinguished was that near Stonehenge in Wiltshire and nicknamed (and later officially designated) Woodhenge (Fig. 56), a most remarkable ritual monument within the class since known as Henges (Cunnington, 1929). These monuments have been discussed as a group by Clark (1936b) and more recently by Atkinson (in Atkinson, C. M. Piggott & Sandars, 1951), and are further dealt with under the head of the Dorchester culture below. Woodhenge falls into the single-entrance class, with a bank and internal quarry-ditch containing an area some 150 ft. across within which were a series of six rings (actually oval settings) of post-holes of various sizes, which I have suggested elsewhere (Piggott, 1940a) may be construed as the post-structure of a building rather than as a series of free-standing uprights. A distinctive form of Rinyo-Clacton ware described below was found in abundance under the bank, in the post-holes and in the ditch silt of the monument, together with Secondary Neolithic flint types.

Similar pottery is represented in other Henge monuments by a sherd apiece from the first phase of Stonehenge, discussed below under the Dorchester culture, from Maumbury Rings and from Dorchester site I (Fig. 56), while we shall see that the 'rusticated' ware in the Henges of Gorsey Bigbury and Arminghall has reason to be regarded as affiliated in some measure.

Associations and stratification

At Orton Longueville, Honington and Edingthorpe, Rinyo-Clacton ware was associated with Peterborough pottery and at the last site with Western Neolithic sherds as well, but at Clacton there was no direct association noted with either the Western Neolithic or the Peterborough ware also found on the submerged land-surface, nor with the *B*-beaker sherds also present. The association with Peterborough pottery at the West Kennet Avenue, Avebury, is not a direct one, while in the West Kennet long barrow a sherd likely to be of Rinyo-Clacton ware (Cunnington, 1927, no. 69) was associated with Peterborough pottery and *A*-beaker sherds. At Stonehenge, the sherd in question was found in the primary silt of the ditch stratified below *B*-beaker sherds, but at Woodhenge the position is confusing. With Rinyo-Clacton sherds beneath the bank were fragments of at least two Western Neolithic bowls (Cunnington, 1929, pl. 25, fig. 2—there is no warrant for the flat base; pl. 32, no. 43), and in the ditch, sherds were in the primary silt beneath those of a *B*-beaker. But in the closely adjacent *A*-beaker burial, Rinyo-Clacton pottery was found in holes under the ploughed-out mound and in the primary silt of the ditch. At West Runton in Norfolk there was again a probable association with *A*-beaker pottery (Gell, 1949), and at Maiden Castle the same situation existed. The alternatives are either a long duration of the pottery style (on conventional views of the sequence of Windmill Hill, Peterborough, *B*- and *A*-beakers), or a cultural rather than an inevitably chronological distinction for the various types of pottery in southern England.

Pottery

While relationship between the pottery of the southern province and that from Skara Brae and Rinyo is clear, and of a sufficiently precise nature to enable us with confidence to assign it to the same cultural background, nevertheless the southern material, and especially that from Woodhenge, is distinctively recognizable in its own right. Basically, the pottery from

339

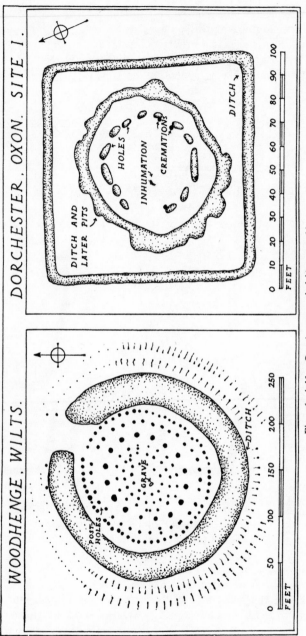

Fig. 56. (*After Cunnington, and Atkinson et al.*)

such sites as Clacton, Pishobury or Creeting St Mary in East Anglia (Fig. 57) is comparable with Rinyo I wares rather than with those of Rinyo II though such features as plastic ornament inside the rim are characteristically southern. In what may be regarded as the southern equivalents of Rinyo II (with greater use of plastic ornament on the body of the pot) complications

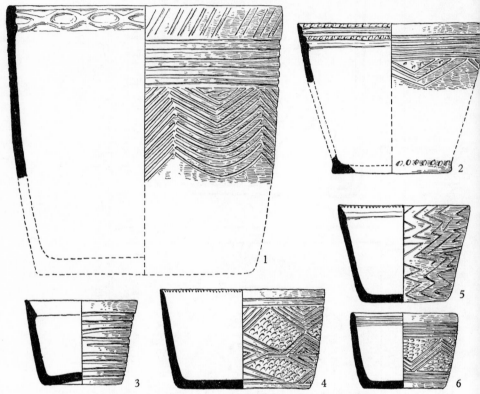

Fig. 57. Rinyo-Clacton culture: pottery. 1, Clacton, 2–3, Pishobury; 4–6, Creeting St Mary. Scale ¼.

are introduced by what seems to be interaction with local styles of plastic and rusticated ornament not present in the northern province and including a free use of finger-tip or finger-pinched techniques.

But the motifs of the Rinyo I style are repeated in the south—channelling, grooving, incision; the use of dotted triangles or lozenges; the absence of cord ornament; the constant use of flat-based pots. Small, fine, applied cordons are characteristic, sometimes notched or incised to form a ladder-pattern, and a small vessel from Woodlands, near Woodhenge, has what appears to be a skeuomorph of knotted network executed in relief over its surface. From this site, too, comes a small pot of very thin ware with small perforated lugs. (Stone, 1948; 1949.)

The plastic element which at Woodhenge is seen in combination with the Rinyo I motifs on the pottery was recognized and discussed by Clark (1936b), who defined a group of 'rusticated wares' which he subdivided into three closely related stylistic groups named from the sites of Arminghall, Holdenhurst and Somersham respectively. All seemed to be associated with the A-beaker culture rather than that of the B class but, as Grimes later suggested (1938), the rusticated styles in question need not represent an integral part of the A-beaker culture, and one may note the association of such pottery at Gorsey Bigbury in Somerset and Fifty Farm in Cambridge-shire with *petit-tranchet* derivative arrowheads proper to the Secondary Neolithic cultures of Britain and abundant at Woodhenge. On the other hand, Clark's Somersham ware does seem to be connected with the Dutch 'pot-beakers', where the appearance of large coarse pots combining features of the Beaker style with rusticated elements represents a late Neolithic tradition which as we have seen has a wide distribution in Europe and in Britain.

The characteristic pottery of the Rinyo-Clacton culture in the southern province as represented at Woodhenge (Fig. 58) (and to a less striking degree on other sites) seems to be a mixture of the Rinyo I style with local and contemporary rusticated traditions within the Arminghall-Holden-hurst-Somersham group. The distribution of these latter wares seems predominantly East Anglian, extending in the north-east to the Scunthorpe region and in the south represented by sites on or near the coast in Sussex and at the mouth of the Hampshire Avon, and one might suggest that contact between the two styles in the Woodhenge region was made by traffic along that river. It is worth while noting the evidence for contact with the sea-coast in the Woodhenge sites: shells of oyster, mussel (*Mytilus*) and scallop in the Woodlands and Ratfyn pits (Stone and Young, 1948; Stone, 1949), and fragments of the shells of *Paphia* and *Mytilis* actually used as grit in the pottery at Woodhenge itself (Dean in Cunnington, 1929). Furthermore, the appearance of carbonized pine-wood at this site, surprising in a chalk area, again suggests contacts with the sandy heathlands of the New Forest at the Avon mouth, where at such sites as Moordown and Holdenhurst rusticated ware appears (Calkin, 1935, fig. 10; Piggott, 1937c).

Stone (1949) has suggested that such Rinyo-Clacton pots in the southern province as that from West Runton should be connected with a series of bowls known from Wessex and the Isle of Wight (Keiller & Piggott, 1936; Piggott, 1938, 98; 1946b) and usually assigned to the Early Bronze Age, and furthermore, to certain small vessels within the incense cup group, usually regarded as early Middle Bronze Age in date. Independently, Scott (1948a) related the Rinyo I style to the Aldbourne cups of the Wessex culture of the Bronze Age, and the whole question is further discussed below when dealing with the European and British relationships of the Rinyo-Clacton culture.

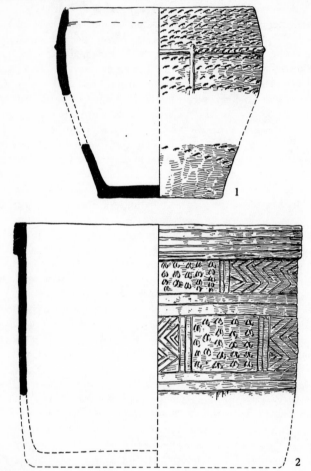

Fig. 58. Rinyo-Clacton culture: pottery from Woodhenge (*after Cunnington*). Scale ¼.

Flint and stone

Axes of flint and greenstone on the Essex coast could not be definitely assigned to the Rinyo-Clacton settlement, but there is a flint axe from Woodlands pit 2 (near Woodhenge) and a *tranchet* axe from Honington. The same Woodlands pit produced a Graig Lwyd axe, and one of Langdale origin came from Sutton Courtenay pit P. At Woodhenge two greenstone axe fragments were found, as well as two ritual axes carved from chalk.

Leaf-shaped arrowheads occurred at Clacton, Honington and Woodhenge, and *petit-tranchet derivatives* were present in almost every site of the culture in the southern province, and are by far the most characteristic stone type associated with it. *Serrated flakes* are again a recurrent type, *scrapers* are frequent, *fabricators* are known from Woodlands and Sutton Courtenay, and a distinctive type from the 'cooking-pits' at Clacton were flint *discs*, some made from polished axes. From one of these pits also came a fragment of a *single-piece sickle* with partly polished edges.

Stone balls occur in flint at Woodlands and chalk at Maumbury, and this latter site also produced several fragments of large *phalli* in chalk.

Bone and antler

Apart from antler picks, scapula shovels and not very distinctive bone points, little is known of the bone and antler equipment in the southern province. A perforated bone 'point' from Woodhenge may, however, be mentioned, as it may have been one of a series worn suspended to form a collar or fringe, as seems certainly the case with the graduated sets of similar objects from a Dorchester-culture burial in Upton Lovel barrow 4 (Hoare, 1812, 75), commented on below (p. 360).

Domesticated animals

The main series of animal bones available for study are those from Woodhenge (Jackson in Cunnington, 1929); here the *ox* was the large-horned form known from the Windmill Hill culture and from Stonehenge I, and distinctively different from the Skara Brae breed. *Pig* was at Woodhenge next in importance, while *sheep* or *goat*, and *dog*, were both scarce: a noticeable contrast to the Orkney evidence and doubtless to be equated with the presence of woodland affording pannage for pigs.

THE RELATIONSHIPS OF THE RINYO-CLACTON CULTURE

Despite the regional styles, the pottery from both the northern and the southern provinces of the culture is sufficiently homogeneous to imply some degree of unity imposed on a background of stone and bone types common to the Secondary Neolithic cultures of Britain at large, and justifies us in regarding the two provinces as related. Of the material equipment other than pottery, that of the southern province is recognizably part of the light industry of the Secondary Neolithic as defined above (p. 285), while elements of this, such as polished-edge knives, are present in Orkney. Here, however, other elements in stone and bone equipment are present, giving a distinctive character to the settlements, while the abundant evidence for houses and their furniture again contributes to make the Skara Brae and Rinyo sites exceptional.

These stone and bone types, as Childe pointed out in his original publication of Skara Brae (1931 *b*), all point to connexions with the Mesolithic cultures of northern Europe and their descendants, and we can now perceive that they (and probably the Skara Brae house-type), also merit at least the partial inclusion of the culture in the north within the ambit of Gjessing's Circumpolar Stone Age. But even among these bone and stone types, certain forms (such as the pins) are without antecedents in the Northern Mesolithic, and these types link the Rinyo-Clacton culture with others within the Secondary Neolithic group (such as the Dorchester culture), and with that of the Boyne tombs. In the southern province, similar links are afforded by the appearance of ritual structures of the Henge monument class associated with pottery which has strong links with that of the Orkney sites.

The origin of the pottery styles obviously constitutes the main crux: there are, as we have seen, two main elements—that of the grooved and incised and 'dotted' patterns of Rinyo I, and the plastic relief-ornament of Rinyo I and II, and its counterpart in the southern province where it can be shown to have connexions with the Arminghall-Holdenhurst-Somersham group of rusticated wares. My original suggestion of an origin in Holland, which involved selecting ornament from one or two pot-beakers and a vague analogy of shape from megalithic *tiefstich* vessels (Piggott in Warren *et al.* 1936), will not in fact stand a close examination, and the total absence of cord- or comb-ornament in the style removes the pit-comb, funnel-beaker and general Danish-north European chambered-tomb pottery series from consideration as a formative influence. Plastic ornament certainly does occur in Dutch Beaker contexts, as we have seen, and even sporadically in the Danish Neolithic series (e.g. Becker, 1948, pl. xxviii, no. 2), but nothing really comparable to the Rinyo I style can be found in that region.

Scott has made a far stronger case for deriving the Rinyo I style from late Western Neolithic and Early Metal Age wares in west France and Iberia, and in such a context the material falls into a reasonable place. The combination of grooved or incised patterns with dotted or *pointillé* triangular and lozenge-shaped motifs is what constitutes the 'Chassey II' style (J. Hawkes, 1934), and one can now separate this style in which the patterns are made in the usual manner, before baking, from the style in which somewhat analogous ornament is scratched or engraved after baking. The engraved ware, probably related to the Italian Matera style, is early in south France but survives to a comparatively late date in the north, as for instance at Catenoy or Fort Harrouard, but the incised Chassey ware is approximately contemporary with beakers in the Rhône mouth and forms the characteristic ware of the 'vase-supports' of Brittany and west France, well-known from such sites as Er Lannic in the Morbihan (le Rouzic, 1930). Comparable ornament appears on pots in a *schnurkeramik* context from Switzerland.

Similarly ornamented pottery is also known from Iberia, where it is represented, in Spanish and Portuguese chambered tombs (G. & V. Leisner, 1943, pls. 153–4; 1951, pl. xxx) and, as in France, it is associated with cups ornamented with pellets or knobs. In Portugal, similar ware, some very reminiscent of that of Rinyo I, has been found in unpublished settlement sites such as Serra das Eguas, Carenque, and the Gruta do Furadeiro, Rocha Forte (Estramadura) (Belem Museum), while from a site at Serra do Monto Junto (Geological Museum, Lisbon, unpublished) comes what appears to be the base of a small clay oven with an internal sub-rectangular area about 8 in. across, of precisely the type of those at Rinyo, and found in association with channelled and incised wares.

Such wares as those described above would form convincing prototypes from which the Rinyo I pottery could be derived as a coarse provincial variant, its imperfections partly due to inadequate fuel in a peat-fired kiln. For the plastic ornament, one might again turn to Iberia, as indeed Childe did in his first report on Skara Brae, illustrating Catalonian 'encrusted' sherds for comparison with the Orkney pottery (Childe, 1929b); the recurrent appearance of such ornament in many regions of Late Neolithic–Early Bronze Age western Europe has already been commented upon. But this same phenomenon of the parallel breakdown of the fine potting traditions of the intrusive Neolithic cultures as the local Mesolithic traditions were absorbed in many areas of Europe could also provide an origin for the plastic ornament in the Rinyo-Clacton culture within Britain itself, just as Hawkes has stressed that the origins of the similar plastic and finger-ornamented wares of the north-west Late Bronze Age 'are the direct outcome of the local Neolithic tradition of North-West Europe between the Rhine, Normandy and Holland', preserved by 'the local substratum-population of Neolithic descent' (Hawkes, 1944; cf. also 1942, 43). While the origins of the incised and dotted patterns in the Rinyo I style are then most likely to be derived from Iberia or west France, the plastic ornament is less localized and could be derived from almost any area of western Europe, or be regarded as a local phenomenon. In the southern province of the Rinyo-Clacton culture, however, there does seem to be some more specific relationship with the rusticated wares allied to the Dutch pot-beakers.

With the pottery it is probable that one should group the bone pins, with their affinities (like those of the Boyne culture), in Iberia. We should have, in fact, an intrusive Iberian or west French element (pottery and pins) imposed on and fusing with local Secondary Neolithic elements, which in the northern province of the Rinyo-Clacton culture were conspicuously allied to Scandinavian Mesolithic traditions and survived in the Circumpolar Stone Age. Presumably one would regard of the colonization the northern and southern provinces, with the introduction of novel pottery styles, as parallel movements, one by the Western Approaches to the Hebrides and the Orkneys, and the other up-Channel to Wessex and East Anglia.

We have seen that both Scott and Stone have connected the Rinyo I pottery style with such vessels as the 'incense cups' usually attributed to the British Early and Middle Bronze Ages, and indeed the relationship of, for instance, the Aldbourne cups with the fine Rinyo I cup from the Unival chambered tomb, a fragment from Tormore and a curious sherd from Rinyo itself (Childe, 1939, 26) seems very close. One might go a stage further and cite the knobbed or pellet-ornamented 'grape cups' of Wessex, contemporary with the Aldbourne series, in connexion with the pellet-ornament idea inherent in Rinyo-Clacton wares, and the elaborate maces or sceptres in Wessex culture graves may not be unrelated to those of Skara Brae or those which we shall encounter in the Dorchester culture. The implication of such connexions is a short chronology, and the whole matter must be reserved for discussion in the last chapter, but it would not be inconsistent with, for instance, the likely equation of some phase of the Boyne tombs with the Wessex culture already commented upon in Chapter VII.

THE RONALDSWAY CULTURE

Recent discoveries in the Isle of Man have shown the existence there of a distinctive culture which comes within the Secondary Neolithic complex as defined above, and which is known from both settlements and cemeteries. Although restricted in area therefore, the Ronaldsway culture is well defined in all its major aspects. The recognition of the culture followed the excavation of a house-site at Ronaldsway (Bruce & Megaw, 1947) and a cemetery at Ballateare (Bersu, 1947): in the light of this evidence it was seen that many sites in the Island represented by chance finds belonged to this culture, including those producing pottery which had been tentatively assigned by Clark (1935 b) to an Ultimate Bronze Age.

Distribution

At least two dozen sites are known from the island, scattered along the coastal fringe. Ballateare, near Jurby, is the most northern site, and Ronaldsway one of the most southerly, about 25 miles away, but a peculiar type of stone axe characteristic of the culture has a slightly wider spread, and is indeed known from several localities outside the Isle of Man.

Settlements

At Ronaldsway an isolated house was found, rectangular with dimensions of 24 by 12–14 ft., slightly sunk into the ground and with post-holes along the edges and forming two internal lines. There was a central hearth area, and what may have been a votive deposit of a small pot in a pit under a flat stone. There was sporadic rough paving on the hut floor, and abundant occupational debris with animal bones, pottery and stone tools. (Fig. 59.)

What appears to have been a similar house, some 30 by 15 ft. in size, was found many years ago at Glencrutchery, though its true character was not recognized at the time. It contained pottery and other objects of the Ronaldsway type.

These two isolated houses suggest that the economy of the culture was based on individual homesteads rather than on hamlets or villages, and the small cemetery to be described below appears to be that of a family community appropriate to such a unit.

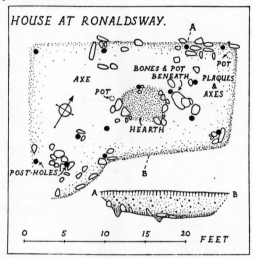

Fig. 59. (*After Bruce & Megaw.*)

Cemeteries

The cremation-cemetery at Ballateare seems to have been confined to an area about 50 by 35 ft., within which were found ten cremated bone deposits, and one cremation in a large pot. In addition, seven similar but empty pots were found, buried mouth upwards, one at least with traces of organic food material encrusting the inside. A miniature cup was found with one cremation, and with that in the large vessel was another such cup, a bone pin and a polished-edge knife. Also associated with the cemetery were various post-holes, some in line, and larger holes containing charcoal, burnt bones, flints and sherds, and considered as *ustrinae* by the excavator. These may be related to the ritual pits discussed below under the Dorchester culture. On the edge of the cemetery area parts of a small shallow ditch were traced, which may have originally enclosed an oval area.

It is probable that other similar cemeteries were found in the past (e.g. a site at Knocksharry), but there are no precise records.

MATERIAL EQUIPMENT

Pottery

The abundant pottery available can be divided into two main categories, and has been discussed in detail by Clark and Megaw. The commonest form is a large, tall, round-based jar, with a rim up to 10 or 16 in. across and a depth which may be twice the rim diameter. The rim itself is of bevelled or

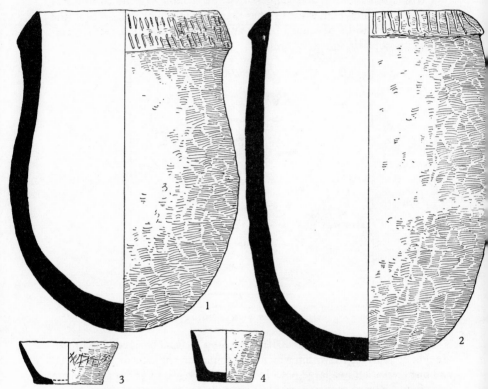

Fig. 60. Ronaldsway culture: pottery. 1, Ballateare (*after Bersu*); 2, Ballahott Quarry (*after Megaw*); 3, 4, Ronaldsway (*after Bruce & Megaw*). Scale ¼.

overhanging section, or is represented by a cordon. There is usually some incised or punctured ornament on the rim bevel, but the body of the pot is plain: no cord ornament is employed (Fig. 60). Both the form of the rims and the ornament suggest derivation from Beacharra forms known in south-west Scotland, e.g. Nether Largie or Rothesay (Callander, 1929, fig. 39), or Rudh' an Dunain (Scott, 1932, fig. 12), and the general form and pro-portions are again seen in at least one unpublished vessel from Eilean an Tighe in North Uist.

From the Ronaldsway house came small flat-based pots, one with roughly scored ornament, of simple forms that could be matched in the unornamented ware from Rinyo or Lough Gur and seem to represent a parallel appearance of flat-based coarse wares late in the Neolithic (Fig. 60, nos. 3, 4). One of the miniature pots from Ballateare was flat-based, but with a bevelled and ornamented rim.

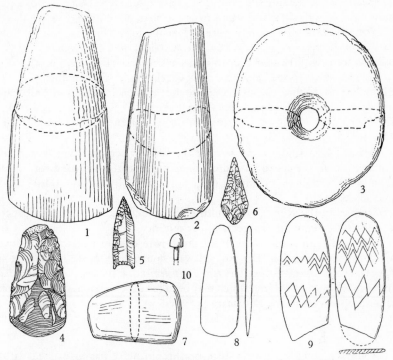

Fig. 61. Ronaldsway culture: stone, flint and bone types. 1, 4, 6–9, Ronaldsway (*after Bruce & Megaw*); 2, 3, 5, Glencrutchery; 10, Ballateare (bone) (*after Bersu*). Scale ¼.

Stone and flint

Axes. The characteristic form of *stone axe* has a thick oval section, a truncated butt, and the peculiar feature of deliberate roughening of the surface for about half the length from the butt-end, the remainder being polished (Fig. 61, no. 1). In the Ronaldsway house seven such stone axes, and four of other less determinate forms were found: the roughened-butt axes are common in the Isle of Man and have been reported elsewhere from Yorkshire, Lancashire and south-west Scotland. It is interesting to note that, although axes of Langdale rock are relatively common in the island, they have in no instance been found associated with the Ronaldsway culture.

Small *flint axes and adzes*, from 3 to 1¾ in. long and partially ground and polished, are again frequent in Ronaldsway culture sites, and their diminutive size may be due to the use of beach-pebble flint (Fig. 61, no. 4).

Gouge. A stone *gouge*, approximating to Gjessing's class of 'curved-back gouges' within the Circumpolar Stone Age, was found at Glencrutchery, apparently associated with the Ronaldsway culture material (Fig. 61, no. 2).

Mace-head. The same site produced a perforated stone object, 3¾ by 4½ in. across and ½ in. thick, which seems to be a form of mace-head (Fig. 61, no. 3).

Arrowheads at Ronaldsway were of lozenge form (Fig. 61, no. 6), but a *petit tranchet* appears to have come from Glencrutchery, together with a curious form with two very small barbs at the base (Fig. 61, no. 5).

Polished flint knives, characteristic of the light flint industry of the Secondary Neolithic cultures, were found at Ronaldsway and Ballateare, as well as at other sites such as Glencrutchery. They form a link between the Ronaldsway culture and that of Rinyo-Clacton, Peterborough and Dorchester (Fig. 61, no. 7).

Serrated flakes and *concave saws* of the 'hollow scraper' type were again common, with the narrow band of lustre distinct from diffused corn-gloss. The latter form is that common in Ulster in the Clyde-Carlingford culture and elsewhere.

Scrapers in the Ronaldsway culture are of a characteristic hump-backed form with a frequently subrectangular outline.

Stone balls similar to those from the Boyne culture and that of Rinyo-Clacton were found in the Ronaldsway house, and miscellaneous stone types include *hammer-stones, grinders* and *polishers*, stone discs used as *pot-lids*, and probable *grain-rubbers*, which may be taken in connexion with at least one grain impression in the Ballateare pottery.

Bone

A broken small *bone pin* with a mushroom head was associated with a polished flint knife in a cremation-burial at Ballateare, and has affinities with the mushroom-headed group (type I) of the Boyne culture (Fig. 61, no. 10).

Schist plaques

In the Ronaldsway house was found a remarkable group of five small schist plaques, of which all but one were broken. The exception is in fact an axe-amulet 2¾ in. long and little over a tenth of an inch thick (Fig. 61, no. 8), but the others all appear to have been oval in shape, and the largest and most complete, originally about 3 in. long, has a fine incised pattern of zigzags and lozenges on each face (Fig. 61, no. 9), while similar ornament is also present on one face of another rather smaller example. The ornament is comparable to that on the Graig Lwyd plaque, and at Skara Brae.

Domesticated animals

The animal bones from Ronaldsway comprised *ox*, of a breed which appears to be nearer to *Bos longifrons* than to the large-horned Windmill Hill-Woodhenge type, *sheep* and *pig*.

THE RELATIONSHIPS OF THE RONALDSWAY CULTURE

While recognizably a member of the Secondary Neolithic group of cultures in Britain, the Ronaldsway culture has a notable insular individuality. The pottery types appear to be of relatively local origin, derived from Neolithic wares known from sites at the head of the Irish Sea, and the absence of cord ornament suggests that the insular development took place before, or at least without any contacts with, the Beacharra C phase in Northern Ireland and the development of Sandhill wares. It is interesting to see the purely local devolution of the pot forms into a tall cylindrical vessel with bevelled or overhanging rim proceeding parallel to that which produced such pots as that from Icklingham (Pl. X, no. 2) and later the Bronze Age cinerary urns, out of the Peterborough stock in Britain, and the comparable pit-comb jars from Finland (Nordman, 1922, 15). Indeed an analogous development can be seen as far away as the Jura, where the later pottery at the Lac de Chalain develops from the earlier Cortaillod forms to produce just such cylindrical round-based forms as those in the Isle of Man. And in the same framework of late Neolithic pottery devolution come the little flat-based pots with their similarities to Lough Gur or the Rinyo-Clacton culture as well as to forms of Horgen or S.O.M. types on the Continent.

Such flint types as the polished-edge knives relate Ronaldsway to the mainland cultures within the Secondary Neolithic group, while the use of cremation-cemeteries is in common with the Dorchester culture described below: in both the foreshadowing of Middle Bronze Age burial rites, including at Ballateare the use of 'pigmy vessels' or 'incense cups', is interesting and important. The long house of the culture may be related on the one hand to Haldon, Lough Gur and Clegyr Boia, and on the other perhaps to Northern Stone Age plans such as those in the Røsnesvalen settlement in Norway (G. Gjessing, 1945, 153).

The plain and decorated plaques seem distinctly Iberian in inspiration, though precise parallels are lacking. Their ornament certainly relates them to the Rinyo-Clacton culture and probably to such elements in the Clyde-Carlingford culture as that represented by the Lyles Hill stone.

THE DORCHESTER CULTURE

Introduction

The most recently identified and least satisfactorily defined of the regional cultures of the Secondary Neolithic group is that which has come to be recognized as a result of the excavations at Dorchester-on-Thames (Oxfordshire) (Atkinson, C. M. Piggott & Sandars, 1951). The name itself is not wholly satisfactory, owing to the possibility of confusion with Dorchester (Dorset), but the only alternative would be the indefensible form Dorocinian (as opposed to Durnovarian), for the Dorchester-on-Thames sites do comprise most of the elements which can be considered to define the culture in question, and no alternative site-name seems wholly satisfactory.

The culture is not distinguished by a consistent pottery style—Windmill Hill, Peterborough or Rinyo-Clacton wares appear in its sites—but it constitutes a distinctive entity defined by certain ritual monuments (including some within the Henge group), cremation cemeteries, and burials under round barrows or cairns. It shares stone types with the Secondary Neolithic cultures at large, and bone-pin types at least with the Rinyo-Clacton culture, while the cremation cemeteries are comparable to those of the Ronaldsway culture just described. It might be possible to consider all the sites here treated under the Dorchester culture as belonging to any or all of the subsidiary groups within the Secondary Neolithic cultures, with an accidental absence of such elements as a distinctive pottery style, but in the present state of knowledge it seems advisable to consider such sites as a distinct group.

Distribution

In addition to the concentration of sites near Dorchester-on-Thames, one should include within the culture the first phase at Stonehenge (Bank, Ditch, Aubrey Holes and cremation-cemetery) among the ritual monuments, and burials in the south of England from Wiltshire, Oxfordshire and Bedfordshire. In northern England there is a noteworthy series of burials in Yorkshire, Derbyshire and Westmorland, while there is a cremation-cemetery with setting of ritual holes in West Lothian. Scattered finds of stone and bone types associated with these sites suggest a probable extension of the culture into north-east Scotland.

Ritual monuments of Henge type

These comprise the sites numbered I and XI at Dorchester, Stonehenge I, and Cairnpapple I. All incorporate cremation burials in addition to settings of ritual pits and, except at Cairnpapple, ditched single-entrance enclosures. The ritual pits have been the subject of much discussion, but there seems little doubt that they never held, nor were intended to hold, uprights of either timber or stone; in certain instances they seem to have been deliberately filled and on occasion (as in the case of some of the Aubrey holes at Stonehenge) this filling was dug into or disturbed at a later date. Their analogies appear to lie with the similar pits already noted as existing under some long barrows (p. 56) and also, for that matter, under many round barrows of the Bronze Age. At Stonehenge and the Dorchester sites, they are set in a circle, and at Cairnpapple in an irregular arc. The Bryn Celli Ddu passage-grave in Anglesey presents remarkable analogies in its enclosing ditch within which the kerb of the cairn was set, and the penannular setting of holes, cremations and pits containing stones within its inner edge (Hemp, 1930). Comparison may perhaps be made with the so-called *ustrinae* in the Balla-teare cemetery mentioned above.

Stonehenge I is by far the largest monument of this group, the Aubrey hole circle having a diameter of 288 ft., with the bank and ditch outside. A cremation cemetery occupied at least the south-east quadrant of the monument, the excavations of 1920–26 producing a large but unrecorded number of cremations in the Aubrey holes, in the bank and in the silt of the ditch to the bottom. Four cremations were accompanied by bone or ivory pins of the Rinyo-Clacton type i (skewer-pins), by flint fabricators, one by a polished stone mace-head comparable to those from the Tormore, Ormiegill or Taversoe Tuack chambered tombs in Scotland, and one by a shallow cup compared by Stone (1949) to a Rinyo-Clacton vessel from Woodlands (Hawley, 1921–28; Stevens, 1933; Piggott, 1951). A sherd of Rinyo-Clacton pottery occurred in the primary ditch silting.

Dorchester site I consisted of a square ditched enclosure with no en-trance, 90–95 ft. across, within which was an oval ditch with internal bank some 58 by 50 ft., containing a penannular setting of thirteen oval holes (Fig. 56), associated with which were four cremations, two with fragments of skewer-pins: there was an inhumation at the gap in the circuit of holes. Scraps of probably Western Neolithic pottery were primary, the oval ditch had been re-cut by people of the Peterborough culture, and there was a sherd of Rinyo-Clacton ware and a scatter of flints including *petit-tranchet* derivatives.

Site XI was complex, with three encircling ditches of as many phases, the outermost about 90 ft. in diameter, and a circle of fourteen holes. There was a single cremation, and a scatter of cremated bones in two of the holes; Abingdon and Peterborough ware occurred in scraps, and a *petit-tranchet* derivative.

The Cairnpapple I monument consisted of an irregular arc of seven holes, about 55 ft. across the chord, with twelve cremations in or near them, two with fragments of skewer-pins. The arc faced a setting of three stone-holes suggesting a structure of the 'Cove' type, which are probably though not certainly of the date of the arc of holes and the cremations, and all are almost certainly earlier than a double-entrance Henge monument with Beaker burials. (Piggott, 1950.)

At Dorchester, in addition to the monuments described, sites IV, V and VI incorporate Henge elements in being single-entrance ditched enclosures, though smaller, with diameters of 20, 35 and 23 ft. respectively. Site II combines features of site I in the ditch of its first phase (about 50 ft.

diameter), but in its later phase it is structurally related to sites IV–VI with their causewayed ditches, which in the three latter sites have the curious feature of post-holes in the bottom. All four sites enclosed cremation cemeteries, and in site II there were central pits, one containing a cremation with a perforated stone mace-head, a flint fabricator, and a bone skewer-pin, and another animal bones. Two of the cremations from the site II cemetery were associated with skewer-pins, but there was none with the cremations in sites IV–VI, which, however, produced *petit-tranchet* derivatives and a fabricator. There were nineteen cremations in the site II cemetery, and two in the central pits; twenty-five in site IV, twenty-one in site V, and forty-nine in site VI.

It will be seen that these monuments of the Henge type, and their derivatives, are distinguished from those already discussed in relation to other subsidiary groups within the Secondary Neolithic complex by the presence of cremation-burials which may form cemeteries, and also by the presence of the curious ritual holes distinct from the true post-holes at such sites as Arminghall or Woodhenge. (There was, however, one cremation at Woodhenge: Cunnington, 1929, 88.) The inherent relationship between the various types of monument within the Henge class under discussion is that of a circular area delimited by a bank derived from a quarry-ditch and having a single entrance: within that sacred area, bounded by its *temenos*, there may have been roofed timber-work structures (Woodhenge), large free-standing posts (Arminghall), upright stones (Mayborough), pits (Stonehenge I and the Dorchester sites) or nothing structural at all (Gorsey Bigbury). Standing stones become a constant accompaniment only in the double-entrance class of Henge monument, which on the present evidence is to be associated with the Beaker cultures rather than any of those within the Secondary Neolithic group.

Burials under round barrows

About a dozen inhumation burials from southern and north-eastern England share characteristics, such as the presence of certain Secondary Neolithic bone and stone types, and the frequent absence of pottery, which justify their inclusion as a distinct group within the Dorchester culture, to which one notable burial of the series is linked by its association with a cremation-cemetery.

In the south of England, at least three burials may be noted, the first being that at Linch Hill, Stanton Harcourt (not far from Dorchester-on-Thames). Here an inhumation of a slightly dolichocephalic female accompanied by a jet belt-slider of the type discussed above under the Peterborough culture, and a polished-edge flint knife, was surrounded by double-ring-ditches which had themselves been cut into by a later grave containing a burial with a *B*-class beaker (Grimes, 1944). A close parallel to this burial is that at Dunstable, where a dolichocephalic female inhumation with a polished-edge knife was found within a ring-ditch under a barrow, the mound of which contained sherds of Abingdon pottery and *petit-tranchet* derivatives, and a Middle Bronze Age secondary burial in a cinerary urn (Dunning & Wheeler, 1931; and unpublished material in Dunstable Museum).

At Upton Lovel in Wiltshire, Colt Hoare's barrow 4 covered a grave 3 ft. deep in which were two inhumations (Hoare, 1812, 75). At the feet of the larger individual were 'more than three dozen' perforated bone points, three flint axes of Seamer-Liff's Low type and stones including a grooved whetstone of a type usually associated with the Wessex culture (Newall, 1931). Boar's tusk blades and natural hollow flint 'cups' were by the legs, and near the chest a further 'two dozen' perforated bone points and a perforated stone battle-axe, again of Wessex culture type. A jet ring, jet and bone beads, a bronze awl, and 'stones and pebbles of various sorts' (including two broken halves of a second battle-axe) were also found in indeterminate association. Although this assemblage has Bronze Age elements, the axes are of similar types to those from Yorkshire and Derbyshire graves described below, and the boar's tusk blades and probably the bone points are again significant: the latter seem likely to have formed some form of necklace or fringe to a garment (see p. 360 below). Among the 'stones and pebbles' are two fragments of Cornish origin, of rocks identical with those from which a great number of axe-blades were manufactured and exported into Wessex (p. 299 above).

In north-eastern England the most remarkable burials of this group were those contained beneath the barrow of Howe Hill, Duggleby, E.R. Yorkshire (Mortimer, 1905, 23–42). This was a very large round barrow, some 125 ft. in diameter and 20 ft. high, though decapitated to form a mill-stance. A central pit-grave 9 ft. deep contained on the bottom the skeleton of an adult male with a bowl, now lost, but apparently of some form of Wind-mill Hill ware (Newbigin, 1937, 206), and in the filling of the grave-pit were unaccompanied skeletons of adults and children. Immediately adjacent was a shallow grave, in and on the edge of which were two adult skeletons, one with a skewer-pin, five *petit-tranchet* derivative arrowheads, boar's tusk blades, beavers' teeth, and flint flakes. The second burial was accompanied by an exceptionally fine polished flint knife. Near these burials, and in a position over the filled-up mouth of the central pit-grave, was another adult male skeleton with an antler mace-head, a chipped and polished flint axe, and a leaf-arrowhead of lozenge outline. (Fig. 62.)

All these burials were under a mound of earthy rubble some 50 ft. in diameter containing at least five other unaccompanied skeletons of adults and children, while also in this, and in a chalk-rubble layer above, were a minimum of fifty cremations, three with skewer-pins in the Dorchester manner and one with a Rinyo-Clacton type ii pin, with perforated lateral bulb. *Petit-tranchet* derivatives were also present. All were sealed by a clay layer (which might have been an old turf-line) covering a mound about 75 ft. in diameter, and this was overlaid by the main body of the chalk rubble mound, in which no prehistoric burials were found in the area excavated by Mortimer. Remains of broken and burnt animal and human bones were found throughout the material of the barrow.

It would be possible to separate the burials in this very remarkable barrow into two groups, the first comprising the skeleton with the probably Windmill Hill bowl at the bottom of the central grave, and the skeletons in the filling of this (H, I, J, K of the original account). The three burials with grave-goods on the old surface (C, D and G) would form a second group, with which must go the additional unaccompanied skeletons and the cremation-cemetery, for it is impossible to dissociate these from one another. But there is no evidence for assuming any long interval between the two series of burials.

Another Yorkshire burial of comparable type is that within the long barrow on Seamer Moor, Scarborough, of which an inadequate account and most of the finds survive. Within the long barrow was a circular cairn, burnt on the top, with pot-sherds (lost), and animal and human bones. In the centre of this were two 'masses' of human bones, with a 'rude flint arrow-head' (lost). Under a flat stone was a deposit of human bones, four polished flint axes, five leaf-arrowheads of lozenge outline, a plano-convex and a fine polished-edge flint knife, two boar's tusk blades and a perforated antler mace-head (or possibly an axe-sleeve). All these survive (Fig. 62), but two 'rude flint spearheads' also found have been lost. (Londesborough, 1848; R. A. Smith, 1927.)

The third important burial of this group is that from Liff's Low, Biggin, Derbyshire (Bateman, 1848, 4–43). This consisted of a male inhumation burial (with a 'fine and intellectual' skull) in an octagonal cist beneath a cairn. Of the grave-goods, there survive a remarkable little vessel of un-certain affinities (Piggott, 1932 *b*, 132), two polished flint axes of the same type as those from Duggleby and Seamer, and a perforated antler mace-head with faceted end, found in the angle of the knees of the skeleton (Fig. 62). The other recorded finds, however, comprise two polished-edge knives (one with the unpolished edge serrated), two flint 'spearheads', two flint arrowheads ('delicately chipped and of unusual form'), two boars' tusks, and pieces of red ochre. The consistent similarity in the assemblages in all these three burials is striking—axes of identical type, polished-edge knives, antler mace-heads, and boar's tusk blades all serve to link them, while the skewer-pins at Duggleby related it to the Dorchester and Cairnpapple cremation-cemeteries as well as to the Rinyo-Clacton culture. A further series of burials from Wiltshire, Yorkshire, and Westmorland, are also clearly related, and confirm the existence of a distinctive culture.

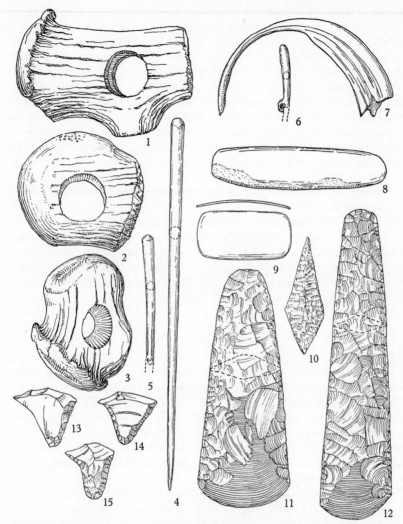

Fig. 62. Dorchester culture: bone, antler and flint types in the north. 1, 8, 10, Seamer Moor; 2, 11, 12, Liff's Low; 3, 4, 6, 7, 9, 13–15, Howe Hill Duggleby (*after Mortimer*); 5, Cairnpapple Hill. Scale ¼.

In Wiltshire, an inhumation burial at Cop Head, Warminster (Hoare, 1812, 68) was accompanied by an antler mace-head (or possibly axe-sleeve) similar to that from Seamer, and at Collingbourne in the same county an antler mace-head was found with a cremation in a barrow which also produced a stone hammer of group I rock from the mound (Lukis, 1867): the former at least has claims for inclusion among the Dorchester-culture burials. In Yorkshire, a barrow at Cowlam (Greenwell, 1877, 214–21) contained a quantity of inhumations, many apparently reburied in skeletal form; with one was a boar's tusk blade, and with another an antler mace-head. There was also a flint leaf-arrowhead among the burials, and sherds of pottery of Heslerton ware (Newbigin, 1937, 205; cf. p. 114 above). At Crosby Garrett in Westmorland, one of several inhumation burials under a round barrow was associated with a perforated-bulb pin (Rinyo-Clacton type ii), a boar's tusk blade and an unworked tusk, and another with an antler mace-head and a pyrites-and-chert 'strike-a-light'. Cremations, some with bone pins, were also found in the mound of the barrow (Greenwell, 1877, 389–91).

A group of Yorkshire burials are associated with skewer-pins—with inhumations at Garton Slack and probably at Wharram Percy and Fimber, and with a cremation at Aldro (Mortimer, 1905, 48, 62, 190, 245). Another series in the same county is accompanied by polished-edge knives: inhumations at Aldro 94 and C 75, and a cremation at Rookdale Farm, Sledmere (Mortimer, 1905, xlii, 74, 82). Finally, an inhumation beneath a round cairn with a boar's tusk blade at Waterhouses, Derbyshire, should probably also be included (Bateman, 1861, 131).

MATERIAL EQUIPMENT

Stone and flint

Perforated stone mace-heads have been found in Dorchester site II (Fig. 63, no. 4) and at Stonehenge (Fig. 63, no. 5) in the cremation-cemetery (Stevens, 1933, 52). Both approximate to the 'cushion-mace' type with central perforation, but the second is also related to the pear-shaped form from the Tormore and Taversoe Tuack chambered tombs in Scotland, and is allied to the stone mace-heads derived from antler forms discussed below. The stone battle-axes at Upton Lovel are likely to be related to the Wessex culture aspect of that burial.

Flint axes of characteristic form, chipped and partially polished, come from burials at Upton Lovel, Duggleby, Seamer and Liff's Low (Fig. 62, nos. 11, 12). As Bruce-Mitford pointed out (1938), the latter axes are allied to those from southern England hoards of flint axes, probably partly connected with flint mining, and at Balcombe, Sussex, one such axe seems to have been associated with a triangular polished knife (Curwen, 1937 *a*, 139), while another accompanied a Beaker burial at Cruden, Aberdeenshire (M. E. S. Mitchell, 1934). Fragments of *stone axes* of Graig Lwyd and Great Langdale origin were found at Cairnpapple, probably though not certainly contemporary with the period I cremation-cemetery and ritual holes.

Leaf-arrowheads of angular lozenge form from Dorchester, Seamer and Duggleby (Fig. 62, no. 10) are similar to others from Yorkshire Neolithic burials of Windmill Hill affinities, described above (p. 118).

'*Petit-tranchet*' *derivative arrowheads* occur in the Dorchester sites, in the mound of the barrow at Dunstable, and at Duggleby (Fig. 62, nos. 13–15). They, like the polished-edge knives, are part of the general Secondary Neolithic flint inventory.

Flint knives polished on the edges or faces, or both, are again a part of the Secondary Neolithic background, and occur at Linch Hill, Dunstable, Duggleby (Fig. 62, no. 9), Aldro, Sledmere, Seamer (Fig. 62, no. 8) and Liff's Low, affording a link with such burials as those in certain Scottish

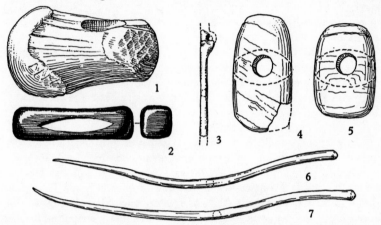

Fig. 63. Dorchester and Peterborough cultures: antler, bone and stone types in the south. 1, Thames at Teddington (*after Smith*); 2, Handley Down (*after Pitt-Rivers*); 3, Windmill Hill; 4, 6, Dorchester-on-Thames (*after Atkinson* et al.); 5, 7, Stonehenge. Scale ⅓.

chambered cairns referred to in Chapter VIII, as well as with that in the Gop Cave with Peterborough pottery. At Stonehenge, *polished-edge scrapers* were found within the area of the monument, though not definitely associated with the first phase.

Plano-convex knives, again known from Scottish chambered cairns, and in Peterborough contexts, are represented only at Seamer: they occur at Stonehenge, but again not definitely related to the first phase.

Fabricators, or similar flaked rods of flint were, however, found in two of the Stonehenge Aubrey holes, and at Dorchester. The occurrence of a chert rod with iron pyrites in one of the Crosby Garrett burials shows that the probable use of many of these objects in the Secondary Neolithic was as elements in a 'flint-and-steel', which is confirmed by the frequent appearance of 'fabricators' and pyrites associated together with Bronze Age burials (cf. Greenwell, 1877, 264–7 for examples).

Antler and bone

Pins of Rinyo-Clacton types i and ii are, as has been shown, a constantly recurring feature of the burials assigned to the Dorchester culture, appearing at Dorchester, Stonehenge, Duggleby (Fig. 63, nos. 6, 7; Fig. 62, no. 4), Garton Slack, Aldro, Cairnpapple (Fig. 62, no. 5) (type i); Crosby Garrett and Duggleby (Fig. 62, no. 6) (type ii). A stray specimen of a type ii pin from the later levels at Windmill Hill is the only specimen known in southern England (Fig. 63, no. 3).

Perforated antler-maces are an extremely interesting feature of the burials under discussion. The mace-heads from Cowlam, Crosby Garrett, Collingbourne, Warminster and Seamer (Fig. 62, no. 1) are all made from the base of a red-deer antler, cylindrically bored but not very elaborately finished, and one may add that from a Bronze Age grave at Lambourn, Berkshire (Greenwell, 1890, 60). The Seamer and Warminster specimens have, in their present state, a hollow cavity which could be interpreted as a socket for a small axe-blade in the manner assumed for the rather similar specimen from Skara Brae already commented upon (p. 333), but it is very probable that in all three examples the hollow is due to the natural decay of the interior tissue of the antler rather than to its deliberate removal. The Duggleby specimen (Fig. 62, no. 3) is better finished, and carefully rounded, while that from Liff's Low has the cut end carefully cut or ground into a series of diamond-shaped facets (Fig. 62, no. 2). At least four similarly faceted antler mace-heads are known from the River Thames near London (Fig. 63, no. 1; Smith, 1918; Lawrence, 1929), and as Smith pointed out, these must be the prototype of similarly shaped and faceted stone mace-heads, one of which again comes from the Thames near London, and others from Quarnford, Staffordshire; Urquhart, Elgin; Bonar Bridge, Sutherland; and Corwen, Merionethshire, the last being a particularly elaborately finished object in white chalcedony (Anderson, 1909).

Boar's tusk blades, made by cutting a long sliver from a large boar's tusk, occur with burials at Upton Lovel, Duggleby (Fig. 62, no. 7), Liff's Low, Cowlam, Seamer, Stonesteads and Crosby Garrett, and may be taken as a type-object of the Dorchester culture. Unworked boars' tusks are also found. Parallels exist in the pit-comb ware cemetery of Västerbjers (Stenberger, 1939; 1943) and in the analogous Visby burials (Nihlén, 1927), both in Gotland.

Perforated bone 'points' up to sixty in number and graduated in size were found in two groups in the Upton Lovel barrow, and can only be interpreted as elements of collars or fringes to garments in which they would hang as a continuous series of pendants, similar to the better-known necklaces of perforated teeth or tusks with an Upper Palaeolithic ancestry and known in the Rinyo-Clacton culture and among modern primitives.

Perforated seals' teeth forming fringes to cloaks or similar garments were found in the burials with pit-comb ware at Västerbjers in Gotland, of late Passage-grave date (Stenberger, 1939; 1943). The six unperforated points from an inhumation burial at Aldro, E.R. Yorkshire (Mortimer, 1905, 76) may have been arranged as a necklace (they were found near the neck of the body), and almost certainly the ten perforated and graduated points from a Middle Bronze Age burial in a cinerary urn at Snailwell, Cambridgeshire, were again strung as pendants in a similar manner (Lethbridge, 1950). A single perforated point of the same type was found at Woodhenge (p. 343). A grave in the Bovila Madurell Neolithic cemetery in Catalonia (no. 33) contained an inhumation with a perforated bone 'double axe' and nine graduated (but unperforated) bone points, possibly analogous (Serra, 1947).

Miscellaneous objects associated with Dorchester culture sites include the jet *belt-slider* from Linch Hill, of a type we have seen to be also associated with the Peterborough culture (cf. Fig. 63, no. 2), *chalk balls* at Stonehenge, comparable with those in the Rinyo-Clacton, the Ronaldsway and the Boyne cultures, and *pottery* finds which include sherds of Western Neolithic wares (as at Dorchester, Duggleby, Aldro, Cowlam and Cairnpapple), Peterborough (Dorchester) or Rinyo-Clacton (Dorchester and Stonehenge). At the latter site, too, was the curious cup related to 'incense-cup' types already commented upon.

THE RELATIONSHIPS OF THE DORCHESTER CULTURE

The affiliations of what has been described above as the Dorchester culture are rendered difficult to assess at the outset by the elusive character of the evidence: in many respects the culture has had to be defined by negatives (absence of a distinctive pottery style, etc.), and there always remains the possibility that what we have attempted to isolate as a distinct culture is in reality, as a whole or in part, a group of residual elements within the Secondary Neolithic complex which have not been assigned to the Peterborough, Rinyo-Clacton or Ronaldsway groups. It is for instance possible that the cremation-cemeteries (which form one of the most definite features of the Dorchester culture) may be those of communities whose settlements would be assigned to one or other of the cultures just mentioned.

To the Henge monuments no European parallels are forthcoming, and it is interesting to note that in the burials two distinct traditions are present —inhumation under a round barrow or cairn, and cremation in cemeteries. The former one would tend to connect with the single-grave burial customs associated with the British Beaker and Food-vessel cultures, the appearance of which in Britain is a parallel event to the arrival of Single-grave and Boat-axe communities in Denmark and Sweden.

N

Cremation is known, exceptionally, in the Ertebølle culture, but the Dorchester culture cemeteries have of course their best British parallel in those of the Ronaldsway culture, and the cremations (with large bone pins) in the chambered tombs of the Boyne culture. A further link with the Boyne culture is afforded by the horse-shoe setting of 'ritual pits' with cremations and stones within the ditch at Bryn Celli Ddu, where Henge monument elements appear incorporated in an otherwise normal passage-grave. The site of Er-Lannic in Brittany, with a cremation-cemetery grouped at the foot of the standing stones of an approximately circular setting, seems to provide an analogy for the Dorchester sites, and at Er Lannic the pottery associated with the cremations was of the decorated Chassey type which we have seen is likely to have been ancestral to that of the earlier phase of the Rinyo wares (le Rouzic, 1930).

The stone types in general belong to the Secondary Neolithic series already familiar from other cultures within the complex, and of the bone types, the boar's tusk blades relate to the Northern Stone Age cultures of Mesolithic derivation and especially to the burials with pit-comb ware at Västerbjers and Visby in Gotland, themselves contemporary with the later phase of the Passage-grave culture in Scandinavia.

The perforated mace-heads of antler and stone buried with evidently ceremonial intent, have a peculiar interest and importance. The former are likely to have Maglemose origins, whether as antler-axes or as perforated axe-sleeves, and elaborate decorated forms are known in Passage-grave times in Denmark (Müller, 1918, fig. 55, from Aa, Fredbjerg), though the specifically British forms do not appear there. A parallel use of the antler-hafted axe as a ritual or ceremonial object is however found in the S.O.M. culture, with its strong Mesolithic substratum, and the remarkable antler or bone double-axe from a Neolithic grave in the cemetery at Bovila Madurell in Catalonia is another comparable example (Serra, 1947). The ultimate connexions with the Minoan world should not be forgotten in this context (Hawkes, 1937). Stone mace-heads of ovoid form were in use by Mesolithic communities in southern England (Rankine, 1949a).

The interest of the Dorchester culture mace-heads in Britain is, however, their relationship with similar objects in Bronze Age contexts. Smith (1918; 1926) showed that the antler mace-heads of the type of Duggleby or Liff's Low were ancestral to a stone series of pear-shaped outline, such as that from the cremation-cemetery at Stonehenge, and these in turn are related to the Tormore-Ormiegill-Taversoe Tuack group already commented upon under the Orkney-Cromarty group of chambered tombs (Chapter VIII); in all instances they must represent burials with which a mace or sceptre has been deposited as a symbol of authority. Now in three well-known graves of the Wessex culture of the Bronze Age, at Clandon in Dorset, Bush Barrow in Wiltshire, and Towthorpe in Yorkshire, maces had again been buried with the dead—at Clandon of jet with gold studs, and at the other two sites of stone (Piggott, 1938; Mortimer, 1905, 3). These must in turn be connected with the ceremonial battle-axes from single-grave burials, and in four instances associated with *A*-beakers (e.g. that near Woodhenge—Cunnington, 1929, 148), and those approaching to the Scandinavian battle-axe form from Wessex culture graves (e.g. Snowshill and Hove). In the Upton Lovel barrow to which attention has already been drawn, with the inhumation accompanied by boar's tusk blades and bone points, there was also a battle-axe of Wessex culture type, while at Lambourn, Berkshire, an antler-mace of Dorchester culture type and another such battle-axe accompanied a cremated burial, two incense-cups and a bronze knife (Greenwell, 1890, 60).

It seems clear then that an overlap can be established between graves of the Dorchester culture and those of the Wessex Bronze Age (and its York-shire counterpart), and that in both cultures the mace is buried with the dead as a symbol of authority, implying some continuity of tradition among the ruling dynasties. The bearing of this on chronology is discussed in another chapter, but we may note in passing that this close relationship which we have been able to establish should also contribute to our understanding of the origins of the cremation tradition in the British Bronze Age.

In assessing the date of the Dorchester culture we have to note the recently determined age-estimate of charcoal from one of the Stonehenge Aubrey holes by means of the breakdown of radio-active carbon (C_{14}), which gave a figure of 1848 B.C.$\pm$275, or a possible range between 1573 and 2123 B.C. This date is further discussed in Chapter XII, and it may be said that a date for the first phase of Stonehenge in the sixteenth or seventeenth century B.C. would be in agreement with the probable estimate arrived at by archaeological means.

A NOTE ON CIRCUMPOLAR STONE AGE ELEMENTS IN SHETLAND

The excavations at Jarlshof near Sumburgh Head in Shetland produced a series of structures and occupation-levels which could be shown not only to be pre-Viking, but also to have elements which related in part to the Late Bronze Age and in part to an Early Iron Age (Curle, 1932–36a; Childe, 1938), and at Wiltrow an actual iron-smelting establishment was found (Curle, 1936b). But throughout these settlements certain stone and bone types were present which have in part parallels within the Secondary Neolithic cultures just described, and in part, as Gjessing perceived (1944, 64), within the Circumpolar Stone Age at large. While in date this material probably all lies within the second half of the first millennium B.C. it deserves a brief reference here.

The *stone types* are normally of slate, in the Circumpolar tradition, and include heavy rough axes or clubs, large hatchets and handled knives, rough saws, sickles and curved blades, and perforated heart-shaped objects. Clark (1947 a, 96) has suggested that these were the blades of blubber-mattocks comparable to those of whale-bone, and of Early Iron Age date, from Foshigarry in North Uist, which have very good parallels among the Hudson Bay-West Greenland Eskimos.

Bone tools include perforated adzes of Skara Brae type, and chisels with or without sockets—types which again occur at Grimes Graves (p. 82) and, like the remainder of the bone equipment, have Maglemose origins (cf. Clark, 1936 a, 110). Other types include scapula-shovels, a perforated mace-head of whale bone, polished bone blades of Skara Brae affinities, points and perforated phalanges—again Maglemose in origin but also occurring in the Lower Dounreay chambered tomb in Caithness (p. 252), and in the settlement of Passage-grave date at Lindø in Langeland (Winther, 1926).

The most remarkable bone object, however, is what appears to be a *girdle-plate* of subtriangular outline with perforations at the apex and the two basal angles, similar to those from the Västerbjers cemetery and from Danish passage-graves (Stenberger, 1943, 92–4; Müller, 1918, figs. 56, 240). It is, however, decorated with a fine incised pattern of zigzags and hatched lozenges, triangles and squares, which as Childe pointed out relate it to the ornament of the Iberian schist plaques and analogous art-styles (Childe, 1938, 362). The combination of these Iberian motifs with an object having its structural affinities with the Northern Stone Age is precisely what might be expected from such a meeting-place of seaborne traditions as Shetland.

CHAPTER XII

THE CONTENT, RELATIONSHIPS, AND CHRONOLOGY OF THE BRITISH NEOLITHIC CULTURES

THE CONTENT OF THE CULTURES

I N the preceding chapters we have studied in some detail the variant cultures which can be grouped as 'Neolithic' within the British Isles. This adjective, as explained in the Introduction, has been used throughout in the sense in which it is generally accepted in current prehistory to denote communities of stone-using agriculturalists which may also have such uniting features as the use of collective tombs for burial. We have seen also that more than one of these cultures is likely to have existed side by side with others possessing knowledge of metals, and at no great distance. Even though the proportion of the population of such communities actually using metal objects may have been very small, there has been common consent in assigning the Beaker culture in Britain, for instance, to the beginning of a Copper or Bronze Age. We shall examine the reality of this division into Neolithic and Early Bronze Age groups later in this chapter, but for the present the traditional nomenclature is retained.

The agricultural economy

There are in fact several constantly recurring features common to all the Neolithic cultures under review which, in spite of diversity in other aspects, justifies us in grouping them into a larger unit. To begin with, they are effectively divided from the Mesolithic cultures by their basis of subsistence, agriculture and stock-breeding. Evidence of grain-growing is available from almost every culture—wheat, emmer and barley in the Windmill Hill culture; emmer, small spelt and probably wheat in that of Clyde-Carlingford; wheat among the builders of the Boyne tombs and barley with those of the Orkney-Cromarty group. Wheat and a saddle-quern come from a settlement with Beacharra and Rinyo I pottery in Bute, and there is a saddle-quern rider from a tomb in the Scilly Islands. There is no direct evidence of corn-growing in the Secondary Neolithic cultures, except for probable grain-impressions on Ronaldsway pottery and the single-piece flint sickles (which might, however, have been used for cutting reeds). But in settlements of these cultures, as with those of the Western group, domesticated animals are well attested. In the south of England, Secondary Neolithic sites such as Woodhenge share the large-horned domestic ox of Windmill Hill type, while in the Orkneys there is a different and distinctive breed.

Both these aspects of mixed farming appear in the British Isles as the result of actual imports of seed corn and of animals for breeding, brought with the first Neolithic colonists as an essential part of their material culture: they are as novel and as intrusive as polished axes and leaf-shaped arrow-heads, or as Windmill Hill or Beacharra pottery. The Secondary Neolithic cultures show how Mesolithic traditions were adopted and incorporated by Neolithic societies after the entrance phase, and hunting was carried on by all groups from the first, but essentially we are dealing with a break in tradition, and the beginning of a new economy.

The settlements

In the extremely incomplete state of our knowledge it is almost impossible to estimate any settlement unit likely to have been common to British Neolithic communities. Where we have information, it is (with one exception) that of individual houses or farmsteads, not grouped into villages or hamlets (Haldon, Clegyr Boia, Ronaldsway, Lough Gur)—the exception is the Rinyo-Clacton culture in the Orkneys, where the Skara Brae and Rinyo sites are in fact agglomerations of huts which either represent large 'undivided' families of thirty to forty individuals, or hamlets of several family groups. Certainly no villages such as those of the Continental Danubian cultures, or settlement sites such as that of Los Millares, have been identified in Neolithic Britain. The distribution of chambered tombs, when studied in restricted areas such as the island of Rousay, strongly suggests the family tombs of individual crofts or farmsteads, and the cremation-cemeteries of the Dorchester culture seem similarly to have been those of small family groups rather than the common burying-place of a village community. The causewayed camps of the Windmill Hill culture can again be reasonably interpreted as the communal product of a number of scattered farmsteads, resorted to seasonally when rounding up the cattle.

Such scanty evidence as there is, then, favours the belief that the distribution-pattern of Neolithic settlements was largely that of self-sufficient farmsteads, probably in many instances accompanied by its appropriate burying-place. The cemeteries of passage-graves which are really only known in the Boyne culture (Fourknocks, Brugh na Boinne, Loughcrew, Carrowkeel and Carrowmore) do, however, suggest a social organization in which members of royal dynasties were brought for burial to traditional cemeteries of great mausolea, and it is probably significant that, as we shall see, these tombs are likely to be contemporary with the Wessex culture of southern England, where comparable barrow-cemeteries with richly furnished graves occur.

Collective burial

A phenomenon common to most, though not all, the Neolithic cultures under review is the practice of collective burial, either by inhumation or cremation, under some form of monumental tomb. With the exception of sporadic or casual individual burials (which may in some instances be regarded as ritual or dedicatory) all the cultures in Britain within the Western Neolithic group at large share this burial rite in some form. In the stone-built chambered tombs, collective burial could be made by successive interments introduced over a period of time to a temporarily closed burial vault: a final blocking was eventually made, for reasons unknown, and the tomb henceforward ceased to be used. In the unchambered long barrows of southern and eastern England, successive burial was made either in an impermanent mortuary house away from the barrow site or, more probably, in such a structure within a *temenos* of some sort on the actual site, later to be covered by the mound of the barrow, which formed the final and irrevocable sealing of the burial deposits.

Grave-goods other than pottery are scanty, or even completely absent, but certain observances outside the entrance to chambered tombs seem to have involved the ritual breaking of pots there, or they may have been left containing offerings of food or drink until broken and scattered by accident. There is some evidence of funeral feasts. The rite is consistently that of inhumation in the Severn-Cotswold group of tombs, while in the Clyde-Carlingford group the Scottish tombs have inhumation and cremation equally divided, but the latter is dominant in the Irish tombs of the culture, and in the Orkney-Cromarty group the rite is again mixed. In the Boyne culture cremation is constant save at Fourknocks, where inhumations were also present.

Collective burial in the Secondary Neolithic cultures takes the form of cremation cemeteries (as in the Ronaldsway and Dorchester cultures), and it is probable that the presence of cremation in the chambered tombs enumerated above may be related to Secondary Neolithic traditions, themselves possibly of Mesolithic origin. Single-grave burials are, however, not uncommon in the Peterborough and Dorchester cultures, where they may owe something to the single-grave traditions of the British Early Bronze Age, where they are almost certainly closely connected with Battle-axe elements.

In at least two instances (Lanhill and Coldrum) the anatomical evidence showed that the tombs had been used for members of a family, and it seems probable that this may be regarded as usual. Burials were made in the tombs without regard to age or sex. What is not known is the status of the families entitled to chambered tombs: were they an *élite*, or the whole population of Neolithic farmers? Any attempt to interpret the tombs and their contents in terms of local population groups, or to estimate even in the roughest terms the size of these communities, is rendered hazardous by these and other unknown factors. Mrs Clifford has made some interesting calculations based on the Cotswold chambered cairns (1950, 33): assuming the use of each tomb to be about a century in duration, and with an average of just over ten burials in the recorded sites, she estimates that, if all the probable total of sixty tombs in the region were in use at one time, a population of only 240 persons could be deduced. But this depends on two very doubtful assumptions—that all the tombs were in fact in use at one time, and that the family unit was not more than four individuals, with an average age at death of 40 years. Atkinson, discussing the same problems in connexion with the Dorchester cremation-cemeteries, gives evidence for a crude annual death-rate of 4 per cent and a family unit likely to have been nearer twenty than ten, with only 30 per cent having an expectation of life of 40 years (Atkinson, C. M. Piggott & Sandars, 1951, 77–9).

General anthropological probabilities would weigh in favour of a large family unit such as that suggested by the Dorchester evidence. The duration of a century or so for the effective use of a chambered tomb seems on the whole to be likely in view of evidence from more than one region, but if the average of ten to fifteen burials per tomb which seems to obtain in the British series as a whole is to be related to a family unit of about fifteen to twenty individuals, a much lower death-rate than that likely at Dorchester would have to be assumed.

Physical anthropology

It is convenient at this point to mention the physical anthropology of the Neolithic colonists of Britain, though only to dismiss it. Daniel had recently summarized the inconclusive evidence from the English and Welsh chambered tombs (1950), which apart from demonstrating the consistent presence of a gracile, slender skeletal form, with a dolichocephalic skull of the so-called 'Mediterranean' type, tells us nothing of the affinities of the immigrants except in the most general way. The Scottish and scanty Irish evidence, not directly reviewed by Daniel, serves to confirm the rest of the chambered-tomb and long-barrow material from the British Isles. It is probable that a new and detailed examination of the whole mass of material by an anatomist guided by a prehistorian as to the precise archaeological contexts of individual finds might produce evidence of varieties of physical type associated with specific divisions based on material culture.

Material equipment

An essential uniting factor throughout the various British Neolithic cultures is, by definition, the use of stone for tools and weapons. The immigrants brought with them as their most distinctive equipment axes with stone or flint blades and the bow with arrows tipped with leaf-shaped flint points. The necessity for abundant axes led to the exploitation of the mined flint from the Upper Chalk in southern and eastern England, and later of the igneous rocks of the west and north, while minor sources of flint supply, such as pebbles from river gravels or the sea-coast, were constantly utilized.

The use of shaft-hole hafting techniques appears only in the Secondary Neolithic cultures, where it is likely to have a Mesolithic origin, though probably also influenced by the introduction of shaft-hole battle-axes by Single-grave immigrants. It is possible that the technically more primitive type of 'hour-glass' perforation may represent the more ancient indigenous tradition (cf. Rankine, 1949 a) and the tubular perforation, made with a hollow drill and sand, the novel Battle-axe contribution.

Primary and Secondary Neolithic cultures

Despite the basic similarities in our Neolithic cultures, it is nevertheless possible to recognize a significant division between those cultures which represent the new traditions introduced from the European continent into Mesolithic Britain, and those which show these immigrant ideas blended with those of the older hunter-fisher population. Of what may be called Primary Neolithic cultures, that of Windmill Hill is perhaps the clearest example of the virtual transference of north French early Neolithic traditions to this country: here is the unmistakable representative of the Western Neolithic represented at Cortaillod, Chalain or Catenoy. The same may be said of the Severn-Cotswold culture, and still more of that of the earlier Clyde-Carlingford settlements in Scotland, where once again the Western Neolithic aspects are stressed not only by the type of collective tomb, but by the channelled ware of west French or Iberian antecedents. The Boyne culture once again, in the architecture and art of its tombs, shows the more or less direct implantation of Iberian or Breton ideas in Ireland, and the other chambered-tomb groups show the same thing, if less completely and strikingly.

But with the group of cultures I have classed as those of the Secondary Neolithic series, the immigrant nature of the various elements is less clearly marked. Already, indeed, in the Boyne culture we have found that the pottery styles represented in the tombs are not those of Iberia or Brittany, but one which seems to be a local development from mixed sources, and when we turn to consider the content of the Peterborough or the Rinyo-Clacton culture we find certain elements which can indeed be regarded as intrusive (Funnel-beaker and Pit-comb wares; derivatives of Chassey ware and Iberian pin-types) but inextricably mixed with other features which have a long local ancestry in Mesolithic cultures, such as *petit-tranchet* derivative arrowheads or stone types of the Circumpolar series. We find, in fact, what we might expect to find—the first impact of the arrival of agricultural communities over, there is a *modus vivendi* established between the newcomers and the old population with hunter-fisher traditions, with a give-and-take of ideas and a consequent series of hybrid cultures growing up in the various regions of the British Isles. The later Neolithic is inevitably a period of cultural diversity, but with a coherence brought about by the incorporation of common traditions.

This concept of the local evolution of Secondary Neolithic cultures may well be found to apply to other regions of Europe. The French 'Campignian', and the Seine-Oise-Marne and Horgen cultures of that country and of Switzerland, seem best interpreted in these terms, and in relationship one to another, as parallel devolutions of the primary Western Neolithic traditions (marked by a degeneration of potting techniques to produce a common level of *kümmerkeramik*) and a complementary resurgence of Mesolithic elements in bone and flint work.

THE RELATIONSHIPS OF BRITISH NEOLITHIC CULTURES

The next stage in our recapitulation must be a discussion of the relationships of the various component cultures of Neolithic Britain one to another. It should be possible then to see the connexions existing between the various regional groups, and to set these into some sort of a relative chronology. The region under consideration is fortunately small enough, and provided with enough natural routes of communication by sea and land for there to be a reasonable chance of contact between communities existing at approximately the same time, and indeed the archaeological evidence of such relationships is considerable.

The contacts of the Windmill Hill culture

The Windmill Hill culture of Wessex and Sussex has in fact less evidence of outside contacts than most of the other regional cultures or groups distinguished in this book, and this, coupled with the close similarities between its pottery and that of the earlier Cortaillod culture and its French representatives, goes to confirm the belief that it represents one of the earliest Neolithic settlements of Britain. In east Sussex, a developed phase can be shown to overlap chronologically, and perhaps to mingle culturally, with the Ebbsfleet phase of the Peterborough culture. The simplicity of the earlier Western Neolithic pottery forms makes it difficult to assess the relationship between Windmill Hill and the simple pot forms from the Severn-Cotswold tombs or from a few of the Clyde-Carlingford and Hebridean groups: these may imply at least an overlap in time, and represent allied colonizing movements contemporary with that which brought the Windmill Hill culture to southern England. Nor is it clear how precisely the west English aspect of the culture (represented by Hembury ware at the type-site and at Maiden Castle) can be placed chronologically with respect to Windmill Hill ware itself. The only indication is afforded by the fragment of an axe of group II*a* in a secondary context at Windmill Hill and another contemporary with the main occupation of Hembury (p. 76 above), which might suggest that the westerly sites were later rather than wholly contemporary with those of central southern England.

Further to the west, there seems likely to be approximate contemporaneity, and some common origins, in such sites as Carn Brea in Cornwall, Clegyr Boia in Pembrokeshire and Lough Gur, Co. Limerick, which may again be broadly contemporary with Hembury and probably partly with the earlier phase of Windmill Hill. A specifically Irish problem is posed in respect of the origins of the shouldered bowls, of types found at Lough Gur and many sites in Eire, and again at Lyles Hill in Ulster. The latter series seems almost inevitably derivative from the very similar Yorkshire pottery, but the more southerly examples are probably rather to be related to the colonizing movements responsible for Carn Brea and Clegyr Boia.

In south-east England, and in the Thames valley, an insular development of the primary Windmill Hill pottery style can be observed, forming the Abingdon, Whitehawk and East Anglian bowl styles: these in their turn seem to be the formative influences in bringing about the evolution of the Mortlake style in Peterborough ware within the Secondary Neolithic group, and at Whitehawk itself this relatively evolved Western style was contemporary with the earlier Ebbsfleet ware of the Peterborough culture. At Dorchester and Abingdon there is evidence of the overlap of the evolved Western wares with the Dorchester culture as well as that of Peterborough.

Typologically, the Lincolnshire and Yorkshire pottery suggests a derivative from the Windmill Hill stock at a fairly early stage (without decoration), and the Peacock's Farm find of analogous pottery in a context early in the local peat stratigraphy supports this. But on the submerged land-surface at Clacton the Windmill Hill culture was represented by sherds of Abingdon and East Anglian bowls, broadly contemporary with the Rinyo-Clacton and *B*-beaker material. In Wessex, however, Rinyo-Clacton and Peterborough pottery occurs (at least at Windmill Hill) above Abingdon ware.

The chambered-tomb groups

Within the various regional groups of collective chambered tombs numerous mutual contacts can be established. As we have seen, there may have been some connexions existing between the Windmill Hill culture and that of the Severn-Cotswold tombs, while typology strongly suggests that some affinities must exist between them and those of Clyde-Carlingford— with this might go the few examples of early style Western Neolithic pots. In both regions the use of the tombs ceases with the local arrival of makers of Peterborough and Beaker pottery.

The Clyde-Carlingford culture can be seen to have contacts in several directions. Lyles Hill ware and the cremation-trench at Dunloy point to the Neolithic of Yorkshire, and here the Hedon Howe chambered barrow may represent a reciprocal interchange of ideas. At least the final blocking of the Dunloy tomb took place when Tievebulliagh axes were in use, and the later pots in this tomb and elsewhere (e.g. Clachaig) are fairly closely related to the Sandhill pottery and probably ancestral to that of the Boyne culture (Loughcrew ware). In Scotland, the final use of the Cairnholy tomb, and probably that of Beacharra also, was at a time when the Peterborough culture existed in some form in south-west Scotland, and at Tormore was a Secondary Neolithic grave-group exactly comparable to examples in the Orkney-Cromarty group of chambered tombs, with a sherd of Rinyo I ware. In this latter group, the tombs of the Yarrows class may, in their crescentic forecourts, imply partial derivation from, or contacts with, the Clyde-Carlingford province.

In the Hebrides, such tombs as Clettraval have architectural and ceramic links with the earlier Clyde-Carlingford series, and the later pottery from this tomb and from Unival is a variant of the Beacharra B type of channelled ware. Other pottery of this style from the Eilean an Tighe potters' kilns is identical to the decorated bowls of Unstan ware in the Orkney-Cromarty region, while the final burial at Unival was accompanied by a Rinyo I cup.

We have already noted the Orkney-Cromarty links with the Hebrides, and probably with Clyde-Carlingford as well. The Quoyness grave-group shows that tombs of the Maes Howe type must be contemporary in part at least with the Rinyo-Clacton culture, and the 'face' motif at the Holm of Papa Westray may show a contact with the Boyne culture also implicit in some of the Loughcrew ware, with its resemblances to that of Unstan and Eilean an Tighe. The grave-groups of the type of Ormiegill and Unstan may relate to the Dorchester culture, or to that of Rinyo-Clacton: in either case they belong to the Secondary Neolithic group.

The Boyne culture has, in Loughcrew ware, an almost certain derivative of the Beacharra C group with other elements which may relate to the Hebrides or Orkneys. The double-spiral 'face-motif' on a sherd of Rinyo I pottery from Skara Brae is precisely similar to those of the Boyne culture carved stones, and the Holm of Papa Westray carving has already been mentioned. The large bone or antler pins in the Boyne and Rinyo-Clacton cultures may also have affinities. A whole series of points of contact may also be established between the Boyne culture and those of the British Bronze Age—the Folkton idols, the Wessex culture pendants and the food-vessels actually present in Boyne tombs are among the most striking, and at Moytira Loughcrew ware was associated with sherds of English B-beakers. At Seskilgreen, too, a grave with a stone battle-axe was decorated with fine Boyne-style engraved stones.

The Bronze Age connexions seen in the Boyne culture become dominant in the Scilly-Tramore group of chambered tombs, where actual bronze has been found as well as faience and glass beads, and pottery of Cornish Middle Bronze Age affinities. The remaining scattered tomb groups give no evidence of interrelations which can be usefully considered.

The Secondary Neolithic cultures

The Secondary Neolithic cultures, as has been stressed in Chapter x, all interpenetrate and cannot be separated from a broad contemporaneity one with another. But outside their own ambit we have already noted contacts with the Clyde-Carlingford and Orkney-Cromarty communities of chambered-tomb builders; with the Sandhill, Beacharra C and Loughcrew wares, employing cord ornament or its coarse imitation; with the Boyne culture, and with a late burial in a Hebridean chambered tomb. Their lateness relative to most of the cultures of Western Neolithic affiliations is demonstrated stratigraphically in many instances, though Ebbsfleet ware is contemporary at least with the developed Windmill Hill pottery of Whitehawk.

The material summarized above can now be examined in order to establish a relative chronology within the various British Neolithic cultures, which in turn can be used as a basis for a discussion of the correlation of any sequence established with that of adjacent regions of the European continent, and for an attempt to interpret this in terms of an absolute chronology.

RELATIVE CHRONOLOGY IN THE BRITISH ISLES

From a study of the foregoing summary of the relationships of the various local Neolithic cultures in Britain it can be seen that they fall into recognizable groups not necessarily linked by geographical proximity but rather by evidence of approximate contemporaneity as shown by trade and other contacts. These groups seem on the whole divisible into three, and for convenience they may be referred to as Early, Middle, and Late Neolithic.

Into the Early phase should go those cultures which show clearest signs of their relationship with early or relatively early Neolithic cultures on the Continent. The first phase of Windmill Hill, represented by the pottery named from the site (in the restricted sense defined above in Chapter II), is the prime claimant for inclusion, and with it may go the western facies of the culture represented by Hembury ware, though a longer duration (and perhaps inception) of these western colonies is suggested by the group II*a* stone axes, primary at Hembury but secondary at Windmill Hill. The Carn Brea and Clegyr Boia sites, and with them the earlier Lough Gur material, may also come into this Early phase, and in south-east England the Peacock's Farm sherds in a Zone VII*a* peat should again be included. The beginnings at least of the Severn-Cotswold culture and of that of Clyde-Carlingford in south-west Scotland, should, on the grounds of the simple pottery types, also come within an Early Neolithic phase. The unchambered long barrows of southern England are certainly likely to begin in Early Neolithic times, but the Bowls Barrow evidence shows that their construction and use persisted into Late Neolithic times.

A Middle Neolithic phase should show signs of increasing contacts between the British communities, and this in fact can be perceived. In southern England this would be the stage of evolution of Western Neolithic pottery represented by the Abingdon, Whitehawk and East Anglian bowl styles, and in east Sussex pottery of this type can be seen as contemporary with the. Ebbsfleet phase of Peterborough pottery, itself related to the Scandinavian Pit-comb and Funnel-beaker traditions. In the north-east, this should be the time of the spread of the Windmill Hill pottery traditions to Lincolnshire and Yorkshire; and the exploitation of Grimes Graves and other flint mines, while perhaps originating in Early Neolithic times, is likely to have grown during this phase. Parallel evolution and settlement in the west would produce the main series of the Clyde-Carlingford and Hebridean tombs, accompanied by the use of Beacharra B pottery, of channelled-ware affiliations, and probably also of the earlier tombs in the Orkney-Cromarty province. In Ireland the Clyde-Carlingford culture would have been firmly established, and also derivatives from the Yorkshire province represented by Lyles Hill pottery; possibly, too, the earlier passage-graves of Tibradden type and some early (but as yet undated) gallery-graves might be included.

The evidence from the submerged land-surface of the Essex coast is of crucial importance at this stage. It should be noted that the Western Neolithic cultures are there represented by pottery at the Abingdon-East Anglian bowl stage of evolution, and also Ebbsfleet ware, in addition to Rinyo-Clacton material in abundance, and B-beaker sherds—all are likely to have been broadly contemporary, and none can be later than the marine transgression which brought an end to human habitation in that region. This transgression, which seems likely to have been the equivalent of the fourth Litorina maximum (LG IV) in Scandinavia (cf. Troels-Smith in Mathiassen, 1943, 162), may in fact be taken as a convenient point at which to make a division between Middle and Late Neolithic.

The presence of B-beaker pottery in this context is again of considerable importance, for it shows that we must regard the makers of this pottery as a component element in the mixed communities comprising our Middle Neolithic cultures. The B-beaker sherds in the mound of the Giants' Hills long barrow in Lincolnshire support this view and, as we shall see later, such an arrangement would fit admirably with the Continental evidence. But it involves a revision of orthodox concepts of the British sequence, since we now proceed to a group of Late Neolithic cultures which are in fact 'post-

Beaker' in conventional terminology! The matter is discussed further later, when the question of the relationship of the *A* to the *B* group of beakers, and of both to the practice of single-grave and barrow burial, is touched upon.

We are now left with a consistent assemblage of cultures representing a Late Neolithic stage, in part involving, as we shall see, what has already been defined as the Secondary Neolithic group. In southern England the Late Neolithic seems marked by the extinction of the Windmill Hill culture except perhaps in the Upper Thames (Abingdon-Dorchester) region, where it may well have had a longer survival than elsewhere. Its place is taken by the Secondary Neolithic cultures such as Rinyo-Clacton and Peter-borough, the latter with the developed Mortlake phase of pottery resulting from Middle Neolithic contacts between the Ebbsfleet and the East Anglian bowl styles. There seems to be a spread of these communities from East Anglia into Wessex, and this may in part be the result of the marine trans-gression referred to above, and in part caused by the arrival of new immi-grants on those coasts. The flint-mining activities seem likely to have increased, and side by side with them, the exploitation of the igneous rocks of the west and north in axe-factories. In Yorkshire, Derbyshire and the south of England, the imperfectly understood Dorchester culture can now be recognized in various forms.

Among the communities building chambered tombs, the final use of the Severn-Cotswold series probably dates from the beginning of the phase, and in the Clyde-Carlingford area the development of later tomb types with Beacharra C and Sandhill wares, possibly beginning in Middle Neolithic times, can be traced: Secondary Neolithic pottery appears in the final phases of the use of tombs in Galloway and the Hebrides, and much of the span of the Rinyo-Clacton settlements and of the tombs of the Orkney-Cromarty region would also fall within the period. Presumably, too, the *B*-beakers of Scotland would be as early as the Late Neolithic as defined here, and possibly some makers of these pots may have arrived by Middle Neolithic times.

In the Isle of Man, this is the period of the Ronaldsway culture, while in Ireland the main period of use of the tombs of the Boyne culture can hardly be earlier. *B*-beakers at such sites as Lough Gur may represent some Middle Neolithic colonization, though at Moytira their association with Loughcrew ware would suggest a slightly later date. In such regions as Yorkshire and Derbyshire it is probable that communities with single-grave burial rites (which included the makers of *A*-beakers) were established by our Late Neolithic times, and that single-grave burial customs were not without their effect on the Secondary Neolithic communities such as that represented by the Dorchester culture.

The Wessex evidence, discussed again in a later section, indicates without much doubt that some part of our Late Neolithic period must connect directly with some part of the Wessex culture of the Bronze Age: certain

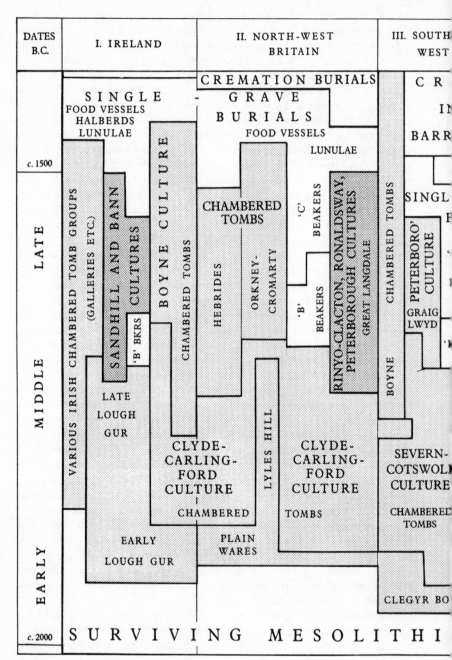

Fig. 64.

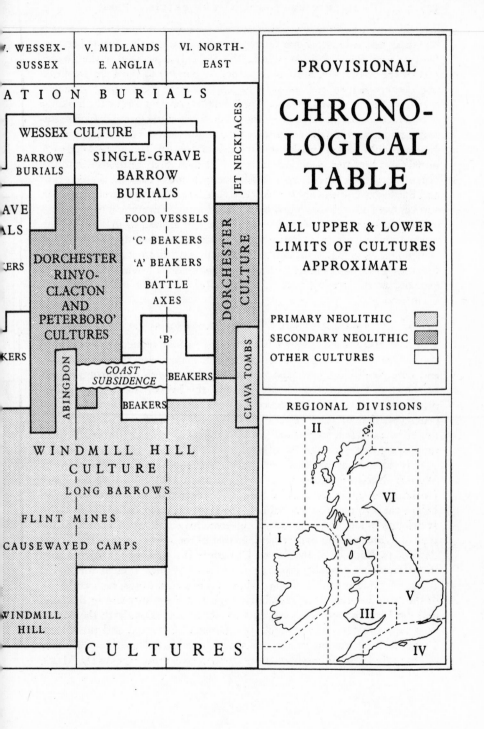

V. WESSEX-SUSSEX	V. MIDLANDS E. ANGLIA	VI. NORTH-EAST		PROVISIONAL

PROVISIONAL

CHRONO-LOGICAL TABLE

ALL UPPER & LOWER LIMITS OF CULTURES APPROXIMATE

PRIMARY NEOLITHIC
SECONDARY NEOLITHIC
OTHER CULTURES

ATION BURIALS

WESSEX CULTURE

SINGLE-GRAVE BARROW BURIALS

BARROW BURIALS

JET NECKLACES

AVE ALS

FOOD VESSELS

'C' BEAKERS

'A' BEAKERS

BATTLE AXES

DORCHESTER CULTURE

ERS

DORCHESTER RINYO-CLACTON AND PETERBORO' CULTURES

'B'

KERS

ABINGDON

COAST SUBSIDENCE

BEAKERS

CLAVA TOMBS

BEAKERS

WINDMILL HILL CULTURE

LONG BARROWS

FLINT MINES

CAUSEWAYED CAMPS

WINDMILL HILL

CULTURES

REGIONAL DIVISIONS

II

VI

I

III

V

IV

incense-cups are intimately connected with Rinyo-Clacton ware, and such burials as that at Upton Lovel (above, p. 355) show clearly a fusion between the two traditions. *B*-beakers certainly, and in all probability the greater part of the *A*-beakers, must be regarded as parallel to the Late Neolithic stage as here defined, and not, as in the past, the mark of a clear-cut boundary between 'Neolithic' and 'Bronze Age'. Single-grave burial and the building of conspicuous round barrows are, however, distinctive customs which represent a tradition wholly alien to any of the components of our large series of Neolithic cultures and, while there is considerable overlapping between such burials and the later Neolithic cultures of Britain, their relationships to the beakers has not in the past been satisfactorily defined. Like the Single-grave and Battle-axe cultures of Denmark and Sweden, and related groups in north and central Europe, they must be regarded as intrusive phenomena whose origins go back to the Russian steppes, and in Britain as in Holland the interaction between these Battle-axe cultures and those of the Beakers must be studied as contacts established between and fusion ensuing from two disparate groups of peoples with widely divergent traditions and origins in east and west, meeting only in south-eastern England and in the Low Countries.

THE SEQUENCE IN ITS EUROPEAN SETTING

The next stage in our inquiry is to test the insular sequence of Neolithic cultures which we have outlined, with its three main phases of Early, Middle and Late Neolithic, against the European cultures with which contacts can be shown to have existed. Geographically, the British Isles are favourably placed at a point where interaction between two great Continental culture-provinces, that of the Western Neolithic and that of the Nordic world, might be expected, so that one set of correlations may, in favourable conditions, act as a check on the other.

It is difficult, as we have seen, to make precise correlations within the Western Neolithic province for our Windmill Hill culture of the Early Neolithic, except in so far as we can reasonably assign its origins to a period before the evolution of specialized (usually decorated forms) of pottery. It belongs in fact to the family of cultures characterized by pottery of the type of Cortaillod I in Switzerland, or that of the lower levels of the Grotte de Bize in Aude or of the Lac de Chalain in the Jura, or the Manio sites in Brittany, and probably represented in Iberia by such sites as the Bovila Madurell cemetery in Catalonia. More specialized features, such as the use of the 'trumpet-lug' as at Hembury, appear in Burgundy and in Brittany, and the long barrows are likely to have some connexions with the Manio type cairns in the latter region. If the Severn-Cotswold and the Clyde-Carlingford settlements were established in our Early Neolithic phase they might again be brought into relationship with such tomb types as the Manio cairns, and the chambered tombs of the Retz group and of the Pyrenees. But the French sites cannot be fitted into a convincing stratigraphical or chronological framework, though in Switzerland it can be shown that the early Cortaillod phase there is earlier than either the Rössen or the Michelsberg sites of the same region (von Gonzenbach, 1949, 69).

This leads to a puzzling correlation which seems to exist between the Windmill Hill culture and that of Michelsberg, implied by the causewayed camps and the antler-combs common to both. As we have seen, they may be parallel evolutions in the two areas, due to the absorption of common Mesolithic ideas, for there would be grave chronological difficulties in the way of making these elements originate in the Michelsberg culture and thence transmitting them to England—if either area is to have primacy, the evidence would suggest the latter as the place of origin.

Contacts between our Early Neolithic and Scandinavia are unfortunately not certainly established, for the long barrow of Julliberries Grave in Kent which contained a thin-butted flint axe of Danish 'dolmen' type could equally well belong to the Middle Neolithic phase. But the presence of Western Neolithic sherds in Zone VII *a* peat at Peacock's Farm, earlier than a marine transgression likely to be the equivalent of LG IV in the Baltic area, would imply approximate contemporaneity of our Early period with the B-type funnel-beakers of Becker's classification and the graves of Virrings type, and perhaps in part with the C-type and the earliest boulder-lined 'dolmen' graves.

With the Middle Neolithic it becomes possible to make a series of interesting correlations. The Beacharra B pottery style belongs to the 'channelled wares' as defined by Mrs Hawkes, and these in the south and west of France can be seen to be in the main contemporary with bell-beakers and tanged copper daggers. Furthermore, the very characteristic channelled-ware ornament of concentric semicircles appears (in applied birch-bark) on a well-known vessel of von Gonzenbach's later Cortaillod phase from Tivoli (1949, pl. 5), and there are other reasons for equating the two cultures. To a similar chronological horizon one must attribute the 'Chassey' pottery with incised and *pointillé* ornament made before firing which is widely distributed in France and has representatives in Switzerland (Cortaillod II at Vallon des Vaux—von Gonzenbach, 1949, pl. 4), and this in its turn is ancestral to the earlier style of the Rinyo-Clacton ceramic series which must, on the evidence of the Essex coast submerged land-surface, go back to Middle Neolithic times in Britain. The well-known Er Lannic site in Brittany, with this decorated 'Chassey' pottery, was itself partly submerged by a marine transgression of uncertain correlation, but possibly to be connected in some way with LG IV.

It is uncertain whether the Boyne culture in the form known from the elaborately decorated and furnished tombs of type II can be set back into the Middle Neolithic, and its correlations are therefore described at a later stage. But with the recognition of *B*-beakers as representing a cultural component first established in our British Middle Neolithic phase, we can see that such associated metal objects as gold ear-rings or tanged copper daggers, known from *B*-beaker graves in England and from chambered tombs in Portugal, would fall naturally into place without the necessity of assuming so short a chronology for the laᵗter as I once thought inevitable (Piggott, 1948).

The Scandinavian correlations made possible by the presence of Ebbs-fleet pottery in this Middle phase are of interest, for we have seen that this pottery should represent a fusion of pit-comb traditions with that of Becker's C group of funnel-beakers. In Scandinavia these are earlier than LG IV, and early in Zone VIII of the peat stratigraphy (equivalent to our VII*b*), again in accordance with their relation to the natural sequence in this country. Into this context, too, would come at least the earlier 'dolmen' graves.

In the Late Neolithic of Britain the main contacts with the western world seem to be those of the builders of passage-graves, though the initial con-nexions may have been established somewhat earlier. The Boyne culture with its Ibero-Breton art, having especially strong affinities to the Los Millares bone idols and a close resemblance to the carvings of the Breton tombs, demonstrates these connexions clearly, as do the bone pins from the Boyne burials with their affinities with the Palmella culture of Portugal—probably in this context, too, come analogous pins in the Rinyo-Clacton culture. The Loughcrew type of pottery appears to be itself derived from that of Beacharra C and the Sandhill sites of Northern Ireland, and this in its turn can be related to the Scandinavian sequence in late Funnel-beaker and early Passage-grave times, at the time of the maximum of the fourth Litorina transgression. This would suggest that the colonization of Britain and Scandinavia by builders of passage-graves was part of a single process, and that settlements were approximately contemporary in the two regions: with this in mind the Bygholm find, with its implied contacts between Alcala and Denmark in early Passage-grave times, would fall into place.

Further Scandinavian contacts may be implicit in the boar's-tusk blades of the Dorchester culture and those from the Västerbjers cemetery of late Passage-grave date, and in general our Late Neolithic period would run parallel with that of the passage-graves and partly with that of the stone-cists in Denmark. Before the end of our Late Neolithic the presence of single-grave burials, frequently with stone battle-axes and sometimes with *A*-beakers or food-vessels, attests the presence of immigrants related to the Corded-ware and Single-grave groups of central and northern Europe: in Denmark the Single-grave invasion takes place after the LG IV marine transgression and may have been broadly contemporary with similar events in this country.

The end of the Late Neolithic in south-west England overlaps with the phase distinguished as the Wessex culture of the Bronze Age, with a great series of richly furnished barrow burials containing in their grave-goods evidence of trade contacts with the central European Bronze Age of Reinecke's A 2 and B phases, which in Scandinavia equate approximately with Montelius's Period I of the Bronze Age, itself overlapping with the stone cists and the later passage-graves which contain bone copies of A 2 bronze types (Piggott, 1938). And with this period an absolute chronology based on established dates in the eastern Mediterranean can be brought to bear on northern and western Europe. Its application to the problem in hand must be reserved for the next section.

ABSOLUTE CHRONOLOGY

The connexion existing between the Late Neolithic phase and that of the Wessex culture is of such vital importance that it is worth while recapitulating the evidence for such an overlap. The close stylistic relationships between the Aldbourne cups from Wessex culture graves and the Rinyo I pottery have been demonstrated by Scott (1950b), and those between certain other contemporary incense-cups and Rinyo-Clacton ware in Wiltshire equally stressed by Stone (1949). There seems little doubt that these two pottery groups cannot be very far removed in time one from another. We have seen that ceremonial mace-heads of antler or stone are characteristic of certain burials of Late Neolithic date which we have included in the Dorchester culture, and in three Wessex culture graves—Clandon in Dorset, Bush Barrow in Wiltshire, and an outlier at Towthorpe in Yorkshire—these symbols of authority once more appear: the Towthorpe mace-head (Mortimer, 1905, fig. 9) is comparable in detail with those from Ormiegill, Tormore or Taversoe Tuack in Scotland, all in Late Neolithic contexts. There is reason to believe that immigrants of the Battle-axe group of single-grave people were already establishing themselves in England during our Late Neolithic phase, and their contribution to Wessex culture burial ritual may be seen in the parallel use of stone battle-axes as emblems of chieftainship in such graves as Snowshill and Hove, and probably in the custom of barrow-burial itself.

The barrow at Upton Lovel in Wiltshire (Hoare's no. 4; above, p. 355) is an outstanding example of the fusion of traditions, with the flint axes and boar's tusk blades exactly as in the Dorchester culture graves of Duggleby or Liff's Low, the bone pendants of similar affinities, and the stone fragments from Cornish axe-factory sources exploited by the Secondary Neolithic cultures. The stone battle-axe also found indicates the single-grave element already referred to, while the bronze awl and the sandstone arrow-shaft smoother are typical of Wessex culture graves. And that the A-beaker element frequently found with that of the Battle-axe group also overlaps with the Wessex culture is shown by the association at Charmy Down, Somerset, of an *A*-beaker with a distinctive type of bead present in the well-known Manton grave-group of the Wessex culture (Williams, 1950, fig. 4; cf. Piggott, 1938, fig. 8).

The Boyne culture contacts with the Wessex culture are in this context hardly surprising, and the mace-pendants known in stone from the former graves appear in amber in Wessex. With this one may take the Boyne art on the Beaker and Food-vessel cists in Scotland and on the Moylough cist which contained a burial with a halberd—represented in miniature in the Wessex culture by the halberd-pendants in the same manner as the maces are reproduced in diminished, but still symbolic, form. The Wessex culture obtained abundant gold from a source almost inevitably that of Ireland, and the Seskilgreen grave, with a cremation and a battle-axe surrounded by stones carved with Boyne art designs, may represent some reflex of this trade.

The date of the Wessex culture can be fairly well fixed by several pieces of evidence which link it through Central Europe to Mycenaean Greece to a period approximately 1500/1450 to 1300 B.C. (Hawkes, 1948; de Navarro, 1950). Whatever its cultural components, it must represent the local aggrandisement of the aristocracy of south English communities who were in a geographical and political position to levy toll on an important series of trade routes between Ireland, Scandinavia, central Europe and the Mediterranean, passing through and converging upon Wessex. As we have seen, there is reason to believe that these communities were in composition a selection or an amalgam of the Late Neolithic cultures we have been engaged in defining, and with the moment of enrichment the phase must come to an end. The date of this event is likely to have been within a generation one side or another of 1500 B.C.

If we can thus fix a lower limit of date for the cultures we have agreed to class as 'Neolithic' in Britain, what of the earlier phases? Here, in the absence of a large series of dates supplied by such physical means as that of radio-active carbon, we are virtually reduced to dead-reckoning or guess-work. Of the two radio-carbon dates available, that of the first phase of Stonehenge, of the Dorchester culture within our Late Neolithic period, would be in accordance with the upper limit determined by archaeological means—1848 B.C. $\pm$275, giving a possible bracket of 2123–1573 B.C. with as much likelihood of the real date lying in the sixteenth as in the twentieth century B.C. Archaeological probabilities, as we have seen, suggest the former alternative. The Ehenside Tarn radio-carbon date, which should on archaeological grounds be broadly contemporary is, however, so divergent (3014$\pm$300 B.C.), and in itself so high, that it is difficult to do more than reserve judgement pending further figures from a long range of archaeologically determined samples.

We have in fact no reliable data by which to estimate the duration of our three phases. It seems on the whole unlikely that the Early Neolithic can be regarded as lasting as long as either the Middle or Late. The not really conclusive estimates that have been made of the duration of use of chambered tombs in south-west Scotland suggest that a century or a century and a half may cover a pottery range which would approximately span our Middle Neolithic period (Beacharra A to Rinyo I, Peterborough and *B*-beakers), and it is difficult to suppose, on *a priori* grounds, that all three phases together could span more than four centuries. It should be possible, in fact, to contain the whole of the British Neolithic cultures described in this book within the first half of the second millennium B.C.

The probable relationships discussed above have been presented in summary form in a provisional Chronological Table (Fig. 64). As in all such diagrammatic representations, definition has been given to chronological boundaries which in their very nature are indefinite and uncertain, but with this reservation the Table serves to show in graphic form the interlocking of the various cultural groups in the different regions of the British Isles. For convenience, six such regions have been defined: I comprises Ireland; II, the west and north coasts of England and Scotland northwards of Wales, and including the Atlantic coasts to the Orkney and Shetland Islands; III, the western coasts of England and Wales including the Cornish peninsula and the Scilly Islands, and also taking in the area of settlement of the Severn-Cotswold people; IV comprises the Wessex and Sussex-Kent regions; V, the Midlands and East Anglia; and VI, a large area stretching from Lincolnshire to the Moray Firth. The Table brings out the increasing diversity and complexity of the cultural groups in the later phases, and the long persistence of cultures rooted in Neolithic traditions side by side with those comprising the beginnings of the British Bronze Age. While obviously open to criticism in detail at almost every point, it is felt that the broad pattern is sound, and that some sort of graphic statement, however tentative, must be attempted in order to provide a basis for discussion.

382

APPENDIX A

THE WINDMILL HILL CULTURE

The documentation of the monuments and finds of this culture, described in Chap. II and summarized on the Maps I–IV, Figs. I and 15, is based on revisions of certain basic lists mainly published in the 1930's.

CAUSEWAYED CAMPS

From the list with references in Curwen 1930 a the following sites are accepted as being now proved by excavation or extremely probable from surface indications.

(a) *Excavated, with evidence of Neolithic occupation*

Abingdon, Berkshire; Combe Hill, Trundle and Whitehawk, Sussex; Knap Hill and Windmill Hill, Wilts.

(b) *Accepted from surface indications or other information*

Maiden Bower, Bedfordshire (site destroyed) (W. G. Smith, 1915); Barkhale, Sussex; Robin Hood's Ball, Wiltshire.

Other sites included by Curwen have been rejected for various reasons.

The following sites, in which large-scale or trial excavations have been made, are additional to Curwen's list:

(a) *Large-scale excavations*

Hembury Fort, Devon (Liddell, 1930–35).

Maiden Castle, Dorset (Wheeler, 1943).

(b) *Trial excavations, 1951*

Hambledon Hill 'Old Camp' (Crawford & Keiller, 1928, 44).

Whitesheet Hill, Mere, Wiltshire (Hoare, 1812, 42).

Habitation sites other than causewayed camps, and stray pottery finds, are noted in the pottery list below.

FLINT MINES

To the bibliography in Clark & Piggott, 1933, add Armstrong, 1934 (Grimes Graves); Curwen 1937 a (Sussex); Holleyman, 1937 (Harrow Hill, Sussex); Stone, 1933a, b, 1935b (Easton Down, Wiltshire and Martin's Clump, Hampshire); Todd, 1949 (East Horsley, Surrey).

UNCHAMBERED LONG BARROWS

The lists used (with minor revisions) are Crawford, 1932 (Wessex); Curwen, 1937a, (Sussex); Greenwell, 1877; Mortimer, 1905 (Yorkshire); Phillips, 1933a, b, 1936 (Lincolnshire). Other individual sites are referred to in the text.

POTTERY FINDS AND HABITATION SITES

To the material listed in Piggott, 1932*b*, revised for Yorkshire by Newbigin (1937), additional sites are given below in tabular form. The following abbreviations are employed:

B	Burial site	EA	East Anglian ware
CC	Causewayed camp	H	Hembury ware
HS	Habitation site	WH	Windmill Hill ware
LB	Long barrow	W	Western Neolithic (subdivision uncertain)
SF	Stray find	U	Unpublished

Site	Type of find	Pottery group	Reference
Barton Mere, Suffolk	HS?	W	U
Carn Brea, Cornwall	HS	H?	Patchett, 1946
Chippenham, Cambs	SF	W	Leaf, 1940
Clegyr Boia, Pembs	HS	H?	U Nat. Mus. Wales
Corfe Mullen, Dorset	HS	H	Calkin & Piggott, 1938
Corhampton, Hants	SF	WH	U Winchester Mus.
Edingthorpe, Norfolk	HS	W	U
Erriswell, Cambs	HS	EA	U Cambridge Mus. of A. and E.
Gayton, Norfolk	SF	W	U Cambridge Mus. of A. and E.
Giants' Hills, Lincs	LB	W	Phillips, 1936
Great Ponton, Lincs	SF	W	Phillips, 1935*b*
Hackpen, Wilts	SF	WH	Piggott, 1937*b*
Hadden Hill, Hants	SF	H	U Brit. Mus.
Haldon, Devon	HS	H	Willock, 1936, 1937
Hambledon Hill, Dorset	CC	WH	U 1951 excav.
Handley Hill, Dorset	B	W	Piggott, 1936*b*
Hayland House, Norfolk	HS?	EA	Leaf, 1935
Hazard Hill, Devon	HS	H	Houlder, 1951
Holdenhurst, Hants	LB	H	Piggott, 1937*c*
Ipswich, Suffolk	SF	EA	U Ipswich Mus.
Maiden Castle, Dorset	CC	H	Wheeler, 1943
Marlow, Bucks	SF	W	U Treacher Coll.
Michelmersh, Hants	HS?	WH?	Piggott, 1934*a*
New Barn Down, Sussex	HS	WH	Curwen, 1934*b*
Peacock's Farm, Cambs	HS	W	Clark, Godwin & Clifford, 1935
Peterborough, Northants	SF	EA	U Peterborough Mus.
Selsey, Sussex	HS	WH	U Chichester Mus.
Snettisham, Norfolk	SF	W	U
Southbourne, Hants	HS	H?	Calkin, 1947
Sutton Poyntz, Dorset	SF	W	U Dorchester Mus.
Thickthorn, Dorset	LB	W	Drew & Piggott, 1936
Whiteleaf, Bucks	B	EA	U Lindsay Scott Coll.
Whitesheet Hill, Wilts	CC	WH	U 1951 excav.
Woodhenge, Wilts	Henge	W	Cunnington, 1929

PETERBOROUGH WARE

The map in Fig. 48 is based on the list of finds in Piggott (1932 *b*) with additions listed below. As it is frequently impossible to distinguish between the Mortlake and the Ebbsfleet types of ware in small sherds, they have not been separated in the list. The following abbreviations are employed:

B	Burial	HS	Habitation site
CT	Chambered tomb	SF	Stray find
LB	Long barrow	U	Unpublished

Site	Type of find	Reference
Ampleforth, Yorks	SF	Willmot, 1938
Badshot, Surrey	LB	Keiller & Piggott, 1939
Barnham, Suffolk	SF	U Thetford Mus.
Barnwood, Glos	SF	Clifford, 1936
Battlegore, Somerset	B	Gray, 1931
Burn Ground, Glos	CT	U
Caesar's Camp, Folkestone	SF	Pitt-Rivers, 1882
Cairnholy, Kirkcudbright	CT	Piggott & Powell, 1949
Cassington, Oxon	HS	Leeds, 1940
Church Dale, Derbyshire	B	*Proc. Prehist. Soc.* IV, 317
Combe Hill, Sussex	HS(CC)	Musson, 1950
Danbury, Essex	SF	Dunning, 1933
Dorchester, Oxon	H	Atkinson, C. M. Piggott & Sandars, 1951
East Kennet, Wilts	SF	U Meyrick Coll. Marlborough
Ebbsfleet, Kent	HS	Burchell & Piggott, 1939
Edingthorpe, Norfolk	HS	U
Fargo, Wilts	B	Stone, 1938
Farnham, Surrey	SF	Clark & Rankine, 1939
Giggleswick, Yorks	SF	Wood, 1948
Glenluce, Wigtownshire	HS	Callander, 1929
Hambledon Hill, Dorset	SF	U 1951 excav.
Hamshill Ditches, Wilts	SF	U
Hinton Ampner, Hants	LB	Grinsell, 1939, 202, fig. 2
Holdenhurst, Hants	LB	Piggott, 1937*c*
Heath Row, Herts	HS	U
Hedderwick, E. Lothian	HS	Callander, 1929
Hedsor/Taplow, Bucks	SF	U Serocold Coll.
Ickburgh, Norfolk	SF	U Norwich Mus.
Iver, Bucks	HS	Lacaille, 1937
Lion Point, Essex	HS	Warren *et al.* 1936
Maiden Castle, Dorset	HS	Wheeler, 1943
Meare Heath, Somerset	SF	Gray, 1936
Newark, Notts	SF	Barley, 1950
Newhaven, Sussex	SF	Field, 1940
North Deighton, Yorks	HS	U York Mus.
Notgrove, Glos	CT	Clifford, 1937
Porton, Wilts	SF	U Salisbury Mus.
Poulton Down, Wilts	SF	U Meyrick Coll. Marlborough
Scremerston Hill, Northumberland	SF	U Nat. Mus. Ant. Scot.
Selmeston, Sussex	SF	Clark, 1934

Site	Type of find	Reference
Selsey, Sussex	HS	White, 1934
Sewells Cave, Yorks	HS	Raistrick, 1931
Shropham, Norfolk	SF	U
Stanton Harcourt, Oxon	HS	Leeds, 1940
Tankerton Bay, Kent	SF	U Maidstone Mus.
Thickthorn, Dorset	LB	Drew & Piggott, 1936
Thorpe, Surrey	HS	U
Walthamstow, Essex	SF	U Brit. Mus.
Whitehawk, Sussex	HS	Curwen, 1936
Winterbourne Dauntsey, Wilts	HS	Stone, 1934
Wylye, Wilts	SF	Passmore, 1940

APPENDIX C

RINYO-CLACTON WARE

The map in Fig. 48 is based on the list of finds of 'Grooved ware' in Warren *et al.* 1936, with additions listed below. The following abbreviations are employed:

B	Burial	P	Pit (perhaps ritual)
CT	Chambered tomb	SF	Stray find
HS	Habitation site	U	Unpublished
	H Henge monument		

Site	Type of find	Reference
Cambridge (near)	P	Frere, 1943
Christchurch, Hants	HS?	U Druitt Mus. Christchurch
Creeting St Mary, Suffolk	HS	U Ipswich Mus.
Dingieshowe, Orkney	SF	Stevenson, 1946
Dorchester, Oxon	H	Atkinson, C. M. Piggott & Sandars, 1951
East Malling, Kent	HS?	U Sidney Thompson Coll.
Edingthorpe, Norfolk	HS	U
Ely (near)	SF	U Cambridge Mus. of A. and E.
Evie, Orkney	HS?	Stevenson, 1946
Glenluce, Wigtownshire	HS	Callander, 1929; Stevenson, 1946
Gullane, E. Lothian	HS	Callander, 1929; Stevenson, 1946
Hedderwick, E. Lothian	HS	Callander, 1929; Stevenson, 1946
Honington, Suffolk	HS	Stone, 1949
Hurn, Hants	SF	C. M. Piggott, 1943
Knappers, Glasgow	HS?	U Ludovic Mann Coll.
Maiden Castle, Dorset	HS	Wheeler, 1943
Maumbury Rings, Dorchester	H	U Dorchester Mus.
Nettlebridge, Somerset	HS	*Arch. N.L.* Feb. 1949
Rinyo, Orkney	HS	Childe, 1939; 1948 *b*
Risby Warren, Scunthorpe, Lincs	HS	U Scunthorpe Mus.
Skara Brae, Orkney	HS	Childe, 1931 *b*
Tormore, Arran	CT	U Nat. Mus. Ant. Scot.
Townhead, Rothesay, Bute	HS	Marshall, 1930
Unival, North Uist	CT	Scott, 1948 *a*
West Runton, Norfolk	P?	Gell, 1949
Woodhenge (near), Wilts	P	Stone, 1949
Wykeham, Scarborough, Yorks	P	U Scarborough Mus.
Wylye, Wilts	SF	Passmore, 1940

BIBLIOGRAPHY

ABBREVIATIONS

The following abbreviations have been used, in addition to those customarily accepted:

Ant.J.	*Antiquaries Journal*
Arch.J.	*Archaeological Journal*
P.P.S.E.A.	*Proceedings of the Prehistoric Society of East Anglia*
P.P.S.	*Proceedings of the Prehistoric Society*
P.S.A.S.	*Proceedings of the Society of Antiquaries of Scotland*
Ant.	*Antiquity*
U.J.A.	*Ulster Journal of Archaeology* (New Series)
S.A.C.	*Sussex Archaeological Collections*
W.A.M.	*Wiltshire Archaeological Magazine*
J.R.A.I.	*Journal of the Royal Anthropological Institute*
J.R.S.A.I.	*Journal of the Royal Society of Antiquaries of Ireland*
P.R.I.A.	*Proceedings of the Royal Irish Academy*
Arch.	*Archaeologia*

ABBOTT, G. W. (1910). The Discovery of Prehistoric Pits at Peterborough. *Arch.* LXII (1910), 333–9.

AILIO, J. (1909). *Die Steinzeitlichen Wohnplatzfunde in Finland.* Helsingfors, 1909.

ANDERSON, J. (1866). On the Chambered Cairns of Caithness, with results of recent Explorations. *P.S.A.S.* VI (1864–66), 442–51.

—— (1868). On the Horned Cairns of Caithness. *P.S.A.S.* VII (1866–68), 480–512.

—— (1886). *Scotland in Pagan Times: The Bronze and Stone Ages.* 1886.

—— (1909). Note on a Group of Perforated Stone Hammers....*P.S.A.S.* XLIII (1908–09), 377–84.

ARMSTRONG, A. L. (1921). The Discovery of Engravings upon Flint Crust at Grimes Graves, Norfolk. *Ant. J.* I (1921), 81–6.

—— (1922*a*). Flint-crust engravings, and associated implements, from Grimes Graves, Norfolk. *P.P.S.E.A.* III, 434–43.

—— (1922*b*). Further Discoveries of Engraved Flint-crust and associated Implements at Grimes Graves. *P.P.S.E.A.* III, 548–58.

—— (1923). Discovery of a New Phase of Early Flint Mining at Grimes Graves, Norfolk. *P.P.S.E.A.* IV, 113–25.

—— (1924*a*). Percy Sladen Memorial Fund Excavations, Grimes Graves, Norfolk, 1924. *P.P.S.E.A.* IV, 182–93.

—— (1924*b*). Further Excavations upon the Engraving Floor (Floor 85), Grimes Graves. *P.P.S.E.A.* IV, 194–202.

—— (1926). The Grimes Graves Problem in the Light of Recent Researches, Presidential Address 1926. *P.P.S.E.A.* V (1927), 91–136.

—— (1934). Grimes Graves, Norfolk. Report on the Excavation of Pit 12. *P.P.S.E.A.* VII (1934), 382–94.

ARNAL, J. (1949). Los dolmenes de corredor con muros de piedra seca, en el Herault (Francia). *Ampurias*, XI (1949), 33–45.

ATKINSON, R. J. C. (1951). The Excavations at Dorchester, Oxfordshire, 1946–51. *Arch. News Letter* (Nov.–Dec. 1951), 56–9.

ATKINSON, R. J. C., PIGGOTT, C. M. & SANDARS, N. (1951). *Excavations at Dorchester, Oxon. Part I.* Ashmolean Museum, 1951.

BAGGE, A. (1941). *Stenåldersboplatsen vid Vivastemålas Västrums Socken, Småland.* Stockholm, 1941.

BAGGE, A. & KJELLMARK, K. (1939). *Stenåldersboplatserna vid Siretorp i Blekinge.* Stockholm, 1939.

BARLEY, M. W. (1950). A Flint Dagger from Staythorpe, Notts. and other finds from the Newark area. *P.P.S.* XVI (1950), 184–6.

BATEMAN, T. (1848). *Vestiges of the Antiquities of Derbyshire.* London, 1848.

—— (1861). *Ten Years' Diggings in Celtic and Saxon Grave Hills....* London, 1861.

BEATON, A. J. (1882). Notes on the Antiquities of the Black Isle, Ross-shire. *P.S.A.S.* XVI (1881–82), 477–92.

BECK, H. C. (1927). Classification and Nomenclature of Beads and Pendants. *Arch.* LXXVII (1927), 1–74.

BECK, H. C. & STONE, J. F. S. (1936). Faience Beads of the British Bronze Age. *Arch.* LXXXV (1936), 203–52.

BECKER, C. J. (1940). Nogle nye Oidsagformer, tilhørende den Ødanske Enkelt-gravkultur. *Fra Danmarks Ungtid* (1940), 93–111.

—— (1945). New Finds of Hafted Neolithic Celts. *Acta Arch.* XVI (1945), 155–75.

—— (1947). Skaeftede Stenalder-Økser. *Fra Nationalmus. Arbjeds.* (1947), 21–8.

—— (1948). Mosefundne Lerkar fra Yngre Stenalder. *Aarbøger* (1948).

—— (1949). Hafted Neolithic Celts II, with observations of a new Funnel-Beaker type from Zealand. *Acta Arch.* XX (1949), 231–48.

BERSU, G. (1936). Rössener Wohnhaüser vom Goldberg.... *Germania*, XX (1936), 229–43.

—— (1947). A Cemetery of the Ronaldsway Culture at Ballateare, Jurby, Isle of Man. *P.P.S.* XIII (1947), 161–9.

BIBBY, H. C. (1940). The submerged Forests at Rhyl and Abergele, North Wales: Data for the Study of Post Glacial History, V. *New Phyt.* XXXIX (1940), 220–5.

BORLASE, W. C. (1897). *The Dolmens of Ireland.* London, 1897 (3 vols.).

BOWLER-KELLY, A. (1935). Silex énigmatiques de Grande-Bretagne. *Bull. Soc. Préhist. Français*, XXXII (1935), 499–506.

BREA, L. B. (1949). Le culture preistoriche della Francia Meridionale.... *Rivista di Studi Liguri*, XV (1949), 21–45.

BREUIL, H. (1934). Presidential Address to Prehist. Soc. E. Anglia, 1934. *P.P.S.E.A.* IV (1934), 289–322.

BRØNSTED, J. (1934). Ein Jütisches Einzelgrab.... *Acta Arch.* V (1934), 290–3.

—— (1938). *Danmarks Oldtid—I (Stenalderen).* København, 1938.

BRUCE, J. R., MEGAW, E. M. & B. R. S. (1947). A New Neolithic Culture in the Isle of Man. *P.P.S.* XII (1947), 139–69.

BRUCE-MITFORD, R. L. S. (1938). A Hoard of Neolithic Axes from Peaslake, Surrey, *Ant. J.* XVIII (1938), 279–84.

BRYCE, T. H. (1902). On the Cairns of Arran.... *P.S.A.S.* XXXVI (1901–02), 74–181.

—— (1903). On the Cairns of Arran—a record of further explorations. *P.S.A.S.* XXXVII (1902–03), 36–67.

BRYCE, T. H. (1904). On the Cairns and Tumuli of the Island of Bute....*P.S.A.S.* XXXVIII (1903–04), 17–81.

—— (1909). On the Cairns of Arran. No. III. *P.S.A.S.* XLIII (1908–09), 337–70.

—— (1940). The So-called Heel-shaped Cairns of Shetland....*P.S.A.S.* LXXIV (1939–40), 23–36.

BUNCH, B. & FELL, C. I. (1949). A Stone-Axe Factory at Pike of Stickle, Great Langdale, Westmorland. *P.P.S.* XV (1949), 1–20.

BURCHELL, J. P. T. (1925). The Shell Mound Industry of Denmark as represented at Lower Halstow, Kent. *P.P.S.E.A.* V (1925), 73–8; Further Report....*Ibid.* 217–23.

BURCHELL, J. P. T. & PIGGOTT, S. (1939). Decorated Prehistoric Pottery from the Bed of the Ebbsfleet, Northfleet, Kent. *Ant. J.* XIX (1939), 405–20.

BURKITT, M. C. (1926). *Our Early Ancestors.* Cambridge, 1926.

BURSCH, F. C. (1928). Silex de Grand-Pressigny en Hollande. *Bull. Soc. d'Anthrop. Bruxelles,* XLIII (1928), 173–5.

—— (1936). Grafvormen van den Noorden. *Oudheid. Meded.* (n.s.), XVII (1936), 53–72.

BUTTERFIELD, A. (1939). Structural details of a Long Barrow on Black Hill, Bradley Moor, West Yorkshire. *Yorks. Arch. Journ.* XXXIV (1939), 223–7.

BUTTLER, W. (1938). *Der Donauländische und der Westische Kulturkreis der jüngeren Steinzeit.* Berlin, 1938.

CALDER, C. S. T. (1936). The Dwarfie Stane, Hoy, Orkney....*P.S.A.S.* LXX (1935–36), 217–22.

—— (1937). A Neolithic Double-chambered cairn of the stalled type on the Calf of Eday, Orkney. *P.S.A.S.* LXXI (1936–37), 115–54.

—— (1938). Excavations of Three Neolithic Chambered Cairns...in the Islands of Eday and the Calf of Eday in Orkney. *P.S.A.S.* LXXII (1937–38), 193–216.

—— (1951). Stanydale. *Arch. News Letter,* III (1951), 111–14.

CALKIN, J. B. (1935). The Bournemouth District in the Bronze Age. *Trans. S.E. Union Scientific Socs.* (1935), 21–31.

—— (1947). Neolithic pit at Southbourne. *Proc. Dorset Nat. Hist. & Arch. Soc.* LXIX (1947), 29–32.

CALKIN, J. & PIGGOTT, S. (1938). A Neolithic 'A' Habitation Site at Corfe Mullen. *Proc. Dorset Nat. Hist. & Arch. Soc.* LX (1938), 73–4.

CALLANDER, J. G. (1924). A Long Cairn near Gourdon, Kincardineshire....*P.S.A.S.* LVIII (1923–24), 23–7.

—— (1925). Long Cairns and other Prehistoric Monuments in Aberdeenshire and Perthshire. *P.S.A.S.* LIX (1924–25), 21–8.

—— (1928). A collection of Stone and Flint Implements from Airhouse....*P.S.A.S.* LXII (1927–28), 166–80.

—— (1929). Scottish Neolithic Pottery. *P.S.A.S.* LXIII (1928–29), 29–98.

—— (1931). Notes on (1) Certain Prehistoric Relics from Orkney....*P.S.A.S.* LXV (1930–31), 78–114.

CALLANDER, J. G. & GRANT, W. (1934). A Long Stalled Chambered Cairn... Near Midhowe, Rousay, Orkney. *P.S.A.S.* LXVIII (1933–34), 320–50.

—— —— (1935). A Long Stalled Cairn, the Knowe of Yarso, in Rousay, Orkney, *P.S.A.S.* LXIX (1934–35), 325–51.

CALLANDER, J. G. & GRANT, W. (1936). A Stalled Chambered Cairn, the Knowe of Ramsay...Orkney. *P.S.A.S.* LXX (1935–36), 407–19.

—— —— (1937). Long Stalled Cairn at Blackhammer, Rousay, Orkney. *P.S.A.S.* LXXI (1936–37), 297–308.

CARDOZO, M. (1950). Monumentos Arqueológicos de Sociedade Martins Sarmento. *Revista da Guimarães*, LX (1950).

CASH, C. G. (1906). Stone-circles at Grenish, Aviemore and Delfour, Strathspey. *P.S.A.S.* XL (1905–06), 245–54.

—— (1910). Archaeological notes from Aviemore. *P.S.A.S.* XLIV (1909–10), 189–203.

CHARLESON, M. M. (1902). Notice of a Chambered Cairn in the Parish of Firth, Orkney. *P.S.A.S.* XXXVI (1901–02), 733–8.

CHILDE, V. G. (1929a). *The Danube in Prehistory.* Oxford, 1929.

—— (1929b). Report on the Excavations at Skara Brae. *P.S.A.S.* LXIII (1928–29), 225–80.

—— (1930). Excavations in a Chambered Cairn at Kindrochat near Comrie, Perthshire. *P.S.A.S.* LXIV (1929–30), 264–72.

—— (1931a). The Chambered Long Cairn at Kindrochat....*P.S.A.S.* LXV (1930–31), 281–93.

—— (1931b). *Skara Brae, a Pictish Village in Orkney.* London, 1931.

—— (1931c). The Forest Cultures of Northern Europe....*J.R.A.I.* LXI (1931), 325–48.

—— (1931d). The Continental Affinities of British Neolithic Pottery. *Arch. J.* LXXXVIII (1931), 37–66.

—— (1932a). Scottish Megalithic Tombs and their Affinities. *Glasgow Arch. Soc. Trans.* III (1932), 120–37.

—— (1932b). Chambered Cairns near Kilfinan, Argyll. *P.S.A.S.* LXVI (1931–32), 415–20.

—— (1932c). The Danish Neolithic Pottery from the Coast of Durham. *Arch. Aeliana*, 4th s., IX (1932), 84–8.

—— (1932d). The Age of Skara Brae. *Man*, XXXII (1932), 191.

—— (1934a). *New Light on the Most Ancient East.* London, 1934.

—— (1934b). Neolithic Settlement in the West of Scotland. *Scottish Geog. Magazine*, I (1934), 18–25.

—— (1934c). Final Report on the Excavation of the Stone Circle at Old Keig, Aberdeenshire. *P.S.A.S.* LXVIII (1933–34), 372–93.

—— (1935a). *The Prehistory of Scotland.* London, 1935.

—— (1935b). Some Sherds from Slieve na Caillighe. *J.R.S.A.I.* LXV (1935), 320–4.

—— (1935c). Le Rôle de l'Ecosse dans la civilisation préhistorique de l'atlantique. *Préhistoire*, IV (1935), 7–21.

—— (1938). Excavations...carried out at Jarlshof in 1937. *P.S.A.S.* LXXII (1937–38), 348–63.

—— (1939). A Stone Age Settlement at the Braes of Rinyo, Rousay, Orkney (First Report). *P.S.A.S.* LXXIII (1938–39), 6–31.

—— (1940). *Prehistoric Communities of the British Isles.* London, 1940.

—— (1942). The Chambered Cairns of Rousay. *Ant. J.* XXII (1942), 139–42.

—— (1944). An Unrecognized Group of Chambered Cairns. *P.S.A.S.* LXXVIII (1943–44), 26–38.

CHILDE, V. G. (1946). *Scotland before the Scots.* London, 1946.
—— (1947). *The Dawn of European Civilization* (4th ed.). London, 1947.
—— (1948*a*). Megaliths. *Ancient India*, no. 4 (1948), 5–13.
—— (1948*b*). A Stone Age settlement at...Rinyo...(Second Report). *P.S.A.S.* LXXXI (1947–48), 16–42.
—— (1949). The Origin of Neolithic Culture in Northern Europe. *Ant.* XXIII (1949), 129–35.
—— (1950*a*). Axe and Adze, Bow and Sling: contrasts in early Neolithic Europe. *Jahr. Schweiz. Gesell. f. Urg.* XL (1950), 156–62.
—— (1950*b*). *Prehistoric Migrations in Europe.* Oslo, 1950.
—— (1950*c*). Comparison of Archaeological and Radiocarbon Datings. *Nature*, CLXVI (1950), 1068.
CHILDE, V. G. & GRAHAM, A. (1943). Some Notable Prehistoric...Monuments.... *P.S.A.S.* LXXVII (1942–43), 31–49.
CHITTY, L. F. (1935). Notes on Iberian affinities of a Bone Object found in County Galway. *Journ. Galway Arch. & Hist. Soc.* XVI (1935), 125–33.
CLAPHAM, A. R. & GODWIN, H. (1948). Studies of the Post-Glacial History of British Vegetation, VIII–IX. *Phil. Trans.* 233 (1948), 233–73.
CLARK, J. G. D. (1929). Discoidal Polished Flint Knives—their Typology and Distribution. *P.P.S.E.A.* VI (1928–29), 40–54.
—— (1932*a*). *The Mesolithic Age in Britain.* Cambridge, 1932.
—— (1932*b*). The Curved Flint Sickles of Britain. *P.P.S.E.A.* VII (1932), 67–81.
—— (1932*c*). The Date of the Plano-convex Flint Knife in England and Wales. *Ant. J.* XII (1932), 158–62.
—— (1934). A Late Mesolithic Settlement Site at Selmeston, Sussex. *Ant. J.* XIV (1934), 134–58.
—— (1935*a*). Derivative forms of the *Petit Tranchet* in Britain. *Arch. J.* XCI (1935), 32–58.
—— (1935*b*). The Prehistory of the Isle of Man. *P.P.S.* I, (1935), 70–92.
—— (1936*a*). *The Mesolithic Settlement of Northern Europe.* Cambridge, 1936.
—— (1936*b*). The Timber Monument at Arminghall and its affinities. *P.P.S.* II (1936), 1–51.
—— (1937). Scandinavian Rock-engravings. *Ant.* XI (1937), 56–69.
—— (1938*a*). A Neolithic House at Haldon, Devon. *P.P.S.* IV (1938), 222–3.
—— (1938*b*). Microlithic Industries from the Tufa Deposits at Prestatyn, Flintshire and Blashenwell, Dorset. *P.P.S.* IV (1938), 330–4.
—— (1945). Farmers and Forests in Neolithic Europe. *Ant.* XIX (1945), 57–71.
—— (1946). Seal-Hunting in The Stone Age of North-Western Europe....*P.P.S.* XII (1946), 12–48.
—— (1947*a*). Whales as an Economic Factor in Prehistoric Europe. *Ant.* XXI (1947), 84–104.
—— (1947*b*). Forest Clearance and Prehistoric Farming. *Econ. Hist. Rev.* XVII (1947), 45–51.
—— (1948*a*). The Development of Fishing in Prehistoric Europe. *Ant. J.* XXVIII (1948), 45–85.
—— (1948*b*). Fowling in Prehistoric Europe. *Ant.* XXII (1948), 116–30.

CLARK, J. G. D. (1949). A Preliminary Report on Excavations at Star Carr, Seamer. *P.P.S.* XV (1949), 52–69.

—— (1950). Preliminary Report on Excavations at Star Carr . . . (Second Season, 1950). *P.P.S.* XVI (1950), 109–29.

CLARK, J. G. D., GODWIN, H. & M. E. & CLIFFORD, M. H. (1935). Report on Recent Excavations at Peacock's Farm, Shippea Hill, Cambridgeshire. *Ant. J.* XV (1935), 284–319.

CLARK, J. G. D. & PIGGOTT, S. (1933). The Age of the British Flint Mines. *Ant.* VII (1933), 166–83.

CLARK, J. G. D. & RANKINE, W. F. (1939). Excavations at Farnham, Surrey (1937–38). *P.P.S.* V (1939), 61–118.

CLARKE, RAINBIRD (1935). The Flint-Knapping Industry at Brandon. *Ant.* IX (1935), 38–56.

CLARKE, W. G. (1916). Are Grimes Graves Neolithic? *P.P.S.E.A.* II, 339–49.

CLARKE, W. G. & HALLS, H. H. (1918). A 'Cissbury Type' Station at Great Melton. *P.P.S.E.A.* II (1917–18), 374–80.

CLAY, R. C. C. *et al.* (1926). *Excavations at Chelm's Combe, Cheddar.* (Conducted under the Excavations Committee of the Somerset Arch. and Nat. Hist. Society.) Sherborne, 1926.

CLIFFORD, E. M. (1936). Notes on the Neolithic Period in the Cotteswolds. *Proc. Cottes. Nat. F.C.* XXVI (1936), 33–49.

—— (1937). Notgrove Long Barrow, Gloucestershire. *Arch.* LXXXVI (1937), 119–61.

—— (1938). The excavation of Nympsfield Long Barrow, Gloucestershire. *P.P.S.* IV (1938), 188–213.

—— (1950). The Cotswold Megalithic Culture: The Grave Goods and their Background. *Early Cultures of North-West Europe* (Chadwick Memorial Studies), 23–50. Cambridge, 1950.

CLIFFORD, E. & DANIEL, G. E. (1940). The Rodmarton and Avening Portholes. *P.P.S.* VI (1940), 133–65.

CLOUSTON, R. S. (1885). Notice of the Excavation of a Chambered Cairn . . . at Unstan . . . Orkney. *P.S.A.S.* XIX (1884–85), 341–51.

COFFEY, G. (1904). Stone Celts and a food-vessel found in Co. Monaghan. *J.R.S.A.I.* XXXIV (1904), 271–2.

—— (1912). *New Grange . . . and other Incised Tumuli in Ireland.* Dublin, 1912.

COGHLAN, H. H. (1943). The Evolution of the Axe from Prehistoric to Roman Times. *J.R.A.I.* LXXIII (1943), 27–56.

COLLUM, V. C. C. (1933). The Re-excavation of the Déhus Chambered Mound. *Trans. Soc. Guernsiaise* (1933), 1–104.

CONWELL, E. A. (1867). Examination of the Ancient Sepulchral Cairns on the Loughcrew Hills, County of Meath. *P.R.I.A.* IX (1867), 355–79.

COOK, N. (1937). Curator's Reports . . . [on sherds from Orpington]. *Arch. Cant.* XLIX (1937), 284.

CORREIA, V. (1921). *El Neolitico de Pavia.* Madrid, 1921.

CRAW, J. H. (1925). The Mutiny Stones, Berwickshire. *P.S.A.S.* LXIX (1924–25), 198–204.

CRAWFORD, O. G. S. (1925). *The Long Barrows of the Cotswolds.* Gloucester, 1925.

CRAWFORD, O. G. S. (1932). *Map of Neolithic Wessex.* Ordnance Survey, 1932.

CRAWFORD, O. G. S. & KEILLER, A. (1928). *Wessex from the Air.* Oxford, 1928.

CUNNINGTON, M. E. (1912). Knap Hill Camp. *W.A.M.* XXXVII (1912), 42–65.

—— (1914). List of the Long Barrows of Wiltshire. *W.A.M.* XXXVIII (1914), 379–414.

—— (1927). *The Pottery from the Long Barrow at West Kennet, Wilts.* Devizes, 1927.

—— (1929). *Woodhenge.* Devizes, 1929.

—— (1931). The 'Sanctuary' on Overton Hill near Avebury. *W.A.M.* XLV (1931), 300–35.

—— (1933). Evidence of Climate derived from Snail Shells and its bearing on the Date of Stonehenge. *W.A.M.* XLVI (1933), 350–5.

CURLE, A. O. (1910). Exploration of a Chambered Cairn at Achaidh...Sutherland. *P.S.A.S.* XLIV (1909–10), 104–11.

—— (1930). Examination of a Chambered Cairn by the Water of Deugh, Stewartry of Kirkcudbright. *P.S.A.S.* LXIV (1929–30), 272–5.

—— (1932). Interim Report on the Excavation of a Bronze Age Dwelling at Jarlshof, Shetland. *P.S.A.S.* LXVI (1931–32), 113–28.

—— (1933). Further Excavations at Jarlshof, Shetland. *P.S.A.S.* LXVII (1932–33), 82–136.

—— (1934). An Account of Further Excavation at Jarlshof, Shetland. *P.S.A.S.* LXVIII (1933–34), 224–319.

—— (1935). An Account of the Excavation of another Prehistoric Dwelling at Jarlshof, Shetland. *P.S.A.S.* LXIX (1934–35), 85–107.

—— (1936a). An Account of the Excavation of a Hut Circle...at Jarlshof, Shetland. *P.S.A.S.* LXX (1935–36), 237–51.

—— (1936b). Account of the Excavation of an Iron Smeltery and of an Associated Dwelling...at Wiltrow....*P.S.A.S.* LXX (1935–36), 153–69.

CURWEN, E. (1928). Notes on Some Uncommon Types of Stone Implements found in Sussex. *S.A.C.* LXIX (1938), 77–91.

CURWEN, E. & E. C. (1926). Harrow Hill Flint Mine Excavation, 1924–25, *S.A.C.* LXVII (1926), 1–36.

CURWEN, E., CURWEN, E. C. *et al.* (1924). Blackpatch Flint-Mine Excavation, 1922. *S.A.C.* LXV (1924), 69–111.

CURWEN, E. C. (1926). On the Use of Scapulae as Shovels. *S.A.C.* LXVII (1926), 37–43.

—— (1927a). Probable Pressure-flakers of Antler from Harrow Hill. *S.A.C.* LXVIII (1927), 273.

—— (1927b). Prehistoric Agriculture in Britain. *Ant.* I (1927), 261–89.

—— (1929a). Excavations in the Trundle, Goodwood, 1928. *S.A.C.* LXX (1929), 33–85.

—— (1929b). Neolithic Camp, Combe Hill, Jenington. *S.A.C.* LXX (1929), 209–11.

—— (1930a). Neolithic Camps. *Ant.* IV (1930), 22–54.

—— (1930b). Prehistoric Flint Sickles. *Ant.* IV (1930), 17–869.

—— (1931). Excavations in the Trundle, Second Season, 1930. *S.A.C.* LXXII (1931), 100–49.

—— (1934a). Excavations in Whitehawk Neolithic Camp, Brighton, 1932–33. *Ant. J.* XIV (1934), 99–133.

—— (1934b). A Late Bronze Age Farm and a Neolithic Pit-Dwelling on New Barn Down, Clapham, nr. Worthing. *S.A.C.* LXXV (1934), 137–70.

—— (1935). Agriculture and the Flint Sickle in Palestine. *Ant.* IX (1935), 62–6.

CURWEN, E. C. (1936). Excavations in Whitehawk Camp, Brighton. Third Season, 1935. *S.A.C.* LXXVII (1936), 60–92.

—— (1937*a*). *The Archaeology of Sussex.* London, 1937.

—— (1937*b*). Querns. *Ant.* XI (1937), 133–51.

—— (1938). The Early Development of Agriculture in Britain. *P.P.S.* IV (1938), 27–51.

DAHR, E. (1937). Studien über Hunde aus primitiven Steinzeitkulturen in Nordeuropa. *Lunds Univ. Arss.* N.F. Ard. 2. Bd. 32. hr. 4. 1937. (Summarized by Clark in *P.P.S.* III (1937), 469.)

DANIEL, G. E. (1937*a*). The 'Dolmens' of Southern Britain. *Ant.* XI (1937), 183–200.

—— (1937*b*). The Chambered Barrow in Parc le Breos Cwm, S. Wales. *P.P.S.* III (1937), 71–86.

—— (1938). The Megalithic Tombs of Northern Europe. *Ant.* XII (1938), 297–310.

—— (1939*a*). On Two Long Barrows near Rodez in the South of France. *Ant.* XIX (1939), 157–65.

—— (1939*b*). The Transepted Gallery Graves of Western France. *P.P.S.* V (1939), 143–65.

—— (1941). The Dual Nature of the Megalithic Colonization of Prehistoric Europe. *P.P.S.* VII (1941), 1–49.

—— (1950). *The Prehistoric Chamber Tombs of England and Wales.* Cambridge, 1950.

DANIEL, G. E. & POWELL, T. G. E. (1949). The Distribution and Date of the Passage-Graves of the British Isles. *P.P.S.* XV (1949), 169–87.

DARBISHIRE, R. D. (1874). Notes on Discoveries in Ehenside Tarn, Cumberland. *Arch.* XLIV (1874), 273–92.

DAVIES, O. (1937*a*). Excavations at Ballyrenan, Co. Tyrone. *J.R.S.A.I.* LXVII (1937), 89–100.

—— (1937*b*). Excavations at Dun Ruadh. *Proc. Belfast Nat. Hist. & Phil. Soc.* 1935–36 (1937), 50–75.

—— (1939*a*). Excavations at Clogherny. *U.J.A.* II (1939), 36–43.

—— (1939*b*). The Horned Cairns of Sardinia. *U.J.A.* II (1939), 158–70.

—— (1939*c*). Excavations at the Giants Grave, Loughash. *U.J.A.* II (1939), 254–68.

—— (1939*d*). Excavations of a Horned Cairn at Aghanaglach, Co. Fermanagh. *J.R.S.A.I.* LXIX (1939), 21–38.

—— (1941). Trial Excavation at Lough Enagh. *U.J.A.* IV (1941), 88–101.

—— (1942). Excavations at Ballyreagh, Fermanagh. *U.J.A.* V (1942), 78–89.

—— (1950). *Excavations at Island MacHugh.* Belfast (Nat. Hist. & Phil. Soc.), 1950.

DAVIES, O. & EVANS, E. E. (1934). Excavations at Goward, near Hilltown, Co. Down. *Proc. Belfast Nat. Hist. & Phil. Soc.* 1932–33 (1934), 1–16.

—— —— (1943). The Horned Cairns of Ulster. *U.J.A.* VI (1943), 7–23.

DAVIES, O. & MULLIN, J. B. (1940). Excavation of Cashelbane Cairn, Loughash, Co. Tyrone. *J.R.S.A.I.* LXX (1940), 143–63.

DAVIES, O. & PATERSON, T. G. F. (1938). Excavations at Clontygora Large Cairn, Co. Armagh. *Proc. Belfast Nat. Hist. & Phil. Soc.* 1936–37 (1938), 20–42.

DAVIES, O. & RADFORD, C. A. R. (1937). Excavation of the Horned Cairn of Clady Halliday. *Proc. Belfast Nat. Hist. & Phil. Soc.* 1935–36 (1937), 76–85.

DÉCHELETTE, J. (1908). *Manuel d'archéologie préhistorique.* T. 1. Paris, 1908.

Degerbøl, M. (1941). Om Kannibalisme i Danmarkes Stenalder. *Dyr i Natur og Museum* (1941), 25–43.

Dickins, Bruce (1930). The Runic Inscriptions of Maeshowe. *Proc. Orkney Ant. Soc.* VIII (1929–30), 27–30.

Dmitriev, P. A. (1934). Hunting and Fishing in the North Ural Tribal Societies. *J.G.A.I.M.K.* (1934), no. 106.

Dobson, D. P. (1938). A Beaker from Somerset. *Ant. J.* XVIII (1938), 172.

Dominguez, J. B. (1929). *Excavaciones en el 'Monte de la Barsella'*. Madrid, 1929.

Drew, C. D. & Piggott, S. (1936). The Excavation of Long Barrow 163a on Thickthorn Down, Dorset. *P.P.S.* II (1936), 77–96.

Dunlop, M. (1939). A Preliminary Survey of the Bridestones, Congleton....*Trans. Lancs. & Cheshire Ant. Soc.* LIII (1939), 14–31.

Dunning, G. C. (1933). Neolithic and Iron Age Pottery from Danbury, Essex. *Ant. J.* XIII (1933), 59–62.

Dunning, G. C. & Wheeler, R. E. M. (1931). A Barrow at Dunstable, Bedfordshire. *Arch. J.* LXXXVIII (1931), 193–217.

Edwards, A. J. H. (1923). Report on the Excavation of a Large Segmented Chambered Cairn...in the parish of Minnigaff, Kirkcudbright. *P.S.A.S.* LVII (1922–23), 55–74.

—— (1929). Excavations at Reay Links and at Horned Cairn at Lower Dounreay, Caithness. *P.S.A.S.* LXIII (1928–29), 138–53.

—— (1935). Rock Sculpturings on Traprain Law, East Lothian. *P.S.A.S.* LXIX (1934–35), 122–37.

Ekholm, G. (1927). Nordischer Kreis, A, Steinzeit, B, Bronzezeit. *Reallexikon der Vorgeschichte*, IX (1927), 6–88.

Elgee, F. (1930). *Early Man in North-East Yorkshire*. Gloucester, 1930.

Europaeus, A. (1930). Die relative Chronologie der steinzeitlichen Keramik in Finland. *Acta Arch.* I (1930), 165–90, 205–20.

Evans, E. E. (1937). The Causeway Water, Co. Down, and its Cairns. *Irish. Nat. Journ.* VI (1937), 241–7.

—— (1938a). Giants' Graves. *U.J.A.* I (1938), 7–19.

—— (1938b). Excavations at Aghnaskeagh, Co. Louth, Cairn B. *County Louth Arch. Journ.* IX (1938), 1–18.

—— (1938c). A Chambered Cairn in Ballyedmond Park, Co. Down. *U.J.A.* I (1938), 49–58.

—— (1938d). Doey's Cairn, Dunloy, Co. Antrim. *U.J.A.* I (1938), 59–78.

—— (1939). Excavations at Carnanbane, Co. Londonderry. *P.R.I.A.* XLV, C (1939), 1–12.

—— (1940a). In *A Preliminary Survey of the Ancient Monuments of Northern Ireland*. Belfast, 1940.

—— (1940b). Lyles Hill—a Prehistoric Site in Co. Antrim. *Belfast Mus. Quarterly Notes*, LXIV (1940).

—— (1940c). Sherds from a Gravel Pit, Killaghy, Co. Armagh. *U.J.A.* III (1940), 139–41.

—— (1945). Field Archaeology in the Ballycastle District. *U.J.A.* VIII (1945), 14–32.

Evans, E. E. & Davies, O. (1935). Excavation of a Chambered Horned Cairn at Ballyalton, Co. Down. *Proc. Belfast Nat. Hist. & Phil. Soc.* 1933–4 (1935), 79–104.

—— —— (1936). Excavation of a Chambered Horned Cairn, Browndod, Co. Antrim. *Proc. Belfast Nat. Hist. & Phil. Soc.* 1934–35 (1936), 70–87.

Evans, E. E. & Watson, E. (1942). 'The Stone Houses', Ticloy, Co. Antrim. *U.J.A.* v (1942), 62–5.

Evans, J. (1897). *Ancient Stone Implements of Great Britain* (2nd ed. 1897).

Farrer, J. (1862). *Notice of Runic Inscriptions... in the Orkneys.* Edinburgh, 1862.

—— (1868). Note of Excavations in Sandy... Orkney. *P.S.A.S.* vii (1866–68), 398–401.

Field, L. F. (1940). Castle Hill, Newhaven. *S.A.C.* xxx (1940), 264–8.

Fleure, H. J. & Neely, G. J. H. (1936). Cashtal yn Ard, Isle of Man. *Ant. J.* xvi (1936), 373–95.

Forde, C. D. (1940). Multiple chambered Tombs in North-western France. *P.P.S.* vi (1940), 170–6.

Forssander, J. E. (1936). Skånsk Megalitkeramik och Kontinentaleuropeisk Stenålder. *K. Human. Vetensk. i Lund. Årsberättelse,* vi (1935–36), 203–353.

Fox, C. (1923). *The Archaeology of the Cambridge Region.* Cambridge, 1923.

—— (1938). *The Personality of Britain,* 3rd ed. Cardiff, 1938.

Fraser, J. (1884). Descriptive Notes on the Stone Circles of Strathnairn and neighbourhood of Inverness. *P.S.A.S.* xviii (1883–84), 328–62.

Frazer, W. (1896). Rude Bone Pins of Large Size... obtained from Cairns of County Sligo, and Lough Crew, County Meath.... *P.S.A.S.* xxx (1895–96), 340–5.

Frere, D. H. S. (1943). Late Neolithic Grooved Ware near Cambridge. *Ant. J.* xxiii (1943), 34–41.

Gell, A. S. R. (1949). Grooved Ware from West Runton, Norfolk. *Ant. J.* xxix (1949), 81.

Gervasio, M. (1913). *I Dolmen e la civiltà del bronzo nelle Puglie.* Bari, 1913. (Conn. Prov. di Arch. e Storia Patria Documenti e Monographie, vol. xiii.)

Gjessing, G. (1942). *Yngre Steinalder i Nord-Norge.* Oslo, 1942.

—— (1944). *The Circumpolar Stone Age.* Copenhagen, 1944.

—— (1945). *Norges Steinalder.* Oslo, 1945.

Gjessing, H. (1920). *Rogalands Stenalder.* Stavanger, 1920.

Glenn, T. A. (1914). Exploration of Neolithic Station near Gwaenysgor, Flints. *Arch. Camb.,* 6th ser., xiv (1914), 247–70.

—— (1915). Prehistoric and Historic Remains at Dyserth Castle. *Arch. Camb.,* 6th ser., xv (1915), 47–86.

—— (1935). Distribution of the Graig Lwyd Axe and its Associated Cultures. *Arch. Camb.* xc (1935), 189–214.

Godwin, H. (1940). Studies of the Post-glacial History of British Vegetation, iii and iv. *Phil. Trans.* ccxxx (1940), 239–304.

—— (1941). Studies in the Post-Glacial History of British Vegetation, vi: Correlations in the Somerset Levels. *New Phyt.* xl (1941), 108–32.

—— (1944). Age and Origin of the 'Breckland' Heaths of East Anglia. *Nature,* cliv (1944), July 1, p. 6.

—— (1945). Coastal Peat-beds of the North Sea Region, as Indices of Land- and Sea-level changes. *New Phyt.* xliv (1945), 29–69.

Godwin, H. & Tansley, A. G. (1941). Prehistoric charcoals as Evidence of former vegetation, soil and climate. *Journ. Ecol.* xxix (1941), 17–26.

von Gonzenbach, V. (1949). *Die Cortaillodkultur in der Schweiz.* Basel, 1949.

Goodwin, A. J. H. (1946). Prehistoric Fishing Methods in South Africa. *Ant.* xx (1946), 134–41.

GRANT, W. G. (1939). Excavations...at Taiverso Tuick, Trumland, Rousay. *P.S.A.S.* LXXIII (1938–39), 155–66.

GRANT, W. G. & WILSON, D. (1943). The Knowe of Lairo, Rousay, Orkney. *P.S.A.S.* LXXVII (1942–43), 17–26.

GRAY, H. ST G. (1931). Battlegore, Williton. *Proc. Som. Arch. & N.H. Soc.* LXXVII (1931), 7–36.

—— (1934). The Avebury Excavations 1908–1922. *Arch.* LXXXIV, 99–162.

—— (1936). Discovery of Neolithic Pottery on Meare Heath. *Proc. Som. Arch. & N.H. Soc.* LXXXII (1936), 160–2.

GREENWELL, W. (1866). An Account of Excavations in Cairns near Crinan. *P.S.A.S.* VI (1864–66), 336–51.

—— (1871). On the Opening of Grimes Graves in Norfolk. *Journ. Ethn. Soc.* II (1871–72), 419–40.

—— (1877). *British Barrows*. London, 1877.

—— (1890). Recent Researches in Barrows....*Arch.* LII (1890), 1–72.

GRIMES, W. F. (1932). Prehistoric Archaeology in Wales since 1925. *P.P.S.E.A.* VII (1932), 82–106.

—— (1936a). The Megalithic Monuments of Wales. *P.P.S.* II (1936), 106–39.

—— (1936b). The Long Cairns of the Brecknockshire Black Mountains. *Arch. Camb.* (1936), 259–82.

—— (1936c). *Map of South Wales, showing the distribution of Long Barrows and Megaliths.* Ordnance Survey, 1936.

—— (1938). The pottery [from Gorsey Bigbury]. *Proc. Univ. Bristol Spel. Soc.* V (1938), 25–43.

—— (1939a). *Guide to the Prehistoric Collections. National Museum of Wales.* Cardiff, 1939.

—— (1939b). The Excavation of Ty-Isaf Long Cairn, Brecknockshire. *P.P.S.* V (1939), 119–42.

—— (1944). Excavations at Stanton Harcourt, Oxon., 1940. *Oxoniensia*, VII–IX (1943–4), 19–63.

—— (1948). Pentre-Ifan Burial Chamber. *Arch. Camb.* 1948, 3–23.

GRINSELL, L. V. (1936). The Lambourn Long Barrow. *Berks Arch. Journal.* XL (1936), 59–62.

—— (1939). Hampshire Barrows. *Proc. Hants Field Club,* XIV (1939), 9–40, 195–229, 346–65.

HAMAL-NANDRIN, J., SERVAIS, J. & LOUIS, M. (1936). L'Omalien. *Bull. Soc. Roy. Belge d'Anthrop. et de Préhist.* (1936), 1–105 of reprint.

HAMILTON, G. A. (1847). [Tumulus near Knockingen.] *P.R.I.A.* III (1845–47), 249–52.

HARRIS, T. A. (1938). Church Dale, Derbyshire (in Notes on Excavations, 1938). *P.P.S.* IV (1938), 317.

HARRISON, J. P. (1876a). On Marks found upon Chalk at Cissbury. *J.R.A.I.* VI (1876), 263–71.

—— (1876b). Report on some Further Discoveries at Cissbury. *J.R.A.I.* VI (1876), 430–42.

—— (1877). Additional Discoveries at Cissbury. *J.R.A.I.* VII (1877), 412–33.

HARTNETT, P. J. (1940). Megalithic Tombs of East Muskerry. *Journ. Cork Hist. & Arch. Soc.* XLV (1940), 71–8.

HASSÉ, L. (1894). Objects from the Sandhills of Dundrum. *J.R.S.A.I.* XXIV (5th ser., IV), (1894), 1–13.

HAWKES, C. F. C. (1937). Current British Archaeology: A Survey of Aims and Needs. *Univ. Lond. Inst. Arch. Ann. Reps.* 1 (1937), 47–69.

—— (1937). The Double Axe in Prehistoric Europe. *Ann. Brit. School Athens*, XXXVII (1936–37), 141–59.

—— (1940). *The Prehistoric Foundations of Europe: To the Mycenaean Age.* London, 1940.

—— (1941). Engraved Plaques of Clay-slate from the Bann Diatomite. *U.J.A.* IV (1941), 19–22.

—— (1942). The Deverel Urn and the Picardy Pin. *P.P.S.* VIII (1942), 26–47.

—— (1944). Problems of the Bronze Age and the beginning of the Early Iron Age in Western Europe. *London Inst. Arch. Occ. Papers*, 6 (1944), 50–7.

—— (1948). From Bronze Age to Iron Age: Middle Europe, Italy, the North and West. *P.P.S.* XIV (1948), 196–218.

HAWKES, J. (1934). Aspects of the Neolithic and Chalcolithic Periods in Western Europe. *Ant.* VIII (1934), 24–42.

—— (1939a). *The Archaeology of the Channel Islands: II, The Bailiwick of Jersey.* Soc. Jersiaise, n.d. (pub. 1939).

—— (1939b). The Significance of Channelled Ware in Neolithic Western Europe. *Arch. J.* XCV (1939), 126–73.

—— (1941). Excavation of a Megalithic Tomb at Harristown, Co. Waterford. *J.R.S.A.I.* LXXI (1941), 130–47.

HAWLEY, W. (1921–28). Reports on the Excavations at Stonehenge, 1920–26. *Ant. J.* I (1921), 19–41; II (1922), 36–52; III (1923), 13–20; IV (1924), 30–8; V (1925), 21–50; VI (1926), 1–25; VIII (1928), 149–76.

HELENO, M. (1933). *Grutas artificiais do Tojal de Vila chã (Carenque).* Lisbon, 1933.

HEMP, W. J. (1927). The Capel Garmon Chambered Long Cairn. *Arch. Camb.* LXXXII (1927), 1–44.

—— (1929). Belas Knap Long Barrow, Gloucestershire. *Trans. Bristol & Glos. Arch. Soc.* LI (1929), 261–72.

—— (1930). The Chambered Cairn of Bryn Celli Ddu. *Arch.* LXXX (1930), 179–214.

—— (1934). The Passage Graves of Antequera, and Maes Howe, Orkney. *Ant. J.* XIV (1934), 404–13.

—— (1936). The Chambered Cairn known as Bryn yr Hen Bobl, near Plas Newydd, Anglesey. *Arch.* LXXXV (1936), 253–92.

—— (1937). Early Rock-cut Tombs in Ireland. *Ant.* IX (1937), 348–50.

HENCKEN, H. O'N. (1932). *The Archaeology of Cornwall and Scilly.* (County Archaeologies, 1932.)

—— (1933). Notes on the Megalithic Monuments in the Isles of Scilly. *Ant. J.* XIII (1933), 13–29.

—— (1939). A Long Cairn at Creevykeel, Co. Sligo. *J.R.S.A.I.* LXIX (1939), 53–98.

HENSHALL, A. S. (1951). Textiles and Weaving Appliances in Prehistoric Britain. *P.P.S.* XVI (1951), 130–62.

HERRING, I. J. (1938a). The Forecourt, Hanging Thorn Cairn...Ballyutoag, Ligoniel. *Proc. Belfast Nat. Hist. and Phil. Soc.* 1936–37 (1938), 43–9.

—— (1938b). The Cairn Excavation at Well Glass Spring, Largantea, Co. Londonderry. *U.J.A.* I (1938), 164–88.

—— (1941). The Tamnyrankin Cairn, West Structure. *J.R.S.A.I.* LXXI (1941), 31–52.

HERRING, I. J. & MAY, A. McL. (1940). Cloghnagalla Cairn, Boviel, Co. Londonderry. *U.J.A.* III (1940), 41–55.

HEWSON, L. M. (1935). Notes on Irish Sandhills. *J.R.S.A.I.* LXV (1935), 231–44.

—— (1936). Notes on Irish Sandhills. *J.R.S.A.I.* LXVI (1936), 154–72.

—— (1938). Notes on Irish Sandhills. *J.R.S.A.I.* LXVIII (1938), 69–90.

HILZHEIMER, M. (1932). Dogs. *Ant.* VI (1932), 411–19. (English version of a paper in *Zeitsch. für Hundeforschung* (1931), 3–14.)

—— (1936). Sheep. *Ant.* X (1936), 195–206.

HOARE, SIR R. C. (1812). *The Ancient History of South Wiltshire.* London, 1812.

HOGG, A. H. A. (1940). A Long Barrow at West Rudham....*Trans. Norfolk Arch. Soc.* XXVII (1940), 315–31.

HOLLEYMAN, G. (1937). Harrow Hill Excavations, 1936. *S.A.C.* LXXVIII (1937), 230–51.

HOLWERDA, J. H. (1912). Neue Kuppelgräber aus der Veluwe.... *Prähist. Zeit.* IV (1912), 368–73.

HOULDER, C. (1951). Excavation of a Neolithic Settlement on Hazard Hill, Totnes. *Arch. News Letter* (April 1951), 165–6.

IVERSEN, J. (1941). Land Occupation in Denmark's Stone Age. *Danm. Geol. Unders.* II, R. no. 66 (1941).

—— (1949). The Influence of Prehistoric Man on Vegetation. *Danm. Geol. Unders.* IV, R. no. 6 (1949).

JACKSON, J. W. (1929). Report on the Animal Remains found at Woodhenge. [In Cunnington, *Woodhenge* (1929), 61–9.]

—— (1934). Prehistoric Domestic Animals. *Compte-Rendu 1st Internat. Congress Prehist. Sciences.* London (1934), 154–7.

—— (1935a). Report on the Skeleton of the Dog from Ash-pit C. [In Stone, 1935b.]

—— (1935b). Report on the Animal Remains from the Stonehenge Excavations of 1920–6. *Ant. J.* XV (1935), 434–40.

JALHAY, E. & DO PAÇO, A. (1941). A Gruta II da Necropole de Alapraia. *Anais Acad. Port. da Historia,* IV (1941), 107–40.

—— —— (1945). El Castro de Vilanova de San Pedro. *Act. y Mem. Soc. Esp. Antrop. etc.* XX (1945), 5–93.

JANSE, O. (1932). *En Stenaldersboplats vid Valdemarsvikens Strand.* Stockholm, 1932.

JESSEN, K. (1949). Studies in Late Quaternary Deposits and Flora-History of Ireland. *P.R.I.A.* (1949), 85–290.

JESSEN, K. & HELBAEK, H. (1944). Cereals in Great Britain and Ireland in Prehistoric and Early Historic Times. *Kong. Danske Videns. Selskab (Biol. Skrift.* III), 1944.

JESSUP, R. F. (1930). *The Archaeology of Kent.* London, 1930.

—— (1939). Further Excavations at Julliberrie's Grave, Chilham. *Ant. J.* XIX (1939), 260–81.

JOLLY, W. (1882). On Cup-marked Stones in the Neighbourhood of Inverness.... *P.S.A.S.* XVI (1882), 300–96.

JONES, J. BRYNER (1934). The Origin and Development of British Cattle. *Compte-Rendu 1st Internat. Congress Prehist. Sciences.* London (1934), 151–4.

JONES, S. J. (1938). The Excavation of Gorsey Bigbury. *Proc. Univ. Bristol Spel. Soc.* V (1938), 3–56.

KEILLER, A. (1934). Excavation at Windmill Hill. *Compte-Rendu 1st Internat. Congress Prehist. Sciences.* London (1934), 135–8.

—— (1936). Two Axes of Presely Stone from Ireland. *Ant.* X (1936), 220.

KEILLER, A. & PIGGOTT, S. (1936). The West Kennet Avenue, Avebury; Excavations 1934–5. *Ant.* X (1936), 417–27.

—— —— (1938). Excavation of an Untouched Chamber in the Lanhill Long Barrow. *P.P.S.* IV (1938), 122–50.

—— —— (1939). Badshot Long Barrow. [In *A Survey of the Prehistory of the Farnham District*, Surrey Arch. Soc. 1939, 133–49.]

KEILLER, A., PIGGOTT, S. & WALLIS, F. S. (1941). First Report...on the Petrological Identification of Stone Axes. *P.P.S.* VII (1941), 50–72.

KELLER, F. (1878). *The Lake Dwellings of Switzerland and other parts of Europe,* 2 vols. (Trans. J. E. Lee.) London, 1878.

KENDALL, H. G. O. (1920). Grimes Graves: Floors 47 to 59. *P.P.S.E.A.* III, 290–305.

—— (1924). The Chalk Carvings from Grimes Graves. *Ant. J.* IV (1924), 46–7.

KENDRICK, T. D. (1925). *The Axe Age.* London, 1925.

KENNARD, A. S. (1935). Report on the Non-Marine Mollusca...from Stonehenge.... *Ant. J.* XV (1935), 432–4.

KERSTEN, W. (1938). Spuren der nordeurasischen Wohnplatzkultur am Niederrhein. *Germania,* XXII (1938), 71–7.

KILBRIDE-JONES, H. E. (1935). Excavation of the Stone Circle at Loanhead of Daviot. *P.S.A.S.* LXIX (1934–35), 168–214.

—— (1939). The Excavation of a Composite Tumulus at Drimnagh, Co. Dublin. *J.R.S.A.I.* LXIX (1939), 190–200.

KNOWLES, W. J. (1887). Whitepark Bay, Co. Antrim. *J.R.S.A.I.*, 4th ser., VII (1887), 104–25.

—— (1891 a). Report on the Prehistoric Remains from the Sandhills of the Coast of Ireland. *P.R.I.A.*, 3rd ser., I (1891), 173–87.

—— (1891 b). Second Report....*P.R.I.A.*, 3rd ser., I (1891), 612–25.

—— (1896). Third Report....*P.R.I.A.*, 3rd ser., III (1896), 650–63.

—— (1903). Stone Axe Factories near Cushendall, Co. Antrim. *J.R.A.I.* XXXIII (1903), 360–6.

LACAILLE, A. D. (1937). Prehistoric Pottery found at Iver, Bucks. *Records of Bucks,* XIII (1937), 287–99.

—— (1948). The Deglaciation of Scotland and the forming of Man's Environment. *Proc. Geol. Assoc.* LIX (1948), 151–71.

LAIDLER, B. & YOUNG, W. E. V. (1938). A Surface Flint Industry from a Site near Stonehenge. *W.A.M.* XLVIII (1938), 150–60.

LANE-FOX, A. H. (1875). Excavations in Cissbury Camp, Sussex....*J.R.A.I.* V (1875), 357–90.

LAUDER, T. D. (1830). *An account of the Great Floods...in the Province of Moray....* Edinburgh, 1830.

LAWRENCE, G. F. (1929). Antiquities from the Middle Thames. *Arch. J.* LXXXVI (1929), 69–98.

LEAF, C. S. (1935). Report on the Excavation of Two Sites in Mildenhall Fen. *Camb. Ant. Soc. Comm.* XXXV (1935), 106–27.

—— (1940). Further Excavations in Bronze Age Barrows at Chippenham, Cambridgeshire. *Camb. Ant. Soc. Comm.* XXXIX (1940), 29–68.

LEASK, H. G. (1933). Inscribed Stones recently discovered at Dowth Tumulus, Co. Meath. (c), *P.R.I.A.* XLI (1933), 162–7.

LEASK, H. G. & PRICE, L. (1936). The Labbacallee Megalith, Co. Cork. *P.R.I.A.* (c), XLIII (1936), 77–101.

LEEDS, E. T. (1922). Further Discoveries of the Neolithic and Bronze Ages at Peterborough. *Ant. J.* II (1922), 220–37.

—— (1927 a). Neolithic Spoons from Nether Swell, Gloucester. *Ant. J.* VII (1927), 61–2.

—— (1927 b). A Neolithic Site at Abingdon, Berks. *Ant. J.* VII (1927), 438–64.

—— (1928). A Neolithic Site at Abingdon, Berks. (Second Report.) *Ant. J.* VIII (1928), 461–77.

—— (1940). New Discoveries of Neolithic Pottery in Oxfordshire. *Oxon.* V (1940), 1–12.

LEHNER, H. (1910). Die Festungbau der jüngeren Steinzeit. *Prähist. Zeitschrift,* II (1910), 1–23.

LEISNER, G. (1934). Die Malereien des Dolmen Pedra Coberta. *I.P.E.K.* IX (1934), 23–44.

LEISNER, G. & V. (1943). *Die Megalithgräber der Iberischen Halbinsel: I. Der Süden* (Römisch-Germanische Forschungen, 17); 1943.

—— (1951). *Antas do Concelho de Reguengos....* Lisbon, 1951.

LETHBRIDGE, T. C. (1950). Excavation of the Snailwell Group of Bronze Age Barrows. *Proc. Camb. Ant. Soc.* XLIII (1950), 30–49.

LIDDELL, D. M. (1929). New Light on an Old Problem. *Ant.* III (1929), 283–91.

—— (1930). Report on the Excavations at Hembury Fort, Devon, 1930. *Devon Arch. Ex. Soc.* (1930).

—— (1931). Report of the Excavations at Hembury Fort, Devon. Second Season, 1931. *D.A.E.S.* (1931).

—— (1932). Report on the Excavations at Hembury Fort. Third Season, 1932. *D.A.E.S.* (1932).

—— (1934–35). Report on the Excavations at Hembury Fort. Fourth and Fifth Seasons, 1934 and 1935. *D.A.E.S.* (1935).

LONDESBOROUGH, LORD (1848). Discoveries in Barrows near Scarborough. *Journ. Brit. Arch. Ass.* IV (1848), 101–7.

LUKIS, W. C. (1866). [Temple Farm 'cistvaen' excavations.] *Proc. Soc. Ant.*, 2nd ser., III (1866), 213.

—— (1867). Notes on Barrow-diggings in the Parish of Collingbourne Ducis. *W.A.M.* X (1867), 85–103.

LYNCH, P. J. (1921). Topographical Notes on the Barony of Coshlea.... *J.R.S.A.I.* L (1921), 119–23.

MACALISTER, R. A. S. (1932). A Burial Cairn on Seefin Mountain, Co. Wicklow. *J.R.S.A.I.* LXII (1932), 153–7.

MACALISTER, R. A. S. (1943). Preliminary Report on the Excavation of Knowth. *P.R.I.A.* (c), XLIX (1943), 131–66.

MACALISTER, R. A. S., ARMSTRONG, E. C. R. & PRAEGER, R. LL. (1912). Bronze Age Cairns on Carrowkeel Mountain, Co. Sligo. *P.R.I.A.* (c), XXIX (1912), 311–47.

MACDERMOTT, M. (1949*a*). Two Barrows at Ballingoola. *J.R.S.A.I.* C (1949), 139–45.

—— (1949*b*). Excavation of a Barrow in Cahercorney, Co. Limerick. *Journ. Cork Hist. & Arch. Soc.* LIV (1949), 101–2.

MACKAY, R. R. (1950). Neolithic Pottery from Knappers Farm, near Glasgow. *P.S.A.S.* LXXXII (1947–48), 234–7.

MACWHITE, E. (1946). A New View on Irish Bronze Age Rock-scribings *J.R.S.A.I.* LXXVI (1946), 59–80.

MAHR, A. (1930). *Brandenburgia*, XXXIX (1930), 56–65. (Kiekebusch Festschrift.)

—— (1937). New Aspects and Problems in Irish Prehistory. (Presidential Address for 1937.) *P.P.S.* III (1937), 262–436.

MANN, L. McL. (1903). Report on the Excavation of Prehistoric Pile-Structures in Pits in Wigtownshire. *P.S.A.S.* XXXVII (1903), 370–415.

—— (1918). The Prehistoric and Early Use of Pitchstone and Obsidian. *P.S.A.S.* LII (1917–18), 140–9.

MAPLETON, R. J. (1866). Notice of a Cairn at Kilchoan, Argyleshire, and its Contents. *P.S.A.S.* VI (1864–66), 351–5.

MARIËN, M. E. (1948). La Civilisation des 'Gobelets' en Belgique. *Bull. Mus. Roy. d'Art et d'Hist.* (1948), 16–48.

MARSHALL, J. N. (1930). Archaeological Notes [on Neolithic habitation site at Rothesay, Bute]. *Trans. Buteshire Nat. Hist. Soc.* (1930), 50–4.

MARTIN, C. P. (1935). *Prehistoric Man in Ireland.* London, 1935.

MARWICK, J. G. (1926). Discovery of Stone Cists at Stenness, Orkney. *P.S.A.S.* LX (1925–26), 34–6.

MATHESON, C. (1932). *Changes in the Fauna of Wales within Historic Times.* Nat. Mus. Wales, 1932.

MATHIASSEN, T. (1943). Stenalderbopladser i Aamosen. *Nordisk. Fortidsmin.* III, 3 (1943).

MAY, A. McL. & BATTY, J. (1948). The Sandhill Cultures of the River Bann Estuary, Co. Londonderry. *J.R.S.A.I.* LXXVIII (1948), 130–56.

MEGAW, B. R. S. (1938). Manx Megaliths and Their Ancestry. *Proc. Isle of Man Nat. Hist. & Ant. Soc.* (n.s.), IV (1938), 219–39.

—— (1939). Corn-Growing in Man 4,000 Years Ago. *Journ. Manx Mus.* IV (1939), 119–21.

MEGAW, B. R. S. & HARDY, E. M. (1938). British Decorated Axes and their Distribution. *P.P.S.* IV (1938), 272–307.

MITCHELL, G. F. (1945). The Relative Ages of Archaeological Objects recently found in Bogs in Ireland. *P.R.I.A.* (c), L (1945), 1–19.

—— (1951). Studies in Irish Quaternary Deposits: no. 7. *P.R.I.A.* (B), LII (1951), 111–206.

MITCHELL, G. F. & O'RIORDAIN, S. P. (1942). Early Bronze Age Pottery from Rock-barton Bog, Co. Limerick. *P.R.I.A.* (c), XLVIII (1942), 255–72.

MITCHELL, M. E. C. (1930). The Nether Largie Chambered Cairn, Kilmartin, Argyll. *P.S.A.S.* LXIV (1929–30), 233–43.

—— (1933). The Prehistoric Antiquities of Benderloch and Appin. *P.S.A.S.* LXVII (1932–33), 320–6.

—— (1934). A New Analysis of the Early Bronze Age Beaker Pottery of Scotland. *P.S.A.S.* LXVIII (1933–34), 132–89.

MOGEY, J. M. (1941). The 'Druid Stone', Ballintroy, Co. Antrim. *U.J.A.* IV (1941), 49–56.

MONTELIUS, O. (1922). *Swedish Antiquities: I. The Stone Age and the Bronze Age.* Stockholm, 1922.

MOREY, J. E. (1950). Petrographical Identification of Stone Axes. *P.P.S.* XVI (1950), 191–3.

MORRISON, J. (1871). Remains of Early Antiquities in . . . The Parish of Urquhart. . . . *P.S.A.S.* IX (1870–71), 250–63.

MORTIMER, J. R. (1905). *Forty Years Researches in British and Saxon Burial Mounds of East Yorkshire.* London, 1905.

MOVIUS, H. L. (1935). Kilgreany Cave, Co. Waterford. *J.R.S.A.I.* LXV (1935), 254–96.

—— (1936). A Neolithic Site on the River Bann. *P.R.I.A.* (C), XLIII 17–40 (1936).

—— (1940). The Chronology of the Irish Stone Age. *Univ. Lond. Inst. of Arch.*, *Occ. Paper*, no. 4 (1940).

—— (1942). *The Irish Stone Age.* Cambridge, 1942.

MÜLLER, S. (1918). *Oldtidens Kunst i Danmark: Stenalderens Kunst.* Copenhagen, 1918.

MULLIN, J. B. & DAVIES, O. (1938). Excavations at Carrick East. *U.J.A.* I (1938), 98–107.

MUNRO, R. (1884). Notice of Long Cairns near Rhinavie, Sutherlandshire. *P.S.A.S.* XVIII (1883–84), 228–33.

—— (1890). *The Lake-Dwellings of Europe.* London, 1890.

MUSSON, R. (1950). An Excavation at Combe Hill Camp near Eastbourne. *S.A.C.* LXXXIX (1950), 105–16.

DE NAVARRO, J. M. (1950). The British Isles and the Beginning of the Northern Early Bronze Age. *Early Cultures of N.W. Europe* (Chadwick Memorial Studies, 1950), 77–105.

NEAVERSON, E. (1936). Recent Observations on the Postglacial Peat Beds around Rhyl and Prestatyn. *Proc. Liverpool Geo. Soc.* XVII (1936), 45–63.

NEWALL, R. S. (1931). Barrow 85 Amesbury. *W.A.M.* XLV (1931), 432–58.

NEWBIGIN, A. J. W. (1936). Excavations of a long and a round cairn on Bellshiel Law, Redesdale. *Arch. Ael.*, 4th ser., XIII (1936), 293–309.

—— (1937). The Neolithic Pottery of Yorkshire. *P.P.S.* III (1937), 189–216.

NEWENHAM, Lt. (1837). On a Tumulus. . . near Rush, County of Dublin. *P.R.I.A.* I (1836–37), 247–9.

NIHLÉN, J. (1927). *Gotlands Stenålders boplatser.* Stockholm, 1927.

NORDMAN, C. A. (1922). Östsvensk Boplatskultur och Finländsk Stenålder. *Finsk Museum* (1922), 1–19.

OAKLEY, K. P. (1943). A Note on the Late Post-glacial Submergence of the Solent Margins. *P.P.S.* IX (1943), 56–9.

O'H-ICEADHA, G. (1946). The Moylisha Megalith, Co. Wicklow. *J.R.S.A.I.* LXXVI (1946), 119–28.

O'NEIL, B. H. ST J. (1942). Excavations at Fridd Faldwyn Camp, Montgomery, 1937–39. *Arch. Camb.* XCVII (1942), 1–57.

—— (1947). The Dwarfie Stane, Orkney, and St Kevin's Bed, Glendalough. *Ant. J.* XXVII (1947), 182–3.

O'RIORDAIN, S. P. (1946). Prehistory in Ireland 1937–46. *P.P.S.* XII (1946), 142–71.

—— (1947). Excavation of a Barrow at Rathjordan, Co. Limerick. *Journ. Cork Hist. & Arch. Soc.* LII (1947), 1–4.

DO PAÇO, A. (1942). As grutas do Poço Velho ou de Cascais. *Comm. Serv. Geol. Portugal*, XXII (1942), 1–44 (of offprint).

PASSMORE, A. D. (1923). Chambered Long Barrow in West Woods. *W.A.M.* XLII (1923), 366–7.

—— (1933). The Giants Caves Long Barrow, Luckington. *W.A.M.* XLVI (1933), 380–6.

—— (1940). Barrow No. 2, Wylye, Wilts. *W.A.M.* XLIX (1940), 117–19.

PATCHETT, F. M. (1946). Cornish Bronze Age Pottery. *Arch. J.* C, I (1946), 17–49.

PATERSON, T. G. F. & DAVIES, O. (1939). Excavation of Clontygora Small Cairn. *U.J.A.* II (1939), 55–60.

PAYNE, G. (1880). Celtic Remains discovered at Grovehurst, in Milton-next-Sitting-bourne. *Arch. Cantiana*, XIII (1880), 122–6.

PEAKE, A. E. (1916). Recent Excavations at Grimes Graves. *P.P.S.E.A.* II (1918), 268–319.

—— (1917). Further Excavations at Grimes Graves. *P.P.S.E.A.* II (1918), 409–36.

—— (1919). Excavations at Grimes Graves during 1917. *P.P.S.E.A.* III, 73–93.

PEAKE, A. E. *et al.* (1915). *Report on the Excavations of Grimes Graves, Weeting, Norfolk, March–May 1914.* [Prehist. Soc. E. Anglia], 1915.

PEAKE, H. J. E. (1937). Some Problems of the New Stone Age. *Mem. & Proc. Manchester Lit. & Phil. Soc.* LXXXI (1937), 37–75.

—— (1938). The Separation of Britain from the Continent. *P.P.S.* IV (1938), 230–1.

PEERS, C. R. & SMITH, R. A. (1921). Wayland's Smithy, Berkshire. *Ant. J.* L (1921), 183–98.

PENNINGTON, W. (1947). Studies in the Post-Glacial History of British Vegetation: VII—Lake Sediments...of Windermere. *Phil. Trans.* CCXXXIII (1947), 137–75.

PÉQUART, M. *et al.* (1937). Téviec. Station-nécropole Mésolithique du Morbihan. *Archives Inst. Pal. Hum. Mémoires*, 18. Paris, 1937.

PÉQUART, M., PÉQUART, S. J. & LE ROUZIC, Z. (1927). *Corpus des signes gravées des monuments mégalithiques du Morbihan.* Paris, 1927.

PERICOT, L. (1950). *Los Sepulcros Megaliticos Catalanes y la Cultura Pirenaica.* Barcelona, 1950.

PHILIPPE, J. (1927). *Cinq Années de Fouilles au Fort-Harrouard, 1921–1925.* Rouen, 1927.

—— (1936). Le Fort Harrouard. *L'Anthrop.* XLVI (1936), 257–301, 542–612.

—— (1937). Le Fort Harrouard. *L'Anthrop.* XLVII (1937), 253–308.

PHILLIPS, C. W. (1933 a). The Long Barrows of Lincolnshire. *Arch. J.* LXXXIX (1933), 174–202.

—— (1933 b). *Map of the Trent Basin showing the distribution of Long Barrows, Megaliths, Habitation Sites.* Ordnance Survey, 1933.

—— (1935 a). A Re-examination of the Therfield Heath Long Barrow, Royston. *P.P.S.* I (1935), 101–7.

—— (1935 b). Neolithic 'A' bowl from near Grantham. *Ant. J.* XV (1935), 347–8.

—— (1936). The Excavation of the Giants' Hills Long Barrow, Skendleby, Lincs. *Arch.* LXXXV (1936), 37–106.

PIGGOTT, C. M. (1943). Three Turf Barrows at Hurn, near Christchurch. *Proc. Hants F.C.* XV (1943), 248–62.

PIGGOTT, S. (1929). Neolithic Pottery and other Remains from Pangbourne, Berks. and Caversham, Oxon. *P.P.S.E.A.* VI (1929), 30–9.

—— (1931). The Neolithic Pottery of the British Isles. *Arch. J.* LXXXVIII (1931), 67–158.

—— (1932). The Mull Hill Circle, Isle of Man, and its Pottery. *Ant. J.* XII (1932), 146-57.

—— (1933). The Pottery from the Lligwy Burial Chamber, Anglesey. *Arch. Camb.* LXXXVIII (1933), 68–72.

—— (1934 a). Neolithic and Early Bronze Age Settlement at Broom Hill, Michelmersh, Hants. *Ant. J.* XIV (1934), 246–53.

—— (1934 b). The Relative Chronology of the British Long Barrows. *Compte-Rendu 1st Internat. Congress Prehist. Sciences.* London (1934), 143–4.

—— (1935). A Note on the Relative Chronology of the English Long Barrows. *P.P.S.* I (1935), 115–26.

—— (1936 a). A Pottery Spoon from the Mendips. *P.P.S.* II (1936), 143.

—— (1936 b). Handley Hill Dorset—a Neolithic Bowl and the Date of the Entrenchment. *P.P.S.* II (1936), 229–30.

—— (1937 a). The Long Barrow in Brittany. *Ant.* XI (1937), 441–55.

—— (1937 b). Neolithic Pottery from Hackpen, Avebury. *W.A.M.* XLVIII (1937), 90–1.

—— (1937 c). The Excavation of a Long Barrow in Holdenhurst Parish, near Christchurch. *P.P.S.* III (1937), 1–14.

—— (1938). The Early Bronze Age in Wessex. *P.P.S.* IV (1938), 52–106.

—— (1939). The Badbury Barrow, Dorset, and its Carved Stone. *Ant. J.* XIX (1929), 291–9.

—— (1940 a). Timber Circles: A Re-examination. *Arch. J.* XCVI (1940), 193–222.

—— (1940 b). A Trepanned Skull of the Beaker Period from Dorset and the Practice of Trepanning in Prehistoric Europe. *P.P.S.* VI (1940), 112–32.

—— (1946 a). The Chambered Cairn of 'The Grey Mare and Colts'. *Proc. Dorset Nat. Hist. & Arch. Soc.* LXVII (1946), 30–3.

—— (1946 b). An Early Bronze Age Vessel from Ashley Hill. *W.A.M.* LI (1946), 384–5.

—— (1948). Relações entre Portugal e as Ilhas Británicas nos começos da Idade do Bronze. *Revista de Guimarães,* LVII (1948), 5–18.

—— (1950). The Excavations at Cairnpapple Hill, West Lothian, 1947–48. *P.S.A.S.* LXXXII (1947–48), 68–123.

—— (1951). Stonehenge Reviewed. *Aspects of Archaeology* (1951), 274–92.

PIGGOTT, S. & C. M. (1944). Excavations of Barrows on Crichel and Launceston Downs, Dorset. *Arch.* XC (1944), 47–80.

PIGGOTT, S. & CHILDE, V. G. (1932). Comparative Notes on a Series of Neolithic Potsherds from Larne. *P.P.S.E.A.* VII (1932), 62–6.

PIGGOTT, S. & POWELL, T. G. E. (1947). Notes on Megalithic Tombs in Sligo and Achill. *J.R.S.A.I.* LXXVII (1947), 136–46.

—— (1949). Excavation of three Neolithic Chambered Tombs.... *P.S.A.S.* LXXXIII (1948–49), 103–61.

PITT-RIVERS, A. (1882). Excavations at Caesar's Camp near Folkestone....*Arch.* XLVII (1882), 429–65.

—— (1898). *Excavations in Cranborne Chase, IV.* 1898.

POWELL, T. G. E. (1938*a*). The Passage Graves of Ireland. *P.P.S.* IV (1938), 239–48.

—— (1938*b*). Excavation of a Megalithic Tomb at Ballynamona Lower, Co. Waterford. *J.R.S.A.I.* LXVIII (1938), 260–71.

—— (1941*a*). Megalithic Tombs of South Eastern Ireland. *J.R.S.A.I.* LXXI (1941), 9–23.

—— (1941*b*). Excavation of a Megalithic Tomb at Carriglong, Co. Waterford. *Journ. Cork Hist. & Arch. Soc.* XLVI (1941), 55–62.

—— (1941*c*). A New Passage Grave Group in S.E. Ireland. *P.P.S.* VII (1941), 142–3.

PULL, J. H. (1932). *The Flint Miners of Blackpatch.* Williams & Norgate, 1932.

—— (1933). *Sussex County Mag.* VII (1933), 810–14.

RADEMACHER, E. (1925). Die Niederrheinische Hügelgraberkultur von der Spätsteinzeit b. z. Ende d. Hallstattzeit. *Mannus*, IV (Ergänzungsband) (1925), 112–39.

RAISTRICK, A. (1931). Excavation at Sewell's Cave, Settle. *Proc. Univ. Durham Phil. Soc.* IX (1931), 191–204.

—— (1932). Prehistoric Burials at Waddington and Bradley, West Yorks. *Yorks Arch. Journ.* XXX (1932), 248–55.

RAISTRICK, A. & BLACKBURN, K. B. (1932). The Late-Glacial and Post-Glacial Periods in the North Pennines: Part III, The Post-Glacial Peats. *Trans. Northern Nat. Union*, I (1932), 79–103.

RANKINE, W. F. (1949*a*). Stone 'Maceheads' with Mesolithic Associations from South-Eastern England. *P.P.S.* XV (1949), 70–6.

—— (1949*b*). Pebbles of Non-Local Rocks from Mesolithic Chipping Floors. *P.P.S.* XV (1949), 193–4.

R.C.A.M.(S) (1911*a*). Royal Commission on Ancient Monuments (Scotland): *Caithness Inventory.* Edinburgh, 1911.

R.C.A.M.(S) (1911*b*). Royal Commission on Ancient Monuments (Scotland): *Sutherland Inventory.* Edinburgh, 1911.

—— (1920). Royal Commission on Ancient Monuments (Scotland): *Dumfries Inventory.* Edinburgh, 1920.

—— (1928). Royal Commission on Ancient Monuments (Scotland): *Outer Hebrides, etc. Inventory.* Edinburgh, 1928.

—— (1946). Royal Commission on Ancient Monuments (Scotland): *Orkney and Shetland Inventory.* Edinburgh, 1946.

REID MOIR, J. (1926). Upper Palaeolithic Man in East Anglia. *P.P.S.E.A.* V (1926), 232–52.

REINERTH, H. (1929). *Das Federseemoor.* . . . Augsburg, 1929.

RICHARDSON, DEREK (1920). A New Celt-making Floor at Grimes Graves. *P.P.S.E.A.* III, 243–58.

RITCHIE, J. (1918). Cup-marks on the Stone Circles and Standing-Stones of Aberdeenshire and part of Banffshire. *P.S.A.S.* LII (1917–18), 86–121.

ROGERS, E. H. (1946). The Raised Beach . . . and the submerged Stone Row of Yelland. *Proc. Devon Arch. Ex. Soc.* III (1946), 109–35.

ROSENBERG, G. (1931). *Kulturströmungen in Europa zur Steinzeit.* Copenhagen, 1931.

ROSS-WILLIAMSON, R. P. (1930). Excavations in Whitehawk Neolithic Camp, near Brighton. *S.A.C.* LXXI (1930), 57–96.

ROUZIC, Z. LE (1930). *Les Cromlechs de Er Lannic.* Vannes, 1930.

—— (1933). Premières Fouilles au Camp du Lizo. *Rev. Arch.* 1933, 189–219.

—— (1934). Mobilier des Sepultures préhistoriques du Morbihan. *L'Anthrop.* XLIV (1934), 485–524.

RYBOT, N. V. L., NICOLLE, E. T. *et al.* (1925). *La Hougue Bie.* St Helier, 1925.

SALISBURY, E. J. & JANE, F. W. (1940). Charcoals from Maiden Castle and their significance. . . . *Journ. Ecol.* XXVIII (1940), 310–25.

SANDARS, N. K. (1950). Daggers as Type Fossils in the French Early Bronze Age. *Univ. Lond. Inst. Arch. Ann. Reports*, VI (1950), 44–59.

SAUER, C. (1949). Catalogue des Instruments Néolithiques en pierre taillée d'Alsace. *Cahiers d'Arch. et Hist. d'Alsace* (1949), 223–34.

SCHWANTES, G. (1934). *Geschichte Schleswig-Holsteins I.* Kiel, 1934.

SCOTT, W. L. (1932). Rudh' an Dunain Chambered Cairn, Skye. *P.S.A.S.* LXVI (1931–32), 183–213.

—— (1933). The chambered Tomb of Pant-y-Saer, Anglesey. *Arch. Camb.* LXXXVIII (1933), 185–228.

—— (1934). External Features of Rudh' an Dunain Chambered Cairn. *P.S.A.S.* LXVIII (1933–34), 194–9.

—— (1935). The Chambered Cairn of Clettraval, North Uist. *P.S.A.S.* LXIX (1934–35), 480–536.

—— (1942). Neolithic Culture of the Hebrides. *Ant.* XVI (1942), 301–6.

—— (1948 a). The Chamber Tomb of Unival, North Uist. *P.S.A.S.* LXXXII (1950), 1–49.

—— (1948 b). Gallo-British Colonies. . . . *P.P.S.* XIV (1948), 46–125.

—— (1951 a). Drift-timber in the West. *Ant.* XXV (1951), 151–3.

—— (1951 b). The Colonization of Scotland in the Second Millennium B.C. *P.P.S.* XVII (1951), 16–82.

SCOTT, W. L. & PHEMISTER, J. (1942). Local Manufacture of Neolithic Pottery. *P.S.A.S.* LXXVI (1941–42), 130–2.

SERRA Y RAFOLS, J. DE C. (1925). Cueva de los Murciélagos. *Reallexikon der Vorgeschichte*, II (1925), 338.

—— (1947). La Exploración de la Necrópolis Neolítica de la Bóvila Madurell. . . . *Museo . . . de Sabadell*, III (1947), 5–23.

SIMPSON, J. Y. (1865). On Ancient Sculpturings of Cups and Concentric Rings, etc., *P.S.A.S.* VI (1865), Appendix.

SIMPSON, W. DOUGLAS (1928). A Chambered Cairn at Allt-nam-Ban, Strathbora, Sutherland. *Ant. J.* VIII (1928), 485–8.

SIMPSON, W. DOUGLAS (1937). [Neolithic pottery from Grantown-on-Spey.] *P.S.A.S.* LXXI (1936–37), 367.

—— (1944). *The Province of Mar.* (Rhind Lectures, 1941.) 1944.

SMITH, E. E. (1947). Flint Implements from Sidmouth. *Proc. Devon Arch. Ex. Soc.* III (1937–47), 167–71.

SMITH, R. A. (1910). The Development of Neolithic Pottery. *Arch.* LXII (1910), 340–52.

—— (1911). Lake-Dwellings in Holderness, Yorks., discovered by Thos. Boynton.... *Arch.* LXII (1911), 593–610.

—— (1912). On the date of Grimes Graves and Cissbury Flint Mines. *Arch.* LXIII (1912), 109–58.

—— (1918). Specimens from the Layton Collection.... *Arch.* LXIX (1918), 1–30.

—— (1925). A Rare Urn from Suffolk. *Ant. J.* V (1925), 73–4.

—— (1926). The Perforated Axe-hammers of Britain. *Arch.* LXXV (1926), 77–108.

—— (1927). Flint Arrow-heads in Britain. *Arch.* LXXVI, 81–106.

—— (1934). Examples of Mesolithic Art. *Brit. Mus. Quart.* VIII (1934), 144.

SMITH, R. ANGUS (1872). Descriptive list of Antiquities near Loch Etive. *P.S.A.S.* IX (1870–72), 396–418.

SMITH, W. G. (1915). Maiden Bower, Bedfordshire. *Proc. Soc. Ant. Lond.* XXVII (1914–15), 143–61.

SPROCKHOFF, E. (1942). Niedersachsens Bedeutung für die Brönzezeit Westeuropas. *Ber. Röm.-Germ. Komm.* XXXI (1942), 1–138.

STAMPFUSS, R. (1929). *Die Jüngneolithischen Kulturen in Westdeutschland.* Bonn, 1929.

STENBERGER, M. (1939). Das Västerbjersfeld: Ein Grabfeld der Ganggräberzeit auf Gotland. *Acta Arch.* X (1939), 60–105.

—— (1943). *Das Grabfeld von Västerbjers auf Gotland.* Lund, 1943.

STEVENS, F. (1933). *Stonehenge Today and Yesterday.* London (revised edition, 1933).

STEVENSON, R. B. K. (1946). Jottings on Early Pottery. *P.S.A.S.* LXXX (1945–46), 141–3.

—— (1950). Notes on some Prehistoric Objects. *P.S.A.S.* LXXXII (1947–48), 292–5.

STONE, E. H. (1924). *The Stones of Stonehenge.* London, 1924.

STONE, J. F. S. (1931 a). Easton Down, Winterslow, S. Wilts, Flint Mine Excavation, 1930. *W.A.M.* XLV (1931), 350–65.

—— (1931 b). A Settlement Site of the Beaker Period on Easton Down, Winterslow, S. Wilts. *W.A.M.* XLV (1931), 366–72.

—— (1933 a). Excavations at Easton Down, Winterslow, 1931–32. *W.A.M.* XLVI (1933), 225–42.

—— (1933 b). A Flint Mine at St Martin's Clump, Over Wallop. *Hants F.C. Procs.* XII, 177–80.

—— (1934). Three 'Peterborough' Dwelling-pits...at Winterbourne Daunstey. *W.A.M.* XLVI (1934), 445–53.

—— (1935 a). Some discoveries at Ratfyn, Amesbury.... *W.A.M.* XLVII (1935), 55–67.

—— (1935 b). Excavations at Easton Down, Winterslow, 1933–34. *W.A.M.* XLVII (1935), 68–80.

—— (1938). An Early Bronze Age Grave in Fargo Plantation near Stonehenge. *W.A.M.* XLVIII (1938), 357–70.

STONE, J. F. S. (1948). The Stonehenge Cursus and its Affinities. *Arch. J.* CIV (1948), 7–19.

—— (1949). Some Grooved Ware Pottery from the Woodhenge Area. *P.P.S.* XV (1949), 122–7.

—— (1950). An Axe-hammer from Fyfield Bavant, Wilts., and the exploitation of Preselite. *Ant. J.* XXX (1950), 145–51.

STONE, J. F. S. & WALLIS, F. S. (1947). Second Report...on the Petrological Examination of Stone Axes. *P.P.S.* XIII (1947), 47–55.

STONE, J. F. S. & YOUNG, W. E. V. (1948). Two Pits of Grooved Ware Date near Woodhenge. *W.A.M.* LII (1948), 287–306.

TEMPEST, H. G. (1949). Bone Objects from an Irish Burial Cairn. *Man*, XLIX (1949), 13–16.

THOMAS, H. H. (1923). The Source of the Stones of Stonehenge. *Ant. J.* III (1923), 239–60.

THURNAM, J. (1861). Examination of a Chambered Long Barrow at West Kennet, Wiltshire. *Arch.* XXXVIII (1861), 405–21.

—— (1868). On Ancient British Barrows, especially those of Wiltshire and the Adjoining Counties. Part I, Long Barrows. *Arch.* LXII, 161–244.

—— (1870). On Ancient British Barrows...Part II, Round Barrows. *Arch.* XLIII (1870), 285–552.

TODD, K. R. U. (1949). A Neolithic Flint Mine at East Horsley. *Surrey Arch. Colls.* LI (1949), 142–3.

TRECHMANN, C. T. (1936). Mesolithic Flints from the Submerged Forest at West Hartlepool. *P.P.S.* II (1936), 161–8.

VARLEY, W. J., JACKSON, J. W. & CHITTY, L. F. (1940). *Prehistoric Cheshire.* Chester, 1940.

VASCONCELOS, L. DE (1922). Encabamento de instrumentos de pedra prehistoricos. *O Arch. Port.* XXV (1921–22), 288–98.

VOGT, E. (1938). Horgener Kultur, Seine-Oise-Marne Kultur und Nordische Steinkisten. *Anz. Schweiz Altert.* XL (1938), 1–14.

VOUGA, P. (1934). *Le Néolithique lacustre ancien.* Neuchâtel, 1934.

WADE, A. G. (1924). Ancient Flint Mines at Stoke Down, Sussex. *P.P.S.E.A.* IV, 82–91.

WAGNER, F. (1928). Prehistoric Fortifications in Bavaria. *Ant.* II (1928), 43–55.

WALSHE, P. T. (1941). Excavation of a Burial Cairn on Baltinglass Hill. *P.R.I.A.* (C), XLVI (1941), 221–36.

WARD, J. (1890). On some diggings near Brassington, Derbyshire. *Journ. Derby Arch. & Nat. Hist. Soc.* XII (1890), 108–38.

—— (1901). Five-Wells Tumulus, Derbyshire. *The Reliquary* (1901), 229–42.

—— (1916). *The St Nicholas Chambered Tumulus, Glamorgan.* Nat. Mus. Wales, 1916 (reprinted from *Arch. Camb.*, 6th ser., XV, 253–320; XVI, 239–94).

WARD PERKINS, J. B. (1942). Problems of Maltese Prehistory. *Ant.* XVI (1942), 19–35.

WARREN, S. HAZZLEDINE (1919). A Stone-Axe Factory at Graig Lwyd, Penmaenmawr. *J.R.A.I.* XLIX, 342–65.

—— (1921). Excavations at the Stone-Axe Factory of Graig-Lwyd, Penmaenmawr. *J.R.A.I.* LI (1921), 165–99.

WARREN, S. HAZZLEDINE (1922). The Neolithic Stone Axes of Graig-Lwyd, Penmaenmawr. *Arch. Camb.* (1922), 1–32.

WARREN, S. H. *et al.* (1936). Archaeology of the Submerged Land-Surface of the Essex Coast. *P.P.S.* II (1936), 178–210.

WHEELER, R. E. M. W. (1943). *Maiden Castle, Dorset.* Soc. Ant. Lond. Reports of Research Committee, XII (1943).

WHELAN, C. BLAKE (1934). Studies in the Significance of the Irish Stone Age: The Campignian Question. *P.R.I.A.* (c), XLII (1934), 121–43.

—— (1938). Studies...The Culture Sequence. *P.R.I.A.* (c), XLIV (1938), 115–36.

WHITE, G. M. (1934). Prehistoric Remains from Selsey Bill. *Ant. J.* XIV (1934), 40–52.

WILDE, W. R. (1857–61). *Catalogue of the Museum of the Royal Irish Academy.* Dublin (two vols.), 1857–61.

WILLETT, E. H. (1872). On Flint Workings at Cissbury, Sussex. *Arch.* XLV, 337–48.

WILLIAMS, A. (1950). Bronze Age Barrows on Charmy Down and Lansdown, Somerset. *Ant. J.* XXX (1950), 34–46.

WILLMOT, G. F. (1938). Neolithic B pottery from Yorkshire. *P.P.S.* IV (1938), 338.

WILLOCK, E. H. (1936). A Neolithic Site on Haldon. *Proc. Devon Arch. Ex. Soc.* II (1936), 244–63.

—— (1937). A Further Note on the Neolithic Site on Haldon. *Proc. Devon Arch. Ex. Soc.* III (1937), 33–43.

WINTHER, J. (1926). *Lindø: en Boplads fra Danmarks Yngre Stenalder.* Langeland, 1926.

—— (1943). *Blandebjerg.* Langeland, 1943.

WOOD, E. S. (1948). Some Current Problems of Yorkshire Archaeology. *Arch. News Letter*, 1948, 13.

WOOD-MARTIN, W. G. (1888). *The Rude Stone Monuments of Ireland (Co. Sligo and the Island of Achill).* Dublin, 1888. (Reprinted from *J.R.S.A.I.* XVII and XVIII.)

ZEUNER, F. (1950). Archaeology and Geology. *S.E. Nat. & Ant.* LV (1950), 5–16.

INDEX